MARX

MARX

ROBERT PAYNE

W. H. ALLEN · LONDON · 1968

PUBLISHED IN GREAT BRITAIN BY
W. H. ALLEN & COMPANY,
ESSEX STREET, LONDON WC 2.

491 00221 1

PRINTED IN THE UNITED STATES OF AMERICA

Karl Marx

CONTENTS

INTRODUCTION

WE LIVE in the age of Marx. A thousand million people, nearly half the world, are ruled by governments which claim to be practicing his teachings and following the path he set for them in *The Communist Manifesto, Das Kapital,* and a host of lesser works. In their eyes he is the new Moses with the tablets of the new law, a figure of prodigious intellectual attainment and moral force. He is the supreme judge, the final court of appeal. To him, and to him alone, was given the gift of prophecy enabling him to foretell the dissolution of entire societies and the coming of the new societies out of the ashes of the old. They claim for him powers which he rarely claimed for himself, and out of that hotheaded and sometimes likable human being they have created an edifice of infallibility. From being a man he became an abstraction.

In the following pages I have attempted to draw a portrait of the man as he was, with his family and friends, and to present him for the first time as a living human being. I wanted to see him walking into the room and to hear him talking about himself. I wanted especially to capture the accent of his voice, the way he formed his words and ideas. His background, his ancestry, his parents, his upbringing, his early essays, his poems and his unfinished poetic drama—for there was a time when he regarded himself as a poet who would take the kingdom of German poetry by storm—seemed to me important in showing the springs of his mind, and where Franz Mehring, his official biographer, devotes scarcely five pages to his ancestry and his childhood and youth, I felt there were good reasons for devoting many more pages to his family and his early years. His ancestors lived on in him, and he never completely escaped from his own youth.

The man described in these pages has very little in common with the infallible oracle worshiped by the Communists. He was human and vulnerable, only too vulnerable. He was far from being a paragon of Communist virtues. He went on monumental pub crawls, speculated on the stock exchange, seduced his maidservant, fathered an illegitimate child, dallied with aristocratic young women, and enjoyed his visits to expensive watering places, where he could consort with the wealthy and the privileged. Bakunin accused him of being a police spy, but this was an understatement, for he delivered the documents of the International into the hands of the British Home Secretary, the head of the police. He exploited everyone around him—his wife, his children, his mistress and his friends—with a ruthlessness which was all the more terrible because it was deliberate and calculating. His tastes were those of a feudal aristocrat. He was one of those who are determined to command, whatever the cost in pain and suffering to others.

Except for a brief period when he controlled the International Working Men's Association, Marx never achieved any position of power in his lifetime. For a great part of his life his mind dwelt on fantasies of power. At moments of depression he would buoy himself up with the hope of becoming the revolutionary dictator of Germany, and he would discuss quite seriously with his friend Friedrich Engels how the next crisis would inevitably bring him to a position of supreme power. It seems never to have occurred to him that the Germans might not want him. Toward the end of his life he suffered from progressive paranoia, and he would talk about the great revolutionary movements he still controlled, when in fact he had no organized following at all.

Marx dreamed of ushering in during his lifetime a new world state based on the dictatorship of the proletariat. He saw this dictatorship as the logical conclusion to which all the forces of history were leading. If it meant that whole classes must be destroyed, and the entire fabric of civilization must be jettisoned, nevertheless the logic of history demanded these sacrifices. He was not one of those who dream small dreams. He dreamed on a massive and breathtaking scale. Sometimes those dreams were close to madness.

Out of the squalor and misery of his life came those insistent fantasies of power, and we shall not understand Marx unless we realize how deeply and pervasively his strange and unhappy life was reflected in his dreams. He announced his doctrines and theories as the result of impersonal scholarship. In fact they derived as much from his private fantasies as from the revolutionary traditions of his time.

In 1917, thirty-four years after Marx's death, Lenin seized power in Russia. The first Marxist state came into existence in a country exhausted by despair, hunger and war. The fantasies which filled the mind of Marx were printed with red-hot irons on the body of a living country. But the dream of the dictatorship of the proletariat was not fulfilled. Instead there was the dictatorship of a single man. Marx would scarcely have recognized the new kind of state which derived its sanction from his writings.

Today nearly all the original documents connected with the life of Marx are in Russian hands. His letters and manuscripts are to be found in the archives of the Marx-Engels Institute in Moscow, and from time to time new editions appear with suitable emendations. The author of a life of Marx must move warily among the official texts, never knowing for sure what documents have been suppressed or distorted.

Nevertheless, from the vast amount of material available, it is possible to draw an authentic likeness of the man. Many who knew him have left accounts of him; there were eyewitnesses of his public career; his private life is revealed in his letters; the real man can be discovered beneath the varnish of the official portrait. In the end the deliberate distortions and suppressions defeat themselves. Sooner or later the real man emerges from behind the screen of propaganda, and as the reader will see, he is far more interesting, more human and more vulnerable than the figure enthroned on the Communist altars.

So this is the portrait of the man who throws the longest shadow over our century. Greatness he had, for a man who changes the climate of the entire world cannot be denied a claim to greatness, but it is a greatness he shares with the tyrants. He never fought on the barricades, never led an army into battle, never commanded a nation; instead, he forged new weapons of tyranny in the silence of his study. That strange, willful genius has left a mark on the world which may take centuries to erase.

THE EDUCATION OF A REVOLUTIONARY

God gave to man a universal goal, so that man and mankind might be ennobled.

A NEST OF GENTLE FOLK

KARL MARX was born at two o'clock in the morning on May 5, 1818, in an elegant town house on the fashionable Brückengasse at Trier in the Rhine province of Prussia. According to the birth certificate he was given the names Carl Heinrich, and the witnesses who signed the certificate were prominent citizens of the city.

In those days Trier, although known as a city, was little more than a large village of about twelve thousand inhabitants. It lived on its past. Once it was the richest city in all Germany, with great towers and archways dominating the banks of the Moselle; and Pomponius Mela, writing about A.D. 41, called it *"urbs opulentissima."* Opulent and powerful, the city commanded all the wealth flowing along the river, and Roman emperors sometimes held court in the great palace. St. Ambrose was born there. The Roman ruins still crowd the once powerful city. An immense hall, thought to be the Roman basilica, still stands, and the Porta Nigra, the Black Gate, is still one of the gateways to the city. This huge gateway of dark stone has an appearance of untroubled power and assurance, as though built by a people who intended to defend the city to the end of history.

But with the coming of the great migrations across Germany, and the decline of Roman power, Trier, then known as Augusta Treverorum, became an obscure township lost to history. It flourished again in the Middle Ages under the rule of a succession of prince-archbishops. The cathedral, built on the ruins of the Roman palace, claimed to possess one of the Nails of the Cross, a portion of the Crown of Thorns, and the Holy Coat, the seamless garment worn by Christ before the Crucifixion. This was said to have been presented to the cathedral by St. Helena, the mother of the Emperor Constantine. In summer pilgrims flocked to Trier for the ceremonial showing of the Holy Coat.

The full force of the Reformation was never felt in Trier, which remained predominantly Catholic. Goethe, visiting the city in 1793, complained that it possessed more religious buildings than any other of comparable size. "The place is burdened, nay oppressed, with churches and chapels and cloisters and colleges and buildings dedicated to chivalrous and religious orders," he wrote, "and this is to say nothing about the abbacies, Carthusian convents and other institutions which invest and blockade it." But the prince-archbishops who surrounded themselves with religious foundations were usually men of wide culture, well-disposed toward Protestants and Jews. There were Protestant churches and a synagogue. The city owed its wealth to the vines on the neighboring hills, and like most wine-exporting cities it was given over to cultivated leisure.

Heinrich Marx, the lawyer whose office consisted of one of the large rooms of his house on the Brückengasse, evidently had no difficulty in making a good living. His fortunes rose and fell with the prosperity of Trier. It so happened that in 1818, the year of the birth of his son Karl, the Prussian government instituted prohibitive duties on foreign wines. Trier, which had become a part of Prussia after the Congress of Vienna, benefited to such an extent that it became once more *urbs opulentissima.* In the following year Heinrich Marx installed himself and his small family in a larger house on the Simeonstrasse, under the shadow of the Porta Nigra.

We would like to know more about that cultivated liberal lawyer. His real name was Hirschel ha-Levi Marx, but he had long since turned his back on Judaism. He was a man of the Enlightenment, who read French as easily as he read German, and he had a special fondness for seventeenth-century French poetry. By all accounts he was a man of grave courtesy and intellectual distinction. His granddaughter, who saw a daguerreotype of him which must have been made very late in his life, describes him as "typically Jewish, but beautifully so." He had a broad, finely modeled forehead, dark penetrating eyes and thick eyebrows; and while the upper part of his face was masculine, the mouth and chin were distinctly feminine. He was gentle by nature, and not easily aroused to anger.

He was born in 1782 at Saarlouis, where his father was rabbi. Indeed his family had produced rabbis in unbroken succession for generations. One of his ancestors was the Rabbi Elieser ha-Levi of Mainz, whose son Jehuda escaped from Mainz during the sack of the city in 1462 and became head of the Talmudic school in Padua, where he was known as Jehuda Minz. Born in 1408, Jehuda died a hundred and one years later. A man of fiery temper, he engaged in a bitter ideological quarrel with Elias del Medigo, a Talmudic scholar from Crete, whose ideas reflected the humanism of the court of Lorenzo de' Medici. Jehuda resolved the quarrel by excommunicating his enemy and banishing him from Italy.

Jehuda's son Abraham engaged in an equally fierce quarrel with another Talmudic scholar called Jacob Pollack, who had invented a subtle hair-splitting method of studying the Talmud. Abraham Minz liked hairsplitting no more than his father liked humanism, and once more there was a battle of wills. Finally they decided to excommunicate each other, and Jacob Pollack retired to Palestine. Abraham Minz, who lived to be eighty-five, continued to be head of the Talmudic school to the day of his death. Some of his descendants became famous rabbis, but for the most part they were obscure men who officiated in small and obscure towns in eastern and central Europe.

Hirschel Marx was the first in his family to rebel against the rabbinical tradition. Soon after his birth his father came to Trier. His childhood seems to have been unhappy, and he had no pleasant recollections of his father, who died when he was sixteen. "I received nothing from my family except, I must confess, my mother's love," he wrote once, and this ambiguous statement provides all the information we have about his feeling for his family.

As a child he watched the French revolutionary army sweeping into the Moselle region, toppling the Prince-Archbishop of Trier, Clement Wenceslaus, from his throne. The ideas of the Enlightenment appealed to him, and from being a Jew destined to spend his years studying the Talmud and superintending his flock, he became for a few years a cultivated Frenchman studying law and the French classics.

During the time of the French Revolution Trier became a small outpost on the frontiers of the French Republic, ruled from Paris. Under Napoleon it belonged to the French Empire, and the youth of Trier went out to fight among Napoleon's legions. Hirschel seems not to have fought in the wars but to have lived quietly in the backwaters, studying for his law degree, identifying himself more and more with Prussia as he grew more and more disenchanted with Napoleon. He admired Prussian order and discipline, and preferred an enlightened Prussian monarch to a French emperor who plundered the German provinces and transformed Europe into his private preserve. He was growing up in a harsh school, and he would say that he survived only by clinging to his "hard principles."

Of his struggles to achieve an education and to practice a profession we know nothing, for all his early history is lost in the confusion of those endless wars. He married late. He was thirty-one when he married Henrietta Pressborck, the twenty-six-year-old daughter of a rabbi from Nymwegen in Holland. The marriage took place according to the Jewish rite at four o'clock on the afternoon of November 30, 1813. We know the hour and the date of the marriage because his wife remembered it vividly, and long before her death she prophesied that she would die at that exact hour on that day. She died at four o'clock on the afternoon of November 30, 1863, exactly fifty years later.

She brought him a dowry and a fierce devotion, and gave him eight children. They came regularly every year or two years. First came Moritz-David, who died in childbirth in 1815. Then came Sophie in 1816, Karl in 1818, Hermann in 1819, Henrietta in 1820, Luise in 1821, Emilie in 1822, Karolina in 1824, and Eduard in 1826. Four of these children died comparatively young of tuberculosis of the lungs. Eduard died at 11, Hermann and Karolina at 23, and Henrietta at 36. The surviving daughters married into their class: one married an engineer, another a lawyer, another a bookseller who emigrated to South Africa. Karl was the only son to survive into middle age.

They were a nest of gentle folk, with wealth and servants at their disposal. There was an indulgent father, a kindly and understanding mother. In later years Karl came to detest his mother, but while he was young he regarded her with deep affection. He called her "angel mother" and "this great and wonderful woman" when he was a student at the university. She was a good housekeeper, careful with money, one of those Dutch housewives who live entirely for their family and have little inkling of anything that happens outside, solid and unimaginative. To the end of her life she spoke German with a heavy Dutch accent and never learned to write a grammatical letter in her adopted tongue. The children spoke Dutch as well as German at home. Intellectually she had nothing in common with her husband, "that real eighteenth-century Frenchman, who knew his Voltaire and Rousseau inside out." So Edgar von Westphalen, the son of the next-door neighbor, described him many years later, remembering him vividly while having nothing whatever to say about his Dutch wife.

It was a leisurely life of ease and bourgeois respectability. The large baroque house on the Simeonstrasse was made for comfort. The lawyer owned land and houses, and the rents supplemented his income from lawyer's fees. There can have been few families in Trier more wealthy, or more well-respected. It was one of those large and happy families where the children grow up as calmly as peaches ripen in the sun.

There was however one shadow, which in the eyes of Hirschel Marx presented no danger and was soon dissipated. When Prussian rule was established in the Rhineland in 1815, he must have known that there would be great administrative changes. In May 1816 the edict went out from the Prussian Ministry of the Interior that no one of Jewish faith could serve as an advocate or an apothecary within the kingdom. Hirschel Marx had long ago abandoned his Jewish faith and broken off all relations with his brother Samuel, now the chief rabbi of Trier. Sometime between that summer and the following spring he formally abandoned Judaism and entered the Evangelical Church as a convert. He took the name of Heinrich, receiving the sacrament of baptism and the certificate which went with it. There was only a small community of Protestants in Trier: in time the Marx family contributed altogether nine new members to the faith.

There is no reason to believe that he suffered any qualms of conscience when he became a Protestant. Like the poet Heine, who spoke of baptism as "an entrance ticket to European culture," he appears to have regarded his apostasy as a relief from the burdens of the rabbinical tradition which dominated his youth. On August 26, 1824, he solemnly gathered up his six children, Sophie, Karl, Henrietta, Luise, Emilie and the baby Karolina, and presented them for baptism. His wife's father was still living, and she therefore postponed her entrance into the Church. She was baptized in November of the following year, after his death.

Heinrich Marx, formerly Hirschel Marx, the descendant of generations of rabbis, had now turned his face resolutely against the past. Nominally a Christian, he was a freethinker who attended church regularly, sang hymns and paid his tithes. Edgar von Westphalen described him as "a Protestant *à la* Lessing," which meant that he was prepared to conform to the outward forms of the Church but did not believe that any faith was superior to any other, that in his view Stoicism, Judaism, Christianity and Hinduism were all equally valid and equally vulnerable. He professed "a pure belief in God, like Newton, Locke and Leibnitz," but that was only to say that he professed a belief in reason. Yet he took his religious duties seriously, and saw to it that all his children went through the proper stages of a Christian education and received the appropriate sacraments including confirmation. So it happened that on March 23, 1834, Karl Marx, then aged fifteen, was solemnly confirmed and received the gift of the Holy Ghost in all His fullness.

The year 1834 was not one which Heinrich Marx was likely to forget. The year began with an extraordinary demonstration at the Casino Club, the large well-lit building in the center of the city where the more intelligent men in the community were accustomed to read French and German newspapers, attend lectures, engage in discussions of all kinds, and put on theatrical performances. The local literary and political clubs also met there. The largest and most influential political club was the Gesellschaft für nutzliche Forschung (Association for Useful Inquiry), founded in 1802. One of the founders was Hugo Wyttenbach, the headmaster of the Friedrich Wilhelm Gymnasium. Heinrich Marx was himself a prominent member of the Casino Club and also of the political society.

On January 12, 1834, the members of the society gave a banquet to honor the newly elected deputies to the Rhineland Diet, especially the deputies who had demonstrated "a liberal tendency." These banquets, which were being held all over southern and western Germany that winter, conformed to a well-known pattern and were intended as sounding boards for political objectives. Heinrich Marx had helped to organize the banquet, and indeed he was one of the principal organizers, for he took his political responsibilities as seriously as he took his religious ones. To him was given the honor of offering a toast to the King of Prussia, the weak and vacillating Frederick William III, the grandnephew of Frederick the Great. He therefore paid a glowing tribute to the king "to whose magnanimity we are indebted for the first institutions of popular representation. In the fullness of his omnipotence he has of his own free will directed that the Diets should assemble so that the truth might reach the steps of the throne." The statement was not strictly accurate, for the king was incapable of doing anything of his own free will; nor was it intended to be ironical. Justizrat Heinrich Marx, who bore the honorary title of Royal Prussian Legal Councilor, was merely employing the time-honored political ruse of flattering the king into granting more liberties to his people. He went on to declare that there had never been a more upright, more noble king, responsible to the just and reasonable demands of the people, and he was certain to hear their appeal and grant their elementary demands. The speech was vociferously applauded, and Heinrich Marx became the hero of the hour.

The speech was reported to the authorities in Berlin, who could take no action against him, for he remained well within the letter of the law. The newspapers in Trier were forbidden to print the speech, but it was printed in newspapers as far away as Paris. For the first time in recent history a voice in Trier was being heard in Europe, and the liberals in the town were understandably delighted. Eight days later, on January 20, they celebrated the anniversary of the founding of the Casino Club with more speeches and toasts. There was a good deal of exuberant singing. They sang the "Marseillaise," the "Parisienne," and "Was ist das deutsche Vaterland," which could be interpreted as an antimonarchical patriotic hymn. This time the authorities were forewarned and careful note was made of every speech, every song, and every toast. An officer denounced Heinrich Marx. "He was one of those from whose attitude we can expect no reconciliation or relaxation of the tensions between Prussia and the Rhineland," he wrote, and the Prussian Ministry of the Interior henceforth regarded him as a man of dubious political beliefs, to be watched carefully and prevented from occupying any position of power. The Casino Club was placed under new auspices, and the local government received an official reprimand for permitting such things to happen.

There was nothing in the least revolutionary about the behavior of Heinrich Marx. He had merely espoused the cause of the liberal members of the Diet elected in the Rhineland, while pointedly omitting any reference to the pro-Prussian members. It was true that he had sung revolutionary hymns like the "Marseillaise," but this was perfectly legal. As a result of these escapades he probably lost some lawyer's fees, but otherwise suffered no harm. He had powerful protectors and was far too important a man to be relegated to obscurity because he had toasted liberty at a drunken spree.

For Karl Marx, who was devoted to his father, such events brightened the dull course of provincial life, and probably gave him luster in the eyes of his schoolmates. He respected his father's learning and intelligence. They were drawing very close to one another. In later years, according to his daughter Eleanor, he would talk endlessly about his father, always with admiration and something approaching awe. Wherever he traveled, he carried with him the daguerreotype of his father, explaining to his children that he never showed it to strangers because it bore so little resemblance to the original. When he died, the daguerreotype was placed in his grave.

At the age of twelve Karl entered the Friedrich Wilhelm Gymnasium, which was originally a Jesuit foundation. There he remained for the next five years. The headmaster, the liberal Hugo Wyttenbach, taught him history. He received excellent marks in Greek, Latin, and German, but showed no great understanding of history, and was weak in mathematics and French. His knowledge of history was to remain defective, and although he prided himself on his French in later years he never reconciled himself to the intricacies of French grammar. As for mathematics, he was generally incapable of solving even the simplest problems accurately, although he claimed many years later to have had a special fondness for mathematical techniques and spoke of having invented a new form of differential calculus.

He was not the most prepossessing youth in the Gymnasium. There was something strange and disturbing in his hard mouth, his brutal chin, dark skin, and mop of uncombed curly black hair. He had rather small hands and feet, and his legs were small in relation to his body. His dark-brown eyes were very fine, and he had a soaring well-modeled forehead, but the general impression was of an awkward pugnaciousness and coarseness. Hair grew on his cheeks, in little tufts in his nose and ears and on his wrists. His thick curling underlip gave him an oddly sardonic expression.

We know very little about his early years except that he was very close to his elder sister Sophie and bullied his younger sisters unmercifully. He was given to making sharp sarcastic remarks, and he was already famous in school for his pungent epigrams describing his schoolmates and the teachers he chose to dislike. He had a quick, jolting mind and a jolting tongue, with the result that he was not particularly popular with his schoolmates, while his teachers appear to have been very long-suffering. There was no denying his classical scholarship or his general intelligence, but he showed no signs of intellectual distinction. He was never at the head of his class. He once received "honorable mention" for compositions in classical and modern languages, but he was only tenth on the list. Hugo Wyttenbach, historian and archaeologist, a humanist with generous impulses, a man quick to appreciate merit, knew the boy well and seems to have been fond of him, but he pronounced no prophetical utterances on his future and regarded him simply as a rather unruly and imaginative pupil who was otherwise quite ordinary.

In August 1835 Karl Marx became an *Abiturient,* a candidate for the final school-leaving examinations. He had decided, or his father had decided for him, that he would become a lawyer and arrangements had been made for him to enter the school of jurisprudence at the University of Bonn. Everything, of course, depended on obtaining his *Reifezeugnis,* that "certificate of maturity" without which no one could enter a university. The long summer was therefore spent in arduous preparation for the final examinations.

JENNY VON WESTPHALEN

When he was in his last year at the Friedrich Wilhelm Gymnasium Marx fell in love with the girl in the house next door.

She was Jenny von Westphalen, the daughter of Baron Johann Ludwig von Westphalen, who had been sent by the Prussian government to act as the chief administrative officer of Trier. He had married twice, the children of his first marriage had long since left his hearth, and he was now living with his second wife and the three children born late in his life. Jenny, who was christened Johanna Bertha Julie Jenny, was the eldest. His son Edgar was the youngest. In between there was another daughter of whom nothing is known, and it is supposed that she died young.

Jenny von Westphalen was born on February 12, 1814, at Salzwedel, where her father was the Landrat, a post corresponding to county sheriff. Her mother, Caroline Amalie Julie Heubel, was the daughter of Julius Christoph Heubel, a minor Prussian official serving in the Rhineland. As a young woman Caroline Heubel was a beauty, but for some reason she married late and she was nearly forty when her eldest daughter was born.

Jenny was always very close to her mother, but she was even closer to her father, whom she worshiped as only young daughters worship aging fathers. In her eyes he could do nothing wrong. He was gentle and calm, and very scholarly; and to a natural distinction of manner he added great physical beauty. Baron von Westphalen was the most distinguished-looking man in all of Trier, and all power flowed through his hands.

His title was Government Councilor, and this meant in theory that he merely advised and offered suggestions to the city government, and reported his findings to the government in Berlin. In fact he was the city government. It was not a very onerous post, and he rarely had to make any difficult decisions. He was more interested in books than in governing, and he had a special gift for languages, speaking English, French, Spanish, Italian, Latin and Greek with remarkable fluency. He had acquired English from his mother, a Scottish woman, and he could never remember a time when English was not spoken in his family.

The barony was created for his father, a man of quite unusual distinction. Born Christian Heinrich Philipp Westphalen in 1724, he emerged out of obscurity to become the confidential secretary of Duke Ferdinand von Braunschweig, and the real power behind the ducal throne. Military historians describe him as an *éminence grise* who worked with great cunning and patience behind the scenes during the years when Russia, Sweden, Austria and France were attempting to dismember the Germany of Frederick the Great. Philipp Westphalen never wore a uniform and never fought in a battle, but he attended the meetings of the general staff and was believed to be largely responsible for the German victories of Bellingshausen, Wilhelmsthal and Minden. He was a gifted writer and left an account of the Seven Years' War which is among the chief documentary sources of the period.

Great Britain was then allied with Germany, and English and Scottish soldiers were fighting beside the Germans. There was much coming and going of families, and so it happened that Jenny Wishart of Edinburgh came to spend a holiday in Germany with her uncle General Beckwith, the commander of the British-Hanoverian army. Philipp Westphalen had recently been ennobled: he was now the Baron Philipp von Westphalen. Jenny fell in love with him, and they were married in the small town of Wesel on October 13, 1765. Jenny was twenty-three, her husband was forty-one.

There were four sons of the marriage. The eldest, Ferdinand, died at twenty-three, but the second son, Heinrich Georg, lived to be over ninety. The youngest son, Johann Ludwig, was his mother's favorite and inherited some of his father's gifts and much of his mother's charm. He inherited, too, his father's self-assurance and intelligence, but was without ambition. Of the third son, Hans, nothing is known.

While Philipp Westphalen rose to the aristocracy on his own merits, Jenny was descended on her mother's side from the Scottish aristocracy and could claim descent from an Earl of Argyll and an Earl of Angus. According to a family tradition cherished by Karl Marx, she was descended from Archibald Campbell, first Marquis and eighth Earl of Argyll, who was beheaded on the orders of Charles II for high treason. A recent examination of the genealogical tree of Jenny Wishart shows that she was descended not from the eighth Earl but from the second Earl, who was killed at the Battle of Flodden in 1513, for her family tree goes back to his second son, known as Archibald Campbell of Skipnish. In those days second sons did not inherit titles, and his descendants were landowners and factors with small estates. Jenny's mother was Ann Campbell of Orchard, and her father was the Reverend Dr. George Wishart, minister of Thron Church in Edinburgh.

The Wisharts were a famous family which had produced many ministers of the Church of Scotland. A collateral branch produced the reformer George Wishart, who was burned at the stake in Edinburgh Castle in 1546.

Karl Marx's future bride, Jenny von Westphalen, the granddaughter of the Scottish lass who came to Germany for a brief visit and stayed for a lifetime, was said to resemble her grandmother. She had the clear Scottish coloring, the green eyes, and the dark-auburn hair of her grandmother. She was not pretty in any conventional way, but she had beauty and grace. A painting made when she was about twenty shows her *en décolletage,* the delicate braids of her auburn hair winding over her bare shoulders, and she wears her hair piled up in an intricate tower in the fashion of the time. The rather long face expresses eagerness as well as serenity, and the features are almost classically Scottish: a high forehead, large widely spaced eyes, a warm mouth, a firm chin. There is something coquettish, too, in the way she loops and curls her hair over an ample forehead. We know on her own testimony that she cared deeply for her beauty and had more than the normal share of vanity. She knew how to dress, and danced well. She was the *belle* of Trier, the daughter of its most powerful and influential citizen, and she was well aware of her position in society.

But there was another Jenny, who took no interest at all in the provincial society of Trier, who was given to brooding and daydreams, and was continually reading the books in her father's library. Poetry was her greatest love, and she dreamed of inspiring some poet to greatness. She wrote well, and her surviving letters are always entertaining, because she pours herself out in them and holds nothing back. She lived much in herself, and her Scottish and German blood were at war within her.

Her greatest friend was Sophie Marx, Karl's serious-minded elder sister. Sophie had all the conventional graces, and was quite easily the most handsome of the Marx children. Jenny and Sophie were constantly exchanging books and carrying on long secret discussions on the nature of life, poetry and humanity. All her life Jenny was passionately devoted to her young brother Edgar, who was a year younger than Karl and sat next to him on the same school bench. Edgar followed in the tradition of his uncles; he never settled down, and was something of a ne'er-do-well. But in his youth he had a quick eager mind and a genuine desire to please, and it seems to have been Edgar who firmly introduced Karl into the Westphalen household.

Baron Ludwig von Westphalen found in Karl a boy after his own heart. Unlike Edgar, Karl possessed a formidable intelligence, a fierce determination to know and understand everything that had been said and written. The old man—he was in his sixties—enjoyed taking the boy for walks in the neighborhood of Trier. They would spend whole mornings and afternoons tramping over the hills and through the woods, while the talk ran from philosophy to science and the art of government and memories of the years when Napoleon's armies swept across Westphalia. The baron had served the Napoleonic kingdom of Westphalia as ardently as his father served the Duke of Braunschweig. He, too, had been fired with the hope of the new revolutionary ideas which followed in the train of Napoleon's victories. He had few illusions about the small kingdoms and duchies of feudal Germany, as later he was to have few illusions about Napoleon. In 1813, when he was still Landrat of Salzwedel, he protested once too often against the system of taxation introduced to pay for Napoleon's never-ending wars. The order for his arrest was signed by Marshal Davout, the most demanding and tyrannical of Napoleon's marshals, and Baron von Westphalen found himself a prisoner in the fortress of Gifhorn near Hanover. There he remained until the abdication of Napoleon in the following year. Two years later he was promoted by the Prussians and given the post of Government Councilor at Trier.

The boy who walked by the side of the old man was learning about history and the art of government at first hand. But Baron von Westphalen was not merely a political officer steeped in history; his cultivated, wide-ranging mind embraced vast areas of literature. He could recite Homer and Shakespeare by heart; he had a well-trained voice, and it pleased him to have an audience when he recited long passages from the poets. He was also interested in social questions, and one day he spoke at length about the doctrines of the Comte de Saint-Simon, who was the first to proclaim the necessity of a socialist form of government. The seed took root, and there is perhaps some irony in the fact that Karl first learned about socialism from the lips of an old aristocrat.

Homer, Shakespeare, Saint-Simon, Lessing, Goethe, Schiller, all these and many more the old baron could recite at length without pausing for a word, for he had a phenomenal memory. Those walks were an essential part of the boy's education, perhaps the most essential part. They broadened his mind, introduced him to the classics, and confirmed his ambition to dedicate his life to some high cause. It was the age of enlightenment, and the baron was an almost too perfect exemplar of that age. New ideas were coming to birth, the barriers were falling, all problems could be solved by careful inquiry and rationalization.

There were however some problems which could not be solved so easily. Although the baron was a liberal and enlightened man, inclined like Lessing, whom he worshiped, to grant a moral superiority to the Jews, he was not disposed to countenance the marriage of his daughter to a Jew. An invisible curtain separated the two houses. Heinrich Marx and his son Karl attended church regularly; they had received the sacrament of baptism; and they regarded themselves as Christians, although the townspeople still regarded them as Jews. Karl had fallen in love with Jenny. In his last year at school there were clandestine meetings arranged with the willing assistance of Sophie, who delighted in her role of go-between. Karl was sixteen, Jenny was twenty, but the disparity in their ages meant nothing to them. There was never a time when Marx was not aware of her presence. He was one year old when the family moved into the expensive house on the Simeonstrasse, next door to the house of Baron von Westphalen. For three or four years he had been in and out of her house, borrowing the baron's books, joining him on long walks, listening attentively to his opinions and his recitals of poetry. He knew the house as well as he knew his own.

During the summer they became secretly engaged. Only Sophie Marx, and perhaps Edgar von Westphalen, were let into the secret. But neither Jenny nor Karl ever doubted that they would get married.

For all the years of his life Karl regarded Jenny as his bride, the one woman who wholly belonged to him. Jenny was just as determined as Karl. If necessary, she would wait patiently for many years, overcoming all obstacles, until at last they were man and wife. Although Karl was something of a philanderer, and any young countess could turn his head, he never seriously thought about any other woman. He was sometimes unfaithful to her, and there were occasions when he treated her harshly, but he never ceased to love and cherish her.

Jenny was beauty, intelligence, aristocracy; the legends grew round her, and she walked through his imagination clothed in dreams. Nearly thirty years later, when visiting his birthplace, he wrote to her with fierce pride: "Every day I make a pilgrimage to the old Westphalen house, which interests me far more than any Roman antiquities because it reminds me of my happy youth and once concealed my dearest treasure. Besides, no day passes but I am asked on all sides about the quondam 'most beautiful girl in Trier' and 'the Queen of the ball.' It is damned pleasant for a man to learn that in the imagination of a whole city his wife is remembered as 'an enchanted princess.' "

But "the enchanted princess" was a woman with a sensible head on her shoulders, and she had not the slightest intention of marrying him until he had settled down to a career and was earning enough to support her. It was decided therefore that he would become a lawyer, and in time he would inherit his father's substantial practice. In the normal course of events he would spend a year at the University of Bonn, which was regarded as a kind of finishing school by many of the Trier students, and then go on to the University of Berlin to obtain his law degree. Then he would return to Trier, marry Jenny von Westphalen, and settle down to the tranquil existence of a lawyer dealing largely with legal questions pertaining to vineyards and the distribution of wine.

It was as though everything had been mapped out to the last detail and nothing of any consequence would ever happen to him. Step by step he would rise in the legal profession until he had attained the same position as his father. He would become a Justizrat and perhaps a town councilor. He would attend political clubs, father many children, and spend his weekends on his country estate. A calm and uneventful life opened out before him. No one could have guessed that he would drag Jenny through a life of turmoil and wild despair and revolutionary dreams.

THREE ESSAYS

Since Karl Marx's ideas were to have such a revolutionary impact on the world, it is important to watch them as they first rise to the surface. Three essays written when he was still a schoolboy permit us to watch the ideas while they are being formed.

These essays were written between August 10 and 16, 1835, during his final examination at the Friedrich Wilhelm Gymnasium. They were therefore written under pressure, in considerable haste, and without sufficient preparation. Nevertheless they show him moving easily among ideas and already in command of a markedly personal style. German piety demanded that these documents should be preserved, and so it happens that in addition to these essays we still have his extemporaneous translations into Latin, his translation of thirty-six lines of Sophocles, his answers to mathematical questions, and much more, together with the corrections, underscorings and comments of the professors. But it is especially in the three essays that he shows himself at his best. We see him wrestling with problems which were of deep concern to him, flexing his intellectual muscles and announcing ideas which sometimes remained with him to the end of his life. He enjoys his power over words, and sometimes he strikes off a memorable epigram.

Already he is writing with muscle and a sense of style, which bears considerable traces of his knowledge of Latin. He obviously enjoyed Tacitus with his hard metallic brilliance, and he clearly enjoyed the rhetoric of Cicero.

The three essays cover a wide area of human experience. One deals with a young man's choice of a profession, and involves a careful study of the purposes of life and man's proper duty to his fellow men. Given free will, a man must strive for a profession in which he can do the greatest good for the greatest number, and he gravely points out the dangers of alienation and self-deception. He writes with passion, as one who is deeply engrossed in the problem and determined to solve it. Another essay, written in Latin, is devoted to Augustus Caesar. It is curiously disorganized, and there are several false starts. He admires Augustus as a man, but cannot quite bring himself to admire the dictator. There are no hesitations in his essay on a young man's choice of a profession, but the essay on Augustus Caesar is alarmingly full of arguments which seem to be deliberately ambiguous. And so, between unreserved praise and a kind of horror at the excesses of the dictatorship, he hovers like a pendulum, moving hesitantly from one to the other.

In the third essay he discusses the nature of Christ and the nature of Communion. The subject was set by the examiner, but he embraces it with the passion of a believer, with skill, devotion and an appropriate reverence. Marx speaks as a Christian in love with the mystery of Christ. The essay was highly praised by his professor, who noted that although it was very thoughtful, fecund and powerful, he had omitted to discuss the real meaning of communion with Christ. He had in fact discussed everything except the essential.

Marx discusses such a broad variety of serious subjects in these essays that they reveal the pattern of his mind, which was to remain virtually unchanged throughout his life. On all these subjects—education, free will, duty, dictatorship, the Christian mystery, the purpose of life—he writes with high seriousness. He is concerned with ultimate meanings, and appears to have been happiest when he is describing things on the boundaries of thought. Except in the rather disjointed essay on Augustus Caesar, in which he simultaneously embraces and rejects dictatorship—in his later writings he did exactly the same—there is no sense of strain. He writes with passionate conviction and concentration, obviously delighting in his own powers of composition.

Because these essays reflect his preoccupations and innermost thoughts, they deserve to be studied at some length. They were not so much the hurried improvisations of the examination room as a welling-up of all his experiences and adventures among ideas. Soviet scholars tend to dismiss these essays as youthful excesses, but a careful reading shows that they are works of mature reflection, and many of the ideas he presented to his professors were to be enlarged and given greater resonance in later years.

Thoughts of a Young Man on Choosing a Profession

With his usual high seriousness Marx impatiently dismisses any idea of discussing particular professions. He is not writing an essay on whether it is better to be a doctor or a lawyer or a priest. He employs the word "profession" almost in the sense of a "professsion of faith." The task given to man is to choose a way of life which will best serve the human race. The theme is one of sacrifice: a man must offer himself up for the greater glory of humanity. Anything less than a supreme dedication to the welfare of humanity is not to be thought of, for God himself has imposed this duty on mankind.

So he begins the essay by asserting man's place in the divine economy and insisting that the choice of a profession involves terrible responsibilities. The choice is fraught with danger, and at the moment of choice a man may have signed his own death warrant. He writes:

> Nature has given to the animals alone a sphere of activity in which they move and quietly accomplish without ever striving to go beyond it or even suspecting that there is another sphere. God gave to man, too, a universal goal, so that man and mankind might be ennobled, and he gave man the power to seek out the means whereby he can achieve this end; and it is left to him to choose the standpoint of society which is most suitable to him and from which he can best raise himself and society.
>
> This choice is a great prerogative given to man above all other creatures, and at the same time it permits him to destroy his whole life, thwart all his own plans, and make himself unhappy.

In this characteristic fashion Marx discusses the choice of a profession in terms of vast abstractions. Free will, the commandments of God, the ennoblement of mankind are all implicated in the theme which will eventually encompass the whole field of human conduct. There is no attempt to chart out a modest corner of the field; he is concerned with the whole landscape.

In this landscape God walks with a measured tread, for He is wholly in command. "The Diety never leaves mortals without a guide," Marx says. "God speaks quietly but surely." Nevertheless the voice of God in men's hearts may be stifled by the importunate demands of the over-leaping imagination. Pride beckons, and ambitions may lead a man away from God and bring about his entire destruction. The danger of ambition, the way in which men are disposed to believe that their ambitions have God's sanction when in fact they are directed against God's will, is well described:

> Our imagination may be inflamed, our emotions may be stirred, phantoms may flit before our eyes, while we stumble eagerly toward the goal which, perhaps wrongly, we imagined that God Himself had set for us; and what we pressed so ardently to our breasts suddenly thrusts us away, and we see our whole existence reduced to nothingness.
>
> We must accordingly examine earnestly whether we really are full of enthusiasm for a calling, asking ourselves whether an inner voice sanctioned it, whether the inspiration is a delusion, and whether what we regarded as a divine summons was not really self-deception. But how can we recognize it when we ourselves are the source of the enthusiasm?
>
> Greatness shines out, its shining light stirs ambitions, and ambition quite easily calls forth inspiration; for if the fury of ambition takes hold of us, then reason may no longer be able to hold it in check, and then ambition hurls us wherever our turbulent instincts call us. A man can then no longer decide his position—only chance and illusion can decide for him.

Only a youth who had pondered the workings of ambition could have written these passages. That he was himself wildly ambitious, and that he was perfectly aware that his ambitions might be dictated by chance or illusion, and were dangerous and might lead him to disaster, would seem to be indicated by the passion behind the argument. Who, then, can advise? He answers that the parents have this power, for they have already experienced the rigors of fate and are in a position to warn their offspring about the snares and delusions of the world. Here Marx was evidently thinking of his father, the wise humanist who was so deeply aware of the world's burdens. But sometimes—and this is evidently Marx raising his voice of dissent in the long dialogue with the father—even the parents are often incapable of forming a just verdict, for "our relationships in society have already to some extent been formed before we are in a position to determine them."

These words, according to Franz Mehring, were like the first flash of summer lightning heralding the coming of Marxian socialism. If so, the idea was quickly dismissed, as Marx went on to declare that there was still another impediment to a man's determination to live the good life. This was a man's physical nature, which "threateningly bars the way." The claims of physical nature, by which he means *personality,* may not be mocked. They, too, determine the course of human conduct. Marx takes the whole man under review, and very seriously and solemnly discusses all the various impediments which can bring about a man's total destruction.

Sometimes, too, a man is confronted with the thought of the uselessness of all his endeavors, and there rises in him a sense of intolerable dissatisfaction and self-contempt, that "serpent which buries itself in the human heart and eternally eats it away, sucking the lifeblood, and mingling with it the poison of despair and hatred of mankind." A man may be filled with self-contempt, and still pass through life with the appearance of having accomplished great works. He receives the approbation of his fellow men, while suffering the torments of the damned.

Damnation, indeed, is never very far from Marx's thoughts. God works in mysterious ways; His voice is not always heard above the clamor of ambitions; and the pitfalls are everywhere. There remains the way of humble service to mankind, which God and history alike have always praised. On this theme Marx writes his most impassioned pages, finding dignity in humility and strength in service. With youthful idealism he announces the perfectibility of man through submission to the common good. Then at last all the traps and pitfalls vanish, for man is then acting in accordance with the will of God:

> The chief directing force which influences us toward a choice of profession is the well-being of mankind, our own fulfillment. One should not presume to let these two things confront one another in deadly combat; one must not destroy the other. The nature of man is such that he cannot accomplish its ultimate aim unless he works for the welfare of the world.
>
> If he acts only for himself he can perhaps become a great scientist, a great sage, an excellent poet, but he can never become a man who is truly perfect and great.
>
> History regards as great men only those who have ennobled themselves for the common good. Experience demonstrates that the happiest are those who make most men happy. Religion itself teaches us that the ideal Being, after whom all strive, sacrificed himself for humanity, and who would dare to oppose such a verdict?

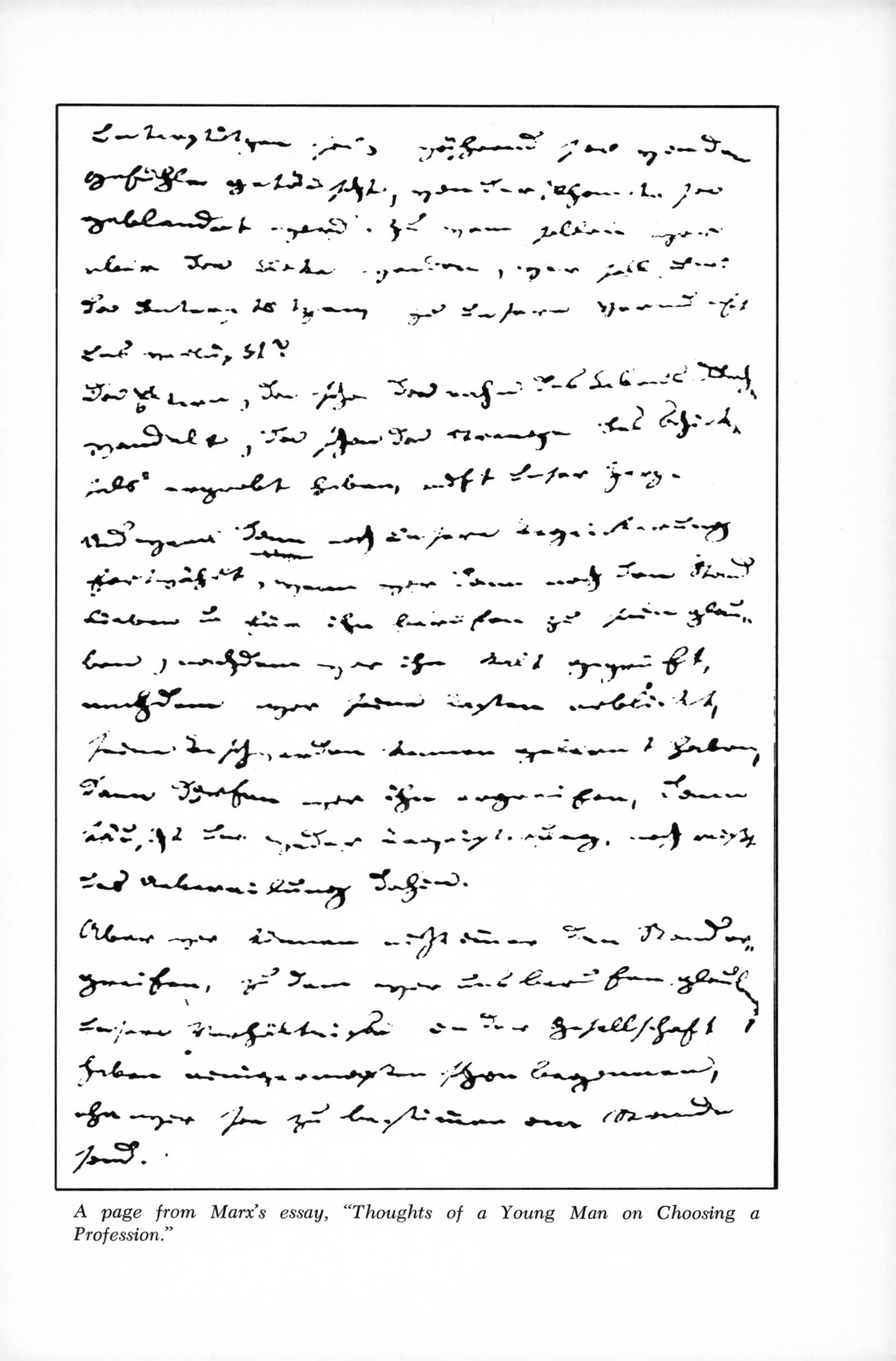

A page from Marx's essay, "Thoughts of a Young Man on Choosing a Profession."

> If we have chosen a position in life in which we can best work for humanity, we shall not bend under its burdens, because this is a sacrifice made for all. Then it is no poor, narrow, egotistical joy which we experience, but our happiness will belong to millions, our deeds will live on silently and effectively through the ages; and our ashes will be watered with the gleaming tears of noble men.

In this way Marx brings his essay to an end, with a paean of triumph, a salute to the good man whose name endures forever. Hugo Wyttenbach commended the essay for the richness of its thought and the organized development of the ideas, while lamenting the "exaggerated search after unfamiliar and picturesque expressions," and the lack of "the necessary clarity, definition and accuracy." Marx might have answered that he was walking in a shadowy landscape, where clarity and definition were beyond his reach. There is the sense of total involvement. Marx was not playing, and meant exactly what he said. If he had to use exaggerated and picturesque expressions, this was only because there is no accepted vocabulary when a man attempts to define the undefinable. He was attempting to penetrate a mystery, and he was doing it with the only words he knew.

"The Thoughts of a Young Man on Choosing a Profession" shows the thrust of a powerful mind. He was thinking his own thoughts about man's proper duty to the world and to God, and saying them in his own way. In a few months God would vanish from his world, leaving him more alienated than ever, but that youthful idealism would remain. We shall not understand Marx unless we realize that when he became a revolutionary, he was carrying out the injunctions of his youthful essay, for he felt that he was choosing the position in life in which he would best serve mankind.

Should the Principate of Augustus Caesar Be Numbered among the Happier Ages of the Roman Republic?

Marx's second essay, which was composed in Latin, deals with problems which have very little interest for modern historians, who are more concerned with weighing facts than attempting to weigh abstractions. There are no scales for weighing happiness, and historical justice is not concerned to judge the satisfactions of a vanished age.

But in Marx's time men were continually pondering the lessons to be derived from Roman history. Schoolboys read Roman history until they were more familiar with it than with the history of their own country. Roman thought, Roman principles of conduct, Roman conceptions of government still possessed a widespread influence over men's minds. In an age when everyone read Plutarch, debates on the relative happiness of different ages of Roman history were commonplace.

Marx opens his essay by offering to cite the opinions of ancient writers concerning the Augustan age, which he will also compare with other ages of antiquity. In fact the promise was never carried out, and he quickly establishes his own rather ambivalent position. Like many others before him, he finds himself caught on the horns of a dilemma. Should he praise the Romans of the time of the Carthaginian wars, who were little more than barbarians with a fondness for virtue and agriculture, or should he praise the age of Augustus, a consummate patron of the arts, of learning, and of luxury? In the end he comes out on the side of Augustus, but with reservations. He wrote:

> His reign was distinguished by its clemency, for the Romans, even when all their freedom and all semblance of freedom had disappeared, still thought they were governing themselves in spite of the fact that the Emperor had the power to alter customs and laws, and all the offices formerly held by the tribunes of the people were now in the hands of one man. They failed to see that the Emperor, under another name, was enjoying the honors formerly granted only to the tribunes, and their freedom had been stolen from them. This is indeed a great proof of clemency, when the citizens cannot discern who is the ruler, or whether they themselves rule or are ruled.

In the last sentence he is clearly ironical, but as he warms to the theme, the irony tends to vanish and the ambiguity is resolved in the contemplation of the Augustan peace. The wars against Germany brought peace to the frontiers in the north, but at the price of fearful massacres. The German tribes acquitted themselves well, and like a good nationalist Marx praised them for conquering the Roman legions by "treachery, ambush and courage," although Augustus finally subdued them by employing the same weapons. Marx is inclined to view the defeat of the German tribes as the inevitable price to be paid for the advance of civilization, but he has no illusions about the civilizing mission of the Romans. The Augustan age was wanting in many respects. Character, freedom and manhood were diminished or wholly demolished, and greed, riotous living, and excesses were the rule.

In later years Marx was sometimes attacked for his German nationalism, which was never far below the surface. He had a deep feeling for German culture, and even for the civilizing mission of the German people. He regarded himself as an internationalist, rising above the narrow temptations of nationalism, and the more he insisted on his internationalism the more nationalist he became. In his eyes the "treachery, ambush and courage" of the German tribes showed that they possessed admirable qualities.

Again and again in the essay Marx returns to contemplate the grandeurs and miseries of the Augustan age. He evidently cannot make up his mind whether the grandeurs exceeded the miseries. Augustus improved the machinery of government and put an end to factional quarrels at the price of reducing the people to slavery and effeminacy. Marx seemed to feel that the logic of history demanded this sacrifice, and that there was no alternative:

> The genius of Augustus and the institutions and laws fashioned by the men of his choosing admirably succeeded in improving the state, which was in a bad way. As a result the confusion which arose out of the civil wars was completely swept away.
>
> By way of example we may observe that Augustus purged the Senate, which very corrupt men had entered, of the last vestiges of crime, and he removed from the Senate many men whose characters were most hateful to his eyes, at the same time appointing men who were outstanding in integrity and ability.
>
> In the reign of Augustus men of outstanding reputation for character and wisdom flourished in the government. Who can name among contemporaries men greater than Maecenas or Agrippa? In this we see the very genius of the Emperor, although it is never displayed by any cloak of pretense nor, as we have said, by any abuse of power. On the contrary he appears to conceal his invisible power under a very mild appearance, and if the state had been just as it was before the Punic Wars, then his attitude would have been most wonderfully adapted to that age, because it aroused minds to great achievements and rendered men objects of dread to their enemies. The state, as Augustus created it, seems to me to have been at the very least admirably adapted to the times, for although the people's spirits were weakened, and they had lost the simplicity of their customs, and although the power of the state was vastly increased, nevertheless the Emperor rather than a free republic was able to give liberty to the people.

Marx's final verdict on the Augustan age was therefore a favorable one, for the reservations tended to vanish the more he contemplated them. The free republic failed to give liberty to the people; it was left to a dictator to grant the "liberty" the people needed. Marx knew that Augustus had merely constructed a façade of liberty, and that in fact the people were entirely at the mercy of the dictator. Nevertheless he seemed to choose dictatorship over any other form of government as leading to the greatest happiness.

Marx's attitude toward dictatorship did not change; he was one of those who regard dictatorship calmly, as a necessary stage in human development. In time he would proclaim the necessity of the dictatorship of the proletariat, and this too would receive historical justification.

But it would not be an "invisible power under a very mild appearance."

The examiners commended Marx for his learning, and noted that toward the end of the essay there were more than the permissible number of errors in Latin. They also noted his "horrible handwriting."

Having discussed the necessity of dictatorship in his second essay, he went on to discuss the necessity of Christ in the third.

On the Union of the Faithful with Christ according to John XV, 1–14, Described in Its Ground and Essence, in Its Unconditional Necessity and in Its Effects.

Characteristically Marx begins the essay with an appeal to history, to the immutable laws written with history's iron pen (*"mit eisernem Griffel"*). Among these laws he singles out two which in his view possess paramount importance: first, even the greatest epochs of history, the ages of triumphant accomplishment, contain within themselves the seeds of corruption; secondly, pagan cultures suffer from the sense of alienation and restlessness, always in danger of provoking the anger of the gods and deeply aware of their own insufficiency and inadequacy. The tragedy of man is his haunting realization that he can never reach fulfillment alone, but needs the presence of a higher Being to give meaning and purpose to his life. Therefore he gives himself to Christ.

For Marx it is not only that corruption and alienation are perennial facts of history, but they are present in mankind to an intolerable and terrifying degree. However much men strive, they know themselves to be incapable of achieving their purpose without divine help. So he depicts man as a creature at the mercy of his vices, saved only by the mercy of God:

> The alluring voice of sin is heard above the enthusiasm for virtue, and sin mocks at us as soon as life allows us to feel its full power, and the lower striving after earthly goods frustrates the effort toward knowledge, and the knowledge for truth is extinguished through the sweetly flattering power of the lie, and so man stands there, the unique being in nature, whose purpose is not fulfilled—the only member of the whole of creation who is not worthy of the God who created him. But the good Creator cannot hate his own work. He wishes Man to raise himself and sent His own Son and allows us to be called through Him:
>
> Now ye are clean through the word which I have spoken unto you. (John XV, 3)
>
> Abide in me, and I in you. (John XV, 4)

As he describes the workings of the divine economy, Marx is clearly following the Protestant evangelical tradition, but the passion is his own, and he will employ the same cadences, the same method of reasoning, the same structural patterns in passages written many years later. He begins with a catalogue of human vices and frustrations, and then quite suddenly the catalogue gives way to the picture of man standing alone under the threatening sky, "the only member of the whole of creation who is not worthy of the God who created him." Such is the preliminary argument. The counterargument is provided by the good Creator, who "cannot hate his own work" and therefore sends His own Son to raise men out of their sinfulness and guilt. With the coming of Christ thesis and antithesis are reconciled in the ultimate synthesis, the union of man with God.

In this dialectical way, with quite extraordinary self-assurance, Marx declares his faith in a living God who alone has the power to bring salvation to mankind. Without God men are helpless; with God they become divine. The ultimate proof of this assertion is found in the words of Christ Himself in the beautiful Parable of the Vine and the Branches.

As Marx proceeds with the argument, we become aware that he is speaking about matters which deeply concern him. What especially concerns him is rejection from the hands of God, and the word "rejection" (*die Verwerflichkeit*) is constantly repeated. He is under no illusions about the nature of man's rejection, for he regards it as the most terrible of all the afflictions imposed on mankind. The angel stands at the gates with heavenly sword, and men walk in the outer darkness in an alien and merciless world; only with God's mercy can men enter into the light again. So he argues that the need for union is absolute, and there is no necessity to look beyond the absolute commandment, because there can be no higher law. Not only the human heart, but human reason and intelligence and history itself proclaim the law:

> Our heart, reason, intelligence, history all summon us with loud and convincing voice to the knowledge that union with Him is absolutely necessary, that without Him we would be unable to fulfill our purpose, that without Him we would be rejected by God, and that only He can redeem us.

The theme of rejection is explored on many levels, but there is one salvation: the willing surrender to God's mercy. Rejection takes many forms, salvation has only one form; only by union with Christ can the blind and erring soul of man reach its fulfillment. At such a moment the soul is filled with the most ardent gratitude and discovers in surrender to God the peace it has always desired.

In later writings, especially in the philosophical manuscripts written nine years later, Marx returned again and again to the theme of man's rejection from the world of men. He believed that the primary need of man was to overcome his separateness, his aloneness, and to become united with others; and the specter of the alienated man, lost in a world which regarded him with indifference, paying no attention to his legitimate desires, transforming him into a cipher, tormented him continually. Many of his most important writings are elaborations on the theme of alienation.

But in the springtime of his life he was aware that there was at least one pathway which led out of the world of alienation into a world of reconciliation. By loving God, he wrote, men find themselves turning toward their brothers and sacrificing themselves for their brothers. Instead of alienation there is the loving bondage of service and sacrifice:

> Thus union with Christ consists in the deepest, most living communion with Him, so that we have Him before our eyes and in our hearts, and while we are penetrated with the highest love toward Him, we turn our hearts at the same time toward our brothers, who are inwardly bound to us and for whom He gave Himself up as a sacrifice.
>
> This love for Christ is not fruitless, it fills us not only with the purest adoration and respect for Him, but also acts in such a way that we obey His commandments and at the same time sacrifice ourselves for others, because we are virtuous, but virtuous only for love of Him.

Virtuous only for love of Him. . . . In this way Marx resolves the theme of virtue by defining it in both divine and human terms, simultaneously bringing divinity down to earth and raising humanity to the level of the divine. Here at last history's iron pen loses all meaning, for virtue dissolves the accidents of history and brings men into the presence of God.

According to Marx, Christian virtue, being free of all earthly attachments, acts as God's agent in the redemption of mankind. By virtue men become divine, while in no way losing their humanity, and in fact virtue makes them only more human, more loving, and more understanding.

So he reaches the peroration where all these themes are triumphantly brought together in a profession of Christian faith written with grave solemnity and sincerity:

> Thus union with Christ contributes to an inner uplifting, consolation in sorrow, a quiet confidence, and a heart which is open to love for mankind and for all noble and great men, not out of ambition or love of fame, but through Christ. Thus union with Christ produces a joyfulness which the Epicureans sought in vain in their frivolous philosophy, their deepest thinkers striving to acquire it in the most hidden depths of knowledge—that joyfulness which is known only to the free childlike soul in the knowledge of Christ and of God through Him, who has raised us up into a higher and more beautiful life.

Quite understandably Soviet scholars have paid little attention to this devotional essay filled with an ardent faith in Christ. The essay however cannot be wished away. It is too urgent, too carefully thought out to be dismissed merely as a contrived performance for the benefit of Christian examiners. Marx was a Christian, and when he turned against Christianity he brought to his ideas of social justice the same passion for atonement and the same horror of alienation which characterize this essay. For him there was always the Garden of Eden, the angel with the flaming sword, and the luckless Adam and Eve walking into their eternal exile.

THE STRUGGLE WITH THE FATHER

On October 15, 1835, at four o'clock in the morning, while Halley's comet shone in the sky, Karl Marx left Trier by river boat for Bonn. His father, mother, sisters, and his seven-year-old brother Eduard accompanied him to the landing stage. In the darkness they could make out the shape of the small yacht, which was called "express," because it would reach Koblenz, at the confluence of the Moselle and the Rhine, in fifteen and a half hours. On the following day he would take the much faster steamboat down the Rhine to Bonn. On the third day, a Saturday, he would enter his name in the books of the university as a student in the faculty of law. Recently Marx had felt curiously estranged from his family; as the years passed, he would become more and more estranged. The long struggle with his father was about to begin.

The University of Bonn was a very small university with about seven hundred students, distinguished by a brilliant faculty. August Wilhelm von Schlegel, the great translator of Shakespeare and of the classics of seven or eight other languages, was living out his long retirement as professor of literature, giving courses on Homer and the elegies of Propertius. Marx took Schlegel's courses, and he also attended the courses on the history of art given by Eduard d'Alton and on the mythology of the Greeks and Romans given by Friedrich Gottlieb Welcker. Altogether he attended six courses in the long winter semester and four in the summer semester. Schlegel and d'Alton reported that he was "industrious and attentive," while Welcker wrote that he was "exceedingly industrious and attentive," suggesting that he was enjoying mythology more than any other subject. He was also taking courses in law, and developing a considerable knowledge of its finer points. He seemed to be reconciled to becoming a lawyer.

While attending classes, he was also enjoying himself. Students from Trier had their own tavern club, at which they discussed all the important matters of the day and rejoiced in phenomenal drinking bouts. There was also a poetry club, which was not however as innocuous as the name suggested. Karl's father was delighted when he learned that his son had become a full-fledged member of the club, imagining that the students spent their time practicing the art of poetry. In fact, they were practicing the art of revolution. All over Germany there had sprung up revolutionary clubs, loosely affiliated to one another, with secret signs and passwords, and there were constant secret communications between the members. The police were alarmed, and attempts were made to infiltrate the clubs with spies and *agents provocateurs*. During the previous year they had succeeded in infiltrating the poetry club of the University of Bonn, only to learn that the rules and articles of association were being well kept with an eye to discovery by the police. They were couched in the language of poetic rhetoric and were chiefly concerned with describing the benefits which would accrue to poets working together. Nevertheless these poetry clubs were revolutionary societies with tentative and amateurish programs, and Marx soon became one of the leading members. The poetry club at the University of Bonn was the first of the many conspiratorial organizations he belonged to.

His letters home have perished, but a number of letters written by his father have survived. It is clear that Heinrich Marx was less than satisfied with his son's behavior at the university. The first letter, written from Trier on November 8, was an exasperated reminder that not a single letter had been received from Bonn although three weeks had passed since he had left the paternal roof. The long silence was driving his mother to despair. "Your mother does not know I am writing this, for I have no intention of increasing her anxiety," he wrote. Marx finally wrote home, enclosing a poem, which his father found completely incomprehensible, and there appears to have been a long account of his relationship with an older man, perhaps a professor, for Heinrich Marx permitted himself a long paragraph on the beauty and nobility of such friendships "understood in the classical sense." He rejoiced that his son had a deep friendship with an older man, and at the same time he felt it necessary to warn him against certain unspecified dangers in such a relationship. "I have not the least doubt that you remain morally pure," Heinrich Marx wrote, and he earnestly reminded his son that the great safeguard for leading a moral life was a belief in God. "On this subject, as you know, I am nothing less than fanatical," he went on, adding that Newton, Locke and Leibnitz had also believed in God. It was a long letter by a dispirited man who already seemed to fear the worst, and there was a kindly postscript from his mother: "Live well my dear beloved Carl be worthy and good and have God and your parents always before your eyes adieu your loving Mother Henriette Marx."

It soon appeared that Marx was in no mood to be good. He was sowing his wild oats, spending large sums of money, writing reams of incomprehensible poetry, and drinking hard. He was warned to put order into his life, and there are ominous appeals to his honor and reminders on the necessity of purity. Heinrich Marx derived very little pleasure from the fact that his son was developing into a poet, and there was some alarming evidence that he was spending far more money than the family could afford. The father was at his wits' end, and he warned that there must be no more high living.

The trouble was that Marx had very little conception of the value of money and he was determined to cut a fine figure among the students at the university. There were many young and wealthy aristocrats attending the university, and they set the pace. By March 1836 he was in debt, and had to be bailed out. In the same month he became one of the five presidents of the tavern club of the students from Trier, a post which demanded that he pay out large sums of money on drinking feasts. About the same time the Trier tavern club became the butt of the young aristocrats who formed the Borussia Korps, and there was some desultory fighting between them, especially in the villages around Bonn. The plebeians would be "jumped" by the aristocrats, manhandled, made to kneel and plead for mercy, and then sent on their way with a warning to respect the aristocracy at all times. Marx appears to have been one of those who were manhandled, and he acquired a pistol as the best means of defending himself. In April he visited Cologne, apparently as an agent of the revolutionary poetry club, and during a police search the pistol was found on him. A pistol being "a forbidden weapon," as distinguished from swords and daggers, which were permissible, he was in danger of arrest and severe punishment. There survives a letter written by Heinrich Marx to a judge in Cologne, pleading as one father to another for leniency for his son. It must have been a very difficult letter to write, but it accomplished its purpose. Prussian officials, citing "higher competence" —no doubt, the intervention of the judge in Cologne—took no further action, although the matter was reported to the officials at the University of Bonn.

Meanwhile the class war between the aristocratic Borussia Korps and the Trier tavern club continued, and there were more and more "incidents" between them. The plebeians were sometimes challenged to duels, and in June Marx fought a duel with one of those young aristocrats. He knew his life was at stake. Several duels among the university students had ended fatally. He was lucky, for he received only a gash over his left eye. Just before fighting the duel he appears to have written a long rambling letter to his father in which he discussed life, death, dueling and philosophy in a manner as incomprehensible as the poems he was regularly sending back to Trier. Heinrich Marx was puzzled and wrote back:

> What is all this mingling of dueling and philosophy? Men fight duels out of respect, and also out of fear of public opinion. And what public opinion? Not always the best, far from it!!! There is so little consistency anywhere among mankind. Do not let this inclination—I would rather say this mania—take root. You might after all end by robbing yourself and your parents of their most beautiful hopes. I believe that a reasonable man would scarcely treat such matters except in a serious way, *tout en imposant.*

The French words were significant, for they mean "while still commanding respect," and they provide a brief summary of the essential beliefs of Heinrich Marx. He believed that it was the duty of man to command respect through his moral behavior and intellectual attainments, not by displays of passion. He knew only too well that his son was at the mercy of dangerous passions. The university authorities also knew it, for they recorded that he was arrested and thrown into the university jail for one day "for disturbing the peace at night with noise and drunkenness." It was not regarded as a very serious offense, and they were more troubled by the strange affair of "the forbidden weapon" which was found on him in Cologne. A considerable dossier, now preserved in the archives of the University of Bonn, deals with this affair, and for some weeks, while official documents were exchanged between Bonn, Cologne and Berlin, Marx's fate trembled in the balance.

Marx spent only two semesters at the University of Bonn. It was decided that he should pursue his studies at the University of Berlin, where the standards were higher and the young aristocrats were less in evidence. When he looked back on his days in Bonn, he would remember chiefly his presidency of the Trier tavern club and the ferocious engagements with the Borussia Korps, the lectures of Schlegel and d'Alton, and the desperate financial straits in which he sometimes found himself. He had been arrested for riotous behavior, fought a duel, waged war against the aristocrats, and been found in possession of a pistol. The pattern of his life was beginning to emerge.

There exists a portrait of him made about this time. It is a very small portrait, for he appears as one of about thirty members of the Trier tavern club disporting themselves outside the White Horse Inn at Godesberg. Such group portraits were common, and the artist usually made an effort to sketch the features of the club members as accurately as possible. Unfortunately Marx is shown in the background—he appears to have been included in the group portrait at the last moment—and all that can be seen is a jowled young man with beetling brows and a thick mane of hair. There is the suggestion of a wispy beard, but no mustache. On the evidence of this tiny portrait Marx's followers have attempted to reconstruct his youthful features, disregarding the jowls and emphasizing the beetling brows and the hair. These attempts to discover the beardless Marx are not very satisfactory. No other portrait of him in his youth survives.

In July 1836 Heinrich Marx drew up an official statement in which he declared that it was not only his wish, but his express desire, that his son should enter the University of Berlin. The authorities at the University of Bonn appear to have been relieved. They gave him a clean bill of health, noted that he had shown diligence in his studies, mentioned briefly the unfortunate arrest for riotous behavior and the incident of the pistol, "which is still under advisement," and found nothing detrimental "in his moral and economic aspects." Marx went off to begin a new life in Berlin.

Bonn had been one of the outposts of the German intelligence, a small frontier town dreaming its life away on the banks of the Rhine. Berlin was the capital of Prussia, already a teeming metropolis with 300,000 inhabitants. It was the hub of the wheel, the center where power was generated and ideas flowed out across the whole of Germany. Here, until recently, Hegel had delivered those lectures which captivated the intellectuals and provided them with philosophical ammunition for a century.

Bonn was a place where a young man might luxuriate in his own intelligence; in Berlin he would be compelled to come to terms with the most formidable intellects of his time.

There was a long-standing tradition at Berlin University that students should give themselves up to intense and unremitting work, as though scholarship were its own reward and books were the only proper companions of a man's life. A famous letter written by Ludwig Feuerbach to his father twelve years earlier describes students who lived like monks, in calm and silence. Duels and drinking bouts were not for them, and they could not be tempted out of their studies by women. "This university is a temple of study," Feuerbach wrote, "and all the others are no more than coffeehouses."

The leading figures at Berlin University were Eduard Gans, who had inherited the mantle of Hegel, and Friedrich Karl Savigny, who was the founder of a famous school of historical jurisprudence. Gans was small and fat, with curly hair; he exuded optimism; and he was concerned that the human spirit should be freed from its fetters. Savigny placed the law above everything. He was a man with lean, narrow, puritanical features and long, lank hair. Between Gans and Savigny there was being fought a stubborn war for the soul of German youth. Marx attended their classes, and both professors found him an apt pupil.

Marx well knew what was demanded of him: unremitting toil, a minimum of outside interests, the determination to succeed. At first his intention seems to have been to become a model student; he attended classes regularly; he read voluminously. But there were hints of trouble to come. He had at last told his family about the secret engagement to Jenny von Westphalen, and his letters home were filled with exalted outpourings on the nature of love. Heinrich Marx recognized the danger signals and warned him that these wild exaggerations might very well have the effect of bringing an end to the engagement. It was not by romantic rhapsodies that he could hope to retain her affections. What was needed was the firm resolve to study and to achieve the respect of one's fellow men. Jenny herself appears to have been frightened by his excessive romanticism, and Heinrich Marx did his best to put her at ease. He wrote to his son on December 28, 1836:

> I have spoken to J. and had hoped to set her fears completely at rest. I did my best, but I did not entirely succeed in reassuring her. She does not yet know how her parents will accept the engagement. The opinions of her relatives and of the world are also not negligible factors. What I am afraid of

> is your sensitivity, which is not always calculated to give you a balanced view, and I leave to you the task of judging the situation. If I had the strength to offer calm and protection to this noble being by the force of my intervention, then no sacrifice would be too great. Unfortunately I am weak in this respect.
>
> She offers you an incalculable sacrifice and demonstrates a self-renunciation which can be understood fully only by cold reason. Woe to you, if you should ever for a moment forget this! You alone must now make the effective steps. You must give her the assurance that in spite of your youth you are a man who deserves the respect of all men and will conquer it with storming strides.

Heinrich Marx seems to have been affected by his son's romanticism. The "storming strides"—*Sturmschritte*—suggested a young and relentless giant who was in no danger of forgoing the world's applause. The father was the first to submit to the legend which the son was busily creating around himself. His sister Sophie, who adored him, burst into tears when he chided her in his letters for not sending him news of his beloved. "I dream and think only of you," she wrote, and went on to tell him how Jenny was constantly visiting the house and weeping over the poems he had written for her.

The family was puzzled and disturbed; he had become a foreigner to them, someone whose letters filled them with apprehension and alarm. Jenny, too, was alarmed and gave way to "involuntary fears and presentiments." In despair, in letter after letter, Heinrich Marx could only hold high the conventional banners of morality and self-respect: hard work, respect for others, obedience to his professors. On the rare occasions when Marx took the trouble to reply, he succeeded only in infuriating his father and once more there would be a stern moralizing letter, in which all the old liberal clichés were repeated. They had reached an impasse. Henceforward there was very little real communication between them.

The reasons for the impasse were not at all complicated: Marx had grown out of his family. He wrote to them when he pleased, at rare intervals, usually to demand money. Their chief service was to keep an eye on Jenny and to report to him faithfully about her affairs. He had discovered two new worlds, which together absorbed all his energy. They were the world of literature—he was writing poems and philosophical essays in uncontrollable spate—and the world of the impassioned university students who debated all night and worked at their studies all day. He was drinking heavily and living the bohemian life, and his letters to his parents seem to have been written in a highly romantic manner in an alcoholic haze. Heinrich Marx wondered whether sobriety was one of his virtues.

Marx had been sending his poems home, and Heinrich Marx began to wonder whether his son's gifts might not be put to better use. It occurred to him that a long epic written on a contemporary subject might bring him to public attention, and he offered some advice on the kind of poem he had in mind:

> It should be an honorable one for Prussia, and should perhaps include an important role for the genius of the Monarchy, and this might be expressed through the spirit of the very noble Queen Louise.*
>
> You might choose the moment of the great battle at Belle Alliance—Waterloo. There was terrible danger—not only for the Prussians, for their monarchs, but for all of Germany etc., etc. The Prussians delivered themselves of a great blow—or perhaps it could take the form of an ode on a large scale, or anything you like, for you understand these things better than I.
>
> It would not be too difficult a task. The important thing is to draw a large picture in a small compass—to describe the great moment joyfully and cleverly. Such an ode, if it were worked out in a patriotic way, full of feeling, and in a German spirit, would be enough to make you famous and establish your name.

It was not, however, by writing odes in honor of Queen Louise that Marx was to achieve fame. Marx was writing, or had written, a tragic drama, which was intended to rival *Faust,* and he had begun work on some philosophical essays. He was gradually coming under the influence of Hegel, and spending whole nights and days reading without intermission, his brain on fire with the new ideas pouring into it. The inevitable result was that he fell ill, and on the advice of a doctor he abandoned Berlin and went to live in the nearby fishing village of Stralau, on the right bank of the river Spree. It was a very small village, no more than a dozen huts, but the country air and the exercise did him good. "It never occurred to me," he wrote later in the year, "that from being an anemic weakling I would develop into a man with a strong and robust body." But so it was; he abandoned his nightlong reading, lived simply, walked every day from Stralau to the university, which was on the other side of Berlin, and back again. He kept regular hours and ate at regular intervals. He had been in grave danger of a nervous breakdown, and he had saved himself just in time. He stayed in Stralau from April 1837 to

* Queen Louise, the wife of King Frederick William III of Prussia, was one of the authentic heroines of the war between Prussia and Napoleon. She upheld her husband's morale at the worst moments of the war.

the autumn, and then returned to his students' lodging house on the Jakobstrasse near the university.

One day, as winter came down on Berlin, he wrote a long detailed letter on his studies and the ideas burgeoning in his brain. The letter was addressed to his father, but it was clearly written under some inner compulsion to satisfy himself that his interminable wrestling with his angels was bearing fruit. He wrote for himself, to see where he had come to. He was not in the least interested in his relations with his father or his family, but only in his ideas, his attitude to the world, his own intellectual achievements. This letter, which covers twelve closely printed pages in the German edition of his early writings, was essentially an expression of his desperate desire to understand the workings of his own mind, and was written under great strain in a mood of ecstatic self-surrender. He began by declaring that he had reached one of those critical moments in life when it is necessary to take stock of oneself, and he therefore proposed to draw up an intellectual inventory of all he had thought during the past year, beginning with the day when he left Trier and set out for Berlin. He wrote:

> When I left you, a new world had opened out before me, the world of love, which began by being a love deprived of all hope and full of frenzied yearnings. Even the journey to Berlin, which would otherwise have delighted me in the highest degree, incited me to the contemplation of nature and inflamed me with the joy of life, left me cold, and in fact depressed me profoundly, for the rocks I saw were no less angular and abrupt than the sentiments of my soul, and the broad cities were no more animated than my blood, and the meals in the inns were not more overloaded or indigestible than the contents of my imagination, and finally art was not so beautiful as Jenny.
>
> When I came to Berlin, I broke all existing ties, made very few visits, and those reluctantly, and sought to drown myself in science and art.
>
> In that state of mind it was inevitable that lyric poetry should be my chief interest, at any rate the most agreeable and the most obvious, but in view of my position and my previous development this was the purest idealism on my part. My love, which equally belonged to the far distance, became my heaven, my art. Everything real grows vague, and all that is vague lacks boundaries, lays siege on the present, produces vast and shapeless expressions of feeling, unnatural, begotten of the moon, the complete opposite of what is and what ought to be, rhetorical reflections instead of poetic ideas, and yet there is perhaps a certain warmth of sentiment and a wrestling with rhythm in the three books of poems I sent to Jenny. The whole extent of a longing which sees no frontiers, assumes multifarious forms, and finds "breadth" in "poetizing."
>
> But poetry could and must only be a casual companion. I had to study jurisprudence, but above all I felt an urgent need to wrestle with philosophy.

> The two were so closely interconnected that I read Heineccius, Thibaut and the sources quite uncritically, more or less like a schoolboy, translating for example the first two books of the *Pandects* into German, and I also attempted while studying law to work out a philosophy of law. In the preface I stated some metaphysical propositions, and in this ill-starred opus carried on the discussion down to the topic of international law—a work of nearly three hundred sheets.

Marx probably meant three hundred pages, for a sheet was a technical term meaning sixteen printed pages. What is certain is that he was engaged in writing at vast length on the subjects that interested him. Having abandoned his philosophy of law, he set out to write an entire metaphysics, until this in turn was abandoned. Meanwhile he was copying out lengthy extracts from Lessing's *Laokoön,* Winckelmann's *History of Art,* and a history of Germany, with his own precise and detailed comments; he was learning English and Italian, "but I have as yet made no progress"; and he was also translating Tacitus' *Germania* and Ovid's *Tristia.* At the end of the first semester he had tried his hand at a novel and a poetic tragedy. In this way, by overworking, he had reduced himself to such a state of ill-health that it became necessary to leave Berlin, and so he went off to the nearby village of Stralau. "I had neglected nature, art, and the world, and I had alienated my friends," he wrote to his father.

He regarded the months spent at Stralau as the real turning point in his life. "A curtain had fallen, my holy of holies had been shattered, and it was necessary to find new gods to put in their place." The new gods did not at once reveal themselves. He wrote *Cleanthes, or the Starting Point and the Necessary Progress of Philosophy,* in which art and science were brought together, as he believed, in an indissoluble union, and went on to write a philosophico-dialectical essay on the nature of the Godhead seen under the aspects of religion, nature and history. This last work pleased him no more than the others, and he spent some days pacing the garden overlooking the river Spree, "which cleanses the soul and dilutes tea," in a mood of utter vexation, unable to think at all, prepared to abandon philosophical inquiry altogether. At last he returned to Berlin for another prolonged immersion among books. The days at Stralau had not been unproductive. There had emerged a new respect for Hegel, though he continued to dislike his "grotesque craggy music," that rough, contorted, deliberately obscure language in which Hegel clothed and concealed his ideas. Already he was hinting that Hegel was profoundly wrong, and the entire Hegelian system would have to be turned upside down. "I proceeded to seek for the idea in the real itself," he wrote. "If in earlier days the gods had dwelt above the earth, they had now become its center."

All his life Marx was addicted to massive reading on a wide-ranging scale. He reported to his father that he had read books on the Franconian kings, on papal letters, on the artistic inclinations of wild animals, on German law, and on the meaning of words. It was all grist to his mill. Somewhere, in one of these innumerable works, he would find the key which turned the lock of the universe.

So he wrote, like a man tortured by incessant frustrations, having abandoned poetry only to learn that all theory was gray and only life was green. The long letter to his father was his *mea culpa,* his confession, his self-advertisement. "My heart," he said, "must often have seemed to you to have gone astray when the travail of my spirit was depriving it of the power of utterance," but while he apologized for his illegible handwriting and terrible style, he made no apologies for sending his father a letter which would inevitably exasperate him. He finished the letter at about four o'clock on the morning of November 10, 1837, when the candle had gone out and he could no longer see what he had written. Almost the last words were: "A deep unrest has mastered me, and I shall not be able to lay the specters that haunt me until I am in your dear presence."

Marx appears to have left this letter on his desk for some days, for a letter written by Heinrich Marx a week later makes no mention of it. Heinrich Marx was disturbed because his son had not troubled to send him a new address—"after all, an address is the first requirement for any correspondence"—and in fact he had not troubled to write any answers to the many questions addressed to him. Heinrich Marx angrily announced that "one does not possess a palace and millions and carriages without hard work and care." He had given his son everything that a fond father could conceivably give to a son, and it was becoming increasingly clear that the son was totally indifferent to the sacrifices made by the family. "Have you not laughed at everything from the time you were in the cradle? Have you not been wonderfully endowed by nature? Have not your parents surrounded you with their lavish love?" They were the usual recriminations, but this time they were uttered with an unfamiliar sharpness. Heinrich Marx was a sick man with only a few more months to live, and his despair over his son's behavior is clearly visible. It needed only another exhibition of tactlessness on his son's part to drive him to fury.

By December 10 Heinrich Marx had had time to digest the monumental letter written by his son a month earlier. This time he took up his pen in a mood of profound disillusion and misery. He wrote in gall. It was a very long letter, and he gave himself enough space to enlarge on all his resentments. He wrote:

> God help us!!! Complete disorder, stupid wandering through all branches of knowledge, stupid brooding over melancholy oil-lamps. Going to seed in a scholastic dressing gown and unkempt hair as a change from going to seed with a glass of beer. Repellent unsociability regardless of all propriety and even of all feelings for your father. The limitation of the social art to a filthy room where perhaps, in all this classic disorder, there may be found the love letters of a J. and the well-meant exhortations of a father written in tears being used as pipe-lighters, which may be better than that they should fall into the hands of a third person as the result of an even more irresponsible disorder. And in the activity of this senseless and purposeless learning, you want to raise the fruits which are to unite you to your beloved! What harvest do you expect to gather from them which will enable you to fulfill your sacred duty toward her!?
>
> In spite of all my intentions I have the feeling that I may be causing you pain and already my weakness comes over me, and in order to help myself, quite literally, I have resort to my real, prescribed pills and swallow them down, because I propose to be harsh again and I will utter my complaints. I will not be weak now, for I feel that I have been too indulgent in the past. I poured out my complaints too rarely, and so, in a way, I am guilty toward you. I will and must declare that you have caused your parents much chagrin and very little—or no—joy.

In this harsh way, holding nothing back, Heinrich Marx wrote his bill of particulars, like a Jewish patriarch raining curses on his son. Nothing had happened as it should have happened. As his sickness grew worse, he was plagued with fears. Even at a very early age, Karl had become estranged from his family, and the family had suffered it in silence. He had piled up debts, driven Jenny to fits of melancholia, taken part in an inexcusable escapade at Bonn, written not a line when his brother Eduard was ill or when his mother was out of her wits with worry because a cholera epidemic was raging in Berlin, and it had never occurred to him to put an end to her fears. "Parents are the forerunners and bearers of their crosses," Heinrich Marx wrote in his agony, showing that he could write as good an epigram as any written by his son.

He could also write in the high sarcastic style which Karl was later to use with merciless effect. Here he is attacking Karl for his midnight labors and for not enjoying the company of friends:

> Meanwhile my clever Karl—so full of talent—keeps awake through the miserable night, with body and spirit exhausted by serious studies, and

> drives away all pleasure in order to devote himself to weighty and abstract studies, but what he builds today, he destroys tomorrow, and at the end the body grows sick and the spirit confused. Meanwhile the common crowd slip ahead undisturbed and reach their goal in a better or at least more comfortable way compared with those who despise their youthful joys and destroy their health in order to snatch at the shadow of erudition, which they would come to possess more easily through an hour's talk with some competent person, and in addition they would have enjoyed the social pleasure of conversation.
>
> I must come to an end now, for I feel my pulse is beating more strongly, and I may fall into writing in a weaker way, but I want today to be without mercy.
>
> I must add here the complaints of your brothers and sisters. One scarcely sees in your letters that you have any feeling for them, and the dear Sophie who has suffered so much for you and for Jenny, and who is so undeviatingly devoted to you—you think of her only if you need her help.

On his sickbed Heinrich Marx continued to ponder the fate of his son. He was dying of tuberculosis, or perhaps of some liver complaint—the doctors appeared undecided, and they seemed to be incompetent. He had lost his appetite and coughed continually. Sometimes Jenny would come from next door and read to him; and her gay spirit brightened the house which was in the throes of so many sicknesses, for three of his daughters were ill, and they were still in mourning over the death of their brother Eduard a few months before.

On February 10, two months after he had taken to his bed, Heinrich Marx wrote his last letter to his son. His hand shook as he wrote, and he needed to be brief. He spoke once more of Karl's peculiar attitude to money, "whose worth to a father of a family you do not seem to have grasped," and he wondered how his son could go on spending money so recklessly when it was obvious that there existed no fathomless treasure chest which could be looted at leisure. "We are now in the fourth month of your law courses, and you have already spent 280 thalers," he wrote. "I have not earned so much through the entire winter." He knew he was dying, and it was necessary at all costs to come to terms with his son. He could not fight any more. He would surrender joylessly, and leave the field to the younger man. He wrote: "I am not blind, and I lay down my weapons only out of weariness. Nevertheless you must believe and never doubt that I carry you in my innermost heart, and you are the greatest hope of my life."

Two weeks later there came a letter from Karl's mother, urging him to write "very tenderly" to his father, who had grown irritable from lying in bed for so long. Jenny was helping to look after the dying man, and her presence made the hours pass more quickly. "She is a darling child, and I hope she will make you really happy," she wrote. In a shaking hand Heinrich Marx added a brief footnote. "Dear Karl, I greet you with these few words, I cannot write any more."

He died on May 10, 1838, at the age of fifty-six. Marx did not attend his father's funeral. The journey from Berlin was too long, and he had other things to do.

THE APES OF GOD

We are chained, shattered, empty, frightened,
Eternally chained to this marble block of Being,
Chained, eternally chained, eternally.
And the worlds drag us with them in their rounds,
Howling their songs of death, and we—
We are the apes of a cold God.

THE POEMS OF KARL MARX

THE YOUNG MARX was passionately devoted to poetry, and took himself very seriously as a poet. He had a feeling for words and rhythms, and a flair for happy improvisations. Marxist scholars have dismissed his poems as youthful indiscretions, not to be taken seriously and quite unrelated to his mature works. In fact they are closely related to his mature works, and when he wrote the poems he did not regard them as indiscretions. Writing to his father he described how he had felt the touch of the magician's wand and seen "the kingdom of true poetry blazing before me like the vision of far-off fairy palaces."

Poetry was the love of his life, the safe refuge from all the turmoils of his revolutionary existence. He could recite page after page of Dante and Goethe by heart, and when he was middle-aged he seriously contemplated a poetic drama to be called *The Gracchi,* which would tell the story of the Roman revolutionaries in dramatic verse. When he was eighteen he wrote the first act of a poetic drama, which he called *Oulanem,* after the name of the hero, which is evidently an anagram of Manuelo. It dealt with satanic possession, homosexuality, seduction, and the ruin of the world. Oulanem visiting damnation on the earth was clearly a self-portrait.

In December 1936 he sent three collections of his poems to Jenny. The first was called *Buch der Lieder* (Book of Songs), the second and third were called *Buch der Liebe* (Book of Love), comprising two separate collections. Of these the first was dated at the end of autumn, and the second and third, which must have come hard on the heels of the first, were dated November. All three collections were tokens of affection for his bride-to-be, and they were all dedicated to "my dear, eternally beloved Jenny von Westphalen." Jenny was deeply moved when she read the poems and gave way to floods of tears.

These three collections had a strange fate. Jenny treasured them all her life, and at her death they passed into the hands of her daughter Laura. When Franz Mehring was collecting Marx's posthumous papers, he asked to see them and Laura lent him the three volumes. When he sat down to

Facsimile title page of Marx's Buch der Liebe.
Meinen teuren, ewiggeliebten
Jenny v. Westphalen
Berlin, 1836
am Ende des Herbstes

study them with the hope of discovering some clues to Marx's thought, he came to the conclusion that they consisted only of romantic ballads about pale lovers, swans, stars and moonlight. They were lacking, he thought, in a proper revolutionary fervor, and he asked rhetorically why Marx concerned himself with moonlight when he had better things to attend to. Marx was writing nine years after the publication of Heine's *Buch der Lieder*. Why, then, did he write such palpable imitations? Mehring was of the opinion that Marx's poems were temporary aberrations. "A spirit such as his," he wrote, "has nothing in common with these moonstruck landscapes, for he was a man perpetually struggling after a blinding clarity." He found only one poem which he thought worthy of Marx, and this was accordingly printed in his edition of the posthumous papers. It read:

Never can I be at peace,
For my soul is powerfully driven.
I must strive and struggle onward
In a restless fury of my own.

I would conquer everything there is,
All the loveliest graces of the gods,
Embracing all the wisdom of the world,
And all the arts and songs.

So shall we move ever onward,
Never quiet, restless always,
Never for a moment standing
Without desire, without determination.

The ignominious yoke
Shall never rest upon our shoulders.
Passion and desire shall lead us,
Action, too—all these are ours!

This poem comes from the *Buch der Liebe*. Essentially it is a love poem, and not, as Mehring supposed, a prophetic statement about the revolutionary future. In the first two verses Marx portrays himself as a man of elemental fury, another Faust determined to possess all the beauty and wisdom of the world, and in the final verses the beloved is caught up within the magic circle of his desires. It is a simple poem, well written, urgent, satisfying, and in the original German there are three or four memorable lines. When Mehring printed the poem in his collection of the posthumous papers in 1903, this was the only poem generally known to have been written by Marx.

As a general rule poets do not hide their light under a bushel, and Marx was no exception. If Mehring had looked more carefully among the literary magazines of the eighteen-forties, he would have found that Marx was sufficiently interested in the fate of his poems to have offered them for publication in the Berlin literary magazine *Athenaeum.* The editors selected two ballads, which accordingly appeared on January 23, 1841, under the title "Savage Songs."

The poems were well named, for there is no attempt to disguise the raw savagery and the yearning for catastrophic destruction in the poet's mind. They are written in the romantic tradition, with all the romantic artifices of spectral horrors. A musician summons up the Prince of Darkness, a lover offers a poison cup to the beloved, and both run headlong to their deaths in a satanic rejection of the world. Marx succeeds in conveying the authentic *frisson,* the terror at the heart of terror. He is not playing games. The poems reek of fire and brimstone, but it is real fire and real brimstone. Here is the first of the two ballads:

THE PLAYER

The player strikes up on the violin,
His blond hair falling down.
He wears a sword at his side,
And a wide, wrinkled gown.

"O player, why playest thou so wild?
Why the savage look in the eyes?
Why the leaping blood, the soaring waves?
Why tearest thou thy bow to shreds?"

"I play for the sake of the thundering sea
Crashing upon the walls of the cliffs,
That my eyes be blinded and my heart burst
And my soul resound in the depths of Hell."

"O player, why tearest thou thy heart to shreds
In mockery? This art was given thee
By a shining God to elevate the mind
Into the swelling music of the starry dance."

"Look now, my blood-dark sword shall stab
Unerringly within thy soul.
God neither knows nor honors art.
The hellish vapors rise and fill the brain,

"Till I go mad and my heart is utterly changed.
See this sword—the Prince of Darkness sold it to me.
For me he beats the time and gives the signs.
Ever more boldly I play the dance of death.

"I must play darkly, I must play lightly,
Until my heart, and my violin, burst."

The player strikes up on the violin,
His blond hair falling down.
He wears a sword at his side,
And a wide, wrinkled gown.

Marx is here celebrating a satanic mystery, for the player is clearly Lucifer or Mephistopheles, and what he is playing with such frenzy is the music which accompanies the end of the world. It is a thoroughly unpleasant poem, at once strident and languorous, but these were precisely the effects the poet hoped to achieve. The pact with the devil is consecrated by the purchase of the magic blood-dark sword, which kills with unerring aim. The blond violinist is not destroying the world because he hates it, but out of mockery and derision, in the knowledge that God has abandoned the world to its fate. Marx clearly enjoyed the horrors he depicted, and we shall find him enjoying in very much the same way the destruction of whole classes in the *Communist Manifesto.* He was a man with a peculiar faculty for relishing disaster.

In "The Player" Marx carefully arranged the stage furniture. On a brightly lighted stage we are presented with a satanic violinist who is seen in three dimensions. The wrinkled gown derives from the Holy Coat in the cathedral at Trier, and no doubt the blood-dark sword possesses Freudian significance. But we do not think of Freud or the Holy Coat; we see the sinister violinist in a dress rarely worn by musicians, with a sword hanging at his waist, and he is very odd and compelling. The theme of destruction develops gradually, and it is only toward the end that we recognize him for what he is.

In "Nocturnal Love," the second of the ballads to appear in the *Athenaeum,* there is no attempt to sketch in the stage scenery. The lovers have the appearance of disembodied spirits plunging headlong into the flames of Hell.

NOCTURNAL LOVE

He pressed her violently to his heart
And gazed darkly in her eyes:
"Darling, thou art on fire with grief,
Thou tremblest beneath my breath."

"Thou hast drunk of my soul!
Mine is thy glowing fire!
Shine, O my jewel,
Shine, shine, O blood of youth!"

"Darling, thou lookest so pale,
Thou speakest so strangely ever.

See how the heavenly choirs
Lift up the world to the skies!"

"Dear one, they are all lifted away!
The stars shine and shine!
Then let us fly away,
And our souls be mingled together!"

So she spoke in gentle whispers
While the terror lay around,
And the light of roaring flames
Shone on her empty eyes.

"Darling, thou hast drunk of poison,
And now thou must depart with me.
Now the night has fallen,
There is no longer any day."

He pressed her violently to his heart,
Death on her breath and breast.
She was pierced by deeper pain,
And her eyes were closed for ever.

It is an ominous and deeply disturbing poem, for a man does not write such things unless he is on the verge of madness or in despair. The poem was evidently addressed to Jenny, who is permitted to speak the second and fourth verses. The doomed lover offers her a poisoned cup and consigns her to the flames of Hell, which are also the flames of his own heart. What is especially disturbing about the poem is its *willfulness*. Realizing that he might never be able to marry Jenny, he destroyed her in his poem. He was taking poetic revenge on the world.

In 1903 these three poems comprised the entire known poetic *oeuvre* of Marx, for no others had been published. It was known that many more existed, for Mehring had discussed the three volumes with mounting horror, declaring that it would be altogether better for Marx's reputation if they remained unpublished. The three books were returned to Laura, and on her death in 1911 they came into the possession of her nephew Jean Longuet. Then they vanished.

David Ryazanov, the Marxist scholar who presided for many years over the Marx-Engels Institute in Moscow, was one of the few who recognized their importance. In 1925 he wrote to Jean Longuet, asking for information about the manuscripts and urging that they be sent to Moscow. He received a surprising answer. Jean Longuet wrote that he had lent them to someone whose name he could no longer remember. He thought perhaps he had sent them to Mehring, who had died in January 1919, but he was not sure; very possibly it had been someone else. He was a lawyer, not overly interested in the affairs of his grandfather, and he was not particularly perturbed by the loss of the manuscripts. It seemed at the time that no further poems by Marx would ever come to light.

Ryazanov was dedicated to the task of searching out every possible document which concerned the life and times of Marx, and as head of the Institute he was in a position to support his researches with ample funds. Soviet scholars were busily following in Marx's footsteps. Thus it happened that in 1926, a year after he heard from Jean Longuet that the manuscripts had probably vanished forever, he received the news that two complete notebooks filled with poems had been found in the Rhineland among the papers left by Dr. Roland Daniels, a close friend of Marx and a member of the Communist League. The discovery was totally unexpected. Dr. Daniels had died in 1855, and no one could have hoped that any documents left in his possession would have survived for so long, nor had anyone guessed that Dr. Daniels had possessed them at the time of his death.

Immediately after the discovery a search was made through the vast files of Marx's correspondence kept in the Marx-Engels Institute. A letter written by Marx to Dr. Daniels in March 1851 seemed to provide the clue. In this letter, written at a time of great privation, family conflicts, and a growing hopelessness with regard to the communist revolution, Marx announced that he saw little prospect of returning to Germany in any foreseeable future. He had left his entire library and some of his private papers with Dr. Daniels in Cologne. He said nothing about the papers, but asked that a good part of the library be sold, and the rest should be sent on to him in London. Ryazanov concluded that the volumes of poetry were probably given to Dr. Daniels as a gift.

One of these volumes proved to be disappointing, for it contained only a lengthy compilation of folk songs which Marx had prepared in 1839 as a gift for his fiancée. The second was full of Marx's poems and included the poetic tragedy *Oulanem*. The collection of poems appeared to be the original or a fair copy of the volume which Marx sent "as a feeble testimony of filial affection" to his father on the eve of his fifty-fifth birthday. Marx mentions the collection in the long letter to his father. Suddenly, after three quarters of a century, the long-lost poems had come to light.

It was a rich feast. Altogether there were about forty poems by Marx and among them were many which explored the mood of "The Player" and "Nocturnal Love," with their visions of a world in dissolution. In a poem dedicated to Jenny, he spoke of how he would hurl a gantlet at the world, and the world would crumble. Then, comforted by her love, he would wander through the kingdom of ruins, his words glowing with action, his heart like the heart of God. In another poem called "The King of the Flowers" he is told that he must tear out his heart before he may become the King of the flowers, but the gods laugh at him, and in his rage he tears out his eyes and digs a grave for himself in the earth. In still another poem a Promethean hero curses the gods and is reduced to beggary; thereupon he swears that in revenge he will construct an iron fortress so strong that no thunderbolts will ever penetrate it. They are all poems of romantic frustration, and they throw long shadows over the future. Those who have lived under the domination of Communism will recognize the significance of the iron fortress.

Not all the poems were romantic elegies. He wrote epigrams to celebrate his discovery that materialism was the answer to all things, and sometimes he would write extended epigrams on poets and philosophers. He celebrated his discovery of materialism in four simple lines:

> Kant and Fichte went roaming in the ether,
> Searching after a distant land,
> While I sought cunningly to seize
> What I found—in the street.

The materialist conception of history could scarcely be expressed more neatly.

The same idea was expressed in more visceral terms in another epigram called "Medical Metaphysic":

> The soul has no existence,
> For the oxen know how to live.
> The soul is pure fantasy.
> It cannot be found in the stomach,
> But should we get to the bottom of it,
> Then we would be able to chase it away with pills,
> And in a vast stream
> The spirits would come streaming from the body.

He could write more satisfying epigrams when he pleased, as in the following poem on Hegel, which is written in hexameters. Hegel is speaking:

> I have taught words in their restless, daemonic confusions,
> And everyone thinks of them as he sees best,
> At least they are never enclosed in a cramped space.
> In a roaring flood they plunge over towering rocks.
> The poet expresses the words and thought of the beloved,
> And what he meditates he knows, and he says what he feels.
> So can each one drink the flowing nectar of wisdom:
> What I teach is All, for which I have taught you is Nothing.

Goethe, too, occupied Marx's thoughts, and accordingly there was another epigram to celebrate him and at the same time put him in his proper place.

> Goethe, too, had a taste for beauty—
> He would rather deal with Venus than with scamps.
> Indeed, he liked to grasp it from below.
> Still one should be compelled to wander in the heights,
> Whereby things can be given quite a sublime form,
> And the poet may altogether lack stability of soul.
> Schiller, however, was probably more correct,
> Since one can read ideals in his words.
> One might say they had been brought low
> Even if one had not gazed into the depths.

In these poems we see the young Marx rejoicing in his powers, saying what he needed to say, now cold and hard, now giving way to romantic despairs. They tell us a good deal about the workings of his mind, but he tells us far more in his strange play in verse.

OULANEM, A TRAGEDY

When a man writes a poetic tragedy, he may be expected to pour into it all his resources of language and feeling. It is not something he undertakes lightly. When Marx wrote *Oulanem,* he was measuring himself against the greatest poet of Germany, for he was attempting nothing less than to write the *Faust* of his own age. He struggled valiantly, but the task was too much for him. He wrote some memorable lines and at least one satisfying dramatic scene; he completed a long first act; sketched out a number of violent and eccentric characters; proved to his own satisfaction that he could make the rafters ring; and then retired from the combat with the certain knowledge that he was incapable of sustaining a poetic mood. He had in fact very little feeling or awareness of tragedy. *Oulanem,* of which only the long first act was written, is a disaster.

Nevertheless it is an interesting disaster, because it reveals some of the springs of his being. We see him in his ruinous youth, splendidly self-assured, spendthrift of his talents and uncertain of his aims. He has not the slightest idea where he is going, but he is determined to go forward at an unrelenting pace. In the tragic drama he exhibits the same faults which can be seen in his mature works: the passionate drive, the flailing of the arms, the abrupt pauses on the edge of the abyss, even the conspiratorial air which attended him on all his journeys. He holds nothing back. He hurls himself into the drama as though his whole life depended on it, but when he comes to the end of his resources he simply walks away, paying no more attention to the creature of his imagination than to a dead bird seen lying on the road. It was a pattern which he repeated throughout his life: total absorption in the act of creation, and then abandonment.

No one would study *Oulanem* if it had not been written by Marx; but precisely because he wrote it, it has an interest far out of the ordinary. It is Marx at his best and his worst, with nothing hidden. All the characters together form a self-portrait. Unscrupulous, harsh, tender, yielding, domineering—all those aspects of the man which were later to become more pronounced are already present in the play. He smiles pleasantly, roars outrageously, consigns the entire human race to damnation, and all the time he is watching himself cynically.

Again and again in the play we come upon themes which will be stated less poetically in his more famous works. The themes of corruption, damnation, doubt, mistrust are continually present, together with a special kind of sarcasm with a rough cutting edge. Sometimes, but very rarely, there are long passages written with the full breadth when he seems to soar outside the world altogether. What is especially remarkable is the presence of a homosexual theme which is not implied but stated directly without any subterfuges.

The setting is a small town in a high Alpine landscape. Two Germans, Oulanem and his youthful companion Lucindo, finding no room at the inn, eagerly accept the invitation of Pertini, an Italian, to stay in his house. In Oulanem Pertini has recognized a former enemy, and he rejoices at the prospect of exacting vengeance.

As he ponders the destruction of his enemy, Pertini soon realizes that Lucindo, Oulanem's youthful lover, provides the perfect instrument for his vengeance. By corrupting Lucindo he will be in a better position to destroy his enemy. But Lucindo is not easily corrupted, and some of the more exalted verses in the play are devoted to his adoring affection for Oulanem:

> A rare alliance joins us to each other,
> One woven in the very depths of our hearts

Blazing, as it were, like glowing torches
And girt around our hearts all shining,
As when the loving demons of the light
Choose one for the other in most tender thought.
So I have known him from the earliest days.
No, scarcely that. Memory speaks softly
Of how we found each other. By the living God
I do not know when it was.

In this way Pertini learns an important truth: the handsome youth is so dazzled by his love for Oulanem that he scarcely knows the man he loves. There is a dark mystery attached to Oulanem, but he will not probe it. Pertini taunts him, presenting himself as a commonplace man who finds it difficult to believe that there are any mysteries in the world. "Take hold of your thoughts as you would take hold of stones and sand," he says, but Lucindo, oppressed by a sudden sense of fatality, demurs. He will take hold of nothing—only fantasies.

For Pertini, himself corrupt and in league with darkness, nothing is simpler than to corrupt the youth. There are well-documented ways of corrupting youths, and he proceeds to embark on the long, slow and cautious process by which Lucindo will become his slave. Lucindo puts up a surprisingly vigorous defense, refuses to yield either to threats or to blandishments, and using Pertini's arguments, goes over to the offensive. Pertini has called him a bastard, a ravening animal, a mere stone fallen from the moon on which someone has scribbled a consonant, and Lucindo replies that Pertini is a scoundrel, a poltroon, an insipid fool incapable of any human thoughts, his heart so impenetrably hard and his mind so withered with age and scorn that he is beyond salvation and must soon appear before the Judgment Seat of God and suffer his just retribution. Saying this, Lucindo leaps away, for he has broken the spell which surrounded him, but when Pertini calls him he returns, abject and quiet now, for he has recognized a greater authority than his own.

It is a long scene, managed with considerable skill, for Marx conveys the hesitations and subtle maneuvers of the adversaries, their withdrawals and sudden obstinacies. The argument is conducted on a high intellectual plane, but there are enough *doubles entendres* to point the way the argument is going. Marx evidently knew a good deal about corrupting boys, or else he had watched the process closely.

As Marx describes Lucindo, there is more than a hint that he is as corrupt as Pertini, only waiting for an opportunity to announce his corruption, alone among mysteries. Indeed, all the characters of the drama are aware of their own corruption, which they flaunt and celebrate with passionate conviction. Lucindo, who has posed as the innocent and troubled lover of Oulanem, now makes advances to Pertini, who accepts them with a proper humility and offers to take him to some secret place where, far from Oulanem, they can commune with one another:

PERTINI

Come with me, I will lead you to quiet places,
I will show you one thing and another, the gorges
Where the volcanic lakes arise, where the waters,
Still and rounded, cradle you to sleep,
Where the skeins of the years rustle quietly along,
And the storms fall away, and there are—

LUCINDO

Stones, creeks, worms, mud? O, everywhere
The rocks and reefs pile up, in every place
We'll see the fountains bursting forth
With overwhelming power, beneath, and more—who knows?
And we are banished slaves chained to the secret places,
Seeing with pleasure how the storms wax in our hearts,
And should the storms increase in violence,
Then 'tis no more than farce, a foolish escapade.
So lead me on, wherever thou willst, and take me—
Without thought, with no wavering—take me far away.

The scene ends with the apparent capitulation of Lucindo, but Pertini has taken the measure of the youth and knows that he has not yet won him completely over. There are battles in store for both of them. So, as they leave together, Pertini flings one last word at the audience. The word is *Misstrauen!* It means "distrust," and is intended to convey agonies of doubt and suspicion.

The third scene opens in a large room in Pertini's house, where Oulanem is working alone at a table, his papers scattered about. Suddenly he rises, paces up and down, and then pauses with his arms folded across his chest in the attitude of Napoleon at St. Helena confronted by the ruin of all his hopes. In this attitude he delivers himself of a highly romantic soliloquy filled with visions of destruction. Oulanem asks himself whether he must destroy the world, which has become too contemptible to be worth contemplating by a man possessed of his great soul. He says nothing at all about Pertini and Lucindo, but they are present by implication. Pertini's last line—that sudden *Misstrauen* thrown at an unsuspecting audience—is now developed and given cosmic significance.

The long soliloquy should be quoted at some length, because it clearly represents the thoughts of Marx as he surrenders to a frenzy of romantic speculation about death, eternity, and man's purpose on earth, and many of these ideas were to remain with him throughout the rest of his life:

> Ruined! Ruined! My time has clean run out!
> The clock has stopped, the pygmy house has crumbled,
> Soon I shall embrace eternity to my breast, and soon
> I shall howl gigantic curses at mankind.
> Ha! Eternity! She is our eternal grief,
> An indescribable and immeasurable Death,
> Vile artificiality conceived to scorn us,
> Ourselves being clockwork, blindly mechanical,
> Made to be the fool-calendars of Time and Space,
> Having no purpose save to happen, to be ruined,
> So that there shall be something to ruin.
> There had to be some fault in the universe,
> The dumb agony of pain wrapped all round her,
> A giant's mighty soul waltzing through the air;
> So Death becomes alive, wears shoes and hose,
> Suffering of plants, the stifling deaths of stones,
> Birds vainly seeking their songs, bemoaning
> The sickness of their airy lives, wars and dissensions
> In blind assemblage shuddering, exterminating
> Itself from its very self in violent clashes,
> Now there emerges a man, two legs and a heart,
> Who has the power to utter living curses.
> Ha, I must bind myself to a wheel of flame
> And dance with joy in the circle of eternity!
> If there is a Something which devours,
> I'll leap within it, though I bring the world to ruins—
> The world which bulks between me and the abyss
> I will smash to pieces with my enduring curses.
> I'll throw my arms around its harsh reality:
> Embracing me, the world will dumbly pass away,
> And then sink down to utter nothingness,
> Perished, with no existence—that would be really living!
> While swinging high within the stream of eternity,
> We roar our melancholy hymns to the Creator
> With scorn on our brows! Shall the sun ever burn it away?
> Presumptuous curses from excommunicate souls!
> Eyes that annihilate with poisoned glances
> Gleam exultantly, the leaden world holds us fast.
> And we are chained, shattered, empty, frightened,
> Eternally chained to this marble block of Being,
> Chained, eternally chained, eternally.
> And the worlds drag us with them on their rounds,
> Howling their songs of death, and we—
> We are the apes of a cold God.

To anyone who has read Marx's later works the soliloquy placed in the mouth of Oulanem has a familiar ring. The annihilating judgment, visited on the world and on men, was never far from Marx's thought. He had little pity for the world or for the men who crawled on its surface, those "apes of a cold God," eternally in bondage. The shattering vision, which belongs wholly to the romantic period, was to endure long after the exultations of romantic poets were forgotten. To the end he would wear scorn on his brows, and the sun would never burn it away.

Oulanem's soliloquy cannot be dismissed cavalierly as a work of Marx's youth and therefore in some mysterious way divorced from his active life. Into that long monologue he poured all his frustrations, his confused yearnings for death and immortality, his penetrating knowledge that there is some fault in the universe which is enshrouded in pain and agony. He will destroy the world, and thus free all those who are "chained, shattered, empty, frightened" from the world's toils. He will squeeze the life out of the world, and then watch it sinking away into utter nothingness. He has become God, and he has consigned the world and all the universes to perdition.

We shall never know whether this speech has any bearing on the rest of the drama, for only one more scene remains. In this scene Oulanem is absent, and we are back again in the corrupt world of Pertini, who is still plotting the destruction of Lucindo. The homosexual theme is now abandoned. He decides to tempt the youth with a woman, the foster daughter of his friend Alwander. The woman's name is Beatrice, and although she lives in this North Italian town she is of German descent. Lucindo immediately falls in love with her, and Beatrice is half inclined to return his love, though she has been promised to another. She is enchanted by his declarations of affection, for he speaks in the authentic romantic tradition and pleads his suit with the proper arrogance and humility. No doubt Marx was thinking of Jenny when he put these words into the mouth of Lucindo:

My God, your virtue casts me to the ground.
You speak as softly as the angels speak,
And I'm ashamed, my heart is torn
By the wild stream of long-forgotten passion.
Your lips say what your lips should seal.
Then look at heaven, which is chastely veiled,
Smiling down through layers of blue cloud,
The colors waving in a sweet glance, and showing
Darkness and light melodiously combined
To form a single portrait, and you so silent—
If lips were ever silent—yet a magic spell
Draws sounds from you . . .

In this ardent manner, with Pertini still present, Lucindo declares his undying love of Beatrice, who mocks him gently. Pertini had not expected this, and as he makes his leave he contents himself with the thought that there are other ways of putting Lucindo in shackles. The lovers are too happy, and he will destroy them. In Pertini's absence Beatrice announces that she has no patience with the laws of ordinary behavior, and will at once give herself to Lucindo, whose romantic speeches have softened her heart. She is about to surrender to him when the door bursts open, and a strange ugly visitor leaps into the room. This is Wierin, to whom Beatrice has been affianced, and as Wierin and Lucindo quarrel Pertini enters to demand that the quarrel be settled by a duel. As the curtain falls Beatrice is heard murmuring softly: "My heart is full of foreboding!"

Marx appears to have abandoned his drama at this point, perhaps because it was already so hopelessly complicated that it was beyond unraveling. It is impossible to guess how it might have been developed, although the presence of a priest in the list of characters suggests that in the last act there might have been a divine judgment and a resolution of the conflicts in Christian terms; but the priest's name is Perto, and like Pertini he would seem to be included among the lost and damned. We gain nothing by peering at the unwritten acts of the drama; it is enough that we have the strange convoluted torso with its thundering curses, homosexual fantasies and tender love scenes, the shadow of corruption falling over every action and every speech.

We have met Oulanem before: he is the mad violinist of "The Player," who has received his sword from the Prince of Darkness and plays his violin in a frenzy, driving the world to destruction. He is Mephistopheles, but not the Mephistopheles of Goethe; he is an altogether lesser creature bereft of dignity, possessing only malice and the desire for vengeance. Vengeance, indeed, is the theme of his long soliloquy in which he celebrates his power to shatter the world through his curses. And one of the major difficulties confronting Marx was that he could think of no hero except Mephistopheles, with the result that the three principal characters, Oulanem, Lucindo and Pertini, are all aspects of Mephistopheles. All are satanic, corrupt, and doomed. Not even the greatest dramatist could construct a successful play about Mephistopheles quarreling with himself.

Marx's drama can be seen as an extended improvisation on the theme announced by Mephistopheles in *Faust: "Alles, was besteht, ist wert, dass es zugrunde geht"* ("Everything that exists deserves to perish"). Marx had a particular affection for this line, which he quoted with relish in *The Eighteenth Brumaire*. It is the romantic nihilist cry reduced to its simplest proportions. "Unless I can have my cup of tea, let the world perish," says Dostoyevsky's underground man. By the time of Dostoyevsky the cry was being uttered with a sordid vulgarity and malevolence, but when Marx made the same demand in the long speech of Oulanem, the words still possessed a down-at-heel nobility, for he was closer to the springs of romanticism.

From his poems and his uncompleted play we learn that Marx was essentially the child of the romantic age, dreaming its dreams and surrendering to its obsessions. Damnation, satanic seductions, curses and excommunications, the ruin of the world—such were his nightmares. What no one could have known or guessed was that more than a century later he would still be visiting his nightmares on the world.

As he turned more and more to philosophy, Marx abandoned the writing of poetry. At rare intervals he would write occasional verses, but never again would there come to him the feeling that he was being touched by the magician's wand. The experience however was not wasted, for the urgency and rhythm of his verses would be channeled into his prose. At rare intervals there would appear in his writings memorable passages, clanging like metal, constructed with deliberate artistry and deriving from his experience of poetry. To the end he remained "something of a poet."

IN FURY RAGING

Who comes rushing in, impetuous and wild—
Dark fellow from Trier in fury raging?

THE YOUNG EDITOR

WITH THE DEATH of his father in May 1838, Marx lost the one man who might have put order and discipline into his life. Those long letters, written in agony and despair by a dying man, might have had an accumulative effect if he had survived for a few more months. With his death, Marx was free of the last vestiges of parental control. He could now live his life as he pleased, devote himself to whatever studies he liked, and continue to act out the role of the bohemian student, who merely regards the university as his camping ground and attends as few lectures as possible. He was a free agent, responsible to no one.

When his father died, he appears to have received a small legacy. It cannot have been a large one, because the family fortune had declined drastically during the time of the lawyer's ill-health and his son's extravagant expenditures. There were five daughters who had to be provided with dowries; Eduard had died of a lingering illness; another son, Hermann, had been indentured to a merchant. Altogether eight people had to be supported on the income from Heinrich Marx's estate. In addition there were the servants, who presumably received legacies from the estate. Heinrich Marx had died before he could assure a sufficiently large capital sum to provide for his family. Inevitably their standard of living had to be reduced.

Meanwhile Henrietta Marx held the purse strings. Like a good Dutch housewife, she appears to have been a capable manager, and she was able to rely on the advice of her brother-in-law Lion Philips, an astute banker and merchant living in Zalt Bommel in Holland. She continued to live with her daughters in the large house on the Simeonstrasse, and from time to time she was able to send money to her son. On October 22, 1838, she sent him 180 thalers, "which you need for your graduation." It is a puzzling gift, for he was not graduating that year. In the past she had written long footnotes to her husband's letters, but the letter accompanying the gift was notably brief. "Let me know when you have received the money. May the good God give you happiness in all your undertakings and lead you along the right path." It was as though she despaired that he would ever follow the right path, as though she wrote the words more for her own comfort than to offer advice to her son.

We know very little about how Marx supported himself during the following years. He lived in the cheap students' lodginghouses, often changing his address—the books of the university record seven changes of address while he was in Berlin—and it is possible that he earned a small income as a theater critic. He attended few lectures, and therefore had considerable leisure for outside employment. In the summer semester of 1838 he attended lectures on logic, geography and Prussian common law, the last being given by Eduard Gans, who reported that he was "exceptionally industrious." In the winter semester he attended a course on the laws of inheritance, perhaps because he was beginning to be anxious about his own inheritance. Eduard Gans died early in the following year and was buried near the grave of Hegel. To many it seemed that a light had gone out in the university, and with his death the age of Hegel had come to an end.

During the remaining three years at the university he attended only two courses. One of these was a series of lectures given by his friend Bruno Bauer on the prophet Isaiah. That he should have attended lectures on the prophet suggests that he still retained some feeling for the faith of his ancestors; and these lectures, offered by someone of whom he was very fond, may have subtly influenced the prophetic role he assumed later. Here and there in his mature works there can be heard, like distant thunder, the echoes of Isaiah's curses, admonitions and conversations with God. *Then said I: Lord, how long? And he answered, Until the cities be wasted without inhabitant, and the houses without man, and the land be utterly desolate.* Such visions of desolation fed into the mainstream of romantic mythology, which he derived ultimately from Goethe.

The last course of lectures he attended was one on the dramas of Euripides given in the winter semester of 1840. Thereafter he appears no more in the official documents of the university until March 1841, when an official résumé of his studies was drawn up by the university authorities. This showed that in five years he had attended altogether thirteen courses, a number which a normally industrious student would attend in a year and a half. They noted, too, that no disciplinary action had been taken against him, and that "with regard to economic matters we may note that there were several complaints about nonpayment of debts."

There was, of course, nothing particularly unusual in such a university career. In all the universities of Germany there were always students who attended few lectures, piled up debts, and frittered their lives away.

So it had been since the Middle Ages, and so it would continue. These students had invented a special jargon, and their own bohemian uniform. They were part of the university, and outside it. They belonged to the no man's land where eccentricities breed and culture goes to seed. Marx appears to have despised most of his professors, and though he attended two universities and acquired a doctorate at a third, he was largely self-taught.

The five years Marx spent at the University of Berlin are the least documented of all. No letters written by him to his family after his father's death have survived, and of his day-to-day affairs we know almost nothing at all. We hear of visits to the salon of Bettina von Arnim in her palace on the Unter den Linden, but we do not know what he said, or whether he said anything at all. We know that he attended Bruno Bauer's lectures and that they were close friends, but we do not know what they talked about. Marx had a habit of turning on his friends, and in later years he would attack Bauer with all the fury of a former disciple who hopes to dethrone his master.

Bruno Bauer, ten years older than Marx, was one of those men who emerge briefly at moments of crisis, wave the banner of revolt, and then abruptly vanish because they can no longer tolerate the revolt they have themselves encouraged. He was a small man with a sharp pointed nose, a high forehead, fine eyes, a well-carved mouth, an air of brooding melancholy which would vanish when he smiled. There was something faintly Napoleonic about his appearance, and like Napoleon he would speak with supreme assurance on matters he little understood. Like his brother-in-law Adolf Rutenberg he believed that all questions submitted to the pure intelligence could be forced to yield true answers. Rutenberg was a journalist who had formerly been a teacher of geography at the Berlin School of Cadets, and had been dismissed for drunkenness.

In his long letter to his father Marx had described Rutenberg as his "most intimate friend," and in the same letter he mentioned that he had joined a Doctors' Club, giving the impression that this was a small, select group of philosophers who debated every subject under the sun. In fact, the club was dominated by Bauer and Rutenberg, and they were a very odd pair indeed. They both possessed intellectual brilliance, but while one pursued a precise academic path, the other waged continual war with the authorities and was continually being thrown into prison. One spoke of revolution, the other was always in revolt. A third member of the club was Karl Friedrich Koppen, a teacher in a Berlin secondary school, who was more interested in history than in philosophy. He was one of those genial, soft-looking men who conceal under a mask of kindliness a ruthless and determined temper. He drank hard, read widely, wrote vehemently. Among his writings was a vigorous defense of Frederick the Great, whose most tyrannical actions he defended. Marx listened sympathetically to Koppen's theories on the necessity of tyranny, and there may be some significance in the fact that when Koppen finally published his book on Frederick the Great, it was dedicated "To my Friend Karl Marx of Trier." The book appeared in 1840, when Marx was twenty-two years old.

The Doctors' Club had altogether about thirty members who met infrequently in the "red room" in the Café Stehely on the Gendarmenmarkt. The "red room" had no revolutionary connotation, for the name derived from the red tapestries hanging round it. Here lectures were heard and debated, newspapers were read, and beer was drunk in profuse quantities. The presence of Bruno Bauer would be the signal for prolonged debates on religion, for he was a theologian who regarded himself as the forerunner of a revolution in Christianity, and the presence of Koppen would immediately bring about debates on the nature of government. Government and religion were the chief subjects debated, and in both these subjects Marx appears to have acquired a debater's skill. He was not however a very good speaker, for at this time he still spoke in Rhenish dialect, which was virtually unintelligible to many Berliners. Wilhelm Liebknecht records that many years later Marx would still slip into the Rhenish dialect. On one occasion, in London, he made a speech in which he continually referred to the *Achtblättler,* which could only mean "a plant with eight leaves." Later it appeared that he had been talking about the *Arbeiter,* the workingman. In addition he suffered from a pronounced lisp, which gave his speech an oddly aristocratic tone. He was always better at thinking out ideas and writing them down than speaking them.

Since he attended few lectures, he could spend as much time as he pleased on the affairs of the Doctors' Club, and he appears to have been its unofficial general secretary, factotum and keeper of the archives. The Doctors' Club was his university, and his teachers were Bauer, the theologian who prophesied a violent revolution in Christianity, Rutenberg, whose brilliant mind was eventually to be corrupted by muckraking journalism, and the learned Koppen, who later became an outstanding authority on Buddhism. They were brilliant teachers, but thoroughly undisciplined; and in their separate ways they reinforced the lack of discipline in their most brilliant protégé, Karl Marx.

Bruno's brother Edgar wrote a poem about the Doctors' Club, in which the leading members were described at some length. The stanza on Marx paints him in a Promethean mood, all frenzy and wild posturing:

Who comes rushing in, impetuous and wild—
Dark fellow from Trier, in fury raging,
Nor walks nor skips, but leaps upon his prey
In tearing rage, as one who leaps to grasp
Broad spaces of the sky and drag them down to earth,
Stretching his arms wide open to the heavens.
His evil fist is clenched, he roars interminably
As though ten thousand devils had him by the hair.

This portrait of Marx was sketched out in 1842 after he had left Berlin, but it looks back to the time when Edgar Bauer knew him well. What men remembered was his wild temper, his impetuosity, his habit of leaping upon his prey. He would clench his fist and roar interminably for the remaining forty years of his life.

By this time the "dark fellow from Trier" had begun to grow the heavy beard which was to give him, with his dark skin, dark glowing eyes, and thick mane of black hair, an even more saturnine aspect. He commanded attention by his appearance as well as by his opinions, and it is unlikely that anyone having set eyes on him would ever forget him.

Bruno Bauer, who admired him this side of idolatry, left the University of Berlin in 1839 to take up a lectureship at the University of Bonn. They kept in close contact. Bauer insisted that Marx should obtain a doctorate and then join him at Bonn. It scarcely mattered how or where he obtained his doctorate, and since it was unlikely that the University of Berlin would provide one, it was decided to apply to the University of Jena, which conferred degrees on external students without submitting them to prolonged examinations or inquiring too deeply into their personal opinions and conduct. Marx wrote a doctoral dissertation on "The Difference between the Democritean and Epicurean Philosophy," in which he came out squarely on the side of Epicurus, the more speculative and visionary of the two philosophers. The book was dedicated to his "dear fatherly friend, Ludwig von Westphalen, in token of a filial devotion."

Marx received his doctorate on April 15, 1841, but by that time Bauer had lost his lectureship at the University of Bonn, and Marx, although playing with the idea of an academic career, turned his mind increasingly toward journalism. He appears to have informed his friends that he was applying for a lectureship at the University of Bonn, for in September Moses Hess, the thirty-year-old son of a Rhineland businessman, wrote an impassioned letter to his friend Berthold Auerbach in which he celebrated Marx as one of the wonders of the world, a man who combined in himself so many philosophical virtues that he was certain to draw the eyes of all Germany on himself. He wrote:

> You will be delighted to meet a man who is one of our friends here, though he lives in Bonn, where he will shortly become a lecturer. He is a phenomenon who has made a tremendous impression on me, although my interests lie in an entirely different direction. In short, you can definitely look forward to meeting the greatest, perhaps the *only real* philosopher now living. Soon, when he makes his *début* (both as a writer and as the incumbent of an academic chair), he will draw the eyes of all Germany upon himself . . . Dr. Marx, as my idol is called, is still a very young man (about 24 years old) and will give medieval religion and politics their last blow. He combines the deepest philosophical earnestness with the most cutting wit. Imagine Rousseau, Voltaire, Holbach, Lessing, Heine and Hegel united in one person, I say *united,* not lumped together—and you have Dr. Marx.

There was not the least doubt that Marx had impressed the impressionable Moses Hess with his intellectual brilliance. Others, too, were impressed. In the following month Georg Jung, a young lawyer who had been a member of the Doctors' Club, was writing to his friend Arnold Ruge that Marx, Bauer and Ludwig Feuerbach were about to produce a theological-philosophical periodical, which would effectively dispel the mists which had gathered around Christianity and thrust God out of his heaven. "Marx calls Christianity one of the most immoral religions, and although he is an absolutely desperate revolutionary, he has one of the sharpest brains I have ever encountered."

Georg Jung was not suggesting that Marx was a political revolutionary; on the contrary he was a theological-philosophical revolutionary, engaged in the revolution of ideas. It had not yet occurred to him that he would become a practical revolutionary attempting to overthrow the entire social system.

Meanwhile he was living in Bonn, and amusing himself by reliving his undergraduate experiences; and Bruno Bauer records how one day while everybody was walking sedately in the street, they suddenly appeared in a donkey cart and caused a commotion. The donkey brayed appropriately, and the townsfolk were suitably alarmed by the appearance of two doctors of philosophy in the cart. They had also collaborated on a strange work called "The Last Trump of Judgment against Hegel, the Atheists and the Anti-Christ," a tract which appeared to be directed against the unbelievers, although on closer examination it proved to be directed against the Christians. Such elaborate conjuring tricks were not unusual in an age of religious pamphleteering, and Bauer and Marx were delighted with their success. They were not particularly surprised when the authorities finally banned the anonymous pamphlet. They had enjoyed their foray against the bourgeoisie, and were well content.

But one cannot make a living by riding in donkey carts or by writing elaborate pamphlets against Christianity. Marx could live off his rich friends, pile up debts, forget to pay his bills, and live like a bohemian, but the day of reckoning was certain to come. His mother still held the purse strings, refusing to give him more than he was entitled to have under his father's will. He was warned that he must earn a living. It was a warning which he would hear at intervals throughout the rest of his life.

Since it was no longer possible to produce the theological-philosophical journal on which he had set his heart, there remained the possibility of journalism. In September 1841 Moses Hess, Georg Jung, Ludolf von Camphausen, Gustav von Mevissen, and Dagobert Oppenheim, all of them people of wealth and influence—Camphausen, for example, was president of the Cologne Chamber of Commerce, Mevissen was an industrialist, and Oppenheim was the brother of a rich banker—put up 30,000 thalers for a new liberal newspaper, to be called the *Rheinische Zeitung*. This would be edited from Cologne, the largest and most important industrial city in the Rhineland, and it would reflect the opinions of the aristocracy of wealth. It was thought that Moses Hess, being the heir to a large fortune, would make a suitable editor, but this plan was dropped when it became known that he had developed a considerable body of socialist and even communist opinions. The economist Friedrich List was approached, but he was too ill to accept the invitation. A certain Dr. Hofken, the editor of the *Augsburger Zeitung*, was given the post. He proved to be unsatisfactory, and in February 1842 the editorship was given to Adolf Rutenberg, Bruno Bauer's drunken brother-in-law.

In this way Bruno Bauer, Moses Hess and Karl Marx captured the *Rheinische Zeitung*, which would henceforth reflect their views and those of their friends and allies. They would pay lip service to the Cologne industrialists, and they would take care not to attack Catholic dogma, or the vested interests of the manufacturers, but their secret intention was quite clear. They would attack everything else. They would produce a genuinely liberal newspaper. Adolf Rutenberg, Marx's intimate friend, was merely the nominal editor. The real editor was Moses Hess.

The Prussian government did not take easily to the new newspaper, and the heavy hand of the censor was felt in nearly every issue. Every second day the newspaper published a supplement which included long, theoretical articles, and these articles were especially frowned upon by the censors. On May 5 and 15 there appeared Marx's first political article. It was on the subject of the freedom of the press, which had been debated by the Rhenish Diet sitting in Düsseldorf. Marx did not agree with their conclusions and wrote a brilliant lawyer's brief attacking them. It was a very long article, and it was written from the point of view of a dedicated liberal who is concerned to establish certain inalienable human rights. Among those rights is freedom of expression, and no government may legitimately take this right away. He quotes with approval the saying of the two Spartans Sperchias and Bucis to the Persian satrap Hydarnes: "You do not know what freedom is! If you had ever tasted it, you would urge us to fight for it, not from afar with spears, but with axes at close quarters!"

Marx's article is a considered defense of a free press. Like Milton he identifies freedom with reason and with the very essence of humanity. Today no authoritarian state would tolerate the publication of this article.

There is no sign of Marx's celebrated fury, his search for the massive blow at the jugular vein. He writes with a kind of compassion, remembering the crimes which have been committed in the name of freedom, while reminding his readers that far more crimes have been committed in the name of authority. The free press is the mirror in which the people see themselves; a censored press is merely a distorting mirror, in which no truth can be observed. The free press is the ever-open eye of the people; tear out that eye, and you have nothing but blindness. He wrote ironically:

> I am humorous in temperament, but the law commands me to write seriously. I am impudent, but the law commands that my style shall be modest. *Gray on gray* is the only justified color of freedom. Every drop of dew on which the sun shines glitters in infinite colors, but the spiritual sun must produce only one, the *official* color, in no matter how many individuals or objects it is refracted. The essential form of mind is *serenity, light,* and you make it appear only as shadow; it is to go dressed in black only, and yet there are no black flowers. The essence of mind is *truth itself,* and what do you make its essence? *Modesty?* Only rogues are modest, says Goethe, and you want to make a rogue of the mind? . . .
>
> The writer is thus a prey to the most *fearful terrorism, the jurisdiction of suspicion.* Laws against *tendencies,* which provide no objective norms, are laws of terrorism, such as were invented by necessity of state under Robespierre and by political decay under the Roman emperors. Laws which have as their criterion not the *action as such* but the opinions of the author of the action, are nothing but *positive sanctions of lawlessness.* Better, like the old Tsar of Russia, to have everybody's beard cut off by official Cossacks than to make this operation dependent on the opinion which has led me to wear the beard.

He was writing with grace and distinction about matters in which he firmly believed. When necessary, he could turn the knife, as when he reminded his readers that Charles I became king through divine right from above, but mounted the scaffold with the help of "divine right from below." He was writing urgently and calmly. The attack on the censorship is one of his most brilliant works.

His ideas had not yet hardened, and he was far from showing any sustained interest in communism. When the *Augsburger Zeitung* accused the *Rheinische Zeitung* of introducing communist ideas, Marx refuted the charge, saying that the newspaper could not accept the theoretical validity of communist ideas, and did not believe they were practical; it remained to submit them to a thorough examination.

Meanwhile Rutenberg had shown himself to be, in Marx's words, "quite impotent," and the time had come to unseat him. Exactly how Marx succeeded in unseating him is unknown, but from a letter written to Arnold Ruge in November, in which Rutenberg is described as an idiot who spent most of his time attending to problems of punctuation, it is clear that Marx was not above employing all the resources of his invective. He had rid himself of Rutenberg, and he proceeded to rid himself of Moses Hess. He was determined, he told Ruge, to prevent "the smuggling into the newspaper of communist and socialist dogmas disguised as theatrical criticism." What he wanted was absolute control of the policy of the newspaper, and for a few months he was able to exercise it.

In October and November Marx wrote and published in the *Rheinische Zeitung* a long study of the laws concerning the theft of wood. This time the tone was sharper. The laws recently introduced by the Diet were so patently unfair that he permitted himself some heat. By immemorial custom the peasants had been gathering fallen branches in the forests and using them for fuel. Now if they gathered so much as a single branch, they could be arrested by the forest keepers, fined, and imprisoned, and in addition they were to pay whatever the forest keeper thought the wood was worth. The fines would not accrue to the state, but to the owner of the forest. If the offender could not pay the fine, he was to be placed in a cell and given only bread and water. One did not need to be a communist to realize that this law was barbaric, and represented only the interests of the wealthy. Marx, like a good liberal lawyer, defended the peasants on the ground of natural right and immemorial custom. The dead branches were not the private property of the landowner; they belonged to the poor. So it had been in all countries and all ages, and so it should remain. In the final words of the article he summed up the whole sorry problem by saying that the dead wood had become nothing more than a fetish for the forest owners: "The savages in Cuba believed that gold was a fetish of the Spaniards. They introduced a festival for it, sang songs around the gold, and then flung it into the sea. If the savages of Cuba had been present at the sittings of the Rhenish Diet, would not they have said that wood had become the fetish of the Rhinelands?"

Marx went on to write more articles on the peasants. He wrote a series defending a correspondent from the vine-growing districts of the Moselle, who had complained that a new customs union had exposed the cultivators to so much competition that their wine was nearly worthless. None of these articles was calculated to endear him to the Prussian government, and a new censor, Wilhelm Saint-Pol, was sent to prevent any similar articles from appearing and to advise on a further course of action. He reported that only the complete banning of the newspaper would prevent Marx from continuing in his chosen path. The decision to ban the newspaper was precipitated by a violent attack on the Russian government written by Marx, which came to the attention of Nicholas I, Tsar of Russia. He protested to the King of Prussia, and the order went out to ban the *Rheinische Zeitung*. On March 18 there appeared the brief announcement in the newspaper: "The undersigned declares that as from today he has resigned from the editorship of the *Rheinische Zeitung* due to present censorship conditions. Dr. Marx."

For about five months he had been the editor in chief of a newspaper, and now it was over. Those months had been eminently productive, for they had given him a taste for public power and they had turned his mind away from liberalism to a harsher way of looking at the world. Some fifty years later, a few weeks before his death, Engels wrote that he had always understood from Marx that "it was his study of the law concerning the theft of wood, and his investigation of the Moselle peasantry, which turned his attention from mere politics to economic conditions and thus to socialism." The decision by Johann Eichhorn, the Prussian Minister of the Interior, to ban the *Rheinische Zeitung* was fraught with momentous consequences. Sickened by Prussian censorship, and free of his editorial duties, Marx now had the enforced leisure to make those studies which were to lead him to communism. Henceforward a new music enters his prose. The tone is more dogmatic, the judgments are harsher, the rhythms are more urgent. The iron had entered his soul.

Not long after the banning of the *Rheinische Zeitung*, an artist drew a picture of Marx as Prometheus chained to his printing press, while an eagle representing the King of Prussia tears at his liver. Marx stands with his head unbowed beside the Rhine, naked except for a pair of white close-fitting drawers. At his feet the seven cities of the Rhineland, Cologne, Aachen, Düsseldorf, Elberfeld, Trier and Koblenz, represented as maidens wearing civic crowns, raise their hands in protestation and supplication. Eichhorn means "squirrel," and accordingly the artist has depicted a squirrel sitting in a window of heaven, manipulating the strings. It is an effective and pleasing political cartoon, and it must have pleased Marx, who liked to think of himself as Prometheus challenging the heavens.

He stands there with a look of defiance, his arms bound, his powerful legs quivering with energy, the iron entering his flesh. Though shackled, he will soon break the chains, topple the printing press, and go on to further adventures. The drawing in which we see him standing outside the White Horse Inn at Godesberg showed him as a youth. Here for the first time we see him as a man.

THE HONEYMOON

For some weeks Marx had been discussing with his friend Arnold Ruge the possibility of editing a magazine to be called the *Deutsch-Französische Jahrbücher* (German-French Yearbooks). The magazine would be published abroad, and since it would have the appearance of a book it would not have to be submitted to the Prussian censorship when placed on sale in Prussia. It would deal with the philosophical and social systems of the day, and would resemble the *Deutsche Jahrbücher,* which had been edited by Ruge and had just been banned by the authorities. Meanwhile Ruge, who possessed independent means, was preparing to publish *Anekdota,* another journal dealing with political questions, in Switzerland. Marx hoped for financial support from Ruge. He knew he was a born editor, immensely hard-working and capable of brilliant improvisations. In the editorial chair he was in his element; removed from it, he was like a lost soul wandering in the wilderness.

Marx saw himself as an editor and as a remorseless critic of society.

Journalism—the day-to-day reporting and weighing of events—was his proper métier, and to the end of his life he was to display the talents of a journalist rather than those of a social philosopher. It was sometimes journalism raised to the height of genius, but it was journalism nevertheless. He was to spend a large part of his life writing articles about events which he had never seen, but interpreted on the basis of newspaper reports. By adopting a consistent point of view, by assuming that the old order was in a state of collapse and that all historical events merely confirmed the corruption at the heart of society, he was able to present contemporary history in the light of apocalyptic doom. It was an attitude frequently to be found among editorial writers.

Meanwhile the dream of creating the *Deutsch-Französische Jahrbücher* was still struggling for fulfillment, and the plans for bringing it out were still being eagerly debated. Neither Marx nor Ruge was sure where it would be published—at different times they thought of Paris, Strasbourg, Brussels and Switzerland—or how it would be financed. Strasbourg offered obvious advantages, as being the capital of Alsace and therefore on the frontiers of France and Germany in the intellectual no man's land between the two countries. Brussels, too, offered the advantages of a pleasant neutrality; and if Switzerland was boring, it had the advantage of a large and cultivated German-speaking population. As for finances, Marx left them entirely in the hands of Ruge, who was more experienced in these affairs.

Marx's own finances were in a state of permanent crisis. He was penniless, living on occasional loans from his friends and from the small sums he was able to borrow from his family. Writing to Ruge in the summer of 1842, he explained that he had been unable to contribute to the *Anekdota* because he was being tormented by financial worries. "The remaining days were wasted and made turbulent by the most unpleasant family controversies," he wrote. "Although they are quite rich, my family has placed difficulties in my way which have temporarily placed me in an embarrassing situation. I cannot possibly disturb you with a description of these stupid affairs, and it is truly fortunate that the state of our public affairs makes it impossible for a man of character to permit his private troubles to irritate him." Translated into a more factual language, the words meant that Marx had had a series of stormy meetings with his family, and especially with his mother, who had finally decided to cut off even the very small allowances he was receiving. He had told the family about his debts, and they had heartlessly refused to pay them. Meanwhile he was brooding bitterly over his fate, irritated beyond measure by his mother's attitude toward him. The break with her was now virtually complete.

How Marx survived during the following months is something of a mystery, for he had few friends he could turn to. Baron von Westphalen had died in the spring of 1842 at the age of seventy-one, and even if he had been living it is doubtful whether he would have come to Marx's assistance. The last months of his life were shadowed by a mysterious quarrel between the two households which had formerly been so friendly, for we find Henrietta Marx complaining that the Westphalens no longer paid any attention to her, behaved haughtily and distantly, snubbed her in public and "showed no family feeling." We hear of a certain Heinrich Schlink, a government official from Saarbrücken, who made it his business to encourage the dissensions. We can only surmise that Frau Marx, with her stubborn Dutch-peasant character, was far less interesting to the Westphalens than her husband had been. It is also very possible that the old baron had lost whatever faith he once possessed in Marx's ability to support his daughter in the manner to which she was accustomed; and the mother had to pay for the follies of her son.

While the baron was alive, he was able to hold a protective hand over Jenny; with his death Jenny's half brother Ferdinand became the head of the family, the inheritor of the title and of a large share of the family estates in Brunswick. Ferdinand was a career official, determined like his grandfather to stand at the very heart of power, and he became the Minister of the Interior in the Prussian government. He was already a powerful figure in Prussian political life, and he had not the least desire to let his half sister marry a man who had been, however briefly, the editor of a revolutionary newspaper. Marx was a Jew, an atheist, a nonconformist; he was spectacularly lacking in aristocratic manners; he professed no loyalty to the Prussian Crown; he showed no evidence of being able to earn a living; and he was physically repugnant. There were enough reasons to forbid the marriage. There followed bitter family quarrels. Ferdinand was determined that the family fortune should not be expended on the support of a wastrel, while Jenny was equally determined to love and cherish and, if necessary, support the man who had filled her dreams for so long.

After her father's death she had moved with her mother to Kreuznach, her birthplace, and she no longer saw Marx except on his very rare visits, but her affection fed on his absence. She was still desperately in love with him. She was nearly twenty-nine, and like many women approaching their thirties unmarried, she was capable of adoring the absent beloved with a passion approaching religious ecstasy. In March 1843, after he paid a brief and hurried visit to Kreuznach, she wrote a fervent letter to him, remembering every detail of his visit and describing him in terms appropriate to a god. She felt "the deepest, most inward love and gratitude to thee, my beloved, good, only, little lord of my heart (*Herzensmännchen*)." She went on more ecstatically than ever:

> I think thou hast never been dearer, nor sweeter, nor more loving, and at thy going, I was in a state of rapture, and if it had been possible to have thee back, then it would be only to tell thee what love, what entire love I have for thee. But this last time was thy victory-departure. I scarcely know how much I love thee in my heart of hearts, when I can no more see thee in the flesh and have only that one faithful portrait standing so vividly before my soul in all its angelic mildness and goodness, grandeur of love and luster of genius. If thou wert still here, my dear Karlchen, what a gift for happiness thou wouldst find in thy little wife, and if thou shouldst demonstrate a still worse tendency and a more *evilly* disposed intention, even then I would still not take any reactionary measures. I would lay down my head patiently, sacrificing it for my evil boy. "What," How?—Light, what, how, light. Dost thou still think of our twilight conversations, our beckoning contests, our hours of slumber? Dear heart, how good, how loving, how indulgent, how joyful thou wert!

In this way she pours out her heart to her beloved, never doubting for a moment that they were made for one another, always adoring, although well aware that he is difficult and demanding. She knows that their lot is "to wait, to hope, to endure, to suffer," but for her he is always "shining, strong with victory" (*glanzend, siegesstark*) and always close to her. He is in Strasbourg, but their thoughts travel over empty space, and it is beyond belief that they will ever be really separated. She invents "a small, tiny thought-speaker" which in her imagination leaves Kreuznach and hovers over him. She scolds him because he bought her a garland of flowers when he could ill afford it, and asks about Ruge, on whom Marx had pinned all his hopes, and the affairs of the *Deutsch-Französische Jahrbücher*. It is a long letter written at full spate, in nervous exhaustion close to hysteria. There had evidently been quarrels, and she patches them up. He had been ill-tempered, and she forgives him. Enemies were conspiring against them, and she brushes them away as though they were of no importance. Above all, she wants him back in her arms again.

Marx's letters to her during this period have not survived, and indeed only a handful of the hundreds of letters they exchanged escaped the holocaust which took place not long after Marx's death when they fell into the hands of his daughter Laura Lafargue. Why she destroyed them is unknown, but we may surmise that she felt there was no need to perpetuate their very human sorrows and joys, their quarrels and reconciliations.

Marx never had any reason to doubt her enduring fidelity. If he had died, she would have remained faithful to his memory to the end of her days. Since he was alive and poor, she was determined to fight his battles for him, to provide for him, and to ward off all the arguments of her half brother, who was supported by an entire army of relatives. She never succeeded in winning Ferdinand over, but she had a useful ally in Edgar and finally succeeded in winning over her mother. Marx, who naturally came to know all the details of Jenny's family troubles, rarely referred to them because they were almost too painful to contemplate. Not long before his marriage he described them very briefly in a letter to Ruge:

> I can assure you without any romanticism that I am head over heels in love, and absolutely serious. We have been engaged now for seven years and more, and my future wife has fought the most bitter battles on my behalf partly against her pietistic aristocratic relatives, to whom the Lord in Heaven and the government in Berlin are equally objects of worship, and partly against my own family in which a number of parsonical individuals and other personal enemies of mine have acquired a measure of influence, and all these struggles have almost undermined her health. For years, therefore, my future wife and I have been compelled to engage in these unnecessary and exhausting conflicts, and we have suffered more of them than many people three times our age who are constantly speaking about their experience of life (which is one of the favorite phrases in our family circle).

In the same letter Marx hinted that after the marriage he would live with Jenny at Kreuznach, in her mother's house, until such time as his financial situation improved. In those days or weeks he would write the articles which would later appear in the *Deutsch-Französische Jahrbücher* "because it is necessary to have something ready before we begin." In tranquillity, with his wife at his side, with no financial troubles, he would contemplate the coming of the revolution.

Everything happened exactly as Marx had hoped. The banns were published, announcing the forthcoming marriage of "Herr Carl Marx, doctor of philosophy, residing in Cologne, and of Fräulein Johanna Bertha Julie Jenny von Westphalen, no occupation, residing in Kreuznach." The wedding took place in the Protestant church at Kreuznach on June 19, 1843. It was a quiet wedding, with only Jenny's mother, her brother Edgar, and a few close friends attending. Most of the Westphalen relatives were absent.

As her wedding portion, Jenny received from her mother the silver dinner service bearing the crest of the house of Argyll, which had come down from her grandmother. There was also some cutlery and bed linen, bearing the same crest. At times of great need the dinner service, the cutlery and the bed linen would be pawned or sold, until the time came when nothing remained.

Many years later, when Jenny wrote a brief autobiography, calling it *A Short Sketch of an Eventful Life,* she began with the words: "June 19, 1843, was my wedding day." It was as though she regarded her wedding day as the real beginning of her life, and all her earlier years were merely a preparation for this day.

It was the custom for young honeymoon couples to visit Rheinpfalz (Falls of the Rhine) in Switzerland, for the same reason that honeymooners in America visit Niagara Falls. They would walk out hand in hand along a narrow gallery jutting over the white foaming waterfalls until they seemed to be cut off from land, alone among the flashing waters. Accordingly the lovers drove by carriage to Schaffhausen in Switzerland, and so to the falls. Then they returned by slow stages through the province of Baden, and made their way back to Kreuznach. Many years later, speaking to her young friend Franziska Kugelmann, Jenny related that they were so completely without any sense of money during their honeymoon that they gave it away. Jenny's mother had received a small legacy. She immediately converted it into cash and placed it in a small double-handled strongbox, which she gave to her daughter and son-in-law for the expenses of their honeymoon. They took the strongbox with them during their travels, and whenever they stayed at a hotel, the box would be left open on a table, so that their friends might dip into it at will. In this way the honeymoon was a perpetual act of charity directed to all those who were less fortunate than themselves. They were too happy to care where the money went, and too careless to count it. Long before they returned to Kreuznach the money had vanished and the strongbox was empty.

Neither Jenny nor Marx had any practical sense about money. All through the remaining years of their lives, they showed an astonishing disregard for its value and its proper uses. Money was a subject they did not understand.

At Kreuznach on their return Marx settled down to work on the first of many essays he intended to write for the *Deutsch-Französische Jahrbücher*. The subject he chose was a recent book by his old teacher Bruno Bauer on the Jewish question. Bauer insisted that the Jewish question was essentially a religious question, incapable of solution unless the Jews were deprived of their faith and entered into the common life of the state as atheists or non-Jews. Marx argued that the Jewish problem was merely an aspect of the social problem convulsing the age, and that the peculiar forms of religious belief practiced by the Jews were merely a social error which would be cured once the socialist state had been brought into existence.

Marx's labored attempts to invalidate Judaism were neither rewarding nor particularly successful, and Marxist critics tend to pass quickly over his arguments, as though they were not to be taken seriously. Marx himself regarded the work with the utmost seriousness, and employed all his resources of logic and vehement oratory in attacking Judaism, as though it were a cancer growing within the state. Given his assumption that capitalism, represented by the rich Jewish merchants, was the principal enemy of human society, the argument proceeds with a brilliant display of reasoning. He is always the counsel for the prosecution, taking pleasure in his own brilliance as he watches his victim shrinking in terror, and it seems never to have occurred to him that the victim might one day parry his terrible thrusts.

The main arguments are deployed on two levels. First, he demonstrates to his satisfaction that all religions are "unreasonable" and have no place in human life. He then demonstrates that the Jewish faith and all other faiths are to be dispensed with, and bourgeois society, supported by the Christians and the Jews, must also be dispensed with. The argument is pursued on a highly emotional level, with a bitter hatred of Judaism and a ferocious delight in scoring off the enemy. He was a Jew conscious of his Jewish inheritance, recently married in a Christian church to a woman who still retained much of her Christian heritage, and as he attacks the Jews he appears to be attempting to compensate for his own inadequacies by the vehemence of his arguments. Consciously or unconsciously, he shows himself biased in favor of Christianity. "Christianity is the sublime thought of Judaism," he wrote. "Judaism is the vulgar practical application of Christianity."

The emotional violence is so high-pitched that he sometimes appears to lack any control. Strange dreams lurk beneath the surface, as when he speaks of the Jewish concern for lavatories, while perhaps half remembering the ritual baths of his ancestors. He writes:

> The monotheism of the Jews is therefore in reality the polytheism of the many human needs, a polytheism which makes even the lavatory the object of divine law. *Practical need, egoism,* is the underlying principle of *bourgeois society,* and is revealed as such in its pure form as soon as bourgeois

society has fully engendered the political state. The god of *practical need* and *private interest* is *gold.*

Money is the jealous god of Israel, beside which no other god may exist. Money degrades all the gods of mankind and changes them into commodities. Money is the universal and self-constituted *value* of all things. It has therefore robbed the entire world, both the human world and nature, of their own proper value. Money is the alienated essence of man's work and existence, and this alien essence dominates him, and he worships it.

The God of the Jews has been secularized, and has become the World-God. The bill of exchange has become the real God of the Jews. His God is only an illusory bill of exchange.

The view of nature gained under the dominion of private property and money is a genuine contempt for, and a practical degradation of, nature, which does indeed exist in the Jewish religion, but only in the imagination.

It is in this sense that Thomas Münzer declares it intolerable that "every creature should be transformed into property, the fish in the water, the birds in the air, the plants on the ground—the creatures too must become free."*

What is stated abstractly in the Jewish religion, the contempt for theory, for art, for history, and for man as an end to himself, is the *real and conscious* point of view, the virtue of the money man. Even the relations between the species, the relations between man and wife, etc., become objects of commerce. The woman is sold off at auction.

If the words seem strange to us, they were less strange in Marx's time when Jews often professed to a defiant anti-Semitism. Marx's anti-Semitism, however, had a virulent quality largely lacking among his contemporaries. In his mind Jews, money, and bourgeois society were seen as aspects of the same nightmare, fundamentally interchangeable. It was not only that he could say nothing in favor of the Jews, but he was determined to permit them no escape from the hell they had chosen for themselves. The massive onslaughts continue in defiance of reason, the subtleties of logic are paraded to demonstrate the truth of an untenable thesis, and the note of self-congratulation is heard above the mechanical reverberations of the epigrams. The careful reader of "On the Jewish Question" has the sensation of being gripped by the throat and choked by an adversary who is determined to kill him unless he yields to the thesis. Marx is not arguing; he is threatening and bullying.

Perhaps only a Jew descended from a long line of rabbis could have written such a work. The agony cannot be expiated; it must be visited

* In 1524, the year before his trial and execution, Thomas Münzer published his diatribe against Luther entitled "Against the Spiritless and Soft-living Flesh at Wittenberg," from which Marx drew the quotation about the freedom of all living things. Thomas Münzer was an Anabaptist priest, who revolted against both Luther and the Roman Church. For a few months he was able to establish a communistic theocracy at Mühlhausen, with himself as the dictator, chief priest, and commander of the peasant army. The Landgrave of Hesse dispersed the army, captured Thomas Münzer and beheaded him.

on all Jews, on all society, and ultimately on the whole world. His deeply personal hatred of the race from which he was descended is dramatized, as he sentences Jews, bourgeois society and money to extinction.

Again and again Marx presents his brilliant, untruthful simplicities, each one more wounding than the last. "Judaism," he says, "reaches its peak with the perfection of bourgeois society, but bourgeois society reaches perfection only in the Christian world." Judaism is incapable of expressing anything new, being wholly passive and self-centered, with no impulse for development until it comes into the stream of Christianity, with its religion of the self-alienation of man from himself and from nature. "Only then could Judaism attain universal dominion and turn alienated man and alienated nature into *alienable,* salable objects subject to the serfdom of egotistical needs and to usury." Christianity, then, is the vehicle by which Judaism has come to power, but it is not itself the prime mover, for "it is too *refined,* too spiritual, to abolish crude material needs except by elevating them into the blue heavens."

All these arguments revolve around a fixed point—the inherent evil of Jewish bourgeois society with its fixed goal of transforming all things into gold. Marx's final conclusion is that the Jew is a "limitation" on society, and must therefore be made "impossible." So he writes:

> It is not only in the Pentateuch and the Talmud, but also in contemporary society that we find the real nature of the Jew as he is today, not in the abstract but in a highly empirical way, not only as a limitation upon the Jew but as a Jewish limitation upon society.
>
> As soon as society succeeds in abolishing the *empirical* nature of Judaism—usury and its preconditions—the Jew becomes *impossible,* because his consciousness no longer has any object, since the subjective basis of Judaism—practical necessity—assumes a human form, and the conflict between the individual as a sensual human being and as a species is abolished.
>
> The *social* emancipation of the Jew is the *emancipation of society from Judaism.*

The argument is given philosophical form, but it remains a cry of rage. In very much the same way Hitler would later pass sentence of death on "the empirical nature of Judaism." With this gratuitous display of uncompromising logic Marx arrives at the conclusion which was already present at the beginning of the essay—*ist der Jude unmöglich geworden* ("the Jew becomes impossible"). This conclusion was a deeply personal one, and scarcely needed to be buttressed by a display of Hegelian pyrotechnics.

At the end of his honeymoon Marx turned from the contemplation of Judaism and bourgeois society to the contemplation of religion, revolution and the emancipation of Germany. All these subjects are discussed in a short essay which purports to be the introduction to a long work on Hegel's philosophy of law. The essay is pieced together from a large number of aphorisms once entered into his notebook and here gathered in a semblance of order. The order however is more apparent than real, and the argument proceeds from aphorism to aphorism.

Although the essay bears the forbidding title "A Contribution to the Critique of Hegel's Philosophy of Law" it has very little to do with Hegel. Marx is launching out into uncharted oceans of ideas, occasionally turning Hegel upside down, but more often pursuing thoughts to their ultimate and sometimes wholly illogical conclusions. The nagging tone of "On the Jewish Question" is absent; he is a free agent, striking out adventurously in search of his own quite personal solutions at whatever the cost. In this short essay, written at the age of twenty-six, we see the earliest formulation of ideas which were to absorb him to the end of his life. Here are some of the aphorisms, which were later to become famous:

> Religion is the opium of the people.
>
> In politics the Germans have *thought* what other nations have *done*.
>
> In France it is enough to be someone in order to desire to be everything. In Germany no one has the right to be anyone without first renouncing everything.
>
> Religion is only the illusory sun about which man revolves so long as he does not revolve around himself.
>
> Philosophy can be realized only by the abolition of the proletariat, the proletariat can be abolished only by the realization of philosophy.
>
> The revolutionary daring which hurls at its adversary the defiant words: *I am nothing, and I must be everything.*
>
> The essence of German morality and honor, in classes as in individuals, is a *modest egoism* which displays, and allows others to display, its own narrowness.

So he wrote in the eagerness of youth, emphasizing by turns his contempt, indignation, and defiance of the world so incomparably dedicated to foolishness. Religion was tossed away with airy disdain, Germany and France were simplified into polar opposites, and philosophy, which hitherto had not burdened itself with the problems of poverty, now found itself permanently chained to the proletariat.

These aphorisms, taken out of context, do not necessarily represent Marx's real thoughts: they are the decorations of his thought, the musical flourishes. He was evidently very pleased with them, but they were not essential to the substance of his argument and sometimes they imperiled his conclusions. "Religion is the opium of the people"—an incantation endlessly repeated by generations of communists—was nearly always thought to refer to religious hallucinations, the pipe dreams of an unreal, heavenly world. The Russian Communists wrote the words in huge letters on the walls of Orthodox churches. But Marx was not talking about pipe dreams; he was talking about an opiate which dulls the pain of living. He wrote:

> *Religious* suffering is at the same time an *expression* of real suffering and a *protest* against real suffering. Religion is the sigh of an oppressed creature, the heart of a heartless world, and the soul of a soulless state of affairs. It is the *opium* of the people.

When Marx in this early essay spoke about religion he was being considerably more merciful and understanding than those who later claimed to be his followers.

Indeed, it was necessary for his argument that he should accept the fact that religion fulfills a real need. He imagined religion as a garland of dead flowers, which men ought to throw away in order to gather the living flowers—the world as it is, and men revolving around their own true sun. There was consolation in the old garland, but there was a greater consolation in the living blossoms.

In saying this, he was saying no more than thousands of other young men brought up on Hegel and Feuerbach were saying at the time. Even when he went on to declare that "the task of history, once the other-worldly truth has vanished, is to establish the truth of this world," he was saying nothing that had not been said a thousand times before. What was profoundly new, and intolerably wrongheaded and dangerous, was the conclusion of the essay which follows a long dissertation on the differences between the political characters of France and Germany. He asks how France and Germany can break their fetters, and answers that France will act dramatically, idealistically, all the classes acting together, while Germany will act epically, egotistically, the classes refusing to act together unless they are moved by immediate needs and material necessities, or unless "the fetters demand it." France will be explosive, splendid, daring; Germany will be lethargic, cautious, mediocre. Nevertheless the time will come when the Germans by virtue of their disabilities will also have their revolution. They will have a philosophic revolution, and this in turn will bring about the abolition of the proletariat.

The theme is worked out with a wonderful display of philosophical jargon and a furious abandonment of logic. Marx will speak in the most casual fashion about "a *total loss* of humanity capable of redeeming itself only by a *total redemption* of humanity," and he will grant to the proletariat completely arbitrary powers, as he summons it from the depths of nonexistence and places it firmly in the realm of philosophy. Here for the first time he performs the magic spell which conjures up the proletariat and its ultimate dissolution. He asks what is the real possibility of bringing about a revolution in Germany:

> *Reply:* In the creation of a class with *radical chains,* a class of bourgeois society which is not a class of bourgeois society, a class which is the dissolution of all strata, a sphere which has a universal character by reason of its universal sufferings, and which does not claim a *particular right* because the wrong it has suffered is not a *particular wrong* but *positively wrong,* and which can provoke no *historical* status but only a *human* status, and which is not in one-sided opposition to the consequences but is in all-sided opposition to the assumptions of the German political system, a sphere finally which cannot emancipate itself without emancipating itself from all the other spheres, which is, in short, a *total loss* of humanity capable of redeeming itself only by a *total redemption* of humanity. This dissolution of society, as a particular class, is the *proletariat.*

Here for the first time Marx announces his theory of the proletariat. With its difficult syntax, its obfuscations, its implicit reliance on absolute words like *total, universal,* and *all-sided,* which beg the question, the paragraph nevertheless possesses a discernible meaning. Some huge and powerful force seems to be emerging through the deadening crust of words, and even Marx seems to be uncertain what it is, but at least he is able to give a name to it. The proletariat comes as a redeemer, the class which is not a class, the dissolution of classes. The redeemer possesses no history and is mysteriously indifferent to the laws of history, having nothing whatsoever to do with the accepted dogmas of German political systems. It is significant that there should have been this summons to a redeemer, for it was precisely this aspect of the theory which would ultimately have the greatest influence on men's imaginations. The redeemer does not come in a fiery chariot, visible to all as he streams across the heavens, but instead he remains invisible, concealed in philosophical robes.

Marx was perfectly aware that in 1843 the proletariat had not yet made its official appearance on the German stage, for there were only a few people who could legitimately be called proletarian. Indeed, in the very next sentence, Marx declares that "the proletariat is only just beginning to come into existence in Germany with the emerging industrial movement." The theory, such as it was, was based on the small cloud appearing over the horizon.

Once Marx had established in his own mind that the proletariat was the wave of the future, and had shrouded it in philosophical wrappings, it was not difficult to reach the conclusion that "the *head* of this emancipation is *philosophy,* its *heart* is the *proletariat.*" Such a formula answered to his own private needs, and had no necessary relation to anything outside himself. What he clearly meant was that the proletariat would eventually bring about a revolution under the guidance of a philosophical revolutionary, who was evidently himself, and this would lead to a classless society in which the proletariat itself would be dissolved. "Philosophy can be realized only by the abolition of the proletariat, the proletariat can be abolished only by the realization of philosophy."

Such arguments could not have arisen in any other language but German. Translated into English or French, or even into Russian, they lose their force. Marx's continual play of antitheses becomes ultimately a vulgar trick, and the essay is full of those clever antitheses which are pleasing to schoolboys. Here, for example, he is seen castigating Luther: "He shattered the faith in authority by restoring the authority of faith. He transformed the priests into laymen by turning laymen into priests. He liberated the body from its chains by placing the heart in chains." Such contrived effects are always unpleasant; they are especially unpleasant when they accompany prophetic utterances. Marx was never more prophetic than when he recognized the power of the emerging proletariat. "A Contribution to the Critique of Hegel's Philosophy of Law" concludes with still another prophecy: "When all the inner conditions have been fulfilled, the *German resurrection* will be heralded by *the crowing of the Gallic cock.*"

This strange and bewildering essay with its brilliant pyrotechnics, prophecies, improvisations, exhibitions of schoolboyish cleverness and philosophical jargon has some importance in history. Here in confused and uncertain terms Marx labored to present a theory of revolution which would have an extraordinary effect on the lives of men living long after his death. With the words, "This dissolution of society, as a particular class, is the proletariat," he rang up the curtain on the long tragedy of modern communism. This was the beginning.

That the words even in the original German are not easily intelligible and were perhaps not completely intelligible to Marx himself does not alter the fact that they lie somewhere near the center of Marx's thought. These words were to become his obsession. He would repeat them continually in different forms to the end of his life. He had found the Archimedean point through which the world could be overturned.

On internal evidence the essay was written in four sittings in four entirely different moods by an author who did not know where his argument was leading him. The last words were dictated perhaps by wish-fulfillment, for he intended to leave shortly for Paris to edit the *Deutsch-Französische Jahrbücher* with Arnold Ruge. In his imagination the revolution would begin in France and then sweep across Germany, and he was determined to be present at the cockcrow.

The long honeymoon came to an end with the coming of winter. In November, armed with the two essays—"On the Jewish Question" and the essay in which he announced the discovery of the proletariat—he left the house of the Baroness von Westphalen at Kreuznach and set out for Paris, taking his bride with him. Never again would he be able to write so quietly and peacefully in an atmosphere of such contentment. At Kreuznach he dreamed his audacious dreams without the compulsions of poverty, which were soon to oppress him. In this small town his slightest wishes were obeyed, a carriage was waiting for him whenever it occurred to him to take a ride into the country, and he was free as the winds. When he left Kreuznach, his days of freedom were over.

One day, talking to Bruno Bauer, he had wondered aloud whether Jenny would be able to endure the rigors of the revolutionary life he was determined to follow. She had always been sheltered. What would happen when she faced privations?

Bruno Bauer was a man with a considerable experience of life and he had taken Jenny's measure.

"Your bride is quite capable of enduring everything by your side," he answered, and then he paused and added: "But who knows what will happen?"

It was as though he had some presentiment of the tormented years ahead.

HEINRICH HEINE

In his *Confessions* the poet Heinrich Heine tells the story of a meeting with the philosopher Hegel. They stood by an open window on a beautiful starlit night, and Heine, who had eaten well and was at peace with the world, heard himself murmuring about the beauty of the stars and how they were perhaps the abodes of the blessed, the promise of eternal life. It was a poetic moment and he expected Hegel to make some sweeping observation on the vastness of the heavens or the grandeur of the starry night. Instead the philosopher glared at him and said: "Future life, eh? So you want a reward because you supported your sick mother and refrained from poisoning your brother?"

This story bears all the signs of having been invented by Heine. It follows a familiar pattern: the innocent gaze, the ironic comment. He wrote at a time when the romantic dream, cultivated for half a century, was coming to an end in tragic despair, the yearning for paradise giving way to frustration and rage. A cold wind was sweeping through the enchanted garden, and soon there would be only the bare boughs and the fallen leaves.

Like Marx, Heine came from a family of some wealth, studied at German universities, and spent most of his active life in exile. Like Marx, too, he suffered from excruciating poverty for long periods, and lived in bourgeois respectability with his wife. But there the resemblance ends. Marx was dogmatic, given to harsh rages, never satisfied until he had dominated his audience. Heine was made of gentler stuff. His character was more French than German. Generous and charming, confident of his genius, he seemed to himself to be a privileged spectator of the human comedy, and it would no more have occurred to him to drown the world in blood because governments were evil than it would have occurred to him to drown his wife when she was unfaithful to him. He celebrated life even when his eyes failed, when every movement of his crippled body was an agony, and his flesh was an open sore.

When Marx came to live in Paris late in 1843, Heine was one of the first people he sought out. There were many reasons for seeking a meeting. As a student Marx had written poems closely modeled on those of Heine, and there was a debt to repay. There was also the fact that Heine had recently engaged in a running battle with the Prussian government, writing satiric poems designed to laugh the Prussians out of existence. In articles written for the *Augsburger Allgemeine Zeitung* Heine had discussed the emerging social forces in France with great penetration, and many Germans were beginning to regard him as a formidable social critic. Above all there was Heine's stature as a poet, as the last survivor of the great period of German romantic poetry. For all these reasons Marx felt there was everything to be gained by arranging a meeting.

Their first meeting came about in December, apparently through the good offices of Moses Hess. There were many subsequent meetings. Heine became a frequent visitor to the small crowded house on Rue Vanneau. He was gallant to Jenny, and long-suffering when Marx went into one of his long harangues. In Marx's eyes Heine lacked the proper characteristics of a revolutionary, but he judged these political weaknesses indulgently, saying that poets were queer fellows and not entirely responsible for their own actions. He would defend Heine against Engels and anyone else who attacked him, claiming that poets could not be measured by standards applied to other men. Marx liked to have poets about him, but Heine was the only authentic poet he ever knew.

Heine's attitude toward communism was one of profound disquiet. He saw it coming and spoke about it with prophetic insight. In letters written for the *Augsburger Allgemeine Zeitung,* he described the coming of the dark hero. He wrote on June 20, 1842:

> Although little discussed today, communism is the dark hero now loitering in hidden garrets on miserable straw pallets—the hero destined to play a great, even if only temporary, role in the modern tragedy, and he is only waiting for the cue to make his entrance. We must never lose this actor from our sight; and from time to time we intend to report on the secret rehearsals at which he prepares for his debut.

Three weeks later, on July 12, Heine, still wearing his prophetic robes, spoke of a coming war, "a most hideous war of destruction," involving Russia, Germany, France and Great Britain. Only Russia and Britain would survive, for the Russians had the advantages of a vast unconquerable territory and the British could always crawl back into their watery lair. But this was only the first act in the terrible drama; new and even more terrible forces were at work:

> In the second act we see the European and the World Revolution, the great duel between the destitute and the aristocracy of wealth; and in this there will be no talk of either nationality or religion; there will be only one fatherland, the earth, and only one faith, that in happiness on earth. . . . Perhaps there will be only one flock and one shepherd, one free shepherd with an iron staff and a flock of human sheep all shorn alike and bleating alike! Wild, gloomy times are roaring toward us, and the prophet who wishes to write the new Apocalypse would have to invent entirely new beasts, and they would be so terrible that the ancient animal symbols of St. John would be like gentle doves and cupids. The gods are veiling their faces out of pity for the children of men, their foster children for so long, and perhaps they do so out of apprehension over their own fate. The future smells of Russian leather, blood, godlessness, and many whippings. I should advise our grandchildren to be born with very thick skins on their backs.

As a visionary Heine saw far beyond his time; as a reporter he saw matters closer at hand. In the summer of the following year he reported that the communists, by which he meant the followers of Blanqui, were the only party in France which deserved attention, and he estimated that there were in Paris about 400,000 persons "who only await the word of command to realize the idea of absolute equality which broods in their rude brains." Revolution was in the air, and he was not prepared merely to watch it from a distance.

About the time that Marx arrived in Paris, Heine was searching for a revolutionary party he could join with a clear conscience. He was impressed by Marx's arguments, and even more impressed by Marx, who looked the part of the Jacobin revolutionary. Dark-skinned, dark-browed, dark-bearded, with flashing eyes and a mane of glistening blue-black hair, he walked with the assurance of his intellectual brilliance and seemed quite naturally to rise above his fellows. What Marx wanted from Heine was a more violent revolutionary poetry, and this poetry was soon forthcoming.

Not that Marx was responsible for the revolutionary character of Heine's poems. Marx would claim, or rather Arnold Ruge would make the claim for him, that he had effectively challenged the poet, saying: "Drop these everlasting complaints about love and show those lyrical poets how it really ought to be done—with the whip!" The words are so much in keeping with Marx's known character that it is almost certain that he spoke in exactly this way, but great poets do not jump to the commands of minor revolutionaries. Heine was already writing a more vigorous and biting poetry when Marx appeared on the scene.

For a few months Heine seems to have basked in Marx's admiration.

We hear of them studying verses together, poring over eight-line poems, discussing each individual word, the rhymes, the rhythms, polishing them until the required smoothness was achieved. Marx's early enthusiasm for poetry revived, and he appears to have started writing poems again.

He was also beginning to move about in the society of revolutionary exiles, sharpening his mind on the opinions and obsessions of others. He was seeing many Russians, including the elegant Pavel Annenkov, who was to write a voluminous book of memoirs in which Marx is depicted with quite astonishing brilliance, and Count Grigory Tolstoy, a legendary *bon vivant,* who publicly proclaimed his adherence to revolutionary causes while secretly dispatching reports on the revolutionaries he met to the secret police in St. Petersburg. He was also seeing a good deal of Mikhail Bakunin, who was later to become his baffled adversary. Bakunin was an aristocratic anarchist, his views already fixed, his talent for improvising revolutions not yet revealed to the world. He enjoyed listening to Marx, and nearly thirty years later he could still remember the strange effect which Marx produced on him—the towering intelligence, the pride, and the wit. He wrote:

> In those days Marx was much more advanced than I was, and he still remains today incomparably more advanced than I—so far as learning is concerned. I knew nothing at that time of political economy, I still had not got rid of metaphysical abstractions, and my socialism was only instinctive. He, although younger than I, was already an atheist, an instructed materialist, and a conscious socialist. It was precisely at this time that he elaborated the first bases of his system as it is today.
>
> We saw each other often, for I greatly respected him for his learning and for his passionate and serious devotion to the cause of the proletariat, though it was always mingled with vanity. I eagerly sought his conversation, which was always instructive and witty, when it was not inspired by petty spite—which, alas, was only too often the case. There was, however, never any frank intimacy between us. Our temperaments did not allow it. He called me a sentimental idealist, and he was right. I called him vain, perfidious and sly, and I was right too.

They were men of such dominating characters that the wonder is that they did not come to blows within five minutes of starting a conversation. Bakunin was the revolutionary *grand seigneur,* Marx the learned pundit of revolution who knew all the answers even before the questions were put. In the eyes of Marx the greatest failing of Bakunin was that he was intolerably ignorant of revolutionary theory. But it was Bakunin who actively took part in revolutions, led the mobs, and lived dangerously.

Marx had no particular appetite for living dangerously. What he enjoyed above all was thinking dangerously, on the edge of thought, beyond the categories of good and evil. He had demonstrated this power in his savage article "On the Jewish Question" written during his honeymoon, and the curiously mistitled "A Contribution to the Critique of Hegel's Philosophy of Law," in which he had tossed so many memorable and barbed epigrams at his readers that they took on the aspect of a barrage of machine-gun fire. To the end of his life he was to remain the *verbal* revolutionary, dreaming vast dreams on paper while never coming close to the barricades.

In all his life he was probably never happier than during the year ne spent in Paris. In February the first, and only, number of the *Deutsch-Französische Jahrbücher* appeared, and he could congratulate himself on having produced a book-length magazine of quite exceptional brilliance. Although the magazine failed to live up to its title—there were no French contributors at all—it gave the impression of being dedicated to all the emerging revolutionary forces in Europe. It was savage, violent, youthful, and sometimes funny. Heine contributed some satiric odes on King Ludwig of Bavaria. Herwegh, Ruge, and Bakunin, the only non-German, were all permitted to sound off either in formal articles or in the letters which were gathered together at the beginning of the magazine, like a highly seasoned hors d'oeuvres. Marx included his two honeymoon essays, and added some letters of his own written with more gaiety than he was normally able to muster.

Much of this gaiety derived from Jenny, who would soon present him with his first child. Occasionally she accompanied him on his visits to the salons of great ladies. Through his friend Herwegh, or perhaps through Heine, he was introduced to the salon of the Comtesse Marie d'Agoult, the daughter of a French officer who had served in Germany. The countess was the mistress of Liszt and a friend of all the musicians, painters, philosophers, and poets of Paris. She was a novelist under the name of Daniel Stern, and being rich, cultivated and liberal in her sympathies, it amused her to gather revolutionaries around her. At one of her musical soirées one might encounter Chopin, Meyerbeer, Sainte-Beuve, Ingres, Heine, Alfred de Musset and Alfred de Vigny, and there would be her daughter Cosima, later to become Cosima Wagner. Adolphe Thiers and Guizot, who dominated French politics for many years, would come late and leave early. Against these two pillars of French society Marx would hurl his thunderbolts with all the more relish because he had met them socially, or at least sat in the same music room with them.

The countess' hotel was a place where intrigues flowered, newspapers were founded, and *agents provocateurs* found themselves side by side with revolutionaries. Though much admired, the *Deutsch-Französische Jahrbücher* had proved to be a failure financially, and Marx, seeking an audience, found it in a German weekly review called *Vorwärts* (Forward), which had its beginnings in one of the countess' soirées. It was financed by Meyerbeer, the composer of flamboyant operas, official *Kapellmeister* to the King of Prussia, a man of many skills. The young Ferdinand Bernays was made editor in chief, and Adalbert von Bornstedt, an Austrian spy and *agent provocateur* in the pay of the King of Prussia, was given the post of editorial assistant. Meyerbeer's intention appears to have been to "smoke out" the German revolutionary exiles in Paris by giving them a platform from which they could give vent to their most resounding threats against the monarchy. In the *Deutsch-Französische Jahrbücher* Marx thundered against the many tyrannies of the Prussian King, and he continued to thunder against them in the pages of *Vorwärts.* Many of his collaborators in the yearbook joined him in these new assaults on the monarchy. Marx wrote an article on the plight of the Silesian weavers, and in the same issue there appeared Heine's "Song of the Silesian Weavers" with its triple curse on the blind God who refused to see their misery, the king who sent his soldiers against them, and the false fatherland which gave them only hunger and shame. Engels, who possessed considerable skill as a translator, later rendered the song into English:

> Without a tear in their grim eyes,
> They sit at the loom, the rage of despair in their faces;
> We have suffered and hungered long enough,
> Old Germany, we are weaving a shroud for thee,
> And weaving it with a triple curse.
> We are weaving, weaving.

The note of terror and doom is sustained through three more verses. Heine had never written more angrily, and both Marx and Engels felt they had acquired a new recruit.

In May Jenny gave birth to her first child, a daughter, who was called Jenny. One day, not long afterward, Heine came to visit the young parents, and found the infant in convulsions with the parents looking on helplessly. Heine took one look at the infant, said calmly: "The proper thing is to put her in a hot bath," and then prepared the bath himself and laid Jenny in it. The child quickly recovered, and Frau Marx wondered for the rest of her life how Heine had come to acquire so much knowledge in so many fields.

Soon she went back to Germany to display the newborn child to her mother and her husband's mother. Two of her letters, written to Marx from Trier have survived. They are strange letters for they seem to be written in joy and despair, with a wild elation and in the grip of fear. The baby gave her a most exquisite joy, but when she thought of the career which Marx had marked out for himself, she gave way to sudden terrified visions of a future too grim to contemplate. "Dear heart, I have so great a feeling of uneasiness about our future," she wrote. "Please calm my fears." But the next moment she is rejoicing in her young strength and tossing all her fears away:

> We talk far too much about a *steady* income. I answer simply with my red cheeks, my white flesh, my velvet cloak, my feathered hat, and my be-ribboned finery. With these I shall strike the best and deepest blows, and if I am laid low, regard it as of no importance. The baby is so marvelously white. . . .

She knew him well, and from the safe distance of Trier she could bring herself to castigate him gently for the ugly violence of his writings, reminding him that an unpretentious French soldier in casual disarray was a match for the stern goose-stepping guards in the Prussian army:

> Please don't write with so much rancor and irritation. Either write factually and deliberately or humorously and lightly. Please, dear heart, just let the pen run lightly over the page, and if the pen should now and then fall and stumble, then those words of yours, your thoughts, stand erect like the Grenadiers of the Old Guard, brave and steadfast, and as they say, *elle meurt mais elle ne se rend pas*. What does it matter if the uniform hangs badly and is not so elegantly tailored? On French soldiers their loose, light uniform looks so pretty! Think of our well-turned-out Prussians—doesn't it make you shudder? So loosen the harness straps and let the scarves fall free and toss away the shako—let the participles run and put the words where they want to be. A race of warriors does not march so correctly. And your troops are still marching in the field?
>
> Good luck then to the general, my black master. Farewell, dearest heart, darling and only life.

So Jenny wrote in June, when the long summer days stretched ahead, and she could forget for a while the ominous thunderclouds. She wrote with gaiety and good sense, showing herself to be an admirable literary critic and a delighted observer of the daily scene. Sometimes when least expected there would come the sudden note of apprehension, the fear clutching at her heart.

When August came, she knew she would soon have to return to Paris and to the strange bohemian life, for which she had no talent. She was frightened of Paris now, and frightened too by the prospect of a second child which would inevitably come when they began living together again. Paris, seen in retrospect, was a place where terror walked in the daylight, and she would find herself weighing "the dark feeling of anxiety, of fear, of menace," which lurked in Paris, against the joy of being in his arms. But mostly she wrote about the baby, healthy and strong and "quiet as a mouse," who spent her days smiling at the patterns on the wallpaper—Jenny was quite sure that this was the most enchanting child who had ever been born. She wrote, too, about all the pageantry surrounding the presentation of the Holy Coat in the cathedral. Rose garlands hung from all the houses, and everyone was buying the little Christ-coats made of ribbons. Everyone was flocking to Trier, the hotels were crowded, booths and tents were being set up in the market place, two hundred new taverns had been opened, and circuses, menageries, dioramas, open-air theaters were all springing up for the entertainment of the pilgrims who came to venerate the Holy Coat. "People seem to have gone mad," she wrote, remembering that Marx disapproved of holy relics with considerable vehemence. "I suppose all hell is breaking loose with you, too."

For once Marx was not suffering any particular hell. He was engrossed in writing the manuscripts which were to become known as "The Economic and Philosophical Manuscripts of 1844," because no title could be found among his papers. These essays were first published in 1932 after nearly a century of neglect. They are in a considerable state of disorder, whole sections are lost, but some ninety pages of close-written inquiry into the nature of alienation remain. They are discursive essays with abrupt changes of tone indicating that they were written at widely different times or in different moods. Occasionally he employs the rhetorical violence of his essay on the Jews, but for the most part he writes with a kind of studied gravity. In the essay on the Jews he attacked the problem sadistically: the Jews were alien, and must be cut off, annihilated, punished for their addiction to the bourgeois vices. Now, in the "Economic and Philosophical Manuscripts," he sees that all men are alienated from life by the circumstances of modern civilization, and no one is more alienated than the workingman, who is enslaved by capital. Once again, as so often in the course of his life, he employs the myth of Prometheus to illustrate his theme. Here he describes the modern laborer alienated from all that makes life worth living:

> Man returns to living in a cave, now contaminated with the pestilential breath of civilization, and he continues to live in the cave *precariously,* for it is an alien habitation which can be withdrawn from him at any moment—if he does not pay for it he can be thrown out at any moment. For this mortuary he has to *pay.* A dwelling in the *light,* which Prometheus in Aeschylus described as one of the greatest boons, so that the savage was trans-

formed thereby into a human being, ceases to exist for the worker. Light, air, etc.—the simplest *animal* cleanliness—cease to be a need for man. *Filth*—the stagnation and putrefaction of man—the *sewage* of civilization (speaking quite literally)—comes to be the *essence of life* for him. Utter, unnatural neglect, putrefied nature, comes to be the essence of his life. None of his senses exist any longer, and not only in his human fashion, but in an *inhuman* fashion, and therefore not even in an animal fashion.

Marx paints the picture as black as possible: the English worker at his treadmill, the Irishman gasping for potatoes, the laborer reduced to a mindless child by the pressures of poverty and a suffocating civilization. He seems to be whipping himself up into a fury, justifying his passionate invective by the purpose he has in view, which is to show that alienation is the common lot of man, and only when private property has been abolished will men rise free from their bondage. Private property derives from alienated man, alienated labor, and alienated life. Abolish private property, and man rises to the fullness of his creativity, free to live in all his individuality. Man should labor freely, not for pay. He should not be bound by the arbitrary and merciless demands of capital. Living as an alien in France, alienated from his religion and his country, Marx writes with passionate conviction about the plight of the alienated worker, himself, impoverished, reduced to gathering crumbs from the tables of the wealthy. There is never a moment when he convinces you that he is talking about real workers. He is not concerned with social progress. What concerns him is the revolution which will take place the moment private property is abolished; at that moment the alien world will give way to a world of freedom.

If this were all, the "Economic and Philosophical Manuscripts" would not deserve careful study. In fact they are central to the long argument which Marx maintained with the world. He rarely spoke about alienation again. It was a subject which he appeared to avoid, because it was one of immense complexity and because it was too deeply involved with his own personal feelings. But it is precisely this sense of alienation which underlies his mature work like a ground swell, giving passion and dimension to his demand for a revolutionary change in society. Long before industrial society reduced men to statistics, he was examining the disproportion between man's desire for freedom and industry's power to enslave. He came to no hopeful conclusions, for he was never able to explain how the abolition of private property would give man the freedom he desired; for if all property became the property of the state, who would protect man from the state?

In September, when he had apparently completed these essays, Friedrich Engels, who had been converted to communism by Moses Hess, came to visit him. They had met briefly when Marx was editing the *Rheinische Zeitung*. Engels was appalled by Marx's dogmatic tone and at that time made no effort to continue the acquaintance. Now, meeting in Paris, they found that they shared a common purpose and a common attitude toward the world. Engels was tall and gangling, with pale-blue eyes, sandy hair, thick lips, and a nose which seemed in some curious way to be unrelated to the rest of his face, with the result that he took a special dislike to any portraits of himself in profile. He was the son of a textile manufacturer in Barmen, and was intended for a business career. There was no question of sending him to a university; he studied in commercial schools, and then served a term of military service in the Artillery Guards, from which he developed a lifelong interest in military strategy. He stuttered when he was excited, but he was rarely excited. Cold, always superbly self-controlled, possessing an almost incredible fluency in many languages, his mind running like a well-oiled machine, he presented an admirable foil to Marx, who was hot-blooded, possessed little self-control, and had no fluency at all, for he wrote and thought with difficulty, chipping each word from his own breastbone. The friendship between Marx and Engels, begun in August 1844, was to endure until Marx's death nearly forty years later.

Marx was impressed with Engels' quick brain and suggested that they should collaborate on a work of destructive criticism to expose the errors of the Berlin Hegelians, especially Bruno Bauer, who had been Marx's teacher. In this way he hoped to clear the ground for a philosophical study of communism to be embarked upon at a later period. Engels was delighted, for it gave him an opportunity to mount a ferocious attack on speculative idealism, but after writing about ten pages he wearied of the task and returned to Barmen to complete his long-projected book *The Condition of the Working Class in England, from personal inspection and authentic sources.* He had studied English factory life in his father's textile mill in Manchester and he was more interested in practical observation than in theory.

They agreed that the book should be called *Critique of Critical Critique / Against Bruno Bauer and His Consorts,* and this title, so heavy with youthful fervor, was designed to suggest the infinite contempt of the young writers for their venerable adversaries. Among themselves they called the book *The Holy Family.*

Although the book covers some 225 closely printed pages in the collected edition of Marx's works, there are scarcely three pages which can still be read with any profit. For the most part it is a farrago of excerpts from Marx's notebooks on every conceivable subject from the novels of Eugène Sue to the philosophy of Spinoza, from the history of the French Revolution to the ideas of Pierre-Joseph Proudhon. A preponderant amount of space is given to the rebuttal of the ideas of a certain Franz Zychlin von Zychlinsky, whose articles in the *Allgemeine Literatur-Zeitung* Marx set out to slaughter with a sledge hammer.

During this year Marx had been giving a great deal of attention to the alienation of the working classes from society, and he now attempted to consider alienation within the framework of Hegelian dialectics. A very simple solution now presented itself. Wealth was the thesis, the proletariat was the antithesis, and the synthesis would come about when the proletariat had effectively dissolved and destroyed wealth. In this way he thought he had discovered the philosophical basis for the revolution which would bring the proletariat to power.

The theory, as Marx stated it, was presented with quite astonishing assurance, and since it represents the first appearance of the theory of Marxist communism, it should be quoted here at some length. Suddenly, in the midst of a commentary on some ideas of Proudhon, Marx inserts a series of categorical statements which seem to have been torn from a single sheet of his notebook. These statements have almost nothing to do with what has gone before or what comes later. They stand in isolation, like mathematical equations inserted in a book of journalistic criticism. He wrote:

> Proletariat and Wealth are opposites. As such they form a whole. They are both forms of the world of private property. What concerns us here is to define the exact position each assumes in opposition. It is not enough to state that they are two sides of a whole.
>
> Private property as private property, as wealth, is compelled to maintain its own *existence* and thereby the existence of its opposite, the proletariat. This is the *positive* side of the opposition, private property satisfied in itself.
>
> The proletariat on the other hand is compelled as proletariat to abolish itself together with its determining opposite, that which makes it the proletariat—private property. This is the *negative* side of the opposition, its restlessness within itself, dissolved and self-dissolving private property.
>
> The possessing class and the class of the proletariat present the same human self-alienation. But the former class finds in this self-alienation its own confirmation and its own good, *its own power,* and possesses in it the *semblance* of human existence. The latter class feels annihilated in its self-alienation, sees in it its impotence and the reality of an inhuman existence. In the words of Hegel, the class of the proletariat is in its abasement indignant at that abasement, an indignation to which it is necessarily driven by the contradiction between its human *nature* and its condition of life, which is the frank, decisive and comprehensive negation of that nature.

Within this opposition, therefore, the owner of private property is the *conservative*, the proletarian the *destructive* party. From the former arises the action of preservation of the opposition, from the latter the action of its annihilation.

Indeed private property drives itself in its economic movement, but only by a development which is independent of and opposed to its will, unconscious, conditioned by the very nature of things; only inasmuch as it produces the proletariat *as* proletariat, that misery conscious of its spiritual and physical misery, that dehumanization conscious of its dehumanization and therefore self-abolishing.

The proletariat executes the sentence that private property pronounced on itself by begetting the proletariat, just as it carries out the sentence which wage-labor pronounced on itself by bringing forth wealth for others and misery for itself. If the proletariat is victorious, it does not at all mean that it becomes the absolute side of society, for it is victorious only by abolishing itself and its opposite. Then the proletariat and its determining opposite, private property, disappear.

In this heavy Germanic manner, with the air of someone pronouncing the ultimate laws which operate on mankind, Marx presented a theory which was to be regarded with the utmost seriousness by his followers, who rarely permitted themselves to observe how many *non sequiturs* and lapses of logic were contained in it. Human poverty and misery become abstractions; the flow of life is converted into a strange trapeze act in the upper air; thesis and antithesis advance toward each other armed with summary judgments; and the final vanishing tricks are performed in full view of the audience by a conjuror who has himself vanished under the weight of his arguments. How or why these categories of wealth and proletariat should act in this manner is never explained. As Marx must have known, he had chosen arbitrary symbols which he maneuvered in an arbitrary way, and with exactly the same reasoning it would be possible to prove that wealth would destroy the proletariat, and then destroy itself.

Desire, not logic, ruled Marx's mind. Determined to find philosophical justification for a revolutionary war between the classes, he devised a theory which involved abstractions piled upon abstractions. Only one statement rang clear. *"Das Proletariat vollzieht das Urteil"*—"The proletariat executes the sentence." The whole edifice of abstractions was designed to justify those five words.

Across all his later works there would fall the shadow of that extraordinary philosophical monologue.

The book in which this outline of communism first appeared was published in Frankfurt in February 1845 under the title *The Holy Family, or Critique of Critical Critique / Against Bruno Bauer and His Consorts.*

Although Engels had written only a few pages, his name appeared first on the title page, a fact which gave him little pleasure. "The new title *The Holy Family* will only lead to family upsets with my pious father, who is now highly annoyed with me, but of course you could not be expected to know this," he wrote, after receiving the brochure announcing the publication of the book. "I see from the announcement that you have put my name first. Why? I wrote hardly any of it, and everyone can recognize your style." But a few days later, when he received the book, he confessed to being amazed by the splendid writing. He had however a few minor objections. The book was virtually incomprehensible to the general public, it was much too long, and there was something abysmally wrong in devoting 352 pages to denouncing some unimportant articles in the *Allgemeine Literatur-Zeitung*. "Nevertheless," Engels added, "the book is brilliantly written, and I laugh until I am ill."

The modern reader finds little to laugh at in *The Holy Family,* which is not so much a book as an obstacle race. The spectacle of Marx lambasting obscure literary critics is not a pleasant one. He buttonholes the reader, sneers, cajoles, interrupts his own arguments with biting commentaries on anything that especially displeases him, and from the heights of his omniscience demands instant obedience to his views. It was his first full-length book and he was very proud of it.

Meanwhile in the pages of *Vorwärts* he was announcing ideas which were considerably more dangerous than literary criticism or philosophical speculation. His constant theme was revolution, the destruction of the old order, the seizure of power by means never precisely indicated because he was still so wrapped up in philosophical terminology that it seemed sufficient to speak of "dissolution" rather than of barricades. "*Socialism* cannot be brought into existence without *revolution,*" he proclaimed. "When the *organizing activity* begins, when the *soul,* the *thing in itself,* appears, then socialism can toss aside all the *political* veils." Hidden among the italics and the philosophical jargon, there can be detected a desire to impose socialism on the people by naked power.

Vorwärts was soon in difficulty with the printer, the censor, and the police. It survived with difficulty, but always appeared on schedule as a result of the herculean efforts of the editorial committee and perhaps of the *agents provocateurs,* in whose interest it was that the newspaper should appear regularly. The editorial committee met in an upstairs room in the Rue des Moulins. They were so noisy that they kept the windows closed for fear that people outside would hear them arguing at the top of their voices and imagine they were killing each other; and since everyone was smoking, they were soon very nearly suffocated. Ferdinand Bernays, the editor in chief, was the first to suffer at the hands of the police. On the technical charge that he had not paid a license fee he was sentenced to two months' imprisonment and ordered to pay a fine of three hundred francs. Meanwhile the government kept a close watch on the newspaper and its contributors, alarmed by their revolutionary fervor and the vehemence of the attacks on King Frederick William IV of Prussia, a mild king who was not particularly pleased to learn from the pages of *Vorwärts* that his assassination would be an excellent prelude to a German revolution. Through his ambassador he asked that measures be taken to suppress the newspaper. It was explained to the ambassador that if *Vorwärts* were brought to trial the case would be decided by a jury, and there was no guarantee that the jury would vote in favor of the King of Prussia.

Heine left Paris for a short visit to his mother in Hamburg. He wrote a long letter to Marx promising to contribute more satiric verses to *Vorwärts*, at the same time complaining against the violent tone of the newspaper and what appeared to be the deliberate attempt by the editors to compromise the contributors. He suspected, with good reason, that strange forces were at work to destroy the newspaper and its contributors, and he seems to have suspected the real purpose behind Meyerbeer's generosity.

The letter to Marx, which has survived, shows that they were on fairly intimate terms and were seeing a good deal of one another. He wrote:

Hamburg, 21 Sept. 1844

DEAREST MARX!

I am again suffering from my distressing eye trouble, and it is only with an effort that I can scrawl these lines to you. Meanwhile the most important thing I want to tell you can wait till the beginning of next month when I can talk to you in person, for I am preparing my departure—after a disquieting hint from Above. I have no inclination to be hunted; my legs have no talent for wearing iron shackles, as Weitling wore them. He showed me the scars. I am suspected of a more important participation in *Vorwärts* than I can boast, and to tell the truth the newspaper displays the greatest mastery in the art of incitement and the publication of compromising material. Where is this to lead? . . .

Let us hope no web of perfidies is being spun in Paris! My book is off the press and will be published within ten days or two weeks, and so there will be no immediate uproar. The proof sheets of the political part—particularly the part with the long poem—I am sending you today by book-post with a threefold intention. First of all to amuse you, secondly so that you can make arrangements right away to campaign for it in the German press, and thirdly, should you so desire, so that you may print the best of the new poems in *Vorwärts*. . . .

Hamburg den 21 Sept. 1844.

Liebster Marx! Ich leide wieder an meinem fatalen Augenübel, und nur mit Mühe kritzle ich Ihnen diese Zeilen. Indessen, was ich Ihnen wichtiges zu sagen, kann ich Ihnen Anfangs nächsten Monat mündlich sagen, denn ich bereite mich zur Abreise beängstigt durch einen Wink von Oben — ich habe nicht Lust auch mich fassen zu lassen, meine Beine haben kein Talent eiserne Ringe zu tragen, wie Weitling sie trug. Er zeigte mir die Spuren. Man vermuthet bey mir größere ~~[illegible]~~ Theilnahme am Vorwärts als ich mich deren rühmen kann und ehrlich gestanden das Blatt beurkundet die größte Meisterschaft im Aufreitzen und Compromittiren. Was soll das geben, sogar Mäurer ist deboardirt! — Wunderlich mich hierüber. Wenn nur keine Verfolgungen in Paris aufgenommen werden. Mein Buch ist gedruckt, wird aber erst in 10 bis 14 Tagen hier ausgegeben, damit nicht gleich Lärm geschlagen wird. Die Aushängebogen der politischen Theile, namentlich wo mein großes Gedicht, schicke ich Ihnen heute unter Kreuzcouvert, in dreyfacher Absicht. Nämlich, erstens damit Sie sich damit amusiren, zweitens damit Sie schon gleich Anstalten treffen können für das Buch in der deutschen Presse zu wirken, und drittens damit Sie, wenn Sie es rathsam erachten im Vorwärts das Beste aus dem neuen Gedichte abdrucken lassen können.

The first page of Heine's letter to Marx, September 21, 1844.

I shall bring the beginning of the book to you in Paris. It consists only of romances and ballads which will please your wife. It is my friendliest request that you greet her heartily for me. I am delighted that I shall be seeing her. I hope next winter will be less melancholy for us than the last. . . .

I am delighted to be coming to you soon. I have already sent my wife to France to see her mother, who is dying. Farewell, dear friend, and excuse this dreadful scribble. I cannot read back what I have written—but we need very few signs in order to understand one another.

Devotedly

H. HEINE

The proof sheets Heine sent to Marx consisted of a long satirical poem called "Germany, A Winter's Tale," written during the previous winter, at times brilliantly brutal, at other times strained and mawkish, as though the poet was unable to come to terms with his despair. Ghosts wander through nightmares of medieval Germany, the axman announces the coming of revolution, the fires burn on the castle walls; and the poet "lying on a hard mattress in the sleepless night of exile" sometimes gives way to clownish horseplay. This long poem, covering over eighty pages, was calculated to give Marx intense pleasure, for it contained the kind of revolutionary poetry he hoped to see. The earlier poems in the book were altogether lyrical, and would please Jenny. Heine enjoyed her company, and looked forward to seeing her on his return to Paris.

He was not to enjoy her company for long. The French government, which had tolerated the presence of German revolutionaries in Paris, was beginning to find reasons to rid itself of an encumbrance. Marx was being closely shadowed by the police, who followed him to obscure lodging houses and taverns, and sent voluminous reports to the ministry. He was also being followed by Prussian spies, and in addition there were at least two spies on the editorial board of *Vorwärts*. He was a marked man, and the question was no longer whether he should be expelled but how the expulsion order would be issued, and by whom. In the normal course of events there would be a show of legality and Marx would be permitted to appeal against the order, with the inevitable delays. Some simpler and more categorical method seemed necessary.

In January 1845 the great scientist Alexander von Humboldt paid one of his periodic visits to the court of King Louis Philippe. He was on intimate and affectionate terms with the French royal family, and in addition he was armed with all the authority which came from being a special envoy of the King of Prussia. Among the subjects raised in conversation was the continued presence of German revolutionaries in Paris. A few days later the Ministry of the Interior issued the order for the expulsion of Marx, Ruge, Bernays, Heine and Bakunin within twenty-four hours. The order was not irrevocable, for it was understood that if they signed a statement promising to take no further part in political activity they would be permitted to remain. In the end only Marx felt the full force of the order, and he left Paris by stagecoach for Brussels at the end of January. In a letter to Heine written on January 12, 1845, when he thought he would be permitted to remain in Paris only for a few more hours, he said: "Dear friend . . . Of all the men I am leaving behind, for me to leave Heine is the most disagreeable of all."

In the following years they exchanged a desultory correspondence. Heine soon became disenchanted with the German communists, and from being half in love with them he came to detest them for their arrogance, their cynicism, and their indifference to the fate of the people they were leading into revolution. Seven years later he wrote:

> I have often pondered the story of the Babylonian king who thought he was the good God, but fell miserably from the height of his conceit to crawl like an animal on the ground and eat grass—of course it might well have been a salad. This story is found in the great and splendid Book of Daniel. I recommend it for the edification of my good friend Ruge, and also to my much more stubborn friend Marx, and also to Messrs Feuerbach, Daumer, Bruno Bauer, Hengstenberg, and the rest of the crowd of godless self-appointed gods.

THE LEAGUE OF THE JUST

BRUSSELS IN THE forties of the last century still resembled a town in the provinces. Belgium had been independent only since 1830, and everything about the country had an air of impermanence and improvisation, as though it were not yet accustomed to seeing itself on the map of Europe and expected at any moment to be swallowed up by its more powerful neighbors. The shadow of the Middle Ages hung heavy over the land, where the peasants wore medieval costumes and the rich burghers sometimes appeared in ermine coats and golden chains of office. Yet changes were rapidly taking place: industrialization was beginning to transform Belgium into a country of smokestacks and factories. Belgium was, in fact, one of the most advanced nations in Europe.

For the refugees who flocked to the Belgian capital there were few comforts. They found it hard to make a living, the Belgians disliked them, and they were kept under observation by the police. They were tolerated as long as they took no part in political affairs, but were usually expelled the moment they were found to be conducting any propaganda. The revolutionary groups therefore found their work severely restricted. There were refugees from Russia, Poland, France and Germany, and most of them were living a hand-to-mouth existence.

Marx traveled from Paris to Brussels in the company of Heinrich Bürgers, one of his closest followers, who had elected to join him in exile. Many years later Bürgers remembered that Marx was particularly gloomy during the journey, seeing himself confronted with the ruin of all his hopes. Jenny had been left behind. To pay the expenses of the journey she sold her furniture and linen, and on scarcely any money at all she would have to wait for some weeks before she was able to rejoin her husband. The Herweghs, who were rich and influential, had pity on her and let her stay in their house. In the stagecoach taking him to the Belgian frontier, Marx would sometimes join Bürgers in singing German songs in his wild and terrible voice, and then he would relapse into a melancholy silence.

They crossed the Belgian frontier at Quiévrain and reached Mons on the afternoon of February 1. On the following night they stayed at the Hôtel de la Gare in Brussels and on the next day set out in search of cheaper lodgings, which they found in the small Hôtel de Saxe, 24 Place du Petit Sablon. From there on February 7 Marx wrote an appeal to King Leopold I, begging for permission to bring his wife and child "to the territories of Your Majesty." He signed the letter: "Your Majesty's most respectful and obedient servant, Dr. Charles Marx." He received no answer to the appeal, and some weeks passed before Jenny and the children finally reached Brussels after a terrible journey in bitterly cold weather.

Marx's movements during his first days in Brussels have been carefully traced. We see him moving quickly from one hotel and lodging house to another, presumably to avoid the attentions of the police. On February 9 he left the Hôtel de Saxe and went to live at 21 Sainte Gudule, a lodging house. A few days later he obtained a furnished room at 7 Rue de Bois Sauvage nearby. All these places were in the center of the city in the shadow of the cathedral. On March 13 he suddenly slipped out of the city and went to live at 35 Rue Pacheco in the working-class district of Ixelles, and on May 1 we find him returning to the city, living at 6 Rue de l'Alliance near the Porte de Louvain, apparently so that he could be closer to the vast municipal library, where he spent most of the day. He was planning to write a *Critique of Politics and Political Economy* in two volumes, and had already signed a contract for it with a Darmstadt publisher and received an advance. According to the contract the book was to be completed by the summer. It was never written. Fourteen years would pass before he published *The Critique of Political Economy,* and twenty-two years would pass before *Das Kapital* was given to the world. The *Critique of Politics and Political Economy* was intended to range over all the territory covered by the two later works. Marx had hoped in a few months to write the work which he would not accomplish in a whole lifetime.

It was in this period, in the spring of 1845, probably during his stay at Ixelles, that Marx wrote his famous *Theses on Feuerbach,* in which he continued the arguments he had pursued in the "Economic and Philosophic Manuscripts of 1844" to their logical conclusions. According to Engels these eleven paragraphs constituted the seed of Marxist communism. "In this document," Engels wrote, "there was laid down for the first time the great seed of the new world view." One may doubt whether those brief theses were of quite such overwhelming importance. Using Feuerbach as a crutch, Marx was merely restating a position which was already implicit in his brief work on the Jews and his "Contribution to a Critique of Hegel's Philosophy of Law," and now, with the economic and philosophic manuscripts in front of him, he was able to arrive at a fixed position. This was stated most clearly in the sixth and eleventh theses:

> The essence of man is not an abstraction inherent in each particular individual. His real nature is the *ensemble* of social relations.
>
> The philosophers have only *interpreted* the world in different ways, the point is to *change* it.

With these statements, unsupported by any evidence, uttered in tones of resounding authority, Marx described a certain philosophical position which was to remain virtually unchanged for the rest of his life. Man vanished into "the *ensemble* of social relations," and philosophy, once a useful tool for the understanding of the world, was relegated to a subordinate position below the art of revolution.

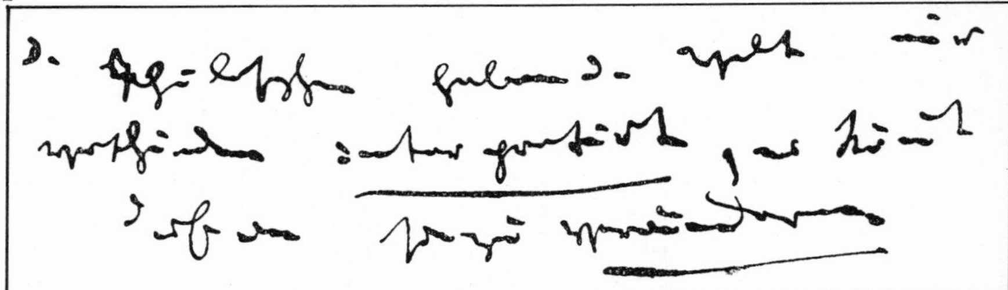

Die Philosophen haben die Welt nur
verschieden *interpretiert*, es kömmt
drauf an, sie zu *verändern*.

The philosophers have only interpreted *the world in different ways, the point is to change it.*

Facsimile of the eleventh thesis of Marx's Theses on Feuerbach.

The *Theses on Feuerbach* are not to be regarded as rational statements so much as improvisations on the theme of revolution, which he seeks to justify at all costs, even at the cost of irrationality. In statement after statement Marx makes entirely arbitrary judgments on society, and he must have known that many of them were patently false and indefensible. The eighth and ninth theses, for example, involve sweeping statements on the nature of society and on the limitations of the bourgeois mentality, and these arguments lead to the triumphal conclusion that only the new revolutionary mentality can deal satisfactorily with human existence. Here are the three utterances:

VIII

All social life is essentially *practical.* All the mysteries which lead theory toward mysticism find their rational solution in human practice and in the understanding of this practice.

IX

The highest form of contemplative materialism—that materialism which does not conceive sensuous existence as practical activity—is the contemplation of isolated individuals and of bourgeois society.

X

The standpoint of the old materialism is bourgeois society; the standpoint of the new materialism is human society or social humanity.

Since Marx had some training in logic, it is difficult to understand how he could make a statement like "all social life is essentially practical" without realizing its falsity. Quite clearly these statements were not intended to be understood literally; he was applying a kind of intellectual rationalization to his own needs, his deeply personal desires. One of his more troubling characteristics was that he was inclined to use the word "all" when he meant "sixty per cent" or "thirty per cent" or even "three per cent." When he wrote: "All the mysteries which lead theory toward mysticism find their rational solution in human practice and in the understanding of this practice," he was dismissing history, philosophy, religion, God, love, sex, the subtle loyalties and traditions which have always worked on men. They no longer existed for him. He was wiping the slate clean, reducing the world to what he regarded as the essentials. There remained "practical man," devoid of mystery and almost of substance. The *Theses on Feuerbach* declared that man existed only as "practical man" and that he had only one duty—to submit to the revolutionary process.

These theses are of crucial importance to the understanding of Marx. Although they are written in a gnomic form, in a kind of shorthand, the meaning is abundantly clear. In the first thesis Marx announces that Feuerbach had some glimmering of this new materialistic approach to mankind, but he had misunderstood the revolutionary process. "In *The Essence of Christianity,* he regards the theoretical attitude as the only genuine human attitude, while practical activity is apprehended only in its filthy Jewish manifestation." Marx proposes to study the practical activity of man in a completely new way, without "its filthy Jewish manifestation."

Out of this confrontation with "practical man" there would emerge the theory of historical materialism, in which man becomes simply the product of economic forces. It was a convenient theory, because it reduced man to insignificance. Many years later Engels would say that Marx had perhaps gone too far in emphasizing the role of economics in the development of human society, but by that time it was too late. A new generation of revolutionaries had arisen who accepted as an article of faith that man was an economic animal and all his activities were dictated by economic laws. It was a simple belief, and the fact that it was demonstrably untrue carried little weight with them.

Meanwhile life in Brussels was relatively calm. Writing some years later, Jenny found herself looking back at a period of comparative tranquillity, remembering her evening excursions to "the pretty cafés" and her contentment amid the small community of German exiles. "The small German colony lived pleasantly together," she wrote, and never again did she speak in this way about German exiles. Heinrich Bürgers lived nearby, and soon Moses Hess came to live in Brussels with his wife. Sebastian Seiler, a Swiss who operated an information bureau, became a close friend, and so too did Joseph Weydemeyer, a former Prussian artillery officer who was a native of Westphalia. Marx's visits to the public library led to a close friendship with Philippe Gigot, a young librarian who dreamed of becoming a revolutionary.

In April, when Jenny was pregnant with her second child, the Baroness von Westphalen sent her own trusted maid to help her. Her name was Helene Demuth, and she was to remain with the Marx family for nearly forty years. Much of Jenny's contentment during those early months in Brussels came from the presence of this young peasant woman who was sweet-tempered, sensible and completely reliable. Jenny had been terrified at the thought of a second child, but now the fear left her.

When summer came, Marx rested from his labors and paid a six-week visit to England in the company of Engels who had some business with his father's mills in Manchester. Marx seems to have spent most of his time in Manchester studying the English economists in the Chetham Library. A quarter of a century later Engels remembered how they had worked together in a small room in the library and saw the English summer through the glow of stained-glass windows.

In London on their return journey they encountered for the first time a remarkable group of revolutionaries, who called themselves the League of the Just. They were mostly Germans who had been living in Paris until they were caught up in the Blanquist uprising of May 1839. Then they scattered, some, like Wilhelm Weitling, taking refuge in Switzerland, while others escaped to London. They regarded themselves as egalitarian communists and were deeply influenced by primitive Christianity. Yet the French revolutionary tradition was strong in them, and they dreamed of guillotines and barricades, of tumbrils and Bastilles.

The League of the Just had no history, for it had developed out of many conspiracies and many failures. It could be traced back to the French Revolution or to Blanqui's secret Society of the Seasons. It changed its name according to its domicile, and in London it was usually known by the more modest name of the German Workers' Educational Society.

The aims of the League were various and at no period did it possess a clear-cut program. While dedicated to the overthrow of existing society, it also aimed to elevate and protect the skilled workmen who joined it. There were perhaps three hundred members in England, Switzerland and Germany. Sometimes the "lodges" took the form of choral societies and athletic clubs, but there was a hard core of determined revolutionaries ruling over them, collecting dues, and preparing for the day of revolution.

In England the League of the Just operated in complete freedom. As the German Workers' Educational Society it was officially inaugurated on February 7, 1840. The three most powerful members, dominating the small conspiratorial committee, were men of considerable revolutionary experience. Karl Schapper, a good-humored giant, tough-minded and capable of acts of great daring, had fought beside Georg Büchner, the revolutionary playwright, in a brief and ill-fated uprising, and had then gone on to join Mazzini in his march on Savoy. Engels thought he detected in him a certain sluggishness of thought, and it is obvious that he lacked Engels' facility. Nevertheless he was one of those men who are made for revolution. He had studied forestry in Germany, and made a living in England as a teacher of German.

Joseph Moll, a watchmaker from Cologne, was a man of grave intelligence, broad-shouldered and strongly built, at least the equal of Schapper in intelligence, if not in daring. He was in charge of most of the foreign correspondence of the League of the Just and acted as the chief diplomat and theoretician. Finally there was Heinrich Bauer, a shoemaker, with the lively wits of a Franconian, small, shrewd, daring. Engels had met these three revolutionaries in 1843 and he now took pleasure in introducing Marx to them.

At these meetings Marx encountered dedicated working-class revolutionaries for the first time. They were artisans, not laborers; they were members of the lower middle class, not proletarians. Any visitor to their weekly meetings could see that they were still searching for a program, although they had already worked out a slender network of communications across Europe. They debated gravely about the problems of the coming communist society: how children should be educated, what position women would occupy, how men should conduct themselves to become worthy members of the new revolutionary society. They were very serious and conscientious people whose only fault in the eyes of a visitor who met them during the following year was a quite remarkable bloodthirstiness, which they would announce very casually. They were like primitive Christians waiting not for the Last Judgment but for the guillotine to be set up on the Place de la Concorde.

The visitor, Hugo Hildebrand, has left a lengthy account of them. He met Schapper and was impressed by his ruddy face, black mustache, and commanding manner. The League's meeting place, like most of the *émigré* meeting places, was above a tavern. There was a long table, a grand piano, an air of calm assurance. The members were orderly and followed a fixed routine of instruction. One evening each week was devoted to studying the English language, another to geography, another to history, another to drawing and physics, another to singing, another to dancing, another to the dissemination of communist ideas. Every half year the subjects of instruction were changed. The atmosphere was thoroughly Germanic; there were regulations to be obeyed, and everyone took his pipe out of his mouth when the speakers delivered their speeches. Some of their statements made Hildebrand's hair stand on end, but afterward he derived some consolation from a serious discussion with Schapper on the subject of his opposition to liberalism. Hildebrand was under no illusions about the nature of the secret conspiratorial organization which directed the affairs of the League.

Marx appears not to have been overly impressed by these German exiles, and there is nothing in his writings to suggest he was aware that the League would play an important role in his life. He did not know, and could not have guessed, that the League would become the parent body of all the communist parties which have proliferated throughout the world.

When he returned to Brussels he was consumed with the desire to write a new book to be called *The German Ideology*. This vast polemic would absorb his energies for the rest of the year and well into the next. The manuscript has survived, written in the handwriting of Marx, Engels and Joseph Weydemeyer, who was evidently brought in as a friendly copyist. Although portions of the book were apparently written by Engels, most of it clearly betrays the dominating mind of Marx with its heavy sarcasms and ferocious passion for argument.

On the whole *The German Ideology* may be described as a relatively good-humored performance. There is little sneering, and the special pleading is maintained on the level of abrasive comment and innuendo. Some of the joy in combat may have come from the birth of his second daughter, Laura, on September 26, and the prospect of an entirely new and hitherto undreamed of way of life, for in October we find him writing to the burgomaster of Trier, asking for a certificate of emigration which would permit him to enter the United States. It was the first of many vague gestures in the direction of America, but nothing came of any of them.

Meanwhile *The German Ideology* was beginning to acquire its voluminous form as a triple-pronged attack against the ideas of Feuerbach, Max Stirner, and the "True Socialists," a coterie of socialists who did not in Marx's view go far enough. The greater part of his energy was expended in demolishing Stirner, the author of *The Ego and His Own,* a book which had achieved remarkable popularity for its celebration of the human ego. Some three hundred and fifty pages were written on Stirner, whose ideas were examined in massive detail. Engels wrote to Marx on November 19, 1844, that Stirner was evidently a man "of great talent, personality and industry, even though he somersaults from idealist abstractions into materialist abstractions, and comes to nothing." The attack on Stirner was accordingly waged with destructive passion, with an unrelenting insistence on his puerility and obscurity, until on the last page Marx reached the triumphant conclusion that "his philosophical lack of thought was already in itself the end of philosophy, just as his unspeakable language was the end of all language." But it is in the earlier discussion on Feuerbach that Marx showed himself to be the resourceful defender of the new communist man who was about to erupt onto the stage of history, and the argument in favor of communism was conducted with considerable force.

Since the book was a polemic against the revolutionary philosophers of his time, it was necessary to put them in their place from the very beginning. This he did in the preface in a carefully worked epigram:

> Once upon a time there was an honest fellow who took it into his head that people drowned in water only because they were possessed with *the idea of gravity.* If only, he thought, they could rid themselves of this idea, by calling it, for instance, superstitious or religious, they would thereby be saved from all danger of drowning. All his life he fought against the illusion of gravity, concerning whose deleterious consequences statistics continually provided him with new and manifold evidence. This honest fellow was the prototype of the new revolutionary philosophers of Germany.

Such weighty epigrams only proved that Marx could be formidable in debate; they did not prove that he could conduct an honest argument. As usual, he comes to conclusions which are totally unwarranted by the evi-

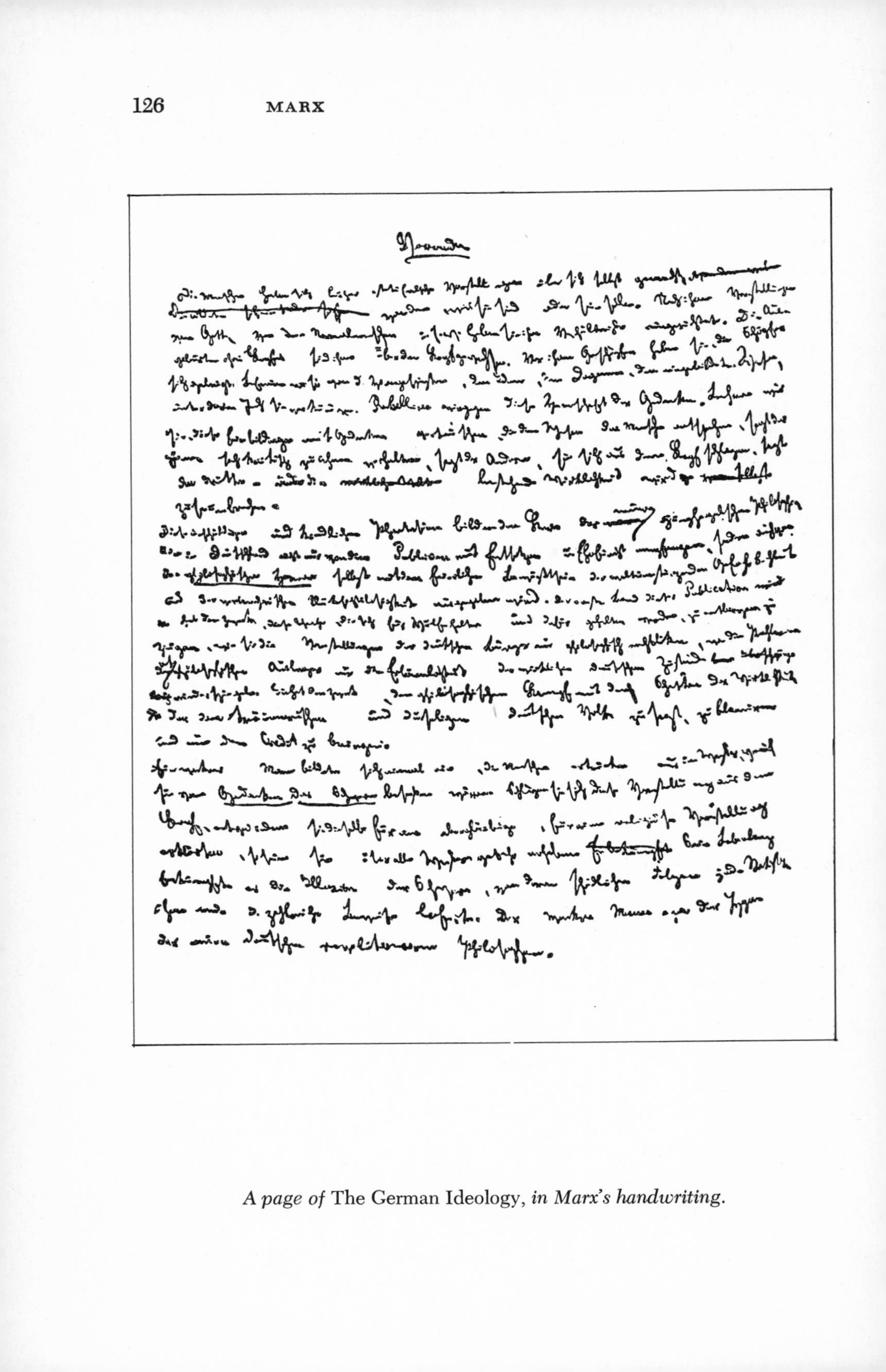

A page of The German Ideology, *in Marx's handwriting.*

dence. He announces that all previous philosophies must be jettisoned in favor of the new philosophy. Hegel's "absolute spirit" is nothing more than a putrefying corpse; only now, at last, with the emergence of "real individuals, their activity, and the material conditions under which they live" can a true philosophy come into existence. In the past German philosophy had descended from heaven to earth; the new philosophy would ascend from earth to heaven. Man himself, by embracing communism, will enter into his proper glory.

Marx's views on communism are still however tentative. He makes sweeping statements about the nature of the society which will come into existence when the communist revolution is successful, but these statements seem to be merely attempts to probe the peripheries of his own thought. When he says, for example, that "communism is empirically only possible as the act of the ruling people all at once and simultaneously, which presupposes the universal development of productive power and the world commerce which depends upon it," we are left in some doubt whether the words have any intelligible meaning. Similarly, when he says that "the proletariat can only exist *world-historically,* just as communism, its actions, can only have a world-historical existence," we are made aware that he is making vast claims for the proletariat, but they are being drowned in their own vastness. Clarity was not one of Marx's virtues.

Yet he is clear enough when he describes the class war which will put an end to classes and the emergence of a new kind of man as a result of the revolutionary conflict. In what is perhaps the most dramatic and terrifying statement in *The German Ideology,* he goes far beyond his earlier statements on the communist revolution, and makes clear that not only is it necessary to change the world but *man himself must also be changed.* He wrote:

> In all revolutions which have taken place up to this time the mode of activity has remained inviolate, so that there has never been anything more than a changed distribution of this activity, with a new distribution of labor to other persons, while the communist revolution is directed against the preceding *mode* of activity, does away with labor, and abolishes class rule together with the classes themselves, the reason being that the revolution is brought about by the class which no longer counts in society as a class, is not recognized as a class, but is the expression of the dissolution of all classes, nationalities, etc., within the present society.
>
> For the widespread generation of this communist consciousness, and for the success of the cause, it is necessary that man himself should suffer a massive change, a change which can take place only in a practical movement, a *revolution;* so that the revolution is necessary not only because the *ruling*

> class cannot be overthrown in any other way, but also because the *overthrowing* class can free itself from its filthy yoke and become capable of founding a new society only in a revolution.

With these words Marx comes much closer to drawing up the blueprint of revolution, demanding, as though in a single breath, that all over the world the proletariat should seize power, abolish national boundaries, put an end to labor, change the nature of man on a massive scale, and found a new society. It was a breathtaking prospect, and even when stated in a prose of quite remarkable awkwardness, the visionary excitement remains.

When Marx spoke of changing the nature of man on a massive scale, he meant exactly what he said. He had no illusions about the inadequacy of man. Like the preachers, he demanded that men should be utterly changed. Indeed, he had much in common with the preachers who wanted men to be "changed in Christ"; Marx wanted them "changed in the proletariat." In a passage which he later canceled out, as though it revealed too many secrets, he wrote that "the communists are the only people through whose historical activity the liquidation of fixed desires and ideas is brought about." By "communists" he meant himself, for there was as yet no communist party, and the desires and ideas to be liquidated were those he disapproved of. In this simple visionary way the world would be made anew.

The canceled passages in *The German Ideology* are often revealing. They show him in his moments of rage, of happy excitement, of sudden leaping enthusiasm. Immediately after writing the long passage on the need for a massive change in human nature, he remembered how Bruno Bauer had once envisaged the eternal joy and bliss which would come about when a real humanism has descended to earth. Marx commented savagely:

> The Holy Father will be greatly surprised when the Day of Judgment overtakes him, the day when all this is to come to pass—the day when the reflection of burning cities is seen in the heavens, marking the coming of dawn, and when the "celestial harmonies" consist of the melodies of the "Marseillaise" and the "Carmagnole" to an accompaniment of thundering cannon blasting his ears, while the guillotine beats time, and the maddened masses scream *"Ça ira, ça ira,"* and "self-consciousness" is hanged on the lampposts.

This is Marx in a state of frenetic anticipatory excitement, seeing already the blood flowing in the streets, the liquidation of desires. That visionary glimpse of the day of revolution was to remain with him for the rest of his life, and at moments of anguish and loneliness his soul would

A page from the manuscript of The German Ideology *in the handwriting of Engels, who also drew the sketch of Marx storming the barricades. The page is here reproduced upside down.*

feed on it. He had said much the same thing in his strange, malignant poem "The Player":

"Look now, my blood-dark sword shall stab
Unerringly within thy soul.
God neither knows nor honors art.
The hellish vapors rise and fill the brain,

"Till I go mad and my heart is utterly changed.
See this sword—the Prince of Darkness sold it to me.
For me he beats the time and gives the signs.
Ever more boldly I play the dance of death.

"I must play darkly, I must play lightly,
Until my heart, and my violin burst."

When *The German Ideology* was finished, Marx tried to find a publisher. No publisher however could be found to publish a polemical work of such massive length. He was not unduly dismayed. "We decided to leave our manuscript to the gnawing criticism of the mice," he wrote, "and we did this all the more willingly because we had attained our chief purpose—self-understanding." The complete work was not published until 1962.

While Marx was writing this book with the help of Engels he was already gathering around him the nucleus of a revolutionary party. It was a very small party. It included Jenny and Edgar von Westphalen, who was working in Brussels as a clerk in the information agency belonging to Sebastian Seiler. Joseph Weydemeyer, a guest in Marx's crowded apartment, also became a founding member. All together, eighteen members are known to have been recruited during the winter of 1845 and the spring of 1846. Very few of the founding members remained in the party, which later came to be known as the Communist League. Among the most important members were Wilhelm Weitling and Ferdinand Freiligrath, both of them being men with established reputations. Weitling was one of the founders of the League of the Just, and Freiligrath was a well-known poet with a considerable following. The overwhelming majority of the members were writers with bourgeois backgrounds, and the only members who could conceivably be regarded as proletarian were two young typesetters, who seem to have been placed on the roster only because it was necessary to have a symbolic proletarian representation.

The original members of the Communist League were:

Karl Marx	Ernst Dronke
Friedrich Engels	Louis Heilberg
Jenny Marx	Georg Weerth
Edgar von Westphalen	Sebastian Seiler
Ferdinand Freiligrath	Philippe Gigot
Joseph Weydemeyer	Wilhelm Wolff
Moses Hess	Ferdinand Wolf
Hermann Kriege	Karl Wallau
Wilhelm Weitling	Stephan Born

The average age of the members was twenty-eight. The oldest was Weitling, who was thirty-seven, and the youngest was Stephan Born, whose real name was Simon Buttermilch; he was twenty-one. Born and Wallau were typesetters, and Wallau was only a year older than Born. Neither of them appear to have taken any part in the discussions of the Communist League.

Such was the small hand-picked group which Marx gathered about him in Brussels, arming his followers with a theory and a discipline which was later to conquer half the world. The group included only three men, Moses Hess, Engels, and Edgar von Westphalen, whom Marx knew intimately. Most of them were recent acquaintances, and many of them were later to be abandoned by the roadside after they had served their purpose. To Wilhelm Wolff, known variously as "Lupus" and "Kasemattenwolff," because he had escaped from a fortress in Silesia where he had been imprisoned for four years for incitement to rebellion, Marx later dedicated the first volume of *Das Kapital.* He was a small clean-shaven man who wore steel spectacles and looked like a professor, but he was in fact a hardened revolutionary with a gift for making fiery speeches.

With the Communist League modeled on the League of the Just Marx made his first step toward bringing about the world communist revolution of his dreams.

THE FIRST PURGE

In those years when Marx was gathering together the small parcels of power which were later to become large and unwieldy luggage, he had already worked out a philosophy of direct action. The party itself must be treated as though it were an enemy; it must be conquered and submitted to his will. He would choose the battleground, prepare the ambushes, outflank the enemy, and wherever possible he would see to it that he had overwhelming firepower. He would make alliances at his convenience. His task was to retain command at whatever the cost in friendship or in exhausting quarrels. All rivals must be suppressed, and in order to assert his supremacy he would attack the strongest and the weakest indifferently.

The strategy had been worked out in great detail, and would be repeated on many occasions with little variation. It was the strategy of the prosecuting counsel who is determined to achieve a verdict of guilty even when he knows that the prisoner is innocent. Marx was supremely indifferent to morality; everything that favored the revolution was right, everything that worked against the revolution was wrong. And when he spoke of revolution, he kept clearly in mind that there was only one possible revolution, the one which he had outlined at vast length in *The German Ideology*, the "historically inevitable revolution" which would follow predestined scientific laws. Anyone who professed not to believe in these laws was automatically excluded from the party. All those who thought that the revolution would break out spontaneously as a result of a sudden uprising of the masses who could no longer endure the presence of intolerable abuses of power were also excluded. In Marx's view only Marxist revolutions were permissible; all others were anathema. So there came about the first of the innumerable purges which have run like a red thread through the history of communism.

That the purges were wasteful, supremely dangerous and ultimately unnecessary seems never to have occurred to Marx. The revolution was a machine; anything that got into the cogs of the machine must be ruthlessly destroyed. Marx could not kill his victims, but he could expel them from the party, blacken their characters, and render them useless for any further revolutionary work. There was no necessity to draw up a bill of particulars; the judgments were summary; the sentence irrevocable.

The first victim was Wilhelm Weitling, the author of a slender volume called *Guarantees of Harmony and Freedom,* which Marx had once regarded with unqualified admiration, saying that nothing in the whole literature of German bourgeois political propaganda could compare with this brilliant pamphlet. Here at last spoke the German workingman with his new-found strength and thundering voice. Marx portrayed him striding forward with seven-league boots, outdistancing the German bourgeoisie in their niggardly and down-at-heel shoes.

Marx had reason to praise Weitling, who was that very rare thing—a true proletarian revolutionary. The illegitimate son of a German laundress by a French officer quartered in Magdeburg during the Napoleonic War, he had grown up in great poverty, never knowing the name of his father. As a boy he was apprenticed to a tailor; as a young man he deserted from the army and led the life of an itinerant revolutionary preacher. In 1839, at the age of thirty, he had taken part in Blanqui's ill-fated attempt at an insurrection in Paris, and in Switzerland, where he took refuge, he was arrested for writing a pamphlet called *The Gospel of a Poor Sinner,* which took the form of an autobiographical fragment in which he appeared as Jesus Christ, "the illegitimate son of a poor girl Mary," and preached communism and the downfall of the state. He was condemned to six months' imprisonment for blasphemy and political unorthodoxy. Thereafter he continued his wandering life; the Chartists fêted him in London, the French workmen collected money for him, and he was usually acclaimed as one of the dedicated leaders of the working-class movement. Thousands came to listen to his speeches and to applaud him. He had one of those long narrow faces with deep-set eyes and stern lips which are to be found among preachers, and indeed he could easily be mistaken for a priest who comforts his parishioners during the week and conducts services on Sundays. He dressed well, and the beard which he wore in a neat fringe only reinforced the melancholy nobility of his features.

This was the man Marx had decided to destroy, and he went about the task of destroying him with exemplary zeal and unaccustomed vigor.

On the evening of March 30, 1846, Weitling, who was passing through Brussels, was invited to attend a meeting of the revolutionary party. Ostensibly the meeting had been arranged in order to discuss the common tactics for the working-class movement. Engels was present, and so was Edgar von Westphalen, Marx's brother-in-law. In addition there were the journalist Louis Heilberg, the former registrar Sebastian Seiler, the former artillery officer Joseph Weydemeyer, and the young librarian Philippe Gigot. Finally there was a young Russian, Pavel Annenkov, a friend of Marx, who had no particular interest in the communist movement. Annenkov was charming and well-traveled, and possessed a flair for vivid description. Many years later Annenkov described the strange scene of Weitling's trial with an incomparable sense of drama. First, he drew a remarkable portrait in depth of Marx, who evidently fascinated him:

> Marx was a type of man all compact of energy, force of character and unshakable conviction—a type highly remarkable in outward appearance as well. In spite of his thick black mane of hair, his hairy hands and crookedly buttoned frock coat, he gave the impression of a man who possesses the right and the power to command respect, although his appearance and behavior might seem somewhat peculiar at times. His movements were awkward, but bold and confident; his manners violated all the accepted social conventions. They were proud and faintly contemptuous. His sharp, metallic voice was remarkably suited to the radical judgments he was continually delivering on men and things. He never spoke at all except in judgments which permitted no appeal, and were rendered even sharper by the harsh and jarring tone of everything he said. This tone expressed his firm conviction of his mission to impress himself on men's minds, to dominate their wills, and to compel them to obey him. Before my eyes stood the personification of a democratic dictator such as might appear in one's mind's eye in a moment of fantasy.

Annenkov's description of Marx, the twenty-eight-year-old "democratic dictator," was written without malice, with kindness and forbearance. Rude, domineering, loud-voiced, and yet oddly attractive, Marx seemed determined to bend the world according to his will, unlike Weitling, who was calm and humble, looking, Annenkov thought, more like a commercial traveler than a stern and embittered revolutionary agitator. Annenkov, who thought that revolutionaries should look like revolutionaries, was surprised by Weitling's air of deference and politeness, his well-cut frock coat and neatly trimmed beard.

There were brief introductions, and then they all sat down at a green table. Marx took his place at the head of the table, "pencil in hand and leonine head bent over a sheet of paper," while Engels, his inseparable companion, rose to address the small gathering on the subject of the common tactics which must be employed throughout the working-class movement and the fundamental doctrines which would serve as the theoretical framework of revolutionary action. Engels emphasized the importance of these doctrines, explaining that they were intended to rally the workers who had neither the time nor the ability to occupy themselves with questions of theory.

As Annenkov describes the scene, Engels rose, "tall and slender, with a grave appearance, and looking like a distinguished Englishman." He spoke about matters which had little interest for Weitling, who believed that revolution came about as a result of the massive discontents of the people. Engels was still speaking when Marx suddenly cut him short, glared at Weitling and said in a harsh, contemptuous voice: "Tell me, Weitling, you who have made such a reputation in Germany with your communist propaganda, you who have won over so many workers with the result that they have now lost their work and their bread, what are your arguments for defending your social-revolutionary agitation, and on what grounds do you propose to defend your agitation in the future?"

Weitling protested that it was not his task to invent arguments in defense of revolutionary agitation; these arguments were to be found in the misery and poverty of the workers, and the wrongs committed against them. The workers had faith in themselves, they did not need doctrines imposed by others. Weitling spoke very seriously and haltingly, with a troubled expression, and sometimes under the thrust of Marx's questions he would become confused, repeat himself, correct what he had said previously, and lose himself in generalities. Annenkov, who was listening carefully, observed that Weitling was confronting a very different audience from the ones he was accustomed to address.

So he went on, becoming more and more nervous, until Marx broke in with angrily contracted brows and announced sarcastically that it was pure fraud to arouse the people without giving them firm foundations for their actions. The awakening of fantastic hopes would never lead to the salvation of the suffering people, but to their downfall. "If you attempt to influence the workers—especially the German workers—without a body of doctrine and clear scientific ideas, then you are merely playing an empty and unscrupulous game of propaganda, leading inevitably to the setting-up on the one hand of an inspired apostle, and on the other of open-mouthed donkeys listening to him!"

At this point Marx turned and made a powerful gesture toward Annenkov, saying: "Here is a Russian! Well, in his country, Weitling, you might find a place for behavior like yours! No doubt in Russia you can build up successful unions with stupid young men and apostles! But in a civilized country like Germany you should realize that nothing can be achieved without doctrine, and up to the present there has been nothing except noise, dubious excitement, and the destruction of the very cause of revolution!"

Weitling, who had been on the defensive for so long, now went over to the offensive. He spoke directly and to the point, his face coloring with excitement. He had had enough, he said, of these innuendoes, and he had not become a revolutionary in order to learn about doctrines invented in the quiet of the study. In the name of Justice, Solidarity and Brotherly Love he had brought men together to advance the cause of the revolution, and in hundreds of grateful letters and declarations by workingmen he had found testimony to his own belief in his cause. Men had come to him from all over Germany, they had demonstrated for him, they had shown abundant faith in him: and why should he therefore submit to the opinions of men who spent their time weaving theories about revolution far from the suffering world, remote from the laboring people? Marx had struck Weitling where he was weakest, and Weitling in turn found the weakest place in Marx's armor. Marx was enraged. Annenkov drew a memorable portrait of Marx roaring like a lion:

> These last words of Weitling so enraged Marx that he struck his fist on the table so violently that the lamp shook. Jumping to his feet, he shouted: "Ignorance has never helped anybody yet!"
>
> We followed his example and rose to our feet, and the conference came to an end.
>
> While Marx was still striding up and down the room in his violent rage, I quickly took my leave of him and of the others, greatly astonished by what I had seen and heard.

So ended the first purge, for Weitling, in Marx's view, was now hopelessly discredited and his only remaining purpose was to serve as a target for abuse and the peculiar kind of vilification of which Marx and Engels were practiced masters. Wherever he appeared, his influence must be resisted, his character assassinated, his speeches denounced. Engels took especial pleasure in denouncing him as "an abject fraud," who had not even written the books which bore his name; they had been written, he said, by a Russian and a group of anonymous and conspiratorial Frenchmen.

Not long after the purge of Weitling, Marx decided that the time had come to purge Hermann Kriege, whose many offenses included his friendship with Weitling and his refusal to follow the party line. He was one of the original members of the first communist party, and at one time Marx had high hopes for him. A few weeks after joining the Communist League, he emigrated to America. There, with the help of some generous

Germans, he published a weekly journal called *Der Volks-Tribun* (The People's Tribune), which purported to be a communist paper. When copies reached Brussels, Marx was incensed to discover that Kriege had his own notions of what communism meant. His ideas of communism evidently derived from Weitling and the League of the Just; he favored brotherly love, justice, women's rights, and private property. *Der Volks-Tribun* advocated that every peasant in America should be granted 160 acres of public land, and Marx answered in a "Manifesto against Kriege" that this was tantamount to making every peasant a king, or queen, or a pope. In the manifesto five articles in *Der Volks-Tribun* were mercilessly pilloried, and Kriege was shown to be a traitor to the communist cause.

As usual there was a board of inquiry to pronounce judgment on the traitor. The board met in May, and consisted of the same members of the League who had sat in judgment on Weitling, with the addition of Wilhelm Wolff. Surprisingly, Weitling, who had refused to take his dismissal seriously, was also a member of the board. He appears to have regarded the proceedings with disgust, for he refused to sign the indictment, which was lithographed and sent to London, Paris, and New York.

The "Manifesto against Kriege" is an astonishing document because it showed a quite extraordinary ignorance of American political conditions. Marx, setting himself up as an authority on American agrarian reform, showed only that he knew nothing at all about it. But what especially annoyed him was Kriege's grotesque ignorance of the historic processes of communism. In a revealing passage he declared that Kriege's ideas about giving land to the peasants would have been more palatable if he had shown some awareness of the fact that the ownership of private property by the peasants was only a stage in the communist revolution, and that afterward the land must be taken from them. In this way, in a document written on May 11, 1846, Marx announced for the first time the terrible thesis that the communists would come to power by promising the land to the peasants, but once in power they would proceed to abolish the ownership of all private property. And in fact in Russia and China the communists did come to power as a result of promising the land to the peasants, and as soon as possible the land was taken from them.

"Kriege's childishly pompous methods are in the highest degree compromising to the communist party in Europe and America," Marx announced in the foreword to the manifesto, adding that Kriege was not a communist but a man given to fantastic and fanatical enthusiasms. Accordingly he was to be regarded as one who had gone over to the enemy, a defector from the ranks of the communists.

Soon other men would feel the weight of Marx's displeasure and find themselves consigned to limbo. Even Moses Hess, who had introduced Engels to communism, felt that he could no longer breathe the rarefied air of the Communist League, and resigned before he could be officially dismissed. The League, which had once had eighteen members, was now reduced to fifteen. There would be more purges as time went on, and nearly all of them came about because the members of the party refused to bow down to Marx's dictatorship.

The purges were not invented in Soviet Russia. They appeared at the very beginning of Marxist communism, and were part of the system.

Sometimes men were purged who did not belong to the party. Marx would embrace a prominent political figure, invite him to join the movement, lay down conditions, and then spew him out if he did not unconditionally accept the terms offered to him. In this way Marx locked horns with Pierre-Joseph Proudhon. The story of their confrontation should be told at some length, because it provided one of the few occasions when Marx came face to face with a man who was his intellectual equal.

PROUDHON

When Marx was beginning to proclaim his socialist faith, the greatest living exponent of socialism was Pierre-Joseph Proudhon, a man of remarkable character and great intellectual integrity. He was born in 1809 at Besançon in eastern France, the son of poor peasants. He had the characteristic mild manner of the Franche-Comtois, and to the end of his life spoke with a heavy provincial accent. Victor Hugo said he resembled a house dog and a monkey—he had a house dog's flat nose and a monkey's beard. His hair was thin and ill-combed, he dressed shabbily, and he had the heavy gait of a peasant. Victor Hugo went on to describe his gestures, which were always small and precise, and his curling underlip, which gave him an expression of timid ill-humor. His eyes however had an appearance of alertness and good humor, and they were notable for their "troubled, steady and penetrating gaze." He had no gift for oratory, but wrote well and had a deep feeling for the French language.

Once someone commended him for his system. "But I have no system," Proudhon answered, and it was true. He despised systems because he felt that humanity could never be committed to anything so hidebound or so unyielding as a series of fixed intellectual concepts. He was selfless and without ambition, in love with moral principles.

In nearly every respect Marx and Proudhon were at poles apart. Marx had been to two universities, and never demeaned himself by working at a trade. Proudhon was self-educated, and made his living as a compositor. Marx was voluble and easily excited; he had married a woman of the aristocracy; he thirsted for violent action; he was at ease among systems. Proudhon was completely incapable of anger; he married a woman of the people; he distrusted all violent action; and systems terrified him. Marx had abandoned moral principles, while Proudhon delighted in them, believing that they alone gave meaning to life. What they had in common was a burning dissatisfaction with society.

In 1840 Proudhon published his most famous book *What Is Property?* It opened with one of those bold statements which were characteristic of the man. "If I were asked, 'What is slavery?' and answered by saying, 'Murder!' my meaning would be clear at once. No further argument would be necessary to demonstrate that by taking away a man's mind, his will power, his personality, power of life and death is being exercised over him, and that to enslave a man is to kill him. And if I were asked, 'What is property?' why should I not then answer, 'Theft'?"

Proudhon's "Property is theft" was to become one of the great battle cries of the nineteenth century, but it was usually misunderstood. He had not intended to suggest that a man's house, his lands, the tools of his trade, his small possessions were theft; by property he meant "the sum of its abuses." He was denouncing the power of the landlords to exploit the peasants, the power of the banks to grant credit at usurious rates, the power of the industrialist to keep his workmen working sixteen hours a day for his own profit.

The famous phrase, and the implications which Proudhon derived from it, had the effect of turning men's minds toward the nature of property, its dangers, abuses and inconsistencies. In October 1842 Marx, who was busy sketching out a study of the fundamental laws of communism, described Proudhon's work in the pages of the *Neue Rheinische Zeitung* as a "supremely penetrating book," adding that it was one of those seminal works which should be analyzed in depth. The analysis came two years later in the pages of *The Holy Family*. It was a curiously haphazard attempt to come to grips with a giant, and took the form of an attack on an article on Proudhon written by Edgar Bauer. The running attack continues for thirty pages, with Marx finding grave faults in Bauer and minor faults in Proudhon, most of them excusable because they are due to his ignorance. On the whole Proudhon comes off well. "Proudhon," wrote Marx, "submits the basis of political economy, *property,* to a critical examination and certainly the first decisive, rigorous and scientific examination. He has made a great scientific progress, a progress which revolutionizes political economy and for the first time makes a real science of political economy possible." Marx never again wrote quite so generously about Proudhon.

They met during the autumn and winter of 1844 when Marx was living in Paris, and many years later, when Proudhon was safely dead, Marx claimed that during interminable conversations in small and cluttered hotel rooms on the Left Bank he had taught Proudhon all he knew about Hegelian philosophy. "I injected him with Hegelianism to his great prejudice," wrote Marx, "for he knew no German and could not study the original texts." The claim however can easily be disproved, for Proudhon already knew a good deal about Hegelian philosophy from his own studies based on translations and from long discussions with revolutionary exiles, especially with Mikhail Bakunin. Arnold Ruge, Karl Grün, Hermann Ewerbeck, and many others had led him through those dark pathways in which men have been known to vanish from sight, and although Proudhon was grateful to them, it was beyond his power to imitate them. He was the master of the clear-cut definition, and the strange processes of dialectic were foreign to him.

We know little more about Marx's confrontations with Proudhon except that they took place and sometimes lasted all night and well into the following morning. Marx evidently retained a high opinion of his friend, for eighteen months later, while living in exile in Brussels, he invited him to become a member of his secret correspondence committee. Marx counted on Proudhon's assistance because he knew that Proudhon delighted in the contemplation of conspiratorial activity and sometimes spoke yearningly of the day when the socialists would acquire supreme power. What Marx did not know was that Proudhon was still the servant of his moral principles and was completely incapable of joining a ruthless conspiracy.

Marx's letter and the reply should be quoted at considerable length because they are of great importance to socialist history and show the cleavage between two opposing forms of socialism. Marx wrote:

May 5, 1846

My Dear Proudhon,

I have often thought of writing to you since I left Paris, but circumstances beyond my control have prevented me until now. Please believe me when I say that the only reasons for my silence are the excessive difficulties of my life and the inconveniences of changing my domicile, etc.

And now let us come immediately *in medias res.* Together with two of my friends, Friedrich Engels and Philippe Gigot (both of whom are in Brussels), I have organized a regular correspondence with German communists and socialists for the discussion of scientific questions and in order to supervise such popular writings and socialist propaganda as one may carry out in Germany by this means. The chief object of our correspondence will however be to put German socialists in contact with French and English socialists, and to keep foreigners informed about the socialist movement in Germany and to inform the Germans in Germany about the progress of socialism in France and England. In this way differences of opinion may come to light; there will be an exchange of ideas and impartial criticism. In this way the socialist movement will have made a step forward in its "literary" character, thus ridding itself of the limitations of "nationality." At the moment of action it is certainly of great interest to everyone to be informed about the state of affairs abroad as well as in his own country.

Besides the communists in Germany our correspondence will include German socialists in Paris and London. Our relations with England are already established; as for France we all believe that it would be impossible to find a better correspondent than you. You know that the English and the Germans have up to now appreciated you more than your own compatriots.

So you see it is only a question of creating a regular correspondence and insuring that it possesses the means to pursue the social movement in the different countries, for the sake of a rich and many-sided advantage, which the labor of any one of them could not encompass.

Should you agree with our proposal, the expense involved in sending letters to you, and your letters to us, will be defrayed here, from sums raised in Germany for this purpose.

The address you will write to here is that of M. Philippe Gigot, 8 rue Bodendrock. He will also be responsible for signing letters from Brussels.

There is no need to add that all this correspondence demands the most absolute secrecy on your part; and in Germany our friends must act with the greatest circumspection to avoid compromising themselves.

Reply soon, and believe in the very sincere friendship of

Your devoted
Charles Marx

This letter, transcribed in the handwriting of Philippe Gigot, was followed by one of those postscripts commonly found in the letters of conspirators. The postscript was a contemptuous attack and denunciation of Karl Grün, one of Proudhon's closest friends:

I hereby denounce M. Grün, of Paris. This man is nothing more than a cavalier of the literary industry, a charlatan who wants to practice a trade in modern ideas. He attempts to conceal his ignorance in pompous phrases and arrogant sentences, and has so far only succeeded in making himself ridiculous with all this gibberish. Moreover this man is "dangerous." He "abuses," thanks to his impertinence, the friendships he has formed with well-known authors in order to elevate himself and compromise them in the eyes of the German public.

In his book on the French socialists he dares to call himself the *Privatdocent* (this is a German academic title) of Proudhon; he claims to have disclosed to him certain important axioms of German science and talks a lot of humbug about his writings. So beware of this parasite. About this individual I may have occasion to speak at a later date.

I take this pleasant opportunity to inform you of the great joy with which I embark on this correspondence with a man as distinguished as yourself. Meanwhile I have the honor of signing myself

Your devoted
PHILIPPE GIGOT

Finally there was a post-postscript from Friedrich Engels declaring his profound respect for Proudhon's writings and the hope that Proudhon would become a member of the correspondence committee:

As for me, I can only hope that you, M. Proudhon, will approve the project we have proposed to you, and that you will have the goodness not to refuse our cooperation.

Assuring you of the profound respect which your writings have inspired in me, I am

Your devoted
FRIEDRICH ENGELS

Such was the famous letter which Marx wrote to Proudhon in the hope that the French socialist would add his weight and authority to the revolutionary organization he had founded in Brussels. This letter, now among the minor treasures of the British Museum, showed that Marx had not taken Proudhon's measure; it was in fact exactly the kind of letter which would arouse Proudhon's suspicions. He noted the ominous phrases scattered here and there—"at the moment of action," "to supervise such popular writings," "demands the most absolute secrecy on your part"—and he was perfectly aware of their significance. He was not pleased to read an ill-phrased denunciation of his friend Karl Grün, and he was sufficiently shrewd and sensitive to observe the authoritarian traits in Marx's character as they revealed themselves in the letter.

Proudhon was a man of great courtesy, and his reply was carefully phrased in a thoroughly conciliatory manner. He knew that Marx was responsible for the letter, and therefore he paid no attention to the request that he should reply directly to Gigot. Instead he wrote directly to Marx, accepting the offer to become a member of the correspondence committee while laying down his own conditions which would, he knew, have the effect of making it impossible for Marx to accept him as a member. At the same time he hoped to retain Marx's friendship, or at least his acquaintance. Writing from Lyons on May 17, Proudhon replied:

> Let us, if you wish, collaborate in trying to discover the laws of society, the manner in which these laws are realized, the process by which we shall succeed in discovering them. But for God's sake, after we have demolished all the dogmatisms *a priori,* let us not of all things attempt in our turn to instill another kind of dogma into the people. Let us not fall into the contradiction of your compatriot Martin Luther, who, after overthrowing Catholic theology, immediately set himself the task of founding, with all the apparatus of excommunication and anathemas, a Protestant theology. For three centuries Germany has been doing nothing else but pulling down the plaster work of M. Luther. Let us not, by contriving any more such messes, add to the burdens of humanity.
>
> With all my heart I applaud your idea of bringing all opinions out into the open. Let us have decent and sincere polemics. Let us give the world an example of learned and farsighted tolerance. But simply because we are at the head of the movement, let us not make ourselves the leaders of a new intolerance, let us not pose as the apostles of a new religion—even though this religion be the religion of logic, the religion of reason. Let us welcome, let us encourage all the protests. Let us condemn all exclusiveness, all mysticism. Let us never regard a question as exhausted, and even when we have used up our last argument, let us begin again, if necessary, with eloquence and irony. Under these conditions I will enter gladly into your association. Otherwise—no!

Proudhon was merely warming to his theme, for he had even more important things to say about the nature of the struggle for socialism. He knew Marx well, better perhaps than Marx knew himself. What disturbed him more than anything else was Marx's attachment to violence, his delight in bloody revolutions. The correspondence committee was clearly not intended to be merely a bureau of information; it had more deadly aims, and Marx had hinted at these aims when he spoke of "the moment of action." Proudhon knew exactly what that meant, and he was not in the least prepared to accept Marx's revolutionary dictatorship. He continued:

> I have also some observations to make to you touching upon those words in your letter: *at the moment of action.* It may be that you are still of the opinion that no reforms are now possible without a *coup de main,* without what used to be called a revolution and is really nothing but a shock. That opinion, which I understand, which I excuse and would willingly discuss, having myself shared it for a long time, is one which, I must confess, my most recent studies have made me completely abandon. I believe we have no need of it in order to succeed, and *consequently* we should not propose *revolutionary* action as a means of social reform, because this supposed

> means would simply be an appeal to force, to arbitrariness, in brief, a contradiction. I myself put the problem in this way: *to bring about the return to society by economic management of the wealth which was withdrawn from society by another economic management.* In other words, through political economy to transform the theory of property against Property in such a way as to engender what you German socialists call *community* and what I will confine myself for the moment to calling *liberty, equality.* Now I believe I know the way to solve this problem with only a short delay. I would therefore prefer to burn Property by a slow fire rather than give it new strength by making a St. Bartholomew's night of the proprietors.
>
> I must also tell you in passing that this seems to be the belief of the French working class; our proletarians have such a great thirst for science that you would receive short shrift from them if you only offered them blood to drink. In short, it is my opinion that it would be bad politics for us to present ourselves as exterminators; there will be enough use of rigorous methods, and the people do not need our exhortations for this.

Proudhon spoke gently, but the words were sharp with anger and dark with prophecy, for he was one of those who saw where Marx's philosophy was leading. He saw Marx as the "exterminator," who was perfectly prepared to drown Europe in blood so long as his cherished theories could be vindicated. Marx was intellectually pitiless, and therefore capable of astonishing improvisations on the theme of destruction. Against the theory of extermination Proudhon set the theory of successive transformations of society, the deliberate but gradual equalization of wealth. The form of socialism he supported was eventually practiced in the civilized countries of western Europe and Scandinavia, while the countries of eastern Europe followed the principles of Marx.

As for the postscript denouncing Karl Grün and ostensibly written by Philippe Gigot, Proudhon pointed out that these words must have been written in hot anger by Marx himself.

> My dear Monsieur Marx [he wrote] I appeal to your calmer judgment. G—— is in exile, with no wealth, with a wife and two children to support, living by his pen. What would you wish him to exploit in order to earn a livelihood, if it were not modern ideas? I understand your philosophic rage, and I share with you the belief that the truth about humanity should not be subject to trade; but I see nothing here except misfortune and extreme necessity, and I pardon the man.

Marx was even more angry when he received the letter; and in his rage at losing a potential conspirator he prepared to do everything possible to destroy him. Henceforth the battle would be waged between giants, or rather since Proudhon rarely wasted his energy on defending himself, Marx would go through all the motions of battle, while Proudhon contented himself with watching from the sidelines. From time to time he would make a few barbed comments or write some barbed sentences in his notebooks, while he left the fighting to Marx.

A suitable occasion for attacking Proudhon occurred a few months later with the publication of *The System of Economic Contradictions, or, The Philosophy of Misery* in October. Writing to his friend Jean-Baptiste Schweitzer nearly twenty years later, Marx announced that Proudhon had written him a long and detailed letter shortly before the publication of the book, saying among other things: "I await the lash of your criticism." No trace of the letter has been found, and it would seem highly unlikely that Proudhon would write in such tones to a confirmed enemy.

The System of Economic Contradictions was a substantial work in two volumes, the first major work to come from his pen since the publication of *What Is Property?* six years earlier. The theme of the book was stated in the title: the built-in economic contradictions which were slowly strangling human society. "Society has provoked the consumption of goods by the abundance of products, while encouraging a shortage by the low level of wages." In this way, and many other contradictory ways, society was reducing itself to economic impotence. Characteristically Proudhon began the work with a dissertation on God, which was followed by a double-edged attack on bourgeois economists and utopian socialists, among whom he counted the German Left-Hegelians. The examination of economic contradictions is pursued ruthlessly, and with great insight into the destructive effects of credit and property. On the title page there was the motto *Destruam et Aedificabo,* I will destroy and I will build.

Marx was enraged with the book and determined to do his utmost to destroy its influence. His polemic, written in French during the winter, was called *Misère de la Philosophie.* It was published in Paris and Brussels in the following June.

Misère de la Philosophie is very largely a series of diatribes against the "infantile ideas" of Proudhon, who is made to appear so stupid that he seems scarcely worth attacking. Marx assumes the roles of judge, jury, chief prosecutor and executioner, and clearly delighted in all these roles. The tone of the polemic can be judged from the two prefatory notes:

> M. Proudhon has the misfortune of being singularly misunderstood in Europe. In France he has the right to be a bad economist, because he is reputed to be a good German philosopher. In Germany he has the right to be a bad philosopher, because he is reputed to be one of the ablest French economists. We, in our capacity of German and economist simultaneously, desire to protest against this double error.
>
> The reader must understand that in this thankless task we have often had to abandon our criticism of M. Proudhon in order to accomplish the same

> purpose for German philosophy, and at the same time offer some observations on political economy.
>
> M. Proudhon's work is not merely a treatise on political economy, an ordinary work: it is a Bible. "Mysteries," "Secrets wrested from the bosom of God," "Revelations," nothing is lacking. But as prophets are discussed nowadays more conscientiously than profane writers, the reader must resign himself to accompanying us through the arid and shadowy erudition of Genesis in order to ascend later with M. Proudhon into the ethereal and fertile realm of *suprasocialism*.

From the beginning Marx showed not the slightest intention of using a rapier when he could more effectively use a battering ram. He had a towering disdain for Proudhon, and was determined to crush him. He regards the enemy as a bourgeois helplessly at odds with himself and his age, obtuse and ignorant, and especially ignorant on the subject of Hegelian dialectics. The sustained diatribe serves to exalt Marx and to debase Proudhon. Marx insists on the intolerable abuse of knowledge committed by all economists up to his time, the grandeur of his own ideas and the insufficiency of Proudhon's. He had comparatively little knowledge of economics, and was taking himself very seriously as an economist.

Although *Misère de la Philosophie* had very few readers, and did not in the least affect the development of economic theory, it was by far the best work he had written. For the first time we hear that metallic vehemence which we shall hear again in the *Communist Manifesto, The Eighteenth Brumaire,* and *Das Kapital:* the harsh music of complaint rising to fever pitch. He was using Proudhon to hammer out his own theories, and at the same time he was exerting his strength to destroy a potential ally. What he wanted was a clear space around him, no allies in sight, himself the lone survivor of the philosophical war, the single knight-errant saving the enchanted Dulcinea. Throughout his career he was continually attacking those who were closest to him.

To destroy Proudhon Marx felt it necessary to erect a number of targets around the enemy; these could be shot down at leisure. Proudhon had never claimed to be a follower of Hegel; he saw the world as light and shade, good and evil, and had no understanding or sympathy for the dialectical flux by which thesis struggles with antithesis to become synthesis. Proudhon saw evil, and thought it should be eliminated. Marx finds this attitude childish, for Proudhon has clearly forgotten his dialectics. Here is Marx explaining that evil cannot simply be cut away:

> M. Proudhon knows no more of the Hegelian dialectic than its manner of speech. His own dialectical method consists in a dogmatic distinction between good and evil.

Well, let us for a moment take M. Proudhon himself as category. Let us study his good and bad sides, his merits and his defects.

If, as compared with Hegel, he has the merit of propounding problems which he proposes to solve for the benefit of mankind, he has also the disadvantage of being attacked by sterility as soon as it is a question of bringing a new category to birth through the dialectical process. What constitutes the dialectical process is the co-existence of two contradictory aspects, their conflict and fusion into a new category. By considering only the problem of eliminating the bad side, the dialectical process is cut short. It is not the category which is posed and opposed to itself by its contradictory nature, it is M. Proudhon, who gets excited, flounders and rages between the two sides of the category.

The argument is presented with all the skill of the professional debater, but it is not particularly helpful, because it omits the essential fact that the dialectical process had nothing to do with Proudhon's argument. Marx plays triumphantly on the theme of Proudhon's ignorance of dialectics. "In spite of all the trouble he has taken to scale the heights of the *system of contradictions,* M. Proudhon has never been able to raise himself above the first two rungs of simple thesis and antithesis; and even these he has mounted only twice, and on one of these two occasions he fell over backwards." In this way, very simply, Marx disposes of Proudhon, relishing the act of execution because it permits him to indulge in epigrams.

But Marx was very serious when it came to establishing his own philosophical theories, which had very little to do with Proudhon's economic theories. In page after page he hammers out his peculiarly German and Hegelian belief in the divine processes of thesis-antithesis-synthesis, and if this belief is sometimes stated in a form which sounds like the croakings of a madman, there are other occasions when a somber music emerges out of the contemplation of a world in the eternal process of becoming. Here, for example, he describes the intricate dance of a thought around itself:

The thought, opposed to itself, splits up into two contradictory thoughts, positive and negative, yes and no. The struggle between these two antagonistic elements comprised in the antithesis constitutes the dialectical process. The yes becoming no, the no becoming yes, the yes becoming simultaneously yes and no, the no becoming simultaneously no and yes, the contraries balancing one another, neutralizing one another, paralyzing one another. The fusion of these two contradictory thoughts constitutes a new thought, which is the synthesis. This thought splits up once again into two contradictory thoughts, which in turn fuse into a new synthesis. Out of this labor of childbirth there is born a group of thoughts. This group of thoughts follows the same dialectical process as a simple category, and has a contradictory group as antithesis. Of these two groups of thoughts is born a new group of thoughts, which is the synthesis of them.

The mind reels at the thought of all problems being interpreted in the light of thoughts splitting endlessly into their contraries, neutralizing and paralyzing one another. Marx sees the world and all its institutions and ideas performing a Dionysian dance, with never a moment of Apollonian calm. Only immortal death can put an end to the dance, and so he writes on one of those pages where we see his mind at work and reaching out toward the extremities of his thought:

> There is a continual movement of growth in productive forces, of destruction in social relations, of formation in ideas; the only immutable thing is the abstraction of movement—*mors immortalis*.

Lucretius had written: "Immortal death has taken away mortal life, *Mortalem vitam mors immortalis ademit.*" It was this tragic vision which Marx imposed on his economic theories. The world, as he saw it, was in a state of permanent revolution, fusion and contradiction. Vast forces had been set in motion, and it was his task to bring order into the illimitable confusions of existence. Order would come about when the proletariat inherited the earth, and he seems to have guessed that this final, immutable order would have much in common with immortal death.

THE COMMUNIST REVOLUTIONARY

A specter is haunting Europe—
the specter of communism.

ON THE EVE

Marx was a voluminous reader of novels, and he especially enjoyed the novels of Eugène Sue. He had no illusions about their worth as literature, but he recognized the novelist's extraordinary skill. Sue knew a good deal about the inner workings of governments, and he had a flair for inventing breathtaking conspiracies which were never completely credible but were always entertaining. The novels were first published chapter by chapter in newspapers and later in book form.

In 1844 there appeared the first of the ten volumes of *The Wandering Jew*. The novel is dominated by the strange figure of Ignatius Morok, a prophet, who lives with a black panther in a village near Leipzig. Long-bearded and red-robed, possessed of a supernatural power to make wild beasts obey his will, Morok is the real ruler of the world. His power resides in his universal correspondence, with headquarters at 11 Rue du Milieu-des-Ursins in Paris, an obscure house in the backwaters, where a certain Monsieur Rodin, dressed in a faded swallowtail coat and shiny black cloth trousers, conducts the affairs of the universal society whose power reaches to the farthest ends of the earth.

Monsieur Rodin's office resembles any unpretentious room in the suburbs, with its white calico curtains and air of faded gentility. It differs from other offices only in having a massive globe studded with thousands of little red crosses, these crosses indicating people who were being closely watched by the agents of Morok. "We are watching people all over the world," observes Monsieur Rodin. "They are far from dreaming that their every movement is known and followed, and from this room we shall send out instructions affecting their most cherished plans and orders will be issued from which there can be no escape or appeal, for what is involved is the destiny of all Europe, nay, of the whole universe!"

Marx could scarcely have avoided reading *The Wandering Jew*, for socialists all over Europe were reading Sue's works, which were deeply colored with socialist thought. Sue was far from being a nonentity; he wrote well, he held the reader's attention, and he could describe with equal facility the lives of the very poor and the very rich. Sometimes he will pause in the middle of a chapter to offer a socialist tract. In *The Wandering Jew,* for example, in a chapter called "The Sister of the Bacchante Queen," he delivers himself of a long sermon on a poor seamstress who earns four francs a week for toiling sixteen hours a day. He describes her existence in great detail, even to drawing up her accounts, so that we know exactly how she spent her pitiful earnings. Marx had read Sue's *The Mysteries of Paris,* and some forty pages of *The Holy Family* were devoted to a study of those mysteries.

But Sue's supreme gift to the socialists was a conspiratorial view of history. He saw conspiracy everywhere; dark and dreadful powers were always emerging from unlikely places; Morok, the tamer of beasts, descending upon Europe from the Arctic wastes of Russia, commanded the destinies of the world. Marx shared this conspiratorial view of history; to the end of his life he saw conspiracies where none existed. Once he described Sue as "a sentimental petty-bourgeois social *phantaisiste,*" but this was to underestimate the novelist's extraordinary gifts. From Sue Marx seems to have borrowed the idea of a network of correspondence societies enforcing the will of the prophet.

With his own correspondence committee in Brussels Marx was already weaving a web of intrigue and conspiracy across Europe. He was in correspondence with the League of the Just, the Socialists in Paris, the Chartists in England, a communist group in Cologne, and another in New York. Soon there would be many more, and a great deal of his time was spent in seeking to establish these correspondence committees and to obtain information from them. When he came to Belgium he was forced to swear on oath that he would refrain from publishing any work on current political questions—the document dated March 22, 1845, has survived, with Marx's almost illegible script followed by a French translation and the signature of the attorney who witnessed the oath—and he was therefore free to pour his energies into the correspondence committee. Ironically the Belgian government which had sought to clip his wings had only succeeded in making him more dangerous.

Marx was not a man to regard an oath as binding, and he did in fact write a number of articles in the *Deutsche-Brusseler-Zeitung,* a twice-weekly newspaper for German *émigrés* in Brussels, which appeared at the beginning of 1847. In one of these articles written in the autumn he bitterly attacked "the social principles of Christianity," announcing that for eighteen hundred years the Christians had encouraged cowardice, humility and humiliation, and all these undoubted virtues were totally foreign to the proletariat, which regarded its pride, courage and inde-

In order to obtain the authorization to reside in Belgium, I hereby declare on my honor that I will refrain while in Belgium from publishing any work concerned with the politics of the day.

Dr. Karl Marx
22 March 1845

Marx's unusually cramped handwriting appears above, with the French translation below.

pendence as being as necessary as daily bread. But the tone of his articles was rarely so moralizing or so high-flown; and in the next article he bitterly attacked Karl Heinzen, who had the audacity to write that the despotic powers of the German princes were the root of all evil. For this, in due course, the communists called him "the prince-killer." Marx attacked him as an imbecile for not realizing that the princes were irrelevant and the real enemy was the bourgeoisie. The general tone of the article was set with a quotation from Shakespeare's *Troilus and Cressida:*

> Thou sodden-witted Lord: thou hast no more brain than I have in mine elbows: an Asinico may tutor thee. Thou scurvy valiant ass, thou art here but to thresh Trojans, and thou art bought and sold among those of any wit, like a barbarian slave. If thou used to beat me, I will begin at thy heel, and tell what thou art by inches, thou thing of no bowels thou.

Marx had a great affection for *Troilus and Cressida,* for it was a thoroughly ill-tempered work and he took pleasure in the violent diatribes between Ajax and Thersites.

In the following year Heinzen published a hundred-page pamphlet called *The Heroes of German Communism,* which he dedicated to Marx. He had taken the measure of the budding communist movement, saying they wanted "to make people happy without making them free." Of Marx he said: "He is one of those who brings up artillery in order to break windowpanes." Nevertheless Heinzen was a born revolutionary, and for a while he worked closely with Marx.

Karl Peter Heinzen was a giant of a man, six feet three inches tall, broad-shouldered and muscular. He was ten years older than Marx and regarded himself as belonging to an older and wiser generation. At first he was a student of medicine at the University of Bonn, but for some reason medicine displeased him and he turned to the less-demanding study of philology. When he was twenty he abruptly left college and sailed as an ordinary seaman to Java, but the East Indies pleased him no better than philology and he was soon back in Germany, where he obtained a post as a tax collector at 240 thalers a year. Annoyed by the behavior of his superiors in the tax office, he wrote a pamphlet against Prussian bureaucracy, and to avoid arrest took refuge in Switzerland. Then he paid a brief visit to America. Restless and embittered, he decided that his true vocation was that of revolutionary.

Marx came to have a fondness for him, recognizing the dedicated revolutionary. Heinzen, who learned to detest him, described him many years later as "a cross between a cat and an ape." There was something feline about Marx, and he was always hairy and dirty. "He had wildly disheveled coal-black hair, and his complexion was dirty yellow," Heinzen reports. "Whether the dirty complexion was as nature made it, or whether the dirt came from outside, can no more be decided than whether his shirt and his clothes were originally made in a dirty color or merely acquired dirt. His forehead, like his features, were lacking in the elements of nobility and idealism." The forehead was knotty, the ears stuck out, the nose was too plump, and he had an unusually thick lower lip. He was so shortsighted that he had to hold a newspaper close to his eyes—those small, hard, penetrating eyes, very dark and full of malice, "spewing out spurts of wicked fire." According to Heinzen the general impression was unpleasant, but he had a merry laugh, and while laughing, his features seemed to compose themselves into an agreeable pattern. But this was the best Heinzen could say of a man he regarded as a born intriguer, who mercilessly exploited everyone who came within his reach, and who suffered pangs of envy over the achievements of others. Heinzen remembered, too, that when he was sitting over a glass of beer, Marx would sometimes tell the same story over and over again, and when he engaged in argument, he liked to stare at his opponent and say fiercely: "I will annihilate you!"

Heinzen's portrait of Marx as an intriguer, an annihilator, a man without any compassion for the people he misled, is not altogether reliable. He wrote his account of Marx in 1860, when there remained only the recollection of revolutionary disasters. He believed that Marx was himself responsible for these disasters, and that innocent people had been sacrificed to Marx's pride and ambitions. He was not therefore a friendly witness, and the portrait should be regarded only as a useful counterweight to the too flattering and respectful portraits by Marx's admirers.

Carl Schurz, who became one of Lincoln's generals, also drew a scathing portrait of Marx. He was attending a congress of democratic associations in Cologne in the summer of 1848 when he met Marx during a conference. He had heard a good deal about Marx's opinions, his learning, and his advocacy of socialist principles, and he expected to see a man who looked like a young professor with an academic manner. Instead he found someone so self-opinionated and domineering that he defeated his own ends. Here is Carl Schurz's description of Marx's behavior at the conference:

> I have never seen a man whose bearing was so provoking and intolerable. To no opinion, which differed from his, he accorded the honor of even a condescending consideration. Everyone who contradicted him he treated with abject contempt; every argument that he did not like he answered

> either with biting scorn at the unfathomable ignorance that had prompted it, or with opprobrious aspersions upon the motives of him who had advanced it. I remember most distinctly the cutting disdain with which he pronounced the word "bourgeois"; and as a "bourgeois"—that is, as a detestable example of the deepest mental and moral degeneracy—he denounced everyone that dared to oppose his opinion. Of course the propositions advanced or advocated by Marx in that meeting were voted down, because everyone whose feelings had been hurt by his conduct was inclined to support everything that Marx did not favor. It was very evident that not only had he not won any adherents, but had repelled many who otherwise might have become his followers.

Many, who were very close to Marx, have reported on his overbearing manner, which they excused on the grounds that he was a genius and therefore permitted to behave as boorishly as he pleased. Carl Schurz, like Heinzen, found it difficult to forgive the unforgivable.

Not that Marx was always boorish; he could be gentle and considerate when he chose, and with his intimates he could be especially charming and well-tempered, although he reserved the right to do most of the talking. Stephan Born, the young typesetter, was struck by the quiet harmony which reigned in the poorly furnished apartment, and Joseph Weydemeyer, who knew Marx better than most people because he was staying in the apartment, was bemused by the bohemian manner in which he lived. He would talk all night with his friends, lie down for an hour or two in the early morning, then go to a nearby tavern for breakfast and spend the rest of the day wandering about in the country with a few chosen companions, returning to Brussels on the last train. According to Weydemeyer, he had a gift for idleness.

In fact he worked prodigiously when he felt the need, and his idleness was merely the leisure he enjoyed after unremitting toil. He wrote countless letters, discussed the political situation with six or seven people every day, attended meetings, gave lectures, and continually pulled strings. One of these strings led to the League of the Just, and there soon arose the question whether the small Communist League in Brussels should join forces with the League in London. In January 1847 Joseph Moll paid a special visit to Brussels to inquire whether Marx would consider cooperating with the revolutionaries in London, and some time later he approached Engels, who was in Paris busily stirring up the French Socialists and attempting to bring them into the communist orbit. These meetings were of quite extraordinary importance for the history of communism, for they led to the publication a year later of the *Communist Manifesto*.

Exactly what happened at these preliminary meetings is unknown, for we have only a one-sided account written by Engels nearly forty years later. Engels claims that he was asked repeatedly and urgently to join the League of the Just. According to his recollection Moll declared that the revolutionaries in London were convinced of the rightness of the communist cause as outlined by Marx and Engels and wanted to abandon "the old conspiratorial conditions and forms." Moll went on to say that if Marx and Engels entered the League, they would be given an opportunity to expound their views before a congress of the League and they would be free to issue a manifesto, which would be regarded as the manifesto of the League. "We would also be empowered to contribute our ideas toward replacing the obsolete organization of the League with one more in keeping with the new times and aims," wrote Engels.

It is extremely unlikely that Moll offered to surrender the entire direction of the League to Marx and Engels. What is much more likely is that Marx and Engels were approached as possible collaborators in drawing up a new program, and it was only much later in the year that the question of the manifesto arose. "We were invited to cooperate in the work of reorganization," Engels wrote. "Could we say *no?* Certainly not. So we entered the League, and Marx organized a League community among our close friends in Brussels, while I visited the three Paris communities."

Engels and Marx were asked to play modest roles in the reorganization. Soon they were to play much more important roles.

The occasion for their emergence as the intellectual leaders of the League of the Just was a conference held in London in the summer. At this conference some twenty or thirty delegates met to decide on a new program. Marx and Engels had already drawn up such a program. It consisted of fifty articles in ten short chapters, and was carefully designed to please the members of the League of the Just, for without changing its goals—it was already a revolutionary society committed to overthrowing the established order—the new program gave sonority and a sense of elaborate organization to the League. New names were given to everything. The League of the Just became the Communist League. The groups forming the society were given the names of communities, circles, leading circles and the central committee, and the table of organization was described in careful detail. The original motto of the League of the Just was "All men are brothers." This was changed to "Proletarians of all lands, unite!" Marx regarded the old motto with distaste, saying there was a vast cross section of mankind for whom he had no brotherly feelings at all.

Article One of the new statutes of the Communist League read: "The aim of the League is the overthrow of the bourgeoisie, the rule of the proletariat, the abolition of the old bourgeois society based on class conflicts and the foundation of a new society without classes and without private property." No further reference was made to the aims of the League, for the remaining articles of the statute referred to organizational matters.

Although Marx was responsible for these statutes, he did not attend the London conference, explaining that he did not have sufficient funds and that he was still suffering from the aftereffects of a bloodletting. The cut had been made in his right arm, and the wound had not healed properly. Marx pleaded extenuating circumstances for his absence. Wilhelm Wolff was sent in his stead. Though absent, and speaking through the lips of Engels and Wolff, he still dominated the conference.

Although Engels was to write later that the statutes of the newly constituted League were designed to make it thoroughly democratic, with elective committees which could easily be voted out of office, thus effectively preventing the rise of a dictator, the statutes were in fact weighted in favor of the five-man executive committee. What Marx called "the communities," the smaller groups within the League, were strictly forbidden to have any correspondence with one another. Communication was vertical. The executive committee received a stream of reports from below, and handed down its orders. Members who earned the displeasure of the committee were to be "rendered harmless." The statutes of this embryo communist government therefore included provisions for dictatorial rule and for purges.

At this time the phrase "Proletarians of all lands, unite!" was known only to the handful of delegates who attended the conference. It was first printed in the *Kommunistische Zeitung*, a fly sheet published in London in September, where it appeared on the masthead. The fly sheet sold for two pence, four French sous, or two German silver groschen. It had been printed at a cost of £25, a substantial sum in those days, on a local press, and appears to have been a complete failure, for no further issues were published. Engels was probably the editor of the newspaper, and he was certainly responsible for the longest and most comprehensive article, "The Prussian Diet and the Prussian Proletariat, together with the Proletariat throughout Germany." He may even have written the introductory article in which special emphasis is placed on the libertarian aspects of communism. "Communists are not out to destroy personal liberty," wrote the anonymous author. "They do not intend to turn the world into one huge barrack or into a gigantic workhouse." He explained that under communism freedom would not be exchanged for equality. On the contrary it was the task of the communist state to preserve freedoms, and "in no social order will personal freedom be so assured as in a society based on communal ownership." Thus with gentle reasonableness in the first of all communist newspapers the communists proclaim their abhorrence of regimentation.

That the question of freedom under communism was raised at all suggests that even in 1847 a good many people were dismayed by the totalitarian aspects of communism.

At the end of November and the beginning of December came the Second Congress of the Communist League. This time Marx attended, having already discussed with Engels a manifesto which would take the form of a catechism. Engels worked on the catechism through most of November. It was an oddly dry and indigestible document consisting of twenty-five questions and answers:

> *Question One: What is Communism?*
>
> Answer: Communism is the doctrine of the conditions for the emancipation of the proletariat.
>
> *Question Two: What is the Proletariat?*
>
> Answer: The Proletariat is that class of society which entirely depends for its means of livelihood on the sale of its labor and not on the profits derived from any capital: whose weal and woe, whose life and death, whose whole existence depend on the demand for labor, on the alternations of good and bad business times, and on the fluctuations which are the outcome of unbridled competition. The Proletariat, or class of Proletarians, is in a word the working class of the nineteenth century.

Such catechisms were familiar to nineteenth-century revolutionaries. In 1825 the Decembrists in Russia produced a catechism, and a considerable number were produced in France. Engels was working on well-trodden ground. He asked all the proper questions—How did the Proletariat arise? How are they to be distinguished from slaves? What form will the new social order assume?—and he answered all of them, or nearly all of them, in a thoroughly lifeless and prosaic way. He did not know, or did not trouble to explain, the difference between the proletarian and the artisan, and he did not explain what would happen to nationalities and religion under a communist regime. These questions were to plague his successors.

Throughout the long catechism nothing is said about the form the communist government would take, although we are left in no doubt that it will be thoroughly authoritarian. Industrial armies will be organized, especially in agriculture. Agriculture and industry will be carried on by the same individuals, with the result that the hostility between the town and the countryside will cease to exist. Schools will be reorganized so that students "will be taught the entire system of production as part of their education, and they will therefore be in a position to pass from one branch of industry to another according as social needs demand or their own inclinations propel." Workers will emerge capable of taking on the entire system of production. Classes, which came into existence through the division of labor, will vanish, because division of labor will vanish. Can the communist revolution take place in one country alone? No, because the world, especially the civilized part of the world, has become so interdependent that whatever happens in one part must automatically affect the rest. In France, Germany, Great Britain and the United States the communist revolution will take place simultaneously. It will be a universal revolution taking place on a universal terrain.

Under communism there will be no more trade cycles, no more unsanitary houses, no more prostitution. Illegitimate children will enjoy the same right of inheritance as legitimate children. Universal industrial planning will take the place of competition between various factories. Finance and credit will be in the hands of the state, and of the state alone.

In this way, making vast claims and wild guesses, Engels sketched out in an intolerably dry manner a state which was not so much a state as an authoritarian principle. No life flowed through those twenty-five questions and answers. On the evening of November 23, 1847, it occurred to him that the catechism should be abandoned and a new document called *The Communist Manifesto* should be drawn up.

Meanwhile others had been attempting to draw up a program. Schapper had attempted to write it, and then given the task to Moses Hess in Paris. Engels took possession of the draft written by Hess, and completely revised it. A few days later he wrote to Marx: "*Just between ourselves* I played a hellish trick on Mosi." The "hellish trick" was the deliberate substitution of his own program for Hess's, which he proposed to send to London "behind the backs of the members of the society." This was the first time Engels had played this particular trick, and it was not the last. In time both Engels and Marx were to become adepts at the game, so that the last-minute substitution of their own programs over those of their adversaries was to become a familiar ritual, an essential part of their strategy.

On November 27 Engels left Paris for London. It was necessary to plan the strategy in detail, and so instead of taking the cross-Channel steamer he made a detour, taking the train to Ostend, where he met Marx that same evening. In a jubilant message announcing their forthcoming meeting, Engels had said: "We shall have it all our own way," writing these words in English and carefully underlining them. They had no doubt that they could capture the newly formed Communist League; the problem was to devise tactics against every eventuality which might occur. Between them, they acted like a pair of pincers, exerting the utmost pressure in unison. Only one thing disturbed them. The secret of the substitution of the documents must be kept. "Even the devil must not know about it," Engels wrote, "otherwise we shall be deposed and there will be a murderous scandal."

They arrived in London on the afternoon of the twenty-eighth, and on the next day they attended a meeting to celebrate the seventeenth anniversary of the Polish uprising. At this meeting Marx encountered the English Chartist leaders George Julian Harney and Ernest Jones for the first time. There were French, German, English and Polish speakers. Marx spoke in German, his words being translated into English by Karl Schapper. He said:

> The old Poland has gone, and we should be the last to wish its restoration. But it is not only the old Poland which has gone, but also the old Germany, the old France, the old England, and the old antiquated society. But the loss of this old society is no loss to those who have nothing to gain from the old society, and the great majority of people in all the countries of the present day are in that position. They have far more to win from the downfall of the old society, which will bring in its train the formation of a new society, no longer resting on class conflicts.
>
> Above all England is the land where the opposition between the proletariat and the bourgeoisie is the most developed. The victory of the English proletariat over the English bourgeoisie is therefore decisive for the victory of the oppressed over their oppressors. Poland will not be liberated in Poland, but in England. You Chartists therefore do not have to offer pious wishes about the liberation of nations. Strike out at your own interior enemies, and you will then have the proud knowledge that you have fought against all the old societies.

Marx did not really believe that the Chartists would succeed in destroying the English bourgeoisie, but it was what they wanted to hear and he accordingly gave it to them. The speech was no more than a decorative flourish; the real work began the following day with the opening of the Second Congress of the Communist League.

The Congress lasted for ten days. There were violent disagreements, with Marx and Engels continually on the offensive. Among the important decisions there were two which would have decisive effect. The headquarters of the League would remain in London and Marx was formally asked to draw up the program. Engels would claim later that both he and Marx were given this task, but in fact it was given to Marx alone. He returned to Brussels, and there in his apartment in the working-class district of Ixelles, at 42 Rue d'Orléans, with Jenny acting as his secretary and copyist, he wrote the document we know as *The Communist Manifesto.*

He wrote it slowly and apparently with great difficulty. The completed version smells of the lamp; he wrote it with extreme care, hammering out each paragraph until it assumed exactly the form he desired, as one writes a poem. Inevitably in the effort to be exact he became repetitious and lost the thread of his own argument. The Central Committee of the Communist League wanted the program urgently, but he kept putting off the date of completion. He always had difficulty in finishing anything, as though he could not bear to part with it.

Some of the delay may have been due to the necessity of discussing each paragraph with Engels, who had returned to Paris. The letters they exchanged on the *Manifesto* have been lost or destroyed, and we do not know how much Engels contributed to the whole. Here and there we can find a few paragraphs which are indisputably in the style of Engels, but the greater part bears the recognizable style of Marx.

The Central Committee had hoped to have the completed manuscript by the beginning of January. At a meeting on January 24, they decided that unless the manuscript was received by February 1, "further measures" would be taken. What these "further measures" would be was not specified, but since the members of the Central Committee were now out of patience and Marx had disobeyed their orders, he was clearly rendering himself liable to suspension or expulsion. The letter sent to Marx on January 26 has survived and reads as follows:

> The Central Committee hereby orders the local committee in Brussels to inform C. Marx that if the Manifesto of the C. Party, which he agreed to draw up at the last Congress, does not arrive in London before Tuesday, February 1, further measures will be taken against him. In the event that C. Marx does not write the Manifesto, the Central Committee requests the immediate return of the documents turned over to him by the Congress.
>
> In the name of the C.C. and by its orders,
>
> SCHAPPER BAUER MOLL

Marx pressed on with the writing of the manifesto, which appears to have reached London just before the deadline, for we hear no more about the "further measures" proposed by the Central Committee. The last two chapters of the *Manifesto* give an appearance of having been

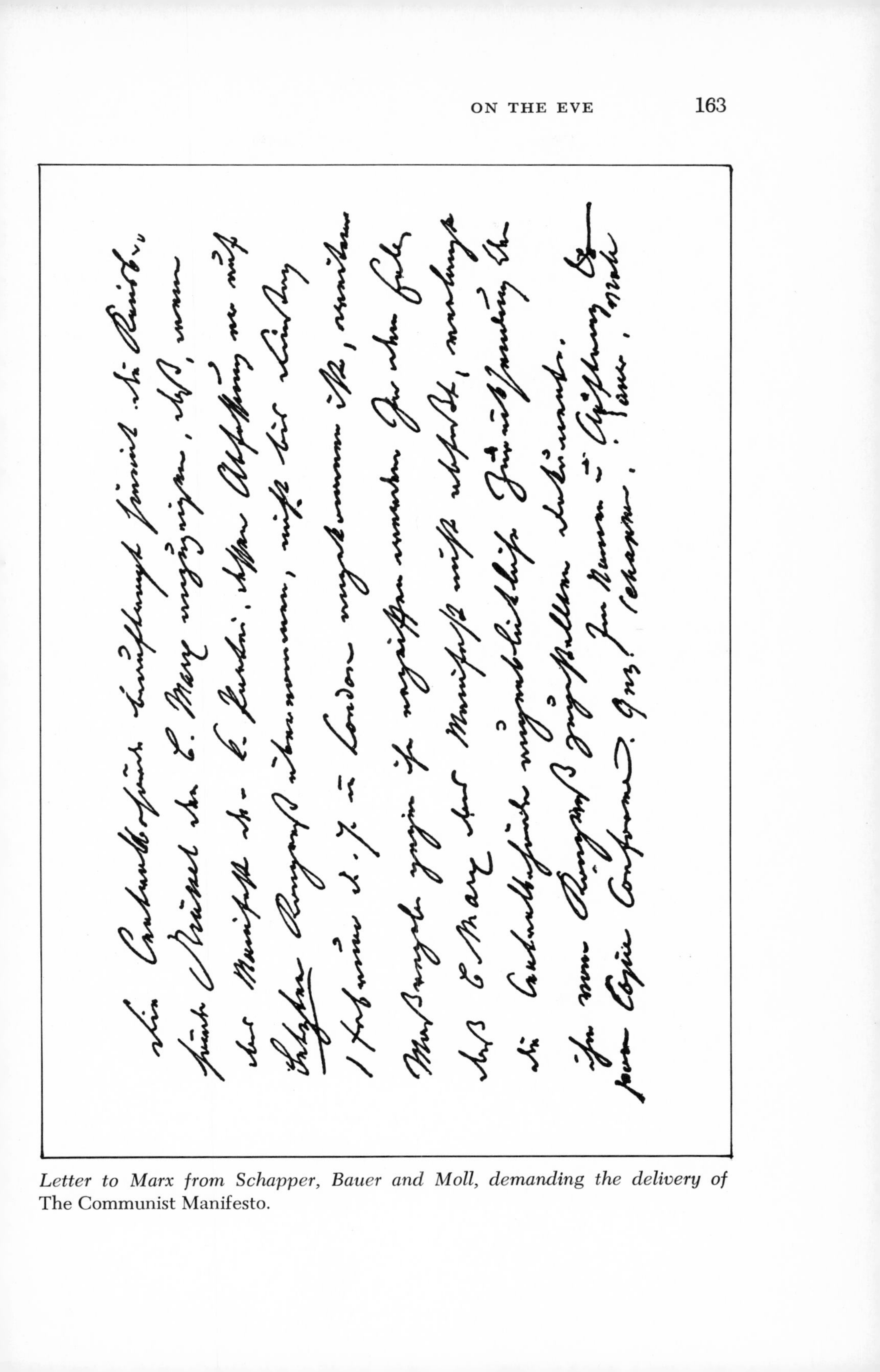

Letter to Marx from Schapper, Bauer and Moll, demanding the delivery of The Communist Manifesto.

written in haste, and these were presumably the ones completed hurriedly during the last days of January.

No one, not even Marx, could have guessed the fate of this strange document written during a desolate winter in a crowded working-class suburb of Brussels. Of all his works *The Communist Manifesto* was to have the widest influence and the most enduring life. It would be translated into more than a hundred languages, and it would be read and studied in countries Marx had never heard of. On or about January 30, 1848, he put it into a mailbox. It was a bomb with a delayed fuse, and in time it would shake the whole world.

THE COMMUNIST MANIFESTO

BECAUSE IT WAS felt that *The Communist Manifesto* should be rushed through the press in the shortest possible time, no attempt was made to send proof sheets to Marx in Brussels. Friedrich Lessner found a small printing shop in Bishopsgate to print the pamphlet, and as the pages were printed he would carry them off to Karl Schapper for a quick proofreading. Schapper was regarded as the most literate member of the party in London, and he evidently did his work well, for there were no misprints. Toward the end of February 1848—the exact date is unknown—the twenty-three-page pamphlet was published. It had a bright-yellow cover, and there was a delicate ornamental border, while the word "*Manifesto*" was printed in a flowery modification of Gothic. So graceful and fanciful a cover might have suggested to a casual glance that it was a book of love poems.

Although it is usually known in English as *The Communist Manifesto,* this was not the title under which it originally appeared. The original title was *Manifesto of the Communist Party,* and it was clearly Marx's intention to suggest that a powerful and numerous party was already in existence, with vast ramifications throughout Europe.

The *Manifesto* owed a great deal to Marx's studies in dramatic form. There is a prologue and four acts. The hero is the proletariat locked in mortal combat with the bourgeoisie, which must eventually fall before

Manifest

der

Kommunistischen Partei.

Veröffentlicht im Februar 1848.

Proletarier aller Länder vereinigt euch.

London.

Gedruckt in der Office der „Bildungs=Gesellschaft für Arbeiter"

von J. E. Burghard.

46, Liverpool Street, Bishopsgate.

Cover of the first edition of The Communist Manifesto.

the greater skill and endurance of its young and formidable adversary. We see the proletariat rising in its youthful glory, at first uncertain of itself, unaware of its own strength, incapable of decision, only gradually exerting its full powers as it becomes aware of its manifest destiny. The theme throughout is the struggle between age and youth, between the corrupt past and the innocence and vigor of the young. And just as in *Oulanem* Marx demonstrated considerable power in his soliloquies, so in the *Manifesto* he soliloquizes continually on the subject of the antagonists, so that they sometimes give the impression of being disembodied forces without recognizable shape or purpose. The aged bourgeoisie and the youthful proletariat have an oddly protean character, and seem to be continually changing their fundamental character.

It is instructive to read Marx's unfinished tragic drama before reading the *Manifesto.* There are some superficial resemblances, but there are also resemblances which go deeper into the confusions of Marx's mind. In *Oulanem* the dramatist shows himself incapable of developing a dramatic crisis, and the characters exist in their own separate worlds, never really communicating with one another, never meeting head-on. The old Pertini, the lost one, and the young Lucindo, who shines with the brightness of the morning stars, shout and rant at one another and never lock horns. There is no logical course of events, the characters are never clearly identified, speeches trail off, the author seems not to know when he is writing well or atrociously—for there are good and sometimes excellent lines buried in those confused soliloquies—and the drama splutters to an end when the author has nothing more to say. The *Manifesto,* too, splutters to an end after the second chapter, for the two remaining short chapters are merely footnotes provided to give ballast to the book.

There are even moments when *Oulanem* reads like a foretaste of the *Manifesto.* Here is the youthful Lucindo prophesying the fate reserved for Pertini:

> Ha, no salvation, no, none! Nowhere!
> Your iron heart so impenetrably hard
> And your withered mind defiled by scorn
> Are mixed with a poison which gathers like the balsam,
> And now, man, smile, perhaps for the last time,
> Grasp it, suck at it, at this last hour,
> In a moment thou shalt stand before the Judge,
> And the long chains of your life will be unloosened . . .

In much the same way, in high romantic tones, Marx addresses the bourgeoisie who can find "no salvation, no, none," their minds being so withered and their hearts so hard that they will never be able to adapt themselves to the new life springing up in the proletariat. The bourgeoisie is damned, the proletariat is blessed. In the *Manifesto* Marx seems at times to be describing an ancient ritual drama, which must be worked out until all the damned are consigned to hell and the blessed take up their abode in heaven.

The theme is outlined chiefly in the first chapter, called "Bourgeois and Proletarians." After the prologue with its famous opening line, "A specter is haunting Europe—the specter of communism," Marx settles down to describe the rise of the bourgeoisie to power and prominence. It erupted, according to Marx, out of the ruins of an oppressive feudal society. Revolting serfs became chartered guild masters in self-governing medieval communes, and these in turn were supplanted by the owners of industrial factories. The guilds collapsed, and the factories took over. With the discovery of America, the rounding of the Cape, and the growing markets in the Far East, vast accumulations of capital came into the hands of the factory owners, and the industrial middle class began to lose its power to the managers of huge industrial complexes. There was only the hard cash nexus, the determination of the industrial managers to exploit the workmen to the uttermost. The bourgeoisie, which had destroyed feudalism, was itself responsible for the rise of the managers, for they came out of the bourgeoisie and were corrupted by it:

> The bourgeoisie, historically, has played a most revolutionary part.
>
> The bourgeoisie, wherever it has got the upper hand, has put an end to all feudal, patriarchal, idyllic relations. It has pitilessly torn asunder the motley feudal ties that bound man to his "natural superiors," and has left remaining no other bond between man and man than naked self-interest and callous "cash payment." It has drowned the most heavenly ecstasies of religious fervor, of chivalrous enthusiasm, of philistine sentimentalism, in the icy water of egotistical calculation. It has resolved personal worth into exchange value, and in place of the numberless indefensible chartered freedoms, has set up that single, unconscionable freedom—free trade. In one word, for exploitation, veiled by religious and political illusions, it has substituted naked, shameless, direct, brutal, aggression.
>
> The bourgeoisie has stripped of its halo every occupation hitherto honored and looked up to with reverent awe. It has converted the physician, the lawyer, the priest, the poet, the man of science, into its paid wage laborers.
>
> The bourgeoisie has torn away from the family its sentimental veil, and has reduced the family relation to a mere money relation.
>
> The bourgeoisie has disclosed how it came to pass that the brutal display of vigor in the Middle Ages, which reactionaries so much admire, found its fitting complement in the laziest indolence. It has been the first to show what man's activities can bring about. It has accomplished wonders far surpassing Egyptian pyramids, Roman aqueducts, and Gothic cathedrals; it has conducted expeditions that put to shame all former Exoduses of nations and crusades.

Marx therefore finds himself caught between admiration for the achievements of the bourgeoisie and detestation of its present chaotic state, for as he sees it the bourgeoisie cannot exist without constantly revolutionizing the instruments of production, thus throwing all human relationships into a state of permanent crisis.

It would appear that for Marx, at this stage of his argument, the enemy is change, for he finds hitherto unsuspected virtues in the easy, simple relations which existed between the feudal lord and the serf. Marx presents himself as the defender of the old order. Under the reign of the bourgeoisie, "all that is solid melts into air, all that is holy is profaned, and man is at last compelled to face his real conditions of life, and his mutual relations with sober eye."

He then recites the crimes of the bourgeoisie at length, making no distinction between the different historical periods in which they were committed. First, the bourgeoisie has destroyed national industry by taking the whole world as its field. "It must nestle everywhere, settle everywhere, establish connections everywhere." Old-established industries fall before it, unable to survive in an age of growing competition. Nationalism is itself endangered, for the bourgeoisie is indifferent to rival nationalisms, and even the intellectual creations of a country soon become the possession of the whole world. Secondly, the bourgeoisie has reduced prices through mass production, and is therefore in a position to sell its cheap goods abroad on a massive scale. "The cheap prices of its commodities are the heavy artillery with which it batters down all Chinese walls." In this way the bourgeoisie compels foreign powers to embrace civilization, and foreigners capitulate to the extent of becoming bourgeois themselves. Thirdly, the bourgeoisie has subjected the rural areas to the towns, vastly increasing the urban population and concentrating the industrial wealth into a few cities. Fourthly, the bourgeoisie has subjected natural forces to its own desires, so that it seems to exist apart from nature, exploiting the earth with the same indifference as it exploits laborers, having such vast forces at its disposition that it has become a sorcerer "unable to control the powers of the subterranean world which he has called up by his spells," and it is precisely this lack of control resulting in a series of unprecedented crises which demonstrates that the bourgeoisie, apparently so powerful, is ultimately powerless. In these crises the bourgeoisie finds itself at the mercy of a force greater than its own:

> In these crises there breaks out an epidemic that, in all earlier epochs, would have seemed an absurdity—the epidemic of overproduction. Society

> suddenly finds itself put back into a state of momentary barbarism; it appears as if a famine, a universal war of devastation had cut off the supply of every means of subsistence; industry and commerce seem to be destroyed; and why? Because there is too much civilization, too much means of subsistence, too much industry, too much commerce. The productive forces at the disposal of society no longer tend to further the development of bourgeois prosperity; on the contrary they become too powerful for these conditions, by which they are fettered, and so soon as they overcome these fetters, they bring disorder into the whole of bourgeois society, endanger the existence of bourgeois property. The conditions of bourgeois society are too narrow to comprise the wealth created by them. And how does the bourgeoisie get over these crises? On the one hand by the enforced destruction of a mass of productive forces; on the other, by the conquest of new markets, and by the more thorough exploitation of the old ones. That is to say, by paving the way for more extensive and more destructive crises, and by diminishing the means whereby crises are prevented.
>
> The weapons with which the bourgeoisie felled feudalism are now turned against the bourgeoisie itself.
>
> But not only has the bourgeoisie forged the weapons that bring death to itself; it has also called into existence the men who will wield those weapons —the modern working class—the proletarians.

Marx's argument necessarily involves the suicide of the bourgeoisie, which dies of a series of self-administered shocks. His theory of crises, although announced with great solemnity, is perhaps the most unconvincing part of the *Manifesto*. It was however one which Marx held to strongly, and for the remaining years of his life he would announce at brief intervals the existence of crises which would surely shatter the bourgeoisie to its foundations. He was equally insistent that the bourgeoisie was its own most fatal enemy. "What the bourgeoisie therefore produces above all is its own gravediggers."

Such an argument leaves little scope for the proletariat, which is reduced to the role of chief mourner without the satisfaction of having vanquished the enemy.

In a few brief pages Marx outlines the entire history of the bourgeoisie from its birth in the feudal age to its death in the proletarian age. In a similar, and rather more perfunctory manner, he outlines the rise to power and prominence of the proletariat. At first there were only a few individual laborers who protested against the encroachments of the bourgeoisie. They formed a small inchoate mass who made ineffective attempts to sabotage industry. "They destroy imported wares that compete with their labor, they smash machinery to pieces, they set factories ablaze, they seek to restore by force the vanished status of the workman of the Middle Ages."

In time, with increasing numbers, the proletariat becomes organized, and the tradition of the Wreckers is continued in riots and social upheaval, which takes the form of a struggle to the death between the classes. The bourgeoisie is continually supplying fuel to the proletariat until at the supreme moment of crisis "a small section of the ruling class cuts itself adrift, and joins the revolutionary class, the class that holds the future in its hands." Meanwhile the greater part of the bourgeoisie—the lower middle class, the small manufacturer, the shopkeeper, the artisan, the peasant—retain their conservative character, and they too must eventually be destroyed. As for the *lumpenproletariat,* the dregs of society, they are likely to be found in the camp of the bourgeoisie, for they are inherently reactionary.

The proletarian victory is assured because the proletariat is by far the largest and most disciplined part of society. Theirs is "the self-conscious, independent movement of the immense majority, in the interest of the immense majority." They regard law, morality and religion as bourgeois prejudices, and therefore they are unconcerned with any ethical questions raised by their revolt. Property is their enemy, and their aim is to take possession of all property. "They have nothing of their own to secure and to fortify; their mission is to destroy all previous securities for, and insurances of, individual property." Their ultimate mission is to wrest power from the bourgeoisie and to establish their own.

In the second chapter Marx studies the relations between the proletariat and the communists. Just as the French Revolution abolished feudal property, so the distinguishing feature of the communist is that he works for the abolition of bourgeois property, by which he means all private property except the household goods of the laborer, the petty artisan and the peasant. "Communism deprives no man of the power to appropriate the products of society; all that it does is to deprive him of the power to subjugate the labor of others by means of that appropriation." To the argument that once property has been abolished everyone will stop working, he answers that if this were so, people would have stopped working long ago under bourgeois society, where "those who work do not acquire property, and those who acquire property do not work."

The arguments always tend toward these simple epigrammatic solutions. They are clever, but not enlightening; and there is never any hint that Marx was aware of the complex relationship between the worker and his employer, the market and the product of human labor. It is not only that the whole of existing society must be swept away, but all the relationships between the worker and his labor must also be swept away;

The only surviving page from an early draft of The Communist Manifesto. *This is an early draft, with two lines at the top written by Jenny Marx.*

and as Marx proceeds with his argument, sweeping society aside, he seems always to be in danger of confronting a vacuum, where there are no workers, no products of their labor, and no one to buy them.

Since property must be swept away, the family, too, must be swept away, for the family is a prime example of bourgeois property. "Bourgeois marriage is in actual fact the community of wives," he declares, noting that it is the chief pleasure of the bourgeois to seduce each other's wives and to force the daughters of the proletariat into prostitution. He is perfectly serious when he demands the abolition of the family; and the argument already used in "On the Jewish Question" is presented with even greater conviction. He has nothing to say on the fate reserved for children under the communist state.

From the abolition of the family he advances immediately to a consideration of the abolition of nations. "The workers have no country," he announces. Nationalism and national boundaries are bourgeois prejudices; the only real nation is the nation of workers, and once the workers have seized power there will be no further hostility between nations. "The ending of class oppositions within the nations will end the mutual hostilities of the nations."

These sweeping generalities are announced without any supporting evidence, as though they were immediately apparent to every unprejudiced observer. Marx seems to have been aware that there was an element of impracticality in these suggestions, and finally announces a practical program of action:

1. Expropriation of property in land and application of all rents of land to public purposes.
2. A heavy progressive or graduated income tax.
3. Abolition of all rights of inheritance.
4. Confiscation of the property of all emigrants and rebels.
5. Centralization of credit in the hands of the State, by means of a national bank with State capital and an exclusive monopoly.
6. Centralization of the means of communication and transport in the hands of the State.
7. Increase of factories and instruments of production owned by the State; the bringing into cultivation of wastelands, and the improvement of the soil generally in accordance with a general plan.
8. Universal and equal obligation to work. Organization of industrial armies, especially for agriculture.
9. Agriculture and urban industry to work hand in hand, in such a way that the distinction between town and country will be gradually obliterated.
10. Free education for all children in public schools. Abolition of factory work for children in its present form. Education and material production to be combined.

What is clear is that Marx had not thought out the nature of the communist state in any considerable detail. His own prejudices colored the new decalogue to a surprising extent, and the ten practical steps had very little relation to the theoretical ideas he had advanced previously. Some of these practical steps seem to have been inserted as afterthoughts, to fill up gaps. "The bringing into cultivation of wastelands, and the improvement of the soil generally in accordance with a general plan," is an idea which appealed strongly to Frederick the Great; it was neither novel nor particularly relevant, since all governments have been partial to land reclamation. The graduated income tax had a respectable ancestry, having been introduced into England in 1799 by William Pitt. "Free education for all children in public schools" was an acceptable and widely publicized platform of all socialist parties. "Confiscation of the property of all emigrants and rebels" was perhaps the most surprising of the new laws, for it honored the expropriated capitalists with the title of "rebels," previously reserved for revolutionaries.

The ten laws announced from Ixelles have a disturbing lack of coherence. Marx was not deeply interested in the practical working-out of details; he preferred destruction to creation. The word "abolition" appears on every page; and after he has "abolished" property, family and nations, and all existing societies, Marx shows little interest in creating a new society on the ruins of the old. He had written in a poem to Jenny that he would throw a gantlet at the world, and watch it crumble. Comforted by her love, he would wander through the kingdom of ruins, his words glowing with action, his heart like the heart of God. The *Communist Manifesto* was the gantlet he threw at the world.

Inevitably a work as important and far-reaching as this bred endless commentaries. Every sentence has been analyzed and scrutinized, with the result that nearly all the ideas have been traced to their source. None of the ideas were original with Marx. "The workers have no country," was said first by Marat, the French revolutionary, who was also the first to say: "The proletarians have nothing to lose but their chains." Blanqui had invented the phrase "the dictatorship of the proletariat." Though Marx wrote: "When the people saw the ancient feudal coats of arms decorating the backsides of the aristocracy, and incontinently dispersed with loud and irreverent laughter," he forgot to remind the reader that he was paraphrasing a verse from Heine's "Germany, A Winter's Tale." Even the most famous phrase of all—"Workingmen of all countries, unite!"—had been borrowed from Karl Schapper and had appeared in print four months earlier. The *Communist Manifesto* was a palimpsest of ideas culled from at least fifteen known sources. Marx had stirred the broth, poured in some coloring matter, and then flung the pot at the faces of the bourgeois. His chief contribution lay in the fact that he gave the old ideas a new resonance and a romantic form, thus making them memorable. The most memorable passage occurs at the end:

> Communists scorn to hide their views and aims. They openly declare that their purposes can only be achieved by the forcible overthrow of the entire existing social order. Let the ruling classes tremble at a Communist revolution. The proletarians have nothing to lose but their chains. They have a world to win. Workingmen of all countries, unite!

THE STORM BREAKS

In the early months of 1848 Europe was suddenly in the throes of revolution, but it was far from being the revolution Marx had been predicting. There was no war between the classes; indeed, all over Europe the bourgeoisie and the proletariat were in alliance. This was a revolution to seize power from the ruling governments and to right the wrongs of centuries. One after another the governments fell, the workers threw up barricades, the bourgeoisie marched on the houses of parliament, and the statesmen went into exile.

It began, as revolutions always do, with some small and unpredictable event which could scarcely have warranted the attention of historians if the consequences had not been so grave and far-reaching. Seven cantons in Switzerland with Lucerne at the head refused to obey the order of the Diet to disband their Jesuit schools. The Catholics and Protestants flew to arms; for a few days there were wild skirmishes; Austria threatened to intervene; and within three weeks Lucerne was captured by a Protestant army and the Jesuits were expelled. This brief war in Switzerland sent shock waves through Europe. Suddenly all over Europe people felt the need to resort to stern measures to put an end to oppression.

The war in Switzerland was not in any real sense a revolutionary war. It was a religious war fought for religious ends, but it had the effect of setting in motion a series of revolutions which exploded like a chain of firecrackers. Austria's threat to intervene was not followed up, and the Italians observed with incredulity that the greatest power in Europe was powerless to influence the ill-armed farmers of Switzerland.

The fighting near Lucerne took place toward the end of November. For more than a month the embers were fanned by revolutionaries. Then in January revolts broke out in Milan and Palermo. Milan was then under the domination of Austria, Palermo under the domination of the Bourbon King Ferdinand of Naples. Neither of these uprisings was successful, but the revolutionary tide swept across Italy with street fighting breaking out in all the principal cities. The sovereign princes of the Italian states, the Pope, the King of Naples and the Grand Duke of Tuscany yielded to the demands of the people and promised constitutions.

The revolutionary tide turned westward and swept across France. King Louis Philippe abdicated after riots broke out in the capital, leaving fifteen people dead in the gardens of the Tuileries. Unharmed, the King was allowed to go into exile in London, while the people proclaimed a republic. Two weeks later, on March 13, the people of Vienna rose and overturned the government of Metternich. The kings trembled; the people rejoiced. The Austrian Emperor conceded that henceforth he would act as a constitutional monarch, and Metternich conceded that the old order had gone forever. "My dear, we are dead men," he told his wife, as he went into exile.

In Belgium the government was determined to ride out the storm. It had its spies among the German exiles in Brussels and knew what they were up to. In particular it had its eyes on Marx, who had just inherited 6,000 gold francs from his father's estate—the only large sum of money he ever inherited—and in the belief that the Belgian revolution was imminent he had given a large portion of this money to a special fund for arming Belgian workmen. In the greatest secrecy he had also lectured to small groups on the art of insurrection. At the same time he was making preparations for a flight to Paris, and he was in touch with some of the members of the Provisional Government, which took power from Louis Philippe. On March 1, Ferdinand Flocon, a leading member of the government, sent him a special invitation to return to the country from which he had been expelled. He wrote:

DEAR AND BRAVE MARX

The soil of the French Republic is a place of refuge for all friends of freedom. Tyranny has banished you; free France opens to you her doors—

to you and to all those who fight for the holy cause of the brotherhood of peoples. In this sense every officer of the French Government understands his duty. *Salut et fraternité.*

FERDINAND FLOCON
Member of the Provisional Government

The letter appears to have reached Marx on March 3, a day which he had cause to remember vividly. On the previous day the Belgian authorities decided to rid themselves of a dangerous revolutionary, the Minister of Justice signing the order for his expulsion. The document, which has survived, takes the form of a royal command from Leopold, King of the Belgians, to all present and to come, greetings. In the king's name "Marx, Charles, doctor of philosophy, aged about 28, born in Trier (Prussia) is enjoined to depart from the Kingdom of Belgium within *twenty-four hours* and forbidden to return." Marx was handed this document at five o'clock in the evening of March 3, and since there was no possibility of any appeal, he spent the rest of the evening preparing for his journey to Paris. He had only a few hours in which to settle all his personal and political affairs, pack his bags, conceal documents, and make arrangements for his wife and children.

He must have known that he was in danger of arrest and of physical harm. The police knew that he spent about 5,000 gold francs on arming the Belgian workmen, and he could expect very little mercy once he was arrested. After a demonstration on the night of February 28, Wilhelm Wolff had been arrested and taken off to the Petits Carmes prison. A day or two later Marx wrote some hurried notes about the ill-treatment Wolff had received:

> Real ill-treatment at the Hôtel de Ville. Blows from all sides. Real ill-treatment first at Police headquarters, where there was a large number of drunken *gardes civiques.* With clenched fist a policeman struck at Wolff's right eye, so that his s—— They tore off his spectacles, spat in his face, kicked him, and cursed him.

One reads these hurried notes with some surprise, for Marx, lost in the realm of revolutionary abstractions, rarely refers to physical violence. He had not seen Wolff being ill-treated, and he had taken no part in the demonstration.

During the night of March 3 the police at last caught up with him. A police captain and a civic guard burst into the apartment with a warrant for his arrest. He was taken to prison. Jenny, who was almost certainly aware of the gravity of his offenses—the gift of money for arming Belgian workmen rendered him liable to execution for high treason—went out

Leopold, Roi des Belges,

A TOUS PRÉSENTS ET A VENIR, SALUT :

Vu les lois des 22 Septembre 1835, 25 décembre 1841 et 23 Février 1846

Sur la proposition de notre Ministre de la Justice,

NOUS AVONS ARRÊTÉ ET ARRÊTONS :

Article Unique

Il est enjoint au nommé Marx, Charles docteur en philosophie, âgé de 28 ans environ, né à Trèves (Prusse) de quitter le Royaume de la Belgique dans le délai de vingt quatre heures avec défense d'y rentrer à l'avenir sous les peines comminées par l'article six de la loi précitée du 22 7bre 1835

Notre Ministre de la Justice est charge de l'exécution du présent arrêté.

Donné à Bruxelles, le 2 Mars 1848

(Signé) LÉOPOLD.

PAR LE ROI

Le Ministre de la Justice

(Signé) De Haussy

POUR EXPÉDITION CONFORME :

Le Secrétaire-Général,

[illegible]

Order expelling Marx from Belgium.

into the night and pounded on the doors of people who might have some influence, but appears to have found only one person who could give her any reassurance. This was Lucien Jottrand, president of the Democratic Association, who offered to investigate. Then she returned to her apartment, only to discover a police sergeant posted at the door. The sergeant told her with exquisite politeness that if she wanted to see her husband, she had only to follow him. Jottrand had arranged that Philippe Gigot should accompany her home, and he now accompanied her to the police station, where a police commissioner began to interrogate her, asking her about her papers and why she had gone to see Jottrand. Gigot was incensed. It was absurd that Jenny should be interrogated in this way, and he spoke a little too loudly about the insolence of police officers. He was thrown into jail. Jenny was also thrown into prison on the grounds that she was a vagabond with no visible means of support. She spent the night on a hard wooden bed in the company of prostitutes; she was sick with fear and misery; and she had no way of knowing what had happened to her husband.

In the morning she caught a glimpse of Gigot, looking cadaverous and mournful in the gray light. He pointed down to the courtyard below, where at that very moment her husband was being led away under military escort. She was now more fearful than ever that he would have to stand trial and suffer a terrible punishment.

About an hour later, with a police escort, she was taken before an examining magistrate. It was now about eleven o'clock. There was a long wait before the judge would receive her, and he appears to have conducted only a cursory examination. Both Marx and Jenny have left accounts of the events of that day, but they have little to say about the interrogation. "The magistrate was somewhat surprised by the fact that the police in their solicitude had not arrested her young children," Marx wrote a few days later for a French paper. "The interrogation could only be a farce, and my wife's only crime was that she shared her husband's democratic opinions, although belonging to the Prussian aristocracy."

By the time the interrogation was over, it was already late in the afternoon and the twenty-four hours had elapsed. Jenny hurried home and finished her packing. A trunk with her silver plate and the best linen was left in the care of a sympathetic bookseller called Vogler, and a few minutes later, with the children bundled up against the bitter cold, the whole family was marched under police escort to the railroad station. The police escort was not removed until they reached the frontier.

In Paris the revolutionary fever was gradually dying away. With the king in London and the Provisional Government making only tentative gestures of ruling, the people seemed to lose interest in the revolution which had been brought about through the secret societies headed by Armand Barbès and Auguste Blanqui. Both Barbès and Blanqui saw themselves as potential Jacobin dictators and dreamed of reviving the Terror. But when Marx reached Paris, there were only the pathetic remnants of the revolution to be seen—heaps of broken glass, overturned horse carriages, a few burned-out buildings, the paving stones lying loose at the street corners ready to be fashioned into barricades again, if they should be needed. What came to be known as the February revolution died out like a spent rocket.

Unpredictable, like a cyclone, the revolution wandered across Europe. On March 10 there were wild demonstrations in the streets of Rome, and the Pope was compelled to grant a constitution and to accept a government in which the churchmen were no longer in full command. On March 13 the people rose in Vienna. On March 18 the barricades went up in Berlin, street fighting broke out, and King Frederick William IV was compelled to pay homage to the revolutionaries who died on the barricades; he bowed deeply before them as they lay outside his palace, and he was forced to grant a new constitution. He was maintained in power only because he was thought to be a liberal, kindly, ineffective man, more useful in Berlin than in exile.

From Paris the German refugees watched the revolution in Germany with feelings of alarm and trepidation. They had hoped to be the agents of revolution, and were merely bystanders. Georg Herwegh, rich and ambitious, saw himself as the commander of the German legionaries who would sweep across Germany and establish a new revolutionary government in Berlin. His German legion was regarded with favor by the Provisional Government, which wanted an excuse to rid itself of so many German refugees in the capital and accordingly paid Herwegh fifty centimes a day for the upkeep of each legionary. He was given arms, barracks, uniforms. The legionaries held parades, marched and countermarched, and with the full blessing of the French government the entire body of the German Legion marched into Germany, where it was roundly defeated.

Marx had no sympathy for such casual adventures. He regarded revolutions with the utmost seriousness, and knew that they had to be prepared and tended with great care, and that propaganda was more damaging than guns. Schapper, Moll and Bauer came to France and set up the headquarters of the Communist League in the French capital. Overnight the Communist League became the Communist Party of Germany. A fly sheet, signed by Marx, Engels, Wilhelm Wolff, Schapper, Bauer and Moll, appeared in Paris toward the end of March; thousands of copies were distributed secretly in Germany with no noticeable effect. The fly sheet however has some importance in the history of communism, for it was written in the form of a manifesto and showed significant variations from *The Communist Manifesto* which had appeared in London the previous month.

The fly sheet, which bore the title *Demands of the Communist Party in Germany,* consisted of a single long strip of paper with seventeen closely printed demands calculated to intimidate the bourgeoisie. The right of inheritance was curtailed; the salaries of all civil servants were to be reduced to the same level; all landed property was to become the possession of the state; the army was abolished, and in its place there was the popular militia with all its members acting as workers in the service of the government when they were not maintaining the security of the state.

Of the seventeen demands there were some which read very oddly today. The separation of church and state, free universal education, a steeply graduated income tax, a guaranteed livelihood for all workers, state ownership of banks and means of transport—these were not particularly revolutionary ideas even in 1848. The manifesto was remarkable for paying considerable attention to the plight of the peasants, who were not usually regarded with sympathy by Marx and Engels. Article Five of the manifesto read: "The legal services shall be gratuitous." Article Ten demanded the gradual abolition of metal coinage in favor of paper, thus releasing gold and silver for foreign commerce. "This measure is ultimately necessary in order to tie together the interests of the conservative bourgeoisie and the revolution." This surprising conclusion reflected a sad ignorance of both revolutionary and financial theory.

Indeed, the *Demands of the Communist Party in Germany* is one of the least impressive documents of the early history of communism. Marx and Engels claimed they wrote it together, but it shows signs of having been written by a committee. It lacks the fire and urgency of *The Communist Manifesto,* and no one could be expected to lay down his life for the principles enshrined in it.

Nevertheless this fly sheet was the chief weapon of the new party. This was their banner, their battle cry, their first salvo. Armed with this document a handful of communists made their way to Germany, Engels claiming later that the party was responsible for sending three or four hundred

Forderungen der Kommunistischen Partei in Deutschland.

„Proletarier aller Länder vereinigt Euch!"

1. Ganz Deutschland wird zu einer einigen, untheilbaren Republik erklärt.

2. Jeder Deutsche, der 21 Jahre alt, ist Wähler und wählbar, vorausgesetzt daß er keine Kriminalstrafe erlitten hat.

3. Die Volksvertreter werden besoldet, damit auch der Arbeiter im Parlament des deutschen Volkes sitzen könne.

4. Allgemeine Volksbewaffnung. Die Armeen sind in Zukunft zugleich Arbeiter-Armeen, so daß das Heer nicht blos, wie früher, verzehrt, sondern noch mehr produzirt, als seine Unterhaltungskosten betragen.

Dieß ist außerdem ein Mittel zur Organisation der Arbeit.

5. Die Gerechtigkeitspflege ist unentgeltlich.

6. Alle Feudallasten, alle Abgaben, Frohnden, Zehnten, rc., die bisher auf dem Landvolke lasteten, werden ohne irgend eine Entschädigung abgeschafft.

7. Die fürstlichen und andern feudalen Landgüter, alle Bergwerke, Gruben, u. s. w., werden in Staatseigenthum umgewandelt. Auf diesen Landgütern wird der Ackerbau im Großen und mit den modernsten Hilfsmitteln der Wissenschaft zum Vortheil der Gesammtheit betrieben.

8. Die Hypotheken auf den Bauerngütern werden für Staatseigenthum erklärt. Die Interessen für jene Hypotheken werden von den Bauern an den Staat gezahlt.

9. In den Gegenden, wo das Pachtwesen entwickelt ist, wird die Grundrente oder der Pachtschilling als Steuer an den Staat gezahlt.

Alle diese unter 6, 7, 8 und 9 angegebenen Maaßregeln werden gefaßt, um öffentliche und andere Lasten der Bauern und kleinen Pächter zu vermindern, ohne die zur Bestreitung der Staatskosten nöthigen Mittel zu schmälern und ohne die Produktion selbst zu gefährden.

Der eigentliche Grundeigenthümer, der weder Bauer noch Pächter ist, hat an der Produktion gar keinen Antheil. Seine Konsumtion ist daher ein bloßer Mißbrauch.

10. An die Stelle aller Privatbanken tritt eine Staatsbank, deren Papier gesetzlichen Kurs hat.

Diese Maßregel macht es möglich, das Kreditwesen im Interesse des ganzen Volkes zu regeln und untergräbt damit die Herrschaft der großen Geldmänner. Indem sie nach und nach Papiergeld an die Stelle von Gold und Silber setzt, verwohlfeilert sie das unentbehrliche Instrument des bürgerlichen Verkehrs, das allgemeine Tauschmittel, und erlaubt, das Gold und Silber nach außen hin wirken zu lassen. Diese Maaßregel ist schließlich nothwendig, um die Interessen der konservativen Bourgeois an die Revolution zu knüpfen.

11. Alle Transportmittel: Eisenbahnen, Kanäle, Dampfschiffe, Wege, Posten, rc., nimmt der Staat in seine Hand. Sie werden in Staatseigenthum umgewandelt und der unbemittelten Klasse zur unentgeltlichen Verfügung gestellt.

12. In der Besoldung sämmtlicher Staatsbeamten findet kein anderer Unterschied statt, als der, daß diejenigen mit Familie, also mit mehr Bedürfnissen, auch ein höheres Gehalt beziehen als die Uebrigen.

13. Völlige Trennung der Kirche vom Staate. Die Geistlichen aller Konfessionen werden lediglich von ihrer freiwilligen Gemeinde besoldet.

14. Beschränkung des Erbrechts.

15. Einführung von starken Progressivsteuern und Abschaffung der Konsumtionssteuern.

16. Errichtung von Nationalwerkstätten. Der Staat garantirt allen Arbeitern ihre Existenz und versorgt die zur Arbeit Unfähigen.

17. Allgemeine, unentgeltliche Volkserziehung.

Es liegt im Interesse des deutschen Proletariats, des kleinen Bürger- und Bauernstandes, mit aller Energie an der Durchsetzung obiger Maaßregeln zu arbeiten. Denn nur durch Verwirklichung derselben können die Millionen, die bisher in Deutschland von einer kleinen Zahl ausgebeutet wurden und die man weiter in der Unterdrückung zu erhalten suchen wird, zu ihrem Recht und zu derjenigen Macht gelangen, die ihnen, als den Hervorbringern alles Reichthums, gebührt.

Das Comite:

Karl Marx. Karl Schapper. H. Bauer. F. Engels.
J. Moll. W. Wolff.

"Demands of the Communist Party in Germany," issued as a flyer.

workers to make propaganda for the communist cause in the homeland, but these figures were figments of his imagination. Only a very small nucleus of dedicated communists made their way back. As for the former members of the Communist League, three quarters of them, on Engels' admission, either abandoned all interest in communism or settled down to start their own revolutionary committees. The conspiratorial arm of the League, which Engels described as "the secret League," vanished. In the course of time it would be built up again with all the inevitable impedimenta of secret codes, invisible ink, and mysterious agents armed with the power of authority given to them by Marx or Engels.

The *Demands of the Communist Party in Germany* had almost no impact on the German working classes. The Communist Party itself was in eclipse; it was represented only by a few stalwarts. Marx went to Cologne in the Rhineland, where he was in less danger of arrest. Wilhelm Wolff went to Breslau. Schapper went to Nassau. Stephan Born made his way to Berlin, where he appears to have been one of those who hoped to acquire a revolutionary movement of his own, for he organized a Workers' Brotherhood in Berlin with himself as the officiating president. "He was in a hurry to become a political figure, and he fraternized with the most miscellaneous rag, tag and bobtail of workers in order to get a crowd together," Engels wrote disapprovingly. What was even worse was that Stephan Born had no sure command of theory, and he was inclined to regard the opinions of Louis Blanc and Proudhon as equally valid as the opinions stated in *The Communist Manifesto.* He was lucky not to be purged. In the end he abandoned communism, and became a schoolmaster in Switzerland. To Engels' disgust he preferred to translate Renan into German than communist theory into practice.

The communists were scattered over Germany. They were in disarray, without a headquarters, without an organization, and without a newspaper. Then at the beginning of June Marx took control of the *Neue Rheinische Zeitung* with offices in Cologne, and once more he was able to dominate the communist movement and give it direction and purpose.

THE MAD YEAR

In later years the communists would find themselves speaking of "the mad year" in Cologne, for it was a year of many contretemps, many frustrations and ignominies. From May 1848 to May 1849 everything seemed to be going wrong. It was a time of smoldering violence and apprehensions of even greater violence, and of a strange waywardness. Marx behaved predictably; Engels for a long period lost his nerve and wandered like a vagabond through France, having no further taste for revolution. The agents of the Communist League vanished into the hinterland, and sent in their reports at their leisure.

There were times during that year when Marx alone seemed to be the Communist League, being its sole member and its only generator. The fortunes of the League revolved around the newspaper and its editorial board which in theory consisted of Marx, Engels, Weerth, Wilhelm Wolff and Ferdinand Wolf, with Heinrich Bürgers in a position of authority second only to Marx. Indeed, the newspaper had been acquired only on condition that Bürgers assumed a responsible post. The first task of the party was therefore to reduce Bürgers to impotence; he was permitted to write one article and then drummed out of the editorial committee. Marx took the title of *Rédacteur en chef*. The other editors merely obeyed his orders.

Engels himself had not the least doubt that Marx was in supreme control, permitting no one else any vestige of authority. The year after Marx's death he wrote an account of the *Neue Rheinische Zeitung,* which betrays a faint note of dissatisfaction. "The organization of the editorial staff was a simple dictatorship by Marx. A great daily newspaper, which has to be ready by a definite time, cannot maintain a consistent policy in any other way. Marx's dictatorship was accepted as a matter of course. It was undisputed and willingly acknowledged by all of us. It was above all his clear vision and firm purpose which made it the most famous newspaper of the revolutionary years."

But this was to claim for the newspaper more than it deserved. It never had a wide circulation, and it was never, except in its last and most famous number, violently revolutionary. In order to exist at all the newspaper had to appear under false colors. "When we founded a great newspaper in Germany, our banner was determined as a matter of course," Engels wrote. "It could only be that of democracy, but in this democracy we emphasized its specific proletarian character at every moment; we were in no position to inscribe the proletariat once and for all on our banner." The task therefore was to appear to be democratic, while preaching communism between the lines, by hints and by subterfuges, and sometimes, as it were, by accident. Marx was a past master in the art of preaching communism by innuendo.

The task was neither so difficult nor so laborious as it might seem. The proletariat scarcely existed, and the liberal revolutionaries who were attempting to rule Germany through the Frankfurt parliament could afford the luxury of being laughed at. The first number of the *Neue Rheinische Zeitung* mocked the Frankfurt parliament, the long-winded speeches of the members, and what Engels called "the cowardly resolutions"—they were cowardly only because they did not accept the seventeen demands of the Communist Party. The *Neue Rheinische Zeitung* could also be accused of cowardice, since the political program of the newspaper consisted of exactly two points: first, a single, indivisible, democratic German republic, and secondly, war with Russia and the restoration of Polish independence. This was scarcely the platform of a revolutionary party, for the entire Frankfurt parliament approved of the first and most Germans regarded a war with Russia sympathetically. The newspaper called itself "an organ of democracy." It was the organ of Marx as he walked a tightrope between his hopes and his fears.

What he feared most of all was the loss of the newspaper, which was continually in financial difficulties. It lost half its shareholders with the opening number; the other half vanished after the publication of Marx's account of the June massacre in Paris, when an uprising of workmen was put down by Cavaignac with extraordinary brutality. The newspaper lived on credit. Some Poles, pleased with Marx's militant attitude toward Russia, contributed two thousand thalers. When a printer refused to print any more, Marx hunted among all the available printers of Cologne until he found another who would print against promises.

Most of the articles in the *Neue Rheinische Zeitung* were designed to be factual or descriptive. Opinion was frowned upon; rhetoric was regarded with distrust. But when the occasion demanded, Marx tossed his own rules aside and railed against his enemies with bitter fury. Here he speaks about Cavaignac's Guards who mowed down the workers and were themselves sometimes mowed down:

> They will ask us whether we have no tears, no sighs, no words for the victims who fell before the anger of the people—those National Guards, Mobile Guards, Republican Guards, and Regiments of the Line.
>
> The state will take care of their widows and orphans, decrees will glorify them, solemn processions will bear their remains to their earthly graves, the official press will declare them immortal, and the European reactionaries will render their homage from east to west.
>
> As for the plebeians, who are torn by hunger, slandered by the press, forsaken by their doctors, abused as thieves, incendiaries and galley slaves by honest citizens, their wives and children plunged into limitless misery, the best of the survivors deported beyond the seas—on their lowered brows may laurel wreaths be placed. It is the *privilege* and the *right of the democratic press* to do this.

At such times Marx would use the word "democrat" as though he were born to it, with no sense of its inadequacy. His aim was to destroy democracy.

Just as he despised democracy, so he despised those who opposed the rightful claims of German nationalism, and he was especially incensed by the behavior of the Danes who objected vigorously to Prussian attempts to take over Schleswig and transform it into a German colony. On this subject there could be no two opinions. The Danes, according to Marx, were nothing more than cutthroats and pirates, and all of Scandinavia was inhabited by barbarians. "Scandinavianism is merely enthusiasm for a brutal, dirty, piratical, Old Norse nationalism, for a deep inwardness which is unable to put its exuberant thoughts and feelings into words, but only in deeds—deeds of brutality toward women, permanent drunkenness, and a tearful sentimentality alternating with berserker rage."

A page or two later, being himself driven by ungovernable rage, he demands a quick solution to the Danish problem. It is a typical Marxist solution: nothing less than a general war between Germany and the three major European powers, Prussia, Russia and England. "Who has been from the beginning on the side of Denmark?" he asks, and he answers: "The three most counterrevolutionary powers of Europe, *Russia, England* and the *Prussian government.*" The counterrevolutionary powers have plotted against Schleswig, against Germany, and against revolution, and therefore they must be obliterated. "Precisely such a war is needed by the slumbering German movement—a war against the three great powers of the counterrevolution, a war which 'brings the Fatherland into danger' and thereby saves it by making a *German* victory dependent upon the victory of democracy."

What Marx meant by this is perfectly clear: he hoped that out of a general conflagration, with all Europe at war, Communism would emerge triumphant. He seemed to know that it could not triumph in any other way.

Marx's article on Scandinavianism and the necessity of a European war appeared on September 10. Three days later he summoned a public meeting in the Frankenplatz in Cologne to protest the brutality of the military, who went about beating up innocent citizens. Wilhelm Wolff and Engels addressed the meeting, protesting in the name of democracy against the outrageous behavior of the garrison troops. A committee of public safety, consisting of thirty citizens, was elected. Their task was to present a formal protest to the military governor, but no protest seems to have been delivered. Marx was elected a member of the committee of public safety, but accomplished nothing.

On September 17 an even more important demonstration took place at Worringen, a village nine miles from Cologne. The site was chosen deliberately, for on the outskirts of this village, in 1288, a battle had been fought between the citizens of Cologne and the army of the Archbishop of Cologne, and the citizens had won. Socialists from all over the Rhineland attended the demonstration. Many came down the Rhine in barges flying the red flag. Ferdinand Lassalle, later an important figure in the rise of German socialism, headed the delegation from Düsseldorf. At this time he was only twenty-three years old. Marx did not appear, but Engels made a speech demanding that a letter should be sent immediately to the Frankfurt parliament urging an immediate declaration of war against Prussia. This was treason, and as a result of this speech it was necessary for him to go into hiding.

The mass meeting in the meadows of Worringen was a success for the communists, who had organized it. Karl Schapper was elected president, and Engels became secretary. According to the description of the meeting which appeared in the *Neue Rheinische Zeitung* two days later, Engels declared for a social-democratic red republic. Among the foreigners who were attracted to the scene was Albert Brisbane, the correspondent of the *New York Daily Tribune*. He spoke German perfectly, and made a short speech.

The excitement was mounting. The military authorities were determined to prevent an uprising, and on September 25 they struck. Moll, Schapper and Wilhelm Wolff were arrested, and most of the leaders of revolutionary organizations fled from the city. Marx stayed at his post. He had not attracted a great deal of attention, and he appears to have been on reasonably good terms with the police. The *Neue Rheinische Zeitung* was temporarily suspended, but resumed publication a few days later. Most of Marx's assistant editors were either in prison or in hiding, but there was a new addition to the staff in the person of Ferdinand Freiligrath, the poet. When he captured Freiligrath, Marx could congratulate himself on a considerable achievement, and indeed he made the announcement in bold letters with every evidence of satisfaction. Although Freiligrath was an original member of the Communist League, he had been a notoriously inactive one, refusing to accept Marx's dictatorship. Now for a few weeks he came under Marx's spell, and Marx rejoiced in having an authentic poet at his service.

Engels, who had attracted considerable attention to himself through his incitements to revolt in the Worringen meadow, slipped out of Cologne and made his way to Barmen and a painful meeting with his father, who intensely disliked the idea of having a confessed revolutionary for a son. There was an order out for Engels' arrest. He had very little money, and few resources. His mother, who had always defended him in the past, now warned him against a course of conduct which could lead only to a final estrangement with his family. He appears to have taken her warnings to heart, for he abruptly abandoned his revolutionary career. Barricades were springing up all over central Europe; the revolution was being fought in Prague and Vienna. Engels slipped out of Germany and went wandering like a vagabond through France, and wrote a charming and lyrical account of his travels.

It was a strange course of conduct for a dedicated revolutionary, and communist commentators who revere Engels only a little less than Marx have had some difficulty in explaining it away. He lost his nerve. He no longer made speeches on revolution; instead, he celebrated the beauty of French women and the delicacy of French wines. He wandered as the spirit willed, happily and aimlessly, and sometimes, being an inveterate taker of notes, he would pause and enter into his notebook some observation on the blue mountains and the shadowy valleys, on the extraordinary hospitality of the peasants who lived so well in a bountiful land, and knew nothing about politics, industry, commerce, or any of the complexities of modern life. He lay with the peasant girls in the fields and sat at the tables of the rich peasants. He found them gay, courteous, and hospitable to excess; and when the time came to put his notes in order, he could not bring himself to forgive them for their ignorance of political movements and their horror of revolution. They especially detested Paris and had no faith in the Parisian workingman. "I have spoken to hundreds of peasants in various regions of France, and they are all ruled by a fanatical hatred of Paris and the Parisian workingman," he wrote. "They would tell me they wished the damnable city of Paris would one day vanish in thin air." It was an attitude which he found perplexing, for he claimed to love Paris more than any other city and to have a special affection and understanding of the Parisian workingman.

Engels had very little gift for dissembling, and his account of his French wanderings reveals a man who can simultaneously love and hate on a scale which takes the breath away. It is not unusual for Germans to love and hate France, but Engels was unusual in the ardor of his love and the ferocity of his hate. He heaps abuse on the French peasants while admiring them this side of idolatry. In the same paragraph he will declare that they are kind, generous, handsome, wonderfully industrious and good, and he will add that they are barbarians, brutally ignorant, and evil. He delights in their company and finds every reason why they must be destroyed.

So he wandered across France in that carefree autumn, alone and penniless, receiving their hospitality and cursing them for their wealth and their solid sense of property, as though owning a farmhouse were the mark of Satan, the ultimate perversity. In slow stages he made his way to Berne, and it was only when he reached Switzerland that he realized that during his absence all Germany and central Europe had been in a state of revolution or near-revolution. In October the workers and students rose in Vienna, hanged the Minister of War from a lamppost, and sent the half-mad Emperor Ferdinand I running for his life. During the following day Windischgrätz collected an army of Slavs and within three weeks he had surrounded the city. Then at his leisure he marched through the gates and executed the revolutionaries en masse. Ferdinand I abdicated, and his young nephew Francis Joseph came to the throne, to rule Austria and its vast empire for nearly seventy years. Soon Hungary was in a state of revolt, and this revolt was put down with the help of Russian soldiers.

But if Engels had lost touch with the revolution, Marx was in fighting trim. He sat at his desk in the office of the *Neue Rheinische Zeitung* continually writing articles which were at once descriptive journalism and incitements to revolt. Twice he was summoned to police headquarters and warned that he would be put on trial for high treason. He merely returned to his desk and wrote bitter and incisive descriptions of the police. In December the King of Prussia dissolved the National Assembly, and Marx threatened dire vengeance. He urged his readers to study the fate of kings who have dissolved parliament, demanded that the people should henceforth refuse to pay their taxes, and hinted that the proper historical answer to the King's action was an *émeute,* a general call to arms. By February 1849 the authorities lost patience. Marx, Schapper and their lawyer, a certain Karl Schneider, were brought to trial for incitement to armed rebellion. The charge was based on an appeal which had appeared in the *Neue Rheinische Zeitung* on November 19, urging the people to organize themselves into armed levies to protest the action of the King of Prussia in destroying the power of the National Assembly. "Those who are without means should procure arms and ammunition at the expense of the commune or from voluntary gifts." The appeal demanded that the authorities should make known their attitude to the National Assembly, or face the consequences. Finally, there was the demand that the Committee of Public Safety should take power if the authorities failed to obey the appeal.

This was a direct incitement to rebellion, and the consequences might have been very grave if the *Code Napoléon* had not been in operation in the Rhineland. The *Code Napoléon* stated very clearly that cases of this kind must be tried by a jury, and Marx took full advantage of the fact. His speech at the trial, which took place on February 8, 1849, was one of his most brilliant efforts, for he was able to show that he had called for an uprising in favor of the legitimate government against the Crown, which had deliberately abrogated the powers of the National Assembly. Far from being a revolutionary, he claimed to be a legitimist faithfully observing the laws; and he suggested to the jury that the verdict, which would assuredly favor him, lay in the hands of history, not in decisions made in the courtroom in Cologne. The incitement to rebellion had been written like a lawyer's brief, permitting him wide scope to interpret it as he pleased. Above all, he presented himself as a defender of the common cause, and pretended to be a little surprised at being prosecuted. He declared:

> The question whether the Crown or the National Assembly is in the right is a historical question. All the juries, all the courts in Prussia taken together cannot solve it. There is only one power which can solve it, and that is history. Therefore I do not understand how it could happen that we should find ourselves by virtue of the penal code on the benches of the accused.

Yet he knew perfectly well why he was in the dock. His task was to show that a call to arms was necessary, inevitable, and historically justified, and if he failed in this, he could always appeal to the fact that no laws existed at the time he wrote the article in the newspaper, for the Crown and the National Assembly were at odds and their laws canceled out.

But for the most part he devoted himself to the necessity of revolution. Like a schoolmaster giving lessons in history, he explained at length how revolutionary movements come into being. The Puritans in England fought Charles I for twenty years before they were able to bring him to the scaffold. He said nothing about the possibility of bringing the King of Prussia to the scaffold, but he wondered aloud whether the King of Prussia's ministers might not one day find themselves in the dock accused of high treason. He went on to give a lesson on the *Code Napoléon:*

> The Code Napoléon, which I am now holding in my hand, did not produce modern bourgeois society. Arising in the eighteenth century and continuing to develop in the nineteenth century, bourgeois society found no more than its legal expression in the Code. The moment social relations no longer correspond to the Code, then it is nothing but a scrap of paper. You cannot make the old laws the basis for the new development of society any more than the old laws made the conditions of the old society.

The laws were in doubt, society was changing, and in the no man's land between the ancient feudal laws of the Prussian Crown and the laws of modern bourgeois society, Marx found a safe hiding place. He could argue on the basis that the Crown was in contempt of the people and had committed treason against the sovereign rights of the people, or—even more energetically—he could argue that the popular will alone flowed through history, and he was the servant of the popular will. A careful examination of the speech shows him parrying imaginary thrusts from all directions, side-stepping, avoiding the main issues and charging head-on in defense of irrelevancies. It was a consummate performance, and he evidently enjoyed his command of the situation. Schapper and Schneider also made speeches in their defense, but they were merely hesitant echoes of Marx. The jury acquitted them, and Marx returned to his desk. The *Neue Rheinische Zeitung* was given a new lease on life. Once more Marx had silenced his enemies.

THE RED NUMBER

Marx was under no illusions about the difficulties confronting him. He had won a victory, but he had also exasperated his enemies beyond endurance. They held a trump card: Marx was an alien on Prussian soil, for he had abandoned his citizenship three years before, and they could therefore expel him at their convenience. Although his trial was reported in the German press and he was famous as a man who had defended himself successfully before the courts, his notoriety had become dangerous. Moreover, the *Neue Rheinische Zeitung* was very nearly bankrupt, and he was in great financial difficulties. His enemies could afford to wait.

In May 1849 there were uprisings in Dresden and the Bavarian Palatinate. Even in the Rhineland there were minor uprisings. The authorities decided to act sternly. On May 11 an official order for his expulsion was signed by a certain Moeller on behalf of the Prussian government:

> In its recent articles the N.R.Z. has published more and more deliberate incitements in contempt of the existing government, aiming at its forcible overthrow and the establishment of a socialist republic. Consequently the hospitality, which he has so scandalously abused, has been withdrawn from the editor in chief, Dr. Karl Marx; and inasmuch as he has not secured permission for further residence in these states, he is instructed to leave within 24 hours. Should he fail to comply with this demand voluntarily, he is to be forcibly removed to the frontier.

Against such an order, there was no possible recourse, and it was merely a question of how quickly the expulsion order would be carried out. Marx appears to have relied on the normal inefficiency of the police, and to have gone into hiding while preparing the last issue of the newspaper. He decided to go down in a blaze of glory. The newspaper would be printed in blood-red ink; it would hurl defiance at the government even more loudly than before. This time there would not be the slightest attempt to remain within the boundaries of the law. Poetry, oratory, fulmination and direct reporting were all pressed into the service of the most bitter attack which Marx had yet mounted against the government.

The "red number" of the *Neue Rheinische Zeitung* is one of Marx's more prodigious achievements as a revolutionary editor. On the front page, immediately below the title, he printed five fiery verses by Ferdinand Freiligrath in which the newspaper is depicted as a revolutionary shouting: "Revolt!" with his last dying breath, a shining dagger clutched in his hand. It is dying "not from an open blow received in honest combat," but through the conniving and trickery of "filthy western Kalmucks." In the manner of a medieval hero the newspaper bids farewell to the world:

Farewell, farewell, O world of battle,
Farewell, O armies locked in combat!
Farewell, O powder-blackened fields,
Farewell, O swords and spears!

Farewell, but not farewell forever!
They cannot kill our spirits, O my brothers!
Soon I shall have rustled my way to Heaven,
And soon I shall return on horseback!

In the last verse the "rebel outlaw" speaks of the day when all the crowns have shattered like glass, and amidst the wreckage of thrones he appears as the savior of the people living on the Rhine and the Danube.

There follows a call to the workers of Cologne to lay down their arms, for nothing was to be gained by a *putsch* against the heavily armed military authorities. "Our last word," said this brief editorial, "will everywhere and always be: *The emancipation of the working class!*"

But this brief editorial was only a foretaste for a longer and more violent diatribe which followed. The theme was revenge—implacable revenge. To the King, to the officials, and to bureaucrats who ruled in the King's name, Marx swears that he will return and exact the last ounce of retribution. *Vae victis!* In that long and bitter denunciation Marx restates the romantic argument of Freiligrath in even more prophetic terms, and in a passage which exhibits the fury of frustration he announces that the royal terrorists will one day meet their fate at the hands of the revolutionary terrorists:

> *We are ruthless, and we ask no quarter from you. When our turn comes, we shall not disguise our terrorism.* But the royal terrorists, the terrorists by the grace of God and the Law are brutal, contemptible and vulgar in practice, cowardly, secretive and double-tongued in theory, and both in practice and in theory they are *without honor.*

Trier during first quarter of nineteenth century SOVFOTO

Marx's birthplace at Trier

Baroness Jenny von Westphalen before her marriage to Karl Marx

Idealized portrait of Marx by Soviet artist I. Grinshtein

Portrait of Marx based on fingernail-sized sketch in Godesberg Tavern Club, pictured opposite

Hegel

The Tavern Club, composed of students from Trier, met at the White Horse Inn at Godesberg in 1836. Marx is below the X.

Eduard Gans

Friedrich Karl Savigny

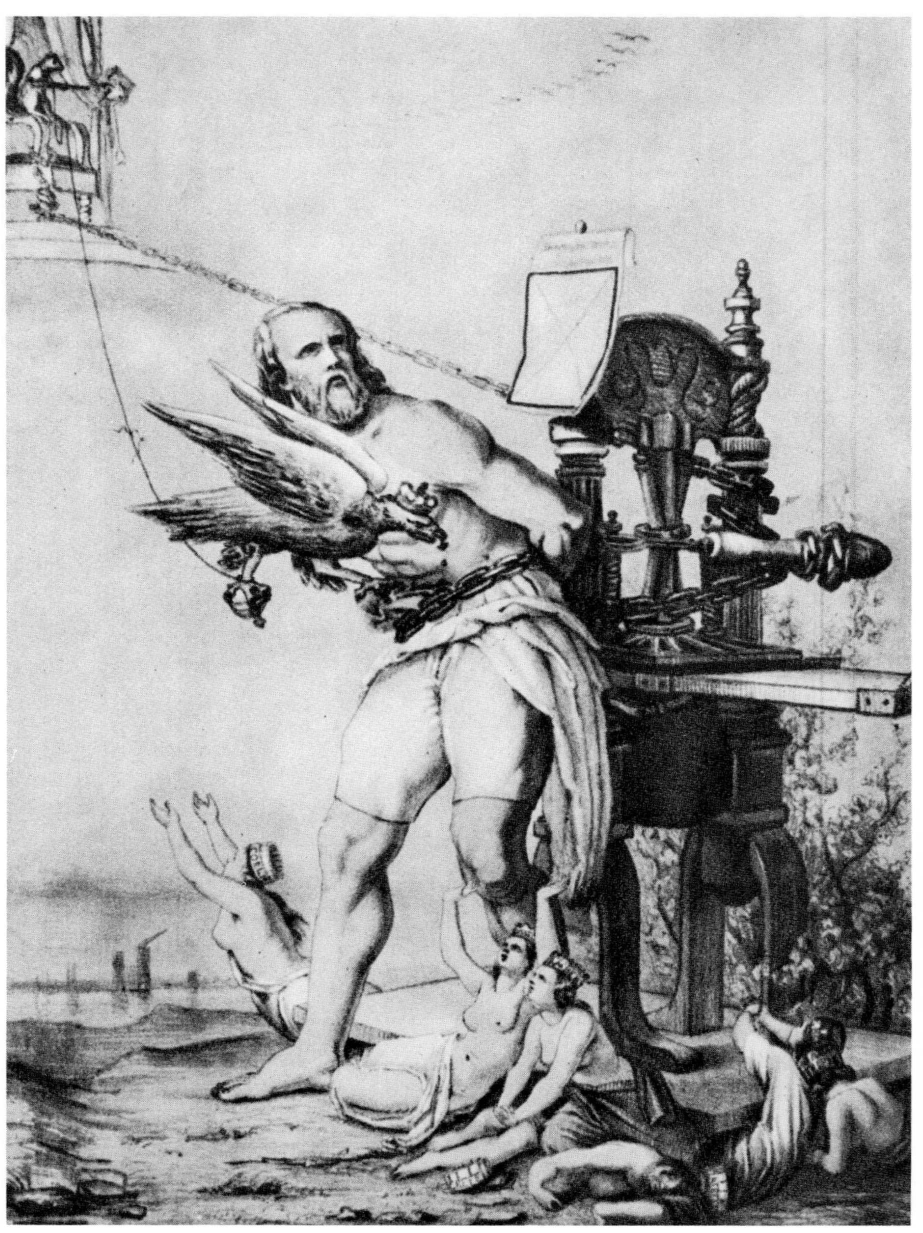

Prometheus-Marx in chains. A drawing made after the banning of the *Rheinische Zeitung*, showing the crowned eagle of Prussia feeding on Marx's liver, while Eichhorn, the squirrel, pulls the strings. At Marx's feet are the lamenting cities of the Rhine.

Helene Demuth—the earliest known photograph, taken shortly after she entered Marx's service

Friedrich Engels, *circa* 1845

Karl Marx, *circa* 18

Heinrich Heine

Ferdinand Lassalle

Pierre Proudhon

Karl Vogt

Joseph Weydemeyer

Wilhelm Liebknecht

Wilhelm Wolff

August von Willich

Wilhelm Weitling

Ludwig Kugelmann

Mikhail Bakunin

28 Dean Street, Soho, where Marx lived from 1850 to 1856. Photograph taken about 1905.

SOVFOTO

Edgar

Laura

Jenny

Eleanor

Marx and Engels, with Marx's daughters Jenny, Eleanor and Laura, *circa* 1861

Marx and his daughter Jenny in 1868. Jenny is wearing the Cross commemorating the Polish Insurrection.

Laura

Eleanor

9 Grafton Terrace, Maitland Park, Haverstock Hill, where Marx lived from 1856 to 1864. SOVFOTO

1867

1872

1876

The Zeus of Otricoli

1 Maitland Park Road, where Marx lived from 1864 to 1875.

Paul Lafargue

Dr. Edward Aveling

Friedrich Engels

Helene Demuth in old age

Jenny Marx—the last photograph

Karl Marx—the last photograph
ROGER-VIOLLET

KARL MARX,
AND KARL MARX,
AND HARRY LONGUET,
THEIR GRANDSON
AND HELENA DEMUTH,
AND ELEANOR MARX, DAUGHTER OF KARL MARX

At the end of the editorial Marx repeats the clarion call which had appeared at the beginning of the year: 1849 must be the year of a revolutionary upheaval of the French working classes and world war. He has not the least doubt that these prophecies are coming to fulfillment. "Already in the East," he wrote, "a revolutionary army is being formed of combatants of all nations, preparing to face the Russian army and bringing about the coalition of old Europe; and already from Paris there comes the threat of 'the red republic.'" But in fact there was no revolutionary army in the East, and no red republic in Paris. One by one the revolutionary armies were going down to defeat.

The expulsion order was sent to the house where Marx was living, but at that very moment he was in Hamburg. Jenny received the order on May 16. Marx did not return until May 18. On that day he had to make arrangements to liquidate the newspaper, to publish the "red number," to raise money to pay his debts, and to go into hiding. There was no time to lose. His assets included a steam printing press, a newly built compositors' office, and some 1,000 thalers received in subscriptions. The office and printing press were sold to pay the newspaper's debts. He borrowed 300 thalers to pay the compositors and the printers, and there was enough left over to help the remaining editors as they took to flight. Some years later Marx told his friend Friedrich Sorge that he made it a point of honor to accept nothing for himself, and he slipped out of the city very nearly destitute.

With Engels he made his way to Frankfurt in the hope that the Frankfurt parliament, which was still in session, might come out on the side of the revolution. This was a vain hope, for all of Germany except Baden and the Palatinate was at the mercy of the Prussian army. Soon, realizing that his efforts to convince the parliamentarians that they had only to summon the revolutionary armies to Frankfurt to win power were leading nowhere, he went off to Karlsruhe and Kaiserslautern, which were still in the hands of the revolutionaries. In Cologne orders for his arrest were issued. There were also orders for the arrest of Dronke and Weerth, who had escaped from the Rhineland. Only Hermann Korff, a young former officer who acted as the manager of the *Neue Rheinische Zeitung*, was arrested. He was not dealt with severely, for he was sentenced to a month's imprisonment and ordered to pay one seventh of the court costs. An order for the arrest of Engels was published in the *Kölnische Zeitung* on June 9, with the following careful and on the whole accurate description:

> ENGELS: Aged 26-28 years, height five feet six inches,* forehead open, hair blond, eyebrows blond, eyes blue, nose and mouth regular, beard reddish, chin oval, face oval, color healthy, stature slender. Special peculiarities: speaks rapidly, and is nearsighted.

When Engels and Marx reached the Palatinate, they discovered, as they had perhaps suspected, that the revolution was faring badly and there were only a few pockets of resistance. Everywhere the leaders of the revolution were giving the same order which Marx had printed on the front page of the "red number" of the *Neue Rheinische Zeitung;* they were appealing to the workers to lay down their arms. In Kaiserslautern Marx had a long talk with Karl Ludwig d'Ester, the deputy representing Cologne at the Frankfurt parliament, and he asked for and received a mandate to represent the German Democratic Party at meetings of the French Social Democratic party in Paris. In effect, this was a mandate to act as a liaison officer between the two revolutionary parties; and since Marx believed, or pretended to believe, that "the red republic" was about to be inaugurated in Paris, he felt that he had placed himself in a position of advantage. He was on his way to Paris with the mandate when he was arrested near Bingen by some Hessian soldiers, who brought him under guard to Darmstadt. This was a serious matter, and he was in danger of being shot out of hand. He succeeded in talking them into sending him to Frankfurt, where he had friends in high places and was released. Then, with Ferdinand Wolf, he made his way to Paris. Jenny, who had accompanied him to Frankfurt, had a less eventful journey, for she made her way with the three children to Kreuznach and the security of her mother's home. There she remained for some weeks, until Marx summoned her to Paris.

Engels, who had some previous experience as a bombardier, joined the revolutionary forces which were still holding out. He became the adjutant of August von Willich, a former artillery lieutenant, "a brave and cold-blooded man in action, who made prompt and accurate decisions, although off the battlefield he was a *plus ou moins* tedious ideologue, one of your 'true socialists.'" So Engels wrote to Jenny Marx, describing briefly the four engagements in which he took part, saying that he was surprised by the lack of any sense of danger on the battlefield, the whistling of bullets being "a quite trifling affair," and people generally being immune to fear. He thought he had seen about a dozen people in a state of panic. What particularly pleased him was that he

* The Prussian foot being slightly longer than the English foot, this corresponds to 5′ 9½″. Engels was in fact nearly six feet tall.

fought as a representative of the *Neue Rheinische Zeitung*, and placed his sword at the service of his revolutionary principles.

Engels spent less than a month with Willich's ragged army, and the final issue was never in doubt. The *coup de grâce* was provided by the troops of the Prince of Prussia, when he stormed the town of Rastatt. The rebels, who were no match for professional soldiers, simply broke and fled, and most of them were later rounded up by the Prussian forces. Only a handful succeeded in escaping to Switzerland, while the rest were simply shot out of hand or thrown into the dungeons of the fortress of Rastatt. Engels was one of the few fortunate ones who reached Switzerland unharmed.

These brief engagements in Baden and the Palatinate were scarcely more than mopping-up campaigns; they left no mark on history, and were soon forgotten. But in a wider historical context they were not forgotten. Engels studied these campaigns during the enforced leisure of his exile in Switzerland, and drew lessons from them, which in turn were studied by Lenin. When the time was ripe, Lenin threw all the weight of his authority behind the doctrines which Engels developed during those forlorn campaigns in southern Germany.

They were very simple doctrines, and they were stated for the first time in the pages of the *New York Daily Tribune* on September 18, 1852, and October 2, 1852, in articles which bore the signature of Karl Marx, though they were in fact written by Engels. The first doctrine related to the nature of the art of insurrection:

> Never play with insurrection unless you are fully prepared to face the consequences. Insurrection is a calculus with very indefinite magnitudes, the value of which may change every day; the forces opposed to you have all the advantages of organization, discipline, and habitual authority; unless you bring stronger odds against them you are defeated and ruined. Secondly, the insurrectionary career once entered upon, act with the greatest determination, and on the offensive. The defensive is the death of every armed rising.

The second doctrine derived from Engels' disgust over the posturing of so many drunken middle-class revolutionaries living in the Donnersberg inn where he was staying during the insurrection. Of these half-hearted revolutionaries he wrote:

> The petty bourgeoisie, great in boasting, is very impotent for action, and very shy in risking anything. The *mesquin* character of its commercial transactions and its credit operations is eminently apt to stamp its character with a want of energy and enterprise; it is, then, to be expected that similar qualities will mark its political career. Accordingly the petty bourgeoisie

> encouraged insurrection by big words and great boasting as to what it was going to do; it was eager to seize upon power as soon as the insurrection, much against its will, had broken out; it used its power to no other purpose but to destroy the effects of the insurrection.

These judgments were final; they were to become welded into the structure of communist thought and propaganda, as though they were eternal truths. In each case it was the last sentence which was burned deeply in Lenin's brain.

While Engels was contemplating the disasters of insurrectionary warfare, he heard the rumor that Marx had been arrested in Paris. In fact, Marx was being hunted by the French police, who had not yet caught up with him, for he was living quietly under another name. The pseudonym he had chosen was Ramboz, an odd name, the first syllable being part of Marx reversed, the second syllable suggesting Boaz. In later years Marx preferred a more conventional pseudonym, and in his conspiratorial correspondence he liked to be known as A. Williams.

Since the "red republic" was largely a figment of Marx's imagination, his days in Paris were filled with frustrations. He was still rejoicing in emphatic prophecies, however. Cholera was raging in Paris, the revolutionary forces were impotent, Prince Louis Napoleon was wielding power with an iron hand. "In spite of everything," Marx wrote to Engels on June 7, "a colossal outbreak of the revolutionary volcano was never more imminent than at this moment. Details later." But there was no outbreak. Demonstrators came out on the streets two weeks later, but they were soon routed by the police. Marx wrote an article for the German paper *Der Volksfreund*, in which he explained that the revolutionaries had failed to mount a *putsch* because they were overconfident; on the contrary, they failed because they were entirely lacking in confidence. The revolutionary leaders, Ledru-Rollin, Louis Blanc, and others, fled to London, leaving their lieutenants to the mercies of the police. Marx took some comfort from these arrests. He wrote to Weydemeyer at the beginning of August: "*Les choses marchent très bien,* and the Waterloo suffered by official democracy must be regarded as a victory. The governments by the grace of God have assumed the roles of executioners and avengers against the bourgeoisie on our behalf." In his bitterness Marx could find no better words for the prisoners in Napoleon's cells than to describe them as "bourgeois puppets."

Monsieur Ramboz, of 45 Rue de Lille, was in fact a deeply embittered man, burdened with an awareness of his own poverty and impotence.

He had written to Weydemeyer in the middle of July: "I tell you, if no help comes to me from anywhere, then I am *perdu,* for my family is here, and already the last piece of jewelry belonging to my wife has found its way to the pawnshop." Soon he was writing to Weydemeyer with the news that still another burden had fallen on him: Jenny was ill, *conséquence naturelle de son état pas trop intéressant.* This was his gallant way of saying that she was expecting another baby.

Wherever he looked, he saw the ruin of his fortunes. Only a few weeks before he had been the brilliant and admired editor in chief of the *Neue Rheinische Zeitung,* the master of the revolutionary epigram, the terror of Cologne. Now the wave of revolution, which had spread across Europe, had been hurled back, and the reaction had set in. He did not know where to turn, or how to earn a living. He wrote to Engels suggesting that the time had come for them to change professions. *"Il faut nous lançer dans une entreprise littéraire et mercantile, j'attends tes propositions,"* he wrote on August 17. The suggestion was clear: they would become publishers, and in some way Engels would finance the business. He asked Engels to remember to address him as Monsieur Ramboz.

On that same day, or perhaps the following day, the police caught up with him. An order of the Commissaire de Police of the Quartier Faubourg St. Germain had already been prepared on August 16, commanding him "to leave Paris without delay and take up your residence in the *département* of Morbihan." The order was addressed not to Monsieur Ramboz, but to Monsieur Marx, Prussian refugee, Rue de Lille.

Evidently the police had known where he was for some time, for Jenny spoke of "a familiar police sergeant" bringing the order of banishment. It was a summary order, and there was no appeal. He asked in what town he was expected to live, and was told that it was Vannes, and he asked too how many more hours he could remain in Paris, and was told that he could stay for twenty-four hours and no more. He made some quick inquiries, and learned that Morbihan was not the most favored *département* in France. The police relented and gave him a few days' grace in order to put his affairs in order, while he debated with himself whether he would remain in France or make his way to England or Switzerland. If he went to England, he would have to cut himself off from his roots. If he went to Switzerland, a country he despised, he would be prevented from taking part in revolutionary activity. The Swiss refused to grant him a passport. He wrote to Engels on August 23: "I have been banished to the *département* of Morbihan, the Pontine marshes of

Brittany. You will understand that I refuse to fall in with this disguised attempt to murder me. I shall leave France. Since I cannot obtain a passport, I must go to London."

One may speculate on what might have happened if England had refused to receive him. Since neither Switzerland, Belgium, Prussia nor the German states would have welcomed him, he would have been compelled to live in Morbihan. It is not an unpleasant place; the sea air is bracing, and the peasants are industrious. He might have ended his days on the coast of Brittany, far from any contacts with revolutionaries. To earn a living he would have become a small farmer or a collector of seaweed; and no doubt he would have turned his attention to the mysteries of the Breton language, for it is not enough to know French in Brittany. One can imagine him in his venerable old age, striding across the sands, his beard flowing in the wind, sustained by the habits of scholarship. He would become a French citizen, and be famous as the compiler of a German-Breton dictionary.

On August 26 he left France, embarking at Boulogne. He was in a mood of profound melancholy, but sometimes he would be buoyed up by the certain knowledge that he could continue his revolutionary career in London. He would edit a new German newspaper, and he would have some part, however small, in the great revolution which, he confidently expected, would break out in England. He did not know that he would never again be the editor in chief of a German newspaper, and there would be no revolution in England. Ahead of him lay years of intense poverty and dubious obscurity. He would see his children dying before his eyes and his wife drawing close to the verge of madness, and sometimes he would follow her along that dangerous road and wonder whether he would return. Griefs, quarrels and frustrations were to be his lot, and misery was his companion.

For the rest of his life he was to remain a Londoner. In that vast and imperial world city, he would acquire some of the habits of the English while remaining a Rhinelander to the end of his days. London engulfed him, and he vanished quietly in its backwaters.

THE DARK NIGHT OF EXILE

One comes to see more and more that the emigration is an institution that must turn everybody into a fool, an ass, and a common knave unless he manages to get completely away from it. . . . It is a pure school of scandal and of meanness.

—ENGELS to Marx, February 12, 1851

THE SATANIC MILLS

When Marx arrived in London in the summer of 1849, he found a country in the high tide of revolution, but it was not the revolution he was dreaming about. The industrial revolution had penetrated every corner of the land. This revolution was based on coal and steel, on steam-driven machinery, on the railroads which penetrated the remote valleys, and on the vast engines which ground up one form of produce to transform it into another. The motive force came from coal, and the color of the revolution was coal-black. Never had so much coal been dug out of the earth—in that year England produced some 36,000,000 tons, considerably more than one ton of coal for every man, woman and child in the country. Everywhere the factories were going up and the smoke was belching from the factory chimneys. The roar of machinery was drowning the human voice.

A small area of central London, known as the City, guided the revolution along its course. There the merchants and bankers issued the orders and the bank drafts which kept the machinery running. In another part of London, known as Whitehall, harried government officials were inquiring into the effects of the revolution on a population wrenched out of their settled agricultural communities and made to serve the demands of machinery. The machine was king; it was driving people into slavery. A government committee in 1841 found that in the lace-making industry the children were not even permitted to return to their homes, but remained at their looms day after day in virtual bondage. The Mines Commission in 1843 reported that children of three years of age were being employed in the mines, and that children and women worked "chained, belted, harnessed like dogs in a go-cart, black, saturated with wet, and more than half-naked, crawling upon their hands and feet, and dragging their heavy loads behind them—they present an appearance incredibly disgusting and unnatural."

But it was not only women and children whose ordinary human rights were being violated; men sometimes worked sixteen hours a day under conditions of squalor so terrible that the government commissioners sometimes drew a veil over their findings, only hinting at the horrors they had seen. They were honest men, and they reported what they had found in a mounting pile of government Blue Books. They realized that the machines had come to stay, and that it had become urgently necessary to curb the power of the industrialists. In 1847 Lord Shaftesbury succeeded in winning the approval of Parliament for the Ten-Hour Act, for which he had fought for fifteen years. In factory legislation England was far ahead of the continent.

As a result of the industrial revolution large areas of London had been transformed into slums. To Dostoyevsky, who visited the city a few years later, London resembled "a biblical picture, something out of Babylon, a prophecy from the Apocalypse coming to pass before your eyes." It was so large, so dark, so filled with human vigor and the noise of engines and machines, and there was so much coal dust in the air, that he felt like someone visiting another planet where all the normal laws of human behavior were held in abeyance. Everything was huge, garish, grimy, strangely menacing at night, curiously beautiful by day. "When the night is over," he wrote, "then a proud and sullen spirit hovers regally over this gigantic city." He called it Baal, and sometimes wondered whether he was not dreaming, for here he was able to touch what previously he had only imagined.

When Marx arrived in London, he hoped in some mysterious way to be the agent of the revolution which would topple the government and usher in the new communist age. "England," he wrote, "is where the next dance begins." Instead of becoming a revolutionary leader, he was merely swallowed up in the vast anonymity of the city, sharing with some five thousand other refugees from the revolutions of 1848 and 1849 the poverty and ignominy which are the badges of exiles. He had no money, and no prospects. Apparently he had no settled address, for the earliest surviving letter written during this period is one asking Freiligrath to send him money in care of Karl Blind, Peterson's Coffeehouse, Grosvenor Square. He spoke of editing a monthly review which would continue the tradition of the *Neue Rheinische Zeitung*, and hinted that there was financial backing, although he must have known that it would be impossible to find backing among the poverty-stricken German refugees. London was strange to him, he had few friends, and Jenny was far away. She was still in Paris, trying to collect enough money to make the journey to England: the police ordered her to leave the country by September 15, and she was able to leave only at the very last moment. Marx did not meet her. Instead, he sent Georg Weerth, his former assistant on the

Neue Rheinische Zeitung, a kindly man who could always be relied upon to act soberly in emergencies. Jenny was ill and nearly eight months pregnant; the three children, Jenny, Laura, and Edgar, who was born in Brussels, were all exhausted by the long journey. Weerth knew little about how to deal with these frightened and half-starving visitors, and was able to find only a single room for them in a lodginghouse on Leicester Square. In the neighborhood of this square most of the German refugees had gathered. Only a few weeks before Jenny had been living in the comfort of her mother's house at Kreuznach, with servants attending her, and with a carriage bearing the Westphalen arms ready to take her wherever she wanted to go. Now she was a lonely stranger in a gigantic, garish, deafening metropolis, imprisoned in a single room, penniless and ill.

While Marx was oppressed by poverty, and numbed by it, Jenny felt it on her flesh and nerves, and the hideous pain of it left scars which never completely healed. There was to be no escape from the nightmare for seven long years.

Many days passed before the family was able to leave the small room in Leicester Square. Finally they found an apartment at 4 Anderson Street in Chelsea, off King's Road, for six pounds a month. Jenny had wanted "a quiet roof over my head" when the time came to give birth to her fourth child; the noise and tumult of central London had become unendurable to her. Anderson Street was one of those small and secretive roads lying in the backwaters of Chelsea, and she had every reason to hope that the birth would take place on a quiet autumn day, with no jarring sounds of traffic or street cries breaking the silence. But in fact her son was born on a day of uproar.

Traditionally November 5 had been celebrated in England as Guy Fawkes Day, commemorating the Gunpowder Plot of 1605, when a handful of Roman Catholics, all of good family and social standing, attempted to blow up the Houses of Parliament. The celebration took the form of fireworks, bonfires, dancing in the streets, and the burning of "the guy." In the early years of the nineteenth century only children celebrated Guy Fawkes Day, but in the forties the celebrations of an earlier age were revived. Enormous "guys," dressed in rags, broomstick heads adorned with ferocious masks, were paraded on donkey carts through the streets, and sometimes they would be lifted up to the second-story windows to frighten the housemaids. Fireworks exploded, German bands played, the drums boomed, clowns turned cartwheels, and dancers in flamboyant costumes and feathered hats whirled down the streets, while masked boys riding on wooden donkeys shouted at the top of their voices: "Please to remember the fifth of November." No one—not even Henry Mayhew, the great historian of London customs in the middle years of the nineteenth century—knew why the celebrations had suddenly become so festive or why there was so much ear-splitting noise.

On the evening of November 5, in the midst of the uproar, Jenny gave birth to her second son. Fifteen years later she could still remember the noise and the strange sight of the boys wearing their "baroque" masks as they rode on their cleverly fashioned wooden donkeys below her window. Marx, who sometimes dreamed of following in the path of Guy Fawkes, found some satisfaction in the thought that a new revolutionary had been born that day. The baby was always called Guido or Föxchen in honor of Guy Fawkes, although his given names were Edmund Heinrich Guy. When Marx registered the birth of the baby a few days later, the unsympathetic registrar transformed him into a young Englishman, and in the huge leather-bound files of Somerset House he is listed as Henry Edward Guy Marx, son of Dr. Charles and Jenny Marx, born November 5, 1849.

Guido was a sickly child from the beginning. Because wet nurses were so expensive, Jenny was compelled to feed the baby herself although suffering from continual pains in the breasts. She suffered, too, from terrible pains in the back, which seem to have been a form of arthritis brought on by the damp London winter. A few months later she wrote to Weydemeyer, who had been a kindly companion to her in Frankfurt, that the child had suffered unendurably since the moment he was brought into the world. "The poor little angel drank in so much distress and silent anxiety that he was always poorly and his days and nights were filled with horrible sufferings. Since he came into the world, he has not slept a single night, at most two or three hours. Recently he has had violent convulsions, so that the child has always hovered between death and a miserable life. In his pain he sucked so hard that my breasts were chafed and the skin cracked, and often the blood streamed into his small trembling mouth."

There were other anxieties, and one of the more troublesome was the sudden arrival of Lieutenant August von Willich, the dashing commander of the revolutionary army which had fought throughout the Baden campaign. One morning he burst into her bedroom in Chelsea, dressed in the appropriate revolutionary attire—a gray doublet with a scarlet sash round his waist, laughing uproariously, eager to engage in a loud debate on communism with Marx. It was very early in the morning; his Prussian horselaughs were unendurable, and perhaps even more unendurable were his brimming energy and good health. He was tall, well-built, with a high forehead, a long thin aristocratic nose, flashing teeth. He looked like a Prussian version of Garibaldi, and he was aware of his immense daring on the battlefield and his success with women. Marx was outraged and succeeded in driving him out of the apartment, but the harm had been done, for Willich appears to have detected the gleam of admiration in Jenny's eyes. And sometimes, when Marx was away, he would come to visit her in order to console her for her poverty, her loneliness, and her brood of ill-fed children. "He would come to visit me," she wrote later, "because he wanted to pursue the worm which lives in every marriage and lure it out."

Other, less demanding visitors came to visit the apartment. There was the small, bespectacled Wilhelm Pieper, a philologist in his early twenties, who served briefly as Marx's secretary, and Wilhelm Liebknecht, also a philologist, who had fought in the Baden uprising and like Engels had slipped across the Swiss frontier. Like Willich, Liebknecht found comfort in Jenny's company, but always worshipfully, timidly, and kindly, without the least desire "to pursue the worm which lives in every marriage." He would run errands for her, buy her small gifts, and look after the children for her. In his eyes she was "a beautiful, noble-minded, high-spirited woman who in a half-sisterly, half-motherly way took care of the friendless fighter for liberty, who had been driven ashore on the banks of the Thames." His mother had died when he was three years old, and he found in Jenny the mother he had always wanted.

In 1849 Liebknecht was twenty-three, thin and gangling, with the sad, angular features of a medieval monk, and a wisp of beard. He had studied in many universities, and there was something about his manner and his voice which suggested the perpetual student. Just as he found ways of helping Jenny, so he would find ways of helping Marx by playing chess with him, by going for walks with him, and by talking quietly and gravely when Marx was in one of his rages. For many years Liebknecht was a daily visitor to the family, an intimate and inseparable companion.

Soon after the birth of Guido, a more important visitor arrived at Anderson Street. This was Engels, who had taken ship from Genoa and had enjoyed a leisurely five-week journey to London by sea. He was in high spirits, full of plans for directing the coming revolution and apparently unconcerned by the failure of so many revolutions during the summer. On the journey, to pass the time away, he had taken careful records of the sun's position, the direction of the wind, the changing seas and the changing coastline. So now, but less carefully, he observed the political weather and the changing shapes of governments, and came to the conclusion, which Marx enthusiastically shared, that revolution was everywhere imminent, and that in a few weeks or months Europe would once more be in flames.

Marx had spoken of a monthly review adequately financed, with a wide circulation in Germany and among the exiled German refugees in France, Switzerland and London, to carry on the tradition established by the *Neue Rheinische Zeitung.* He would have preferred a newspaper, but this was now out of the question, although in time, if the magazine was successful, he thought it might be possible to transform the monthly magazine into a weekly, and the weekly into a daily. But all that was for the future. For the moment it was necessary to bring out the first issue of the magazine, which they decided to call the *Neue Rheinische Zeitung, Politisch-ökonomische Revue,* thus retaining the name of the newspaper for future use. Since there was no money, or very little, behind the review, a fly sheet was distributed inviting subscribers to pay 50 francs for a year's subscription, while the bookseller in Hamburg who printed the review was guaranteed half the gross proceeds.

From the beginning the new review fell on stony ground. There were few readers, and the subscription list was never filled. Five issues were printed, including a final double issue, which appeared at the end of 1850 and was intended to have the same effect as the "red number" of the *Neue Rheinische Zeitung,* being a final salute to the adversary. Jenny believed that the Hamburg bookseller had been bribed by the government not to distribute the review, and that in general he had acted negligently and carelessly. It is much more likely that the review was ill-timed and ill-conceived, and addressed to an audience which was no longer in any mood to subscribe to its opinions. Most of the surviving revolutionaries were too busy licking their wounds and attempting to earn a living to enjoy Marx's insistent appeals to revolt against the government.

The weight of intolerable poverty hung over the refugees, who took the most menial jobs and quarreled incessantly among themselves. Committees were organized to help them, and Marx became the prime mover of the fund for aiding the Social Democratic refugees. The response to his appeals was meager. Five shillings came from the office of the Chartist newspaper *Northern Star,* a shilling came from a German merchant in London, nine shillings and sixpence from another. Heinrich Bauer, now a shoemaker, formerly a revolutionary, raised seven pounds, and eighteen pounds came from an unknown source in Stettin in Prussia, but such windfalls were rare. "In clothes torn to shreds half a nation begs at the gates of strangers," wrote Marx in his appeal. It was a characteristic exaggeration, but it reflected the urgency of the times. In much the same spirit Jenny spoke of "thousands of refugees" arriving daily, although never more than a hundred or so arrived each week, to find lodgings in the already overcrowded slums. Soho, with its tortuous alleyways branching off Leicester Square, attracted them like a magnet. Men with skilled trades could survive; the rest went to the wall. Poverty was so acute among the political refugees that many of them lost their revolutionary fervor. A few escaped to America, and others found jobs in the provinces.

In the long sleepless night of exile many of the refugees lost their mental balance. Living in dreams, deprived of accurate sources of knowledge, they lost the power to make sensible judgments and to think out a logical course of action. It was not only Marx who thought that Europe was on the eve of a great revolutionary upsurge. Fantastic plans were concocted by the refugees for the reconquest of Germany, Hungary, Italy and France. They dreamed of violence, and to their horror all Europe was peacefully mending its wounds. The horror lay precisely in the fact that Europe had had enough of bloodshed.

While nearly all the refugees suffered from poverty, Marx and his family suffered more than most. Neither Jenny nor her husband were temperamentally equipped to deal with it; they had never learned, never wanted to learn the desperate little tricks, the daily subterfuges, which the poor have to learn in order to survive. They continually acted like helpless children, turning in all directions for money which rarely came. They would make long and difficult journeys abroad to plead for money, which was scarcely ever given to them; and the expenses of the journey would bring them still closer to the verge of destitution. Marx refused under any conditions to take a job, asserting that he had more important things to do. No doubt this was true, but the hardship it involved for his family was beyond anything Jenny dreamed of in her worst nightmares.

There are many levels of poverty; each level has its own coloration, its own nausea. Only a few pennies separate shabby gentility from utter destitution, and there is only a step between destitution and the unmarked grave. In the following months Jenny came to know all the levels of poverty so well that none was a stranger to her.

One of the grimmest blows occurred in April, six months after they had rented the small apartment on Anderson Street. They had paid five months' rent regularly, largely out of money Jenny had received from her mother, but when April came, they owed the landlord £5. Every effort to raise the money had failed, and the landlord decided to evict the entire family and take possession of all their property, beds, linen, clothes, the baby's cradle, even the better toys of the girls. He sent the bailiffs in. He promised that in two hours, unless the full rent was paid, everything would be removed. Konrad Schramm, who was living in the same house, offered to go to town to seek help from other refugees. He took a cab, the horses bolted, and he jumped out, falling headlong into the road. Bleeding, he was carried back to the house, where the children were weeping and Jenny was almost out of her mind with despair. It was a bitterly cold day, and it occurred to her that she would have to spend the night on the bare floor "with my freezing children and my aching breast." But at the last minute the bailiffs retreated, and they were allowed to spend their last night in their own beds.

The rest of the story should be told in her own words written a few weeks later when the memory of the horror was still fresh. She wrote to her friend Joseph Weydemeyer in Frankfurt:

> The following day we were forced to leave the house, it was cold and rainy and dreary, my husband looked for a place for us to live, no one would take us in when he spoke of the 4 children. At last a friend came to our rescue and we paid what we owed, and I quickly sold all my beds to pay the chemist, the baker, the butcher and the milkman, who were alarmed by the scandal of distraint and suddenly besieged me with their bills. The beds I had sold were taken out through the door and loaded onto a hand-cart—and then what happened? It was now long after sunset, and English law forbids moving furniture so late. The landlord rushed up with some constables, maintaining that some of his property might be on the cart, we might be escaping to a foreign country. In less than 5 minutes there were 2 or 300 people loitering outside our door, the entire mob of Chelsea. The beds were brought back again, and could not be delivered to the purchaser until after sunrise the next morning. And then when we had sold all our goods and chattels, we were able to pay our debts to the last farthing, and I took my little darlings to our two small rooms in the German Hotel, 1 Leicester Street, Leicester Square, where for £5½ a week we were given a human reception.
>
> Forgive me, dear friend, for describing to you so lengthily and in such detail a single day of our life here. It is indiscreet, I know, but this evening my heart is pouring into my trembling hands, and once at least I must pour out my heart to my best and oldest and truest friend. Do not imagine that these paltry sufferings have bent me, I know only too well that our struggle is no isolated one, and that I in particular belong to the chosen ones, the favored and fortunate, for my beloved husband, the mainstay of my life, is still at my side. The only thing that really crushes me and makes my heart bleed is that he is obliged to endure so much pettiness, that so few people have come to his aid, and that he who has so willingly and gladly come to the aid of so many, should be so helpless here.

When Jenny wrote these proud words, she was not telling the truth. Her spirit had been crushed, and she was already brokenhearted. What she called "paltry sufferings" was the stuff of tragedy, and she would never completely recover from it.

They stayed for two months at the German Hotel, and then took a small apartment at 64 Dean Street nearby. During the summer they were close to destitution again, and Jenny decided upon extreme measures. Instead of writing to Karl's Dutch uncle, Lion Philips, a rich industrialist living in Zalt Bommel, who at various times had shown sympathy for her growing family, she decided to intercede with him in person. She was pregnant now with her fifth child, and it may have occurred to her that a rich Dutchman could scarcely refuse a pregnant and despairing woman.

In this she was wrong, for Lion Philips was a man of strong character and determined opinions. He knew that Karl had been fomenting revolution and he had apparently read the *Communist Manifesto*. He was in no mood to help the family of a struggling revolutionary, who threatened his business affairs and his peace of mind. His sons were in business, and they too were threatened. Lion Philips showed her to the door, giving her only a small present for little Guido, who was continually ill. She returned from Holland empty-handed.

When winter came down on London, tragedy struck at the family. Little Guido, who suffered from occasional convulsions and always survived them, was laughing and playing in the small apartment in Dean Street when he died without warning of a seizure. To Engels, who was now working in his father's factory in Manchester, Marx wrote the same day: "This morning at ten o'clock our little Föxchen, the gunpowder plotter, fell dead." The doctor was called in, and pronounced that death was due to "dental irritation and inflammation of the brain." Föxchen was only a year and fourteen days old.

The years of desolation had begun.

A LETTER FROM THE EARL OF WESTMORLAND

On May 24, 1850, the Earl of Westmorland, the British ambassador in Berlin, received a confidential report from the Prussian Minister of the Interior, Baron Otto von Manteuffel. It was a lengthy document written in German, in that curiously stilted language employed by secret agents when they are describing matters of great consequence, and it purported to be a full description of the German revolutionary movements in London as seen by someone who had succeeded in infiltrating them. The Earl of Westmorland, an old soldier who had taken part in the Napoleonic campaigns, read the document the same day, and immediately ordered that it should be translated and sent by diplomatic pouch to Lord Palmerston. He had very good reason to act quickly, for the document was of the highest importance, involving the safety of the British Crown. According to the secret agent a plot was being engineered by Marx, Wolff and Engels to murder Queen Victoria.

The Earl of Westmorland was one of those superbly cultivated men who from time to time rise to high position in the British Army. He had fought in the Hanoverian campaign and served under Wellington in the Peninsular War; he had marched with the Allies to Paris in 1814; he had been offered and had accepted great military positions in Sicily and Egypt; and he was a musician of accomplishment married to a lady who had a considerable reputation as a painter. He was not a man to be fooled easily, and when he sent the document to London he was perfectly aware that Palmerston distrusted Manteuffel's motives and detested reading long reports. Nevertheless he acted with great speed, convinced that there was some substance in the report and that at the very least the police should inquire into it.

The report survives in the archives of the Foreign Office. In thirteen handwritten pages the secret agent of the Prussian government gives a quick sketch of the revolutionary movements, concentrating chiefly on the group which gathered around Marx. He writes from London on May 2:

There exist here 4 Socialist Republican Societies—two German, one Polish and one French, besides a Blood Red English secret Chartist Society.

A. One of the German Societies under Marx, Wolff, Engels, Vidil, meets at No. 20 Great Windmill St. on the first story. It is divided again into three Sections. The Society B. is the most violent. The murder of Princes is formally taught and discussed in it. At a meeting held the day before yesterday at which I assisted and over which Wolff and Marx presided, I heard one of the Orators call out "The Moon Calf will likewise not escape its destiny. The English Steel Wares are the best, the axes cut particularly sharp here, and the guillotine awaits every Crowned Head." Thus the murder of the Queen of England is proclaimed by Germans a few hundred yards only from Buckingham Palace. The secret committee is divided again into two Sections, the one composed of the Leaders and the other of the so-called "Blindmen" who are from 18 to 20 in number and are men of great daring and courage. They are not to take part in disturbances, but are reserved for great occasions and principally for the murder of Princes. 4 of these men are at Berlin. The German society A is in communication with Paris and with the Secret Chartist Society in London, of which Wolff and Marx are members. Wolff declared in the meeting of the evening before last "The English want what we do, an Orator (of the Chartist Society) has loudly proclaimed, we want not only the Social Democratick Republick, *but something more*. You therefore see (said Wolff) that the English Mooncalf with Her Princely Urchins must go the way we mean to send all crowned Monarchs." Upon which one well-dressed man cried out "You mean hanging, Citizen—another the guillotine."

The month of May or June was spoken of for striking the chief blow at Paris. Before the close of the meeting Marx told his audience that they might be perfectly tranquil, their men were everywhere at their Posts. The eventful moment was approaching and infallible measures are taken so that not one of the European crowned Executioners can escape. . . .

With all its hesitations and sudden changes of direction, and with its very amateurishness, this report is oddly convincing. There is no doubt that Marx was at this time engaged in a conspiratorial movement of considerable scope, reaching down among groups of communist workmen in Germany, France and England, and that he believed that a new European revolution was imminent. When the secret agent puts into Marx's mouth the words: "They might be perfectly tranquil, their men were everywhere at their Posts . . . not one of the European crowned Executioners can escape," he was employing the authentic Marxist jargon, and we have only to translate the words back into German to realize that this is very much how Marx would have spoken. That Queen Victoria should twice be described as "a Moon Calf"* appears surprising until we learn

* In Elizabethan times "moon calf" meant "an abortion." So in *The Tempest* we find Stephano addressing the strange and deformed Caliban: "Moon calf, speak once in thy life . . ." In the circle of Marx and Engels "moon calf" was used of crowned heads of both sexes. Engels, writing to Marx on December 3, 1851, speaks of "the moon calf Louis Napoleon," who had just brought about a *coup d'état* and established himself as the dictator of France.

London 2 May 1850

There exist here 4 Socialist Republican Societies, — two German One Polish, and One French, besides a Blood Red English secret Chartist Society.

A. One of the German Societies under Marx, Wolff, Engels, and Seidel, meets at No 20 Great Windmill St on the first story. It is divided again into three sections, the Society B. is the most violent. The murder of Princes is formally taught and discussed in it. At a Meeting held the day before yesterday at which I assisted and over which Wolff and Marx presided, I heard one of the Orators call out "The English Moon Calf will

will likewise not escape its destiny
The English Steel Wares are the best
the axes cut particularly sharp
here, and the guillotine awaits
every Crowned Head." Thus the
murder of the Queen of England
is proclaimed by Germans a few
hundred yards only from
Buckingham Palace. The secret
committee is divided again
into two sections. the one composed
of the leaders and the other of the
so called "Blindmen" who are
from 18 to 20 in number and
are men of great daring and
courage. They are not to take
part in disturbances, but are
reserved for great occasions
and principally for the murder
of

First two pages of the Foreign Office's translation of the confidential report from Von Manteuffel.

that these words also belonged to the conventional Marxist vocabulary. The secret agent, whoever he was, had caught the precise accent of the revolutionary oratory at Great Windmill Street.

During these months Marx was living in a state of feverish excitement and enthusiasm. For perhaps the first time he was tasting the delights of revolutionary command, seeing himself as the self-appointed leader of the masses in their long-awaited uprising against their feudal rulers. According to the secret agent there were between 300 and 350 workmen's organizations in Germany, all ready to come out in open revolt. These numbers were no doubt exaggerated, but even if only a hundred workmen's organizations existed, each with its own secret conspiratorial arm, these would be enough to provide the core of a revolutionary army. The secret agent goes on to say that only a few of these workmen were "initiated in the more immediate views of the Chiefs, and thus their measures are directed with more secrecy and certainty," and we know that this was precisely the kind of revolutionary organization of which Marx approved. Peter Roser, in Cologne, was being urged to establish as many secret communes in the Rhineland as possible; emissaries were continually being sent to Germany to fan the flames; every day the prospects became more inviting. Soon "the Blindmen" would strike down the kings of Europe, and the armed workmen would come into their own.

If Marx had drawn up a balance sheet of his revolutionary designs, he would have found very little to suggest that he was on the eve of a catastrophe. Everything seemed to point in his favor. In April his own party had formed a confederation with the French revolutionaries and with the Chartists. His intellectual dominance was being acclaimed in revolutionary circles. He had already worked out in great detail a theory of the coming revolution based on his studies of the abortive revolts of 1848. Only one thing disturbed him: all his appeals to the German comrades to provide money to pay for the cost of running the Central Committee went unanswered. The revolution was in desperate need of funds.

The secret agent had depicted Marx and Engels as violent men who would stop at nothing to bring the revolution about. There was some justice in the accusation. In March a secret call to arms, written by Marx and Engels, was distributed to the German members of the Communist League. It was called *A Plan of Action against Democracy* and took the form of an appeal to revolutionary terrorism. Bourgeois democracy, according to the plan, would receive its deathblow at the hands of the armed and awakened proletariat. The revolutionaries were ordered to form open and secret conspiratorial groups, both acting on orders from above. Their first task was to ally themselves with the bourgeois democrats in order to seize power from the ruling princes; once the princes were dethroned and exterminated, the revolutionary proletariat was ordered to turn pitilessly against the democrats and destroy them.

A Plan of Action against Democracy, although little known and rarely studied, is one of the most important and seminal documents of the nineteenth century; it is also one of the most chilling. It had very little influence in its time. It acted like a bomb with a delayed fuse, exploding only in the twentieth century.

Step by step Marx and Engels described a plan of action which was to become only too familiar after 1917. They had no illusions about the strengths and weaknesses of bourgeois democracy. They explained in great detail how a popular front should be formed, and they showed that the moment of victory was dangerous for the proletariat, which was likely to continue to ally itself with the bourgeoisie. On the contrary the proletariat must strike hard against its former allies. The destruction of the princes was merely the prologue; the real drama consisted in the destruction of democracy.

Neither Marx nor Engels had any objection to terrorism. The assassination of leaders and the burning of public buildings, the murder of countless hundreds of people and the entire destruction of the machinery of the state, were all encouraged as being necessary and inevitable to bring about the dictatorship of the proletariat. There could be no half measures. What ordinary people called "revolutionary excesses" were the proper instruments of revolutionary progress. Here in an extraordinary appeal to naked violence Marx and Engels describe the stages the revolution will pass through:

> It is obvious that in the bloody fighting that lies ahead, as in the fighting of the past, the workers will be victorious chiefly through their own courage, determination and self-sacrifice. As in the past the petits bourgeois will, as long as possible, show themselves in the mass to be hesitant, inactive and indecisive in the fighting; but when the victory has been secured, they will make it their own, inviting the workers to remain quiet and to return to their work, thus avoiding so-called excesses and snatching from the proletariat the fruits of their triumph.
>
> It is not in the power of the workers to prevent the petits bourgeois democrats from acting in this way, but it is in their power to render their growth more difficult as against the armed proletariat and to dictate such conditions to them that the rule of the bourgeois democrats will from the outset carry the seeds of its own downfall and their subsequent suppression by the rule of the proletariat will be considerably facilitated.
>
> Above all, the workers must during the present conflict and in the subsequent fighting work against appeasement by the bourgeois as much

> as possible and they must compel the democrats to carry out their present terrorist designs. They must so direct their labors that direct revolutionary agitation will not be suppressed following the victory. On the contrary it must be maintained as long as possible.
>
> Far from opposing the so-called excesses, those examples of popular vengeance against hated individuals or public buildings which have acquired hateful memories, we must not only condone these examples but lend them a guiding hand.

The call to arms went on to describe the need for the workers to establish simultaneously with the bourgeois government their own revolutionary workers' government, and to compromise the bourgeois democrats as much as possible. The bourgeois government must be placed in a position where it feels threatened and menaced by the authorities who command the workers. The workers must be armed with guns, carbines and cannons, and formed into militant revolutionary groups under their own elected officials. At the decisive moment the Central Revolutionary Committee will arrive in Germany from abroad—evidently the committee consisted of Marx and Engels—and they would then assume supreme power. There was no question now of a dictatorship of the proletariat; all power would be gathered in the hands of the Committee, which would rule by dictatorial decree.

This blueprint for a communist revolution written in the spring of 1850 was carried out to the letter in the autumn of 1917. Lenin had read *A Plan of Action against Democracy,* and he knew exactly what had to be done. The last words of the plan were the most terrifying of all, for they offered no relief from the iron rule of the Central Revolutionary Committee—*The battle cry must be: The Revolution in permanence.*

A Plan of Action against Democracy, which was also known as *An Address from the Central Committee to the League,* derives of course from Jacobin sources colored by the ideas of Blanqui. In time Marx would moderate his views, saying that the plan was unrealistic because the revolutionary proletariat could not acquire power through a short and savage confrontation with the enemy but only after many years of constant struggle. But when the plan was written he felt supremely confident. Revolution was in the air, and the defeated revolutionaries of 1848 had gained their second wind.

With the utmost seriousness the English, French and German revolutionaries in London drew up a statement of revolutionary aims on behalf of a new organization called the Universal Society of Revolutionary Communists. In theory this organization was to govern all the European revolutions which were expected to break out in the summer. The statutes of the Universal Society were drawn up by Marx and Engels. The first restated some of the arguments of *A Plan of Action against Democracy*, while the remaining five statutes have a curiously improvised and ineffective appearance, as though they were added in an afterthought by men who found it too much trouble to draw up serious statutes for an organization which was not likely to have any future whatsoever. The six statutes read:

1. The aim of the society is the overthrow of all the privileged classes, and to submit these classes to the dictatorship of the proletariat by maintaining the revolution in permanence until the realization of communism, which will be the last organizational form of the human family.
2. For the attainment of this aim the society will form bonds of solidarity among all sections of the revolutionary communist party by breaking down the barriers of nationality in conformity with the principle of republican fraternity.
3. The founding committee of the society constitutes itself the Central Committee. Wherever it is necessary to carry out the appointed tasks, there will be established local committees in direct communication with the Central Committee.
4. There is no limit to the number of members in the society, but no one may be a member who is not elected by a unanimous vote. But on no account may the vote be secret.
5. All members of the society are obliged by oath to observe unconditionally the first article in the statutes. Any changes, which may conceivably have the effect of weakening a member's deliberate intention to follow the first article, releases the member of the society from his obligations.
6. Decisions of the society will be always arrived at by a two-thirds majority of the votes.

The statutes of the Universal Society were originally written in French in the middle of April 1850, about a month after *A Plan of Action against Democracy*. The signatories were Marx, Engels, Willich, George Julian Harney and Adam Vidil, a representative of the Blanquists. While *A Plan of Action against Democracy* can still chill the blood with its battle cry for a permanent revolution and its detailed analysis of provocations and treacheries, the statutes appear curiously remote and unreal. There is no bite in them. The five self-elected leaders of the conspiracy, regarding themselves as the future dictators of Europe, had merely sketched out a vague and uncertain program leading to the last organizational form of the human family.

Nevertheless they were in earnest. The spring and summer were full of revolutionary excitement. While the English Chartists were merely toying with thoughts of revolution, the Blanquists were deliberately preparing for an armed uprising in France and there were small but powerful groups in Germany which could be expected to come out in revolt. Marx confidently expected to see a European revolution in the summer or at the very latest in the autumn when, according to his prognostications, there would be a general economic collapse.

Nearly all the documents of the short-lived Universal Society are lost. For a brief moment Blanquists, Communists and Chartists made common cause, believing that they had only to utter the word and all of Europe would be scorched with revolutionary flames. All crowned heads would be killed, all who opposed the Universal Society would be trampled underfoot. When the autumn came, the revolutionaries learned that the revolution would have to be postponed indefinitely—Europe was economically secure, world trade was developing at an extraordinary pace, and the discovery of gold in California was visibly improving the economic health of the world. The people of Europe had put revolutions behind them.

The Earl of Westmorland's confidential report to Lord Palmerston was accurate in all its essentials. In that feverish spring the revolutionaries were determined on extreme measures. They spoke of mass insurrections, the creation of vast revolutionary armies, and the assassination of the crowned heads of Europe, as though all these things were inevitable and desirable. They thought they had prepared the ground and were only waiting for the signal to plunge Europe into revolution. The signal never came.

A DUEL AT ANTWERP

There were, as Marx well knew, many reasons why the signal never came, and the most important reason was that the revolutionaries no longer possessed any deep roots among the people. During the summer power—the power to act decisively—slipped out of their hands. They no longer represented a social force; from being men possessing great authority they became the lost and abandoned rejects of society. History had marched over them and trampled them into the ground.

Marx himself appears to have realized the hopelessness of any further revolutionary activity sooner than most, for he possessed a profound sense of history. What he had not foreseen was that the exiled revolutionaries in London would give way to every imaginable kind of stupidity, and that he himself would be drawn into an unsavory quarrel which should never have taken place. There are different versions of how the quarrel began, but there is general agreement about its outcome—a duel fought on the sands outside Antwerp between a soldier who could shoot a man through the heart at a hundred paces and a young revolutionary who had never in his life held a pistol in his hand.

One evening at the end of August or the beginning of September there was a meeting of the German revolutionaries in the upstairs room in Great Windmill Street. There was a bitter quarrel between Marx and Willich, which sprang apparently from the fact that Marx had abandoned all hope of an imminent revolution in Germany, while Willich was determined to bring revolution to Germany, if necessary by "the power of the guillotine." Marx had a violent temper, Willich's temper was even worse. They shouted at each other, and Marx found himself to his surprise described as a "traitor," while Willich was described as a "nincompoop." Finally, Willich shouted that there was only one way to resolve the issue and that was by fighting a duel. Marx replied in his lofty way that he had not the slightest intention of engaging in "the frolics of Prussian officers," although he was an experienced fencer who had fought a duel in his youth. At this point Konrad Schramm, Marx's faithful young assistant, jumped up and shouted that he would take Marx's place, and it was only a question of choosing the place and the weapons. Schramm was a hothead—Marx called him "the Percy Hotspur of our Party"—and he refused to be dissuaded. It was agreed that they would fight with pistols, and since dueling was outlawed in England and duelists were likely to receive heavy punishment, it was decided that they would take the night boat to Antwerp and stage the duel nearby on the seacoast.

Marx appears to have made no serious attempt to prevent the duel, and his attitude appears to have been one of cynical indifference. He liked Schramm, and he had come to detest Willich, but he seems to have felt that the idea of fighting a duel was too stupid to be worth his attention.

The date was fixed: September 3. Schramm chose as his second a young Polish officer, Henryk Miskovsky, while Willich chose two seconds, Lieutenant Gustav Techow and a French *émigré* called Emmanuel Barthélemi, a strange man who looked the part of a French revolutionary to perfection with his broad shoulders, dusky pallor, brilliant piercing eyes, dark curly hair, mustaches and goatee. He was a man of ferocious violence, and was credited with many murders. He had a deep sonorous voice, and he would explain in his slow, measured way that revolution and extermination went hand in hand and were indeed inseparable. When he came to the Dean Street apartment, Jenny had taken one look at his dark eyes and prayed that he would never come again. Her prayers were not answered, for on the evening of September 4, when Marx was away and only Jenny and Helene Demuth were in the apartment, Barthélemi knocked at the door. Helene Demuth let him in. He bowed stiffly. Jenny asked whether he brought any news.

"Yes," replied Barthélemi. "Schramm has a bullet in his head."

He said nothing more, bowed again, and went out into the street.* Jenny, half unconscious with fright, felt that her unreasoning fear of him had at last received its justification, and when Marx and Liebknecht, who tells the story, arrived an hour later, they discovered her in tears and learned that Schramm had died somewhere on the barren coast of Belgium.

They were both sorry, for Schramm was an engaging companion, not very intelligent, but always prepared to serve the cause of revolution by running errands and performing those useful and dangerous tasks which must always be done by the assistants of revolutionaries.

On the following day, while they were mourning him, there was another knock on the door. This time it was Schramm himself, a little pale and ghostly, with a bandage round his head, looking as though he had returned from the dead. What was even more surprising was that he was laughing gaily. He told them he had received a glancing shot in the head, and had lost consciousness. When he woke up, he was alone with Henryk Miskovsky and a doctor. Willich and his seconds had vanished.

Lieutenant Techow, in a letter which was later to become famous in German revolutionary circles, gave a slightly different version of the story.

* The subsequent fate of Barthélemi and Marx's reaction to it are interesting. Barthélemi conceived a plan to kill Napoleon III with deer shot steeped in sulphur, and if this failed he was determined to stab the Emperor to death. He had obtained by some unknown means an admission card to a ball at the Tuileries, where the Emperor was expected to be present. With his mistress, who appears to have been a secret agent of the French government, he was about to leave London when he decided to call on a refugee naval officer, Frédéric Cournet, who owed him some money. There was a quarrel. Barthélemi shot Cournet and killed him, and a few moments later killed a police officer and wounded another. He was arrested and brought to trial in January 1855 and was hanged after a sensational trial.

Marx wrote to Engels on December 15, 1854: "Barthélemi's end is glorious. At the preliminary inquiry (or rather at the coroner's inquest) it was said that some important documents which however had nothing to do with the assassination were found on him. It would be highly annoying if they found among these old papers some indications of our former relationship with this fellow, especially since he liked to boast that he had 'reserved' a bullet for us if we ever returned to Paris."

He tells how the two adversaries fired their pistols, and Schramm received a bullet in the head which "if it had been half an inch deeper would have blown out the light of his life." While Techow was loading the pistols for the second round, Schramm asked Willich for his hand and assured him that he had no personal animosity, but had acted only because he felt the party should not give ground and because he felt that Willich's actions were harmful. He asked for "a full and loyal reconciliation," and they then shook hands. Techow, who half despised Schramm for never having been an army officer, was inclined to suggest that Schramm begged for mercy. "Willich's shooting was extraordinarily good," he wrote. "An absolutely direct shot, only half an inch too high."

There is not enough difference between the two accounts of the duel to suggest that anyone was consciously lying. Schramm may well have lost consciousness after his brief conversation with Willich, and it is likely enough that Willich would abruptly turn away and leave the wounded man in disgust. He was a Prussian, Schramm came from southern Germany, and there was no love lost between them.

So ended the duel, but in fact nothing had been ended. The left and right wings of the Central Committee had split so wide apart that there could no longer be any question of "a full and loyal reconciliation." The time of compromise was over. There was to be a final meeting to preside over the obsequies.

The meeting took place on September 15, and was attended by Marx, Engels, Schramm, Pfänder, Heinrich Bauer, Eccarius, Schapper, Willich, and Albert Lehmann, an obscure German workman living in London. All except the last three supported Marx, who therefore possessed a majority of the votes. Marx had come prepared with a thunderbolt, exactly the same thunderbolt which he was to hurl twenty-three years later at the Hague Congress. He decided to destroy the Central Committee by proposing that its seat of operations be removed to Cologne. By transferring the headquarters of the League to Germany, he was depriving it of its most powerful leaders and its motive force. Nothing would be left except a few quarrelsome workmen and intellectuals who had not yet established a name for themselves. As Marx well knew, he was presiding over the dissolution of the Communist League.

Karl Schapper, an unruly giant with considerable gifts as a speaker, objected violently. This was neither the time nor the place for making arbitrary decisions; and he proposed that there should be a clear understanding that the aim of the Communist League was to produce revolutions, not debating societies. Marx had even suggested that Willich's minority group might establish its own committee owing allegiance to the Central Committee in Cologne, leaving Marx's majority group free to pursue its own course. This course was eventually agreed upon, but not before Marx delivered an earnest harangue on the dangers of Willich's appeals for immediate revolution. He said:

> You are insisting that sheer *will power* rather than the facts of the situation are the driving wheel of the revolution. While we tell the workers: You have fifteen or twenty or fifty years of bourgeois war to go through, not just to alter existing conditions but to alter yourselves and qualify for political power, you on the contrary tell them: We must take over political power *at once* or else we may lie down and go to sleep.

This did not mean that Marx had abandoned all thoughts of direct action in the immediate future, but it did mean that he had grown more cautious and no longer possessed any real faith in the small conspiratorial groups in Germany. Willich might dream of becoming dictator of Germany; he spoke of assuming power in Berlin and then marching on Paris at the head of a great revolutionary army. But such dreams no longer seemed to be worth dreaming. Many years later Engels, writing an evasive and not altogether truthful short history of the Communist League, described Willich and Schapper as men who had become nothing more than "bourgeois-democratic artificers of revolution." And since both "bourgeois" and "democratic" were terms of abuse, he meant that they had gone over to the enemy and no longer served any real revolutionary purpose.

Henceforth the history of communism was to contain a separate chapter entitled the "Willich-Schapper Schism." Marx and Engels would rage about this small minority group which defied their authority and refused to acknowledge its errors. Among their crimes, as Marx made clear in his speech, was that they used the word "proletariat" as though it has some sacred meaning, exactly as the democrats used the word "people." Their greatest crime was that like the democrats they substituted revolutionary phrases for revolutionary progress. Marx attacked them unmercifully, and it was not until many years later that he recognized that he had perhaps attacked them a little too mercilessly. In 1875, when all his battles were over, he spoke of how among the exiles even the most able revolutionaries "become as it were irresponsible after a longer or shorter time." Exile weighs so heavily on men that they can no longer make sound judgments. He remembered that he had gone to see Schapper on his deathbed five years before, and the dying revolutionary had spoken with bitter irony about "the clumsiness of the exiles." This clumsiness, however, was culpable. "In these moments of crisis," Marx commented severely, "to lose one's head becomes a crime against the party which demands public expiation."

Yet it was Marx who lost his head in this crisis. There was no elasticity in him. He could not tolerate opposition, and by transferring the Communist League to Cologne he effectively killed it, when it would have been perfectly possible to keep it alive. Henceforth, until the founding of the International, he was to be a man without a party, alone in the wilderness. At intervals he would write to Engels and declare that nothing delighted him more than his obscurity, his lack of responsibility, his calm amid so many crises. On February 11, 1851, he wrote: "This open and authentic isolation in which we two, you and I, find ourselves pleases me very much. It is entirely in accordance with our position and our principles. The system of mutual concessions, of half measures tolerated for decency's sake, and the necessity of bearing one's share of ridicule in the eyes of the general public together with all the other donkeys in the party have come finally to an end." But the truth was that he detested his isolation, hating it with a bitter hatred. Engels might agree with him and say that the chief advantage of isolation was that they were now responsible for no one but themselves, and when the revolutionaries eventually turned toward them for assistance, they would be able to dictate their own terms. But in the foreseeable future there was no likelihood that the revolutionaries would turn to them. The wilderness claimed them.

About the same time that he lost a party, Marx lost what may have been even more valuable to him—a vehicle for expressing his opinions. The last number of the *Neue Rheinische Revue* appeared in November 1850. It was more notable for a book-length study of the medieval peasant wars in Germany by Engels than for anything Marx wrote in it. Engels, basing his work on an earlier study by Wilhelm Zimmermann, had come to the conclusion that the revolution of 1848 and the peasant war of 1525 sprang from the same causes. It was an untenable conclusion, but he labored earnestly to prove it, and in the process he was able to quote some of those romantic spine-chilling utterances of the peasant leader Thomas Münzer, "the man with the hammer," who threatened destruction upon all his enemies with all the abandonment of a Hebrew prophet, saying:

> All the world must suffer a big jolt. There will be such a game that the ungodly will be thrown off their seats and the downtrodden will rise up.
>
> Beware, I have put my words into thy mouth. I have lifted thee above the people and above the empires that thou mayest uproot, destroy, scatter and overthrow, and that thou mayest build and plant. A wall of iron against the kings, princes, priests, and for the people hath been erected. Let them fight, for victory is wondrous, and the strong and godless tyrants will perish.

There were many more of these sayings in the works of Thomas Münzer, and Engels quoted them with glee, for they suited his mood in the summer of 1850 when there was still a lingering hope of bloody revolution sweeping across Europe. *The Peasant War in Germany* is one of his more rewarding works, for he was chiefly concerned to tell the story of the medieval uprisings and his theoretical conclusions are reserved for the last chapter of the book. He had a deep affection for Thomas Münzer, who was the enemy of Luther, and he had nothing but scorn and indignation for Franz von Sickingen and Ulrich von Hutten, the bloodthirsty nobles who put down the peasant revolts with ferocious violence, with the result that the book sometimes reads like a boy's story.

Marx never showed any interest in medieval peasant wars. Indeed, he showed little interest in any period of the past except the immediate past, for he was essentially a journalist. He could look back three or four years to survey the development of a revolutionary process, but he lacked the full sweep of the historical imagination. What concerned him most was the future, and in a note to a short article by Eccarius in the *Neue Rheinische Revue* he stated his position with the utmost clarity. There was no need for rousing speeches, manifestos, debates, medieval histories, even parties, but there was a great need for an intellectual justification for the coming revolution. "Before the proletariat wins its victories on the barricades and on the battle fronts, it announces the coming of its rule with a series of intellectual victories."

In due course he proposed to present his intellectual victories to the world.

THE HOUSE IN DEAN STREET

For all the remaining years of his life Marx would be haunted by Dean Street, feeling for it a kind of desperate affection mingled with horror. The street became a part of him, and was woven into the fabric of his soul and into the books he wrote. Its miseries became his miseries, and the raucous, sweating people who lived on it provided the background for his thoughts and wildest dreams. Once it had been a fashionable, much-sought-after street, but the days when neighboring Soho Square was the hub of fashion had passed away long ago. Mozart had played in one of the fine houses, the sculptor Nollekens was born in another. But already in the eighteen fifties the plaster was peeling from the bright façades. Then as now it was a seedy street, long and narrow, with some good eighteenth-century mansions standing cheek by jowl with plain jerry-built houses which would have become sprawling tenements if they had been permitted to grow larger. The rich and the poor lived together, and watched each other warily.

For a hundred years foreigners had been coming to live in Soho, bringing their poverty with them. A man walking in Soho might hear ten languages in as many minutes, and he would be able to eat for a month in a different restaurant without stepping out of the bounds of that small corner of London. Every dialect was spoken, and every kind of continental food could be found. There were seven restaurants on Dean Street alone. There was also the Royalty Theatre, and every night there would be flocks of carriages pouring into the narrow street. The street was noisy with traffic on the cobbled stones and with the perpetual cries of the street vendors. In the evening the prostitutes came out, sauntering up and down between the gas lamps; and when the crowds had entered the Royalty Theatre the dull roar of London grew quieter. Then in the light of the flickering yellow gas lamps the street possessed a kind of remote air of respectability, as of a place which had known wealth and saw no reason to bemoan its poverty and vulgarity.

For the greater part of six years Marx lived on this street, and if his circumstances had been different, he might have reflected that it was a good street for a philosopher to live on. Circumstances however dictated that he should spend most of those six years in grinding poverty, in hideous rooms, with the threat of the bailiff always present, his wife an invalid, his children ailing. Three of his legitimate children died in this street, and his illegitimate son was born there. In a small upper room halfway down the street he did much of the research for *Das Kapital,* wrote his book-length pamphlets *The Eighteenth Brumaire of Louis Napoleon* and *Herr Vogt,* and innumerable articles for the *New York Daily Tribune.* From here he sent off streams of begging letters to Engels in Manchester and to his relatives in Holland and Germany. From here, too, over long periods he made his daily eight- or nine-minute walk to the British Museum on Great Russell Street.

Soon after little Föxchen died, they moved from No. 64 Dean Street to No. 28, apparently because it was absolutely necessary to remove Jenny from the place where her son had died. She was in a state of near-collapse, and six months pregnant. Marx wondered whether she would survive, for she seemed to have no stamina. He wrote to Engels toward the end of November: "My wife is in a truly dangerous state of nervous excitability and has suffered a breakdown." The doctor came, but he could do little for her. To go into a new apartment, even if it was on the same street, might prove to be a distraction, and accordingly all their small goods and chattels were moved at the beginning of December to the new apartment.

Nothing is left of No. 64, which was demolished long ago, but No. 28 still stands. The room where Marx labored on a crooked table is now part of the office of a restaurant called the Quo Vadis owned by Mr. Peppino Leoni, who remembers the famous day in 1936 when he found under the stairway a battered tin trunk filled with hundreds upon hundreds of sheets of paper covered with small neat handwriting in a language he could not read. He found the trunk when he was remodeling No. 28, which he had taken over in order to enlarge the restaurant. The hinges of the trunk had burst, the paper was thick with dust and spiderwebs, and he saw no reason to pay any further attention to the battered trunk, or its contents; he ordered that it should be thrown away. Some months later he mentioned his discovery of the trunk casually to one of the guests in his restaurant, and learned that he had destroyed an entire library of Marx's papers. Presumably Marx had hidden the trunk under the stairway at a time when he feared arrest, and they were accidentally left behind when he took his family to live in Hampstead.

Marx would probably still recognize these small rooms if he returned to them today. The stairway has vanished, but the three narrow windows remain unchanged. The room where the Marxes spent their waking hours was fifteen feet wide and twenty-four feet long, and behind this there was a tiny bedroom. The kitchen was wherever the stove happened to be, and the lavatory was down the stairs. The front room served as parlor, nursery, dining room, reception room, study and library. The tiny bedroom served as washroom, pantry and scullery; there was a sink with running water, which was sometimes cut off because Marx was not always able to pay the water rate. At night the rooms were illuminated by gaslight, and the gas was sometimes cut off. These two rooms reeked of stale food, tobacco, unwashed clothes, and the peculiar smell of people living in close proximity to one another. They were like a prison. Jenny spent a good deal of her time in bed, her refuge from the sights and sounds of the world which she had learned to fear; she left all the practical affairs of the apartment in the hands of Helene Demuth, who did the shopping, washed the children, prepared the meals, and saw that the bills were paid if there was any money to pay them; and when there was no money, she would wander down the street to the pawnbroker at the corner. It was a squalid, dirty, miserable place, but all of them came in time to have a feeling of belonging. It was their home, the only place they could call their own.

A police spy, whose secret report on Marx came to light in 1921 in the archives of the Prussian government, has provided a vivid portrait of Marx and his family when they were living in those two wretched rooms. It should be quoted at some length because, unlike most reports by police spies, it is written with warm humanity and sympathy:

> At the head of the party is Karl Marx; his lieutenants are Engels, who lives in Manchester where there are thousands of German workmen; Freiligrath and Wolff (known as Lupus) are in London; Heine in Paris; Weydemeyer and Cluss in America; Bürgers and Daniels were his lieutenants in Cologne, and Weerth in Hamburg. All the rest were merely party members. The shaping and moving spirit, the real soul of the party, is Marx; therefore I will describe his personality so that you will have a better idea of him.
>
> Marx is of middle height, 34 years old. Although in the prime of life, he is already turning gray. He is powerfully built, and his features remind you of Szemere* very distinctly, only his complexion is darker, and his hair and beard quite black. Lately he does not shave at all. His large piercing fiery eyes have something demonically sinister about them. The first impression one receives is of a man of genius and energy. His intellectual superiority exercises an irresistible power on his surroundings.
>
> In private life he is an extremely disorderly, cynical human being, and a bad host. He leads a real gypsy existence (*il mène une vie à la bohémien de l'intelligence*). Washing, grooming and changing his linen are things he does rarely, and he is often drunk. Though he is often idle for days on end, he will work day and night with tireless endurance when he has a great deal of work to do. He has no fixed times for going to sleep and waking up. He often stays up all night, and then lies down fully clothed on the sofa at midday and sleeps till evening, untroubled by the whole world coming and going through the room.
>
> His wife is the sister of the Prussian Minister von Westphalen, a cultured and charming woman, who out of love for her husband has accustomed herself to his bohemian existence, and now feels perfectly at home in her poverty. She has two daughters and one son, and all three children are truly handsome and have their father's intelligent eyes.
>
> As father and husband, Marx, in spite of his wild and restless character, is the gentlest and mildest of men. Marx lives in one of the worst, therefore one of the cheapest quarters of London. He occupies two rooms. The one looking out on the street is the salon, and the bedroom is at the back. In the whole apartment there is not one clean and solid piece of furniture.

* Bartholomeus von Szemere (1812–1869) was prime minister of the short-lived Hungarian revolutionary government. He was a friend of Marx.

> Everything is broken, tattered and torn, with a half inch of dust over everything and the greatest disorder everywhere. In the middle of the salon there is a large old-fashioned table covered with an oilcloth, and on it there lie manuscripts, books and newspapers, as well as the children's toys, the rags and tatters of his wife's sewing basket, several cups with broken rims, knives, forks, lamps, an inkpot, tumblers, Dutch clay pipes, tobacco ash—in a word, everything topsy-turvy, and all on the same table. A seller of secondhand goods would be ashamed to give away such a remarkable collection of odds and ends.
>
> When you enter Marx's room smoke and tobacco fumes make your eyes water so much that for a moment you seem to be groping about in a cavern, but gradually, as you grow accustomed to the fog, you can make out certain objects which distinguish themselves from the surrounding haze. Everything is dirty and covered with dust, so that to sit down becomes a thoroughly dangerous business. Here is a chair with only three legs, on another chair the children are playing at cooking—this chair happens to have four legs. This is the one which is offered to the visitor, but the children's cooking has not been wiped away; and if you sit down, you risk a pair of trousers. But none of these things embarrass Marx or his wife. You are received in the most friendly way and cordially offered pipes and tobacco and whatever else there may happen to be; and eventually a spirited and agreeable conversation arises to make amends for all the domestic deficiencies, and this makes the discomfort tolerable. Finally you grow accustomed to the company, and find it interesting and original. This is a true picture of the family life of the Communist chief Marx.

Although there is not the slightest doubt that the police spy infiltrated into Marx's household, he seems not to have been a frequent visitor. He gets a few unimportant things wrong. It was not true, for example, that Jenny accustomed herself to a bohemian existence and felt at home in her poverty. Nor were Marx's eyes black—they were brown. Nor was it true that Heine was Marx's Paris representative, for Heine had long ago lost interest in the communist movement. But in all essential matters the spy was intelligently recording what he saw and knew, with detachment and quiet good humor. His meeting with Marx seems to have taken place in the autumn of 1852.

Humor, indeed, was one of the saving graces of life in those squalid rooms. From time to time Marx and Jenny would find themselves convulsed with laughter. It was often Germanic humor, rather heavy, rarely devoid of *Schadenfreude*. Marx himself was continually making jokes, but they were rarely tender except when he was joking with his children. He liked to tell amusing stories at length, pausing to make dramatic gestures, and all the time keeping his eagle eyes on the listener.

One of his stories concerned his first meeting with Louis Blanc, the French revolutionary leader and former member of the Provisional Government, in the apartment at Dean Street. Louis Blanc is little remembered now, although he has considerable importance in the history of modern revolutions. He was the first to announce the slogan: "To everyone according to his needs, from everyone according to his abilities." He was also the first to convoke a council of workers' delegates, the precursor of the Russian soviets. He was the author of a massive *History of the French Revolution,* and a man of quite unusual intellectual distinction. Marx disliked him, as he disliked most French revolutionaries.

As Marx told the story, Louis Blanc came to the apartment one morning, and was properly received by Helene Demuth, who invited him into the parlor. Marx quickly dressed himself in the bedroom. The door connecting the two rooms had been left slightly ajar, and he was therefore able to catch a glimpse of his visitor, who was behaving in a very odd way indeed. The great historian and politician was a little man, not much taller than an eight-year-old boy, and he was excessively vain. He had found a mirror and was preening himself, but since the mirror was high up on the wall he had to stretch himself to his full height, with the help of his high-heeled boots. As he gazed at himself in the mirror, he contemplated himself affectionately, smiled, assumed imposing attitudes, and behaved like an amorous March rabbit. Jenny was also watching through the crack in the door, bursting with silent laughter, and Marx, in the intervals of completing his toilet, was also watching. Meanwhile Louis Blanc continued to pose and simper at himself. At last Marx decided that he had had enough of the comedy. He cleared his throat noisily, and had the pleasure of watching Louis Blanc retreating from the mirror in a hurry and immediately performing a fanciful French bow.

Liebknecht who tells the story as he heard it from Marx's lips was careful to add a moral. "Nothing," he says, "was so foreign to Marx as posturing and play-acting. And so it happened that 'little Louis'—as the Parisian laborers called him in contradistinction to Louis Napoleon—soon behaved as naturally as he was capable of doing."

Among very close and trusted friends Marx did in fact behave with "naturalness," and he was perfectly at ease when imposing his "naturalness" on Louis Blanc. But Liebknecht underestimated the complexity of Marx's mind and his behavior. Marx postured and play-acted a good deal. He was the master of the subtle art of flattery and condescension, and he knew how to intimidate and mislead. He had a coarse blunt humor, a vitriolic tongue and a profound knowledge of invective, and he could stimulate artificial rages at will. He was a man who wanted power, and such men are never immune from the poisons of play-acting and self-dramatization.

The Prussian police spy was a man of unusual discernment; he had taken Marx's measure; he knew what he was dealing with. Marx was not merely a revolutionary philosopher lost in dreams of catastrophes, but he was also actively helping to bring the catastrophes about. After describing the apartment on Dean Street, he continues:

> Marx is, after Mazzini, indisputably the most capable and most suitable man to be the head and leader of a conspiracy. He is extraordinarily cunning, crafty and reserved, and it is only with difficulty that one can gain access to him, but once he has given a man his trust, he will make himself responsible for this man and defend him through life and death, and he will never admit that he can be deceived by a man he has tested. He is jealous of his authority as head of the party; against rivals and adversaries he is vindictive and inexorable; he will not rest until he has ruined them. The dominating trait of his character is a limitless ambition and love of power. In spite of communist equality, which he keeps up his sleeve, he is the absolute ruler of his party. It is true that he does everything on his own, and he gives orders on his own responsibility and will endure no contradiction. All this, however, concerns only his secret activity, and the secret sections. At public meetings of the party, he is on the contrary the most liberal and the most popular of them all.
>
> So far his greatest, and one might say his exclusive task has been the overthrow of his rivals and the destruction of their parties. To him, every means to do this was good; sometimes he would intrigue secretly; sometimes he would try to make the leaders of the other party look ludicrous and contemptible by speaking publicly about their faults and weaknesses; sometimes again he would incite the members of one faction against another, and in so doing he would cause a split; and then again he would try to insinuate some of his own secret companions into the inner circle of his opponents, and order them to inform him about their plans, which he would thwart secretly; and then after they had failed, he would scourge them publicly with his fearsome satire.
>
> Marx never regarded Ruge's party and the Revolutionary Alliance in America as dangerous, and accordingly he treated it always with contempt. He never thought it worthwhile to have a serious battle with them, and at most he would now and again make them seem amusing, so that the majority of the members renounced the League with feelings of shame. Marx had a double purpose in mind with this maneuver: (1) He had his revenge on his rivals and was able to overthrow them. (2) While the parties were being reduced to ineffectiveness and the members were scattered, he would draw all the useful elements in them to himself and so strengthen his party. In a word the unique purpose of his endeavors was to be at all times, without any rivalry, the single German head of the revolution of any significance.

The police spy's report on Marx's political aims is a quite extraordinary document for many reasons, not the least of these reasons being his psychological insight. Writing with a feeling for character and the peculiar graces of the revolutionary mind, and with a considerable knowledge of the German revolutionary parties in London, he was able to show exactly how Marx went about acquiring power by setting the parties at one another's throats, by infiltrating them, by suborning them, and by reducing them to impotence once he had discovered their secrets. The history of the quarrels between the revolutionary parties can never be written, because the documents are lacking. Here and there we can make out the shapes of conflict; we hear protests and cries for help; and sometimes, writing to Engels, Marx will proclaim his obscure victories. But the police spy was the first to depict the mechanics of Marx's strategy. It is a strategy which has become more familiar to us today, because it has been pursued with the same vigor by communists in their rise to power.

As Marx well knew, the strategy was double-edged and therefore dangerous. Although he had become one of the leaders of the German revolutionaries in London, and therefore in the running for the position of dictator if the new German revolution broke out, he was feared more than loved, and actively disliked by many who counted themselves among his followers. He was ruthless and intolerant of any opinion but his own. He had a ferocious temper, and a brilliantly sarcastic tongue which made many people avoid him. He did not mingle easily with ordinary people, and he usually entered into a debate with the Olympian air of a man who descends from the heavens in order to instruct. All his life he was a pedagogue sternly pointing to the blackboard on which he had chalked his irrefutable formulas. Those who refused to accept the validity of the formulas were dismissed from the class.

There was another side to him which was rarely mentioned by his friends: he was a bully. He bullied his wife and the maidservant Helene Demuth, as later he would bully his daughter Eleanor. The maidservant would often fight back, but she was his chattel to be exploited unmercifully. She accepted her slavery meekly out of loyalty to Jenny. The police spy makes no reference to her and perhaps was not aware of her presence, for she was one of those who cling to the shadows and hover in the background. Yet she was an important member of the household, and something should be said about her in any biography of Marx.

DEAR, FAITHFUL LENCHEN

When Helene Demuth, the servant in the Marx household, looked back on her early life, she could remember only that it was bleak and troubled. She had been born into a peasant family in one of the villages near Trier, and when she was eight or nine she went to earn her living as a nurse. It was a time when child labor was commonplace, and there was nothing unusual in a child becoming a nurse. She worked in one of the well-to-do houses in Trier, looking after a troublesome baby which had to be rocked in its cradle all night and carried about all day. She remembered that the baby was very heavy, and that she suffered greatly during the long nights when she had to remain awake beside the cradle. One day the Baroness von Westphalen came to call on her employers, took one pitying glance at the child-nurse, and decided to adopt her, or rather to employ her as a servant.

From being an overworked drudge Helene Demuth, at the age of eleven or twelve, became a maidservant in the Westphalen household with time on her hands and no heavy duties to perform. She was rather small, with delicate features and winning ways, and the baroness was fond of her. She was born on January 1, 1823, and therefore was nine years younger than the baroness' daughter Jenny and four years younger than her son Edgar. She became a familiar presence, an essential part of the household. Her duties seem to have been no more arduous than carrying messages, cutting flowers and running to open carriage doors.

In those days a servant who entered an aristocratic family could expect to remain in their service for life. All her decisions would be made for her; when the time came to marry a suitable footman would be chosen for her; she would live all her life in the shadow of the ancestral mansion, and her children and her children's children would sometimes live under the protection of the master of the house. Although she was an unpaid bondslave, she nevertheless possessed certain inalienable rights. It was not necessary for her to wonder where her next meal was coming from, because this was always given to her, and she would make her own clothes from cloth given to her by her mistress. Entertainment was provided at Christmas, feast days, and especially the great pre-Lenten *Karneval* when all the Rhinelanders came out on the streets in masks.

When Karl Marx and Jenny von Westphalen were married in the summer of 1843, Helene Demuth was twenty years old and had been in the service of the baroness for eight or nine years. She was too precious to give away, and it was not until April 1845, nearly two years later, that the baroness decided that her daughter was living so difficult a life that it was necessary that Helene should come to her help. One child had been born, another was on its way. A previous German maid called Gretchen had proved unsatisfactory. In the spring of 1845, when the baroness sent Helene Demuth to Brussels, saying she was "the best she could send, the dear faithful Lenchen," the calm life of the maidservant was exchanged for the hard life of exile. Never again was she to enjoy the settled peace of Kreuznach.

Of all the people Marx ever knew this Westphalian peasant woman was perhaps the one who shed on him the most light and grace. She possessed a delicate beauty when young, and had no lack of admirers. Yet she remained faithful to the Marx family, and never left their service. She carried to the grave many of the secrets he had entrusted to her.

An early photograph has survived, showing her at the age of about twenty-four. She dresses well, wears her hair in a chignon, and knows exactly the right kind of earrings to set off the grave and placid beauty of her face. She carries herself with the air of a woman who knows her place in the world but sees no reason to adopt a humble attitude. She has evidently learned a good deal from the baroness.

It is a memorable portrait and worth studying, because it sheds some light on her employer. We see the peasant girl, but there is more than a touch of native refinement. She has large blue eyes, a broad forehead, fine cheekbones, delicate lips, a small but firm chin. She dresses with taste and even elegance, and she can arrange ribbons and bows to happy effect—witness the white collar and the silk bow at her throat, with the silver locket lying against the ribbons. We know that she had a fine figure, laughed easily, and like all Rhinelanders she enjoyed her wine. There was some earthiness in her, and much nobility, so much indeed that Russian writers on Marx have often printed her portrait under the mistaken impression that it was a portrait of Jenny von Westphalen. Many years later Eleanor Marx described her as "the most tender of beings to others, while throughout her life a stoic to herself."

Helene Demuth had scarcely entered the household of Marx when she was thrown into the misery of poverty. Marx was an improvident husband, Jenny a careless mother with no skill at managing a rapidly growing family. What little money Marx could scrape together was usually entrusted to the maidservant, who held the purse strings. She dominated Marx, stood no nonsense from him, and went about her affairs as though she were the mistress of the house looking after difficult and capricious children. Wilhelm Liebknecht, who knew her well, said that while Jenny remained the mistress of the house, Helene Demuth was the dictator; it was always her will that prevailed. Time after time that "stern and strong will" saved the family from disaster. The "dear, faithful Lenchen" ruled the family with delicate and determined hands.

Her relations with Marx were subtle, ambivalent and curiously compelling. He was never more than the theoretical head of the family, and when Liebknecht described Jenny as the mistress of the house, he was granting her more power than she ever possessed: she had long since abdicated that position. Helene Demuth ruled the family without appearing to do so. She went about her work with calm assurance, knowing at all times what had to be done. By hints and suggestions, by doing her work without waiting for orders or permission, she imposed her own orderly character on the disorderly life of Marx, his aristocratic wife, and their turbulent brood of children.

Her position in the family is important because it has some bearing on Marx's attitude to power. She was the embodiment of "the dictatorship of the proletariat." She cooked, cleaned, made the beds, swept the floors, sewed their clothes, fed the children, prepared all the meals, lit all the fires, did all the washing, and carried the coal into the house. When there was no money in the house, she simply wrapped up some object of value and marched off to the pawnbroker, "the uncle with the three balls." This was a task which Marx could never bring himself to face. He let her do this, as he let her do all the other unpleasant things about the house, and he never paid her a penny.

She ran all his errands, took his letters to the post office, and bought all the food that came into the apartment. She nursed him when he was ill, and when the children were young, she was more a mother to them than their real mother. No work was too menial for her. In her childhood she had been a drudge, and now that she was grown up, she was a drudge again, but this time with a difference—the drudge was a dictator. She was one of the very few proletarians known to Marx, yet she belonged to the peasantry, and all his life he had an unreasoning and ferocious hatred of peasants. He exploited her shamelessly, as he exploited nearly everyone who came in contact with him. He was the *grand seigneur* demanding that everyone should bow before his relentless vanity, but she was one of the few who refused to bow.

He took care not to annoy her or cross her path, for the inevitable consequence would be a tongue-lashing. Jenny had a quick and savage tongue, and used it freely. Marx was terrified of her outbursts, but he was even more terrified of the rarer outbursts of the servant. He had taken her measure. Sometimes he would describe her in three simple words: *Demuth, Wehmuth, Hochmuth*—humility, sorrow, pride.

Liebknecht has described how she would storm at him when she felt it was necessary:

> Marx submitted like a lamb to her dictatorship. They say that no man is a hero to his valet. Neither was Marx a hero to Lenchen. She would have sacrificed her life a hundred times for him, for Frau Marx, for the children, if it had been necessary and possible—and she did indeed sacrifice her life for them—but Marx could not inspire *her* with awe. She knew him with all his humors and weaknesses, and she could twist him round her little finger. He might give way to explosions of ill temper, storming and raging, keeping everybody else at bay, but Lenchen would go into the lion's den, and if he growled, she would give him such a piece of her mind that the lion became as meek as a lamb.

She had a weapon so powerful that she scarcely ever had to use it: she could threaten to leave him. With her strong hands, good figure and appealing face she would never have any difficulty obtaining another job. She stayed with them from feelings of family loyalty, but also out of pity. Pity was the badge of her servitude.

Wherever they went, she was by their side. She accompanied them to Paris, Brussels and London; she fed them when everything was pawned; she watched over the births and deaths of the children; she cheered them when they were downcast; and she was the last person to see Marx alive. In any portrait of Marx she deserves to occupy a special place.

The worst years were the early years in London, when the family's survival depended on her unaided efforts. The small dark apartment on Dean Street saw the doom of their hopes. In the autumn of 1850 Marx reached the lowest ebb of his fortunes. He was politically ruined, for he had lost control of his party, and he had antagonized so many of his friends that he was very nearly friendless. He had no income, no hope of money from any source, and he was confronted with starvation. Only a few months before he had been riding high as the potential dictator of revolutionary Germany, giving orders to party chieftains in twenty different German towns and debating with himself which officers would command the vast revolutionary army which would sweep across Europe. The ruins of his shattered dreams lay all around him, and he was wondering how he could raise the fare to go to America, a country he despised.

As winter came down, new and more terrible shocks came to shake him almost out of sanity. First, little Föxchen died, then Jenny suffered the inevitable nervous collapse. In his despair and desolation he turned to the only person who still had pity for him. Helene Demuth became his mistress.

It is possible that she became his mistress almost from the day she entered his service, for he had no moral scruples whatsoever. As the *grand seigneur* of a desperate and impoverished household, he would take his comfort where he could. That she was virtually his bondslave was a matter of entire indifference to him. It was enough that she was available to serve his sexual needs at a time when Jenny was too ill to satisfy them. We shall probably never know whether he raped or seduced the servant, though the large number of images concerned with rape in his later writings suggest that it was rape rather than seduction. In due course a child was born.

Jenny, too, was pregnant during that terrible winter. In the two-roomed apartment on Dean Street two women were pregnant by him. At least five people were living in huddled discomfort in the two rooms, for the three surviving children, Jenny, Laura and Edgar were with him.* Soon there would be two more.

For Marx this was a period of unrelenting anxiety, of brutal and terrifying urgencies. At all costs he must conceal Helene's pregnancy from Jenny, who was scarcely likely to tolerate a husband who had fathered a bastard. The heavy skirts of the period would conceal the pregnancy for a while. For Marx it was almost as important that he should conceal the pregnancy from the German revolutionaries in London, who would inevitably rejoice over his downfall. He dared not think what would happen when Helene's child was born. There would be articles in the German press, satiric poems would be written, there would be whispered jokes in the public houses they frequented, and small boys would bawl at him in the streets. His revolutionary reputation, which he had nurtured over so many years, was at stake. "The great revolutionary has fathered a bastard on a house servant." It took no particular knowledge of the Ger-

* In a census return of 1851 Marx appears as Dr. Charles Mark, philosophical author, and the family included a German servant and an English nurse. The nurse was probably taking care of Jenny. This would suggest that six people were living in the two rooms.

man revolutionaries to know that they would pour all kinds of filth on his head.

Marx confronted the problem by going into seclusion. Every day, from nine o'clock in the morning to seven o'clock at night, he vanished into the reading room of the British Museum where he studied economics for his long-projected *Critique of Political Economy.* He read interminably, copied out lengthy extracts from all the English economists and sociologists, dipped into Roman and medieval history, and studied banking and agricultural chemistry. He would occasionally pick up a German or French book, but most of his reading was in English. Although he sometimes reminded Engels, who was living in Manchester, that all this vast amount of reading was necessary for his own book, he was in fact giving himself up to an orgy of reading in order to drown out the sounds of the world outside. Reading his books he could forget his miseries. The British Museum was his opiate, his refuge, his rock of salvation.

I have read the "DIRECTIONS respecting the Reading Room,"
And I declare that I am not under twenty-one years of age.

1833 Karl Marx, 1 Modena Villas, Maitland Park

Marx's signature on his application for an admission ticket to the British Museum Reading Room. The application had to be renewed periodically. This one was dated March 16, 1874.

Wilhelm Pieper, who still acted as his occasional secretary, wrote to Engels in January: "Marx is living in complete isolation, his only real friends being John Stuart Mill and Loyd.* When you pay him a visit, you are received not with greetings, but with economic categories."

During this period Marx carefully avoided the meeting places of revolutionaries, and he was never seen in the public houses. He had become a hermit, remote from the world as in a grave. His following was no more than a handful, perhaps seven or eight people. In poverty and in silence, with aching wounds, he passed his days in the shadows.

Meanwhile the revolutionaries were still holding their meetings, and he would read about them in the newspapers or send Schramm or Pieper to attend them as his emissaries. On February 24, 1851, to honor the anni-

* Samuel Jones Loyd, Lord Overstone (1796–1883) was a well-known banker and economist.

versary of the February Revolution of 1848, Willich organized a banquet which was held somewhere in central London. It was attended by about seven hundred people, with large deputations from France and Germany. Willich and Louis Blanc made speeches. Marx reported to Engels that the speeches were uniformly terrible, "and in spite of all their claim to *fraternité* the dew of boredom gathered on their faces and on their tongues." This information however came at second hand. It came in fact from Wilhelm Pieper who had attended the banquet with Konrad Schramm. They had scarcely taken their seats when they heard cries of "Spy! Spy!" Everyone knew that Marx had sent them. They were roughly manhandled, and thrown bodily out of the banquet chamber into a courtyard, where they were kicked and beaten by a mob of Germans and Frenchmen. At one o'clock in the morning Pieper knocked on the door of the Dean Street apartment. His clothes were torn, his hair was in disarray, and he resembled a soldier returning more dead than alive from the battlefield. Breathlessly Pieper poured out a long recital of the events of the evening. Marx was left to ponder the fate that would have awaited him if, instead of sending his emissaries, he had attended the banquet himself.

Because he was deeply wounded, he took refuge in dreams. One of his major pleasures was to dream of public trials at which his enemies were compelled to appear before the bar of justice. There, trembling in the dock, they would listen to the pitiless judge handing down impressive and memorable sentences. In the days that followed, Marx decided that he had sufficient cause to demand the punishment of all the principals who had attended the banquet. Willich, Louis Blanc, Karl Schapper, Ernest Jones, George Julian Harney, Emmanuel Barthélemi, and many other revolutionaries who had been his close friends six months earlier would all be brought to trial. Pieper and Schramm were ordered to draw up affidavits. Witnesses were asked to describe what had happened in the banquet hall and in the courtyard outside. Ironically, Marx proposed to charge his enemies with attempted murder.

As the days passed, Marx became more and more obsessed with the forthcoming trial. Whatever the result of the trial, whether or not the defendants were given long prison sentences, he felt that all the advantages would accrue to his side. He could scarcely wait to see the full reports which would appear in *The Times*. Louis Blanc would be irremediably ruined, Willich would be seen in his true light, the newspaper which Jones and Harney hoped to publish would never come off the presses, and Barthélemi, the ex-convict, would be imprisoned for life, since he had been the most abusive and the most dangerous. By bringing the case to court, Marx thought he would sow so much dissension in the ranks of the revolutionaries that they would never again raise their voices against him.

It was a pleasant prospect, and he was understandably elated at the spectacle of his enemies cast into outer darkness. In his letters to Engels he expatiated at length on the necessity of bringing matters to a head at the earliest possible moment; the lightning must strike; there must be an end to the imbecilities of these *soi-disant* revolutionaries. Engels advised caution. After all, he would have to pay the costs of bringing the case to court. He spent a few days in London, and there was no more talk of a public trial. Engels warned Marx that public quarrels among the refugees could only lead to new, repressive laws against them. It was the year of the Great Exhibition, and the British government wanted no trouble from the refugees. Willich had the last word. He announced derisively that when he was installed as military dictator of revolutionary Germany, he would summon Karl Marx to Cologne at forty-eight hours' notice, and if he argued against the order or gave way to unseemly witticisms he would be sentenced to death. Marx would be appointed commissar of finance and social reform in the new revolutionary government. Since he could not be trusted with the finances, he would have a personal guard consisting of an officer and six soldiers.

Such sallies were not calculated to amuse Marx, who was accustomed to deliver barbs rather than to receive them. The joke about finances was in bad taste. He was in desperate poverty and confronted with a distressing domestic crisis. His two pregnant women were approaching their terms. Only Wilhelm Pieper had answered his urgent call for assistance, giving him ten pounds, which went to pay off an old debt. When he begged his own mother for help, she answered that she had already given him more help than he deserved and she would permit no more bills of exchange to be signed in her name. An appeal to the Baroness von Westphalen was equally unsuccessful: some money which had been set aside for Jenny had been taken by her brother Edgar to pay the expenses of his emigration to Texas. Wherever he turned, Marx was surrounded with a wall of indifference and scorn.

On March 28, 1851, Jenny gave birth to a daughter, who was given the name of Franziska Aveline. "The delivery was easy, but she remains very ill in bed more for domestic than physical reasons," he wrote to Engels. "I have literally not a farthing in the house, but there is no shortage of bills from the shopkeepers, the butcher, the baker, etc." In the same letter he spoke of his unavailing efforts to raise money while the German revolutionaries were proclaiming that he lived off the fat of the land, exploited the workers unmercifully, and proposed to make himself dictator of Germany. He wrote at the end of the letter: "To round off on a tragicomic note, I shall reveal to you a *mystère en très peu de mots*. But no, I have been interrupted and must go to my wife's sickbed." He added that he would tell Engels about the secret in his next letter.

The secret was probably connected with the interesting condition of Helene Demuth. Something would have to be done, and done urgently. He needed advice, money, the assurance of a friend. "I am saying nothing about the *mystère*," he wrote in his next letter. "I must absolutely see you before the end of April. I'll leave here in about eight days." He did in fact spend a few days in Manchester in the middle of April. Nothing is known about the decisions that were made, and the *mystère* is never mentioned again in their surviving letters.

In May there came another of those devastating shocks which were now coming with increasing frequency. Peter Nothjung, an emissary of the Communist League, was arrested in Leipzig on May 10. Papers were found in his possession indicating the existence of the League, and the names and addresses of its members. Some thirteen or fourteen members were arrested by the police; twelve were kept in jail for a year and a half before being brought to trial. Among the documents found by the police was the inflammatory pamphlet written by Marx and Engels called *A Plan of Action against Democracy*, urging an immediate uprising and encouraging every manner of revolutionary "excess." This pitiless and brutal document later became widely known, for the police arranged for its publication in German newspapers for the edification of their readers.

Although Marx and Engels were to claim that they were the chosen leaders of the Communist League with unchallenged authority over its actions, it appears to have retained its autonomous character and to have acted on its own responsibility, turning to them only for occasional advice. Engels claimed that it was the only authentic revolutionary party in Germany, and he was delighted when he learned that the newspapers had published the pamphlet, for he felt that they were disseminating the communist program at no cost to himself. In this he was probably wrong. The pamphlet was published in order to demonstrate the extraordinary brutality of the communist program and its absolute amorality.

Marx was staggered by the arrest of the members of the Communist League, for he was left without a base in Germany. Some of his closest friends had been arrested. Heinrich Bürgers, who had accompanied him during his long, lonely journey to Brussels in 1845, young and charming, and completely guileless, was among the first to be arrested. Dr. Roland Daniels, always one of Marx's more fervent admirers, was arrested about the same time. He scarcely knew the young tailor Peter Nothjung, but he had the most agreeable memories of another tailor, Friedrich Lessner, who was arrested in June. As he surveyed the ruin of his hopes, it may sometimes have occurred to him that the Prussian government would demand exemplary punishment for its prisoners, for it would inevitably bring them to court on charges of high treason. There was nothing to prevent them from demanding the death penalty.

Ostracized by the German revolutionaries in London, without any money, his friends in Germany in prison, and with little hope of regaining his former influence, Marx may have reflected that life could scarcely impose any further burdens on him. He had reached the end of the road.

It was at this moment in the summer of 1851 that he received the blow that he had been long expecting. On June 23 Helene Demuth gave birth to his child in the small and cluttered apartment in Dean Street. There was no possible way to conceal the birth from Jenny. She knew only too well what was happening, and although sworn to secrecy, she could not prevent herself from mentioning in her memoirs that there occurred during the early summer "an event which I shall not dwell upon further, although it brought about a great increase in our private and public sorrows." This was the birth of Henry Frederick Demuth.

The private sorrow endured for the rest of Jenny's life; the public sorrow was short-lived, for only their closest friends came to learn of the birth, and they could be trusted. The existence of the child was carefully concealed and innumerable stratagems were employed to prevent its being known. Inevitably there were rumors. The German revolutionaries heard about it, and made inquiries, only to meet Marx's categorical denials. At intervals the rumor would be revived, only to die a natural death. For the rest of his life Marx was to be haunted by the thought that at any moment one of his enemies would make a public statement about his bastard son.

Among the heavy leather folios in the General Register Office at Somerset House there can be seen the child's entry of birth. The government did not insist in those days that the name of the father should be given, and there is a blank where the father's name would normally be. The mother's name is given as Helene Demuth, and the place of birth is given as 28 Dean Street. It is possible that the birth was a difficult one and that Helene Demuth was seriously ill, for more than five weeks passed before she appeared before the Registrar of the Sub-district of St. Anne, Westminster, in the County of Middlesex to announce that she had given birth to a son, whose father she refused to name. Someone must have told her that there were severe penalties for disobeying the English laws concerning the registration of births. One imagines that she put on her bonnet and walked out of the Dean Street apartment alone, making her way to the Registrar's office. She needed no help from anyone.

For Marx, wrapped up in his dreams of revolution and power, the birth of a bastard son was an unmitigated tragedy, a shadow falling over all the remaining years of his life. His life was devoted to the creation of a revolutionary legend of heroic proportions; in this legend the rape of a servant girl could have no place. He therefore repudiated the child, refused as far as possible to have anything to do with it, and made no attempt to support it. Many years later he met his son, but it was a very brief meeting. The son did not know he was seeing his father.

For Jenny, the birth of Marx's bastard son led to a hysterical collapse and long months of nervous prostration. She had possessed an infinite trust in her husband, whom she had always regarded as a heroic figure waging a selfless war on behalf of the dispossessed; now she knew that he had all the frailties of ordinary mortals. If he had fathered a son on almost any other woman, she might have been more tolerant, but that it was her beloved Lenchen was almost beyond endurance. For the rest of her life the mere presence of the maidservant would remind her of her shame. In a letter to Engels, Marx speaks of the sobbing which continued all night and the recriminations of the daytime. "And you know I am naturally not very long-suffering and even a bit hard, and so it happens that from time to time I lose my equanimity."

On the day following Helene Demuth's visit to the Registrar's office, Marx unburdened himself in a long letter to his friend Joseph Weydemeyer, who was then staying in Zurich. He spoke of "the unspeakable infamies which my enemies are spreading about me" and how they were all gleefully crying "Marx is finished." "Of course, I should laugh at all this filth," he continued. "I should not let it interfere with my work for a moment, but you understand, my wife is ill, and she has to endure the most unpleasant bourgeois poverty from morning to night, and her nervous system is disturbed, and she gets none the better because every day some idiotic talebearers bring her all the vaporings of the democratic cesspools. The tactlessness of these people is sometimes colossal."

So it was, and it may sometimes have occurred to him that he had only himself to blame for the misfortunes which were raining down on him.

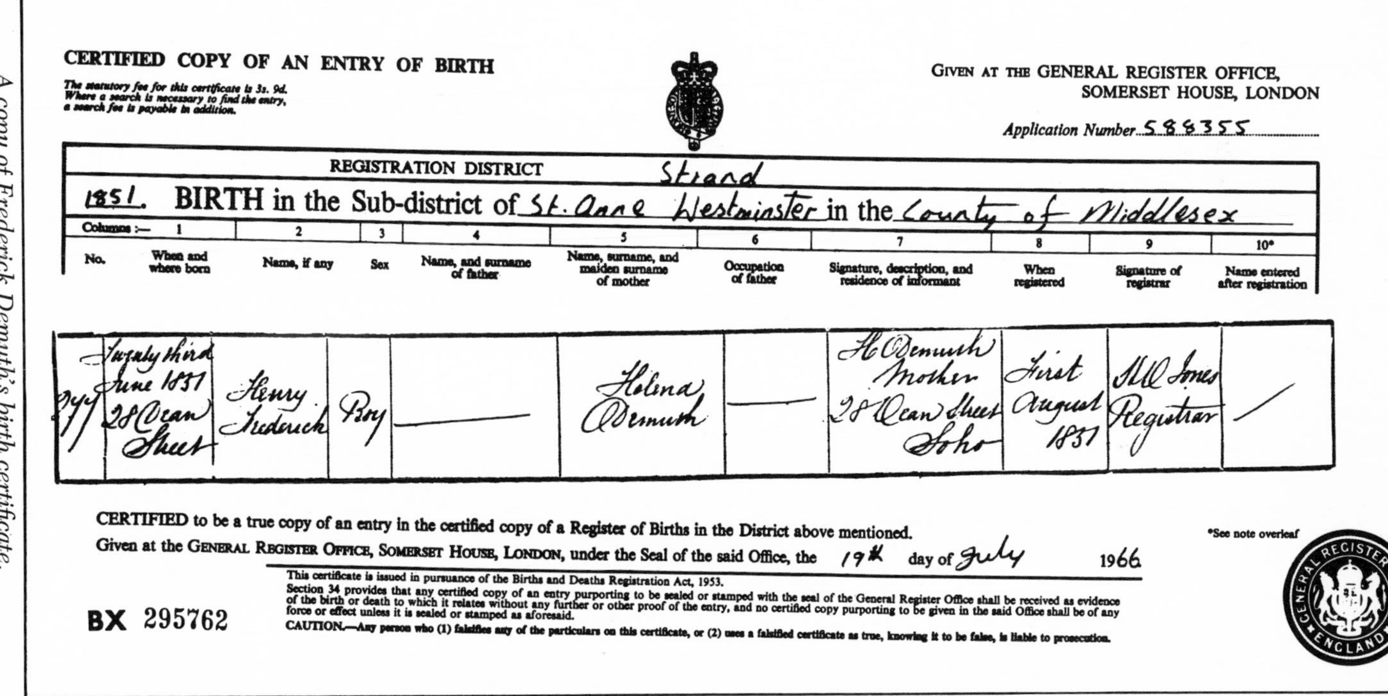

CERTIFIED COPY OF AN ENTRY OF BIRTH

The statutory fee for this certificate is 3s. 9d. Where a search is necessary to find the entry, a search fee is payable in addition.

GIVEN AT THE GENERAL REGISTER OFFICE, SOMERSET HOUSE, LONDON

Application Number 588355

REGISTRATION DISTRICT Strand

1851. BIRTH in the Sub-district of St. Anne Westminster in the County of Middlesex

Columns:—	1	2	3	4	5	6	7	8	9	10*
No.	When and where born	Name, if any	Sex	Name, and surname of father	Name, surname, and maiden surname of mother	Occupation of father	Signature, description, and residence of informant	When registered	Signature of registrar	Name entered after registration
[illegible]	Twenty third June 1851 28 Dean Street	Henry Frederick	Boy	—	Helena Demuth	—	H Demuth Mother 28 Dean Street Soho	First August 1851	[illegible] Registrar	—

CERTIFIED to be a true copy of an entry in the certified copy of a Register of Births in the District above mentioned.

Given at the GENERAL REGISTER OFFICE, SOMERSET HOUSE, LONDON, under the Seal of the said Office, the 19th day of July 1966

*See note overleaf

This certificate is issued in pursuance of the Births and Deaths Registration Act, 1953.
Section 34 provides that any certified copy of an entry purporting to be sealed or stamped with the seal of the General Register Office shall be received as evidence of the birth or death to which it relates without any further or other proof of the entry, and no certified copy purporting to be given in the said Office shall be of any force or effect unless it is sealed or stamped as aforesaid.
CAUTION.—Any person who (1) falsifies any of the particulars on this certificate, or (2) uses a falsified certificate as true, knowing it to be false, is liable to prosecution.

BX 295762

A copy of Frederick Demuth's birth certificate.

His own "colossal tactlessness" had led him from one disaster to another. The evidence of his failure lay all around him—in his abysmal poverty, his wife's nervous prostration, his friends in jail, his ineffectiveness as a revolutionary, his unwanted child.

THE EIGHTEENTH BRUMAIRE

At this moment of great need help came from a totally unexpected quarter—the United States of America.

Marx had been hoping for a miracle to happen, for his efforts to raise money had proved unavailing. Engels was in no position to aid him, the bankers Simon and Louis Bamberger had finally rejected his application for a loan, and there was simply no source of income in sight. Two children had been born to him within the space of three months, and there must have been doctor's bills and extra expenses during that spring and summer. He was heavily in debt to the extent of at least £100, a formidable sum in those days.

Suddenly at the beginning of August Marx received a letter from Charles Anderson Dana, one of the editors of the *New York Daily Tribune,* suggesting that he become the European political correspondent of the newspaper. Dana, who had been a follower of Robert Owen at Brook Farm and a student of revolutions, was particularly anxious to have articles on the current revolutionary crises. He had an ironic turn of mind, and it may have amused him to employ as his "correspondent on revolutions" a man who might one day become the architect of the European revolution. Payment was one pound for each article, and if Marx wrote two articles a week he would have earned a substantial sum by the end of the year. It was an enticing prospect and he accepted at once, being especially pleased because the *New York Daily Tribune* had the largest circulation of any newspaper in the world and could therefore provide him with an adequate forum for his ideas.

The newspaper was ten years old, lively and adventurous. It had been founded in April 1841 by Horace Greeley, a printer from New Hampshire, on $2,000 of his own money and $1,000 borrowed from a friend. He described it as "a New Morning Journal of Politics, Literature and General Intelligence," aimed at "advancing the interests of the people, and promoting their Moral, Political and Social Well-being." Greeley intended to produce a newspaper which exactly fitted these qualifications. He aimed to abolish slavery, prohibit the sale and consumption of liquor, and establish utopian socialism. He was not afraid of social revolution, and spoke quite openly of the need to reconstruct society at all levels. He gave such an impetus to his newspaper that it lasted for 125 years, coming to an end only in 1966.

When Marx became the chief European political writer and occasional editorial writer, Greeley was perfectly aware of his views. Marx was under no compulsion to change or modify them, and he wrote his articles very much as he pleased, making no effort to conceal his bias. They were weighty and ponderous articles, sometimes penetrating, written with great care, and usually there would be a passage of intricately wrought sarcasm in which the enemy of the week would be slaughtered. In the following week the same enemy might be slaughtered a second time. These articles are not among Marx's greatest productions, but they have the merit of showing his mind working amid passing events, deftly elaborating and explaining the causes of all things. Since he possessed a conspiratorial view of history, seeing skeletons in innumerable closets and governments formed from cabals of traitors, he was able to make his articles exciting, even if they were not always reliable.

Altogether over a period of ten years Marx sent nearly five hundred article to New York. A careful examination of the articles shows that he wrote about 350 of these, while Engels wrote about 125, and about a dozen were written in collaboration. Engels assumed the burden of writing about military affairs, while Marx contented himself with discussing social and political affairs. At first the articles appeared under Marx's signature, but later they appeared anonymously.

Although he rejoiced at the idea of becoming the European political correspondent of an American newspaper, he claimed to be too busy studying political economy at the British Museum to be able to write two articles a week. There was a very simple solution at hand. Engels would write the articles, and Marx would receive payment. It seems not to have occurred to him that Engels was overwhelmed with work at the factory in Manchester or that there was anything in the least immoral in signing articles which he had not written. "Because my hands are full with my political economy," he wrote in his characteristic fashion on August 14, "you really must help me out. Write a series of articles on Germany from

1848 onward. Make them as spirited as you please. These gentlemen are exceedingly daring when it comes to foreign affairs."

Obedient as always, Engels committed himself to writing the articles Marx demanded. From time to time there would come plaintive appeals against the heavy load of work the articles entailed. "So little time, and the work has to be done to order, and my almost total ignorance of the newspaper and its readers, and therefore the sheer impossibility of making an orderly plan," he wrote a few days after receiving Marx's peremptory command. Nevertheless he wrote during the following year a long series of articles on revolution and counterrevolution in Germany under Marx's name and the secret was so well-hidden that Eleanor Marx published them later as written by Marx. Engels was a superb ghost writer and he could sometimes imitate Marx's style.

For eleven years, from 1851 to 1862, Marx received an income from the *New York Daily Tribune*. It was not a large or even a regular income, but it remained his principal means of support except for the money which Engels sent him at first in very small sums and later in large benefactions. Sometimes he was able to arrange simultaneous publication of the same articles in England and on the continent, but this did not happen very often. He was proud of his connection with the New York newspaper and he was well aware that his articles were carefully studied in American government circles. When he settled down to write the articles himself late in 1852 he worked prodigiously hard to improve his English, and for this purpose he carefully studied the leading articles in *The Times* of London. *The Times* indeed was his chief source of information, and he would often begin an article with a quotation from this newspaper, which he affected to despise. Although he was immersed in English books in the library of the British Museum, and although he learned to read English with ease, the style and thought of his articles remained heavily Germanic, and the arguments proceeded circuitously in the manner of a scholar who surrounds the problem and then triumphantly attacks it from all sides. He was a relentless and determined counsel for the prosecution even when he was writing newspaper articles.

These articles raise a number of problems. As the Russian scholar David Ryazanov soon learned when he began to study them, it is not always easy to discover exactly how much of an article was written by Marx even when it is signed by him. The editorial hand was at work, and the New York office was not always in entire agreement with its correspondent. Changes were made, the articles were sometimes rearranged, shortened, or tampered with in other ways. Sometimes, of course, the style is so transparently Marxist that there can be no doubt about the author. Here, for example, he discusses an election day in England:

> Days of general election in Britain are traditionally the bacchanalia of drunken debauchery, conventional stock-jobbing terms for the discounting of political consciences, the richest harvest times of the publicans. As an English paper says, "these recurring *saturnalia* never fail to leave enduring traces of their pestilential presence." Quite naturally so. They are saturnalia in the ancient Roman sense of the word. The master then turned servant, the servant turned master. If the servant be master for one day, on that day brutality will reign supreme. The masters were the grand dignitaries of the ruling classes, or sections of classes, the servants formed the mass of these same classes, the privileged electors encircled by the mass of the non-electors, of those thousands who had no other calling than to be mere hangers on, and whose support, vocal or manual, always appeared desirable, were it only on account of the theatrical effect.

The article on "Corruption at Elections" appeared under Marx's signature in the *New York Daily Tribune* on September 4, 1852, and was therefore one of the earliest written directly in English. It tells us something of his attitude toward servants, and his difficulties with the language. But it is also an example of his ineradicable tendency to employ theatrical effects at every opportunity. For him politics was always a form of theater, with the grotesque villains at war with the equally grotesque heroes.

Again and again in his articles we find him deliberately seeking grotesque theatrical effects. We never see him leaning back and surveying the problem calmly; he is always leaping onto the stage and wielding a battle-ax. Most of his articles—those in which we recognize the authentic voice of Marx—are written in controlled fury. The relentless pursuit of his enemies at last becomes wearisome, for they are all described in much the same way. Of Lord John Russell he declared: "His whole life can be viewed either as a systematic sham or as one uninterrupted blunder." Lord Palmerston is described as a man who regarded history as "a pastime expressly invented for the private satisfaction of the noble Viscount Palmerston of Palmerston." The cutting edge of the ax has been blunted from too much use.

Marx reserved his most vitriolic attacks for Napoleon III, and the long diatribe against the Emperor, known as *The Eighteenth Brumaire,* is remarkable for its total fury. These articles, originally intended for a weekly magazine to be published by Joseph Weydemeyer in New York, appeared under curious circumstances. Weydemeyer was unable to bring out the weekly, and many weeks passed while the manuscripts gathered dust. There was no hope of finding a publisher, and Weydemeyer was too poor to publish the articles himself. Finally, in April, when he had lost hope of ever seeing the articles in print, a casual acquaintance, a German tailor who had only recently immigrated to America, offered to put up his entire life savings amounting to forty dollars so that *The Eighteenth Brumaire* could be printed. To the unknown German tailor Marx owed a debt he was never able to repay.

Exactly a thousand copies of the pamphlet were printed, about two thirds of them being distributed in America and the remainder in England and Germany. The pamphlet purported to be the first issue of a magazine called *Die Revolution,* and consequently many copies were confiscated by the German police.

On December 2, 1851, Prince Louis Napoleon, President of France, with the assistance of his half brother the Count de Morny and some disaffected generals, staged a *coup d'état.* It was a *coup d'état* in the modern fashion, designed to create so much popular confusion that the people would welcome the emergence of the dictator if only because he might be expected to put an end to the disorder he had himself created. On the previous night the government printing works had printed thousands of posters announcing that the Assembly was dissolved, universal suffrage established, a state of siege proclaimed, and that there would shortly be elections to approve or condemn the act of the President of France, who would soon proclaim himself the Emperor of the French. The Parisians woke up to learn that the *coup d'état* was a *fait accompli,* and there was very little they could do about it because the generals and the army were on the side of Louis Napoleon. The Second Empire was born in corruption and false promises, and it was to die nineteen years later on the muddy battlefields of Sedan.

The news of the Prince's *coup d'état* reached England the same day, and on December 3 Engels wrote a long letter to Marx in which he discussed the events taking place in Paris in a mood of scorn and lofty detachment. Prince Louis Napoleon was an imbecile, the National Assembly consisted of incompetents, and the people of Paris had shown themselves to be puerile idiots. The *coup d'état* was a travesty of the Eighteenth Brumaire, when Napoleon Buonaparte, fresh from his disasters in Egypt and Syria, seized power and made himself First Consul. "What we have now," wrote Engels, "is the Consulate without a First Consul."

As he warmed to the task, becoming more and more vituperative and exasperated at the thought of the Parisians being hoodwinked by Louis Napoleon, it occurred to Engels that the history of the Eighteenth Brumaire was being repeated in the form of a farce. He wrote:

> After what we have seen yesterday, the people are no good for anything, and it really looks as though old Hegel in his grave is directing history like the spirit of the world, ordaining most conscientiously that everything should be spun out twice over, first as great tragedy and then as lousy farce.

Marx appears to have brooded over these words of Engels, for *The Eighteenth Brumaire* opens with the same idea expressed more succinctly:

> Hegel observes somewhere that all the facts and personages of great importance in world history occur, as it were, twice over. He forgot to add: the first time as tragedy, the second time as farce.*

With these words Marx states the theme which he will pursue relentlessly through the most brilliant hundred pages he ever wrote. From the beginning he assumes that the *coup d'état* partook of the same nature as a stage farce, the implausible characters carrying on their implausible conspiracies in implausible surroundings, stretching credulity to the limit, obeying the laws of farce rather than the laws of history. The actors portray their masks; they scarcely know what they are doing, and certainly do not care. Like sleepwalkers they move back and forth across the stage in the darkness of their own indifference. They have no living breath, no heart, yet they are not puppets. A spark of volition lives inside them; they desire to be doomed.

As Marx depicts the conspirators who brought about the December *coup d'état,* it becomes increasingly clear that he moves these creatures of his imagination across the stage exactly as he pleases and he is in full command of the stage machinery. *The Eighteenth Brumaire* has very little to do with history; it is an improvisation on the theme of an outrageous and vulgar seizure of power, and it amuses him to make it even more outrageous and even more vulgar than it was. He caricatures the characters in the play, and since they already possessed some of the qualities of caricature, he finally produces caricatures of caricatures.

In this world of caricatured caricatures Marx's imagination was perfectly at home. He could give free rein to any imaginative reconstruction he pleased. While contending that Louis Napoleon's seizure of power was merely a pale facsimile of his uncle's successful effort to pervert the whole meaning of the French Revolution, he could, and did, amuse him-

* The same idea appears in a slightly different form in Marx's *Contribution to the Critique of Hegel's Philosophy of Law,* written in 1843. He wrote:

> The last phase of a world-historical form is *comedy.* The gods of Greece, already made to suffer a tragic death in the *Prometheus Bound* of Aeschylus went on to endure a comic death in the dialogues of Lucian. Why should history move in this way? So that men shall cut themselves serenely from the past.

self by insisting that Napoleon Buonaparte was no better than his nephew. The farce was being played twice over; there was no tragedy.

The lunatic actions of the conspirators are discussed in considerable detail with relish and malice, and if this were all, *The Eighteenth Brumaire* would have long since been forgotten. What gives the book its enduring quality is the passion behind the invective, the underlying ferocity. Marx rages at these creatures of his imagination, and from time to time, like a stage manager who finds the behavior of his actors intolerable, he steps forward and announces his views on the subject of revolution—real revolution, not the shoddy imitation practiced by Louis Napoleon. And these asides, which often have very little to do with the *coup d'état*, have the effect of a play within a play. They are sometimes penetrating, and they are always theatrical. Here, for example, he compares the revolutions of the eighteenth and nineteenth centuries:

> Bourgeois revolutions, like those of the eighteenth century, storm swiftly from success to success, their dramatic effects outdo each other, men and things glow with the brilliance of fire, and ecstasy is the spirit of every day; but they are short-lived, and as soon as they have reached their height a kind of drunken depression seizes hold of society before it learns soberly to assimilate the results of a period of Storm and Stress. On the other hand, proletarian revolutions, like those of the nineteenth century, criticize themselves constantly, interrupt themselves continually in their course, return to the apparently accomplished in order to begin afresh, deride with unmerciful thoroughness the inadequacies, weaknesses and wretchedness of their first efforts, seem to hurl down the adversary in order that he may gain new strength from the earth and rise before them more gigantic than ever, and constantly recoil from the vague monstrousness of their own aims, until at last a situation arises from which there is no turning back.

Here, as in so many other places, Marx gives the impression of someone *playing* with revolution. His ideas are disclosed in sentences of prodigious length and complexity, and uttered with an air of extraordinary authority. He has not the slightest doubt that there is one law for the eighteenth century, and another for the nineteenth. On closer examination these laws prove to be fallacious. It was simply not true that the revolutions of the eighteenth century were always short-lived; the revolutionary fire blazed for many years during the American and French revolutions, and these revolutions were not followed by periods of exhaustion and depression. Nor were there any proletarian revolutions in the nineteenth century.

Here and there we can detect a note which appears rarely in Marx's works—the note of suppressed sexual excitement. Of Odilon Barrot, who waited twenty years before becoming Prime Minister, he wrote: "At long last he led his bride home, but not until she had become a prostitute." The sexual theme becomes more explicit when he writes: "All that was needed was a bayonet thrust to burst the bladder, so that the monster could leap into the light of day." He may have been thinking of Helene Demuth when he wrote: "Neither a nation nor a woman can be forgiven for the unguarded hour in which a chance comer has seized the opportunity for an act of rape."

Marx forgives no one. It is his habit to be unforgiving, and he confronts the world with a stern and implacable countenance. Engels had said "the people are no good for anything." Marx takes an exquisite pleasure in underscoring the incompetence of all Frenchmen from the Prince-President to the dregs of the *lumpenproletariat.* The bourgeoisie and the peasantry are consigned to perdition, and even the proletariat receive little encouragement. Louis Napoleon is depicted as a clown, an elderly *roué,* "an adventurer whose trivial and repulsive features are concealed under the iron death mask of Napoleon." That a man cannot simultaneously wear the features of a clown and an iron death mask seems never to have occurred to Marx, who rejoices in bringing together the ultimate extremes. Throughout *The Eighteenth Brumaire* we look in vain for any man with normal human impulses.

In Marx's world bedlam is always breaking loose, catastrophe is always near, dreadful murders are about to be committed at the turning of the road. There is no refuge from sensationalism. Clowns, murderers and ruffians of all kinds parade across the stage, and if the spirit moves him, Marx provides a catalogue of the spear-carrying extras who from time to time make their appearance. Here he describes the hangers-on in the court of Louis Napoleon:

> Together with decayed *roués* possessing dubious means of existence and of dubious origin, and alongside ruined and adventurous offshoots of the bourgeoisie, there were vagabonds, discharged soldiers, discharged galley-slaves, discharged jailbirds, swindlers, mountebanks, *lazzaroni,* pickpockets, tricksters, gamblers, *macquereaux,* keepers of bordellos, porters, *literati,* organ-grinders, ragpickers, knife grinders, tinkers, beggars, in short, the whole indefinite, disintegrated mass, tossed hither and thither, which the French call *la bohème.*

Such catalogues are amusing and captivating on a program note, but they are out of place in a serious study of a *coup d'état.* Misled by his own catalogue of ruffians, Marx arrived at the conclusion that Louis Napoleon derived his greatest strength from the *lumpenproletariat,* the dispossessed dregs of humanity. He saw the Prince moving at ease among the scum of society, "the only class on which he could base himself unconditionally." It was an outrageous and breathtaking perversion of the truth, and it can be understood only as an indication of Marx's seething hatred of Louis Napoleon and his almost total incapacity to see him in historical perspective. In fact, the Prince's strength came from his own legend, his command of the army, his friendship with bankers, and his thoroughly bourgeois character. Marx saw the *coup d'état* as the defeat of the bourgeoisie, when it was their triumph. No civilization has ever been so bourgeois as the Second Empire.

As always, Marx preferred the romantic view. It pleased him to see the dregs of society in alliance with the nephew of Napoleon Buonaparte. In this way he could defend his thesis that the *coup d'état* was a farce. It was not a farce. It was another tragedy.

In the same brilliant, wrongheaded and casual way Marx took the utmost pleasure in indicting the entire French people after indicting the emperor they voted into office. Characteristically—for he was then living in England—he was able to employ a metaphor derived from an English madhouse. Here he describes the French people at the time of the *coup d'état:*

> The entire people, who believed that through revolution they had acquired an accelerated power of motion, suddenly found themselves thrown back into a dead epoch, and so that there should be no deception about their return to the past, the old dates rose again, and so did the old chronology, the old names, the old edicts, which had long become the subject of antiquarian research, and there were also the old constables, who, one would have thought, had long ago decayed.
>
> The nation came to feel like that mad Englishman in Bedlam, who believed he was living in the time of the ancient Pharaohs and daily complained against the hard labor he was compelled to perform in the gold mines of Ethiopia, deeply immured in his subterranean prison, a dimly burning lamp fastened to his head, while behind him there stood the overseer of the slaves with his long whip and at the entrances there gathered a confusion of barbarian mercenaries, who understood neither the forced laborers in the mines nor one another, since they speak no common language. "And they are asking me, a freeborn Englishman, to mine gold for the ancient Pharaohs," the mad Englishman sighs. And the French people also sigh, saying: "We have to pay the debts of the Buonaparte family—"

The elaborate portrait of the mad Englishman and the barbarian mercenaries in the Ethiopian gold mine has very little to do with the *coup d'état* of Louis Napoleon. They have their place in the argument only because Marx felt an obscure compulsion to introduce them, perhaps because he saw himself in the mad Englishman mining gold for the ancient Pharaohs. He often used images of people and animals burrowing under the earth, and his own work must often have seemed to be a form of subterranean endeavor with little hope of ever emerging into the sunlight.

These long and carefully wrought imaginative passages are characteristic of Marx at his best, for there was always some vestige of the poet in him. The passage quoted above ends in bathos, for the sighs of the entombed miner were clearly of greater intensity than the sighs of the French people. But when he chose, Marx could write with quite extraordinary brilliance and penetration when he was dealing with subjects which profoundly affected him. He writes best about death, corruption and vengeance.

The most memorable single paragraph in his work comes at the beginning of *The Eighteenth Brumaire.* He was discussing the dead weight of the past, the death which corrupts the living. "Death seizes the living"—"*Le mort saisit le vif*"—these words of the French poet were quoted in the introduction to *Das Kapital.* In his eyes capital was the dead weight pressing down on the living productions of men. But history, too, was a dead weight, and so he wrote in *The Eighteenth Brumaire:*

> Men make their own history, but they do not make it just as they please. They do not make it under circumstances chosen by themselves, but work upon circumstances as they encounter them, as they are transmitted and handed down from the past. The tradition of all the dead generations weighs like an incubus on the brain of the living. And just when they seem to be engaged in revolutionizing themselves and things, when they seem to be creating something entirely new, in precisely these periods of revolutionary crisis they anxiously conjure up the spirits of the past to their service, borrowing from them names, battle cries and costumes in order to present the new scene of world history in this time-honored disguise and this borrowed language. Thus Luther donned the mask of the Apostle Paul, the revolution of 1879 to 1814 draped itself alternately as the Roman Republic and the Roman Empire, and the revolution of 1848 could find nothing better to do than to parody, now 1789, now the revolutionary traditions of 1793–1795. So does someone beginning to learn a new language find himself always translating it back into his mother tongue. But he can never completely assimilate the new language in its spirit nor can he freely express himself in it until he learns to forget the old usages and uses the new instrument without thinking of the old.

In this way Marx ruminated on the past which continually confronts the present, and found no consolation in it. He wanted to fashion a new instrument, a new society, even a new kind of man, and long before his death he must have known that it was beyond his capacity. In the revolutions which finally came about, as though spun from his brain, the ancient traditions lingered on, and those who thought they had found something new woke up to discover that they had merely restored the old tyrannies.

THE BOURGEOIS GENTLEMAN

ALTHOUGH MARX WAS above all the dedicated revolutionary, never happier than when he was plotting the downfall of kingdoms, his habits were those of a bourgeois and in his private life he was the conventional Victorian husband. He saw himself as the kingpin around which the whole family revolved; his word was law; he ruled from the Olympian heights; and he walked with the majestic tread of the typical Victorian paterfamilias. The great bearded figure who sat at the head of the table was not a man to be trifled with.

He was Victorian, too, in his attitude toward conventional morality. He would spend hours in the British Museum searching for some small erotic bauble to present to Engels, he enjoyed singing student songs about the downfall of young maidens—he could not keep a tune in his head, and he would simply shout the songs tunelessly—and he liked to tell dirty stories in the political clubs and saloon bars, but in the presence of women and children, he would blush like an English governess if there was so much as a whisper about sex. At such times he would squirm in his chair, look anxiously around, ponder various courses of action, his face growing redder and redder as he became more flustered. Finally there would come from somewhere in the depths of his being a harsh command for silence.

Wilhelm Liebknecht tells the story about a gathering of young German refugees in the Dean Street apartment. They were all sitting round the table in the front room when one of the refugees, with a fine voice, began to sing a German folk song, "*Jung, jung, Zimmergesell*" (Young, young, carpenter boy), a song which was not notable for its celebration of chastity. Jenny had gone out, otherwise no one would have dared to sing the song. It was assumed that Lenchen and the children were also out of the apartment. The refugees were still shouting and singing at the top of their voices when Marx thought he heard someone moving about in the back room, and there occurred to him the awful possibility that Lenchen and the girls were still in the house, that they were listening, and that fearful knowledge was being imparted to them. Liebknecht observed the familiar symptoms. Marx was squirming in his chair, his face reddening, his hands moving in a strange flustered dance, his whole body reeling. At last, when he could bear it no longer, when the full extent of the impropriety dawned on him, he suddenly jumped up from the table, his face glowing beet-red, and hissed: "Hush! Hush! The girls will hear you!"

Liebknecht was a little puzzled by the scene, for it occurred to him that the girls were of tender years and would have found the song incomprehensible. This thought may also have occurred to Marx during the long interval while he made up his mind, and it is possible that he was not so much concerned with the children as with Lenchen, his occasional mistress, who must be treated with the same propriety as a wife.

There was something else which Liebknecht found strange in Marx's behavior. When he was discussing politics, Marx habitually used the strongest and most cynical expressions; he consigned whole classes, whole nations, to oblivion; the aristocracy, the bourgeoisie, the peasantry were so much filth to be consigned to the dust heap of history; he approved of political murder and every kind of dubious political expedient; and he rejoiced in character assassination as a fine art. But in the bosom of his family the thunderer cooed like a dove, and he was almost fawningly gentle toward his wife, Lenchen and the children. He was like a man split down the middle: kindly and malevolent, harsh and sweet-tongued, calm and wildly passionate. He was given to terrible rages, but they would die down as soon as Lenchen entered the room. She alone had the power to tame his savage breast.

In all private matters Marx was a conformist, and this attitude was largely dictated to him by Jenny, who inherited the character of her Scottish Presbyterian ancestors. "She had a look that made a word freeze to your tongue, if you showed any signs of boldness," Liebknecht relates, and since he possessed a thoroughly undisciplined mind and was always talking out of turn, he must have suffered from her rebukes. "This dignity, this aloofness," Liebknecht says, when discussing Jenny; and although he came to know her well, he appears never to have been perfectly at ease in her presence.

Among Marx's closest personal friends was Ferdinand Wolf, the fiery journalist usually known as Red Wolf. He was one of the select few who were always welcome at the Dean Street apartment. Exile in Paris had given him a taste for picking up women in the streets, and his work as a journalist had made him exceedingly shortsighted. One evening when he was wandering in the streets of Soho, he was attracted to a woman who walked with remarkable grace and wore a hat with a veil. He encircled her several times, but she paid no attention to him. Growing bolder, he went right up to her and peered at her face through the veil. The next morning, in a state of shock, he hurried to Liebknecht's lodgings in Church Street, where he related the incident at length.

"Hol' mich der Deuwel!" he exclaimed. "The devil take me! It was Frau Marx!"

"Well, what did she say to you?" Liebknecht asked.

"Nothing at all, that's what's so devilish!"

"And what did you do? Did you say you were sorry?"

"Hol' mich der Deuwel! I ran away!" Wolf said miserably.

Liebknecht thought a simple apology was called for; Jenny would be gracious in circumstances like these. Red Wolf, however, felt that he had committed the unpardonable sin. For six months he could not be induced to enter Marx's apartment, even though Liebknecht interceded for him and obtained a pardon. Whenever he remembered the incident, the usually imperturbable Wolf suffered agonies of remorse. Like Marx he was a confirmed cynic, and like Marx he learned that cynicism failed in the presence of Jenny.

Sometimes even Marx found Jenny's imperious manner too much for him. At such times he would wander off with his bosom companions on a monumental pub crawl. A German pub crawl was a very serious affair undertaken with deliberation and with a proper respect for the convention that nothing less than a full glass of beer must be drunk at every public house they passed. Only one pub crawl by Marx has been recorded at any length. It ended, not surprisingly, with a shattering of glass and a wild chase by the police.

It began one evening when Edgar Bauer, whom Marx had attacked bitterly in *The Holy Family* many years before, suddenly descended on Soho from his place of exile in Highgate. In a letter to Engels written about this time, Marx describes Edgar Bauer as a man who has become prematurely old, resembling a pedantic professor, with his high forehead and air of remoteness from the world, but on this occasion Bauer was in high spirits. He proposed a pub crawl from Oxford Street to Hampstead Road, a distance of about a mile. It was an area of London with a vast concentration of public houses, and only the boldest spirits could be expected to endure such a prolonged exertion. Bauer, Marx and Liebknecht took part in this endurance test. They succeeded in reaching the end of Tottenham Court Road without incident, and then came upon a public house where members of the Order of Oddfellows were having a reunion.

There was nothing odd about the Oddfellows. They were working-class men organized in a society for mutual aid, and they had elaborate rituals. They were intensely patriotic, kindly, hospitable, and convivial, and when they saw Bauer, Marx and Liebknecht—three men who were only too obviously refugees from Germany—they invited them to join their reunion. Speeches were made in honor of the refugees, who were commended for having abandoned the despotism of Germany for the freedom of England. The German princes and the Prussian nobility were consigned to the devil by these happy Oddfellows, who were not entirely clear where Prussia was situated, because they kept referring to the Russian nobility. Toasts were drunk, and the Germans were called upon to drink to the health of the Oddfellows. Swollen with drink, and halfway through a hilarious evening, they scarcely knew what they were saying.

There is a stage in drunkenness when the mind turns sour and speech turns to bile. Suddenly the three Germans began to abuse their hosts. Stung by a chance remark, Bauer accused the English of snobbishness, while Marx, not to be outdone, launched into a bitter denunciation of British science and music—especially music. What had the British done to promote civilization? What musicians could compare with Beethoven, Mozart, Handel and Haydn? The British, lacking music, were incomparably below the Germans in culture, and in all other matters the Germans would be superior if it were not for the appalling political and economic conditions in Germany which have prevented them from accomplishing their destiny. Nevertheless, Marx shouted, the time would come when Germany would rise above all other nations and demonstrate her vast and triumphant power.

He was in a ranting mood, all his old antagonism to the British flowing out in this, his first address to the London working class. His German nationalism was never very far below the surface, while his contempt for British culture was real, profound, and enduring, being based entirely on his own unconquerable ignorance, for he knew scarcely any Englishmen, had never studied English history, and had chosen to ignore the culture of the country which had given him sanctuary.

So he went on, carried away by the fury of denunciation and mischief, never at a loss for a biting word or a sarcastic phrase. The outburst was provoked by fear, his own poverty and insularity, the knowledge that he was living in a country which paid no attention to the just claims of refugees; and as he solemnly denounced the Oddfellows for their cultural immaturity compared with the Germans, it never occurred to him that he had chosen the wrong audience at the wrong time and in the wrong place. The Oddfellows were normally good-humored and they made allowances for the strange habits of foreigners, but when their country was attacked they were likely to be dangerous.

Liebknecht, too, was caught up in the fever of denunciation, and when Marx had completed his sermon, he launched into a scholarly dissertation intended to prove that political conditions in England were no better than in Germany, the only difference being that the Germans *knew* their governments were miserable, while the English simply did not know how miserable their government was: whence it followed that the Germans surpassed the English in political intelligence.

By this time the Oddfellows were growing restless, or as Liebknecht describes it, "their countenances were growing darker." Unhappily the Germans were too drunk to stop, and Edgar Bauer took this opportunity to bring up his heavy guns and to enlarge on the subject of English cant. Some of the long-suffering Oddfellows began to murmur, there were cries of "Damned foreigners!" and these grew louder and more menacing. Fists were being clenched. The Germans finally realized that they were in danger and chose the better part of valor by beating a hasty retreat. It was a difficult maneuver, but they accomplished it without too much difficulty —the Oddfellows were probably glad to see them go.

The first part of the unhappy evening was over, and normally they might have been expected to continue their pub crawl in a more chastened mood, but they were still determined to create trouble. Here Liebknecht recounts the last stages of that famous night:

> We had now had enough of our "pub crawl" for the time being, and in order to cool our heated blood, we began a forced march, until Edgar Bauer stumbled over a heap of stones used in paving the roads. "Hurrah, I have an idea!" he shouted, and remembering his wild student antics, he snatched up a stone, and with a terrific clatter the glass panel of a gas lamp was smashed to smithereens. This madness was contagious. Marx and I were not to be left behind, and we smashed four or five street lamps—by this time it was two o'clock in the morning, and consequently the streets were empty. The noise however attracted the attention of a policeman who promptly signaled his colleagues in the area. Soon answering signals could be heard. The position became critical. Happily we took in the situation at a glance, and happily we knew the district well. So we stormed ahead, with three or four policemen pursuing us in the distance. Marx displayed an agility that I would not have attributed to him. After the wild chase which lasted several minutes, we succeeded in turning down a side street and so into an alleyway —a back yard running between two streets—and in this way we came in the rear of the policemen who were pursuing us and had lost the trail. We were safe now. They had no description of us, and so we arrived at our homes without any further adventures.

So ended the monumental pub crawl which was intended to take the three travelers from Oxford Street to Hampstead Road. This was the only occasion, so far as is known, when Marx was pursued by the London police.

Since he was generally law-abiding, and took care to avoid the attentions of the police, he was never in any real danger of arrest. Once the police saved his life, or at least prevented him from being beaten within an inch of his life. Again it is Liebknecht who tells the story, that wholly unimaginative Liebknecht who was incapable of embroidering upon any facts that came to his attention, and is therefore always reliable.

One day Marx and Liebknecht were riding along Hampstead Road in the box of a horse-drawn omnibus when they saw a commotion outside a public house. It was one of the regular stopping places of the omnibus. When a woman began to scream "Murder! Murder!" Marx, who was always sympathetic to women in distress, jumped down from the box and hurled himself into the crowd, closely followed by Liebknecht, who was more concerned for Marx than for the woman. "I tried to hold him back," Liebknecht wrote, "and it would have been easier to catch a flying bullet with my hands." The crowd closed round them, and soon Marx, who had no idea that he was in grave danger, began to ask what had happened. A moment later he realized that he had blundered into a family quarrel and was about to pay the price demanded of all those who blunder into such quarrels. A drunken woman was screaming "Murder!" at her husband only because he wanted to take her home. They had been fighting like scorpions, but the moment they saw the strange-looking Marx and his even stranger companion they forgot their own quarrel and advanced on the newcomers. The drunken woman was especially infuriated by the sight of Marx's magnificent black shining beard. She grabbed at it. No one troubled to grab at Liebknecht's beard, which was thin, unimpressive, and scarcely entitled to be called a beard. The crowd began to shout: "Damned foreigners!" Marx was in danger of losing his beard, and perhaps his life. The crowd was becoming more turbulent, and the two Germans were in very real danger. They were saved when two strong constables advanced through the crowd and saved them from further molestation. They took the next omnibus home. "On later occasions," commented Liebknecht, "Marx was inclined to show more caution before attempting to intervene in quarrels."

Caution, indeed, was his watchword. He obeyed the law, took no part in public demonstrations, and avoided any entanglement with officers of the Crown. Outwardly, he gave the impression of a sedate Victorian husband whose most daring escapades consisted of occasional pub crawls. The inner man, however, was given over to lawlessness. He liked to say: "The mind of the criminal has more grandeur and nobility than the wonders of the heavens." He seethed with plans for destroying European civilization at the roots, for demolishing all existing governments, for banishing elective offices and reducing democracy to scorn. He was consumed by the rage for destruction, and by a passionate desire to elevate the proletariat to its proper place in the sun. But it was only in these chance meetings at public houses that he ever saw the proletariat in action.

While he dreamed of destruction, he pursued the bourgeois life with unabated pleasure, as though he could conceive of no other form of life, as though he fully shared the desires of the bourgeoisie. His instincts were bourgeois, though his mind was predatory, capricious, and obsessed with violence. In many respects he was more bourgeois than the bourgeoisie, so that he was almost a caricature of respectability and Victorian propriety.

On Sundays, like any proper Victorian father, Marx led his family on a solemn excursion into the London parks. Usually they went to Hampstead Heath. These excursions were carefully planned and talked about during the week, but they were nearly always the same excursion. They would start off around eleven o'clock, all dressed in their Sunday best, the women and the girls in their bonnets, Marx in his top hat. Sometimes they were a little late, because there was a last-minute hitch—Marx had overslept or Helene Demuth had not yet prepared the hamper. The hamper, indeed, was the supreme object of veneration. Liebknecht, who often accompanied the Marx family on these Sunday excursions, calls it "the holy of holies."

It was an oversize hamper which had once belonged to the Westphalen household in Trier. Helene Demuth was always in charge of the hamper, which contained the Sunday roast, a tablecloth to be spread out on the grass, plates, cutlery, glasses, all the various odds and ends which go to make a Sunday feast. There were cannisters of tea and sugar, and usually some fruit to serve as a dessert. Hot water, milk, bread, butter and cheese could be obtained at Jack Straw's Castle, a tavern overlooking the Heath, and therefore none of these were carried in the hamper. And if Marx or Liebknecht were in funds, they could buy shrimps, periwinkles and watercress. Periwinkles were delicacies eaten with the help of a pin.

Hampstead Heath is a good five miles away from Soho, with much of the journey uphill. By walking at a spanking pace they could reach Jack Straw's Castle in an hour and a quarter.

These Sunday promenades resembled route marches, and they had their own tables of organization. The two daughters Jenny and Laura went ahead with Liebknecht, setting the pace. Then came Marx and his wife together with the special Sunday guest, who might be a German or French political refugee. Helene Demuth, carrying the heavy hamper, brought up the rear.

After a brief call at Jack Straw's Castle, they trooped off to some shady spot on the Heath, spread out the tablecloth, and settled down to Sunday lunch. When the lunch was over, Marx would read the Sunday newspapers they had bought during the journey, while the girls went off in search of other young girls to play with. Sometimes there were organized games—races, a wrestling match, or putting the shot, the shot being stones. Once they found a chestnut tree loaded with ripe chestnuts. Someone shouted: "Who can bring down the most?" There was a good deal of shouting and clamoring for position, as they began to knock down the chestnuts. Marx rolled up his sleeves and went into action. "He was like a madman," reports Liebknecht, who was present on this famous occasion, "but surely the looting of chestnuts was not his strong side." Nevertheless Marx behaved with commendable perseverance and inexhaustible energy, until the time came when there were no more chestnuts on the tree. He worked so hard at bringing down chestnuts that for a week he was unable to move his right arm.

In those days Hampstead Heath was even wilder than it is now, so that a man could easily be lost in it. The memory of the eighteenth-century highwaymen still lingered over the place. There were dark groves of oak trees, heather-covered slopes, hidden valleys and meadows, winding pathways through the woodlands. Above all there was a sense of spaciousness, with few houses in sight. It was so popular on Bank Holidays that a hundred thousand people had been known to picnic on the Heath, but on any normal Sunday there were perhaps three or four thousand people taking the air.

Already it was becoming commercialized. The costermongers sold their wares, small booths were set up, and there were donkeys for hire. For Jenny and Laura Marx a donkey ride was the supreme enjoyment, the perfect reward for a week's good behavior, and they were never happier than when they were riding their donkeys at full gallop. Marx, who considered himself an expert rider on the ground that he had once taken riding lessons as a student and had once ridden to hounds with Engels in Manchester on a horse so gentle that it was commonly supposed that it was drugged, proved to be a thoroughly incompetent rider on donkeys.

He knew nothing whatsoever about riding, but would launch into long discourses on the subject, proving to his own satisfaction that no one had ever ridden more skillfully. With his heavy body and short legs, he had difficulty keeping a seat; he did not know how to hold the reins; and he was deadly serious. The children laughed at him, but only when they were at a safe distance.

The table of organization was reversed on the journey home. By this time the children were exhausted, and they therefore came last, usually walking with Helene Demuth, who could attend to them more easily now that she was no longer burdened with a heavy hamper. Marx enjoyed singing during these long journeys in the gathering darkness, and Sunday evening strollers on Haverstock Hill and Chalk Farm Road were sometimes surprised to hear Marx's tuneless rendering of German patriotic songs. He especially liked to sing *"O Strassburg, O Strassburg, Du wunderschöne Stadt."* The children would sometimes join in, but they preferred minstrel songs—bands of Negro minstrels were playing all over London. Jenny and Laura were both accomplished dancers and they would imitate the minstrel dances on the way home. On one of those evenings Jenny, who was walking with her mother, began to act strangely. Her eyes were shining, and her small face was lit with a wild excitement as she spoke about another world far away in the stars with such passion that she seemed to have escaped from the present world. Her mother was terrified. She appealed to her husband. "No child should talk like that at her age," she said. "So much precocity isn't healthy." Jenny was describing life in the stars with absolute conviction in a strange poetic language, as if "the spirit came over her." Marx was less surprised than his wife, and Liebknecht good-humoredly suggested that after the spirit came over the Pythian goddess at Delphi, she stepped down from her tripod and became a normal, laughing girl. It had been a long and tiring excursion to the Heath, and Jenny was probably suffering from nothing more serious than excitement and exhaustion.

Marx himself liked to sing or chant during the journey, and he especially liked to roar out long passages of *Faust*. In the middle years of the nineteenth century Englishmen were noisier and more demonstrative than they are today, and these loud homecomings caused little surprise. While the upper middle classes strained toward an aristocratic refinement, the lower middle classes were as boisterous and unruly as the workmen. Everywhere there was a bedlam of noise. Street vendors shouted their wares, blew on trumpets, rang bells, twirled rattles, and attempted to drown out their neighbors. There was the continual clatter of horses' hoofs on the cobblestones. Hurdy-gurdies, organs, and brass bands paraded through the streets, pausing outside the public houses; fiddlers played at the street corners; Scottish pipers played the bagpipes; there were ballad singers and Negro minstrels; every variety of sound abused the ears of Londoners. Mayhew records that there were no fewer than 250 brass bands marching through the streets of London. Amid such a babble of sounds Marx's strident chanting of *Faust* would not have seemed unusual.

London in the middle years of the nineteenth century was noisier, rowdier, dirtier, and far more dangerous than it is today. The smell of alcohol hung in the air, and it was not uncommon to see workmen reeling drunkenly through the streets. The poor looked ill; only the middle classes and the rich were healthy. In spite of the constables, London was still a lawless place, like a frontier town. It was also a great imperial city addicted to pageantry and great parades, huge crowds forming in the streets to watch the processions of foreign kings, or of the heroic dead on their way to burial at Westminster Abbey or St. Paul's Cathedral.

On September 14, 1852, the Duke of Wellington died at Walmer Castle. More than two months passed before all the arrangements for his burial in the crypt of St. Paul's Cathedral were completed. On November 18 the immense catafalque moved through the streets of London at a snail's pace, while the crowds watched in silence. For days people had been gathering from all over England to watch the procession of splendidly equipped soldiers and sailors, the dignitaries from foreign lands, all marching to a muffled drumbeat.

Marx had not the slightest intention of watching the procession, but his daughters Jenny and Laura, then eight and seven years old, were determined to see it. The pale scholarly Liebknecht, whom they called "Library," because he was always carrying books, was asked to accompany them, and since he adored the girls he was only too willing to do so. The funeral procession would pass along the Strand and up Ludgate Hill, and it was therefore not a question of a long journey from Dean Street.

When he arrived at the apartment that morning, Marx was still asleep. Frau Marx and Helene Demuth had already seen that the girls were ready, and it took only a few moments to climb the stairs, claim them, and return to the street. "Be careful with the children, and don't go in the crowds," Frau Marx said, and Liebknecht was aware of his heavy responsibility.

He decided to make his way to Temple Bar, where he thought he would find a good vantage point for seeing the procession. He had no money, and therefore could not buy a space in a window overlooking the procession. The streets were not too crowded, and he was able to find some steps overlooking Temple Bar, and posted the children on a higher step while he stood below them. It was, he thought, a wonderful solution to the problem, for no possible harm could come to them; and in fact they saw the whole procession with its huge towering catafalque and the gold-braided horsemen and the solitary horse with the Iron Duke's boots reversed, as though they were sitting in a box at the theater.

Writing more than forty years later Liebknecht could still remember the horror of the next few minutes: how many minutes he did not know, perhaps six, perhaps a whole quarter of an hour. It was the most terrible few minutes he had ever lived through:

> Suddenly there was a shock—a sudden storming forward of the mass of people behind us, all wanting to follow the procession. I held them back with all my strength, trying to protect the children so that the crowd would rush past without touching them. It was all in vain. No human strength can prevail against the elemental power of the masses. One could more easily brave the ice floes in a frail canoe after a hard winter. I was forced to give way, pressing the children against me, endeavoring to escape the main thrust of the human stream. I thought I had succeeded and was beginning to breathe more easily, when suddenly a new and more powerful human wave poured down on us from the right; we were swept into the Strand, and the thousands and hundreds of thousands who had massed there in that great thoroughfare endeavored to rush after the funeral procession in order to enjoy the spectacle again. I clenched my teeth and tried to lift the children on my shoulders, but the crowd was pressing me too close. I grabbed madly at the children's arms, but the whirlpool drove us on, and suddenly I felt it wedged between the children and myself—I clasped one of their wrists in each hand—but the force which has come between me and the children forges onward like a wedge—the children are torn from me, and all resistance becomes useless—I had to release them, or else I would break or dislocate their arms. It was a terrible moment.
>
> What now? Before me rose Temple Bar Gate with its three passageways—the middle one for carts and horses, the side ones for pedestrians. Along the walls of this gate the human flood had piled like water rising up the piers of a bridge—I had to get through! If the children had not been trampled underfoot—and the agonized screams all round showed me they were in great danger—then I hoped to find them on the other side, where the pressure would be lighter. So I hoped, and worked frantically with my chest and elbows. But in such a turmoil a single man is like a straw swimming in a whirlpool. I fought and fought—a dozen times I thought I was in the passageway, but was hurled aside. At last a shock, a terrible crush of people flung me through the passageway and out on the other side, where I was free of the wild crowds. I looked round, running hither and thither. Nothing! My heart was gripped with fear. Then there came two clear childish voices—"Library!" I thought I was dreaming. It was the music of angels. The two

girls stood before me, smiling and unharmed. I kissed and hugged them. For a moment I was speechless. Then they told me how the human wave that tore them away from me carried them safely through the gate and threw them aside under the shelter of the same walls which had caused so much pressure on the other side. There, remembering my instructions to remain exactly where they were or as close as possible if they ever got lost in any of our excursions, they simply posted themselves behind a projection of the wall.

We returned home in triumph. Frau Marx, Marx and Lenchen welcomed us jubilantly, for they had been very apprehensive. They had heard that there had been terrible crowds, and many people had been hurt and killed.

As Liebknecht tells the nightmarish story, we are aware that the strange events of that day were in some way symbolical of the lives of the exiles. He told many stories about the Marx family, but never again did he tell a story at such length in such hallucinatory detail. He seems to have found some special meaning in that asphyxiating crush of humanity at Temple Bar, the murderous and nerveless mob rising like an elemental force and dashing itself against stone walls. Among that mob, as he continually repeated, he felt like a straw in a whirlpool, doomed to vanish without a trace.

For the German exiles in London, living in poverty and misery, were also straws in a whirlpool, nearly all of them doomed to vanish without a trace. Life was unbearably hard for them, and they survived only by a succession of miracles. At least three times Marx was on the verge of suicide, and his wife was often close to madness. The apartment in Dean Street was their prison, their refuge, the breeding ground of many strange and passionate dreams. Above all, it was their home, and they had a brooding affection for it.

They seem to have got on well with their neighbors. Living in the same house was an Italian confectioner called John Marengo and an Irishman, Peter Morgan Kavanagh, a teacher of languages and occasional author. He wrote a long and quite unreadable novel called *Aristobulus* about Palestine in the time of Christ, and an even longer study of mythology called *Myths Traced to Their Primary Source through Language,* both books being published while Marx was staying in the house. From him Marx rented the small apartment, and when he wrote to Engels about his pressing financial problems, he would mention his debts to the tradesmen, the butchers, the bakers, the milk vendors, and many more, but he never mentioned, during all the time he lived at Dean Street, that he was in danger of being evicted for nonpayment of rent. Peter Morgan Kavanagh was a kindly man, and Marx got on well with him, while Jenny Marx got on well with his bedridden wife and his daughter Julia, who was to become a well-known novelist.

Through Mrs. Kavanagh and her daughter Jenny came to know some of the English women writers of her time and many of them remained her friends when she went to live in another part of London. All the Kavanaghs wrote books, but no one any longer reads Peter Morgan's studies of mythology or Julia's novels *John Dorrien, Daisy Burns,* and *Madeleine, A Tale of the Auvergne.* Today, if they are remembered at all, it is because they were the kindly protectors of the Marx family during the early years of their stay in London.

THE DEATH OF THE LITTLE FLY

OF ALL HIS CHILDREN Marx loved his son Edgar most. There was something strange about the boy, who was never well and whose head was too big for his body: a strangeness which seemed to come from some hidden knowledge, for he was wiser than his years. He was affectionate, and yearned for affection, and was very gentle. He was three years old when a friend drew a portrait of him, showing that he had inherited his father's forehead and eyes and his mother's mouth. The eyes especially attracted attention, being deep-set beneath heavy curving eyebrows. They called him Musch, from the French *mouche,* a fly, because he was so small, but as he grew older they called him Colonel Musch, because he was vigorous and commanding and self-contained.

There were times when he seemed to possess overabundant energy, immune from illness and disease, certain to outlive his sisters. At the age of four he was a chubby and handsome boy already engaging in serious discussions with his father, with a passion for singing, quick at his lessons, capable of amusing himself quietly for hours at a time. Jenny found him wonderfully companionable. Writing to Joseph Weydemeyer in the spring of 1850 when Edgar was a little more than three years old, she described him as "a little goblin who sings his comic songs with enormous feeling and huge voice all day long." Freiligrath had written a revolutionary call to arms during the previous year, with two memorable lines:

O Juni, komm und bring uns Taten,
Nach frischen Taten lechzt das Herz.

Come, June, and bring us deeds,
For fresh deeds our hearts are languishing.

Jenny wrote proudly that Edgar, who had probably learned the words from his father, roared out these lines "in a terrifying voice" which shook the whole house. She did not normally enjoy full-throated singing, but she approved of Edgar's songs. They showed at the very least that he had powerful lungs.

Marx had always wanted sons, and regarded his daughters as charming but not altogether necessary members of the household. He had the Jewish feeling for male progeny, the patriarch made more powerful by the presence of powerful sons. So he watched over Edgar as he never watched over his daughters, noting carefully every advance in speech and reading and intelligence. "Children must educate their parents," he used to say, and it was from Edgar that he expected to acquire his most enduring education.

We have only a few brief glimpses of Edgar, who was born one day in December 1846 in Brussels—the exact date of his birth in unknown—and who died a little more than eight years later in London. Very early in his life he learned that the family was living in dire straits. In the spring of 1853 Jenny was writing one of her occasional begging letters to Engels, saying there was no money in the house and almost no food. Marx had gone off to the City, to try to raise some money from the Jewish banker Isidor Gerstenberg, and in his absence the baker had called to demand an accounting. The baker caught sight of Edgar playing in the street outside the house, and asked: "Is Mr. Marx at home?" Edgar had the quick-wittedness of the Cockney boys with whom he played. "No, he ain't," Edgar said, and quickly removing three loaves of bread from the baker's tray he vanished up the stairs.

Such triumphs, however, were rare, and like the rest of the children he often went to bed hungry. Yet at moments of crisis it was his gaiety which kept Marx and his wife from falling into utter despair. Edgar adored Engels, who taught him songs and sometimes wrote him notes in Italian addressed to "Signor Colonello Musch." It was probably Engels, who was nicknamed General, who gave him his rank of colonel.

The year 1855 opened ominously, the whole family being ill. At the beginning of the year Edgar began to show signs of the illness which would carry him away in the spring. Jenny was in one of her more hysterical and despondent moods—"My wife is marching with firm strides toward a catastrophe," Marx announced laconically to Engels on January 12, forgetting to mention that she would soon be giving birth to another child. Five days later he wrote that on January 16, between six and seven in the morning "my wife gave birth to a *bone fide* traveller—unfortunately of the 'sex' *par excellence*—I would have been happier if it had been a male creature." But he was happy enough with the new daughter who was called Eleanor. She was plump and beautiful, and at first caused little trouble, for it had been an easy birth and Jenny quickly recovered. Franziska had died on April 14, 1852, having lived little more than a year. The new baby promised to bring joy to a household which had known too much grief.

Then as the cold winter wore on, the small apartment in Dean Street began to look more and more like a hospital. Nearly everyone was ill. There were the usual money problems. Jenny was making plans to go to Trier to sign the legal documents concerning a small legacy. It was vital that she should go, but with so many people in the family sick, she remained a prisoner in the apartment. At the beginning of March Marx wrote to Engels:

> Today I am sending you only these few lines to explain the reason for my silence.
>
> First. Musch is suffering from a gastric fever which has not yet reached the critical phase (this is the most serious).
>
> Second. The baby grew worse every day, throwing the whole household upside down, and making it necessary a few days ago to change the nurse.
>
> Third. Although my wife had a superb recovery from childbirth, she has a kind of blister on the index finger of her right hand. It gives her little pain, but the deep irritation affected her. It was operated on yesterday.
>
> Fourth. The trouble with my eyes is now more or less over, but I had such a wretched cough that I swallowed several bottles of medicine and had to keep to my bed for several days.
>
> So you see the house has become a sort of hospital.
>
> The doctor says I must have a change of air, because for two years I have not left the precincts of Soho Square. I would like to come to Manchester before my wife leaves for Trier. If you don't have any room in your house because of your father's coming, or for any other reason, I could rent a room in M. In any event—naturally I shall first have to wait until everything is in order here—I shall simply have to leave this place for a short while, because this corporeal stupidity is stultifying my brain.

The weight of human flesh, and all its pains, was Marx's most crushing burden. *Die leibliche Verdumpfung,* corporeal stupidity, was to pursue him to the end of his life, giving him no rest. This characteristic letter, one of several in which he describes the catastrophes menacing his family and then announces that he must escape before he goes mad, was written when there was still some hope that the family would survive intact. Indeed, a few days later the doctor thought he saw a remarkable improvement in Edgar's condition and promised that he would be well again in a week's time. Marx was overjoyed, and began to look forward to a few weeks of repose in Manchester. Furthermore, there had come news of the opportune death of Jenny's ninety-year-old uncle Heinrich Georg von Westphalen. In his rather ghoulish fashion Marx was inclined to view all deaths in the senior branches of his own and his wife's family with expressions of satisfaction. He described Uncle Heinrich's death as "a very happy event." Uncle Heinrich was a pensioner of the Westphalen estate, and his pension, amounting to perhaps £100 a year, would hopefully revert to Jenny. There was also the question of an original manuscript on the Seven Years' War, which had been written by the Duke of Braunschweig. The Duke had given the manuscript to Jenny's father and it had passed into the hands of her half brother Ferdinand, now Minister of the Interior in the Prussian government. It appeared that he was planning to present the manuscript to King Frederick William IV, "the romantic on the throne," but Jenny was loudly demanding that there should be no outright gift, for she, too, possessed rights over the manuscript. There were other and even more complicated sources of income arising from their German relatives, and Marx was elated by the prospect of new riches falling into his hands.

Meanwhile the condition of Edgar was improving, growing worse, improving again. The crisis had not yet come; there was still hope; Jenny was on the verge of collapse; had collapsed; and Marx dared not think what would happen if Edgar was taken from them. All through that month they waited in hope and apprehension.

On March 27 Marx reported that Edgar was responding to treatment, and the doctor was more hopeful than ever that he would soon be convalescent. Then it would be necessary to send him into the country, away from the fog and dirt of London. He was pathetically weak and very thin, but there was no more fever and there was less hardening of the stomach —the doctor had detected signs of "tuberculosis of the intestines."

Three days later Marx knew the worst. There was no hope, for the boy was visibly fading before their eyes. Jenny, too, had given up hope. For a week she had been lying in bed, surrendering to despair, for she had known long before the doctors that she would lose her son. "The disease," wrote Marx, "has finally taken on the character of a phthisis of the lower stomach, which is inherent in my family, and the doctors have given up all hope. As for me, my heart bleeds and my head burns, although of course I have to keep control of myself. During his illness the child has not for a single moment acted out of harmony with his original, good-natured, and independent character."

Edgar possessed a strong constitution, and for nearly a week he fought on. He had the courage of a lion, and they were all in awe of him. Finally, on April 6, between five and six o'clock in the morning, when Marx was cradling him in his arms, he died. It was Good Friday, and soon the church bells were ringing all over London.

On the following day the Registrar of Deaths in the Sub-district of St. Anne, Westminster, in the County of Middlesex, noted that Edgar Marx, male, eight years old, the son of Charles Marx, Doctor of Philosophy, had died of mesenteric disease in the presence of his father.

Liebknecht came to console the family, which was inconsolable. He found Jenny silently weeping, bent over the body of her son. Helene Demuth was sobbing beside her, and Marx was in a state of wild excitement, vehemently, almost angrily, rejecting all consolation. The two older daughters clung to their mother's skirts, and sometimes Jenny would take them convulsively in her arms, as though to protect them from the angel of Death who brooded over the family.

Two days later came the funeral. Edgar went to join Guido and Franziska in the churchyard of Whitefield's Tabernacle in Tottenham Court Road.* Only a few of Marx's friends were present at the funeral. Neither Engels nor Wilhelm Wolff was able to come down from Manchester, and only Liebknecht, Lessner, Pfänder, Konrad Schramm and Ferdinand Wolf accompanied Marx to the graveside. Liebknecht rode in the carriage with Marx. He sat there like someone who had been struck by lightning, with his head in his hands, and from time to time Liebknecht would stroke his forehead.

"Mohr," he said, "you still have your wife, your daughters, and us—and we love you so much!"

Marx refused to be consoled.

"You can't give my boy back to me!" he groaned, and then they rode in silence the short distance to the churchyard.

* Nothing remains of the graves. Whitefield's Tabernacle was bombed in World War II, and rebuilt in 1957. Where the churchyard was there is now a small rose garden.

The coffin seemed strangely large, for Edgar had grown considerably during the three months of his illness.

When the coffin was about to be lowered into the grave, Marx made a step forward as though he wanted to hurl himself onto it, and Liebknecht took the precaution of moving to his side.

Marx returned to the lonely apartment on Dean Street, more determined than ever to leave it. Two of his children had died there, and he feared for his three surviving daughters. There seemed to be a curse on the house, and he himself was accursed, and he wanted to leave London and never return.

A few days later he wrote to Engels:

> The house is desolate and orphaned since the death of the beloved child, who was its living soul. It is impossible to describe how we miss him wherever we turn. I have suffered every kind of misfortune, but now for the first time I have learned what real unhappiness is. I feel broken down. As luck would have it, since the day of the funeral I have suffered from such desperate headaches that I can no longer think and see and hear.
>
> Amid all these fearful miseries which have afflicted me during these days, the thought of you and your friendship, and the hope that we may still have something worth while to do in the world, has kept me going.

The memory of Edgar haunted him through all the remaining years of his life. It was no consolation to him that Eleanor was thriving, for he remembered that she was born about the same time that Edgar fell ill. He had no son now to carry on his name, and sometimes he would give way to ungovernable rage at the thought of this final misfortune, the last of so many. To Lassalle, who wrote a letter of condolence, Marx wrote:

> Bacon says that really important men have so many contacts with nature and the world, and have so much to interest them, that they easily get over their loss. I am not one of these important men. My child's death has shattered my heart and brain, and I feel the loss as keenly as on the first day. My wife is completely broken down.

His friends gathered round him, urging a change of scene, for that shattering of his heart and brain was only too evident. They urged him to immerse himself in his work, and warned him that surrender to grief was a form of treachery to his son. He was to learn, as Jenny learned, that grief can endure for a lifetime. More than ten years later Jenny would write to a friend: "The longer I live without the boy, the more I think of him, and the grief only grows greater." She would gaze at the children playing around her and suddenly her face would go blank as she remembered Edgar. Marx, watching her, would see the telltale signs, and he had no need to ask her what she was thinking.

Leaving the three daughters in the hands of Helene Demuth, Marx and Jenny spent nearly three weeks in Manchester as the guests of Engels. The days passed too quickly, and soon they were back in Dean Street in an apartment which had become strange and foreign to them. Jenny was ill, and the weather was atrocious. Marx drowned his grief in work, writing articles for the *New York Daily Tribune,* while Jenny remained in bed, silent and wide-eyed.

Wherever Marx looked during that lonely summer, he saw only the ruins of his hopes. The money he had hoped to raise in Germany failed to arrive, the doctor who had attended Edgar was dunning him, Konrad Schramm was dying of tuberculosis. He was suffering from atrocious headaches and toothaches, and there seemed now no purpose in continuing the long debate with society which had engrossed him for so long. He was like a ship without sails or rudder. Engels was writing for *Putnam's Monthly Magazine* a series of articles on the armies of Europe, and Marx was acting as a research assistant, working in the British Museum and ferreting out all those little-known statistics which properly decorate the pages of magazine articles. It was work that dulled the brain, and mercifully prevented him from thinking about himself. In this way he was able to inform Engels that his researches on the army of the Kingdom of the Two Sicilies had produced a surprising result. Thirty years ago some Swiss mercenaries had been enrolled for a thirty-year period in the King's army. Since there was no native army, and the Swiss had presumably returned to Switzerland, Engels in his tabulation of the armies of Europe could properly announce: Number of soldiers in the army of the Kingdom of the Two Sicilies = 0. It was a game which Marx liked playing, for many of his equations tended to end in zero.

From time to time Marx felt the need to rise from his labors and survey the English revolution. It was not going as well as he expected, but it could not be said that it was altogether dormant. On June 25, 1855, there were riots in Hyde Park. The Chartists summoned the working classes of London to demonstrate against the New Sunday Bill prohibiting the publication of newspapers and the opening of places of entertainment, restaurants and barbershops on Sundays. The bill, according to the Chartists, was aimed entirely at the working classes, for the rich could always feed themselves and amuse themselves pleasantly on Sundays, whether the restaurants and barbershops were open or not. They called for a mass meeting at three o'clock in the afternoon in Hyde Park, between the Serpentine and Kensington Gardens. This was precisely the area where the Victorian upper middle classes liked to disport themselves on a Sunday afternoon. The Chartists posted their proclamations all over London, and large crowds came to Hyde Park. Marx knew many of the Chartist leaders, and decided to investigate.

Many speakers denounced the new bill, and there was some good-humored heckling of the fashionable men and women who rode by on horseback or in carriages. The police, too, were heckled, and there were occasional clashes. There was nothing remotely resembling a revolution, although Marx, in an article written the next day for the *Neue Oder Zeitung* announced solemnly in italics: "*Yesterday the English revolution began in Hyde Park.*" The wish was father to the thought. He had seen a police charge, and was convinced that the English working classes were about to rise against their oppressors.

The article was written in a state of considerable excitement. The mood of *The Eighteenth Brumaire* is imitated and sustained in this account of a small riot on the fringes of Hyde Park. There are the same organ notes and peals of bells as he describes weightily the overwhelming importance of this moment of revolutionary history. He begins with a solemn warning:

> There is an old and historically established doctrine that obsolete social forces nominally still in possession of all the attributes of power, continuing to vegetate long after the basis of their existence has rotted away—for the heirs are quarreling over the inheritance even before the obituary notice has been printed and the testament read—these forces once again summon all their strength before the death agony, pass from the defensive to the offensive, challenge the enemy instead of giving way, and seek to draw the most extreme conclusions from premises which not only have been questioned but have already been condemned. Such is the English oligarchy, and such is the Church, its twin sister.

So, in a very similar manner, Marx had described the downfall of Louis Philippe and the dubious rise of Prince Napoleon, establishing the formula by which corruption entered the modern state, insisting against all the evidence that society was in its death throes. In Hyde Park he saw the English oligarchy in its insolence parading in full view of the revolutionary rabble, while in his mind's eye the trees were decorated with hanged aristocrats. But alas, the English rabble was singularly uninterested in punishing its oppressors. Instead, the rabble merely shouted itself hoarse, blowing off steam in a characteristically English way. Marx was deafened by the noise; and being a German, with no insight into normal English behavior, he was inclined to attribute to the noise a revolutionary and Mephistophelean significance. Here is Marx describing the noisy confrontation between the riders on Rotten Row and the infuriated proletariat:

> These unwilling actors in the play, the elegant ladies and gentlemen, "commoners and Lords," in their high coaches-and-four with liveried lackeys in front and behind, together with some old fellows slightly under the weather from the effects of port wine, were not now passing in review. They were running the gantlet. There rose a Babel of sneering, jeering, evil-sounding complaints, of which no language is so rich as English, bearing down on them from both sides. As it was an improvised concert, they were lacking in instruments. The chorus had only its own organs at its disposal and was compelled to confine itself to vocal music. And what a devil's concert it was: all grunting, hissing, whistling, shrieking, groaning, rattling, snarling, growling, croaking, rasping, howling and gnashing! It was a music which could drive men mad and put consciousness into stones. A strange mingling of outbursts of genuine Old-English humor and seething wrath long contained within themselves and now bursting forth. But the only articulate sound which could clearly be heard was: "Go to church!" One lady soothingly offered a prayerbook bound in the orthodox manner in her outstretched hand, leaning from her carriage. And the thousandfold echo roared back: 'Give it to your horses to read!"

One may doubt whether the thousandfold echo roared back precisely those words—Marx was not a trained reporter, and there is some doubt whether he was in Hyde Park that day. He enjoyed the sound he was making. He also enjoyed attacking the Church, which was clearly behind the formidable bill which permitted so few enjoyments to the poor on Sundays. Indeed, the article gave him the excuse to coin one of his most brilliant and bitter epigrams. The poor, he explained, were paid late on Saturday and therefore expected to make their small purchases on Sunday, and it was precisely this relief which the government and Church refused to grant them. So he wrote:

> In the eighteenth century the French aristocracy said: For us, Voltaire, for the people the Mass and the tithes. In the nineteenth century the English aristocracy says: For us, pious phrases, for the people the practice of Christianity. The classical saints of Christianity mortified *their* bodies for the salvation of the masses; the modern, educated saints mortify *the bodies of the masses* for their own salvation.

It was very clever, but it did not really advance his argument. As so often, these epigrams had an eighteenth-century flavor, and the exact balancing of thesis and antithesis tended toward a kind of epigrammatical conformity which was far from his intention. In much the same way he had written epigrammatical verses in his youth.

On the following Sunday the Chartists again called out the workingmen of London. By half past two, according to Marx, 150,000 people were surging along both banks of the Serpentine, waiting to greet the aristocracy and their liveried lackeys. This time the artistocrats were forewarned: they made no appearance; instead, there was the London constabulary in full force. There were so many of them, and they were so determined to make their presence felt, that *The Times* the next day described them as being more effective than the British soldiers fighting in the Crimea, a remark which Marx, who derived most of his knowledge of the riots from the newspapers, gleefully reported. Marx was especially impressed by the fact that the police had taken the place of the terrified aristocracy:

> Last Sunday the ruling classes showed their fashionable physiognomy; this Sunday they showed their government physiognomies. Behind the old gentlemen with the friendly smiles, the stylish fops, the genteel superannuated widows, the beauties arrayed in cashmere, ostrich feathers and diamonds, scented with garlands of flowers, there stood the constable with his waterproof jacket, greasy oilskin hat and truncheon. This was the reverse side of the medal. Last Sunday the masses were confronted with the ruling class as individuals. This time the ruling class appeared as government power, the law, the truncheon. This time resistance was insurrection.

These were satisfying words—*Diesmal war Widerstand Insurrektion*—but unhappily there was no insurrection. A few arrests were made, and the police good-naturedly rounded up a few pickpockets. When the paddy wagons drove off, there was some hissing and jeering, and Marx, who heard the hissing or learned about it, knew perfectly well that it was a poor substitute for revolution. The resistance took the form, as Marx phrased it, of "passive resistance with the men phlegmatically maintaining their battle positions."

The two articles on the two Chartist demonstrations have some importance because they provide the rare spectacle of Marx watching, or claiming to have watched, Englishmen giving way to revolutionary violence. He had no profound faith in their revolutionary capacity, but he was always hopefully looking forward to the time when they would storm the Houses of Parliament. Eleven years later there was another near-riot in Hyde Park, and Marx lamented bitterly that the workers did not tear down the railings and use them to attack the police. "What the Englishman needs," he announced to Engels, not for the first time, "is a revolutionary education. One thing is certain, these thickheaded John Bulls, whose brain pans seem to have been specially manufactured for the constables' truncheons, will never get anywhere without a really bloody encounter with the ruling powers."

In Marx's view the English suffered from an inexcusable revolutionary incompetence. They were the first to bring about the Industrial Revolution, but the English working classes had singularly failed to proceed to the revolution in which they took possession of industrial power and turned it against their class enemies. He saw the revolution in romantic and Germanic terms: a vast upsurge of primal energy, a *Götterdämmerung* set against vast spaces lit with dying fires. The English workingmen had no patience with romantic fictions. They preferred to hiss at paddy wagons and phlegmatically maintain their battle positions.

Yet Marx never quite despaired of the English workingmen. He would explain that they had revolution in their blood—had they not cut off the head of Charles I?—and in their time they had brought about many revolutions. They needed to have their blood heated up, and he sometimes saw himself as the man destined to inflame them into action.

He did not however think very often of his role as a revolutionary leader. More and more he was coming to regard himself as a catalytic agent who influenced the struggle merely by his existence. He was the theoretician who moved universes by his thoughts, sometimes descending from the heights to view the importunities of men. More and more he took shelter in the British Museum.

Even the British Museum could not shelter him from his creditors. The butcher, the baker, the milkman, the greengrocer, the tea vendor and the doctor were all sending in their bills, demanding immediate payment. The doctor who had attended Edgar was Dr. Freund, and Marx wrote bitterly to Engels about "the charming, friendly Dr. Freund," who was making his life intolerable. He was able to rake up some scandal about the doctor, but the bills had to be paid. "This Jew is making these demands because he is himself at the very brink of bankruptcy," Marx noted. The ugliness and Jewishness of Dr. Freund became an offense in Marx's eyes, and it appears to have been in order to avoid the doctor that he decided on flight as the best remedy for his financial ills.

His friend Peter Imandt, a former revolutionary, made a living as a teacher. He had suddenly received a teaching post in Scotland and no longer needed his small apartment at 3 York Place, Denmark Road, Camberwell. In those days Camberwell was a quiet and sleepy place on the outskirts of London. One day in July the whole family slipped out of the Dean Street apartment and went to live in York Place, and there they remained in hiding from their creditors until September. Then Jenny and the children returned to Dean Street, and Marx, in fear of Dr. Freund, removed himself to Manchester. It was not a very satisfactory solution to a pressing difficulty, but it was the best they could do until they received the small legacy from Uncle Heinrich Georg von Westphalen.

Jenny was glad to return to Dean Street, for she had developed an affection for those two small rooms, the only place on earth she could call a home. She liked the sounds of central London; and the silence of Camberwell, which then resembled a country village, seems to have oppressed her. Yet she realized better than Marx that they could not go on living in Dean Street—"our dear old Dean Street headquarters"—if only because Edgar had died there and too many ghosts lingered in the air. She, too, had firmly decided to leave Dean Street at the first opportunity.

For Marx it was a bad year, and he would think of it sometimes as the worst year of a life which seemed dedicated to misery. He had lost his beloved son, and had no dwelling place he could call his own. He was a fugitive from his creditors, living in a small rented room in Manchester, far from his family, alone with his dreams. He did not know and could not guess that there would be a change in his fortunes the following year.

THE DEMONS

All the houses of Europe are now marked by the mysterious red cross. History is the judge: its executioner, the proletariat.

THE HOUSE ON GRAFTON TERRACE

WHEN MARX RETURNED to London in December, he was confronted with the same problems as before. He still lived, as he said, "from hand to mouth," paid his debts when he could, and gave way to the endless grief of poverty. Once more his shelter was the British Museum, from which he would sometimes emerge to make speeches and conduct small study groups among German refugees; and Liebknecht has recorded how Marx would fix his students with an eagle eye and demand exact answers from them, putting them sternly through their paces. But little money came from these speeches and tutorials, and he lived on his hopes.

In March a certain Gustav Levy, a delegate from the Düsseldorf workers, came to London and suggested that the time was ripe for another uprising in Germany, and perhaps Marx and his friends would lead the uprising. Marx reported his conversation with Levy to Engels. Of the Düsseldorf workers he said that "they quite naturally feel the need for political and military leaders." He had counseled caution, saying that "if conditions permit, we shall join the workers of the Rhineland, but if they make an uprising on their own account without any initiative coming from Paris, Vienna or Berlin, they will be imbeciles; if Paris gives the signal, then they should immediately risk everything, for then even a momentary defeat could have bad consequences only for a moment." He suggested that they should send an emissary in due course and keep him in touch with the situation. He evidently brooded on the possibility of the uprising, for a month later he wrote excitedly in a mixture of English, French, and German: "*Wir, die* so enlightened *sind über unsere braven frères von jenseits des Rheins!* The whole thing in Germany *wird abhangen von der Möglichkeit,* to back the proletarian revolution by some second edition of the Peasants' War. *Dann wird die Sache vorzuglich.*"* When he mixed his languages, he was nearly always in a state of uncontrollable enthusiasm.

About this time the Chartist newspaper *The People's Paper* celebrated

* We who are so enlightened about our worthy brothers on the other side of the Rhine! The whole thing in Germany will depend on the possibility to back the proletarian revolution by some second edition of the Peasants' War. Then the affair will be splendid.

its fourth anniversary with a supper at the Bell Hotel in the Strand. Marx was pleased to learn that he was the only refugee to be invited, and he was invited to make the first toast on the subject of the proletariat of Europe. He prepared his speech carefully—it would be a rousing summons to proletarian vengeance. In the speech he reviewed the history of recent revolutions and explained why they had come to grief, and pointed to the English workingman as the standard bearer of the coming revolution. It was one of his strangest and most spine-chilling speeches, and should be quoted at some length:

> The so-called revolutions of 1848 were but poor incidents, small fractures and fissures in the dry crust of European society. However, they denounced the abyss. Beneath the apparently solid surface, they betrayed oceans of liquid matter, only needing expansion to rend into fragments continents of hard rock. Noisily and confusedly they proclaimed the emancipation of the proletarian, i.e. the secret of the nineteenth century, and of the revolution of that century . . .
>
> There is one great fact characteristic of this our nineteenth century, a fact which no party dares deny. On the one hand there have started into life industrial and scientific forces which no epoch of the former human history had ever suspected. On the other hand there exist symptoms of decay, far surpassing the horrors recorded in the latter times of the Roman Empire. In our days, everything seems pregnant with its contrary. Machinery, gifted with the wonderful power of shortening and fructifying human labor, we behold starving and overworking it. The newfangled sources of wealth, by some strange, weird spell, are turned into sources of want. The victories of art seem bought by the loss of character. At the same pace that mankind masters nature, man seems to become enslaved to other men or to his own infamy. Even the pure life of science seems unable to shine but on the dark background of ignorance. . . .
>
> We know that if the newfangled forces of society are to work satisfactorily, they need only be mastered by newfangled men—and such are the workingmen. They are as much the invention of modern time as machinery itself. In the signs that bewilder the middle class, the aristocracy, and the poor prophets of regression, we recognize our old friend Robin Goodfellow,* the old mole that can work in the earth so fast—the revolution.
>
> To take vengeance for the misdeeds of the ruling class there existed in the Middle Ages in Germany a secret tribunal called the *Vehmgericht.* If a red cross was seen marked on a house, people knew that its owner was doomed by the *Vehm.* All the houses of Europe are now marked by the mysterious red cross. History is the judge; its executioner, the proletariat.

Marx delivered this speech on April 14, 1856. With this appeal to lynch law, he was merely ringing the changes on a theme he had presented many times before: the theme of the coming terror. He hoped to make their flesh creep, and to remind them of their responsibility to destroy the

* Robin Goodfellow was the sprite who turned the milk sour and tumbled the village maids. He had nothing to do with subterranean affairs.

old order, but just as he was wrong in depicting Robin Goodfellow as the presiding spirit of the English revolution, so he was wrong in depicting the *Vehmgericht* as the instrument which punished the ruling classes in medieval Germany. In fact, the *Vehmgericht* was the secret tribunal of the medieval freebooters, who punished their private enemies and were especially concerned to mark the houses of wealthy Jews. Out of some confused memory of medieval history Marx constructed an image of the terror in its most bloodcurdling form, with all the romantic trappings. The Chartists printed the speech in *The People's Paper,* but their influence was already waning. Within a year they had become an almost forgotten force in English social history.

But for Marx the story of the *Vehmgericht* may have had a much deeper personal significance. The house in Dean Street seemed to have been marked by a red cross. His enemies were not the hooded swashbucklers who murdered with their three-pronged daggers, but the more commonplace enemies of poverty, disease, insecurity and misery.

By the summer he was ill again, and living alone in the house with only Helene Demuth to wait on him, for Jenny was in Trier with his daughters, sitting at the bedside of the old Baroness von Westphalen. For some time the baroness had been paralyzed in the right arm, and Jenny, who loved her mother deeply, felt that it was among the greatest of her afflictions that she no longer received her mother's letters. The baroness was eighty-two years old, and visibly sinking. She died on July 23, and Jenny remained in Trier with her brother Edgar to superintend the division of the effects. She would receive a small legacy, which pleased her. But the shock of watching her mother die was too much for her, and many months passed before she recovered her nervous stability.

During her absence Marx had been working on the text of one of his most extraordinary writings. It was nothing less than an examination of Russia's historical role in the light of some documents he had discovered in the British Museum. He had discovered the documents in 1853 and pondered them at great length to curious effect, for he had come to the conclusion that Great Britain, far from being the enemy of Russia, was her friend and secret supporter through the centuries, and Lord Palmerston, who claimed to be the enemy of Russia, had sold himself to the Russian Crown. This theory had been advanced by David Urquhart, a rich and adventurous Scot, who became pro-Turk after prolonged residence in Turkey, but Marx claimed to have arrived at the same conclusion independently.

The articles written by Marx and collected under the title *Secret Diplo-*

matic History of the Eighteenth Century showed, or pretended to show, that ever since the time of Peter the Great the British and Russian cabinets had been in secret collusion. There was, of course, considerable evidence to the contrary; the Crimean War scarcely supported the untenable thesis. In his effort to come to grips with the problem Marx wrote a long article on the nature of Russian power, examining the unchanging Russian policy from the time of Rurik to the present day. The article was written in Marx's strange and curiously contrived English, which always reads like a translation from German. It was written with power and brilliance, and since his conclusions were not likely to please the Russians, it has not been reprinted in his collected works.

Marx's thesis was that the Tatar invasions, which lasted for two hundred years, reduced the Russians to slavery, and when the Tatars were overthrown they accepted slavery under the Tsars, who themselves possessed the mentality of slaves. Slavery was a Russian disease. Ivan the Terrible was not the august and terrifying personage depicted in the history books but a man who hid behind his own fears and "succeeded in hiding under a mask of proud susceptibility and irritable haughtiness the obtrusiveness of the Mongol serf." In Marx's eyes Ivan the Terrible was a craven theatrical figure, possessing only those virtues which are granted to slaves. He was a cunning mass-murderer, a deceitful ally, an obtuse politician. Peter the Great was little better, for he merely brought Ivan the Terrible up to date. Here is Marx's summing-up of Russian policy since the time of Peter the Great:

> Peter the Great is indeed the inventor of modern Russian policy, but he became so only by divesting the old Muscovite method of encroachment of its merely local character and its accidental admixtures, by distilling it into an abstract formula, by generalizing its purpose, and exalting its object from the overthrow of certain given limits of power to the aspiration of unlimited power. He metamorphosed Muscovy into modern Russia by the generalization of its system, not by the mere addition of some provinces.
>
> To resume. It is in the terrible and abject school of Mongolian slavery that Muscovy was nursed and grew up. It gathered strength only by becoming a *virtuoso* in the craft of serfdom. Even when emancipated, Muscovy continued to perform its traditional part of the slave as master. At length Peter the Great coupled the political craft of the Mongol slave with the proud aspiration of the Mongol master, to whom Genghis Khan had, by will, bequeathed his conquest of the earth.

These words were printed in *The Free Press*, an obscure news weekly published by David Urquhart in Sheffield and London. Marx's study of Russian policy appeared in the news weekly at intervals. Eleanor Marx later collected the articles and they were published under the title of *Secret Diplomatic History of the Eighteenth Century.* For some reason she deliberately excluded the passage quoted above with its orchestrated denunciation of Russian policy.

Marx had read widely about Russia in the British Museum, and very little that he read gave him any satisfaction. He regarded Russia with intense fear and loathing. It was a phantom power, swelling like a gas, poisonous and deadly because it seemed to have no limits. A passage at the beginning of his short history of Russia breathes a peculiarly modern disenchantment:

> The overwhelming influence of Russia has taken Europe at different epochs by surprise, startled the peoples of the West, and been submitted to as a fatality, or resisted only by convulsions. But alongside the fascination exercised by Russia, there runs an ever-reviving skepticism, dogging her like a shadow, growing with her growth, mingling shrill notes of irony with the cries of agonizing peoples, and mocking her very grandeur as a histrionic attitude taken up to dazzle and to cheat. Other empires have met with similar doubts in their infancy; Russia has become a colossus without outliving them. She affords the only instance in history of an immense empire, the very existence of whose power, even after world-wide achievements, has never ceased to be treated like a matter of faith rather than like a matter of fact.

Such statements were to be found in Marx's articles to the *New York Daily Tribune,* and were by no means unusual. What he feared above all was that Russia would spill over her frontiers and infuse Kalmuck blood into Europe. There was, he believed, only one way to deal with Russia—to oppose her fearlessly.

The *Secret Diplomatic History* had three printings in the nineteenth century. It was published in installments in Urquhart's *Free Press* of Sheffield between June and August 1856 and then again in the *Free Press* of London between August 1856 and April 1857. More than forty years later came Eleanor Marx's bowdlerized version. The Bolshevik historian David Ryazanov rediscovered it in 1908, and then it was forgotten again.

These same ideas were being included in articles to the *New York Daily Tribune.* In some fourteen or fifteen articles Marx dissected the Pan-Slavism of his day, only to learn later that the articles never appeared in print. A Pole, Count Adam Gurowski, once condemned to death by the Russians, had caught the ear of the New York editors and strongly objected to their publication.

Such disappointments were the commonplaces of Marx's life, but now at last there came a brief moment of intense satisfaction. In October, with the help of some money advanced from the estate of the Baroness von Westphalen, the family was able to leave Dean Street. The legacy amounted to "a few hundred thalers," large enough to permit them to pay their debts and remove their linens from the pawnbroker. The new house was near Hampstead Heath, which was particularly cherished by the Marx family. For two weeks, from morning to night, Marx had wandered in the neighborhood of Haverstock Hill in search of such a house, and the one he found at 9 Grafton Terrace, Maitland Park, Hampstead Road, fulfilled all his expectations. Instead of the two small ugly rooms on Dean Street he now had seven rooms. There was a large living room, a kitchen, three bedrooms, a basement, and servants' quarters. Seven steps led up to the front door, and there were stone decorations around the windows. It was such a house as a minor civil servant might own. The rent was £36. They were able to furnish it from top to bottom for £40, finding most of their furniture in junk shops. Nevertheless for Jenny the house and all its furnishings possessed a princely beauty.

She loved the house passionately and spoke of it with awe, as something she had never hoped to possess. The children could wander over Hampstead Heath; they were high above London, far from the noisy traffic of the streets. But Jenny had not recovered from her mother's death, and the solitude frightened her. In one of the most moving passages in her memoirs she recounts the dreadful isolation of her life in that first winter in Hampstead:

> We spent that winter in great seclusion. Nearly all our friends had left London; the few who remained lived far away; and besides it was not easy to reach our small neat house, which in spite of its diminutive size seemed to be a kind of palace compared with the places where we had lived before. There was no smooth road leading to it, a good deal of building was going up, we had to pick our way over accumulations of rubbish, and when it was raining the red clay clung to the soles of our boots, so that it became a tiresome struggle to lift our hundredweight boots into the house. And when the darkness fell over this barbaric district, rather than spending the evening in a struggle with the dark, the rubbish, the clay and the heaps of stones, we preferred to gather round the warm fireside. All that winter I was very ill, always surrounded by a whole battery of medicines. It was a long time before I became accustomed to the complete solitude. I often missed my long walks in the crowded West End streets after my meetings, our clubs, and the familiar public house with the cosy conversations, which had so often helped me to forget for a while my worries.

To her surprise she felt uprooted and insecure now that she possessed a house of her own, and she was grateful that Marx was still writing his articles for the *New York Daily Tribune* because it was her task to copy them out in her clear handwriting, and in this way she felt she was in touch with the world.

Their entire income apart from the gifts of money which came from Engels derived from New York and the occasional articles which Marx was able to place in German and English papers. Soon they had exhausted the legacy received from Jenny's mother. The *New York Daily Tribune* was not publishing all the articles he sent them, and they were not paying for the ones they did not publish. By January he was complaining to Engels that he had no money, he was utterly and profoundly miserable, the family quarrels were starting up again, and he was in a more desperate situation than he had been at any time during the past five years. He wrote on January 23, 1857:

> It is truly disgusting when one is condemned to regard it as a favor when such a piece of blotting paper takes you on board. To pound and grind up bones and make a soup out of them, as paupers do in the workhouse, this is the sum total of the political work to which one is generously condemned in such an undertaking. Although I am only an ass, I am conscious of having given these rascals, I will not say recently, but in former years, too much for their money.

In the past the *New York Daily Tribune* had been his sheet anchor. Now the editors rejected his articles so cavalierly that he demanded explanations, and it was arranged that henceforth they would pay him for only one article a week. He was enraged when he recognized on a returned manuscript the hand of the censor, Count Adam Gurowski.

At this time Dana was bringing out the *New American Cyclopaedia*, and it occurred to him that Marx might contribute some articles on great military leaders. Marx was dubious about his ability to write about men whose craft he little understood and half despised. With immense difficulty, he forced himself to write articles on General Jozef Bem, the Polish patriot who fought against the imperial Austrian armies in 1848, on Bolívar, and on four of Napoleon's generals—Bessières, Brune, Bernadotte and Bugeaud. These six articles were his only contributions to the *New American Cyclopaedia.*

Meanwhile he worked on his long-projected *Critique of Political Economy,* which went on so slowly that he despaired of ever finishing it. As he contemplated the mounting pages of his manuscript, a feeling of helpless dissatisfaction swept over him. It was a feeling he knew well, for nearly all his books were written with prolonged labor pangs, and the endless delays drove him nearly out of his mind. These delays were of his own making. He lacked the power to concentrate fully. He would plead poverty, misery, headaches, boils, his old liver complaint, but he knew only too well that these were no more than excuses. The truth was that fear had a place in the workings of his mind—fear of his own capacities, fear that the book would not be the masterpiece he had hoped for, fear that it would be forgotten the moment it was published. On this book he proposed to stake his reputation.

As he worked, he was buoyed up by the hope of a crash which would destroy all the governments of western Europe. He had indeed been prophesying crashes for many years. Long ago, in 1844, he had predicted revolution following the uprising of weavers in Silesia. In 1848 he had surrendered to some weeks of joyful expectation as revolutions broke out in many of the capitals of Europe, only to collapse before the forces of the reaction. In the first number of the *Neue Rheinische Revue* he predicted a European revolution "by August 1850 at the latest." Afterward he saw it coming in 1851, in 1853, and again in 1854 at the time of the Crimean War. These prognostications were shared by Engels, who wrote in 1855 that a general trade crisis would bring about the total ruin of European industry, glut the markets, and reduce the bourgeoisie to the level of the proletariat. In the following year he repeated the same dire prophecies with even greater urgency. There would be a crash of phenomenal proportions such as the world had never known before; and Marx was of the opinion that his role as a spectator would soon come to an end. "The mobilization of our persons is at hand," he wrote, meaning that at any moment he expected to direct the fortunes of the European revolution, with Engels as commander in chief of the revolutionary forces and himself as dictator.

The first great crisis in the capitalist world did in fact shake the European governments, but not in the manner that Marx and Engels had predicted. In the autumn of 1857 there was an economic crisis of quite extraordinary proportions, beginning in America and extending to England, France and Germany. Engels, observing the strange aberrations of the Manchester stock exchange, prices plunging down, bankruptcies taking place every other minute, confessed to a sense of wonderful wellbeing at the prospect of disaster. He wrote to Marx on November 15, 1857:

> Physically the crisis has done me as much good as a swim in the sea. In 1848 we said: Now our time is coming, and in a certain sense it came, but this time it is really coming, now it will be a fight for life. This at once makes my military studies more practical, and I will immediately throw myself into the existing organization and elementary tactics of the Prussian, Austrian, Bavarian and French armies, and beyond this nothing but riding, i.e. fox hunting, which is the real school.

Engels preparing himself for revolutionary war by fox hunting was no more surprising than Marx suddenly working himself to the bone in order to complete his book before Europe erupted in flames. He wrote at the beginning of December: "I am working like mad all through the night to put my economic studies together so that I may at least have the outlines clear before the deluge comes." In a fever of physical contentment Engels continued to go fox hunting, strengthening his body for the perils ahead. He wrote on the last day of the year:

> Last Saturday I went fox hunting, 7 hours in the saddle. This kind of thing makes me hellishly excited for a few days, it is the greatest physical pleasure imaginable. In the whole field I only saw 2 who rode better than I, but they had better mounts. This brings my health really to a peak. At least 20 fellows fell from their horses or were thrown, 2 horses were ruined, 1 fox was killed—I was in at the kill.

But Engels' hopes to be in at the kill of Western civilization were to be sadly disappointed. The crisis was a spectacular one, but it was not mortal. The markets recovered, and Marx's repeated fears that he would be unable to finish his book before the revolution caught up with him proved to be illusory. The great crash had not come; in the following years he would prophesy again and again that it was about to come, and would inevitably take place in a week or in a few months. Prophecy had become a habit. What he wanted to happen became the subject of a prophecy, whether it was rational or not.

These oracular utterances were always made with fervor, and then quietly forgotten. A quite fantastic number of these prophecies appear in his letters, and the only explanation would seem to be that he did not expect them to be fulfilled, did not keep a close record of them, and had grown accustomed to failure. His prophecies were an indulgence and a recreation, like chess. Banks would crash, armies would march across Europe, emperors would fall, there would be barricades in the streets and the red flag would fly from the government offices; at all costs there must be the glimpse of disasters on the horizon.

It was a hard winter, for he was alternately buoyed up by wild hopes and cast down by deep depressions. Among his many burdens was the discovery that his mathematical calculations in the *Critique of Political Economy* were hopelessly inaccurate; it became necessary to learn mathematics all over again. He decided to embark on a course of algebra. One of the immediate results was the discovery that the hitherto accepted doctrine of profit was based on inadequate mathematical foundations, and he was soon writing to Engels: "I have overthrown the entire doctrine of profit as it has existed up to this time." A few days later he decided that he must overthrow Hegel. Freiligrath, having found some volumes of Hegel which had once belonged to Bakunin, sent them to Marx as a present. He read them, and decided that the time had come for a new critique of Hegel. The mood quickly passed, and soon he was once more at work on his great book on political economy, working all night with a jug of lemonade at his side and his cigars always within reach. He complained that the nights were cold, for he did not have enough money to buy coal. Once more misery had settled on the family—the misery of unpaid bills, and no hope of ever rising above a meager level of subsistence, and even the level of subsistence was almost beyond hoping for. He wrote to Engels:

> If this condition goes on, then I would prefer to lie 100 fathoms below the earth rather than vegetate in this way. To be always dependent on others, and to be always tormented by these little filthy worries, this cannot be endured for long. Personally, I can always break through my misery by means of work and by a rigorous attention to general concepts. My wife, of course, lacks these resources.

So, indeed, she did, for she had not yet recovered from the birth of a stillborn baby the previous July and was a prey to profound and intolerable anxieties. She was fighting on behalf of her children, attempting to see that they obtained a proper education, grew up in good health, and behaved like gentlewomen. Jenny, her eldest daughter, was fifteen, and already behaved like a mature and responsible young woman, with her dark round cheeks, dark shining eyes, and dark hair. Sometimes she seemed almost too mature for her age, unlike Laura, who was thirteen, but looked younger, because she was fairer, lighter, and altogether delicate. She had wavy chestnut-colored hair which fell down her back in cascades. Jenny was especially good at drawing and had a drawing master who delighted in her work; Laura, who could not draw well, was removed from his class. As for Eleanor, the youngest, she was the joy of the family, and her mother sometimes wondered whether there was anywhere on earth a more lovable, pretty, simple and good-humored child. Her passion was telling stories and listening to them. They read to her all the fairy tales of the Brothers Grimm, and then read them over again, and woe betide anyone who left out a sentence, for she had a remarkable memory. In this way she came to know the legends of the Noisy Goblin, King Brosselbart and Snow White and the Seven Dwarfs. To the end of her life her imagination was to be filled with the horrors and delights of Gothic fairy tales.

When the spring came, life at Grafton Terrace became more endurable. There was no longer the feeling of living in some remote backwater, far from the bustle of central London. They walked on Hampstead Heath with Liebknecht, who had a passion for discovering the first spring flowers. Near a small tree-shaded lake he would point out the first wild forget-me-nots, and in the corner of a dark velvety-green meadow he would show them bewildering clusters of hyacinths—they bewildered him because he thought wild hyacinths grew only on the shores of Lake Leman in Switzerland and in the Mediterranean countries.

There were pleasures to be found even closer than Hampstead Heath. There were gardens, meadows and wastelands near the house, and sometimes an observer might see a short heavily bearded man marching across them, singing lustily and carrying on his shoulders a small thin-legged girl whose thick hair was crowned with blossoms. In the evening he would return to his study, the green lampshade, the sheets of paper piling up, the heaps of letters which remained unanswered because there was no time, dreaming of revolutions and catastrophes and sometimes pausing to reflect on his own misery and poverty with anguish in his heart.

THE DEMONS

There were times when Marx seemed to be possessed by demons, when rage overflowed in him and became poison, and he seemed to enter into a nightmare. From the days of his youth he rejoiced in the barren landscape of romanticism, the ghostly apparitions rising for a moment on the blasted heaths only to vanish under the magician's spell; and sometimes he was the magician, and more often he was the apparition. In his early poems and in the unfinished drama *Oulanem* he had displayed his rage for destruction and his essential nihilism: there was no cause worth fighting for, no heaven worth seeking. *Und wir, wir Affen eines kalten Gottes* ("And we—we are the apes of a cold God"). So Oulanem long before had spoken in the silence of his study, and sometimes the same words seem to burn through the interminable pages of Marx's works on economic theory. He was a man who wore his despair close to his skin.

That rage which was so natural to him appears to have had its roots in his early childhood: the mother who was remote and strange, the long illnesses of his brother and sisters, the loneliness of the large house, the sense of alienation as a Jew in a predominantly German town. There was rarely a moment when he felt at ease in the world, unless it was when he was in Jenny's arms. His daughter Eleanor wrote that he was profoundly disturbed by the death of his younger brother Eduard, and still more disturbed by the death of his father, whose photograph he cherished and carried with him wherever he traveled. At an impressionable age he felt the intolerable weight of grief. With his father's death he suddenly found himself without a family, for his mother meant nothing to him. When he thought of her at all, it was always cold-bloodedly; she was the woman who prevented him from reaching his full flowering because she controlled the family fortune and refused to part with it. The sullen, smoldering rage against his mother, as it appears in his letters, is not pretty to contemplate.

That Marx should have spent so much of his life in a helpless rage against the world is less surprising than the fact that he seemed unaware that he was driven by it, and made no effort to moderate it. In letter after letter he roars his disgust at the world and at people, with unbridled malevolence, drawing on the resources of gutter language in order to emphasize his passionate rejection. Friends of many years suddenly become enemies of the moment, and he exhausts the vocabulary of vituperation in denouncing them. Frustration, no doubt, played a large role in those interminable diatribes: the frustration of a man who felt himself under a great compulsion to govern and command, and found too few people willing to obey him. Sexual frustration also played a part, for we have his wife's testimony that at least on one occasion she left his house because she was mortally afraid of bearing any more children, and in her *Short Sketch of an Eventful Life* she carefully records the occasions when she went off to an English seaside resort without him. At such times she was free of his oppressive presence. For years they were at daggers drawn, and Marx speaks of her coldness and her sharp tongue quite openly in his letters to Engels. It was not a happy marriage; nor was it unhappy; there was always the memory of their early years to sustain them.

As Marx grew up, the characteristics which were noted in him in his childhood and youth were reinforced. There was a cruel streak in him. He enjoyed acting the tyrant over his sisters, and he used to take them up the Marcusberg at Trier, tie ropes round their arms, and pretend they were horses and himself the driver. He also enjoyed making "cakes" out of dirty dough, kneading them with his dirty fingers and making his sisters eat them. Eleanor, who heard these stories from her aunts, never doubted their truth, saying that Marx's sisters obeyed him because they felt sufficiently rewarded by the stories he told them.

Marx seems never to have recognized the source of his frustrations and rages. They went too deep; they were too intimately woven into the fabric of his being; and he was powerless before them. Some clue, however, is provided by an interminable story he liked to tell his children during their Sunday walks to Hampstead Heath. It concerned an imaginary character called Hans Röckle, who kept an enchanted toyshop, and was always in debt. The shop was full of the most wonderful things: men and women made out of wood, dwarfs and giants, kings and queens, masters and journeymen, four-footed beasts and birds as numerous as those which entered Noah's Ark, tables and chairs, carriages and boxes of every shape and kind. Hans Röckle was a magician, but his powers were limited, for with the best will in the world he was unable to meet his obligations to the devil. He was always having to sell off his toys. He sold them piece by piece with a fierce reluctance, holding onto them to the last moment. But he had made his pact with the devil, and there was no escaping from it. Some of the stories he told about Hans Röckle were wryly humorous, but others made the children's hair stand on end. Eleanor, who remembered the stories and regretted that they were never written down, says that sometimes they were as terrible as any of the stories of E. T. A. Hoffmann.

There can be very little doubt that those interminable stories were autobiographical, and that Hans Röckle, who bought and sold wooden men and was always in danger of losing them to the devil, was Karl Marx presiding over the fortunes of economic man. The pact with the devil was the central theme of *Oulanem* and appears in various disguises in many of his early poems. It was a subject on which Marx had brooded frequently, not only in his youth. Goethe's *Faust* was his bible, the one book which he regarded with unreserved admiration, and he liked to roar out the verses of Mephistopheles, just as he liked to sign himself "Old Nick." He had the devil's view of the world, and the devil's malignity. Sometimes he seemed to know that he was accomplishing works of evil.

If we isolate the images he employs in his works, the images which constantly recur and which he uses with ferocious effect, we find that they are nearly always concerned with mutilation or death, torture, ruptured wombs, the executioner advancing out of the darkness with leisurely tread. His mind moved at ease among images of corruption and damnation, of sudden sprawling deaths and agonies. He had no visual imagination, and therefore he was compelled to describe his nightmares in general terms. He attacked his enemies with searing force, in gutter language and with strange sexual symbols which arose out of the depths of his being. But strangely he was always most inclined to attack people who offered to help him—he heaped curses on Lassalle, who found him a publisher for the *Critique of Political Economy* and offered his assistance in various other ways—or people who were scarcely worthy of his venom. His most ferocious polemic was directed against an obscure professor at the University of Berne.

Karl Vogt, who was to receive the full weight of Marx's vituperation, sought no quarrel with Marx. He was quietly teaching in Switzerland when an obscure German refugee newspaper in London accused him of being a paid agent of Napoleon III. The matter might have been forgotten if Liebknecht had not sent the accusation to the *Allgemeine Zeitung*, which was published in Augsburg. Liebknecht was the London representative of the German newspaper. The *Allgemeine Zeitung* published the story. Vogt was incensed, sued the newspaper for libel, and although the case was dismissed, he was able to claim a technical victory. He suspected, quite wrongly, that Marx was behind the attack. In fact Marx found little pleasure in the affair which dragged on for many weeks, and he was relieved when it was over.

Matters might have rested in the peace of exhaustion, but late in 1859 the bitterness flared up again. A small book appeared in Geneva bearing the title *Mein Prozess gegen die Allgemeine Zeitung*. It was Vogt's account of his lawsuit against the *Allgemeine Zeitung* with a stenographic record of the court proceedings and whatever explanatory and contributory documents the author could lay his hands on. Vogt was a scientist, and he took care that the documents should be quoted with exemplary accuracy. Occasionally he would give initials rather than full names, but he was careful not to tamper with anything else. Here, finally, was the full evidence for Marx's treachery and duplicity as revealed in precise and objective testimony. There were no appeals to the gallery, only the documents. Vogt's presentation was masterly, and no one reading the book casually could imagine that it would be possible to rebut the evidence.

When Marx with great difficulty succeeded in obtaining a copy of the book, for Vogt despised him too much to send him a copy, he was outraged beyond measure. Never before had a book excited him to such a state of overwhelming horror. He had received some preliminary warnings. A German refugee called Julius Faucher, an avid reader of polemical books, went out of his way to inform Marx that Vogt had treated him with an exquisite contempt, as though he were the scum of the earth. The book claimed, among other things, that Marx lived in luxury at the expense of the working class. In describing all this to Engels, Marx added that on no account must Jenny learn the bad news.

Marx was exasperated because he could not put his hands on a copy of the book. None of the German bookstores in London were selling it, and no one except Faucher seemed to have read it. Marx kept asking his friends, his former friends, and even his enemies to lend him the book, but they all disclaimed any knowledge of it. He even approached the poet Ferdinand Freiligrath, whom he had once admired, regarding him as the greatest of German poets, though he was now deprived of any vestiges of his former glory. They met briefly, and Marx amused himself later by describing their melancholy dialogue:

MARX
(*with great solemnity*)
I have come to ask you whether you could lend me a copy of the pamphlet about the lawsuit against the Allgemeine Zeitung. I have looked for it everywhere in all the bookshops. Your friend Vogt must surely have sent you a copy.

FREILIGRATH
(*in the most melodramatic tone*)
Vogt is not my friend!

MARX
Then you don't have a copy of the pamphlet?

FREILIGRATH
No!

MARX
Good evening!

Then they parted with a "Westphalian handshake."

For Marx they were days of dreary expectation, as he prepared himself for the worst. There was no comfort in fighting an invisible enemy. He wanted desperately to grapple with this strange book, which seemed to have no physical existence, being no more than a pillar of cloud suspended over his head. Two long leading articles, based on the book, appeared in the Berlin liberal newspaper *National Zeitung*, but they were too diffuse to give him an idea about the more devastating aspects of the book. "From what I hear, Vogt is obviously trying to make me into a wretchedly insignificant bourgeois clod," Marx complained to Engels. He insisted that there must be a *grand coup*, a tremendous barrage of arguments, another trial. At the very least it would be necessary to sue the *National Zeitung* for defamation of character. It would not be expensive; Germany was filled with lawyers who would be only too willing to appear on his behalf; there was not the least doubt that the trial of the newspaper would cause a great sensation; nor was there any doubt that the suit would be won, for he had found in the second of the two leaders so many clear-cut instances of defamation of character that the defense would necessarily "go *kaputt.*" It was Marx at his very worst, the enraged legalist searching among all the letters of the law for the one which was most suitable and consoling. He raged intolerably, sent off letters to seven German newspapers announcing that he was about to sue, engaged a Berlin lawyer, and prepared for the forthcoming trial by assembling all the documents which could be of service to him. When the London *Daily Telegraph* finally reported that there had been two editorials in the *National Zeitung* with some uncomplimentary references to Marx, he sent them a threatening letter, demanded a retraction and threatened to sue them if they refused. He was pursuing the *National Zeitung* so hotly that he had almost forgotten Vogt. When the book finally reached his hands in the middle of February, he was too exhausted to pay much attention to it. "It is nothing but shit and fooling around," he wrote, adding that all the offensive passages had been published by the *National Zeitung,* which therefore laid itself open to juridical attack.

Vogt's book was not just "fooling around." On the contrary it was a carefully thought-out polemic in the guise of selected documents. It represented Marx as a contemptible revolutionary vagabond, domineering and unprincipled, a blackmailer, a thief, a philosophical mountebank with a penchant for the aristocracy, a Karl Moor who ranted ungovernably about the destruction of all the existing forms of government. There was a sediment of truth in these accusations, and Marx's anger was aroused by these desolate truths as much as by the manner in which they were expressed. Vogt had hurt him to the quick and he would not be satisfied until he had exacted retribution.

Among the documents in Vogt's book was a letter written by Lieutenant Gustav Techow, who had been Willich's second at the time of the duel with Konrad Schramm. In 1848, he had been one of the commanders of the Berlin arsenal, and when it was stormed by the people, he surrendered it to them. For this he was sentenced to fifteen years' imprisonment in a fortress at Magdeburg. He escaped, made his way south, and became one of the leaders of the Baden uprising. With the survivors he slipped over the Swiss frontier and soon reached London where for a brief while he was on familiar terms with Marx who wanted him to be one of the commanders of the new revolutionary army. It appeared that Willich had already been chosen as the general in command of the revolutionary forces, and Marx, who had some qualms about Willich's loyalty to himself, was seeking another general who would act as a counterweight. Techow was accordingly asked by Marx whether he would agree to become a member of the Central Revolutionary Committee. He hesitated, and promised to give a final answer in a few days. The conversation took place on August 21, 1850, and a few days later Techow wrote a long account of the meeting to a friend in Switzerland.

Techow's portrait of Marx was reproduced in Vogt's book. It was brilliant, damaging and only too credible. He wrote:

> First we drank port, then claret which is red Bordeaux, then champagne. After the red wine Marx was completely drunk. That was exactly what I wanted, because he became much more openhearted than he probably would have been otherwise. I found out the truth about certain things which would otherwise have remained mere suppositions. In spite of his drunkenness Marx dominated the conversation up to the last moment.
>
> The impression he made on me was that of someone possessing a rare intellectual superiority, and he was evidently a man of outstanding personality. If his heart had matched his intellect, and if he had possessed as much love as hate, I would have gone through fire for him, even though at the end he expressed his complete and candid contempt for me, and had previously indicated his contempt in passing. He was the first and only one among us all to whom I would entrust leadership, for he was a man who never lost himself in small matters when dealing with great events.
>
> Yet it is a matter for regret in view of our aims that this man with his fine intellect is lacking in nobility of soul. *I am convinced that a most dangerous personal ambition has eaten away all the good in him.* He laughs at the fools who parrot his proletarian catechism, just as he laughs over the communists *à la* Willich and over the bourgeoisie. *The only people he respects are the aristocrats, the genuine ones, those who are well aware of their aristocracy.* In order to prevent them from governing, he needs his own source of strength, which he can find only in the proletariat. Accordingly he has tailored his system to them. In spite of all his assurances to the contrary, and perhaps because of them, I took away with me the impression that the acquisition of personal power was the aim of all his endeavors.
>
> E[ngels] and all his old associates, in spite of their very real gifts, are all far inferior to him, and if they should dare to forget it for a moment, he would put them in their place with a shameless impudence worthy of a Napoleon.

At various times many people had attempted to draw a portrait of Marx in words, but few succeeded so brilliantly as Techow, who wrote calmly, without animosity, and even with a kind of pity. Marx emerges as a revolutionary pontiff, capable of every subterfuge and every lie, determined to achieve power at whatever the cost. Techow had some admiration for him, remembering that he had once in Brussels poured his entire personal fortune into the revolution. What he could not forget was Marx's contempt for humanity and especially for that section of it which he called the proletariat. To hear Marx talking about "all that class shit" was to recognize the full measure of his cynicism.

All this and much more was contained in Vogt's book, which dwelt especially on the events of the year 1850 when Marx was desperately attempting to revive his revolutionary fortunes. Vogt spoke of the hundreds of blackmailing letters demanding specified sums of money which were sent out by Marx's revolutionary committee, and there is little doubt that letters of this kind were sent. Vogt portrayed Marx as "the directing intelligence" of a band of revolutionary ruffians, ignoble and unworthy of anyone's trust.

Although Lassalle protested, pointing out that a lawsuit against the *National Zeitung* would open Marx to further attack, he decided to press on with his lawsuit at all costs. He was in a mood for vengeance, and kept busily supplying his Berlin lawyer with documents proving his own innocence and Vogt's venality. When the case finally came up for trial, the Prussian court immediately threw out the lawyer's brief on the grounds that the *National Zeitung* had committed no crime in printing "mere quotations from other persons." The case was then taken to the court of appeals, and was again rejected, this time on the grounds that there was nothing in the least insulting in calling Marx "the leader of a gang of blackmailers," for it was no more than the truth. Not unnaturally Marx detected political motivation in the statement handed down by the court of appeals.

In a state of unrestrained fury Marx sat down to write his own bitter counterblast against Techow, Vogt, the *National Zeitung*, and everyone else who had incurred his displeasure. All his resources of vituperation, innuendo, sarcasm, and spite were poured into a long polemical work which fills three hundred closely printed pages of his complete works. From April to October 1860 he collected letters and affidavits from his friends in support of his contention that Vogt had acted with diabolical cunning. At intervals he would set these documents in order and write a withering commentary. He quoted extensively from Shakespeare, Virgil, Plautus, Schiller, Dante, Walther von der Vogelweide, Byron, and twenty more great authorities from the past in order to lay the intolerable ghosts. He devoted a whole chapter to Techow's famous letter and another chapter to the trial before the Prussian court. In 1849 the Frankfurt parliament had elected Vogt to be one of the five Reichsregents with full powers to rule over Germany, and accordingly there was a bitter chapter on his regency. Vogt had written a number of books and these were pilloried in a chapter called "Da-Da Vogt and his Studies." For reasons which had very little to do with his argument he launched into a brutal attack on the Hungarian revolutionary Lajos Kossuth. Some of his most bitter comments were reserved for Moses Joseph Levy, the editor of the *Daily Telegraph*, who had had the impudence to discuss the two long articles which appeared in the *National Zeitung*. Marx poured all the vials of his wrath on the offending editor. He found it intolerable that someone born Levi should change his name to Levy. In his heavy-handed way he pointed out that "not one of the twenty-two thousand people of the tribe of Levi who were counted by Moses on the journey through the desert were called Levy." But not only was his name offensive; everything about him stank to high heaven. Here is Marx describing the precise odor associated with the name of Levy:

> By means of a hidden and artificial sewer system all the lavatories of London spew their physical filth into the Thames. By means of the systematic pushing of goose quills the world capital spews out all its social filth into the great papered central sewer called the *Daily Telegraph*. Liebig was quite right when he severely criticized this senseless waste, which deprives the waters of the Thames of their purity and the English countryside of manure.
>
> Now Levy, the proprietor of that central sewer made of paper, is not only an expert in chemistry; he is infallibly an alchemist. Having transformed the social filth of London into newspaper articles, he transforms the articles into copper, and finally the copper is transformed into gold. Over the gates leading to this central sewer made of paper there can be read these words written *di colore oscuro: "hic . . . quisquam faxit oletum,"* or as Byron so poetically expressed it: "Wanderer, stop and — piss!"

Having begun a massive assault on Levy, Marx cannot let go. It is bad enough that he has changed his name from Levi to Levy, but it is even worse that he should be a Jew intent on appearing to belong to the Anglo-Saxon race and therefore regularly attacking the Jew Disraeli, who did not change his name to Disraely. Levy's newspaper columns, according to Marx, were filled with inaccurate accounts of sensational crimes, and more than once he had been brought to court for defaming innocent people. "Just as you can read on the walls of London the words *Commit no Nuisance*, so you can read over the gates of the English law courts: *Commit Levy*."

In his unrelenting determination to run Levy to the ground, Marx pursues him through Shakespeare ("Get thee to a nunnery, Levy") and *Tristram Shandy* ("I have been at the promontory of Noses; and have got me one of the goodliest and jolliest, thank Heaven, that ever fell to a single man's lot"). Levy's nose becomes the subject of a learned dissertation. It was not, Marx notes, something that could be concealed, for it was written in the most extravagant black-letter type in the middle of his face. Nor did it in any way resemble the nose in *Tristram Shandy,* which was a matter of discussion at the Strasbourg fair for more than a week; Levy's nose was a matter of discussion in the city of London all the year round. He continues in the same ferocious manner:

> There was a Greek epigrammatist who described the nose of a certain Castor, which served all kinds of purposes. It could be used as a shovel, a trumpet, a sickle or an anchor. The epigram concludes with the words:
>
> Thus Castor possessed a tool of many uses,
> Which could be manipulated for any kind of work.
>
> Nevertheless Castor would never guessed the uses to which Levy placed his nose. The English poet came closer to the truth when he said:
>
> And 'tis a miracle we may suppose,
> No nastiness offends his skillful nose.
>
> The great art of Levy's nose consists in the fact that it caresses foul odors, and that it can sniff them out over a hundred miles and attract them. Levy's nose serves the *Daily Telegraph* as an elephant's trunk, an antenna, a lighthouse, a telegraph. Without exaggeration one may say that Levy writes his newspaper with his nose.

Moses Joseph Levy was only a minor actor in the drama; Marx was using a steam hammer to kill a fly. By dealing exhaustively with Levy's nose, employing a machinery which was totally disproportionate to the theme, Marx demonstrated his inability to conduct a polemic with civilized grace. He writes with a sneer, employs excremental images wherever possible, and always loads the dice. The book is such an obviously unfair presentation of a case that his champions have carefully avoided translating the work into English.

The attack on Levy's nose seems to have arisen as a result of deep-seated forces over which he had no control. Sexual nightmares and frustrations, his aversion to Jews, his perpetual consciousness of his own Jewishness, his loneliness and physical weakness, his manic depressions, his urge to destroy everything he admired or envied—he had always imagined himself as the editor of a great newspaper—all these things appear to be involved in that unpleasant diatribe. And beyond and above all this there was the knowledge that he was descended from a long line of rabbis called Levi.

As the work progressed, Marx took pleasure in reading it aloud to Jenny and to his friends. Jenny called it "a fine piece of drollery," Liebknecht reveled in "this laughing humor," Engels thought it was his finest polemic, and even Lassalle wrote later that it was a work of art which had given him inestimable pleasure. Time has amended these verdicts. The jangling, sneering tone is heard throughout, and becomes finally unendurable.

As the time for the publication of the long, unwieldy manuscript came closer, Marx became increasingly preoccupied with the question of the proper title to be given to the work. *Karl Vogt* was not, he felt, a suitable title: his own name would appear below on the title page, and there was something faintly ridiculous in the appearance of the two Karls at war with one another, each with his short four-letter surname, in carefully balanced opposition. Accordingly the obvious title was dismissed, and Marx went in search of a title which would somehow suggest the stupidity and fallibility of his enemy. He considered *Ex-Reichs-Vogt,* until Engels pointed out that there was little to be gained by reminding the reader that Vogt was a former Reichsregent. Then he decided that *Da-da-Vogt* was a title which would amuse and delight the philistines. It had the proper air of mystery, and tripped easily on the tongue. To this suggestion Engels answered with a severe lesson on the technique of inventing titles. They should be simple, descriptive and accurate. Why invent a title which will only bemuse the reader? Why raise up obstacles between the author and his public? "You should choose a title which the public can understand without having read the work," he wrote sensibly, adding that there was something to be said for including Napoleon III somewhere on the title page. And when Marx insisted on *Da-da-Vogt* because it suggested the mockery and contempt which Vogt deserved, Engels pointed out that the reader scarcely needed to be confronted with mockery and contempt on the first page; he would find it soon enough in the book.

The question of the title obsessed Marx, and he continually returned to it. He was in a mood to strike hard, and wanted the title page to be a trumpet blast announcing the coming battle. So ferociously did he fight in defense of his title that Engels was compelled to seek the counsel of Wolff, who agreed with him that the most deplorable titles are those which can only be understood when the reader has read half the book. Marx was appalled. Should he put some nebulous, empty title on a book of fiery wrath and fearful denunciation? Since Engels had sought the counsel of Wolff, Marx sought the counsel of Jenny, reporting that his wife had come out openly on the side of *Da-da-Vogt,* saying it was a splendid title and it was impossible to think of a better. "She pointed out to me from the depths of her classical learning that there are Greek tragedies with titles which seem at first sight to have little connection with their subject matter." He seems to have known that he was defeated, for in the same paragraph he acknowledged that he had decided to follow Engels' latest suggestion—he would call it *Herr Vogt*.

While the curious war of the titles was continuing, Marx was engaged in a pleasant correspondence with Lassalle, who had promised to contribute heavily to the publication of the book. They were discovering larger and larger areas of agreement, and the tone of their letters was uniformly polite, affable and intelligent. Lassalle spoke highly of Marx's works, and Marx in turn congratulated Lassalle on the formative ideas he expressed in his letters. Among these ideas there was one which held a special place in Lassalle's mind, for it offered a solution to many of the problems which haunted him. It was nothing less than a holy war to be fought by the Germans against Russia. At some length he explained the logical advantages to be gained by a victorious war against an entrenched tyranny, and Marx found himself in happy agreement. Together with Engels he had made over many years a profound study of Russian diplomatic documents, and their study had led them to an inexorable conclusion—the absolute necessity of war against Russia. He wrote:

> Everywhere in Germany there is this hatred of Russia, and as far back as the first number of the *Neue Rheinische Zeitung* we proclaimed that the war against the Russians was the revolutionary mission of Germany. But hatred and understanding are two very different things.

Marx did not elaborate on the difference between hatred and understanding, and went on to discuss the publication of his own works in a mood of cautious appraisal. There was nothing particularly surprising in his verdict on Russia. For him Russia was the eternal enemy.

Meanwhile there were enemies nearer at hand, innumerable and infinitely perplexing, liable to spring up when least expected. Jenny had scarcely finished making the fair copy of *Herr Vogt* to be sent to the printer when she came down with what was at first thought to be typhoid fever. Marx offered to run for the doctor, but she refused, fearing the day when they would have to pay the doctor's bill. The doctor came two days later, decided that it was typhoid and counseled the utmost care, for he thought she was dangerously ill. Three days later he realized he had made the wrong diagnosis—she was suffering from smallpox.

The children were immediately sent off to stay with Liebknecht, while Helene Demuth and Marx cared for her as best they could. For Jenny the worst moment was when the children trooped out of the house, taking their few belongings with them. From time to time they would be made to stand in the street outside the window, so that she could feast her eyes on them from the open window upstairs. With the help of money from Engels, Marx was able to employ a nurse. He was inclined to believe that she must have caught the germ in a shop or in the horse omnibus, her nervous system weakened by the dreadful excitement which came from incessant poverty.

In a letter to a friend Jenny described vividly the agonies of those days:

> I got worse from hour to hour, pockmarks broke out fearfully. I was in great suffering. I had severe burning pains in my face and was completely unable to sleep. I was mortally anxious about Karl, who took the most tender care of me. In the end I lost all use of my outward senses although I was fully conscious all the time. I lay constantly by the open window so that the cold November air would blow over me, while there was a raging fire in the stove and ice on my burning lips. I could hardly swallow, my hearing was getting weaker, and finally my eyes closed, so that I did not know whether I would be enveloped in eternal night!
>
> My constitution, helped by the tenderest and truest care, took the upper hand, however, and so I am sitting here now in perfect health but with my face disfigured, covered with scars, and dark red—quite *à la hauteur de la mode couleur de Magenta.* The poor children were not allowed to come back to the family home until Christmas Eve—they had yearned for it so long. The girls were overwhelmed with emotion and could scarcely hold back their tears when they saw me. Five weeks before I had looked quite respectable beside my healthy-looking girls. Surprisingly I had no gray hair and my teeth and figure were good and therefore people used to include me in the ranks of well-preserved women—it is all a thing of the past now! I seem to myself to be more like a kind of rhinoceros which has escaped from a zoo than a member of the Caucasian race.

So Jenny wrote about her griefs with accuracy, humor and spirit, without rancor. She had always been proud of her aristocratic features and her delicate skin, but she knew now that she would remain disfigured to the end of her life. Her beauty had been ravished, her courage broken. Unlike Marx, who raged against the insults of fortune, she accepted them with grace.

While Jenny watched herself being transformed into "a kind of rhinoceros," Marx complained bitterly of his own ills. He suffered a recurrence of his old liver complaint, a tooth extraction left him with a swollen face and swollen throat, sleeplessness and misery had so weakened him that once more he began to think of suicide as the sole means of escape; and he thought broodingly about the dictum in Hegel's *Logic* that "pure thought and pure being and *nothingness* are all identical." He could not concentrate on his work, and he complained that Jenny, as she slowly recovered, demanded too much of his time.

Meanwhile *Herr Vogt* had at last been published on a small German press in London. The book had an ugly appearance, for to save money the long text amounting to 120,000 words was crowded into 192 pages. Printed at his own expense on borrowed money, the book had so small a circulation that it was without any notable influence on public opinion, and only his stanchest friends could bring themselves to read it. Marx had expected an uproar; instead there was indifference. And though he consoled himself with the thought that there was a deliberate plot to suppress the work, "the base, cowardly, mercenary press" having decided to ignore it out of existence, he was deeply wounded. He went to immense efforts to see that the book was properly distributed and that notices went out to forty German, Swiss and American newspapers and magazines, but his efforts were unavailing. *Herr Vogt,* on which he had expended more than six months of his life, sold forty-one copies in the first week of its existence.

Eleven years later Marx had his ironical revenge. Among the charges he had leveled at Vogt was the unsubstantiated accusation that he was a spy in the pay of Napoleon III. During the Paris Commune the archives of Napoleon's government were found in the Tuileries and a special revolutionary commission was appointed to examine the documents. Then it was discovered that in August 1859 Vogt had signed a receipt for 40,000 francs given to him out of the secret funds of the Emperor.

FERDINAND LASSALLE

THE FAILURE OF *Herr Vogt* was a source of great bitterness to Marx, who had hoped in some mysterious way that his polemic would bring him immediate fame. He had wielded a big stick, brought it firmly down on the dragon's head, split open its skull, and shown himself to be a redoubtable warrior. There had been a polite murmur of applause from his closest friends, and nothing more. Jenny would say that with a single blow he had refuted "the calumny which was being peddled *con amore* from town to town and village to village by the entire German press," but this was to misinterpret Marx's effectiveness. His "seven blows in one" proved to be completely innocuous and the German press refused to acknowledge that they had ever been delivered.

For consolation he turned to Darwin's *Origin of Species,* which was written, he thought, in crude English, although he found much to admire in it. "The book contains the basis in natural history for our view," he wrote approvingly to Engels. He was also reading the historian Appian's account of the Roman civil wars, taking some pleasure in the fact that he could read it in the original Greek. Appian spoke highly of the military prowess of the rebel leader Spartacus, and Marx therefore cast an approving eye on him. He was now reading novels and biographies, and every book he could lay his hands on. Reading was his drug.

But the reading of books, especially books which had nothing to do with money or revolution, could not go on indefinitely, and since he despaired of making any money from his books he decided to go to Holland to try to raise a loan from his Dutch uncle, Lion Philips, and then to go on to Germany to discuss the founding of a new review with Lassalle. He was also seriously thinking of settling down in Germany, for he saw no future for himself or his family in England, and the new King of Prussia on coming to the throne in January 1861 had proclaimed an amnesty. With money from Engels Marx set off at the end of February in pursuit of a fatherland and a source of income.

Lion Philips was the founder of the business concern which was eventually to become the worldwide Philips Electrical Company. He had married one of the sisters of Henrietta Pressborck, Marx's mother. He lived in a large house at Zalt Bommel, with a small estate; and though he lived well, he took no interest in living ostentatiously. He disapproved of Marx, though on occasion he could be cordial enough for the family's sake. Marx paid four visits to Zalt Bommel, and was usually greeted kindly. The story was told that on one occasion he so infuriated his host that it became necessary to summon the footman to boot him down the steps. Mr. August Philips, who is Lion Philips' great-grandson, is inclined to think the story is untrue bcause to his certain knowledge there was no footman in the house and there were no steps. But Marx may well have been an infuriating guest. There is a tradition in Zalt Bommel that he attracted attention to himself by going around in a silk shirt and red tie, and was genuinely disliked by the townsfolk.

He cannot have been disliked by Lion Philips, for he was a house guest for more than two weeks. When Marx raised the question of finances, he was able to borrow £160, this sum being an advance on his share of his mother's estate. The money would enable him to pay off outstanding debts. It also permitted him to pay for his extensive travels in Germany, for he visited Berlin, Elberfeld, Barmen, Cologne, and Trier, where he spent two days with his seventy-four-year-old mother and learned to his satisfaction that she had canceled his old debts. For some reason this did not endear her to him, for he continued to speak about her with contempt.

The highlight of Marx's stay in Germany was his visit with Lassalle in Berlin. Lassalle lived in a sumptuous apartment on the Bellevuestrasse, and this was placed at Marx's disposal. There was an expedition to Potsdam, they attended a debate at the Landtag, and in the company of Lassalle and the Countess von Hatzfeldt he spent an evening at the theater where he was amused to find himself close to the royal box. He did not enjoy his visit to the theater and complained that it was not possible to look at the ballet for three hours with any satisfaction. But he enjoyed the company of the countess, saying that she was politically far more advanced than Lassalle. She was a red-haired, middle-aged woman on whose behalf Lassalle had engaged in a divorce suit against her estranged husband. The lawsuit had lasted for such a long time, so many skeletons had emerged from so many cupboards, and so much heat and passion were involved that both Lassalle and the countess had become well known all over Germany.

In the apartment on the Bellevuestrasse, surrounded by the rare and beautiful objects which Lassalle had gathered during a journey to the Near East, Marx felt perfectly at home. The countess was wealthy, and Lassalle possessed a fine cellar and served exquisite meals. There was a constant stream of visitors. Marx held court, interrogating high officials and generals on the state of the country. He wrote to Engels that he found Berlin depressing and frivolous, but he wrote in terms which clearly indicated that he was enjoying himself; and he especially enjoyed the visits of people of title and power. One reason why he was concerned with meeting important dignitaries was his desire to resume his Prussian citizenship and to find men who could vouch for him. Accordingly, he wrote many letters to the authorities, urging that his citizenship should be restored. In these letters he would claim that he was a loyal servant of the King and the Church. "I was born on May 5, 1818, in Trier in the Prussian Rhineland, and I profess the evangelical religion . . ." In these formal terms he solicited the aid of the Prussian bureaucracy.

The police however were unrelenting; they saw no reason to grant Prussian citizenship to a convinced enemy of Prussia, and his application was firmly rejected. His plans to edit a newspaper or a review with Lassalle also ended in failure. Marx insisted that Engels and Wilhelm Wolff should also be editors, and Lassalle took fright. He asked that his vote should be considered the equivalent of the combined votes of Marx and his followers, and Marx took umbrage. Was Lassalle so proud that he considered himself the equal of three men?

Outwardly the relations between Marx and Lassalle were cordial. Their old antagonism vanished in the contemplation of the victories they hoped to accomplish together, and a strange euphoria settled on them. Always gallant, Lassalle wrote to Jenny, who was eating out her heart in London, saying that everything was going well, Marx was in the best of health, and he looked forward to the time when she would return to Germany. Jenny replied in one of those letters which are transparently clear and honest, reflecting the movements of her troubled soul, and although she was always inclined to be generous in her letters, she could not forget that Lassalle had failed to come to Marx's defense at the time of his bitter controversy with Karl Vogt. She wrote:

> I thank you from the bottom of my heart for your kind letter and for your friendship to my lord and master, which you have proved once more during his stay in Berlin.
>
> I have always thought of you as one of our oldest, truest and best of friends, and have never doubted the sincerity of your sympathy and kindness. Only once was I really angry with you, and that was when the loathsome campaign started against my husband. I counted on your impulsiveness, I thought you would descend upon that wretched rabble with fire and sword—the one living voice in a silent world. But you too were silent. Only later did I learn that you had no hand in that filthy campaign and only kept silent because you had no platform from which to speak. Now it is all over, and I must forget that little grievance and offer you my hand in friendship.
>
> You offer glowing prospects of my early return to the Fatherland! But the truth is that I have lost this "dear" Fatherland. I have searched in all the corners and hidden places of my heart without finding it. Also, I don't want to show myself to my old friends as I am now, for I have grown so ugly and so strange, but there is my pretty little daughter. . . . Don't keep the Moor too long. I would let you keep anything else, but not him. This is the one point where I become truly demanding, selfish and jealous; at this point my human feelings come to an end and they are replaced by naked egotism so strong that it cannot be uprooted.

Jenny's letters are nearly always like that: quietly urgent, sensible and free-flowing. Marx's letters were more contrived, for he wrote them with difficulty, even though he carefully noted down in advance what he wanted to say and then carefully assembled his ideas in the proper order. Afterward he would scratch out whole paragraphs impatiently, begin again, and revise the letter until he was satisfied. Finally he would make a clean copy with no erasures, written in a tight crabbed handwriting which was so difficult to read that even Engels, who received more letters than anyone else, sometimes found difficulty in deciphering them.

When Marx finally left Berlin he carried with him a small treasure chest of gifts from Lassalle. There was an expensive atlas for Engels, and dresses for Jenny and all her daughters. Jenny was overjoyed, immediately put on her dress, and paraded up and down the room, while Eleanor cried: "You're just a peacock!" What especially pleased Jenny was that these new clothes gave her distinction in the eyes of the neighbors and with luck might induce the local shopkeepers to extend her credit. "A dress like that impresses our philistine neighbors," she wrote to Lassalle, "and it gives us prestige and credit."

Marx, too, was filled with gratitude for the unexpected kindness of the man he had always distrusted and whose writings he despised. Lassalle had lent him money—some £40, and this in itself was an act of considerable friendship. In his letter of thanks Marx wrote that he was considering a much longer visit to Berlin if his naturalization papers came through, but London had a great attraction for him and he was not at all certain that he wanted to be uprooted. He concluded his letter: "And now, *mon cher,* I must close with the heartiest thanks for all your kindly friendship in taking me in and looking after me and bearing with all my tiresome ways. You know I had a head full of miseries as well as suffering from my liver. The great thing is that we found a lot to laugh at. *Simia non ridet.*" The Latin tag means "apes do not laugh," and Marx appears to have intended a kind of backhanded compliment. He was suggesting that nothing useful had been accomplished, but they had enjoyed themselves.

To Engels he had another story to tell, for he wrote to Manchester about the same time:

> Lassalle is so dazzled by the reception of his book *Heraklitos* and the attention of certain parasites who enjoy his dinners and wines that he does not realize his bad reputation in the world at large. Then there is his being always right, and his attachment to "speculative ideas" (the fellow is even dreaming of a new Hegelian philosophy raised to the second power, and he will write it himself). Also his infection with the old French liberalism, his itch to write about everything, his self-assertiveness, tactlessness, etc. Under strict discipline he might render service as one of the editors, but otherwise he would only be an embarrassment.

In this way Lassalle was summarily committed to limbo, a shadow of a shadow, to be consulted only in emergencies and even then to be held at arm's length. Not long afterward the Prussian authorities finally rejected Marx's application for naturalization on the grounds that "his convictions are republican, or at any rate not royalist." The dream of being editor in chief of a Berlin newspaper was therefore abandoned.

One by one the other dreams also perished. His long connection with the *New York Daily Tribune* was coming to an end, *Die Presse* of Vienna which had been buying his articles no longer showed much enthusiasm for them, and the debts were mounting until they threatened to drown him completely. At the end of the year he could write to Engels: "If the New Year is like the old, then it can go to the devil." Not long before he had reported to Engels that he owed £100 to the pawnbroker. This was a crippling debt, and there were many others.

The future had never appeared darker, the present more threatening. Early in 1862 his favorite daughter Jenny fell ill. She was old enough now to realize the full weight of their misery, and Marx recognized that her illness was more psychological than real. To his horror he learned that she had approached a dramatic coach in the hope of finding a job on the stage. "Take all in all, it is not worth while to lead the life of a louse," Marx wrote in despair; and he was only a little relieved when Engels sent him eight bottles of Bordeaux, four of Rhine wine, and two of sherry, to strengthen the blood of his ailing daughter. Now once again money became a problem over all other problems, and in the summer Marx claimed that for seven weeks not a penny had entered the house.

Frau Marx was in an agony of despair as she watched the collapse of their fortunes. "Every day my wife tells me she wishes she was lying in her grave with the children," Marx reported to Engels. "I cannot blame her, for it is impossible to describe the humiliations, sufferings and horrors which must be gone through in this situation." Nevertheless Marx was now working as well as he had ever worked, with astonishing powers of concentration. Many of the posthumous manuscripts edited by Engels were the fruit of this period. Notebook after notebook was filled; chapters were added to the manuscript which would eventually become *Das Kapital;* the work progressed so well that Marx, accustomed to plodding progress, was himself surprised, saying that "it is quite extraordinary how amid all these miseries my brainpan functions better than it has for years." Suddenly these intellectual labors were interrupted by the arrival of Lassalle, who came to stay at the house on Grafton Terrace as their guest.

Into their poverty Lassalle came like the breath of splendor and riches, the herald of the revolutionary spring. He stayed at their house for nearly three weeks, ate their food and drank their wine, talked interminably, and failed to observe that the entire Marx family was living on the edge of penury, having taken to the pawnbroker nearly everything that could not be nailed down.

Marx had been entertained royally by Lassalle the previous year, and he now attempted to return the honors. Although he could no longer look forward to being editor in chief of a Berlin newspaper with Lassalle as his willing assistant, he could still hope for many favors. Lassalle was at the height of his power and influence. There could be some working arrangement between them, an alliance, or at the very least a compromise. But as the days passed, it became only too evident that Lassalle regarded himself as the sole arbiter of the destinies of the German workingman. "He is now posing not only as the greatest scholar, the profoundest thinker, the most brilliant investigator, etc., but also as a Don Juan and a revolutionary Cardinal Richelieu. And in addition to all this there is his everlasting chatter, his unnatural falsetto voice, his unpleasant demonstrative gestures, and didactic tone." This was bad enough, but Lassalle had recently lost a large sum of money and was in no position to lend Marx more than a few pounds.

Jenny reacted to the spectacle of Lassalle with the same unreasoning hatred and scorn. In her memoirs she wrote about him with a savagery which is completely unexpected and curiously hysterical, as though she too envied his position in the German working-class movement, detesting him because he occupied the position which should rightfully have belonged to her husband. She wrote:

> In July 1862 Ferdinand Lassalle came to visit us. He was almost crushed by the weight of the fame he had achieved as scholar, thinker, poet and politician. The laurel wreath lay fresh upon his Olympian brow and ambrosian locks, or rather on his stiff, bristling Nigger's *chevelure*. He had just brought his Italian campaign to a triumphant end—a new political *coup* was being brought about by great men of action—and fierce battles were being fought in his soul. There were still many fields of knowledge he had left unexplored. He had made no advances in Egyptology. "Should I therefore astonish the world as an Egyptologist, or should I demonstrate my versatility through my actions as a politician, a warrior, or a soldier?" It was a terrible dilemma. He wavered between the ideas and sentiments of his heart, and often expressed this inner warfare in sardonic terms. With all his sails flying he swept through our rooms, orating and gesticulating so loudly, his voice rising to high C, that our neighbors became alarmed by the terrible uproar and asked what was happening. It was the inner struggle of the great man breaking out in shrill discords. The news of his father's serious illness made him leave London. He departed with Lothar Bucher, his poodle, the man who during the Exhibition of 1862 performed for him the duties of errand boy, messenger, informer and *maître de plaisir*. I must say that on a tour to Windsor and Virginia Waters, which we undertook together, he "comported" himself very well and showed himself completely worthy of the honorary title of "governor."

Lassalle hurried away when he discovered that we had little sympathy for the ideas of so great a man. In Switzerland he found people more receptive to him, and there amid the society of great men he received the warm admiration which his soul hungered for. In the society of spongers and sycophants he found a congenial atmosphere. He returned to Berlin and there, instead of demonstrating his prowess as an Egyptologist, or as a soldier, or as a politician, or as a poet, or as a thinker, he chose to follow a yet untrodden path—he became the Messiah of the workers.

Although Jenny is here writing with spleen and venom, and sometimes catching the authentic splenetic accents of her husband, she demonstrates a humor which Marx never possessed. She writes quickly, giving herself free rein, rising above the page, while Marx always digs into the page, the pen biting deep. Though she detested Lassalle, she could not paint him all black and she remembered that he had been kindly during an excursion to Windsor and Virginia Waters.

Soon after Lassalle left for Berlin, the entire family except Marx went off to the seaside. He remained alone in the house, working at *Das Kapital* and writing occasional articles. The American Civil War interested him deeply, and in his correspondence with Engels he would sometimes correct the younger man's simple notions about how war should be engaged. Engels sometimes wrote as though he thought the South should win, and Marx gently chided him for his simple faith. He wrote to Engels in September:

As for the Yankees, I am as certain as ever in my opinion that the North will win in the end, or perhaps the civil war will continue through many episodes, and there may be an armistice, and it may take a long time . . . The way the North is conducting the war is only what might have been expected from a *bourgeois* republic, where fraud has been enthroned king for so long. The South, an *oligarchy,* is better adapted to it, especially an oligarchy where the whole productive work falls on the niggers and the 4 million "white trash" are professional filibusters. All the same I would wager my head that these fellows will get the worst of it, in spite of "Stonewall Jackson." It is possible of course that before this happens there may come a sort of revolution in the North itself.

As usual, Marx was measuring America by the yardstick of Europe; the hoped-for revolution in the North did not take place; and there was no armistice. He was far from being an accurate purveyor of prophecies about the course of the war, but he was a more accurate judge than Engels.

Meanwhile he was so pleased with his progress with *Das Kapital* that he thought the end was already in sight, and at the end of the year, in a letter to Dr. Ludwig Kugelmann, he even announced that he had completed it. The doctor was a friend of Freiligrath, and he had written to Marx expressing his warm interest in the *Critique of Political Economy.* Marx replied with a long letter of appreciation. He informed his newfound friend that *Das Kapital* would have about 480 pages, and must be regarded merely as the successor of the earlier volume, developing certain ideas which had already appeared. He emphasized that it was not a work which could stand alone, but needed to be read in the context of the earlier work. With Dr. Kugelmann's letter there began the lengthy correspondence which was to continue for twelve years. Then quite suddenly, as the result of a few words spoken by the doctor as they were walking through a pine forest at Karlsbad, the friendship came to an end.

When Marx wrote that *Das Kapital* was already completed, he was merely giving way to a natural ebullience with regard to his work. The springs were flowing again. In spite of poverty, he was now writing at his best, in complete command of his medium. It was a year in which he wrote few articles and engaged in few polemics; he was free to concentrate on the most important contribution he had to make to revolutionary theory—*Das Kapital.*

Yet all through the year disasters had followed close on one another's heels. At the end of the year Jenny made a sudden dash to Paris in the hope of raising a loan from a rich banker, arriving a few hours after the banker had a paralytic stroke. Everything went wrong. She caught a bad cold, an omnibus she was riding in overturned, a hackney coach taking her to Grafton Terrace was struck by another, and when she reached her house, she learned that the second maidservant, Marianne Demuth, Helene's sister, who had come to join them when they first moved into the house on Grafton Terrace, had died of a heart attack only a few hours earlier. A strange fatality seemed to hover over the family. It was a fatality which could be measured in terms of money. "The funeral will take place at two o'clock on Sunday, and I must find £7 + ½ to pay the undertaker," Marx wrote on Christmas Eve to Engels.

MARX AND ENGELS

THE RELATIONSHIP BETWEEN Marx and Engels was a complex and enduring one. It was a marriage of opposites, and the course of true love did not always run smooth. They quarreled frequently, and were not always charitable to each other's errors. There were frequent storms, sudden cries of anguish, and prolonged sighs. Yet they remained close friends because they needed each other.

Engels was by nature cold and withdrawn, invariably polite, incapable of losing his temper, accustomed to wealth and deference, taking his pleasures where he found them. For twenty years of his life he lived the life of a respectable industrialist, finding his friends among the industrialists and stockbrokers of Manchester. He had fastidious manners, and a crisp military mind; he was perfectly aware of his intellectual superiority. When Marx was on leave of absence from the *Neue Rheinische Zeitung,* Engels had taken his place in the editorial chair, and at once provoked serious objections by his disturbing arrogance, and this arrogance led to incessant quarrels with people like Eccarius and Hermann Jung, whom he regarded as his intellectual inferiors. The Bolshevik scholar David Ryazanov describes Engels as "hopelessly dry and cold."

In Manchester he maintained two residences, one where he entertained his business friends, the other in which he installed his Irish mistress Mary Burns and her sister Elizabeth. He was accustomed to living *en grand seigneur,* and it amused him that he should be a successful businessman secretly engaged in revolutionary affairs. He wrote in a simple uncomplicated prose, with no feeling for the rhythm of words or the orchestration of sentences. Marx, on the other hand, was absorbed by the music of words, and he was not in the least amused by his own pretensions to revolutionary leadership. He detested immorality, and excused Engels' lapses only because he was in no position to offend his benefactor, and because he was sufficiently aware of his own singular lapses from conventional sexual behavior. Where Engels was cold and withdrawn, Marx was hot-headed and outgoing, seething with continual rages which were likely to explode in his writing or on the people around him. Marx was a volcano, Engels an iceberg. Between them there was little fundamental sympathy. They were yoked to each other by their common desire to bring about a world revolution, to establish its theoretical base and then to lead it to a successful conclusion, seeing themselves as the two chosen revolutionary dictators who held the destiny of the world in their hands.

These were dreams so dangerous that they were often in danger of stepping out of the normal world altogether. Madness was always lying in wait for them at the turning of the road.

That they survived was due very largely to the help they gave each other, for they were able to console each other in a variety of ways. The revolution which would shake the world and bring them to power was always about to happen; in letter after letter they would announce that their prognostications had proved correct, that capitalist society was about to founder, and that the inevitable revolution was about to take place. In thirty years they foresaw forty revolutions, none of which took place. They were not disheartened. They resumed their theoretical work and prepared themselves for the next revolution which would take place in six months' time.

But while they consoled each other, they saw with the unerring eyes of lovers each other's weaknesses and took advantage of them. They flattered one another, and it was a matter of accepted doctrine that they alone possessed the keys to the mystery; they were continually reminding each other of their happy discovery. Flattery became a game, which they played so frequently and incautiously that it lost its savor, so that heavier and heavier doses became necessary. In their letters they kept as strictly as possible to the subject of the revolution; their private lives were to be regarded as unworthy of discussion in comparison with the grandeur of the revolution. Marx liked to assail his real or imaginary enemies with epithets derived from his vast vocabulary of denunciation, and Engels, to humor him, would deliberately imitate him, using the same epithets which Marx had coined, but without conviction and without enjoyment. Engels despised the rough language of Marx and felt uncomfortable in the role of imitator.

Their greatest differences arose from their respective attitudes toward money. Marx had no understanding of money and no aptitude for earning it. He was a congenital spendthrift, a confirmed beggar, and an incompetent investor, whose occasional sallies in the stock exchange usually ended in disaster. Engels on the other hand possessed a broad understanding of the nature of money, and knew how to direct it into his own pockets. Marx was continually begging money from him. Day after day, week after week, there would come pressing demands for the ready cash which Marx needed in order to pay the rent, the groceries, the doctor's bills, and the children's clothes. Only those who have been constantly badgered for money know the strains which arise from these negotiations, and how demand feeds on demand, and how finally the giver feels so vulnerable that he is tempted to give away everything he possesses if only to put an end to those demands. Marx could not hide his envy of Engels' wealth. He was always urgent and uncompromising. He seemed to be holding a pistol to Engels' head and saying that the money must come, or else.

On one occasion Marx was so brusque in his demand for money at a time when Engels was overwhelmed with a private grief that their relationship almost came to an end.

On January 6, 1863, Engels' mistress Mary Burns died suddenly of a heart attack. Engels wrote a brief letter filled with the agony of grief to Marx, who replied by the next post:

> DEAR ENGELS,
>
> The news of Mary's death has surprised and dismayed me. She was very good-natured, amusing, and deeply attached to you.
>
> The devil knows that there is nothing but rotten luck in our circles. I simply don't know any more whether I am standing on my head or my feet. My attempts to raise money in France and Germany have failed, and it is only to be expected that the £15 will hold off the avalanche for no more than a week or two. Apart from the fact that no one will give us any more credit, except the butcher and baker, and they will only give us credit to the end of the week, I am being dunned for school expenses, for rent, and by the whole pack. The few to whom I have paid a little on account have pocketed the money slyly, and will fall upon me with redoubled vigor. And then, too, the children have neither clothes or shoes, for going out. In a word, there is hell to pay. . . .

There was a great deal more self-commiseration, as Marx described the desperate straits in which he found himself. Jenny had been screaming at him, and as he told Engels, the only weapon left to him was a stoic silence. It was a weapon which he was temperamentally incapable of using for long. He had no strength to go on. In two weeks, with all his possessions at the pawnbroker's and the debts unpaid, he would be faced with irretrievable ruin. "It is abominably egotistical of me to retail all these *horreurs* to you at such a moment," Marx continued. "But the remedy is homoeopathic—one disaster cancels another." He added in a postscript: "How will you arrange your household affairs? It must be extraordinarily hard for you, because Mary gave you a home, completely free and far from all the filth of humanity, as often as you wanted it."

It was a strangely ambiguous letter, but not an unfeeling one. When Marx's daughter Franziska had died, Engels noted the fact in passing, expressed his sorrow briefly, and passed on to more weighty affairs. Marx had not expected otherwise; death was a familiar presence; he did not want to be reminded of its existence. He had himself just spent a week caring for his servant girl Marianne Demuth, Helene's sister, and watched her die, and wondered how he would pay for a coffin. Jenny had just returned from Paris, vainly hoping to borrow money from the rich Jewish banker who had been stricken with apoplexy a few minutes before she reached his house; she was now in London, sick, distraught, bitterly complaining. Despair was something he could seize and hold in his clenched hands. Must he therefore despair because a man's mistress had died?

Engels waited five days before replying. He wrote in frigid outrage a letter even more remorseless than that written by Marx.

> DEAR MARX,
>
> You will find it natural that my own distress and your frosty attitude toward it have made it positively impossible for me to answer your letter sooner.
>
> All my friends, including acquaintances among the philistines, have on this occasion, which indeed touches me deeply, shown more sympathy and friendship than I expected. You alone have chosen this passing moment for a display of the superiority of your frigid way of thinking. So be it!
>
> You know how my finances stand. You know, too, that I have done everything to drag you out of your misery. But the considerable sum you mention is beyond my present power, as you well know. . . .

In the same frosty manner Engels suggested that Marx should apply to a loan society. He promised to send £25 in the following month, and offered to sign a note for £60, payable in July. Beyond this he refused to go, and Marx was perfectly aware that nothing would be gained by pursuing the subject. He had escaped a disastrous break in their friendship only by a hairbreadth.

Henceforward a new note can be heard in their correspondence. They are like lovers who have been estranged, and now speak warily to one another. Now more than ever they offered one another little compliments, and sometimes they poured compliments with a heavy hand. Rereading Engels' *The Condition of the Working Class in England* nearly twenty years after it was written, Marx can scarcely find words enough to praise it. "How freshly and passionately, with what bold anticipations and without any learned and scientific doubts did you deal with the matter," he wrote, adding that it possessed a warmth and vivacious humor which did honor to the author. Engels in turn would find reasons for complimenting Marx on his penetrating mind, his brilliant foresight, his towering genius. That Marx was a genius was now accepted as a matter of course, and when his friend Dr. Kugelmann offered the hope that he would devote himself solely to the completion of *Das Kapital,* Engels remarked: "That men of genius must eat, drink, have lodging and pay for it, such a thought never penetrates the minds of these upright Germans." Marx may have shared Dr. Kugelmann's enthusiasm for the book, but there was little need to remind him that food, drink and lodging had to be paid for.

Marx was in such desperate straits that he was now contemplating a course of action he had never previously considered seriously, though from time to time he had discussed it with Jenny. He would abandon his bourgeois existence altogether. First, he would declare himself bankrupt, thus avoiding the importunities of his creditors. There was a lien on his furniture, and this would be lost, but he felt that something would be gained by punishing the butcher and the baker. Helene Demuth would be dismissed; a place would be found for her in another household. His two older daughters would become governesses to the children of his friends the Cunninghams. With his wife and youngest daughter he would take up his lodging in a workmen's dwelling house in central London. As far as he could see, no other solution was possible, and he was quite seriously contemplating the move when Engels, in a mood of profound disenchantment and knowing the risks he was running, arranged to send him a postdated check for £100, although he knew it was not properly secured. He relied on the fact that the general audit would not take place until the summer and by that time he would have accumulated enough money to balance the account.

Long ago Engels had realized that as long as he lived he would have to be the main support of the Marx family. Marx could not, or would not, earn a living. Only once in his life was he known to have applied for a job. This was in September 1862, and the job he applied for was that of a railroad clerk. He was not particularly distressed when he learned that his application had been rejected on the grounds that his handwriting was too poor. Even if he had accepted the job, it is unlikely that he would have tolerated it for long.

Although Engels held an important position in his father's cotton-spinning factory in Manchester, he was not yet a wealthy man. His expenses were heavy. He had to keep up appearances with other Manchester merchants; he went out riding regularly; he entertained frequently, kept a good cellar and ate like a trencherman; and there were the two residences to maintain. His earnings until the time of his father's death in 1860 appear to have been about £500 a year, and in addition there was income from his investments on the Manchester stock exchange. After 1860 his situation improved. He received a legacy from his father's estate. In 1864 he became a full partner, and his income was considerably increased. Five years later he sold out his interest in the firm and became a free man. With his investments and the capital sum received from the sale of his good will, he was now sure of an income of about £800 a year. This was a princely sum in the middle years of the nineteenth century, and now at last he was able to offer Marx a pension of £350 a year. If it was not as large as Marx had hoped for—he calculated that his expenses ran to about £500 a year—it was at least sufficient for his immediate needs. During the last fifteen years of his life he was never in need.

Ironically Marx became solvent only when his best work was accomplished. In 1863 he was still struggling for survival. One could not say his fortunes were at their lowest ebb, for they were no better and no worse than they had been since he arrived in London. In spite of Engels' generosity he was continually in debt. Although he spent most of his waking hours thinking about money, he had very little understanding of the risk attached to borrowing. He would sign bills of exchange at high interest and wonder how he had brought himself to such a pass when the bills fell due. He was improvident and oddly childlike in financial matters. He had no gift for making money and none for spending it.

From the time of his marriage poverty had been the thorn in his side. Now there was to be added another affliction. For a good deal of his life he had suffered from boils. As he struggled with the last chapters of *Das Kapital,* they came with increasing frequency and urgency, demanding attention. He writhed in agony and cursed the Egyptian plague which had been visited on him.

THE BOILS

"So went satan forth from the presence of the Lord, and smote Job with sore boils from the sole of his feet unto the crown."

Marx may sometimes have felt that the sufferings of Job were no greater than his own. He, too, had seen his body festering, covered with sores and with gaping holes, exuding a stench which drove people away.

For more than twenty years of his life he was tormented by these boils and carbuncles which the doctors seemed incapable of curing, for as soon as one was removed, another would break out in another place. There were periods of quiescence, and other periods when his whole body seemed to break out in ulcerous sores. Like Job he protested vehemently, accusing the fates of reserving a special malediction for him alone.

Strangely, no one else in his family suffered from them. All his children suffered from a variety of diseases: diphtheria, tuberculosis, scarlatina—these were the commonplaces of their lives. Jenny suffered a terrifying attack of smallpox in middle age; it permanently disfigured her and left her more and more isolated from the world. For Marx there was reserved an equally terrifying fate, for his whole body—face, arms, chest, back, buttocks, thighs, even his legs—was pitted with the marks left by boils. He was continually consulting doctors, experimenting with various ointments, reading up medical dictionaries; nothing availed. The agony and misery of boils was an ever-present accompaniment of most of his active life.

We begin to hear of them quite early during his stay in London. One of the most painful occurred in the spring of 1854, when he was living in Dean Street. It was very large, and grew between his nose and upper lip, making it difficult for him to speak. "My face has reached a crisis," he wrote to Engels. "For fourteen days the devil has been hurling shit at my head." The doctor ordered him to stop reading and smoking, but he was in a state of nervous collapse, the whole family ill around him, and it is unlikely that he obeyed the doctor.

The worst of many attacks occurred in October 1863, when he was forty-five. It was a time of intolerable frustration, his work going badly, *Das Kapital* uncompleted, his hopes of a settled income and an established position as remote as ever. In Germany he was eclipsed by Lassalle; in England there was only a handful of followers. He slept badly, smoked more than was good for him, and took far too many pills against his bilious attacks. For a long time his liver had ceased to function properly, and in his more somber moments he thought it would cease to function altogether. But it was not his liver which failed him in that autumn. A boil appeared on his back, and grew to be the size of a fist. It drained him of energy, kept him awake at night, and reduced him to a quivering jelly, for the pain was terrible, his mind seemed to collapse under the weight of pain, and he was as close to death as he had ever been.

Jenny had not the faintest idea how to deal with this situation. She thought that it might have something to do with his drinking, for he consumed enormous quantities of fourpenny ale; she made him drink lemonade instead. It had no effect. At last, on November 10, she called in Dr. Allen, the family physician. The doctor knew the family well, and took in the situation at a glance. Jenny, Eleanor and Helene Demuth were all crowding round the patient. He motioned to Jenny and Eleanor to leave the room, for he was afraid they would become hysterical, but he knew he could rely on the faithful Lenchen, who was ordered to hold Marx down on the bed while he cut out the abscess. He cut deep, and there was a gaping wound, with blood streaming over his naked back. "He was very quiet and still, and did not wince," Jenny reported proudly to Wilhelm Liebknecht two weeks later.

There followed days and nights of turmoil and anxiety. The wound had to be attended to, the bandages changed frequently, the patient comforted. During the first days after the operation Jenny was almost beside herself with worry; then it was Lenchen's turn to collapse. Somehow they managed to look after him round the clock. Marx was in fearful pain, and someone had to be awake at all hours of the day. Jenny slept on the floor beside his bed.

The wound gradually healed, and Marx recovered. Dr. Allen ordered him to take three or four glasses of port and half a bottle of Bordeaux a day to increase his strength, and because he had been eating so little he was ordered to eat four times as much as before. But though his health improved, he could not sleep. He was oppressed by waking dreams, by thoughts of his imminent end, by the knowledge of his failure to complete *Das Kapital.* Engels sent cheerful letters. "Stick to drinking and meat, that's the main thing," Engels wrote; it was not the kind of advice which a brooding hypochondriac needed.

Marx was still in pain on December 2, when a telegram arrived from Trier. It said simply that his mother was dead. At once Dr. Allen was summoned. Marx wanted to know whether he was in a fit state to travel. The doctor was inclined to believe that a change of air would do the patient good, but the wound had not completely healed and for seven weeks Marx had kept to his bed: the verdict was that the advantages of a change of air probably outweighed the inconveniences. Marx had been on his feet for only three days, and for half an hour each day he had been allowed to go for a walk. His head was still swimming and his knees were weak.

Marx wrote to Engels, asking for money for the journey and explaining the circumstances: it was essential that the matter of the inheritance should be cleared up. "I myself have one foot in the grave," he wrote.

"Under the circumstances I am more necessary than the old woman." As for the difficulties of the journey, he was sure he would be able to find some good female Samaritans who would be only too willing to bathe and bandage his wound. Quite obviously nothing would stop him, and Engels replied at once with the gift of a case of port and £10 for the journey. In thanking him Marx mentioned that he was now drinking 1½ liters of the strongest London stout a day; it was a hopeful sign, and he felt that full recovery was just round the corner.

He did not leave for Trier until December 7. The weather was bitterly cold and he was in no shape to travel. At Trier he stayed at the Gasthaus von Venedig, and saw much of his younger sister Emilie, who was married to the engineer Johann Jakob Conradi. He learned that most of his mother's personal possessions had been bequeathed to Emilie. He also learned that his mother had died at four o'clock in the afternoon of November 30, exactly fifty years to the day and hour after her marriage to Heinrich Marx, whom she had survived by a quarter of a century. She had prophesied the hour and day of her death. Marx notes her strange prophetical gift, and passes on to other affairs. He was himself a man who prophesied often, but never did he look into the future with such a clear and untroubled gaze.

For the biographer Marx's mother remains a dimly lit figure hovering in the background, shapeless and ill at ease. No portrait of her survives, and we know little more about her than that she spoke German with a heavy Dutch accent, was a good housewife, passionately loved her husband, and never forgave Karl for spending so much of the family fortune when he was a student. She was hard, stubborn and unforgiving. She never understood Karl, whose brilliance she seems to have resented, and whose incapacity to earn a living seemed to her an indication of his general irresponsibility. In these last years Marx's attitude toward her was a very simple one: he hoped she would die so that he could come into his inheritance. It was a feeling he shared with Jenny, who wrote to Frau Liebknecht that it would be hypocritical of her to feel any sorrow at the news of her mother-in-law's death.

The executor of the will was Lion Philips, and after spending some days in Trier and paying a brief visit to Frankfurt to see two aunts, Esther Kosel and Babette Blum, from whom he hoped eventually to receive some small legacies, he accordingly went to Zalt Bommel. Lion Philips was able to arrange an advance of 1,000 Dutch gulden against a final settlement of the inheritance, and it was clear that little more could be expected. In 1861 Lion Philips had advanced £160. The new advance, amounting to rather less than £100, was disappointing, for he had hoped for more. His mother, however, had been scrupulously fair, for there survives in Marx's handwriting a tabulation of the legacies to the four surviving children, Sophie, Karl, Louise and Emilie, showing that they all received equal amounts, although some, notably Karl and Sophie, had already drawn heavily on their legacies and received correspondingly smaller sums after her death.

Marx had no sooner reached Zalt Bommel when the boils began again, more painful and more widespread than ever. They erupted on his back, stomach, neck, armpits, arms, legs and buttocks. He could not stand or walk or sit down; and he noted that his urine, usually cloudy, now became absolutely pure. He complained that he could not sleep, and that life had dealt him a blow which he could scarcely endure. It was *eine christliche perfide Krankheit,* a Christian perfidious sickness: so he wrote to Engels, forgetting that boils were more appropriate to Job than to Christ. He raged against this sickness in a fury of despair, and sometimes he realized that he was lucky to be in Zalt Bommel among relatives who tenderly bathed his wounds.

Old Lion Philips had pity on him, saw that he received the best medical attention, and found himself acting the role of a nurse, for he sometimes applied the bandages and the poultices. His daughter Henriette had married the local doctor, and there were endless consultations. Another daughter, Antoinette, who was Marx's favorite, also bathed the wounds, and Marx always looked forward to the times when she acted as nurse, "her dark eyes shining dangerously as she pampers me, and no one could do it better." Dr. Anrooy offered no hope of a speedy cure, and thought they would not be cured until the end of January. In fact, he was in no state to leave Zalt Bommel until the middle of February.

What especially annoyed Marx was the boil on his buttocks. He wrote to Engels that it was the most troublesome and painful of all, even more horrible than the one he suffered in London. "So you see, *mon cher,* how nature in her wisdom afflicts me," he wrote in the authentic accents of Job. "Wouldn't it have been more reasonable to send these trials of patience to some good Christian, someone like Silvio Pellico? Apart from the boil on my backside, you should know there is another on my back and the one on my breast is not yet healed, so that like a real Lazarus (alias Lassalle) I am being attacked in all directions."

Surprisingly he had been reading Renan's *Vie de Jésus,* and though it was scarcely the kind of book he could approve, being filled with "mystico-pantheistic daydreams," he commended it to Engels' attention, saying that it was at least an improvement on German versions. "Naturally," he added, "it is entirely based on German researches."

Meanwhile he was confronted three or four times a day with the dreadful evidence of physical corruption. The appalling odors, the red sores, the swelling and the pus were all revealed when the bandages were removed, and there seemed to be no way of keeping them under control. It was evidently a staphylococcal infection, which could be treated before the invention of the sulpha drugs only in the most elementary way. The infection was able to spread because he was physically run down, smoked too much, had eaten highly spiced foods for many years, and was a prey to overwhelming nervous crises. He took almost no exercise except on Sundays, and rarely took baths. He was therefore in no state to resist the ever-present staphylococcal germs, and indeed it is surprising that he did not suffer from boils many years earlier.

As the years passed, he was to grow accustomed to them until every part of his body bore the indelible traces of those small explosions which burst through his skin; and when he surveyed himself naked, he showed more wounds than many soldiers. He took a kind of pride in them. In letter after letter he described them to his correspondents, and sometimes he would go on to describe the various medicaments he was employing, or their size and frequency. They came unannounced at all seasons; there was no pattern in their progress. Ten years after the massive outbreak at Zalt Bommel he was still writing: "A carbuncle broke out on my right cheek . . . I am now using quicksilver ointment at the first hint of carbuncle irritation and find it works quite specifically." Previously he had taken the arsenic cure. Later he took sulphur. A good deal of his waking life was spent in warding off the remorseless invasions of the staphylococcal germs.

There was scarcely any place of his body which they left untouched. In October 1867 he reported to Engels that he was suffering from insomnia and almost incapable of working because "I have had the pleasure of watching two carbuncles blossoming in the region of the penis. Happily they have now faded away." These boils appear to have produced considerable sexual excitement, for he immediately took to reading the erotic verses of the sixteenth-century French poet Mathurin Régnier and quotes them at length in the letter to Engels. Two of these poems should be quoted here as an indication of the kind of erotic verse which he found pleasing:

Mon cas, qui se lève et se hausse,
Bave d'une estrange façon;
Belle, vous fournistes la sausse,
Lors que je fournis le poisson.

Las! si ce membre eut l'arrogance
De fouiller trop les lieux sacrez,
Qu'on luy pardonne son offence,
Car il pleure assez ses péchez.

Fluxion d'Amour

L'amour est une affection
Qui, par les yeux, dans le coeur entre,
Et, par la forme de fluxion,
S'éxcoule par le bas du ventre.

These boils in so vulnerable a part of the body disturbed him deeply, and at the most he was able to work only two hours a day. In time, however, he came to have a kind of affection for his boils, and he liked to say that they were "really a form of proletarian sickness." If so, it was one of the few things he had in common with the proletariat.

Many of the subterranean fantasies which appear in his writings may derive from his boils. Madmen lurk in the underground gold mines, moles carve tunnels underneath the earth, and there is always the sense of danger underfoot. He had dedicated his life to a searching examination of the corruptions of society, and his body was like a map marking the corruptions of the flesh.

He would tell lies about his boils, even to doctors. Shortly after the appearance of two boils near his penis, he wrote to Dr. Kugelmann that he had suffered from them only for a few years. Before that they had been a stranger to him. In fact, he had been suffering from them for at least fourteen years. Sometimes the boils provided excuses for not seeing visitors: many of the boils occurred on his face, which would immediately be wrapped in plasters. He had boils in his eyes, in his mouth, in his ears: no place was immune, and there was no time when they were not lying in wait for him. It became almost a habit to be lanced and cut, so that he came to resemble those men of the middle ages who were continually being bled by barbers. In a letter to Dr. Kugelmann written early in 1868 he described the process as though it were a daily event:

> Cut, lanced, etc., in short treated in every respect *secundum legem artis.* In spite of all this, the thing is continually breaking out again so that with the exception of two or three days I have been lying fallow for eight weeks. Last Saturday I went out again for the first time. On Monday came a relapse. I hope it will come to an end this week, but who will guarantee me against new eruptions? Moreover it sharply attacks my head.

He made the same complaint to Engels: the boils were in some way connected with his brain. He could never explain it, just as he could never find anyone who would guarantee him against new eruptions.

Boils were not his only plagues. His long-standing liver complaint continually tormented him, and had to be watched carefully. The medicines for it were repeatedly changed, and never had the slightest effect. He suffered from chronic stomach disorders, interminable headaches, sleeplessness, nervous exhaustion. The first grave attack of digestive trouble occurred in 1857, when he was only thirty-nine, and thereafter the attacks recurred every spring. To ward off insomnia he took to wearing a black veil over his eyes in bed, for any chink of light would instantly make him wide awake.

Although Marx in his letters had provided a fairly complete account of his various illnesses and complaints, and we are never left in doubt about what particular ailment he is suffering from at any moment, it is difficult to track the course of his medical history. So many things were wrong that the picture tends to become confused. Above all, there were psychological disorders which can only be guessed at. He was a tyrant in his home, and tyrannical in his works, and such men are usually believed to be compensating in adult life for the indignities suffered in their childhood. Yet there is no evidence that Marx had an unhappy childhood. On the contrary it appears to have been an idyllic one, surrounded by a worshipful family, among the bourgeois comforts of an upper-class home.

For most of his adult life he was a sick man, physically and spiritually. In England, the country he adopted, he felt himself an alien, and was never at ease. His ferocious arrogance, his flaming temper, his continual sarcasm and sadistic behavior point to psychological defects which lay at the root of his being and influenced his thought. In the last five or six years of his life he descended into the calms of a premature old age, and even then the explosive temper would sometimes erupt, and his rage was something to wonder at.

But the boils were his chief torment, his constant plague. "You see," he once wrote to Engels, "I am the object of plagues just like Job, though I am not so God-fearing as he was." The boils were especially prevalent while he was writing *Das Kapital.* He wrote this work in spleen and anger, in the hope of bringing down the entire capitalist system and of undermining the whole of existing society; he knew its destructive force and reveled in it, and he seems to have suspected that the boils were in some mysterious way connected with it. In another letter to Engels he wrote: "Whatever happens, I hope the bourgeoisie, as long as they exist, will have cause to remember my carbuncles." For another hundred years the bourgeoisie may have cause to remember them.

DEATHS AND ENTRANCES

When Jenny looked back on her life, she always remembered vividly the houses she had lived in. There was the quiet baronial mansion at Kreuznach and the elegant town house with the arched courtyard at Trier, and later there came a succession of small cramped apartments in Paris, Brussels and London. These apartments filled her with dread; they were the caverns in which she spent the best years of her life. The house on Grafton Terrace had pleased her because it provided her with space and sunlight, but it was small and mean in comparison with the houses nearby. What she wanted above all was a house more in keeping with her husband's position in society, with all the middle-class comforts. In March 1864, with the aid of his mother's legacy, Marx was able to provide her with exactly the house she wanted.

In those days the house was known as No. 1 Modena Villas, but four years later it was renamed No. 1 Maitland Park Road. The new house was only a stone's throw from Grafton Terrace, but it represented a leap from the lower middle classes to the upper middle classes. It was elegant and spacious, and their neighbors were doctors, lawyers and civil servants who rose early and took the horse bus to the city. In such a house no one would be ashamed to entertain distinguished guests or hold musical soirées.

The family had scarcely entered the new house when disturbing news came from Manchester. Wilhelm Wolff was dying. He was one of the few men for whom Marx entertained feelings of profound friendship, and although he no longer played an active revolutionary role, he could always be relied upon for advice and comfort. He was now a teacher and one of the guiding spirits of the Schiller Anstalt, a society dedicated to the spreading of German culture in England. He was fifty-five, but looked much older.

His illness began with fearful headaches, strange lapses of memory, sleeplessness, stabbing pains in the feet. Engels, who visited him frequently, was at his wits' end, because he distrusted the doctors and Wolff himself, driven half mad with sleeplessness, was beyond caring. The doctor treated him for gout and bled him, and then diagnosed meningitis and inflammation of the brain. Another doctor diagnosed uremia or a general anemia affecting the entire nervous system. It was obvious to Engels that the doctors were incompetent, and since the patient was sinking rapidly while the doctors quarreled, Engels insisted that his own universal remedy should be applied. Accordingly Wolff was given two beer mugs of champagne daily and his soup was spiked with brandy. He seemed to recover a little.

So the days passed, while Wolff gradually became a strange tormented ghost of himself, sometimes hurling himself out of his bed, crying out in his delirium, and even when he seemed to be conscious he could not recognize the people gathered around his bed. Engels realized that even if the patient recovered his physical health, it was likely that his brain had been burned away in the fever; and instead of the gentle Lupus he had known, there would be a raving idiot. He was busy with the affairs of his company, but he usually managed to see Wolff early in the morning and again at night. On the evening of May 2 he sent a hurried note to Marx, urging him to come at once, or at least to arrange to send a male nurse from London, for none seemed to be available in Manchester.

Marx hurried to Manchester to preside over the deathbed of his friend. He had many reasons for making the journey. He wanted, of course, to see Wolff, but he also wanted to consult Engels' doctor about his own boils, which were becoming unusually troublesome, and he wanted to get away from his family, which was going through one of its periodic invasions of illness. He had a deep affection for Wolff, although they had quarreled violently in the past, and if necessary, he would himself act as male nurse and bully the doctors and see that his friend's last hours were attended with the least possible pain. There was also another matter of great importance. Wolff had made no secret of the fact that he intended to bequeath some money to Marx. By going to Manchester Marx hoped to ensure a quick settlement of the legacy.

Although Wolff had been a resourceful revolutionary, he was also a very cautious and methodical man with all the characteristics of his Silesian forebears. His will had been written with a scrupulous attention to detail. There were legacies of £100 each to Marx, Engels, his doctor, and the Schiller Anstalt, and there followed a comprehensive and exact summary of the properties to be inherited by Marx:

> THIS IS THE LAST WILL AND TESTAMENT OF ME JOHANN FRIEDRICH WILHELM WOLFF of Chorlton upon Medlock in the County of Lancaster Teacher of Languages . . .
>
> I give devise and bequeath and appoint all my books furniture and effects debts and moneys owing to me and all the residue of my personal estate and also all real and leasehold estates of or to which I may die seized possessed or entitled or of which I have power to dispose by this my Will unto and to the use of the said Karl Marx his heirs executors administrators and assigns according to the nature thereof respectively for ever or for all my estate term and interest therein for his and their absolute use and benefit provided that if the said Karl Marx shall die in my lifetime then I direct that the estates and effects hereinbefore devised and bequeathed to him shall go to and be divided equally among his children living at my decease who shall attain the age of twenty-one years or be married and if but one such child then the whole to such one child. . . .

With the exception of three small legacies, Wolff's entire estate was to pass into the hands of Marx or in the event of Marx's death into the hands of the surviving members of his family. This princely gift was to bring Marx more money than he ever earned from his books, and it enabled the family to live briefly in bourgeois ease and splendor.

When Marx reached Manchester on the evening of May 3, he went at once to see Wolff, who was unconscious. The small man with the benevolent round face had changed remarkably, and was almost unrecognizable. Marx stayed by the bedside for a while, and then went off to spend the evening with Engels. The next morning he returned to the bedside with Engels and the two doctors, and for a brief and precious moment Wolff emerged from the dreary landscape of illness to say a few words in a weak and trembling voice. Marx was deeply moved, for he imagined that there was still some hope for his friend. So the days passed, while Wolff seemed to rally and then sink back again into a state of profound apathy, remote from the world as in a grave. He died quietly during the afternoon of May 9, having been unconscious for three days.

That evening, not long after Wolff's death, Marx wrote to his wife, telling her about the distressing circumstances which attended those last days, raging furiously against the doctor who had wrongly diagnosed Wolff's illness, and promising more news on the following day. This news, of course, concerned the will, and with some satisfaction Marx was able to tell Jenny that the greater part of the estate amounting to more than £600 "has been bequeathed to me, and to you and the children, in the event that I die *before* them." The will had been read by Wolff's notary, and it remained only to fulfill the legal formalities, which in Marx's view would be a matter of only a few days.

The burial took place on Friday, May 13, with Marx saying a few words of farewell over the grave. About thirty people attended the burial, and he was a little puzzled by the presence of half a dozen merchants and some twenty members of "the lower classes," all of whom made the long journey to the cemetery on foot. Afterward Dr. Borchardt, who had so singularly failed to help Wolff as he lay dying, invited Marx to dinner. Marx said sternly that he had no intention of dining out on the day he was burying his friend.

A few days later Marx left for London, leaving to Engels the task of liquidating Wolff's affairs. There were lawyers to see and papers to sign, and these affairs went slowly. In his sternest tones Marx began to bombard Engels with letters demanding an accounting. Why had the money not come? He had expected it in the beginning of June, and it was now July, with no money in sight. Marx worked himself into a fury with the predictable result that he was once more attacked by boils and carbuncles, and for ten days he remained in bed. Then he took Jenny and Eleanor to Ramsgate to escape the heat of the London summer, but the heat followed him to the seaside. There was no escape from it, no escape from his boils, no escape from the presence of his daughters. In one of his more misanthropic moods he wrote to Engels: "The Philistines here and their better halves and their female offspring are lording it over everything here. It makes me sad to think that that old Ocean, the first of the Titans, permits these pygmies to dance on his nose and use him for a pastime."

In the intervals of contemplating the ocean's nose, Marx was sometimes moved to contemplate his blessings. This year had seen a dramatic change in his fortunes. There was the new house, there was the promise of money from Wolff's estate, and in addition he had been speculating on the London stock exchange. He was no longer a poor man. He was, in fact, becoming a passably rich man as the result of these dubious speculations. At the end of June he was able to announce to his uncle Lion Philips that since the doctor had refused to let him work because of his illness, he had spent his time profitably in speculating with American funds and English joint-stock shares, "which this year are growing out of the earth like mushrooms." He had realized a profit of over £400, and he was proposing to reinvest the money, or at least to continue with his speculations, "because the complexities of the present political situation offer new scope." At this time he had very nearly finished writing *Das Kapital.*

Marx made no secret of these speculative affairs, and he must have discussed them at considerable length with Engels in letters which have vanished or been suppressed. He wrote to Engels on July 4, asking for a final accounting of the Wolff legacy by July 15. "If I had had the money during the last ten days," he wrote, "I would have been able to make a good deal on the stock exchange. The time has now come when with wit and very little money one can really make a killing in London."

The full details of Marx's speculations on the stock exchange are lost to history. He seems to have been an incautious and improvident investor, for within a year he was reduced to begging from Engels. As for the Wolff legacy, the final accounting came only in March 1865, although most of the money had long since passed into his hands. He received £235 on June 8, 1864, less than a month after Wolff's death. A further £235 reached him at the beginning of July, and there was another payment of £200 at the beginning of November. The total amount of the legacy was £824, a considerable sum in those days. Marx, who kept a watchful eye on the legacy, noted that £40 had not been accounted for. He therefore sent a peremptory letter to Engels demanding that the £40 be sent by return of post.

Engels had many crosses to bear, and not the least of them were those peremptory letters from Marx, which came with every post. He answered coldly that he had no time to look into his books for the missing £40, but if Marx said they were owed to him, then it must be so, and he would send the money in due course.

For Jenny especially this new-found financial independence came as a godsend. She loved giving presents, and now she was able to indulge herself in an orgy of gift-giving. In the small circle of her friends everyone received a gift, and Engels received a carving knife and a fork. Since she was ill at ease in his presence, and never quite forgave him for being the main support of her husband, there may have been some unconscious symbolism in her gift.

In later years she would remember that summer and autumn with affection and longing. It was the year when the clouds lifted, when the oppressive nightmares seemed about to vanish forever, when the flowers came out and the winds died down. For the first time in her married life she was able to go off on a vacation alone for no other purpose than to bask in the sunshine. She went to Brighton for fourteen days, abandoning her husband and her children, who were sometimes too much for her.

On her return to London she was able to enjoy one of the supreme events of her life—she gave her first ball. In her youth she had been a passionate dancer, attending all the balls that were given in Trier, dancing tirelessly, never at a loss to find a partner. Through all the years of misery and exile she had dreamed of the day when she would herself give a ball. She was fifty now, and aging rapidly; it was time to satisfy a whim. Marx was passably rich; she could at least permit herself an evening of perfect enjoyment. A small select list of friends and social acquaintances was drawn up and invitations were sent out. Somewhere, in some forgotten love-chest, there may still be in existence a gold-bordered invitation bearing the words:

Dr. Karl Marx
and Frau Dr. Jenny Marx
née von Westphalen
invite the pleasure of your
company
at a ball to be given at their residence
1, Modena Villas, Maitland Park, Haverstock Hill,
London, N.W.
on October 12, 1864

The ball was a success, and Jenny luxuriated in her role as hostess. For the occasion she had bought a ball dress, paid for the musicians and the frock-coated servants, and provided an impressive supper for her guests: these were the least of the decorations at a Victorian ball. It is possible that Marx did not appear, for he was suffering from a new outbreak of boils. Indeed, we know very little about the ball. We do not know the names of the guests, or why that particular day was chosen. We know only—on the testimony of Jenny herself—that the ball took place, and was followed by others.

Marx, too, was enjoying his triumphs. All that summer and autumn he was in a mood of exaltation, as though he firmly believed that the finger of fate, so long hidden behind the clouds, would suddenly reveal itself and point unerringly in his direction. He had accomplished wealth; soon he would accomplish power. He did not know how it would happen, but there were many obscure portents. He studied them with the air of a man who has been deceived before and may well be deceived again, but knows in his heart that the fates will eventually bend to his will.

On September 1, six weeks before the ball at 1, Modena Villas, Marx received a letter from Freiligrath with some extraordinary news. Lassalle, his only enemy, "the pseudo dictator," "the Jewish Negro," "the *canaille,*" had fallen mortally wounded in a duel in Geneva. Freiligrath supplied only the sketchiest account. It appeared that Lassalle had fallen hopelessly in love with Helene von Dönniges, the daughter of a high Bavarian official, who opposed the match vigorously. One of Helene's former fiancés, a Wallachian prince, had entered the affair, there was an exchange of letters, finally an act of provocation followed by a duel. "He was shot in the abdomen and now lies at the Hotel Victoria, hovering between life and death," Freiligrath wrote. "Unfortunately the ball is so deeply lodged in his body that the wound may be easily infected with gangrene. I went to see him as soon as I arrived here, and found him dictating his will, very quietly, looking death in the face."

Marx was thunderstruck by the news. Never in his wildest moments had it occurred to him that Lassalle would die in a commonplace duel over a girl. He sent off a telegram to Engels, who was equally astonished and strangely saddened. "He was certainly one of the most eminent men in Germany," Engels wrote. "For us he was an uncertain friend, and a certain enemy in the future, but it hurts a man to see how Germany kills off all its more or less capable men of the extreme left." As the days passed, more information came to light, and it became clear that Lassalle had been infatuated by the girl to such an extent that he lost control of himself, fell helplessly into the traps prepared for him by his enemies, and in the manner of a romantic hero encompassed his own downfall. His opponent, Janko von Rakowitz, was a nonentity; Helene von Dönniges was so beautiful, with her flaming-red hair and doelike eyes, that the middle-aged Lassalle might almost be excused for falling hopelessly in love with her; and Wilhelm von Dönniges, her father, was a cold and ruthless conspirator who went about the business of destroying Lassalle with no more compunction than he would have in destroying a wild boar on his estates. They were all characters in a romantic play, curiously unreal, brightly colored, dancing into the limelight for a brief moment, then vanishing forever.

But as Marx well knew, this was far more than a romantic play. The duel in Geneva was to have fearful repercussions on the German working-class movement, now deprived of its acknowledged leader. On that morning in late summer Lassalle had simply stood there on the dueling ground, a sad mischievous smile on his lips, waiting to be killed; it was observed that he did not lift his pistol; his death had been a form of suicide. The more Marx contemplated the mystery, the more uneasy he became, for there were no simple explanations. During the following months they would debate the mystery at great length, seeking for a motive or at least a credible explanation of his strange behavior. Engels mentioned Lassalle's "extraordinary mingling of frivolity and sentimentality, of Jewishness and chivalry," but this was merely a clever attempt to patch up a wound. Marx was more deeply disturbed, and wrote to Engels on September 7:

> L.'s misfortune has been going damnably through my head all day. In spite of everything he was one of the *vieille souche*, and an enemy of our enemies. Besides, it all happened so unexpectedly it is hard to believe such a noisy, stirring, pushing man is now dead as a mouse and must altogether hold his tongue. With regard to the cause of his death, you are quite right. It was one of the many tactless acts which he committed in the course of his life. With all that I am sorry that during these last years our relationship should have been so clouded, although it was his own fault. . . . The devil knows, our crowd is always getting smaller, and there are no new ones coming along. I am certain, however, of one thing—if L. had not been living in Switzerland among military adventurers and revolutionaries in yellow gloves, this would never have happened.

A few days later, still evidently under great strain, Marx wrote a letter of condolence to Countess von Hatzfeldt. The words come haltingly, crudely, but there is no doubting the passion behind them. "I know what he was to you and what his loss will mean. But rejoice in one thing—he died young, in triumph, like Achilles."

Some weeks later he wrote to her again, saying that he could not bring himself to believe that Lassalle was really dead. He had been so young, and to think of him lying in the stillness of death was to find oneself in the presence of a confused and monstrous nightmare, beyond imagining. He spoke, too, of the very real respect they had had for one another:

> You are quite right in feeling that I, more than others, could appreciate his greatness and importance. He was the first to acknowledge this, as his letters to me attest. As long as we were in correspondence, I always expressed the warmest appreciation of his achievements and always very frankly criticized any point that seemed to me wrong.
>
> In one of his last letters he told me in his own forceful way what satisfaction this gave him. But quite apart from his accomplishments I loved him *personally*. The unfortunate thing is that we concealed it from one another, as if we were going to live forever.

At such moments Marx was able to exorcise the demons. The years of bitter envy and tormented jealousy had come to an end with a strange death and a strange silence. He knew himself to be the logical successor, the man who by right of intellectual ability should have stepped immediately into Lassalle's shoes, but he could only ponder in silence the fate which left him a permanent exile, beyond the pale, powerless to rule the German workers because he could not enter Germany without being arrested. He knew now that there had been a *Brüderschaft* between them, and their hatred for one another was mingled with love. If they had fought side by side, instead of quarreling continually, they might have brought about a revolution in Germany.

He had played the game of denigration with the utmost ferocity, and he realized now that he had gained nothing by it. "The greasy Jew from Breslau," "Yiddle Brown," and "Baron Itzig" had all vanished. In their place there was a youth lying in some forgotten garden in Switzerland, beautiful and unassailable. It was a strange metamorphosis, but one entirely in keeping with Marx's sympathies; for he could show kindness to his enemies when they were dead.

For the rest of his life Marx continued to speak of Lassalle with affection and respect. Occasionally—and this happened especially when he was talking to Engels—some remembered slight or the memory of the immense power which Lassalle exercised over the German workers would send him into a splutter of rage, but the rage would pass, and he would find himself defending Lassalle even against Engels. Sometimes he spoke of "the immortal service rendered by Lassalle," and how singlehandedly Lassalle had awakened the German working classes from a fifteen-year slumber. And to those who derided Lassalle's achievements he would ask peremptorily what they had done in comparison with "the dead lion," who had fought for the German workers when they were incapable of fighting for themselves. In later years, when power seemed almost within reach and he found himself measured against Lassalle, the bitterness would break out again, but never for long. In the last years of his life it may have occurred to him that both in their different ways lacked the essential qualities of revolutionary leadership.

For Marx the year 1864 was another *annus mirabilis*. He had entered a new and more spacious house, inherited a small fortune from Wolff, engaged in successful speculations on the stock exchange, and learned of the death of his most powerful rival. A ball had been given in his house, and he had enjoyed several vacations by the seaside. But the most dazzling of his exploits was still to come. In the same month that he learned of Lassalle's death he attended a meeting at St. Martin's Hall, Long Acre, and watched the birth of the International Working Men's Association. He would take it into his hands, shape it, make it obedient to his will, so that it became his personal machine for the advancement of revolution in Europe. Then in eight years' time, he would wring its neck and throw it contemptuously away.

THE YEARS OF TRIUMPH

***Things are moving, and in the next revolution, which is perhaps nearer than it seems,* we *(i.e. you and I) have this powerful machinery* in our hands.**

—Marx to Engels, September 1867

THE BIRTH OF THE INTERNATIONAL

According to the Marxist mythology, history is wholly the product of social and economic forces. The blueprint has already been established; the movements of history follow preordained paths, and the careful student can calculate to a hairbreadth the exact course which history will pursue, for the various classes obey unalterable laws and emerge according to fixed patterns. Such was the view of history which Marx derived from Hegel and Aeschylus, and his own remorseless studies. He was not however a historian, and there is no reason to believe that history follows the laws invented by Marx.

It would be more true to say that history is lawless and follows its own wayward path. There is something strangely obsessive in the way history searches for the insignificant events which summon great dramatic changes in their train. A politician trips over a shoelace and dies; on the following day the stock market collapses, banks fail, governments are overturned, dictators emerge. Just as a shoelace can affect the destiny of a nation, so a battle may be lost when a wind changes direction, or a whole civilization may come to an end because a guard at the frontier fell asleep at his post and let the barbarians pour in. There was no historical necessity for the barbarians to overrun the empire; one man fell asleep, and this was enough.

In the life of Marx the accidental was continually playing its part. In September 1864 he was at the lowest ebb of his political fortunes, an obscure German *émigré* living in isolation, often ill, writing little—he had not published anything for nearly two years—and completely out of touch with the labor movement in Britain and with only a tenuous contact with the labor movement in Germany. He was a capitalist unashamedly investing in the stock market. He had no followers, no newspaper, no developed revolutionary theory. The *Communist Manifesto* had joined thousands of other manifestos in the limbo reserved for ephemeral political publications, and his books were unread and largely unknown. A few Frenchmen might still remember the savagery of his attack on Proudhon in *La Misère de la Philosophie*, and if so, they remembered it with distaste, for Proudhon was still a powerful force to be reckoned with in the French labor movement. Marx was no *éminence grise* directing a revolutionary conspiracy; he was a man at the end of his political resources, and it might be expected that he would vanish forever into a decent obscurity.

It was at this juncture that Victor Le Lubez, an obscure teacher of the piano and of the French language, came to call on Marx to ask him whether he knew of a German worker who would speak at a forthcoming congress to be held at St. Martin's Hall, Long Acre. No one could possibly have guessed that such a simple request would have such momentous consequences.

Le Lubez's visit to Marx took place about September 20, and appears to have been quite brief. Marx answered that he could recommend a worker, Johann Georg Eccarius, a tailor from Thuringia, who had formerly been one of his followers. Eccarius was a good but not particularly brilliant speaker, but he would serve well enough as a representative of the German working class. Significantly Le Lubez had not asked Marx to speak: the congress was to be essentially a congress of delegations of workmen unencumbered by too many intellectuals.

Marx asked the purpose of the congress and learned that it was designed to establish a fraternal organization of European workmen to protest against Russian tyranny in Poland—the Polish uprising the previous year had been quelled with extraordinary cruelty by the Russian army—and to take whatever other measures were necessary to ensure that the working classes of Europe acquired political power. Similar congresses had been held in the past, and nothing came of them. Marx appears to have asked whether he could attend the congress, but Le Lubez was in no position to offer a formal invitation. This came later, on the very eve of the congress, at almost the last moment, in a letter from William Randall Cremer, one of the organizers. It was so very formal a letter that it suggests that Cremer had never met Marx and was not particularly interested whether Marx attended or not. The letter, which was found among Marx's papers, read:

31 Gt. Titchfield Street,
September 28, 1864

SIR,

The Committee who have organized the meeting as announced in the enclosed Bill respectfully request the favour of your attendance. The production of this will admit you to the committee room where the Committee will meet at half 7.

I am, Sir, yours very respectfully,

W. R. CREMER

The enclosed bill showed that the meeting at St. Martin's Hall was essentially a rally of French and English workingmen, and that the French were expected to submit a plan "for a better understanding between the peoples." It was to be a public meeting, and anyone, including Marx, could have a seat in the main hall. Marx wanted a seat on the platform, and he obtained permission to be seated there only a few hours before the congress opened, presumably through the intervention of Le Lubez.

Everything about Marx's attendance at the meeting suggests that he was neither particularly welcome nor encouraged to take any active part. He was merely tolerated.

The congress opened at eight o'clock in the evening of September 28. About two thousand people were crowded into the hall. According to the official minutes there was "a numerous body of German, French, Italian and Polish workmen," but there appear to have been very few Poles, and most of the Germans were members of the choral group which sang patriotic songs at intervals during the evening.

On the motion of Richard Dennis Butler, an English typesetter, Edward Beesly, professor of history and political economy at the University of London, was invited to act as chairman. He was a well-known radical, very popular among workingmen, and his appearance in the chair was greeted with applause. He welcomed the delegations, called for an Anglo-French alliance "to secure and maintain the liberties of the world," and asserted that intellectuals had no place in the movement of fraternization, which should grow out of the needs of the workingmen themselves. He was followed by George Odger, Secretary of the London Trades Council, who reminded the audience that they had come to protest the cruelties inflicted by Russia on the defenseless Polish people, and he pointed to the working classes as the defenders of human freedom, "who must come forth and legislate for the rights of the many, and not the privileges of the few." Odger was a shoemaker, a sensible man feeling his way toward a political role for the working class. They must come forth and legislate, but he did not suggest how they should seize power.

Then it was the turn of the French delegation led by Henri-Louis Tolain, a Paris engraver, who was considerably less interested in defending human freedom than in developing his Proudhonist views on the laws of supply and demand, and on the protection of the small farmer and the artisan from the growing power of capitalism. Marx, who was standing on the platform, must have regarded this speech as one of his heavier crosses, for he still detested Proudhon, and it was clear that the entire French delegation regarded Proudhon with respect. Tolain, a tall man with an immensely high forehead, a skilled and resourceful orator with a thunderous voice, dominated the meeting; and if he said little of importance, and nothing at all about the cause which had brought them together, he spoke with revolutionary fire and showed once again that the French workmen were in love with their barricades.

So the speeches went on, with the speakers all assuming recognizable and well-defined attitudes, although nothing much was being said. Marx's protégé, Eccarius, made a speech on behalf of the German working classes, but it appears to have been a perfunctory one which had no visible effect on the audience, for no one troubled to report it. It was not until George Wheeler, an English trade unionist, got up and formally moved the establishment of an international association of workingmen that the meeting began to show signs of moving in a practical direction. The motion was carried by acclamation, and at that moment the International, which was to play an extraordinary role in European history and to father two more Internationals, came into existence. As yet it had no name, no program, no statutes, and no clearly defined aim. The program and the rules would be provided in due course by Marx, who had remained mute throughout the congress. His decision to capture the International was probably made while the congress was meeting.

The last business of the congress was to appoint a committee of workingmen to draw up the rules and regulations. Of those who were appointed twenty-seven were Englishmen, and there were three Frenchmen, two Germans, and two Italians. The Poles went unrepresented. These thirty-four members were to constitute the General Council. All except Marx and the two Italians, one a soldier and the other a doctor, were workingmen. In the list of names Marx came last, and he appears to have been co-opted as an afterthought.

The International was far from being international. The English trade unionists vastly outnumbered the rest, and they may have thought they were in overwhelming control, but within a few weeks Marx had all the strings in his hand.

On November 4, 1864, five weeks later, Marx mentioned these events for the first time in a long letter to Engels. After explaining why the meeting had been called, he went on:

> A Public Meeting in St. Martin's Hall was summoned for September 28 '64 by Odger (shoemaker, president of the Council here of all London trade-unions, and also especially of the Trade Unions Suffrage Agitation Society, which is connected with Bright) and Cremer, mason and secretary of the masons' union. . . . A certain *Le Lubez* was sent to ask me whether I would take part *pour les ouvriers allemands*, and especially if I could pro-

> vide a German worker to speak at the meeting, etc. I provided them with Eccarius, who came off splendidly, and ditto was present myself as a mute figure on the platform. I realized that real "powers" were involved both on the London and the Paris side, and I therefore decided to waive my usual standing rule to decline any such invitations.

What is remarkable in this letter is how much Marx got wrong. He was evidently out of touch with the trade unions, for his descriptions of the two important working-class leaders are inaccurate. Odger was secretary, not president, of the London Trades Council. Cremer was not a mason, but a carpenter, and he had never been a trade-union secretary. It is unlikely that the speech of Eccarius came off splendidly, because, as we learn from a letter he wrote to Marx the day before the meeting, he had not the slightest idea what to say and was having the greatest difficulty in understanding Odger's suggestions for themes he might discuss in his speech. Finally, Marx was being extremely disingenuous when he said he had waived his usual standing rule to decline invitations of this nature, for he had gone out of his way to ask for an invitation and had received it only on the day before the meeting opened. But he was speaking the truth when he said he detected real "powers" emerging from this meeting. He had a nose for "powers."

Marx's tactics were the same as those he had employed during the days of the Communist League. He intended to write the charter, draw up the rules, appoint his own delegates to the General Council, and at each of the meetings he would, as far as possible, dictate the subjects to be discussed. His success was all the more remarkable because he was dealing very largely with English trade unionists, whose ideas were often diametrically opposed to his own, and because he still spoke a defective English and was not always understood.

The first step was to write the charter. This proved to be surprisingly easy, although he was absent through illness from the first two meetings of the subcommittee appointed to draft a declaration of principles and provisional statutes. Originally the task was given to Luigi Wolff, a former adjutant of Garibaldi, now a police spy working for Napoleon III, although this was of course unknown to the committee. This version was unsatisfactory, and another version was prepared by John Weston, a carpenter and formerly a follower of Robert Owen. This new version was too long and too ineffective to meet the wishes of the members, and was referred back to the subcommittee. At a meeting of the General Council held on October 18, it was decided to jettison the versions prepared by Weston and Wolff and to substitute a third version prepared by Le Lubez, who had retained many of Wolff's resounding phrases in favor of a central European government of the working classes, but also included some of Marx's ideas. This was not satisfactory, but it was the best they could come up with. Cremer proposed and Marx seconded the motion that this version should be accepted, and this was agreed with only a few dissenting voices from the English workmen on the committee. William Worley, an English printer, wanted to strike out the words "capital and land in the hands of the few," and he also wanted to strike out all references to the class war. He was overruled. The matter was then referred back to the subcommittee to polish the version of Le Lubez, so that it could be submitted to the approval of members at the meeting to be held the following week. The instructions to the subcommittee were "to put into a definite form the preamble and rules and submit the same to the next meeting of the General Council." The subcommittee was specifically ordered to retain the sentiments of the Le Lubez version. All that was needed now was to put it into acceptable English.

This was Marx's opportunity. Although he had approved in committee of the version approved by Le Lubez, and knew that nothing more was demanded than that the declaration should be written in a more acceptable form, he determined to sabotage it. At all costs it was necessary to prepare a fourth version which would be entirely his own. He was determined to rewrite the declaration in a form as close as possible to the *Communist Manifesto*. It would be watered down; here and there he would make insignificant compromises for the benefit of the English workingmen who comprised the majority of the committee and were not susceptible to communist ideas; he would disguise his true purpose, but he would not permit himself to depart from his own conception of the International under any condition. He would draw up a declaration for a communist International.

It was a brilliant maneuver, and he carried it off with complete success. He was perfectly aware that he was playing a conspiratorial trick on his fellow members. He knew too that the communist International he envisaged was far from being the fraternal International which the English workers envisaged. In his letter to Engels Marx explained exactly how he went about hoodwinking the other members of the subcommittee. He wrote:

> On October 20 there was a meeting at my house attended by Cremer for the English, Fantana (Italy) and Le Lubez. (Weston could not come.) Hitherto I had never had physical possession of the documents (written by Wolff and Le Lubez), and so I could not prepare anything, but was firmly

determined that if possible not one single line of the stuff should be allowed to stand. In order to gain time I proposed that before we "edited" the preamble we should "discuss" the rules. This was done. It was an hour after midnight before the first of the 40 rules was agreed to. Cremer said (*and this was what I was aiming for*): We have nothing to show the Committee, which meets on October 25. We must postpone the meeting to November 1. But the subcommittee can get together on October 27 and attempt to reach a definite conclusion. This was agreed to, and the "documents" were "sent back" for my opinion.

I saw that it was impossible to make anything out of the stuff. In order to justify the extraordinarily strange way in which I proposed to present the "sentiments" which were already "voted," I wrote "An Address to the Working Classes" (which was not in the original plan: a sort of review of the adventures of the working classes since 1845); on the pretext that everything material was included in this "Address," and that we ought not to repeat the same things three times over, I altered the whole preamble, threw out the *déclaration des principes*, and finally replaced the forty rules with ten. In so far as international politics come into the "Address," I speak of countries, not of nationalities, and denounce Russia, not the *minores gentium*. My proposals were all accepted by the subcommittee. Only I was obliged to insert two "duty" and "right" phrases in the preamble, ditto "truth, morality, and justice"; but these are placed in such a way that they do no harm.

At the meeting of the General Council my "Address" was greeted with great enthusiasm (unanimously). . . .

At the meeting of the General Council held on November 1 Marx arranged that three of his followers, Karl Pfänder, Friedrich Lessner and Hermann Jung, should be elected members—four more Englishmen and one Frenchman were elected at the same time—and then he read out his "Address to the Working Classes," which he had previously sent to Cremer. "There are one or two words, which I fear will not be understood by the mass," Cremer replied in a brief note. In fact only two words were deleted at the meeting. Marx had spoken about the "frightened avarice of profitmongers," and William Worley had jumped up and demanded that "of profitmongers" should be struck out. Of the twenty-one members present, eleven voted for the amendment, which was accordingly passed. Marx could comfort himself that this was a small price to pay for so large a triumph.

In this way, with calculated effrontery, by delaying tactics, dubious pretexts and deliberate subterfuges, Marx put forward the document which came to be known as the "Inaugural Address," as though he had delivered it at the inaugural meeting of the International. He confessed to Engels that it had not been easy to prevail over the opinions of the other members of the committee, and he had evidently employed all his oratorical skill and all his powers of persuasion to ensure their approval. He admitted that he had compromised with his own ideas, and regretted he could not employ all his old boldness of speech when talking with English workingmen. He quoted the old Roman adage: *fortitur in re, suavitur in modo* ("strong in deed, smooth in manner"). He had worked upon the members of the committee so smoothly that they came to believe that he had merely rephrased the ideas of Weston and Le Lubez. They passed a vote of thanks to Marx, Weston and Le Lubez for producing so admirable a document, although the credit belonged to Marx alone.

The "Address" shows Marx in his customary prophetic role. His special hobby horses are dragged from their stables and presented as brilliant discoveries: the economic crisis is at hand; the British government is criminally conspiring with Russia to oppress the working classes of all Europe; the laws designed to improve the lot of the working class are merely the devices of the ruling class to impose their will upon the poor. The oppressive theme of murder returns again and again. There had been a strange epidemic of garroting in London at the beginning of the sixties; Marx insisted that the convicted garroters fared better at the hands of the British government than the agricultural laborers of England and Scotland. British industry, vampirelike, was sucking the life blood of children. "In olden times, child murder was a mysterious rite of the religion of Moloch, but it was practiced on some very special occasions only, once a year perhaps, and then Moloch had no exclusive bias for the children of the poor." Once more, as in the days of the *Communist Manifesto,* Marx was presenting himself as the old bogieman determined to make people's flesh creep.

What Marx was seeking to do against all the evidence was to prove that the lot of the English workingman, far from having improved in the sixteen years since the 1848 revolutions, had in fact deteriorated to such an extent that only another revolution, fiercer and more far-reaching, would bring about conditions which permitted the workingman to earn a living wage.

While Marx indicted the British government, he reserved his most sonorous passages for the industrial crisis which had spread throughout Europe. *Everywhere* the great mass of the working classes was sinking down to the lowest depths; *nowhere* was there the last hope of amelioration. The language of rhetoric was pressed into the service of social philosophy. He declared:

> In all countries of Europe it has now become a truth demonstrable to every unprejudiced mind, and only denied by those whose interest it is to hedge other people in a fool's paradise, that no improvement of machinery, no appliance of science to production, no contrivances of communication, no

new colonies, no new emigration, no opening of markets, no free trade, nor all these things put together, will do away with the miseries of the industrious masses; but that, on the present false base, every fresh development of the productive powers of labour must tend to deepen social contrasts and point social antagonisms. Death of starvation rose almost to the rank of an institution, during this intoxicating epoch of economical progress, in the metropolis of the British empire. That epoch is marked in the annals of the world by the quickened return, the widening compass, and the deadlier effects of the social pest called a commercial and industrial crisis.

Wherever Marx looked, he saw evidence of the crisis, which arose out of the ancient and obsolete law of supply and demand as instituted by the bourgeoisie, and which would end only when the working classes took power and managed the economy with "social foresight." With "shameless approval, mock sympathy, or idiotic indifference" the ruling classes had watched the Russians devastating the Caucasus and drowning Poland in blood, and it was the task of the working classes to protest vehemently against the immense encroachments of that barbarous power, "whose head is in St. Petersburg, and whose hands are in every cabinet of Europe." Russia, too, must bear some share of responsibility for the ever-widening crisis, and he urged on the members of the International that they master the mysteries of international politics and challenge the diplomats of their own governments. "The fight for such a foreign policy forms part of the general struggle for the emancipation of the working classes. Proletarians of all countries, unite!"

The provisional rules, which followed immediately after the address, began with some general considerations of the nature of the revolutionary struggle confronting the working classes. These considerations form a preface to the ten rules, and continue in a more dogmatic form the arguments announced in the address. The opening words are especially significant, because they reflect the beliefs which Marx shared with the English workingmen who founded the International:

Considering,

That the emancipation of the working classes must be conquered by the working classes themselves; that the struggle for the emancipation of the working classes means not a struggle for class privileges and monopolies, but for equal rights and duties, and the abolition of all class rule;

That the economical subjection of the man of labour to the monopoliser of the means of labour, that is the sources of life, lies at the bottom of servitude in all its forms, of all social misery, mental degradation and political dependence;

That the economical emancipation of the working classes is therefore the great end to which every political movement ought to be subordinate as a means;

That all efforts aiming at that great end have hitherto failed from the

> want of solidarity between the manifold divisions of labour in each country, and from the absence of a fraternal bond of union between the working classes of different countries;
>
> That the emancipation of labour is neither a local nor a national, but a social problem, embracing all countries in which modern society exists, and depending for its solution on the concurrence, practical and theoretical, of the most advanced countries . . .

Since Marx had drawn up the rules and was their sole interpreter, he was in a powerful position to dominate the society. He attended most of the meetings, drew up many of the reports, and saw to it that his own creatures were elected. He had dreamed of power, and now power was at his finger tips. He was determined to make the International so strong that it would become the vehicle for his attack on all the European governments.

The work, although arduous, gave him enormous satisfaction, and in his correspondence he was inclined to boast about the influence of the International and his own predominant role. In March 1865—five months after the original meeting in St. Martin's Hall—he was complaining to Engels that he was exhausted with his labors, which took nearly all his time, but he had concluded that it was well worth his energy, because he was in fact the head of the whole affair. There was a new tone in his letters. They became less argumentative; he was no longer laying down opinions, but standing in judgment. Curt, efficient, unmistakably in command, he explains what has to be done in the tones of a man accustomed to being obeyed.

In his own eyes the power of the International extended across England, France, Belgium, Switzerland and Italy. Only in Germany did he feel that the International was being resisted, and he put the blame squarely on the successors of Lassalle. The power and importance of the International continually fluctuated, but Marx's own power was continually increasing. In the 1866 Congress only four countries sent representatives—England, France, Germany and Switzerland—but at the Congress held three years later there were nine countries, with delegates arriving from the United States, Austria, Belgium, Spain and Italy. No accurate calculation of the numbers of members was ever made. Newspapers published by the International claimed fantastic numbers: the figure of seven million was not considered excessive. The police, who had their own reasons for exaggerating the number of members, were inclined to place the figure at five million. In fact there were never more than a million members, and there were years when the number was considerably less.

In the eyes of Marx the International was a revolutionary secret society preparing to take over the governments of Europe. "Things are moving," he wrote to Engels in September 1867, "and in the next revolution, which is perhaps nearer than it seems, *we* (i.e. you and I) have this powerful machinery *in our hands.*" In the following year he wrote to Dr. Kugelmann: "If I were to leave here at this critical hour, the whole labour movement, which I influence from behind the scenes, would fall into very bad hands and go the wrong way." At such moments Marx appears to be suffering from delusions of grandeur; and there was never a time when the International could have assumed power in Europe.

The European governments were vividly aware of the activities of the International, and were not particularly afraid of it. Most of the documents of the International fell into the hands of the police; they were stolen or copied out by police spies; vast dossiers accumulated. Oscar Testut, a lawyer from Lyons, working with the assistance of the French police, published three volumes of documents, which are among our chief sources for the workings of the International. Except for a curious habit of omitting occasional phrases, Testut compiled a scrupulously accurate record of the proceedings of the International. Against the continual encroachments of the police the International was powerless.

Marx himself attended none of the Congresses of the International except the last, which was held at the Hague. He lived quietly in London, pulling strings, writing innumerable letters, embarking on a thousand intrigues, while continuing to work on *Das Kapital.* Every Tuesday evening, when his health permitted, he attended the meetings of the General Council which were held in an upstairs room at 18 Greek Street, Soho. The minute books have survived, and they show him to have been a resolute proposer of motions, always advancing the cause of the German branches of the International, but prepared to assume any duty and to take on any difficult and onerous task. When it was decided to draw up an address for presentation to the people of America congratulating them on having elected Abraham Lincoln to the Presidency, it was Marx who assumed the responsibility of writing the address. He never acquired a knowledge of idiomatic English, and so the address was written in that strange and passionate Germano-English which reads better when translated into German:

To Abraham Lincoln, President of the United States of America

SIR,

We congratulate the American People upon your Re-election by a large Majority.

If resistance to the Slave Power was the reserved Watchword of your first election, the triumphant Warcry of your Re-election is Death to Slavery.

To Abraham Lincoln

President of the United States

of America

Sir

We congratulate the American People upon your Re-election by a large Majority.

If resistance to the Slave power was the reserved Watchword of your first election, the triumphant Warcry of your Re-election is, Death to Slavery.

From the commencement of the Titanic American Strife, the Working men of Europe felt instinctively that the Star spangled Banner carried the Destiny of their class. The Contest for the territories which opened the dire epopee, Was it not to decide whether the virgin soil of immense tracts should be wedded to the Labour of the Emigrant, or prostituted by the Tramp of the Slave Driver?

When an Oligarchy of 300,000 Slaveholders dared to inscribe, for the first time in the annals of the World, Slavery on the Banner of Armed Revolt; when on the very spots where hardly a century ago the idea of one great democratic Republic had first sprung up, Whence the first Declaration of The Rights of Man was issued, and the first impulse given to the European Revolution of the 18th Century; When on those very spots counter revolution, with systematic thoroughness, gloried in rescinding "The Ideas entertained at the time of the formation of the old Constitution" and maintained "Slavery to be a beneficent Institution, indeed the only solution of the great problem of the relation of Labour to Capital"; and cynically proclaimed property in Man "The corner stone of the New Edifice"; Then the Working Classes of Europe understood at once, Even before the fanatic partisanship of the Upper Classes for the confederate gentry had given its dismal warning, That the Slaveholder's Rebellion was to sound the tocsin for a general holy Crusade of Property against Labour, and that for the Men of Labour, with their hopes for the future even their past conquests were at stake in that tremendous Conflict on the other side of the Atlantic. Everywhere they bore while before the Negro, mastered and sold without his concurrence, they boasted it the highest prerogative of the white skinned Laborer to sell himself and choose his own Master; they were unable to attain the true Freedom of Labour or to support their European Brethren in their struggle for Emancipation, but this barrier to progress has been swept off by the red sea of Civil War.

The Working Men of Europe feel sure that as the American War of Independence initiated a new era of ascendency for the Middle Class, so the American Anti-Slavery War will do for the Working Classes. They consider it an earnest of the epoch to come, that it fell to the lot of Abraham Lincoln, the single-minded Son of the Working Class, to lead his Country through the matchless struggle for the rescue of an enchained Race and the Reconstruction of a Social World.

Signed on behalf of The International Working Men's Association

The Central Council.

Le Lubez (corresponding French Secretary)
F. Rybczinski / Pole
Emile Holtorp (Pole)
B. Bocquet
H. Jung corresponding secretary for Switzerland
Morissot
George Wm. Wheeler
J. Denoual
P. Bordage
Le Roux
Talandier
Jourdain
Dupont
R. Gray

D. Lama
C. Setacci
F. Solustri
P. Aldovrandi
D. G. Bagnagatti
[illegible]
G. P. Fontana Corresponding Secretary for Italy
P. Lake
J. Buckley
G. Howell
J. Osborne
J. D. Stainsby
J. Grossmith

G. Eccarius
Frd. Lessner
L. Wolff
K. Kaub
Henry Bolleter
Ludwig Otto
N. P. Hansen / Dane
Carl Pfaender
Georg Lochner
Peter Petersen
Karl Marx, Corresponding Secretary for Germany
A. Dick
J. Wolff

J. Whitlock
J. Carter
W. Morgan
William Dell
John Weston
Peter Fox
Robert Shaw
John H. Longmaid
Robert Henry Side
William C. Worley
Blackmore
R. Hartwell
W. Pidgeon
B. Lucraft
J. Nieass

Geo. Odger President of Council

William R. Cremer Honorary General Secretary

> From the commencement of the Titanic American Strife, the Working men of Europe felt instinctively that the Star Spangled Banner carried the Destiny of their class. The Contest for the territories which opened the dire epopee, Was it not to decide whether the virgin soil of immense tracts should be wedded to the Labour of the Emigrant, or prostituted by the Tramp of the Slave Driver? . . .

The tribute to Lincoln, "the single-minded Son of the Working Class," was inscribed on parchment and signed by fifty-eight members of the International, Marx describing himself as the "Corresponding Secretary for Germany." It was handed to Charles Francis Adams, the American Minister to the Court of St. James, and in due course William Cremer, the secretary of the International, received a letter from the Minister indicating that Lincoln had received the address and approved of its sentiments and hoped "to prove himself not unworthy of the confidence which has been recently extended to him by his fellow-citizens and by so many of the friends of humanity and progress throughout the world." Marx was delighted with Adams' reply, saying it was the only Presidential response to a congratulatory message which "was not merely a *formal* confirmation of receipt." He seemed to believe that President Lincoln had read the address carefully and told Adams what to say.

The work of the General Council was rarely exciting, and very few presidents or prime ministers deigned to reply to the addresses or threats of the International. Reports came in, and were duly filed. Routine questions were discussed, and set aside. They debated whether Cremer should receive a salary, or how they would raise the money to pay for the use of a meeting room in the Hotel New York. The affairs of the International were conducted on a level of humdrum expediency, without any particular urgency. The revolution was still a long way away.

THE HOUSE ON MAITLAND PARK ROAD

As he grew older, Marx's habits became more regular and more temperate. He no longer worked through the night and slept during the morning. The old bohemian ways were abandoned, as he became more affluent. He lived quietly, according to a fixed schedule, rarely going out, working hard at his correspondence and his books during the morning and afternoon, receiving visitors over a bottle of port in the evening. Except for the regular Tuesday evening meetings in Greek Street, he rarely ventured into central London.

The days when he had gone pub-crawling through Soho and Bloomsbury were now over, and he rarely visited the German clubs or took part in their debates. He had become a creature of habit, a solid and respectable citizen, who read *The Times* over breakfast and spent the rest of the day in very much the same way as any other man of scholarly tastes and independent means.

No one arriving at the new house on Maitland Park Road would mistake it for a workman's lodging. It was spacious and handsome, with cornices over the windows and elegant Corinthian columns at the head of the steps, with a small garden in front and a larger one at the back. Like nearly all the columned houses in London, this house gave an impression of subdued affluence. A doctor, a local magistrate, or a businessman who worked in the city would not have been out of place in it.

There was a hallway lit by a fanlight over the door, and just inside the door there was the usual mahogany umbrella stand. Steps led down to the basement, and the stairway led straight up to the first floor where Marx's study adjoined the master bedroom. The children's bedrooms were on the second floor, and the dining room and parlor were on the ground floor.

Altogether there were eight or nine rooms in the house, the largest being Marx's study on the first floor overlooking a small park. The walls, from floor to ceiling, were hidden by bookshelves, and since the shelves could not hold all the books there were tables piled high with them. Facing the window, near the door, was the leather sofa where Marx sometimes rested. Bookshelves surrounded the fireplace; on the marble mantelpiece there were more books, together with the miscellaneous gatherings of half a century: keepsakes, letters, matches, cigars, tobacco boxes, paperweights, photographs of Engels and Wilhelm Wolff, and of his wife and daughters. The Marxes were inveterate visitors to photographic studios and regularly sent out photographs of themselves, and just as regularly received the photographs of their friends. The mantelpiece was crowded with photographs. The decoration of mantelpieces is now a lost art, but in Victorian England it was cultivated with assiduity and a quiet passion.

In the middle of the room, gathering the full light from the windows, was the small wooden desk with the wooden armchair at which Marx regularly worked. The desk could hold little more than a sheet of notepaper and a few books, for it was only three feet by two feet. It resembled the small desks used by schoolboys. There was an inkwell, an assortment of steel pens, pencils, a box for stamps, gum, gutta percha, and a paper cutter. Marx usually wrote in India ink, and the tart smell of the ink hung over the room.

At first sight Marx's study gave an impression of violent disorder, and this impression was increased by the piles of newspapers on the floor, in the bookcases and on the tables. The bookshelves, too, looked distressingly disorderly, for the books were not displayed according to size or bindings or subject matter, but according to Marx's very personal ideas of relevance. Government pamphlets were wedged in beside books on economic theory, British Blue Books were everywhere, folded newspapers were stuffed into some books and others when they were opened would pour out cascades of neatly written notes. There were rows of French novels bound in yellow paper—Marx had a curious passion for Paul de Kock's novels about the *grisettes* and cabarets of Paris—and there were bound volumes of Balzac, whom Marx regarded so highly that at one time he planned to write an extensive critique of *La Comédie Humaine*. He had a strange theory that Balzac possessed prophetic powers, describing during the reign of Louis Philippe characters which did not fully emerge into history until the reign of Napoleon III.

Marx's study was really a workshop, an engine room for generating those turbulent ideas which were to determine the course of history; the schoolboy's desk at the center of the room was his command post. There he sat hour upon hour, a small hunched figure with heavy shoulders and small dangling legs, so shortsighted that he wrote with his nose close to the paper even though he wore steel-rimmed spectacles. In public he was more likely to sport a monocle. The monocle permitted him to make those stern gestures and assume those quizzical expressions which could still paralyze his friends. A stupid question, or one which did not meet with Marx's approval, would be greeted with a quick stare, a puffing of the cheeks, and the slow fixing of the monocle under the beetling eyebrow. It was a weapon of offense.

Through this workshop a straight path, uncluttered by books or newspapers, had been cleared from the door to the window, skirting the desk. Along this narrow path Marx would often pace restlessly up and down, his head bent forward, his hands clasped behind his back. A strip had been worn out on the carpet, as clearly defined as a track across a meadow.

There was a narrower and fainter strip leading to the leather sofa against the wall.

Marx's attitude toward his books was that of an engineer surrounded by the expendable tools of his trade. He had no feeling for books as works of art or as possessions of value. He would turn down the corners of the pages, or insert matchsticks, to mark important passages. He scribbled on the margins, underlined sentences in ink, and wrote on the end papers. He confronted passages with which he disagreed with enormous question marks, or he would write: "This is rubbish!" When he was old and dying, he told Eleanor that she would find much to amuse her on the margins of his books. In his memoirs on Marx, Paul Lafargue asserted that he never wrote on books but merely underlined a few notable passages, but this was an expression of filial piety. A book, after Marx had gone through it, looked as though it had been swallowed and digested, and then regurgitated.

The disorder and confusion of the study exactly mirrored the disorder and confusion in his mind. Those tables heaped with British Blue Books and ancient newspapers, those bulging shelves, those mounting towers of books on the floor, those volumes scattered on the window ledge and the mantelpiece, suggested a mind which had never completely escaped from the convulsions of adolescence. He treated books as he treated people, abusing them unmercifully, never demonstrating the least sign of repentance. "They are my slaves," he said, "and they must serve my will." He had no affection for them; they were foreign territory to be raided and conquered as he pleased, and he was perfectly serious when he spoke of them as slaves.

Although the study seemed to bend under its load of books, hemming him in on all sides, so that it was almost impossible for him to move about except along the two clearly defined roads, there was method in this madness. The small space in the center of the room was consecrated to his writing, while all the rest of the room was sacrificed to books. It was as though he needed to be strictly confined to a very small and secure area where he alone was master. The study therefore served as a womb, a prison, a place of refuge, an ivory tower. It was characteristic of the man that he received his visitors in this crowded room where there was scarcely space to sit down, and that he enjoyed leading the subject of conversation to ideas which derived from books. At such times he would dart to the shelves and produce a volume which would triumphantly vindicate his own opinions. It was also characteristic of him that he permitted no one to remove a book from the shelves, and even Helene Demuth was never permitted to dust them.

In this confusion, with cigar butts lying about, his large assortment of pipes scattered on whatever would support them, matchboxes everywhere—he was a large consumer of matchboxes, for he struck an incredible number of matches in order to keep a cigar or a pipe alight—and with the air filled with the decaying smell of tobacco, he passed his working hours in supreme contentment. He enjoyed writing, even though it was always difficult for him, and he enjoyed wrestling with ideas. He could not afford a large and extensive library, and at no time did he possess more than a thousand books. But in a hundred notebooks he preserved the important passages from the books he had read in the British Museum, and the library therefore represented only a part of his available literary resources. He was an inveterate note-taker, and the habit grew even more pronounced as he grew older.

What Marx did not know was that this mode of life was slowly killing him. It was not only that he smoked too much, but he spent eight or nine hours a day breathing tobacco smoke in a room where, except on calm summer days, the windows were permanently closed. He was taking less and less exercise, and less and less sensible food, for now that he was reasonably affluent he was indulging himself more and more with highly seasoned foods. The only physical exercise came from the Sunday walks on Hampstead Heath, but these were neither so frequent nor so prolonged as in the days when he was younger. Sometimes he would go for a short stroll on Hampstead Heath in the evening.

His day began around nine o'clock in the morning, with breakfast consisting only of a roll of bread and black coffee. He would read *The Times,* make some observations on the weather, and then vanish into his study in a cloud of cigar smoke. He was one of those men whose minds grow clearer as the day advances, and he was not at his best in the early morning. Once he had reached his study, his first task was to deal with his extensive correspondence, which threatened to engulf him, so that he was continually apologizing to his correspondents for his delay in answering their letters. Eleanor or his wife would sometimes be called in to take dictation, or if Paul Lafargue was visiting London, he too would be called in to act as an assistant secretary. So many letters flowed out of the house that the cost of postage stamps seriously interfered with the family budget.

The workday was interrupted only by meals, with lunch in the early afternoon and dinner around seven o'clock. Sometimes he would take a nap after lunch, and after dinner he liked to read to Jenny whatever he had composed during the day. By common consent weighty subjects were rarely discussed at dinner, which Marx regarded as a sacred feast, a time of communion with his family; only very rarely were visitors invited to share this feast. Helene Demuth usually sat with them at the table, which was served by a parlormaid.

Because the children were growing up, the long years of dependence on Helene Demuth came to an end. She was no longer the kingpin, making all the vital decisions which enabled the family to survive economic disasters. She did the shopping, sewed the children's dresses, saw that the bills were paid, and superintended the household, but her effective power had diminished. She had more leisure, and being a heavy drinker, she had more time for secret drinking. She was growing old rapidly, and she had lost the fragile beauty of her youth.

In March 1864, when Marx first began to live in Maitland Park Road where he was to remain for the rest of his life, his daughter Jenny was nearly twenty, Laura was eighteen, and Eleanor, the late-comer, was nine. Jenny, with her dark eyes and jet-black hair, took after her father. She had a lively disposition and thought of herself as a budding actress, with the result that she learned long passages of Shakespeare by heart and declaimed them at every opportunity. She had inherited something of her father's coloring and much of her mother's beauty. Laura had the misfortune of inheriting her father's hard mouth, and her face seemed to be composed of two separate halves. She had her mother's fine green eyes, dark-auburn hair, and rosy coloring, and in some lights, when her face was lowered and the lines of her mouth were in shadow, she too could give an impression of adolescent beauty. She was less vivacious than her elder sister, more cautious, and more philosophical. Jenny was gifted in drawing, and at one time there had been some talk of sending her to art school, but Marx could not tolerate the thought of his daughters living away from him, and so a drawing master was employed to come to the house and give her lessons. Laura showed no talent for drawing, and her drawing lessons were discontinued shortly after they had begun. She was given to long fits of brooding and evidently suffered from the presence of a more brilliant older sister. Very early she learned that there could be no rivalry for her father's affection, for Marx clearly adored Jenny above all his daughters.

Eleanor, who was so much the youngest, enjoyed all the advantages of her age, and was granted freedoms never permitted to her older sisters. She, too, had her father's dark-brown eyes and jet-black hair, and though she possessed none of Jenny's nobility of expression, and was never beautiful, she had an appealing nature and was by far the most daring of Marx's daughters. Jenny was too shy to go on the stage; Eleanor took every opportunity of appearing in amateur theatricals. She demanded attention, and was never happy without it. There was always something theatrical in her gestures and in her speech, and like her father she was inclined to see herself as a tragic actor in a romantic drama.

Just as Marx adored his eldest daughter almost to the exclusion of the others, so his wife adored her youngest daughter, remembering that she had been born just about the time that Edgar died. She chattered incessantly as a child, and she was always telling stories derived from the romantic fables of the Brothers Grimm. She was very close to Helene Demuth, with whom she spoke German, and was the only one of Marx's daughters who spoke and read German fluently. Gay, impudent, and charming, she grew up into a rather willful and determined exponent of her father's ideas, which she scarcely understood.

Everyone in the family had a nickname, and most of them had a variety of nicknames. Eleanor was Tussy, Quo-quo or Dwarf Alberich, the powerful treasurer of the *Nibelungenlied*. Alberich wore a cloak of invisibility until it was wrested from him by Siegfried. Eleanor gloried in this nickname through most of her childhood, becoming Tussy only when she was an adolescent. Laura, perhaps because she was the fairest of Marx's daughters, had the nickname of Hottentot, but she was more often called Kakadu, after a fashionable tailor in an old novel. Jenny, being the eldest and the most aristocratic in appearance, took the name of Emperor of China, or Qui-qui, or Di. Marx himself was generally called Moor, Devil, or Old Nick by his children in tribute to his dark beard, dark complexion, and faintly sinister appearance. Sometimes he was called "Challey," the Marxist equivalent of "Charlie." His wife was called Möhme, which was merely the Germanic form of the English "Mum." Helene Demuth had the nickname of Nym or Nimmi. The children had originally called her Mimi or Minni, but as they grew older they settled on a slightly less sentimental name. The short clipped "Nym" reflected perhaps the no-nonsense quality of the servant who ran the household with quiet efficiency.

On the whole it was a happy family except on the days when poverty opened the doors and took command of the house. At such times a neurotic terror descended on them, and for a few days or weeks they found themselves in the grip of a misery so great that it tore them apart and left them helpless. The children were carefully protected, but they learned very early to recognize the face of poverty; they heard their mother weeping and they knew when Helene Demuth was hurrying off to the pawnbroker. At various times all three daughters suffered from nervous diseases which perhaps derived from the pervading sense of insecurity.

The house on Maitland Park Road hinted at affluence. The wide windows, the high, columned doorway, the endless stairways and the spacious rooms suggested an upper-middle-class family living in cultivated ease, with many servants attending them, and in fact there were never fewer than two servants. Jenny especially enjoyed the house, and spoke of "this new, friendly, sunlit house with the bright and airy rooms." For her it was almost paradise.

A SHORT SKETCH OF AN EVENTFUL LIFE

In the summer or autumn of 1865 Jenny Marx sat down to write a brief and informal account of her life, perhaps to sustain herself in her hours of loneliness or simply because she felt there was a need to record her strange and unhappy life for posterity. It was not a long work, for it covered only thirty-seven closely written pages, of which some twenty-nine have survived. The manuscript was not published in her lifetime, nor in the lifetime of her children. For a century it existed in a kind of limbo, gathering dust. It was a relic, too holy to be touched, too intimate a document to be shown to any except the most privileged. Liebknecht and Eleanor both quoted a few sentences, and Franz Mehring, Marx's first biographer, permitted himself a whole paragraph, but until the publication of a bowdlerized version in the Soviet Union in 1958 it was not known whether the manuscript had survived. Finally the complete text was published for the first time in Leipzig in 1965, a hundred years after it was written. Then at last Jenny was permitted to show herself as she was.

There were, of course, excellent reasons for concealing the document, and no doubt the eight missing pages were torn out for good cause. Jenny liked to speak bluntly, and though she loved her husband to distraction there was never any period of her life when he appeared to her as the living embodiment of a legend; for her he was human, all too human. Like Liebknecht, who described Marx with warm humanity, happily recounting his pub crawls and his delight in throwing stones at gas lamps, his ill temper when he lost a game of chess and his incessant talk of impending crises which never happened, Jenny depicts a Marx with ordinary human failings. When she speaks of herself there is no trace of the legendary "comrade in arms of the great fighter for the world proletarian revolution." Instead she describes herself as a woman who never completely disassociated herself from her aristocratic background, loved dressing in expensive clothes, delighted in the society of cultivated middle-class people, adored the comforts of life, and was oppressed by her husband's incapacity to earn a living. She was especially anxious that her children should be brought up in an atmosphere of refinement, with the best available tutors in singing, music and languages. She liked giving balls and entertaining guests, and she was proud when her friends could stay in her house. Her greatest happiness came when they were able to find "a pretty and healthy house, which we furnished very comfortably and rather elegantly." All this appeared in her manuscript, which was kept secret for so long.

When the bowdlerized version was published in the Soviet Union, all the aristocratic and bourgeois traits in Jenny's character were scrupulously omitted by the simple process of censoring out all the passages in which she speaks of her love for fine clothes, balls, comforts, the refinements of life. The Soviet government was in a strong position, for it had acquired the unpublished document from the Longuet family, which had inherited it from Eleanor. The original manuscript now reposes in the archives of the Marx-Engels-Lenin Institute in Moscow, where no one except the most dedicated Marxist scholars are permitted to see it. It is therefore impossible to check whether the version published in Leipzig is complete in all essentials, although there is some internal evidence to suggest that it is virtually complete except for the eight missing pages. These pages were probably destroyed by Eleanor, who was determined that nothing should be known about the quarrels and dissensions of her parents.

Jenny's manuscript deserved a better fate, for she wrote with her heart's blood. She begins simply on her wedding day, the day which she always regarded as the beginning of her mature life:

> June 19, 1843, was my wedding day. We journeyed from Kreuznach over the Ebernburg to Rheinpfalz and then by way of Baden-Baden returned to Kreuznach, where we stayed until the end of September. My dear mother returned to Trier with my brother Edgar. At the beginning of October Karl and I went to Paris, and we were met by Herwegh and his wife.

So she writes, always a little disjointedly, never allowing herself to pause very long over any incident, never describing a person, at ease among names and dates, curiously detached. She evidently wrote with a diary in front of her, but the diary was sketchy and she sometimes omits important incidents in her life entirely. Perhaps she had forgotten them; perhaps there were so many miseries that she preferred to forget them. There emerges the portrait of a woman who had suffered greatly and was dedicated to her children above all. She especially remembered the dull, gray days when tragedy flowered:

> At Easter 1852 our poor little Franziska fell ill with severe bronchitis. For 3 days the poor child wrestled with death. She suffered much. Her little lifeless body rested in the small back room; we all wandered out into the front room, and when night fell we made our beds on the floor, and the three living children lay with us, and we wept for the little angel who lay cold and lifeless nearby. The death of our beloved child took place at the time of our bitterest poverty. Our German friends could not help us just then. Ernest Jones, who was then paying us long and frequent visits, had promised to help us, but he could give us nothing. Bangya, a Hungarian colonel who had insinuated himself at this time into our group, having asked Karl to correct a manuscript for Szemere, promised his immediate assistance, but he was incapable of helping.
>
> With anguish in my heart I ran to a French *émigré* who lived near us and used to visit us. I begged him for help in our terrible need. He at once gave me £2 with the friendliest sympathy, and with the money the small coffin was bought, and there my poor child now slumbers peacefully. She had no cradle when she came into the world, and for a long time she was refused a last resting place.

From Jenny's memoirs we learn that her greatest satisfaction when she was living in Dean Street was to escape from the small apartment into the ladies' saloons of the local bars, where she could drown her sorrows in London ale. She enjoyed the "cozy conversations" in the public houses, the air of conviviality, the noise and the banter. Walking, too, was one of her great pleasures, and she speaks of her long lonely walks through the crowded West End streets after attending meetings at the German clubs and after her solitary visits to the public houses. These walks became less frequent as she grew older. We learn from other sources that she had a passion for the theater, but she does not mention it in her memoirs, perhaps because the Royalty Theatre was almost opposite the apartment on Dean Street and was therefore an intimate part of her life, so familiar that it was scarcely worth noting.

She records the pains and miseries of exile, sicknesses and deaths, her daughters growing up, the happy Christmases when a friend came to decorate the tree and the children were loaded with presents. She remembers, too, the long summers when visitors came to stay with them—one year it was the revolutionary Georg Eccarius, another year it was her friend Lisa Schöler, a governess, who was beloved by the children and was gentle with everyone.

About Helene Demuth she says surprisingly little, but she has more to say about Helene's youngest sister Marianne. Marianne was about twelve years younger than Helene, a sturdy hard-working peasant girl, who did the ironing and all the menial work in the house, serving as kitchen maid and parlormaid, and running errands. She was cheerful and lively, and suffered from heart disease.

Jenny tells the story of Marianne's death, which took place in London shortly before she returned from one of those brief and unavailing visits she made to rich bankers in search of money to support her family. It had occurred to her that she might obtain a loan from a certain Abarbanel, a Jew living in the outskirts of Paris. She traveled to France alone and in despair, almost out of her mind because Marx had been incapable of raising any money in London and the children were destined to have a poverty-stricken Christmas. Everything went wrong during the journey. She sailed from Folkestone to Boulogne in a storm, and saw a ship foundering before her eyes. There was an accident on the railroad near Paris. Outside Paris she took an omnibus which overturned, and when at last she returned to London her hackney carriage drove into another and she had to make the rest of the journey on foot. But when she remembered that tragic Christmas, she forgot all the excitements of the journey in the contemplation of a dying banker and a dead servant girl. She wrote:

> There came a fairly long period of sorrow, want, privation and illnesses. To put a temporary end to these well-nigh unbearable conditions I traveled to Paris at Christmas 1862 to get help from a former acquaintance, who had grown rich in the meantime but remained generous. I reached this good friend's house in bitterly cold weather, full of cares, only to find that he had suffered a stroke and was scarcely recognizable. He died a few days after my arrival. I returned home in a state of hopelessness, and I had scarcely entered the house when I heard the terrible, melancholy news that Lenchen's sister, our dear, good, faithful Marianne, had died of a heart attack a few hours before. She had been a gentle and happy person, like a big child. This good, faithful, gentle, hard-working girl had been with us for 5 years. I had so won her love and depended so much upon her that her loss distressed me deeply. I lost in her a faithful, dependable, friendly being, whom I shall never forget.

In her memoirs Jenny never wrote about anyone else with such brooding affection.

All through *A Short Sketch of an Eventful Life* Jenny shows herself to be the aristocrat, proud of her lineage, her beauty and her instinctive generosity. She hated poverty because it removed from her the opportunity to be generous; and she hated squalor because it removed from her the opportunity to wear beautiful clothes. While she loved her husband passionately, she seems never to have been completely at ease in his presence: the seeds of distrust were sown very early. For her he was a stranger who had to be known afresh each day. In the end she became accustomed to him, as one becomes accustomed to strangers. Her real love was for her children.

She was one of those women who scarcely have any existence unless they are surrounded by servants. It was her good fortune that Helene Demuth came into her service very early in their married life. Without the "dear, faithful Lenchen" she would have gone mad under the strain of living with Marx.

For Marx, Jenny was the symbol of all that he prized most in the world. She represented the aristocratic tradition, the lost splendors of the past, the traditional graces. Her letters were signed "Jenny Marx, née Baronne von Westphalen," and there is no doubt that her aristocratic descent gave Marx an exquisite pleasure. On her envelopes and note paper there appeared according to the fashion of the time the letters *J* and *M* intertwined. In this elegant way she announced that she belonged wholly to the husband she worshiped and half feared.

Gradually after 1865 she begins to vanish from the scene. She became more than ever a recluse, rarely venturing out, a shadowy figure whose greatest happiness was an occasional visit to the seaside. The years passed, and her two older daughters left her side; Marx would embark on further revolutionary adventures; *Das Kapital* would be launched; the Paris Commune would surprise the world with its testimony of the strength and weakness of the revolutionary movement; but Jenny remained in the shadows. Pockmarked and prematurely old, she was now only the husk of the woman she had been.

THE BIRTH PANGS

As Marx gazed at the mounting manuscript of *Das Kapital,* he felt that he was at the mercy of a monster which was slowly destroying him. All his energy, all his hopes were in this book, which came to birth so slowly. He struggled with it as a man struggles with his demon, and sometimes he would retire for weeks and months into baffled silence, exhausted by the combat.

All his life he had the habit of writing hopeful letters in which he would announce that in a few weeks or months he would bring some great project to fulfillment, and he would write these letters more as goads to himself than as promises. Inevitably he shamed himself by his repeated failures; and sometimes it was as though he desired to feel the brand of shame on his face. These failures were sometimes acts of self-torture, and the pain was all the greater because he felt that *Das Kapital* would crown his lifework.

In his eyes the book already possessed historical significance. Here at last, displayed for all to see, there would be a book of majestic proportions announcing the inevitable destruction of the old order and the coming of the new. With immense learning and scholarship he would demonstrate the sources of capitalist power and show that they were tainted. He would prove step by step that capitalist society no longer had any reason to exist, and that a new, simpler, more egalitarian society under the dictatorship of the proletariat would inevitably replace it. This book would be the trumpet blast shattering the walls of the old Jericho. He would open the way, and the revolutionaries would take the city by storm.

In November 1864 he was in a prophetic mood as he wrote to his friend Dr. Kugelmann. "I believe," he wrote, "that during the next year my work on capital (60 sheets) will at last be ready for the press." In the same letter he spoke of a forthcoming Austro-Franco-Italian war which would have a disastrous effect on the socialist movement in England and France. Both prophecies remained unfulfilled, and they were perhaps not intended seriously. Prophecy was the world he lived in, and he was accustomed to failure.

Eight months later, in a long letter to Engels, he wrote as though he was already close to finishing not only the first volume, but two other volumes. "As regards my work I will tell you the absolute truth about it," he wrote. "There are still 3 chapters to write in order to make the theoretical part (the first 3 books) ready. Then there is still a 4th book to write, the historical-literary one, which will be for me relatively the easiest part, since all the problems have been solved in the first three books, so that this last one is more in the nature of a recapitulation in historical form. But I cannot make up my mind to part with any of it until I have the whole in my hands. Whatever shortcomings they may have, it is the merit of my writings that they form an artistic whole, and this can only be attained through my method of never sending anything to the press unless *the whole* lies before me." So the months passed, and it was not until the beginning of 1866 that the whole book lay before him in such a state that he believed he was ready to make a fair copy. It was becoming a nightmare, and he wanted to finish it off quickly. He wrote to Kugelmann on January 15: "As for my book, I am working twelve hours a day at writing out a fair copy. I expect to take the manuscript myself to Hamburg in March, and shall then have an opportunity of seeing you."

March came, and the manuscript was only a little more advanced. Delay was driving him out of his mind. In the excitement new boils emerged, this time on his buttocks, and his complaints about poverty became more urgent. "If I had more money," he wrote to Engels on February 13, "that is, if I had more than minus zero for my family, and if my book was ready, then it would be all the same to me whether today or tomorrow I was tossed into potter's field, *alias* went down the drain." Once more there was a balance sheet. "As regards the 'damned' book, this is how matters stand. It was *completed* at the end of December. The discussion of land-rent alone, the penultimate chapter, forms one book in itself, or very nearly so." It was already so vast a book that the labor of copying and recopying it terrified him. The style had to be improved, references had to be looked up, he had to be sure to copy it accurately, and no one could help him. At first he enjoyed "licking the infant clean after so many birth pangs," but this enjoyment vanished after a few days. There was trouble with the boil on his buttocks, which refused to heal. "If I am going to bring this thing to an end," he complained, "I must at the very least be able to *sit down*."

Many more weeks passed before he could sit down with ease, and all through the spring he merely made a few inconsequential changes in the manuscript, and the furious labor of copying was abandoned in the contemplation of minutiae.

So the days passed, while he seemed to be dissolving into the manuscript which he could never bring himself to complete, and the echoes of the outside world rarely reached him. On May 7 a shot was fired at Bismarck as he was walking along the Unter den Linden. The shots were fired by a youth standing only a few feet away. Bismarck had been ill, but he had the courage of a lion and he leaped at the youth and grappled with him. Some soldiers came to the rescue, and soon Bismarck was able to return to his own house, having lost, as he said later, "only a few hairs from my chest." There were bullet holes in his coat, overcoat, waistcoat and shirt. Altogether five shots had been fired at close range. The youth was arrested, and on the following day he hanged himself in prison.

Bismarck regarded his miraculous escape as a sign from heaven, and from that moment his popularity increased. He was cheered wherever he went. Marx regarded the incident more philosophically. The name of the youth was Ferdinand Cohen-Blind, and he was the half-English stepson of Karl Blind, a German refugee living in London. Marx had known the youth well when he was younger, for the boy had been the playmate of little Musch. "I had a special fondness for the boy, though he was not particularly intelligent," Marx wrote to Engels. He was harsher toward Karl Blind, who publicly displayed his grief and wrote about the sacrifice of his son's life in various public newspapers. Marx commented: "He has a fine eye for business." About Bismarck he wrote: "He must have been wearing a coat of mail, no doubt about it. He probably got it from his friend Napoleon. As you know, these coats are made to be very thin, but they are immensely strong."

These improvisations were not among Marx's best. Bismarck had not been wearing a coat of mail, and Karl Blind did not have a fine eye for business. But both Marx and Engels were agreed that the attempted assassination had been disastrous, for Ferdinand Cohen-Blind had made Bismarck the most popular man in Germany.

When summer came, Marx's health improved: the boils and the headaches vanished, and he was no longer taking arsenic pills. He began to work steadily, went off to Margate for a holiday, attended meetings of the General Council of the International Working Men's Association, and showed himself in his letters to be in fine good humor, although he was incapable of maintaining an equable temperament for long. He still complained, still poured out his vials of wrath, but for the first time in a decade he seemed to be in high spirits. Partly, this was due to the knowledge that Laura had found a potential fiancé in Paul Lafargue, a handsome twenty-four-year-old medical student of good family and considerable prospects. In his heavy-handed way Marx called him "Negrillo" or "Gorilla," because he had some Negro blood, but Paul Lafargue was incapable of taking offense.* His father was the owner of sugar plantations in Cuba, and the son had stirred up so much revolutionary excitement among the students in the French medical school he attended that he had been barred from attending lectures. He was now studying in London, but intended eventually to acquire a medical degree from Strasbourg University.

Paul Lafargue was a constant visitor to the house, and no one could have been kinder or more considerate. Laura was not sure she was in love with him, but he was quite sure he was in love with her. He had first visited the house in order to pay his respects to Marx, but gradually an attachment to the father had come to include an attachment to the daughter. Although understandably nervous—Marx had no experience in marrying off his daughters—he approved of his future son-in-law, and at once got down to business. What exactly were his prospects? He wrote to the young man's father, who was living in Bordeaux, to ask for an exact statement. The father answered courteously, assuring Marx that the family was solvent, indeed more than solvent, indeed passably rich, and perfectly prepared to settle an income on the young couple. Marx thereupon wrote to Engels to seek his advice, adding that the father had officially demanded on behalf of his son the hand of Laura in marriage. Everything was satisfactory except for the fact that Paul Lafargue was a little too ardent, and the further fact that Laura "liked him, as usual, in a rather cold way." Marx hoped that Laura would come to like her suitor more warmly, and that Paul Lafargue would learn to curb his ardor. "I told this Creole of ours that he must adopt the calmer English way," Marx wrote to Engels in August. "I warned him that unless he did this, Laura would send him packing without any ceremony at all. He must definitely understand this, otherwise we shall have nothing to do with him."

* Paul Lafargue had in interesting ancestry. He had French, Jewish, Carib Indian and Negro blood. His paternal grandmother was a mulatto from St. Domingo, who took refuge in Cuba during the revolutionary uprising of Toussaint L'Ouverture. His paternal grandfather was a French officer who was killed during the insurrection. On his mother's side, his grandfather, Abraham Armagnac, was a Jew of French origin. His maternal grandmother was a Carib Indian. Although Marx liked to call him "Gorilla," all the surviving photographs show a man of distinguished appearance with characteristically French features.

As usual, Marx was holding the leading strings. The hot summer had brought on more boils, he was working hard on *Das Kapital,* and he was not in the best of tempers. One thing particularly worried him: the Lafargues must be kept in ignorance about his own insolvency. Nevertheless he succeeded in concealing the full extent of his poverty from the suitor by more borrowing and by more urgent requests to Engels. As for the marriage, he decided that it must wait until Paul Lafargue had passed all his examinations and was ready to embark on a career.

These decisions coincided with a momentous discovery: the work on *Das Kapital* had advanced so far that the early chapters could be sent to the publisher. In a letter to Engels in November Marx announced that he was sending "the first batch" during the following week. Engels replied that he would drink a special toast to Marx to mark the occasion, but he was under no illusions concerning the finished work. There would, he knew, be more delays, more appeals for money, more and more excuses. The publisher did not want the preliminary pages; he wanted the entire book.

Finally, at the end of March 1867, Marx claimed that the book was ready and he intended to take the complete manuscript to Hamburg, where it would be published, the following week. Unfortunately, he was suffering from more boils, could not sit down, and was in desperate need of money. His watch and much of his clothing were at the pawnbroker. "Nor can I leave my family in their present state, without a *sou,* and with the creditors becoming more insolent every day." Engels answered good-naturedly: "An irrepressible hurrah! came from my lips when I read at last in black and white that the first volume is really ready, and that you are about to leave for Hamburg with it." He added the usual *bénéfice* in the form of seven five-pound notes, which were intended to defray the expenses of the journey and to keep the Marx family fed during his absence in Germany.

The sea journey was thoroughly unpleasant, and Marx described it to Engels with an unpleasantness equal to his theme. For some reason the journey through a storm made him feel "as cannibalistic as five hundred sows." Most of the women kept to their cabins; one proud woman, however, refused to go below. She was old and toothless, and in her delicate Hanoverian accent she liked to talk about raising the level of the working classes. Marx disliked her on sight. Since she insisted on remaining in the lounge where a handful of men were waiting out the storm, she became a butt for their jokes. They laughed uproariously when she was pitched out of her chair and thrown across the lounge, and they amused themselves by telling scatological jokes for her benefit. There was a German who had spent fifteen years in Peru, "where the eating of human flesh is still practiced." It was this German who related everything he knew about the strange sexual customs of the Peruvians in the presence of the old lady. He spoke of coming to an Indian hut where a woman had just given birth to a child, and the afterbirth was cooked and given to him. Marx was enormously amused by the horror of the old lady.

Otto Meissner, the Hamburg publisher, proved to be "a good fellow, a bit of a Saxon," who knew exactly how to put an author at his ease. He promised everything—the manuscript would go to the printer in a few days, every detail would be immediately attended to, the edition would be ready in the shortest possible time. When Marx suggested that there was something to be said for compressing the last chapter dealing with history, the publisher replied that it was exactly that chapter which would have the greatest appeal for the readers and that he himself, in his capacity as a bookseller, agreed with the ultimate judgment of the public. The manuscript was removed to the safety of the publisher's vault, and it was made clear to Marx that no more treasured volume had ever passed through a publisher's hands. "Thereupon we clinked glasses, and he declared himself 'overwhelmed' to have made my esteemed acquaintance." With some satisfaction Marx wrote to Engels: "We now have a publisher who will do everything we want him to do."

Alas for Marx's hopes! The dealings between author and publisher are rarely so amicable. Meissner promised that the typesetting would be completed in four or five weeks, in Hamburg, with his own proofreaders working on the manuscript. It soon became evident that he could not print the work on his own presses, but would have to farm it out to the printer Otto Wigand in Leipzig, and the Leipzig printer could not begin printing at once. Wigand took his own time and more than six weeks passed before Marx received the proofs of the opening pages. Meissner, too, was demonstrating that he was his own master. Marx had promised that *Das Kapital* would appear in three volumes, and now Meissner was insisting that he should keep to the promise; the second volume must be placed in his hands in the autumn, and the third in the following spring. Marx had no alternative; he had to agree to these provisions, and wrote hopefully to Engels that he intended to complete the second and third volumes during the winter. When the spring came, the entire work would be out of his hands.

Such were his hopes when the first printed sheets lay before him in Hanover, where he was a guest in the house of Dr. Ludwig Kugelmann.

Now that his book was actually going through the press, he felt uplifted by a new and hitherto unsuspected strength. He was sure he would complete the two remaining volumes in the stipulated time. In fact, these volumes were never completed, and for the remaining years of his life he would be forced to invent one excuse after another to explain the interminable delay.

Meanwhile Marx was enjoying the bourgeois comforts of Dr. Kugelmann's house. The doctor was a gynecologist, with a pretty young wife and an eight-year-old daughter. He was thirty-eight years old, but he was already established as one of the leading gynecologists in the country, consulted by specialists, his fame reaching into the medical academies in Berlin. Marx was enchanted with the doctor, and the doctor in turn was enchanted with Marx. "He is a fanatical supporter (and to my mind too Westphalian an admirer) of our doctrine and both our persons," Marx reported to Engels. "He sometimes bores me with his enthusiasm, which is in contradistinction to his frigid manner as a doctor. But he *understands,* and he is *basically sound,* uncalculating and self-sacrificing, and what is most important *convinced.*" He had a large library, which included most of the published works of Marx and Engels. Marx was able to discover a copy of *The Holy Family,* a book which was lacking in Engels' library. Accordingly the doctor's copy went off to Engels.

Marx was still staying with Kugelmann when he received a curiously worded letter from Engels. It was such a letter as would at any ordinary time make him pause, for all of Engels' pent-up anger, frustration and weariness were being subtly indicated. After mentioning that at Jenny's request he was sending her ten pounds, and at the end of the month he proposed to send another ten pounds to one of Marx's creditors, he wrote:

> It has always seemed to me that this damned book, at which you have been toiling for so long, was the root cause of all your rotten luck, and that you never would and never could get over it until you were able to shake off this incubus. This eternally unfinished thing crushed you to the earth physically, spiritually and financially, and I can well understand that now you have shaken off this nightmare, you will become quite another fellow, especially since the world, which you are now entering again, will look to you less dreary than before. Especially now that you have a publisher as wonderful as M. appears to be.

Engels was pointing out, as clearly as he could, that the publication of the book must be regarded as the beginning of a new way of life, a new attitude to the world. He was weary of paying Marx's debts, and most of all he was weary of Marx's querulous temper, his carping ways, his self-pity, and his strange delusions about money. He was not issuing an ultimatum, but there was more than the hint of a warning. He was saying that he hoped Marx would pull himself up by his bootstraps and become a more intelligent human being.

Marx was dimly aware that he was being rebuked, but he was in no mood to accept a large share of blame. He was confident that *Das Kapital* would bring him a large amount of money, that his days of penury were almost over, and that life would now blossom out in all its glory, and at the same time he knew that he was doomed to poverty, that he would never complete his works in time, and that his family life, outwardly so calm, would continue to be strained and stormy. He wrote back:

> I hope and am firmly convinced that in the course of the next year I shall have acquired sufficient money to enable me to reform my economic situation from the ground up and at last stand once again on my own feet. Without you I would never have been able to bring my work to an end, and I assure you that it has always been a heavy load on my conscience that it was chiefly for my sake that you had to squander your splendid energy, letting it rust in a commercial career, and into the bargain you had to share all my *petites misères*.
>
> On the other hand I cannot conceal from you that I have a year of trial before me. I have taken a step on which much depends, and it depends on acquiring from the only source possible several hundreds of pounds. There are quite good prospects of success, but for about 6 weeks I shall remain in suspense. A definite decision will not reach me before that date. But what chiefly fills me with fear—quite apart from this other uncertainty—is my return to London, which must take place in six to eight days. My debts are important and the Manichees [creditors] "most urgently" await my homecoming. And then once more, instead of sitting down freely and freshly to work, there will be family troubles, domestic collisions, the hunters after their prey.

Marx, of course, had no illusions about what awaited him at home, for Jenny had never shown herself indifferent to his long absences and there could be no relief from the creditors. "Family troubles, domestic collisions, the hunters after their prey" were familiar ghosts which had never been laid to rest. All these were absent in that large and well-run house in Hanover, where his slightest wishes were instantly obeyed and his comforts were continually being attended to. "The Kugelmanns rarely leave me alone 'to wander through the desolate regions of my own ego.' " So he wrote to Engels, praising their charm and their generosity, their providential kindness and their solicitude for his welfare.

It was not only that he was living a life of ease and luxury, without responsibilities, but he was enjoying the respect of the bourgeoisie. People would come up to him and compliment him on his works. An official from the Bureau of Statistics in Hanover came to see him and spoke at some length on the subject of money; it was a subject that had inordinately puzzled him, but the reading of one of Marx's books had thrown such a dazzling light on it that he felt he now understood the subject in all its ramifications. The chief of the local railway came to compliment him, and Marx noted with some misgiving that "our influence has spread among the functionaries far more than among the working classes." It was an oddly prophetic remark, for communism throughout its earthly career was to remain largely in the possession of "functionaries."

Not only did the officials and functionaries of Hanover come to greet him, but the very highest people in the land were waiting upon him. "Von Bennigsen is coming tomorrow to pay his homage to me," Marx announced casually in a letter to Engels, and it cannot have escaped Engels' knowledge that Rudolf von Bennigsen was one of the most powerful figures in Germany. According to Marx an even more powerful figure was making secret advances to him. Bismarck himself had sent an emissary, the lawyer Ernst Warnebold, to learn whether Marx would place "his person and his great talents at the service of the German people." Marx urged Engels to keep this visit secret, and there is some doubt whether there was any meeting between Marx and Bismarck's emissary.

But there was no doubt that Marx was riding high in his own estimation. He knew he had written a masterpiece, a book of explosive power and extraordinary violence, and he seems to have guessed that it would be studied and used by men hoping to bring about great revolutions in the future. To his friend Johann Philipp Becker he wrote from Hanover: "It is certainly the most terrible missile which has ever been hurled at the bourgeois (including the landowners)." He wrote in German, but used the English word "missile" which more precisely conveyed the sibilant ferocity of his thought.

To another friend, Sigfrid Meyer, who had recently arrived in New York, Marx wrote more explicitly about his emotions when he was writing the book:

> You ask why I have not replied to your letters. It is because I was constantly hovering over the edge of the grave. So I had to make use of EVERY moment when I could work in order to complete my book, to which I have sacrificed health, happiness, and family. I trust this explanation will need no further postscript. I laugh at the so-called "practical" men and their wisdom. If one chose to be an ox, then one could of course turn one's back on the sufferings of mankind and care only for one's own skin. But I would have really regarded myself as *impractical* if I had conked out without completely finishing my book, at least in manuscript.

In this way he would return again and again to the reasons which compelled him to write the book. There were private and public reasons; there were reasons which had little enough to do with his real intentions, and there were reasons which he deliberately concealed. Once he wrote to Kugelmann that he had submitted the work to the public "in order to raise the party as high as possible and to disarm even the vulgar by the manner of presentation," and there was perhaps more truth in this explanation than in most of the others. *Das Kapital* was intended to give dignity and substance to the communist party, and at the same time it was to be a work of art, existing in its own right. In Marx's mind this second reason was at least as important as the first.

But while he was editing and proofreading the manuscript Marx seemed to be living far above the conflict. In those calm days in Hanover, while a light mist clung to the earth and spring gave way to a glorious summer, he was living like a man of leisure in bourgeois comfort. A friend of the Kugelmanns, a certain Frau Tenge, Italian by birth, thirty-three years old and the mother of five children, became his constant companion. She spoke English, French and Italian, and played the piano magnificently. Marx wrote about her so enthusiastically that Laura inquired whether he was conducting a "flirtation." He answered that he would have to be a bold man to do such a thing, and he found her more entertaining than beautiful. She was the wife of a rich Westphalian landowner, and he liked her well enough to embark on a correspondence with her when he returned to London.

He delighted too in the company of Dr. Kugelmann's wife, Gertrud, whom he nicknamed "Madame la Comtesse," and her daughter Franziska, who was the apple of her father's eye. And whenever he wrote to Dr. Kugelmann in later years, he would always ask to be remembered to them with more than the usual warmth and affection.

Although he was happy in the company of these women, his chief happiness was in the company of Dr. Kugelmann, who was kind, considerate and worshipful, treating his guest with infinite respect. At the doctor's suggestion Marx rewrote a particularly difficult chapter of *Das Kapital:* it was the only substantial change he made in the text. Like most of Marx's friends, the doctor received a new name—he became Wenzel after he had told a story about making a trip to Prague and being bored by a guide who spoke about the two Wenzels, one good, the other bad, one a saint, the other the murderer of St. John of Nepomuk. And if the doctor was in a high good humor, he would be called "good Wenzel," and if he frowned, Marx would say: "There's the bad Wenzel."

It was a game which Marx played nearly all his life, so that there was scarcely anyone among his close friends who did not receive a nickname. His acquaintances were called by their proper names.

In the doctor's house there was a large and beautiful music room with five windows looking out on a garden. Around the room, according to the fashion of the time, stood busts of Greek and Roman divinities, with pride of place going to the majestic Zeus known as the Zeus of Otricoli from the small Italian town where it was discovered. This powerful and massive head, with magnificently thoughtful brows, leonine glare, and superb air of authority, portrayed the king of the gods at a moment of pure abstraction. He meditates, creates, gazes approvingly and defiantly at his creation. It was a statue especially beloved by the Germans at this time, and many philosophical fantasies were written about it.

The resemblance of Marx to the Zeus of Otricoli was sufficiently striking for the doctor to comment on it. Marx spent a good deal of time in the music room, and he had many opportunities to study it. He became very enamored of it, so much indeed that he came to imitate it. Until he came to Hanover, he had always worn his hair long, but not so long that it concealed his ears, and it was his custom at rare intervals to trim his beard. From this time onward he let his hair and beard grow until they assumed the shape of the hair and beard of Zeus, the thick curling mane falling in great waves and mingling with the heavy, untrimmed beard. The face began to change, and a new mask was presented to the world.

Because Marx so coveted the Zeus, Dr. Kugelmann sent him a bronze copy later in the year as a Christmas present. Thereafter it always dominated Marx's study, always within view, a perpetual reminder of the uncanny resemblance between the ancient king of the gods and the living philosopher. The statue arrived in London two days before Christmas, while the whole family was engaged in stirring the Christmas pudding. As Jenny wrote in a letter of gratitude to Dr. Kugelmann, it came as a total surprise and was attended by all the proper auspices. They heard the sound of a cart outside, then secret footsteps and strange noises as the crate was unloaded and carried into the house. No one had the remotest idea what was in the crate. Then suddenly they heard shouts: "A huge statue has come!" They were all dumfounded, for statues came rarely to the house on Maitland Park Road.

Only a few days before, some Irish revolutionaries had stormed Clerkenwell Prison, throwing a bomb and killing many of the guards in an attempt to release some prisoners belonging to an Irish-American revolutionary secret society known as the Fenian Brotherhood. Jenny wrote that she was as surprised as if she had heard the ominous cry: "Fire, fire, the Fenians are here!" She was overwhelmed by the sight of "Jupiter Tonans in all his ideal purity and colossal magnificence." The whole family gazed at it in wonder and astonishment, and they guessed the doctor's intention. It was the highest tribute he could pay to the man he described in a letter to a friend as "the scholar compared to whom all the scholars since Aristotle are no more than pygmies, the thinker who deserves to be called the consciousness of the nineteenth century."

The statue became the most prized of Marx's possessions. The more-than-life-size bust was the first thing that any visitor saw when he entered the study; and many visitors were bemused by it, and some so far forgot themselves as to mention the resemblance.

For Marx this month-long stay in Hanover was perhaps the most tranquil of his entire existence. His heavy hand was felt rarely; he was amusing and sociable. When the doctor, referring to the gods and goddesses in the music room, remarked: "The classical gods are eternal rest without passion," Marx replied: "On the contrary, they are eternal passion without any unrest." It was a description which had the merit of defining his desires.

The gods, of course, formed an endless theme for conversations. Once Dr. Kugelmann remarked that it would please him more if Marx imitated the Zeus of Otricoli by hurling his occasional lightnings and thunderclaps at the world, but removing himself completely from daily agitation. Marx disagreed, pointing out that daily agitation was an essential part of a revolutionary's life and he could not escape from his responsibilities.

There was a statue of Minerva Medica attended by her owl, and it pleased Marx to compliment Gertrud Kugelmann by exclaiming on her resemblance to the goddess. The doctor's wife was a sensible woman. "No, it's not me at all," she answered. "I am only the little screech owl that sits listening at her feet." Thereafter she was sometimes called "my dear little owl," and later the same name was given to her daughter Franziska, who liked to sit on his knees and listen to his stories.

The courteous eighteenth-century banter sometimes went on all day. They would all gather together in the early morning, and then when the doctor vanished into his office to see his patients, Gertrud Kugelmann liked to sit and talk with Marx over a coffee table. She adored philosophy and he became her patient tutor, telling her about Kant, Fichte and Schopenhauer. Many years later she recalled that he told her the quip spoken by Hegel: "Only one student understood me. This was Rosenkranz, and he got it wrong." Later in the morning Marx would spend an hour or two correcting proofs. In the afternoon he might take a walk with Franziska, and in the evening he would listen to Frau Tenge playing the piano in the music room. He especially liked to listen to her playing at dusk.

His relations with her were probably platonic, but he was very much smitten by her. She was born to wealth and position; her husband was not merely a wealthy landowner, but one of the richest in the country. But she was one of those women who are bored by wealth and crave new excitements. Not long after Marx had come to stay in their house, Gertrud Kugelmann wrote to her friend and announced that they had acquired an extraordinarily interesting visitor who moreover was actually sleeping in the room usually reserved for Frau Tenge. The words were a summons. Frau Tenge arrived the next day, was given another bedroom, and immediately set to work to charm Marx, who offered no resistance. He recited poetry to her; she played the piano for him. On the grounds that he was occupying her bedroom and could therefore be rightly considered as her guest, she offered him her visitors' book and demanded an inscription. He had been reciting poems in Spanish to her, for he had brought along some plays by Calderón and was learning them by heart. Calderón's famous line *La vida es sueño, un frenesí, una ilusión* had especially pleased her and accordingly he wrote in her visitors' book:

> *La vida es sueño, un frenesí, una ilusión,*
> So Master Calderón tells us.
> I regard it as the most beautiful illusion
> To take up my residence in Frau Tenge's book.

In the original Spanish and German the verses rhymed, or at least there was an illusion of rhyme. The expression was gallant and hinted at improprieties. Some days later Gertrud Kugelmann found a loose sheet of paper on which Marx had written an earlier and longer version:

> *La vida es sueño, un frenesí, una ilusión,*
> So Master Calderón tells us.
> Yet when thy hand skims over the sea of sound,
> Then might I dream for all eternity.
>
> This feminine spell, this noble harmony
> Tames the wild frenzy of life.
> I regard it the most beautiful illusion
> To take up my residence in Frau Tenge's book.

This earlier version was intended to remind Frau Tenge of his enjoyment of her music, and he appears to have abandoned the middle lines to convey a more direct implication. Dr. Kugelmann himself thought he had abandoned the middle lines because they took up too much space in the book.

Marx had stopped writing poetry after he left the university, and these verses to Frau Tenge are the only ones he is known to have written in later life.

He spoke a great deal about poetry while he was staying with the Kugelmanns. Both the doctor and the social philosopher could recite whole pages of ancient Greek poetry; they rivaled one another in recitations of Goethe, but Marx had the advantage when it came to modern languages. He knew, or claimed to know, Russian and Spanish so well that he could translate from them at sight. He explained that he learned Russian "as a diversion" when he was suffering from boils. He was of the opinion that Turgenev wonderfully rendered the peculiar characteristics of the Russian soul, and he thought Lermontov's descriptions had never been equaled.

He appears to have known very little Russian at this time; his serious study of the language came in the seventies. But when he spoke about Heinrich Heine, whom he had known briefly, he could speak with greater authority. He had a strange theory that Heine was very unsuccessful with women and led a miserable married life. He told the story of visiting Heine in Paris, while the bedsheets were being changed. Because the poet could not bear to be touched, the nurses lifted him into the bed in a sheet. "See, my dear Marx," Heine said in a thin voice, "the ladies still carry me aloft."

So the days passed while he told jokes, boasted of his languages, discussed science and art, danced, sang in his throaty voice, and enjoyed the bourgeois comforts of the house, where a study and a bedroom had been set aside for his sole use. There was only one subject which he refused to discuss with casual visitors who came to the house: his doctrines. But these doctrines were discussed at length during the meetings held in the doctor's study, where communists from all over Germany came to listen to Marx's plans for a communist seizure of power. For a few weeks the doctor's house was the secret headquarters of communism in Germany.

At last the enchanting holiday came to an end, and Marx returned to Hamburg for a last visit with Meissner. All his life he was to remember the month he spent in Hanover: the homage, the women, the theaters, the walks through the park on a spring evening to listen to the band and Frau Tenge playing the piano. Now it was all over, and he felt desolate at the prospect of returning to London. Sometimes he would find himself dreaming of a time when he could live in Hanover, where living costs were cheaper and life was simpler and he was regarded with the veneration due to a great leader and a man of culture.

This time the seas were calm, and no scatological jokes were told for the benefit of aristocratic old ladies. They were sailing across the North Sea when Marx struck up an acquaintance with a young woman who had attracted his attention by her quick military stride as she paced up and down the deck. She was aristocratic in appearance and Prussian by accent, and when she explained that she was traveling from London to Weston super Mare that evening, and was wondering how she would take her luggage across London—it was Sunday, and no porters were available—Marx offered to act as her porter and guide through the mazes of London traffic. First, there was the question of which railroad station she would have to go to. She was carrying a little card on which a friend had scribbled: "Northwestern Station." Since Marx lived in northwest London, he offered to accompany her to her train. She accepted the offer gratefully, and he was looking forward to the prospect of being her *cavaliere servente* when it occurred to him that the Northwestern Station was an unlikely starting point for Weston super Mare, a seaside resort on the Bristol Channel. He went to consult the ship's captain, and learned to his dismay that she would have to leave from Paddington Station. It was now too late to withdraw. When the ship docked, he accompanied her to the station, only to learn that her train was not leaving until eight o'clock in the evening. He spent a long afternoon with her in Hyde Park, and from time to time they would pause and eat ice creams.

Marx was sufficiently amused by this adventure to give a long account of it to Dr. Kugelmann in a letter written three weeks later. He could still remember all the details of his encounter with the young woman whose name, he learned, was Elizabeth von Puttkamer. The surname was familiar, for Johanna von Puttkamer had married Bismarck, and Elizabeth was his niece. "I learned that she had just spent a few weeks with Bismarck in Berlin," Marx wrote. "She had the whole Army List at her finger tips, for her family has been abundantly providing our "brave army" with gentlemen of honor and fine figures. She was a merry, well educated girl, but aristocratic and "black-white"* to the tip of her nose. She was not a little

* "Black-white"—the traditional colors of the Prussian army.

astonished when she learned she had fallen into "*red* hands, but I assured her that our rendezvous would pass without bloodshed."

This was not quite the end of the story, for Elizabeth wrote him a graceful letter of thanks, and in due course her parents wrote from Berlin to thank the learned doctor for taking care of her. Marx had always had an eye for aristocratic young women.

The family troubles and domestic collisions, which he had feared while in Germany, broke out as soon as he returned, and he fled to the hospitality of Engels in Manchester. They had much to discuss. Above all, there were questions involving the revival of the party in Germany as a result of the imminent publication of *Das Kapital;* the soil was more fertile than Marx had expected. There was a list of names to be carefully examined; future plans must be worked out; Engels, too, must make a journey to Germany to knit together the emerging forces of communism. Once more Marx was in a fever of expectancy. He was planning English and French translations of his work: not one missile, but three were to be hurled at the heads of the bourgeoisie. In this happy frame of mind he stayed with Engels for two weeks, correcting proofs, discussing the minute details of his theories with Engels, and sometimes being entertained at tea by the learned Dr. Karl Schorlemmer, who taught chemistry at Manchester University. Then at last, the long holiday over, he returned to his family at the beginning of June.

Now more than ever he was confronted with financial difficulties. The letters to Engels become more urgent: he needs money to pay his debts, to pay the interest on the pawnbroker's tickets, to pay the quarterly installment of the rent. His three daughters had been invited by Lafargue *père* to spend a summer holiday in Bordeaux. He could not refuse them, but the fare alone amounted to £30, not to speak of their small possessions which must be rescued from the pawnbroker. The Lafargues must never know that the Marx family was perpetually on the verge of bankruptcy; and as he put the finishing touches to the proofs of *Das Kapital,* he was feverishly attempting to conceal his poverty from his future son-in-law.

At last, at two o'clock in the morning of August 16, 1867, his labors over *Das Kapital* came to an end as he made the last corrections on the last of the proof sheets, and immediately sent off a letter of joy and gratitude to Engels, who had supported him royally through all the long years. The letter was written in German, but eight words—"Dear Fred," and "I embrace you, full of thanks"—were written in English:

2 o'clock at night, 16 Aug. 1867

I shall only
want the corrected proofs *when the whole book has appeared*

DEAR FRED,

Have just finished correcting the *last sheet* (49th) of the book. The appendix—*form of value—printed in small type,* takes 1¼ sheets.
Preface ditto corrected and sent back yesterday. So *this volume is now finished.* To *you* alone goes my thanks that this was possible! Without your sacrifices for me I could never possibly have accomplished the enormous work for the three volumes. I embrace you, full of thanks!
Enclosed 2 sheets of corrected proofs.
The £15 received with best thanks.
Greetings, my dear, beloved friend!

Your K. MARX

For Marx this was a moment of unalloyed happiness—perhaps the purest happiness he ever knew. Never again was there to be a letter reflecting so much joy and gratitude. He would dedicate the book to his friend Wilhelm Wolff, "intrepid, faithful, noble protagonist of the proletariat," but he knew, and would always know, that Engels had helped him more than anyone else.

DAS KAPITAL

THE BOOK ON which Marx had spent so many years of his life was now finished and launched upon the world. He would make small alterations in the French version which appeared later, write new introductions, and here and there he would find reasons to quarrel with it, but in its essentials it was complete and final, and there was no turning back. He was fully aware of its importance, and he was shocked to learn that few people troubled to buy it. It was published on September 14, 1867, and six weeks later he was complaining that there were still no reviews.

Although *Das Kapital* seemed to vanish into that limbo which is especially reserved for immensely long works on economics and sociology, it was destined to become one of the most widely read books of all time. In some thirty languages and in hundreds of thousands of copies it would

Ich brauche die Reinabzüge zurück, sobald das Buch ganz erschienen ist.

2 Uhr Nachts. 16 Aug. 1867.

Dear Fred,

Eben den letzten Bogen (49.) des Buchs fertig corrigirt. Der Anhang — Werthform — kleingedruckt, umfaßt 1¼ Bogen. Vorrede ditto gestern corrigirt zurückgeschickt. Also dieser Band ist fertig. Bloß Dir verdanke ich es, daß dieß möglich war! Ohne Deine Aufopferung für mich konnte ich unmöglich die ungeheuren Arbeiten zu den 3 Bänden machen. I embrace you, full of thanks!

Beiliegend 2 Bogen Reinabzug.

Die 15 £ mit besten Dank erhalten.

Salut, mein lieber, theurer Freund!

Dein K. Marx.

Marx's letter to Engels on the completion of Das Kapital *(August 16, 1867).*

be published in the Soviet Union and in other communist countries; and students would pore over a systematic inquiry into the economics of Victorian England as though they were reading a book of revelations which contained the answers to the world's misery. In fact, there were few answers. *Das Kapital* was far from being a textbook on the art of revolution or on the science of utopia. Slow-moving and cumbrous, it resembled a heavy clogged mill wheel grinding capitalism to powder. It enumerated one by one the perversities of capitalism, but it did not offer any workable alternative. It attempted to destroy, but did not build. In Marx's eyes it was a work comparable with Dante's *Inferno,* and he hoped to show that the world of capital was one of unspeakable evil.

Like all great works of art *Das Kapital* was deeply personal, reflecting the experiences, obsessions and longings of its creator. It was an intensely autobiographical work, recounting his own desolate adventures in the unexplored landscape of capitalism, his own pilgrimage to the source, and his absolute determination to take the enemy castle by storm. Capital had destroyed him; therefore he would destroy capital. He had lived a life of many privations, and he was determined to show that the system rather than his own inadequacies was responsible for his sufferings. These intimately personal considerations were never expressed or admitted, but they were never far below the surface. A work of such vast complexity and urgency must in the nature of things spring from innumerable complex and urgent causes; and as Marx sought to explain and justify himself, to find reasons for the book's existence, continually shifting his ground and discovering new and always more enticing explanations, the ultimate explanation always eluded him, and it never seems to have occurred to him that there was any autobiographical content in the work. On the contrary he insisted that *Das Kapital* was a purely objective description of the world as it was.

Because it was so personal a work, and was charged with so much passion, and had been labored over for so long, the book inevitably assumed the dimensions of an autobiography which must be read on many levels. The Russian novelist Gogol wrote a long sardonic novel called *Dead Souls* in which he described how an unscrupulous adventurer bought up dead serfs, and under the title he wrote: *A Poem. Das Kapital,* too, is a poem dealing with a world which was already dead or dying when it was written. Marx walks through the enchanted forests of an ancient heroic world in which the villains are the possessors of gold and the heroes are the innumerable alienated wage slaves who serve their masters in fear and trembling. The colors are painted in stark black and white. There is no

Das Kapital.

Kritik der politischen Oekonomie.

Von

Karl Marx.

Erster Band

Buch I Der Produktionsprocess des Kapitals.

Hamburg

Verlag von Otto Meissner.

1867

New-York: L. W. Schmidt, 24 Barclay-Street.

Title page of the first German edition of Das Kapital.

shading. The destiny of the wage slave is to be ground to powder while the possessors of gold grow daily richer, more powerful, and more uncompromising.

Marx's thesis was a very old one; what was new was his passionate insistence on the intolerable injustices of the capitalist system, the tract couched in the form of a scientific inquiry, the passion disguised in quotations from parliamentary records, the fury coming to the surface in sudden explosive comments which flare up like red-hot metal. It is as though Marx, having trained himself to maintain a scientific composure, could endure it no longer. He will discuss elaborate technical matters quite calmly, and suddenly a rage will come over him, and then the rage will pass and once more he will be writing a scientific treatise. The habits of the polemicist are not easily abandoned, and vituperation is continually interrupting the flow of exposition.

Marx's gifts did not develop in the direction which leads toward the logical organization and deployment of large masses of material. Indeed, his mind moved tentatively and awkwardly among facts, and he was happier with vast generalities. *Das Kapital* is a strangely ill-organized work, which seems to have no beginning or end. The chapter on the genesis of capital, which should properly be at the beginning of the book, comes toward the end. The long chapter called "The Working Day" with its searing description of the exploitation of English laborers, comes about a third of the way through the book and has no logical connection with the preceding chapters. It is a bravura performance based on the finding of English parliamentary commissions, to show that the condition of the laborers is unendurable and past praying for. But Marx never mentions that the parliamentary commissions were appointed to right these wrongs and legislation had already been introduced for this purpose. He sees all history as though it were some vast criminal conspiracy, and the fact that the parliamentary reports from which he quotes are already out of date is of no concern to him. The long chapter is drawn up like a brief for the prosecution. Here are the crimes committed by the capitalists, he says, and he forgets to add that the capitalists were busily attempting to change the social atmosphere and to punish the criminals.

Marx had a special affection for this chapter, which covers some seventy pages of the printed text. Writing to Dr. Kugelmann, he pointed out that there were three chapters which he would like Mrs. Kugelmann to read. They were the chapters on "The Working Day," "The Division of Labor and Machinery," and "Primitive Accumulation." These were the most discursive chapters, dealing largely with historical events as seen through the eyes of a disenchanted sociologist, with the emphasis on human exploitation. In these chapters he acts out the role of the prosecuting counsel who assembles the damning evidence and offers it to the bewildered jury with an exquisite self-righteousness. There are no extenuating circumstances. The crimes have taken place in broad daylight, and innumerable witnesses were present. The judgment he demands is death to the entire civilization which produced such monsters.

In the introduction to the first edition, Marx presents himself as another Perseus the dragon-slayer. "Perseus wore a magic cap that the monsters he hunted down might not see him," he wrote. "We draw the magic cap over our eyes and ears as a make-believe that there are no monsters." But it is clear that he does not regard himself as one of those who wear the magic cap of make-believe. He has seen the monsters with his own eyes; they are everywhere, always lying in wait for the unwary. They come out of the remote past and with their sharp teeth bite deep into the living flesh of the present. "*Le mort saisit le vif,*" he cries, and that theme, which is repeated constantly in his work, echoes throughout *Das Kapital.* "Death lays its hand on the living."

This, too, was part of his romantic heritage: the awareness of death as a profound force moving through life and laying claim on it. The ghosts of the past feed on the present and exact their tribute, being monsters with inexhaustible appetites. They are not to be placated with gifts of honey and cakes. They demand the sacrifice of the living. Only when the revolution comes, offering a new dispensation to men, will the spell of the monstrous past be lifted from men's brows. Then suddenly, as in a moment, there will be no need to expiate the ancient crimes; and salvation will come through immersion in the blood of revolution.

In Marx's peculiar attitude toward history time has no place. The coal miners of England are coeval with the temple prostitutes of Phoenicia; the slaves of ancient Rome are the brothers of the peasants of France suffering under the exactions of the tyrannical Sun King. Empires rose and fell, new continents were discovered, virgin territories were opened up by explorers, but Marx seems incapable of seeing the movements of history. All through history he sees only the titanic oppressor, the lord of the earth, surrounded by his mindless laborers. It is as though history had become merely a series of anecdotes about human oppression.

Marx had no clearly worked out philosophy of history, and in his attitude toward historic events he resembles the medieval scholars who saw history *sub specie aeternitatis.* Much of his strength derives from this scholastic vision, his sense of the earth's impermanence, of some more permanent existence which lies beyond the realm of ordinary human life. He has the medieval scholar's attachment to the unseen Paradise which will be disclosed in God's good time. Like Dante, whom he is always quoting, he finds the restless activities of men scarcely worth his attention unless he can place them in their proper categories in the circles of hell.

Sometimes, too, he speaks in the authentic accents of the medieval scholar. He will deliver himself of long meditations anchored in the classics, making learned jokes, rejoicing in the subtleties of his own mind. He has most of the classics at his fingertips, and he will quote Homer, Plato, Sophocles, Isocrates and Athenaeus when it pleases him. It is not enough to say that modern society is in love with gold. Instead he translates the idea into the language of the medieval schoolmen, introduces the Holy Grail, quotes an obscure phrase from the *Deipnosophists* of the third-century grammarian Athenaeus, and invents a complex epigram which might please a professor but would remain completely incomprehensible to a workman. He wrote:

> Modern society, which soon after its birth pulled Plutus by the hair of his head from the bowels of the earth, greets gold as its Holy Grail, as the glittering incarnation of the very principle of its own life.

Such recondite allusions are by no means rare in *Das Kapital.* Marx enjoyed his learning and saw no reason to conceal it, even when instead of clarifying his ideas it made them more opaque. In much the same way he discusses the value of iron in relation to gold. One might have thought he would find a simple equation between the two metals, but he succeeds in reducing them to philosophical abstractions with the aid of Hegel, St. Jerome and Dante. Here is his perplexing account of an imaginary transaction:

> In order, therefore, that a commodity may in practice act effectively as exchange-value, it must quit its bodily shape, must transform itself from mere imaginary to real gold, although to the commodity such transubstantiation may be more difficult than to the Hegelian "concept," the transition from "necessity" to "freedom," or to a lobster the casting of its shell, or to Saint Jerome the putting-off of the old Adam. Though a commodity may, side by side with its actual form (iron, for instance), take in our imagination the form of gold, yet it cannot at one and the same time actually be both iron and gold. To fix its price, it suffices to equate it to gold in imagination. But to enable it to render to its owner the service of a universal equivalent, it must be actually replaced by gold. If the owner of the iron were to go to the owner of some other commodity offered for exchange, and were to refer him to the price of the iron as proof that it was already money, he

would get the same answer as St. Peter gave in heaven to Dante, when the latter recited the Creed:

Assai bene e trascorsa
D'esta moneta gia la lega e'l peso
Ma dimme se tu l'hai nella tua borsa.

The reader who does not know his Dante by heart may find himself gliding swiftly over the quotation from the *Paradiso,* wondering why he should be expected to recognize verses in thirteenth-century Italian. Marx however knew Dante well, and he expected his reader to be equally learned. St. Peter had been summoned by Beatrice to interrogate Dante on his faith, and Dante affirmed his utmost belief. St. Peter, impressed by the scholastic form in which Dante expressed his faith, then asked him whether he truly possessed it, saying:

Excellently have you discussed
The alloy and the weight of this coin,
But tell me whether you have it in your purse.

Dante answers that he does indeed possess such a coin; it is bright and round, and there is not the least doubt of its value. It is a heavenly coin, and therefore outside the realm of Marx's investigations.

Not that Marx was totally indifferent to heavenly matters. Since he had introduced St. Jerome in his discussion on the relative value of iron and gold, he added a footnote to explain his allusion to the Old Adam. "Jerome," he wrote, "had to wrestle hard, not only in his youth with the bodily flesh, as is shown by his flight to the desert with the beautiful women of his imagination, but also in his old age with the spiritual flesh. 'I thought,' he says, 'I was in the spirit before the Judge of the Universe.' 'Who art thou?' asked a voice. 'I am a Christian.' 'Thou liest,' thundered back the great Judge, 'thou art nought but a Ciceronian.' "

Marx appears to have had a great liking for St. Jerome, who was waspish and hot-tempered, roaring like a lion when he felt an injustice had been done. Jerome protested vigorously against usury, and Marx shared his belief that it was the source of most of the evils of his time.

When Marx introduced Hegel, St. Jerome and Dante into his argument, he was perhaps admitting defeat. They did not help him to solve the problem; on the contrary they helped to make the problem even more complex, more unyielding, and more diffuse. He never came to any satisfactory conclusion on the subject of value, though he wrote about it endlessly. He will cover page upon page with abstruse technical verbiage, losing the thread of the argument, endlessly repeating those basic axioms which are always dubious, interjecting here and there a precise "therefore" or a more devious "it is evident that," restlessly surveying the economic development of the world from the time of the building of the pyramids to the latest available figures on market crises. The effect is of a kind of baroque conflagration, an edifice so heavily ornamented with examples and footnotes that it takes the breath away.

Although Marx's economics are irrelevant in the age of computers and the atomic bomb, his savage indignation still has power to quicken the heartbeat. *Das Kapital* is essentially a work of moral philosophy. He wrote when preaching was still a fine art, and the great preachers of the day, Ruskin, Carlyle and Kingsley, roared out imprecations in thundering tones of outrage. It was a full-bodied age. A preacher did not stand calmly in the pulpit. He shook his fists at heaven and at his audience, assumed vivid postures, lowered his voice to a whisper and then bellowed with all the force of his lungs; and men dabbed at their eyes, while women fainted and children screamed. In the Victorian age men demanded more from a preacher than that he should make sense. They demanded that he should possess the powers of a tragic actor and the voice of a prophet.

When Marx exhibits his indignation, he pulls out all the stops and roars like any lion. It is not enough to say that capital is inherently evil; instead, he describes it in all its physical squalor:

> If money, according to Augier, comes into the world with a congenital bloodstain on its cheek, capital comes dripping from head to foot, from every pore, with blood and filth.

Again, when he discusses the adulteration of food, he will launch into a catalogue of horrors with every word carefully placed for its maximum effect:

> Englishmen, always well up in the Bible, knew well enough that man, unless by elective grace a capitalist, or landlord, or sinecurist, is commanded to eat his bread by the sweat of his brow, but they did not know that they had to eat daily in his bread a certain quantity of human perspiration mixed with the discharge of abscesses, cobwebs, dead black-beetles, and putrid German yeast, without counting alum, sand, and other agreeable mineral ingredients.

Such ferocious improvisations run like a thread through *Das Kapital;* they hold it together. But it is perhaps worth remarking that they are not entirely original, for he was rearranging and adapting observations made by others. Marie Augier had spoken of money with a congenital bloodstain on its cheek; Marx had gone one better. The description of the adulterations in bread had been provided for him in an official report presented to Parliament in 1863. He had merely rearranged the order of the ingredients, placing "the discharge of abscesses" first, because this was a subject on which he was an authority.

In *Das Kapital* there is room for everything. Old battles are refought, old enemies chastised, old friends rewarded. Like Gibbon he reserves some of his choicest barbs for the footnotes, and he enjoyed complex Victorian epigrams balancing neatly on a point, as when he described in a footnote the uproar at the opening of Parliament: "The bull-like bellow of the landed proprietors at the opening of Parliament in 1866 showed that a man can worship the cow Sabala without being a Hindu, and can change himself into an ox without being a Jupiter." He had a great contempt for Jeremy Bentham, "that insipid, pedantic, leather-tongued oracle of the ordinary bourgeois intelligence of the nineteenth century." But it is not enough to demolish him in the text; he must be demolished further in a footnote:

> Bentham is a purely English phenomenon. Not even excepting our philosopher Christian Wolff, in no time and in no country has the most homespun commonplace ever strutted about in so self-satisfied a way. The principle of utility was no discovery of Bentham. He simply reproduced in his dull way what Helvétius and other Frenchmen had said with *esprit* in the eighteenth century. To know what is useful for a dog, one must study dog nature.

There is a good deal more of this oddly ill-tempered abuse, and Marx finally arrives at his conclusion: "Had I the courage of my friend Heinrich Heine, I should call Mr. Jeremy a genius in the way of bourgeois stupidity." Jeremy Bentham fares better than the philosopher Destutt de Tracy, who is dismissed briefly as "the fish-blooded bourgeois doctrinaire."

There are flaws everywhere in this flawed work, but the grandeur of the conception makes even the most ill-tempered passages endurable. As the preachers pointed their shaking hands at the devil, so Marx pointed all the resources of his knowledge at capital, which he regarded as far more dangerous and cruel than any devil dreamed up by theologians.

When the book was safely launched, he seemed to withdraw from the world. He attended meetings of the International, but more and more irregularly. The boils came again, there were prolonged sicknesses in the family, Laura and Paul Lafargue were married and went off to live in Paris. From time to time he would dream of becoming a British citizen, so that he could travel again on the continent, and sometimes, even more vividly, there would come dreams of revolution. He was aging rapidly. He was only fifty-one when he published *Das Kapital,* but already he had the look of a man in his sixties.

One day in 1868 he wrote to his daughter Laura: "Dear child, you must surely imagine I am very fond of books, because I am always bothering you about them at inconvenient times. But you are wrong. I am a machine condemned to devour books and then to hurl them transformed onto the dunghill of history."

THE COLLAPSE OF THE INTERNATIONAL

The task of the International is to organize and unite the powers of the working classes in the coming struggle.

THE PARIS COMMUNE

The Paris Commune was established on March 18, 1871, and went down to defeat seventy-two days later. Quite suddenly, under almost laboratory conditions, so that the forces at work could be traced cleanly and there was never the slightest doubt what the revolutionaries were attempting to do, a new and hitherto unknown form of revolutionary government claiming to represent the people had emerged in Paris. The leaders of the revolution were followers of Blanqui steeped in the Jacobin tradition. What they wanted above all was a federal republic with each municipality possessing its own independence. They wanted a more egalitarian society, an end to the power of the Church and the Army, the destruction of the existing power structure. They called their government the Commune in conscious imitation of the free communes of the Middle Ages and the revolutionary Commune of Paris inaugurated in 1789 immediately after the fall of the Bastille. They called themselves the Fédérés, while their enemies called them the Communards.

Following the disaster at Sedan, the German armies like a huge unwieldy machine rumbled up to the gates of Paris. For five months of siege the Parisians endured intolerable privations, while the Provisional Government which had taken power after the surrender of Napoleon III debated ignominiously in the security of Bordeaux. The government had lost touch with the people and seemed concerned only with the problem of perpetuating its own existence. Finally, the government signed an armistice with the Germans in January 1871, agreeing to the surrender of Alsace-Lorraine and the payment of a crushing indemnity. In the eyes of the government, which consisted largely of men who had served the Emperor, the time had now come for the old order to be re-established, but the Franco-Prussian war had set in motion new social forces which could not be ignored. War creates social revolutions, and the France of 1871 was in no mood to restore the Second Empire, even a Second Empire deprived of its Emperor.

When Adolphe Thiers, the chief executive of the Provisional Government, returned to Paris from Bordeaux, he found the Parisians in an ugly mood. He was a small, gnomelike man, a veteran of many government offices and the author of many historical works, a supreme realist who loved power for its own sake; and he knew where the sources of power lay. Returning to Paris he ordered the National Guard to surrender their guns, and when they refused he concluded rightly that Paris was on the eve of insurrection. He slipped out of Paris and made his way to Versailles. On the same day the insurrection began.

The revolutionaries had no Dantons or Robespierres among them. There was no single person capable of dominating the stage and leading them in the chosen direction. Auguste Blanqui, the spiritual father of the insurrectionary movement, was in prison. Charles Delescluze, a veteran of 1848 and the prisons of French Guiana—a man of great generosity of spirit and single-mindedness—was too old and too ill to offer effective leadership. The men who rose to prominence during the Commune were mostly intellectuals, middle-class tradesmen, and a scattering of genuine workers. It was a revolution without a head, but with a heavy, powerful, instinctive body.

As soon as the revolutionary government was installed in the Hôtel de Ville, it decreed the abolition of the police and the army, with a popular militia taking over their power and functions. Rents were remitted, the Church was expropriated, the people were given the right to elect their magistrates, and no public official was to be paid more than 6,000 francs a year. Lenin was deeply impressed by these early decrees, and when he returned to Russia in April 1917 from his exile in Switzerland, he modeled his revolutionary program on them. What especially delighted him was the beautiful simplicity of the decree which abolished the army and the police in one stroke of the pen.

Inevitably the army and the police remained: the army was needed to defend Paris, and the police were needed to keep revolutionary order and punish the counterrevolutionaries where they could be found. Tragically, the police were headed by a murderous buffoon, Raoul Rigault, who took a savage joy in prosecuting priests. A Jesuit priest was brought before him, and the following interrogation took place:

RIGAULT. What is your profession?
PRIEST. Servant of God.
RIGAULT. Where does your master live?
PRIEST. Everywhere.
RIGAULT (*to a secretary*). Take this down. So and so, describing himself as a servant of someone called God, a vagrant.

Under Rigault's orders the scholarly Monsignor Darboy, the Archbishop of Paris, was arrested and shot.

Just as tragically, the army was placed under the command of men who had little experience of revolutionary warfare and little understanding of its strategies. Three Polish officers, refugees from the 1863 uprising against Russia, were given important commands on the defensive positions around Paris. The best fighters were the common people of Paris who dug up the paving stones and mounted the barricades. They were rarely well-led but they fought magnificently.

The Paris Commune was not alone. All over France short-lived Communes appeared. Bakunin presided briefly over the Commune at Lyons, the most traditionally revolutionary of all French cities. There were Communes at Marseilles, Narbonne, Cette, Perpignan, Toulouse and Limoges. The revolutionary flame flared sporadically in the south and then went out. Paris was a revolutionary island surrounded by a sea of torpor.

Almost from the beginning the revolutionaries seem to have known they were doomed to defeat. They were strangely hesitant, afraid to march on Versailles for fear of provoking civil war and afraid to impose a dictatorship for fear of bringing forth another Robespierre or another Napoleon. They scrupulously refrained from requisitioning the vast sums in the National Bank, and took care to buttress all their actions with a show of legality. They restored the red flag, which was the first flag of the French revolutionaries in 1789, and they ordered the destruction of the Vendôme column, which fell after interminable delays with a satisfying crash amid clouds of rubble, while a band played the "Marseillaise" and an American girl in a hotel overlooking the scene sang "Hail Columbia." Everyone was wearing a red scarf, red banners were raised, and all the public buildings were festooned with sheets of red silk. Paris was bathed in a sea of red, and the dyers were working overtime.

Meanwhile more serious affairs were taking place. The revolutionary army was being drilled and trained. The forts surrounding Paris, which had defied the Germans for six months, were placed in a state of preparedness, to defend the capital against the army of Thiers. From time to time Thiers would order an attack on the outer fortifications, but these were repelled. The more violent and sinister revolutionaries planned to put Paris to the flames if the army of Thiers entered the gates. Among their ranks *agents provocateurs,* spies and traitors abounded. The revolution was disintegrating long before the national army broke through an undefended gate.

From London Marx and Engels watched the progress of the Commune with stupefaction. It was not moving in an orderly Germanic way, or in any way that was intelligible to them. "Unquestionably," Engels wrote later, "the Commune is the intellectual child of the International," but he knew it was not so, and in the same letter to Sorge he admitted that the International had contributed nothing whatsoever to the strange events happening in Paris. No letter from Marx or Engels shows the slightest indication that they knew it was about to come into existence, or that they guided it in any way, or understood it. In later years Marx claimed that he wrote hundreds of letters to his agents in Paris and all over Europe in an effort to bring the utmost assistance to the embattled Communards. In fact he wrote very few letters and contented himself with ineffectual gestures, while claiming always that "our party" was responsible for the revolution.

He sent two emissaries to Paris to make contact with the handful of members of the International who were taking part in the Commune. They were Auguste Serraillier, a shoemaker, and Elizabeth Dimitrieva, the revolutionary daughter of a Tsarist cavalry officer. Serraillier's task was to make contact with Leo Frankel and Eugène Varlin, who were members both of the Commune and the International. Dimitrieva's task was to organize an *Union des Femmes* to aid the Commune and to act as a private *reporteuse* to Marx. In his letters Marx mentions a certain N. Eilau, a German businessman, who also acted as his agent, passing in and out of Paris at will. This mysterious businessman hovers like a shadow over Marx's enterprises in Paris, and nothing more was ever heard of him.

To his friend Dr. Kugelmann, on whom he had been depending for medical advice, Marx wrote on April 12 a paean in praise of the revolution, which was also an affirmation of his own brilliance and foresight. Never was he more self-regarding or more pleased with his own success. He wrote:

> If you will take a look at the last chapter of my *Eighteenth Brumaire*, you will see that I claim that the next attempt of the French revolution will be no longer, as before, to transfer the bureaucratic-military machine from one hand to another, but to *smash* it, and this is essential in every true popular revolution on the Continent. This is exactly what our heroic party comrades in Paris are attempting. What elasticity, what historical initiative, what capacity for sacrifice in these Parisians! After six months of starvation and ruin caused more by internal treachery than by the external enemy, they rise beneath Prussian bayonets as though there had never been a war between France and Germany, and the enemy were not at the gates of Paris!
>
> History has no like example of a like greatness! If they go down to defeat,

> the blame rests with their "good nature." After first Vinoy and then the reactionary section of the Paris National Guard had left the field, they should have marched on Versailles. The right moment was missed from scruples of conscience. They did not want to begin a *civil war,* as though that mischievous abortion Thiers had not already started the civil war with his attempt to disarm Paris. Second mistake: the Central Committee surrendered its power too soon, to make way for the Commune. Again from a too "honorable" scrupulosity!
>
> However that may be, the present uprising in Paris—even if it is crushed by the wolves, swine and low curs of the old society—is the most glorious achievement of our party since the June insurrection in Paris. Compare these heaven-stormers of Paris with the heavenly slaves of the Germano-Prussian Holy Roman Empire with its posthumous masquerades reeking of the barracks, the Church, cabbage-Junkerdom, and above all, of the Philistine.

So he raged, like another Don Quixote at war with windmills, while dreaming of victories. If Dr. Kugelmann took the trouble to look up the last chapter of the *Eighteenth Brumaire,* which deals mostly with the French peasantry, he would have searched in vain for the prophecy that the next attempt of the French revolutionaries would be to smash the bureaucratic-military machine; this idea belonged more to Bakunin than to Marx. As usual, Marx proposed simple solutions. To say that the Central Committee surrendered its power too soon to make way for the Commune was to misunderstand the forces at work: the Central Committee had no legal existence in the eyes of the Parisians who were determined even under revolutionary conditions to enjoy the benefits of elective government. Marx saw revolutions conducted by central committees dominated by one man, just as he dominated the General Council of the International. The French had other ideas on how to make revolution.

Already the myth-making process was in full operation. Although the history of the Commune was well reported in the British press, Marx saw it, as he saw most political events, in the light of his own prejudices and theories, his determination to make events fit into the pattern he had prescribed for them. The Paris Commune became the work of "our party." The statement was untrue, but it pleased him to believe it was true. Writing to Eduard Bernstein many years later, Engels concluded that Marx "improved the unconscious tendencies of the Commune into more or less conscious projects," adding that these improvements were "justified, even necessary, in the circumstances." Engels was claiming that history may be distorted for revolutionary purposes.

Marx would have been in a still more powerful position to distort history if he had succeeded in gaining possession of the archives of the Commune. On May 13, when the Commune was already doomed, he wrote to

Frankel and Varlin urging them to transfer all the documents which compromised Versailles to a safe place. He attached enormous importance to documents compromising other people, and he had himself built a considerable library of them. But these documents, which he hoped to see in his own archives, passed into the possession of the French government, and his history of the Commune was written on the basis of newspaper reports.

His attitude toward the Commune was one in which joy, envy, and hopelessness were mingled in equal parts. He liked to imagine that it was a proletarian uprising led by socialists and members of the International, but he came in time to realize that the uprising had almost nothing in common with the revolutions demanded by his theories. Ten years later, writing to Domela Nieuwenhuis, he as much as admitted that it had no place in the real revolutionary struggles of the time, and rather surprisingly suggested that all would have been well if the Commune had come to an accommodation with Versailles. "The war was merely the rising of a city under exceptional conditions, and the majority of the Commune was in no sense socialist, nor could it be," he wrote. "With a small amount of sound common sense they could have reached a compromise with Versailles useful to the whole mass of the people—the only thing that could be reached at that time."

To describe the Commune as merely a rising of a city under exceptional circumstances and to suggest against all the evidence of history that a compromise could be worked out between determined enemies was to show how little he understood what was at stake. Since the Commune had paid no attention to his ideas, he could safely disregard it and, like Pilate, wash his hands of it.

But as long as it served his purpose, he took care to identify himself with it and he was not above taking full advantage of his frail connections with some of its leaders. On May 30, two days after the collapse of the Commune in a welter of blood and horror, he read out at a special meeting of the General Council of the International in London a long speech in which he praised the leaders of the Commune for their heroic resistance against their oppressors, noting that "the greater part of the members of the Commune" could be counted among "the most active, intelligent, and energetic minds of the International Working Men's Association." "It was but natural," he said, "that members of our association should stand in the foreground." It appeared that the Commune would never have come into existence except for the leadership provided by the International. Benjamin Lucraft and George Odger, both founding members of the International, resigned in protest against the many evident untruths contained in Marx's speech.

The speech, which came to be known as "The Civil War in France," is not one of his major works. Covering some thirty closely printed pages, it reads like a parody of the *Eighteenth Brumaire* with Thiers, "the parliamentary Tom Thumb," taking the place of Louis Napoleon. There is a good deal of adolescent rhetoric, but there is never any awareness of the terrible tragedy which had been played out on the streets of Paris. Cleverness is always butting in. Debating points are made, and the counsel for the prosecution waits once again for the applause of the gallery. Observing that the Church was disendowed by the Commune, he says: "The priests were sent back to the recesses of private life, there to feed upon the alms of the faithful in imitation of their predecessors, the Apostles." In much the same way, with balanced Ciceronian phrases, he castigates "that monstrous gnome Thiers":

> A master of small state roguery, a virtuoso in perjury and treason, a craftsman in all the petty stratagems, cunning devices and base perfidies of Parliamentary party warfare; never scrupling, when out of office, to fan a revolution, and to stifle it in blood when at the helm of the State; with class prejudices standing him in the place of ideas, and vanity in the place of a heart; his private life as infamous as his public life is odious—even now, when playing the part of a French Sulla, he cannot help setting off the abomination of his deeds by the ridicule of his ostentation.

Such calculated rhetorical devices belong to an earlier age, and although they evidently pleased Marx, it is doubtful whether they had any effect whatsoever on the workingmen of the International. The speech smells of the lamp; no human emotions seem to be involved; even when he talks of the dead he observes them at a distance, looking out from the windows of his study. "The Civil War in France" suffers, like so many of his writings in English, from a defective knowledge of the language, with the result that when he is attempting his most carefully contrived effects, they nearly always fall flat. Here, for example, he describes Paris after the conquest as seen by the followers of Thiers:

> The Paris of M. Thiers was not the real Paris of the "vile multitude," but a phantom Paris, the Paris of the *francs-fileurs,* the Paris of the Boulevards, male and female—the rich, the capitalist, the gilded, the idle Paris now thronging with its lackeys, its blacklegs, its literary *bohème,* and its cocottes at Versailles, Saint-Denis, Rueil, and Saint-Germain; considering the civil war but an agreeable diversion, eyeing the battle going on through telescopes, counting the rounds of cannon, and swearing by their own honour and that of their prostitutes, that the performance was far better got up than it used to be at the Porte St. Martin. The men who fell were really

> dead; the cries of the wounded were cries in good earnest; and, besides, the whole thing was so intensely historical.

So it was, but Marx's labored sarcasms were no more endearing to his audience of workingmen nearly a hundred years ago than they are today. He never gets to grips with the terrible last days of the Commune. There is nothing to suggest that he felt it on his nerves or on his mind. We see some well-dressed gentleman gazing at the battle through a telescope, and there is more than a suspicion that the gentleman is Marx himself, seeing it all at a great distance from the safety of the middle-class residence in London. Bakunin had flung himself into the battle; Marx merely read about it in the London *Times.*

The most charitable explanation for "The Civil War in France" is that Marx was completely out of touch with the social forces of his time. He had formed certain theories over many years at great expense of intellectual toil, and he was not prepared to sacrifice them because the Commune invalidated them. So he spoke continually of the "proletarian revolution," even though he was aware that it was not a proletarian revolution at all, and he continued to depict the enemy as gnomes, monsters and dandies, when they were in fact ruthless and determined reactionaries who behaved with the simple logic of their class. "I shall be pitiless," said Thiers, and he carried out his promise to the letter. The Communards killed 150 hostages. The government executed about 30,000 men, women and children in reprisal, and exiled 7,000 to New Caledonia.

The myth of the proletarian Commune survived long after the death of Marx. Lenin read "The Civil War in France" and was deeply impressed by it. He was especially impressed by Marx's statement that it was "essentially a working-class government, the product of the struggle of the producing against the appropriating class, the political form at last discovered under which to work out the economical emancipation of Labour." That single sentence was the basis for his own experiments in government. The Bolshevik revolution was patterned on the Commune, not as it was but as Marx thought it was, and Lenin regarded himself as the successor of the Communards. When he died one of the embroidered red flags of the Commune was placed in his tomb.

As the years passed, Marx seemed to disassociate himself more and more from the Commune, rarely spoke about it, and scarcely ever mentioned it in his writings. It was one of those nightmares which are best forgotten, because they are altogether too terrible to contemplate. He had not really confronted it in "The Civil War in France," and he saw even less reason to confront it in later years. Sometimes he would make hints about the lessons to be derived from the Commune, and then pass on to other things.

One of these hints appeared in the introduction to a new German edition of *The Communist Manifesto* published in the summer of 1872. He noted that "to a certain extent" the manifesto was "out of date." In particular there were lessons to be drawn from the Commune, "where the proletariat held political power for the first time." The chief lesson to be drawn was that "the working class cannot simply lay hold of the ready-made state machinery and wield it for its own purposes." Marx did not pursue the argument further. Lenin, writing *State and Revolution* while he was hiding in Finland on the eve of the October Revolution, with a copy of "The Civil War in France" beside him, drew the logical conclusion. "The working class must *shatter* the ready-made state machinery," he wrote, and a few weeks later he shattered the state machinery of Russia.

Of all Marx's works "The Civil War in France" is perhaps the least rewarding. Strident and formless, written in great weariness, it says nothing which was not said better by the writers of his time. But in terms of human history that speech, which later appeared as a brief pamphlet, was to have a special place. Lenin studied it at a time when his studies were to have a decisive influence on the course of history. "The Civil War in France" was the bridge between the Commune and the Russian Revolution.

A LETTER TO THE HOME SECRETARY

After the fall of the Commune, the General Council of the International began to organize help for the refugees who were expected to arrive in large numbers. There were mass meetings and pledges of assistance, and John Stuart Mill sent a message deploring "the horrors now being perpetrated in Paris." The massacres in Paris were regarded by the English workingmen with horror and detestation. They had never experienced massacres like these, and could scarcely understand how a civilized nation could permit them. It was as though some strange and hitherto unknown ritual bloodbath was being enacted, and they searched eagerly for an explanation.

Marx's "Civil War in France" offered an explanation which at least had the merit of being vivid and sensational, even if it was careless of the facts. It was widely reprinted and much discussed, and Marx found himself in the unfamiliar limelight. "It is making the devil of a noise, and I have the honor to be at this moment the best calumniated and the most menaced man in London," he wrote to Dr. Kugelmann. "This really does one good after a tedious twenty years' idyll in my den." Three editions appeared in two months in London, and it was translated into German, Dutch, Italian, Spanish and Russian. It was the one work of Marx which had a wide distribution in his lifetime, and it was far better known than *The Communist Manifesto.*

This brief incursion into fame occurred at a time when Marx was in need of stimulation. He knew—he must have known—that the fall of the Commune was a revolutionary disaster of the first magnitude, and at the same time he felt compelled to regard it as the justification of his theories, the triumph, however temporary, of his revolutionary prophecies. He therefore busied himself with work on behalf of the refugees, attended meetings of the International, and cheerfully accepted responsibility for the Commune, which he had been unable to guide and which had never listened to his pleas. "The work of the International is immense," he wrote in another letter to Dr. Kugelmann, "and in addition London is overrun with refugees, whom we have to look after. Moreover, I am overrun by other people—newspaper men and others of every description—who want to see the *monster* with their own eyes."

Meanwhile he was beginning to realize that fame has its dangers and the very existence and survival of the International was at stake. On June 6 Jules Favre in the name of the French government had dispatched a memorandum to all the European governments urging that the International should be outlawed. Lord Aberdare, the British Home Secretary, was asked to give his opinion on the matter. There was little public support for the demand in England, but it was not a question which could be lightly dismissed, and it was necessary for the government to acquire some information about the workings of the International. While the French and German governments possessed ample dossiers, there appear to have been no comparable dossiers in the possession of the British government.

Henry Austin Bruce, the first Baron Aberdare, was a man with liberal sympathies. The discovery of coal on his family estates made him a rich man, and he had a deep knowledge of and sympathy for his Welsh coal miners. He wrote essays and delivered speeches on such subjects as "The Present Condition and Future Prospects of the Working Population in the Mineral Districts of South Wales" and "On Amusements as the Means of Continuing and Extending the Education of the Working Classes." These essays were well thought out, and although couched in a rather pompous Victorian prose, they demonstrated that he was a forthright, intelligent and kindly man, who weighed his ideas carefully. If he was asked whether the International should be permitted to have its headquarters on British soil, he would study the matter at length and give his considered opinion.

When Lord Aberdare undertook to study the International, he asked his private secretary to obtain the relevant documents. His private secretary was a man called Albert Osliff Rutson, a graduate of Magdalen College, Oxford, about thirty-two years old, personable and hard-working. "I like Rutson very much, and am quite satisfied with my choice," Lord Aberdare wrote in December 1868, shortly after Rutson became his secretary. Rutson knew that Professor Beesly was one of the founders of the International, and accordingly he asked Beesly for a list of the documents published by the International and where they could be obtained. Beesly referred him to Marx, who thereupon sent him a copy of nearly all the official documents he had prepared for the General Council of the International. With the documents went an accompanying letter:

12 July 1871

DEAR SIR,

Together with this letter I am sending you the following publications of the General Council of the International.

(1) The Inaugural Address and Provisional Rules.
(2) Rules of the International Association of Working Men, as finally agreed upon at the Geneva Congress in 1866.
(3) Resolutions of the Geneva Congress of 1866 and the Brussels Congress of 1868.
(4) *The Times,* 9 September 1868. Report of the General Council of the Brussels Congress.
(5) On the Belgian Massacres.
(6) Address to the National Union of Workers of the United States.
(7) Report of the Fourth Annual Congress in Basle.
(8) The Question of the Irish Amnesty.
(9) The Lockout of the Building Workers of Geneva.
(10) Program of the Fifth Annual Congress. NB. The calling of the Congress was prevented by the Franco-German War.
(11) Two addresses on the Franco-German War.
(12) Address on "The Civil War in France." (Second edition)

The address "Mr. Washburne, the American Ambassador" is now at the press, and I will send it to you tomorrow.

Yours truly,
KARL MARX

A. O. Rutson, Esq. 7 Halfmoon Street, W.

P.S. I am enclosing a handwritten copy of the Address to Abraham Lincoln and his reply.

It was a strange letter for a revolutionary to write, for Marx was sending important documents belonging to the International for the approval of the Home Secretary. Some of the documents like the Inaugural Address and the Provisional Rules were public property, and had been widely published; others like the reports of the Congresses were secret, even though they had already fallen into the possession of the French police. Marx did not know Rutson, and he had never met Lord Aberdare. On his own responsibility he was entering into secret correspondence with the enemy. He was not dealing with some miserable police spy: he was dealing directly, through Rutson, with the head of all the police in England.

A revolutionary in secret correspondence with the police incurs grave risks if the correspondence becomes known. Marx obviously took care that his correspondence with Rutson should be kept secret. Members of the International who were not well disposed to Marx appear to have got wind of it, and somehow the news seems to have reached Bakunin, who described Marx as a man "who exposes himself before the public in the role of a sneakish and calumniatory police spy." There was some truth in the charge. The letter to Rutson was testimony of the fact that he was perfectly capable of giving documents to the police.

Marx's intention was to show that the International was a legitimate and law-abiding society, which presented no dangers to the British Crown. Lord Aberdare came to the conclusion that the International was harmless, and while realizing that it might be potentially dangerous, he was inclined to the belief that it needed only "education with some religious training" to become thoroughly respectable. Speaking in the House of Commons, he laughed at the fears expressed by some members of Parliament, who imagined that the International was a dangerous revolutionary organization, and he noted that the total paid-up membership in the International in England was only eight thousand. In his characteristically British fashion he was not prepared to be alarmed by bogiemen.

One would like to know more about Rutson, who was far from being a colorless private secretary. He was a man with strong opinions, as he showed when he published, in the year before he joined Lord Aberdare at the Home Office, a long essay called "Opportunities and Shortcomings of

Government in England" in a book called *Essays on Reform.* He found very little good to say about the British governmental system. He objected vehemently to British rule in Ireland, attacked the political power of the aristocracy, and noted that "the great want of the country is a House of Commons that will give a fair field to statesmanship." Of the British working classes he wrote: "The danger of the enfranchisement of the working class is smaller in England than in any other country of the world. In England the power of capital is so great that labour obtains its bare rights with difficulty." He published nothing more in his lifetime, and it has been impossible to trace in the records of the Home Office any further papers connected with his correspondence with Marx.

Marx himself had no illusions about the International. He regarded it as the revolutionary arm of the working class, the most powerful weapon ever devised for the overthrow of bourgeois governments. In due course he would throw this weapon contemptuously aside, but in 1871 it still seemed to him to be the hope of the future.

On September 25, 1871, a banquet was held to celebrate the seventh anniversary of the founding of the International. All the members of the General Council were invited with their families, and in addition there were some of the most distinguished refugees from the Commune. Wilhelm Liebknecht and August Bebel were invited, but could not come for lack of money. Six Belgians arrived, and from Switzerland came Nikolay Utin, who played some part in helping Marx to uncover the curious role played by Nechayev. The International had survived the seven climacteric years, and called for a very special celebration.

The banquet was prepared by the Communards, who were able to demonstrate the virtues of French cooking. A former wine merchant, who was also a former member of the Ministry of Public Works under the Commune, made himself responsible for the wine. As for the meats, they were of every kind; and as his eyes traveled over the loaded tables, Marx observed that there was roast beef, mutton, ham, veal and roast leg of lamb. Indeed, a large roast leg of lamb was lying on the table in front of him.

Among the refugees from the Commune the most impressive was Yaroslav Wroblewski, the Polish patriot who fought magnificently at Butte-aux-Cailles and escaped from Paris by a miracle at the last moment. He was a man of distinguished appearance, tall, handsome, elegantly dressed, with a magnificent silky beard and luminous deep-set eyes; he looked like a tragic actor in a play. There was also a certain Colonel Dombrowski, the brother of the ill-fated commander in chief of the army of the Commune, who fell on the barricades and whose body, lying on blue silk sheets in the Hôtel de Ville, was briefly an object of worship by the Communards. These two refugees were given the place of honor beside Marx, and as though to cement the friendship between Marx and the Commune, Jenny and Laura also sat beside the Poles.

The banqueters were all sitting at their tables when the question arose as to who would preside over the feast. Someone cried: "Karl Marx!" and this cry was taken up by others. Marx pretended to be surprised. He explained that he could not preside because he was perfectly incapable of carving the roast. On the other hand he was the oldest member of the General Council, having reached the respectable age of fifty-three, and therefore had perhaps some claim to the presidency. In a mellow mood Marx went on to declare that he had carved up several governments in his time, but there remained the question—the insuperable question—of the roast, and he greatly feared that his own inexpertise would be fraught with serious consequences to the banqueters. He was in good humor, enjoying his Pickwickian role. The question of the roast was satisfactorily settled when Colonel Dombrowski offered to be the carver. Marx said later that he carved so well that one might have thought he had spent his whole life carving meats.

After the dinner there were toasts and speeches, with Marx acting as president and master of ceremonies. General Wroblewski rose and made a characteristically Polish speech, saying that he had dedicated his sword to the red flag and he would continue to fight the good fight whenever called upon to do so. He assured all his friends that he would not have the slightest hesitation in unsheathing his sword for a good cause. Another Polish refugee jumped up and declared that Poland had given many generals to many revolutions, and would continue to do so in the future. "Intelligent Poles," he declared, "were always ready to march in the ranks of the most advanced democracies of Europe, for they had broken completely with the past and abandoned all their old prejudices."

These gentle reminders of Poland's existence were not out of place at a meeting celebrating the seventh anniversary of the International. Some of the banqueters may have remembered that the International had its birth when British and French delegations of workingmen met to protest the bloody suppression of the Polish uprising in 1863. During the following years Poland had rarely been mentioned in the discussions of the International.

Marx, of course, made the speech of the evening. He was in a benign and reminiscent mood, and therefore capable of making statements which he must have known were untrue. The International, he declared, was founded by workingmen for workingmen, and therein lay its novelty. No politicians, no intellectuals, had any hand in its making; it was a completely spontaneous movement. The International had no credo. Its task was merely to organize the forces of the working class, to unite and coordinate the different trends, and it had triumphed over all persecutions precisely because it was a spontaneous movement. Like the early Christians, they had suffered persecution, but the concerted plans to destroy them had resulted only in increasing their strength; and just as the early Christians, though few in numbers, had overwhelmed the massed might of the Roman Empire, so the International was the destined instrument for overthrowing the oppressive weight of capitalism.

He was now warming to his theme: the theme which had dominated his thoughts for so long—the dictatorship of the proletariat. He described how the revolution of 1848 had opened the way to the revolutionary forces which came to maturity in the Paris Commune. He said:

> There have been many misunderstandings about the Commune. It was unable to bring about a new form of class domination. In destroying the existing conditions of oppression by transferring the means of production to the productive workingmen, thus compelling everyone capable of working to work in order to live, they had also destroyed the single basis of class domination and oppression. But before such a change can fully take place, it is necessary that there should be a dictatorship of the proletariat, and the first condition of such a dictatorship was the formation of a proletarian army. The working classes must conquer on the battlefield the right to their own emancipation. The task of the International is to organize and unite the powers of the working classes in the coming struggle.

In the past Marx had rarely spoken about the International in these terms. In the "Inaugural Address," seven years before, he had suggested more modest aims. The vision of vast proletarian armies achieving power by victories on the battlefield derived from the Paris Commune; never before had it occurred to him that proletarian armies might seize power, establish a dictatorship, and sweep away the last vestiges of bourgeois power. Ironically the vision came to him at a banquet. He had eaten well, had drunk copiously, and was basking in the admiration of the crowd.

They drank a silent toast to him, and soon a young Frenchman rose and offered a toast to the devotion and heroism of Polish women who preferred to see their sons go to the scaffold rather than live in slavery, and there were more toasts, and at the end they all sang the "Marseillaise."

For Marx it had been an extraordinary experience, for he was one of those who belong to the silence of the study and he was not accustomed to public acclamation. He rarely presented himself as a jovial master of ceremonies, and there were few banquets in his life. This banquet had a special significance: they were celebrating the International and its future victories. They did not know that the International was dying and had only a few more months to live. Marx himself would deliver the death-blow.

A LETTER FROM NECHAYEV

Of all the Russian revolutionaries of the nineteenth century there was none who inspired more dread than Sergey Nechayev. Small, ugly, dark-featured, nervous, always dressed shabbily, he was immune to fear and capable of the most reckless and brutal acts, but it is not for his recklessness and brutality that he is remembered so much as for his astonishing power to convince others that he was the leader of a revolutionary movement which had no existence except in his fertile imagination. He was himself a revolutionary movement determined to bring about the downfall of Tsarist Russia. He had discovered a simple truth: one man, provided that he is absolutely ruthless, can destroy a state. It was a lesson which was learned by Lenin, who studied his works and passionately admired the cruel simplicities of Nechayev's mind.

Nechayev stands at the threshold of the modern world—the dedicated terrorist determined to destroy existing society, with no thought of the consequences. While Marx concerned himself with vast and complicated theories on the nature of capitalist society and the inevitable emergence of the dictatorship of the proletariat, Nechayev contented himself with the simple thesis: society must be destroyed.

At the age of twenty-one Nechayev was already a legend among the students in St. Petersburg. With only a small following of students, he formed a network of determined revolutionaries in the Russian universities. He had a secret printing press, a widespread intelligence system, considerable funds from sources which have never been traced, and clear-cut ideas about how the general uprising could be brought about. It was

1868, the year after the publication of *Das Kapital.* In May 1869 he expected the uprising to take place.

In fact there was no uprising, because the police were able to arrest some of the students acting as runners between St. Petersburg and Moscow. Nechayev disappeared, having first arranged that a penciled note should fall into the hands of a young revolutionary friend, Vera Zasulich. "They are taking me to the fortress," it read. "Do not lose heart, beloved comrades." By "the fortress" he meant the Peter and Paul Fortress in St. Petersburg, the most terrible prison in Russia. The ruse succeeded; his legend grew. He went underground, vanishing without a trace. In March 1869 he slipped out of Russia on a false passport and made his way to Geneva to teach the art of revolution to Bakunin. He was twenty-two, Bakunin was fifty-five. He was unknown outside of Russia, and Bakunin was the most famous revolutionary of his age.

To the tolerant and credulous Bakunin the arrival of Nechayev was a matter for rejoicing. Nechayev was a great spinner of tales. He told how he had been captured by the Tsarist police, thrown into a dungeon in the Peter and Paul Fortress from which he escaped by throwing a general's cloak over his shoulders, and then in slow stages, always closely followed, making his way to Rumania and freedom. There had been terrifying encounters, sudden confrontations with the police, ambuscades. For many weeks he had lived in deadly peril, nursing his secret plans for a revolution which would shake Russia from end to end. The Secret Revolutionary Committee had sent him to Geneva to demand the blessing of Bakunin for the projected revolution. In a few weeks he would return and lead the revolution to victory.

Nechayev's brilliant improvisations pleased Bakunin, who was capable of equally outrageous improvisations. What attracted him to Nechayev, however, was his youth, his vigor, his absolute determination and dedication. "He is one of those fanatics who doubt nothing and fear nothing," he wrote to his friend James Guillaume.

Together they wrote a number of revolutionary manifestos. In the shadow of Bakunin Nechayev wrote his chilling *Revolutionary Catechism* with its promise of "terrible, total, merciless and universal destruction." In twenty-six formal articles the *Revolutionary Catechism* described how a successful revolution could be carried out by employing all the arts of subversion, intimidation and murder. In August, armed with his pamphlets and a considerable sum of money, Nechayev returned to Russia on a Serbian passport.

He organized more student cells and made plans to capture the Imperial Armory at Tula. He soon had his own agents inside the armory, where cannon and rifles were manufactured. He drew up a list of high officials to be assassinated, and announced to his fellow conspirators that a general uprising would take place on the ninth anniversary of the liberation of the serfs.

In November he made one of those grave and stupid mistakes which revolutionaries sometimes make when they are exhausted or dazzled by their own arbitrary power. He murdered a student called Ivan Ivanov, who refused to obey his orders. The murder took place just outside a grotto in the Petrovsky Park in Moscow, and the body was thrown into an ice-covered pond. A few days later the body rose to the surface, and the police were hot on the heels of the murderer.

During the following days they began to uncover the details of a conspiracy which extended as far as Tula and the remote universities of Russia. They found and deciphered the *Revolutionary Catechism,* which was later printed in full in the *Government Courier.* They arrested 152 persons, most of them students, and kept them in jail for a year and a half before bringing them to trial. Orders were issued for the arrest of Nechayev. About the middle of December he fled across the border, and in January he was in Switzerland. Once more he was explaining to Bakunin that Russia was on the eve of a bloody revolution.

Meanwhile Bakunin had been suffering his usual financial reverses. A student called Lyubavin took pity on him. Knowing a publisher who urgently wanted to publish a translation of *Das Kapital* into Russian, he suggested that Bakunin, who knew German extremely well, would make an admirable translator. It was an ironical choice of translator, for Bakunin was engaged in a protracted war with Marx for control of the International, passionately detested Marx while recognizing his ability, and was temperamentally incapable of understanding Marx's ideas, especially in the baroque form they assumed in *Das Kapital.* He was in such financial straits that he would have agreed to almost any proposition, and accordingly he offered to make the translation for 1,200 rubles to be paid in installments. On September 28 Lyubavin sent him the first installment of 300 rubles and four days later Bakunin wrote a receipt. Since the contract had been made out in Lyubavin's name and Bakunin was notoriously resistant to fulfilling contracts, a heavy responsibility rested on the student.

For a month Bakunin did nothing whatsoever with the translation. He was busy with his own writings and preparing to leave Geneva for Locarno. Toward the end of October he wrote to his friend Alexander Herzen a long letter in which he set out his reasons for admiring and detesting Marx. There was no meanness in him, and he discussed Marx fairly, with a careful weighing of the evidence. "Leaving aside all the filth he has vomited at us," he wrote, "we cannot fail to recognize—at least I cannot fail to recognize—his enormous services to the cause of socialism during the twenty-five years I have known him, and in all this he has undoubtedly left us far behind." He admitted Marx's great services to the International, his careful strategies, his inflexible purpose. All this was on the credit side. On the debit side there was his adoration of state communism, a form of perpetual slavery, and his fatal defects of character, especially his *Schadenfreude,* his malicious joy in the suffering of others. When he wrote this letter *Das Kapital* was gathering dust on his shelves.

The days passed, and Bakunin was in no hurry to pay his debt to Lyubavin. At the beginning of November he wrote that he was winding up his political affairs, and he would really set down to work the following day. Translators tend to be procrastinators, and Bakunin was one of the most accomplished procrastinators of his time. To a friend he wrote later in the month that he could perhaps manage three pages a day—there were nearly eight hundred pages in the original German edition of *Das Kapital*—and under favorable conditions he might be able to manage five pages a day, or even ten. He sent a few pages to Lyubavin in December, and seems to have felt reasonably satisfied that the work was progressing.

Suddenly in the middle of January Nechayev returned to Switzerland. A few days later he was in Locarno, telling Bakunin about all his extraordinary adventures in Russia, injecting his own poison into the revolutionary atmosphere. The dark stranger had returned, and nothing would ever be the same again.

When Nechayev learned that Bakunin was translating *Das Kapital,* he decided to take the matter in his own hands. He liked simple solutions, and he devised a simple way to prevent Bakunin from doing any more hack work. He wrote a threatening letter to Lyubavin, forbidding him to have any further dealings with Bakunin under pain of death.

The letter has some considerable importance, because it came into the possession of Marx and was used as a powerful weapon against Bakunin at the Hague Congress held in 1872. At this congress Marx and his handpicked delegates placed Bakunin on trial, the letter written by Nechayev being put forward as evidence of Bakunin's diabolical duplicity and treachery. In fact, there is no evidence that Bakunin was responsible for the letter in any way, and it is unlikely that he ever saw it. The letter read:

25 February 1870

To the student Lyubavin residing in Heidelberg.

SIR,

In compliance with the orders of the Bureau, I have the honor to inform you:

We have received from the Committee in Russia a document which, among other matters, concerns you.

Here are the passages concerning you:

"It has come to the knowledge of the Committee that a few young Russian gentlemen, dilettantes of liberalism, living abroad, have decided to exploit the knowledge and energy of certain people of well-known views by taking advantage of their difficult material circumstances. These beloved personalities, compelled to work the treadmill by these dilettantes who have the mentality of extortioners, are thereby deprived of the opportunity of consecrating their energies to the emancipation of mankind. Thus a certain Lyubavin—(Heidelberg, at the house of Widow Wald, Sandgasse, 16)—has recruited the famous Bakunin in order to translate a work by Marx, and like a proper bourgeois extortioner succeeded in exploiting his financial distress by giving him an advance, and insisting that he complete the said work without delay. In this way Lyubavin, the untried colt, concerned to bring enlightenment to Russian eyes by putting others to work, has prevented Bakunin from working for the supremely important cause of the Russian people, for which he is indispensable. The behavior of Lyubavin and others like him conflicts with the cause of the freedom of the people and those who fight for it, and is so bourgeois, immoral and contemptible that it can scarcely be distinguished from the behavior of a police spy. This must be clear to everyone who is not a scoundrel."

The Committee has entrusted the Foreign Bureau with the following message:

"That if he and other parasites of a similar ilk are of the opinion that translating Marx is important to the Russian people at the present time, then they should do the work themselves, consecrating to the task all their pitiful strength, instead of studying chemistry with a view to obtaining a fine sinecure in the government schools.

"That Lyubavin must immediately inform Bakunin that in accordance with the decisions of the Russian Revolutionary Committee he is exempt from the moral duty to continue the work of the translation."

There follow a number of points which it would be premature to disclose to you, since we are counting to some extent on your perspicacity and prudence. Recognizing with whom you are dealing, you will therefore do everything necessary to avoid the regrettable possibility that we may have to address ourselves to you *a second time in a less civilized way.*

We therefore propose:

1. As soon as you receive this letter, you will telegraph B. releasing him from the moral obligation of continuing the translation,

2. You will send him an explanatory letter immediately, and you will enclose this document and the envelope which contained it.

3. You will write at once to those agents of ours who are nearest to you (even if it is only the address you know in Geneva), informing them that you have indeed received the document of the Bureau bearing such-and-such number, and that you have accepted its demands and carried them out.

We are always rigorously punctual, and we have calculated the exact day on which you will receive this letter. You, in turn, should be no less punctual in submitting to these demands, so that we shall not be placed under the necessity of having recourse to extreme measures which will prove to be a trifle more severe.

Assuring you that our appreciation of you and your conduct will be infinitely more tolerable, and that it depends entirely on you whether our relations become more amicable and a firmer understanding is created between us or whether our relationship takes an unpleasant course.

I have the honor to be, Sir, yours truly,

AMSKY
Secretary to the Bureau

The signature of this monumental essay in blackmail was not very legible, and "Amsky" is merely an educated guess.

Lyubavin received the letter on March 3 and at once wrote to Bakunin, accusing him of the basest kind of duplicity and demanding an explanation. Bakunin was deeply offended and broke off all relations with the student. He was old and tired, engaged in a number of difficult and complex stratagems for raising money to support his wife and her illegitimate children. Nechayev had left him, and was wandering from one hiding place to another, for the Russian government had demanded his extradition as a common murderer. For more than two years Nechayev was to live the life of a fugitive. Then the Russian police would drag him from Switzerland to the Peter and Paul Fortress in St. Petersburg, where he would die in his chains.

Marx learned about the letter a few weeks later from his friend Herman Lopatin. He called it "the letter of a swine." He was properly incensed, and though he knew it was written by Nechayev, he placed all the blame on Bakunin, whom he regarded as his inveterate enemy, busily attempting to dethrone him from his place of power in the International.

Marx never recognized the strange power of Nechayev. He knew the *Revolutionary Catechism,* and since he was filled with undying hatred of Bakunin, he came to the conclusion that only Bakunin could have written it. He wrote a history of Nechayev's relationship with Bakunin, and since he relied entirely on Russian refugees who detested Bakunin, nearly all his facts were wrong. He tells a curious story of Ivan Ivanov, who is depicted as a rich man's son busily financing the escapades of Nechayev until suddenly it occurred to him that there were better ways of spending his money. According to Marx, Ivanov was murdered for his wealth. In fact he was a poor agricultural student who was murdered because he had the good sense to refuse to obey arbitrary orders.

The letter which Nechayev wrote to Lyubavin was to have a strange influence on history. Armed with that letter, Marx would strike down Bakunin and at the same time destroy the International.

THE HAGUE CONGRESS

FOR MANY MONTHS Marx had been feverishly preparing for a conference which would, he hoped, settle once and for all whether the International would follow his program or become merely a sectarian organization at the mercy of disruptive forces. He embarked on a vast correspondence, continually sought out allies, maneuvered his friends, attacked his enemies, always in the hope of strengthening his own domination within the International, which no longer possessed effective power. The International was dying before his eyes, and all his efforts to pour life into it seemed to end in failure. For many years it had been split by internal rivalries, and had lost any real contact with the working classes.

For Marx the continuation of the International was a matter of the very greatest importance, because it provided him with his one fulcrum of power. Through the International he was able to speak above the heads of the leaders of the socialist factions, and to have a finger in every socialist pie. He could, and did, dominate the International by the power of his own personality, but increasingly it had become clear that he was manipulating the members of the General Council as though they were pieces on a chess board. He was surprised when they rebelled, and still more surprised when he realized the general ineffectiveness of the International to move events in the direction he desired. The International had shown itself to be powerless at the time of the Paris Commune; could it be expected to be more effective if another revolutionary wave broke across Europe?

The first broadside on behalf of the Hague Congress was fired in the spring of 1872 with the publication of a circular printed in Geneva under the title *Les Prétendues Scissions dans l'Internationale* (The Alleged Schisms in the International). The circular was written by Marx and

Engels in reply to a bitter attack on Marx by the followers of Bakunin, who saw in the International merely the perpetuation of a personal dictatorship, with one man dictating terms and regarding all who disagreed with him as heretics. Marx answered in his best polemical manner, violently attacking the heresies which had grown up in the revolutionary movement and insisting on the rightness of his cause. The circular concluded with a long tirade against anarchism, "the great show horse" of Bakunin, which sought to deprive the socialist movement of its orderly progress toward power by a deliberate disorder, an anarchic confusion. There were no real schisms in the International; there was only a handful of intriguing heretics, of whom Bakunin was the most ludicrous and self-serving. Bakunin replied contemptuously that the circular was "not a sword, but Marx's habitual weapon, a heap of filth."

To defeat Bakunin, to reduce him to impotence, now became Marx's overriding passion to which all other passions were subordinated, for Bakunin represented the greatest potential threat to his domination of the revolutionary movement in Europe. He had, of course, been attacking Bakunin for some time, but always with distaste, as though the enemy was scarcely worthy of his steel. It puzzled him that anyone could take Bakunin seriously—this man who had long ago established that all authority was evil, and therefore the state was evil, and therefore a ship's captain or an engine driver was evil, and anyone in any position of authority was evil, and even the majority was evil when it voted against the minority. In this way Marx reduced the anarchist hatred of any central authority to a string of nonsensical statements which seemed to be uttered by a buffoon. But Bakunin was not a buffoon, and Marx always underestimated his power and influence.

Essentially it was a quarrel between two attitudes of mind, two opposing philosophies which could never be reconciled. Bakunin opposed all authority; Marx opposed all authority except his own, and his authoritarian temper fed on intrigue and the small measure of power he was able to enjoy. Bakunin detested Germans and Jews as people more prone to authoritarianism than any other, while Marx viewed the Russians as a people congenitally incapable of orderly thought, half savage and politically incompetent. Bakunin's anarchism appealed to the workers of Spain, Italy and southern Europe, where the state which demanded taxes was hated as much as the landowners who demanded rent.

It was a strange battle, for there could be no fixed battleground, no point of contact. There were manifestos and circulars and strident calls to arms, and there were guerrilla raids into each other's territory. At the end of 1871 Marx had sent Paul Lafargue to Madrid in order to establish a branch of the International and to uncover the machinations of Bakunin in Spain. Paul Lafargue spoke Spanish perfectly, and he was able to obtain copies of Bakunin's secret dispatches to the Spanish revolutionaries. There was not the least doubt that Bakunin was seeking to undermine the International and to capture it. Marx, carried away by enthusiasm, now looked forward all the more eagerly to a direct confrontation with Bakunin at the forthcoming Congress, for he had evidence enough that Bakunin had acted with duplicity and bad faith. In a shattering speech, he would finally demolish Bakunin and cast him into outer darkness. The entire working-class movement would come to know that Bakunin was a buffoon and an intriguer. Marx had demolished many men before, and he would have no difficulty in demolishing Bakunin.

The more he thought of the danger arising from Bakunin's intrigues, the more determined he became to compile a complete dossier of the crimes committed by his enemy. The Hague Congress would open on September 2. In the middle of August it occurred to him that one of his most effective weapons would be the letter which Nechayev had written to Lyubavin demanding on pain of death that no further effort should be made to force Bakunin to continue working on the translation of *Das Kapital*. Blinded by anger, and viewing this personal quarrel with Bakunin as a deeply significant incident in the history of the revolutionary struggle, he decided to offer the letter as prime evidence of perfidy at the Congress. The letter, he knew, was still in the possession of Lyubavin. He therefore wrote to his friend Nikolay Danielson in St. Petersburg and asked as a matter of the utmost urgency that the incriminating document be sent to him. Apparently under the impression that the Russian censors knew no foreign languages, he wrote in English, signing himself with his *nom de guerre* A. Williams. Many years later Danielson presented this letter together with many others received from Marx to the British Museum, and we can therefore read it in the original manuscript:

15 August, 1872

DEAR SIR,

I hope you have received the first part of the second German edition which I have sent you a few days since. I shall also send you the first 6 *livraisons* of the French edition which will be out in a few days. It is necessary to compare *both editions* because I have added and changed here and there in the French edition.

Your interesting letter I have received and shall answer to it in a few days. I have also received the manuscript and the article of the *Vestnik*.

Today I write in all haste, for one special purpose which is of the *most urgent* character.

10

15 August, 1872.

Dear Sir,

I hope you have received the first part of the second German edition which I have sent you a few days since. I shall also send you the first 6 livraisons of the French edition which will be out in a few days. It is necessary to compare <u>both editions</u> because I have added and changed here and there in the French edition.

Your interesting letter I have received and shall answer to it in a few days. I have also received the manuscript and the article of the Bestnik.

To day I write in all haste, for one special purpose which is of the <u>most urgent</u> character.

B—n has worked secretly since years to undermine the International and has now been pushed by us so far as to throw away the mask and <u>secede openly</u> with the foolish people led by him — the same man who was the manager in the Y. of affair. Now this B. was once charged with the ~~translation~~ Ausgabe of my book, received the money for it in ~~advance~~

Marx's letter to Danielson, August 15, 1872.

11

and instead of giving work, Netchaieff had sent to Lubavin
(I think) who transacted for the publisher with him the
affair, a most infamous and compromising letter. It
would be of the highest utility for me, *if this*
letter was sent me immediately. As this is a mere
commercial affair and as in the use to be made of
the letter no names will be used, I hope
you will procure me that letter. But no
time is to be lost. If it is sent, it ought
to be sent at once as I shall leave
London for the Hague Congress at the
end of this month.

Yours very truly

A. Williams

B——n has worked secretly since years to undermine the International and has now been pushed by us so far as to throw away the mask and *secede openly* with the foolish people led by him—the same man who was the manager in the N——ff affair. Now this B. was once charged with the Russian translation of my book, received the money for it in advance and instead of giving work, sent or had sent to Lubavin (I think) who transacted for the publisher with him the affair, a most infamous and compromising letter. It would be of the highest utility for me, *if this letter was sent to me* immediately. As this is a mere *commercial* affair and as in the use to be made of the letter no names will be used, I hope you will procure me that letter. But no time is to be lost. If it is sent, it ought to be sent at once as I shall leave London for the Haag Congress at the end of the month.

Yours very truly

A Williams

As Marx well knew, the statement that "as in the use of the letter no names will be used" was untrue. He proposed to conceal nothing. The letter would be used to the hilt to prove that Bakunin was capable of the most infamous threats and the most perfidious conduct.

Five days later Marx's letter was safely in the hands of Lyubavin in St. Petersburg. Lyubavin replied with a long letter to Marx explaining the circumstances under which he had received Nechayev's threats, and he enclosed the original copy of Nechayev's letter. With the documents furnished by Lafargue in Spain and this letter Marx set out for the Hague, jubilant in the knowledge that he had sufficient evidence to drum Bakunin out of the International.

The Congress met in a shabby hall in the working-class district of the Hague. It was one of those small ill-ventilated and ugly buildings used for dances and amateur theatricals, political meetings and workingmen's clubs, and was without any pretensions to grandeur. Tables had been arranged in a horseshoe, there was a gallery along one side, and iron columns supported the roof. This colorless and joyless building, next door to a prison, was called Concordia Hall.

There was, however, very little concord in the Congress, even though it was wholly dominated by Marx and his supporters. Quarrels were continually breaking out, charges were continually being leveled, and for about half the time the delegates were in a state of uproar. The atmosphere was charged with venom, as the followers of Bakunin shouted against the followers of Marx and were themselves shouted down. There were only six followers of Bakunin, but they made up for their lack of numbers with the strength of their lungs.

The great majority of the delegates had been hand-picked by Marx, who was thus assured of victory before the debate began. There were altogether sixty-four delegates, of whom eighteen were French, fifteen German, seven Belgian, five English, five Spanish, four Dutch, four Swiss, two Austrian, one Hungarian, one Danish, one Irish, and one Polish. The Belgian, Dutch, Swiss, and most of the English and Spanish delegates were opposed to Marx, a few because they were followers of Bakunin, a larger number because they intensely disliked his authoritarian manner. Marx's strength lay in the solid bloc of French and German delegates.

Writing to Dr. Kugelmann in the summer Marx said: "The international congress is a life-and-death matter for the International. Before I resign I would like at the very least to protect it from disintegrating elements." But as the Congress opened, he did not appear to be waging a life-and-death struggle. He was affable and self-possessed, dressed in a black broadcloth suit, smiling indulgently whenever a foreign comrade was presented to him. At such times he would press a monocle to his right eye and examine the comrade with a paternal and faintly quizzical look. He was well aware that he was the principal actor in the unfolding drama and that all eyes were turned to him. The destiny of the Congress was in his hands and he could direct it in whatever way he pleased.

To his surprise and disgust Bakunin had failed to appear. The entire Italian delegation had also failed to appear, out of sympathy with Bakunin. Instead of the head-on collision which he desired, the battle of giants, there was to be a strange indecisive war against a pygmy who refused to be silenced and who continued to mock at the pretensions of Marx and his followers until the end of the Congress. This pygmy was James Guillaume, a schoolteacher and journalist of great charm and ability, who represented an anarchist federation of workers in the Jura mountains. Guillaume's lieutenant was Adhémar Schwitzguebel, a watchmaker from the Canton of Berne.

The opening days of the Congress were spent in continual wrangling about the credentials of the delegates. There was an especially violent dispute on the seating of Marx's son-in-law Paul Lafargue, who claimed to represent Madrid and whose claim was denied by the Spanish followers of Bakunin. It was learned that an English cobbler represented a section of Chicago, a city he had never visited. Thomas Mottershead, an English trade unionist, asked how this had come about, and was told by Marx that it was none of his business. "He is not one of the leaders—a nobody," Mottershead said; and Marx replied: "It is to his credit not to belong to the so-called leaders of English workingmen, for they have all more or less sold out to Gladstone." In this way Marx could have justified a mandate to anyone he chose. An American called West, a small man with a bald head, thin features and a billy-goat beard, claimed to represent a section in New York. He was a voluble talker with a gift for dramatic gesticulation, and he somehow held the floor for nearly an hour as he defended himself against the charge, brought by Marx, that he had not paid his dues and belonged to the heretical sect of bogus reformers, middle-class quacks and proponents of free love and spiritualism which had been organized by Mrs. Victoria Claflin Woodhull, a candidate for the Presidency of the United States of America. Marx delivered a harangue against the New Yorker, adding some unflattering comments on Mrs. Woodhull.

This was the first international congress that Marx had attended and he was beginning to enjoy the opportunity for invective. The question of West's credentials was put to the vote, and since no one voted for him, all the followers of Marx voting against him and the Bakuninists abstaining, he was unceremoniously ejected. For the rest of the week he sat in the gallery, gazing wistfully at the delegates below and talking to anyone who cared to listen about his four-thousand-mile journey from America to attend an ungrateful congress.

One reason why Marx never attended congresses now became clear. He was neither an arresting speaker nor a forceful debater. Theodor Cuno, one of his most loyal and admiring followers, remembered that "he was not very fluent, and there was nothing in him of the practiced speaker." He remembered too that Marx, while speaking, would permit his monocle to drop from his eye and there would be a long and painful delay while he carefully inserted it again. Nor was Engels a very convincing speaker, for he spoke conversationally in the casual sarcastic tones of a college student making quick debating points. He was "a tall, bony man with sharp-cut features, long, sandy whiskers, ruddy complexion and little blue eyes." Cuno was impressed by the fact that Engels had learned twelve languages for the sole purpose of carrying the communist faith into as many countries as possible.

Gabriel Ranvier, one of the heroes of the Commune, was elected president. Predictably he sang the praises of the Commune, defended it against its enemies, and proclaimed that the first task of the Congress was to appoint a permanent committee on barricades. He had been the mayor of Belleville, and it was his voice which proclaimed that the Commune had come into existence. He had also issued the last of the four hundred proclamations that the Communards issued in the space of two months. This was an appeal to the people of Belleville to march out against the enemy. They marched, and were mowed down.

James Guillaume had no more affection for Ranvier than he had for Marx. When he took the floor on the afternoon of September 5 he lashed out at the authoritarian rule of the International. There were two opposing forces, one that believed in the centralization of power in the hands of the few, the other that believed in free federations. The working-class movement did not need a General Council, a single brain controlling it. Had it ever organized or conducted a class war? Had it ever advanced the economic position of the workers? Had it ever built barricades? What use had it been anywhere in the world? "If it is asked: 'Does the International require a head' we answer, 'No,'" he declared. Like the other Bakuninists, he felt it might be worthwhile to retain the General Council, but merely as a center for correspondence and statistics, without power to make binding decisions. The argument for reducing the powers of the General Council until it was nothing more than a letter box was advanced by the Belgian delegate Désiré Brismée, who felt that this was a modest proposal, for an equally good argument could be made for abolishing the General Council altogether. By the "General Council" he meant "Marx," and Marx was perfectly aware that he meant this. Charles Longuet, the future husband of his daughter Jenny, and Paul Lafargue, the husband of Laura, were therefore thrown into the battle to defend him. Longuet defended the General Council on the ground that it fulfilled an absolutely indispensable role, and Lafargue argued that those who attacked the General Council for its despotism were themselves despots.

Then it was Marx's turn to denounce his adversaries, the windbags, ultra radicals and *agents provocateurs* who always endangered the movement and were forever compromising individual members. He laughed at those who said the General Council possessed the powers of a Negro prince or a Russian tsar. On the contrary, it was powerful only in the measure that it possessed the consent of the members, for it had no army, no budget, no power to make members conform unless they wanted to. The General Council was a moral force, and if it was reduced to being a letter box, then it would be wholly meaningless and might as well be abolished. "We would rather abolish the General Council than follow Brismée's wish and transform it into a letter box," Marx said. "In that case the leadership of the association would fall into the hands of journalists, that is, mainly nonworkers." It was a strange argument, for the leadership had never been in the hands of the workers in the past. And why, Marx continued, should there be a letter box, for it was certain that there would be no letters or at best only the exchange of stale news. No, the important thing was to maintain the General Council at all costs and to give it even greater powers. Especially it should have the power to suspend any section or federation it pleased, and in this way exert its full weight in the affairs of the International.

Since Marx had the votes to maneuver the Congress in any direction he pleased, the voting was a mere formality. The General Council was granted increased powers by 36 votes against 6, with fifteen abstentions.

With the voting completed, and the General Council now more powerful than ever, an extraordinary event occurred. A heavy, thickset German suddenly made his way into the meeting place, shouting that he had been threatened by one of the delegates and was in danger of his life. He talked very rapidly, and at first no one could understand what he was saying. He said he was not afraid of death, had fought before, and would fight again. By this time all the delegates had leaped to their feet and were shouting themselves hoarse. The stranger went up to Marx and asked why he had been condemned to death, and Marx, who had never seen the man before, said it was all a mistake, no one had been condemned to death, he was sure everything would come out all right. It appeared that Theodor Cuno had a personal quarrel with the German, who had been the Prussian consul at Milan when Cuno was arrested there. Cuno had not threatened him with death, but had attacked him angrily in words that had found their way into a local newspaper. One of the stranger aspects of the Hague Congress was that it was believed to be a meeting of terrorists engaged in a conspiracy to overthrow the governments of Europe, with a blacklist of officials and politicians already condemned to death. In the sensational press it was regarded as a powerful revolutionary instrument, but it had long ago become powerless.

When the uproar over the appearance of the German consul had died down, Marx sprang his *coup de théâtre*. He had acquired all the powers he wanted for the General Council, and now he proclaimed that the time had come to abolish the General Council and the entire International. He did not say this in so many words. What he said—or rather what Engels said, for Engels read the speech prepared by Marx—was that he had decided to transfer the General Council to New York, where the documents of the International would be kept in greater safety and where so many working-class men from so many countries were living that it would be possible to find sincere and dedicated men ready to carry on the work. Here at last it would be possible to avoid the party frictions which endangered the movement in London. Marx was adamant. It was New York or nothing: he refused to consider any alternatives. He demanded an immediate vote. There were 26 votes in favor of New York, 23 against, and nine abstentions. Many who had voted against Marx were among his faithful supporters. They realized that by moving to New York, the General Council would have no further influence on the working-class movement in Europe, that Marx himself would retire from the scene, and that the International had received its death blow.

Marx had made the decision to retire earlier in the year, for in May 1872 we find him writing to his friend Danielson:

> Ich bin so overworked, and so much interfered within my theoretical studies, that, after September, I shall *withdraw* from the *commercial* concern, which, at this moment, weighs principally upon my own shoulders, and which, as you know, has its ramifications all over the world. Mais, est modus in rebus, and I can no longer afford—for some time at least—to combine two sorts of business of so very different a character.

The decision was final and irrevocable. It was as though Marx could no longer tolerate the existence of the International unless he stood at the helm. It must work for him, obey his commands, disseminate his doctrines, or perish. The decision to destroy it was his and his alone.

Meanwhile there remained one final task of great importance—Bakunin and his anarchist followers must be officially condemned by the dying International. A select committee had been appointed to examine the documents which Marx brought to the Congress and to pronounce a verdict. There was no doubt what the verdict would be. The select committee concluded that Bakunin had deliberately attempted to sabotage the International and that he had embezzled money from Marx's publisher. They urged the Congress to expel Bakunin, Guillaume and Schwitzguebel from the International. Bakunin's expulsion was carried by 27 votes against 7, with eight abstentions, and his two most prominent followers were also expelled. At the Congress Marx had accomplished everything he desired, and the meeting was accordingly declared closed. With his wife and his daughter Laura he went off the next day to Amsterdam for a meeting of local party officials.

At this meeting he was in an expansive mood, for he was pleased with his successes and a good deal of attention was being paid to him. Once more he spoke of the need for a great centralization of power in the General Council, and for strong and vigorous propaganda to prepare for the day of revolution. Above all there must be solidarity, for the Paris Commune had proved that without solidarity revolutions fail.

These thoughts of solidarity and revolution were always on his mind, and he repeated them now perfunctorily, almost mechanically, for he was about to enter into retirement. He could afford to be generous, and so he reminded his listeners that violent revolution was not always the key to social progress. "We do not deny that there are countries like England and America, and—if I am familiar with your institutions—Holland, where labor may attain its goal by peaceful means." There would be no barricades in North America, he declared, but there were still many countries where revolution offered the sole hope for change, and these included "most countries on the continent." If the workers did not seize power, they would fare like the early Christians who never saw their kingdom realized in this world. It was a strange comparison, for the early Christians had never hoped to establish an earthly kingdom.

This was his last public speech, his valedictory to the working-class organizations over which he had presided for so long. It was also, in a very real sense, his valedictory to revolution, for there could be no hope of revolutionary fervor in New York, which was now to become the headquarters of the International. As far as he was concerned, the future revolutions in Europe would occur without benefit of the International, which had outlived its usefulness. A new International might arise; new forces would emerge from among the working classes; new leaders would take power. For himself he was content to spend his remaining years working on the remaining volumes of *Das Kapital.*

At about the same time Bakunin also stepped down from the position he had so long occupied in the revolutionary movement. The indomitable old agitator was mortally weary of the struggle against Marx, and now that Marx himself had retired from the combat he felt that nothing was to be gained by continuing a debate which must of necessity be unproductive. Yet there was still some fire in him, and he wrote for the newspaper *Liberté* in Brussels a long and reasoned attack on Marx, which was intended to be at once an act of self-vindication and a final attempt to dethrone Marx from his place of eminence. He accused Marx of being a man of infinite ambition, who regarded himself as the chief architect of the European revolution, humorless and pitiless, more German than the Germans, and wholly devoted to authoritarianism. If such a state as Marx envisaged could be brought into being, it would consist of "slavery within and interminable war without." It would not be a state that served the people, but on the contrary it would serve only its masters. He wrote:

> I regard Marx as a very serious, if not always very sincere revolutionary, who really desires to bring about the revolt of the masses; and I ask myself how he can fail to see that the establishment of a universal, collective or individual dictatorship, a dictatorship designed to carry out as it were the work of a chief engineer of world revolution, directing and guiding the insurrectionary movement of the masses in all countries exactly as one might direct a machine—the establishment of such a dictatorship would alone suffice to paralyze and falsify all the popular movements.
>
> What man, or what group of men, however richly endowed with genius, could venture to flatter themselves that they alone could grasp and understand the infinite concerns, trends and activities which are so different in every country, every locality, every profession, all this immense whole, being united without possessing any uniformity, moved by great common aspirations and by certain principles which have now entered into the consciousness of the masses, forming the future social revolution?

In Bakunin's eyes Marx's "universal dictatorship" was nothing more than the age-old dream of world empire which had driven so many popes and emperors to despair, but this time the dream was even more dangerous because it was impelled forward by a particularly harsh, German and mechanical mind.

When Bakunin learned the terms of his expulsion from the International, he had no doubt that Marx had written them, for they bore the indelible imprint of his style. "Whereas citizen Bakunin has made use of deceptive tricks in order to appropriate a larger or smaller part of other persons' fortune, which constitutes fraud, and whereas, further, he or his agents have had recourse to threats lest he be compelled to meet his obligations . . ." So read the clause which most directly revealed the hand of Marx, and to Bakunin these words merely reinforced the opinion he had long professed—that Marx was ultimately a bourgeois, concerned with the small profit and loss, and anxious to be under the protection of the police.

Although Marx had convinced himself that the incriminating letter written by Nechayev was the work of Bakunin, it was not so. Lyubavin himself had clearly explained the situation in the letter he wrote to Marx. "I must impress upon you," he wrote, "that the evidence against him is not of so clear-cut a nature as you perhaps have believed," and he explained all the circumstances which led up to the letter at great length, very patiently. His final conclusion was that the letter might very well have been written without Bakunin's knowledge. Marx chose to ignore this conclusion, for he had his own well-defined opinions on the matter. As for Nechayev, he was in no position to say anything. Two weeks before the opening of the Congress Nechayev was arrested by the Swiss police and handed over to Tsarist gendarmes at the frontier. For the remaining ten years of his life Nechayev was the personal prisoner of the Tsar, consigned to a damp cell in the Peter and Paul Fortress in St. Petersburg, where he was kept in solitary confinement and shackled to the wall.

Toward the end of the year Marx remembered the famous letter and wrote an acknowledgment to Danielson, saying it had accomplished its purpose. He wrote:

25 Nov. 1872

MY DEAR FRIEND,

The letter sent over to me has been duly received and has done *its work*.

If I have not written earlier, and if, even at this moment, I do not send but these few lines, it is because I want you to send me another—if possible—*strictly commercial address*, under which I may write to you.

In consequence of the extradition of N. and the intrigues of his master B., I feel very anxious on your behalf and that of some other friends. Those men are able of every infamy.

I cannot enough express my gratitude for the interest taken in my work and labours by you and other Russian friends.

Yours most sincerely
A. WILLIAMS

Please reply to these lines as soon as possible.

About the same time that Marx was writing this letter, Bakunin was writing his final summary of Marx's character from his sickbed in Switzerland. "Marx does not believe in God," Bakunin wrote, "but he believes much in himself, and makes everyone subservient to himself. His heart is not full of love, but of gall, and he has very little sympathy for the human race."

As it happened, Marx was full of the milk of human kindness now that he was free of a grave responsibility. There was still another reason for him to be happy. In October, soon after returning from the Hague Congress, he attended the wedding of his favorite daughter Jenny to Charles Longuet, a revolutionary journalist who had edited a newspaper during the Paris Commune and taught at London University while in exile.

12

25 Nov. 1872

My dear friend,

The letter sent over to me has been duly received and has done its work.

If I have not written earlier, and if, even at this moment, I do not send but these few lines, it is because I want you to send me another — if possible — strictly commercial address under which I may write to you.

In consequence of the extradition of N. and the intrigues of his master B., I feel very anxious on your behalf and that of some other friends. Those men are able of every infamy.

I cannot enough express my gratitude for the interest taken in my work and labours by you and other Russian friends.

Yours most sincerely

A. Williams.

Please reply to these lines as soon as possible.

Marx's letter to Danielson, November 25, 1872.

Marx hoped that Charles Longuet would become a communist; instead he remained a socialist. Ten years later Marx, writing to Engels, dismissed both of his sons-in-law as nincompoops. "Longuet is the last of the Proudhonists," he wrote, "and Lafargue is the last of the Bakuninists—may the devil fly away with them!"

THE BARREN YEARS

My head feels so stupid, like a mill-wheel going round and round.

—Marx to Engels, August 3, 1881

THE CURE AT KARLSBAD

INTO THE LIVES of nearly all men who struggle against the current of their time there comes a moment of truth, a sudden realization that the game cannot be played indefinitely with the weapons they have chosen. Sooner or later they realize that they have done all that it is in their power to do. Dimming eyesight, faltering speech, the infirmities of the flesh and the mind's incapacities remind them that the dream to which they have dedicated all their energies and hopes will not come into existence in their lifetime. They see the young outstripping them, and their own early struggles become a footnote in history. Such men do not yield gracefully. The knowledge that they are redundant does not leave them with peace of mind. Instead they fight back furiously, capriciously, disastrously. In this struggle they sometimes destroy themselves.

For Karl Marx the moment of truth came in the English watering town of Harrogate in Yorkshire toward the end of 1873. He had been in failing health since the early spring, suffering from headaches and unaccountable fits of nervous depression. He sometimes trembled like a leaf, and for no reason at all he would break out into violent tirades against those who were closest to him. Eleanor, who had accompanied him to Harrogate and loved him this side of idolatry, seemed to have lost the ability to calm him. It was clear that he was suffering from a nervous disease which had little or nothing to do with his past medical history. It was no longer a question of carbuncles or a defective liver; the brain itself and the entire nervous system of the body were affected. Hurriedly, she arranged that he should be taken to Manchester and placed under the care of Dr. Gumpert, who ordered a complete cessation of work. Previously he had been permitted to work up to four hours daily; now he was forbidden to work or read newspapers, and he must not speak about anything except the bare necessities of life. He was under doctor's orders to become the one thing he dreaded most of all—a vegetable.

Eleanor and Engels shielded him; no one must know that he had suffered a complete collapse. In later years Marx himself would dwell broodingly on this period of terrible depression and insomnia, saying that it was brought about as a result of his superhuman endeavors in writing *Das Kapital* and in his work on behalf of the International. In September the doctor thought he had suffered from a stroke, and by the end of the year they were sure he was suffering from nervous exhaustion. Engels was wondering whether he would survive for more than a few months.

At the height of the crisis, while he was still staying with Eleanor at Harrogate, Marx wrote that he had been reading Sainte-Beuve's *Chateaubriand,* and there were scarcely words enough in his vocabulary to express his hatred of the work. What especially annoyed and exasperated him was that Sainte-Beuve had acquired so much fame in his own country. He wrote:

> If this man has become so famous in France, it can only be because he is in every respect the classical incarnation of French *vanité;* and this *vanité* does not present itself in the light and frivolous garments of the eighteenth century, but instead wears romantic robes and prides itself on newfangled forms of expression, false profundity, Byzantine exaggerations, sentimental coquetry, play of colors, word painting, theatrical, sublime—it is in fact a mixture of lies never hitherto equaled in form and content.

Such diatribes were among the commonplaces of Marx's writings, but here the effect is almost one of self-parody. The mind seems to have slipped its gears in his horror of Sainte-Beuve's fame; and as he describes with mounting indignation the long catalogue of vices, he seems unconsciously to be describing his own, for he too had written in the high romantic style, theatrical, sublime. He appears to have hated Sainte-Beuve because he recognized his own style in the writings of the French critic.

We hear the same note of exasperated naked rage again in a letter he wrote a few days later to Dr. Kugelmann, who had read a report on Marx's ill-health in the *Frankfurter Zeitung,* and wanted to know whether it was true. Marx answered that there was another boil on his right cheek; it had been operated upon; there had been a few more minor ones, but he was taking quicksilver ointment and hoped he had seen the last of them. Then he upbraided the doctor for paying attention to rumors:

> You shouldn't worry at all about newspaper tripe, and *still less should you answer it.* I myself allow the English newspapers to report my death from time to time, without giving a sign of life. Nothing annoys me more than appearing to supply the public with reports on the state of my health through my friends (*you are the greatest sinner in this*). I don't give a farthing for the public . . .

This was rage of a kind he had rarely permitted himself, directed against one of his most loyal and long-suffering friends. It was the rage of a sick man who strikes blindly at everyone around him.

Although he had no more financial troubles, for Engels sent him his pension of £360 a year regularly, he was oppressed by his state of health and even more oppressed by the fact that he was unable to work. "Not to be able to work is a death sentence for any man who is not a beast," he wrote to his friend Sorge in America. In spite of the doctor's orders he would occasionally spend a day over his papers, working hard, making up for lost time; then there would be the inevitable relapse. His liver complaint returned to plague him. Eleanor, too, was ill. She was physically run down, overworked, suffered from insomnia, and was desperately in love with a French refugee called Prosper-Olivier Lissagaray. Marx had already made it clear that he disapproved of an engagement between his daughter and the aristocratic revolutionary, but she was still maintaining a secret correspondence with him. Caught between love for Lissagaray and adoration of her authoritarian father, she was on the verge of a nervous breakdown.

When Dr. Gumpert considered the best treatment for Marx, he always came to one conclusion. Marx must be moved bodily from London, away from his books, writings and correspondence, away from all the pressing problems which engrossed him. Karlsbad, the fashionable watering place in Bohemia, occurred to him as a likely place where he could enjoy a complete rest and obtain relief from his liver complaint. Accordingly Marx began to make tentative arrangements for the journey into forbidden territory, for he knew that he was liable to be arrested the moment he set foot on the territory of the Austro-Hungarian Empire. He was a self-proclaimed revolutionary, his name was widely known, and he had bitterly attacked the rulers of the empire in his articles. Dr. Gumpert was insistent that he should go to Karlsbad as soon as possible—Karlsbad and nowhere else—and the problem was how to cross the border and return in safety. A solution to the problem finally presented itself during the summer, when Marx decided to become a British citizen and to travel abroad under the protection of the British Crown. He consulted his solicitor. It appeared that naturalization was the right of any foreigner who had lived in England for one year and could produce favorable recommendations from four householders of impeccable reputation. On August 1 the four householders solemnly presented themselves at the solicitor's office, swore out affidavits stressing the excellent civic qualities of Karl Marx, and went on their way. These affidavits together with the solicitor's letter and various other documents obtained from the local magistrate were then taken immediately to the Home Office. Marx was under the impression that it was a purely formal matter and would be settled in a few days.

The Home Office, however, had other ideas. It knew of the existence of Karl Marx and had been watching him closely for many years. The affidavits were therefore handed over to Scotland Yard, which was asked to give its opinion on whether Marx deserved to be naturalized. The wheels ground slowly and more than two weeks passed before Scotland Yard rendered its verdict:

> CARL MARX–NATURALIZATION
>
> With reference to the above I beg to report that he is the notorious German agitator, the head of the International Society, and the advocate of Communistic principles. This man has not been loyal to his own King and Country.
>
> The references Messrs. "Seton," "Matheson," "Manning," and "Adcock" are all British born subjects, and respectable house-holders. The statements made by them with reference to the time they have known the applicant are correct.

By the time the Home Office received this letter from Scotland Yard, Marx had already left England, apparently in the belief that all the formalities had been complied with and the certificate of naturalization would catch up with him in Karlsbad. In fact the Home Office rejected the application. On August 26, 1874, a curt letter was sent to R. Willis Esqre, 18 St. Martin's Court, Leicester Square, informing him that the Secretary of State had decided to decline to grant Marx a certificate. The solicitor protested in a letter to the Secretary of State, demanding the reasons for the rejection. Once more there was a brief letter, saying that the Secretary "must decline to give his reasons for refusing a certificate of naturalization to Mr. Carl Marx." Marx never knew that the real reason why he was refused a certificate was contained in a secret report from Scotland Yard: "This man has not been loyal to his own King and Country."

Because Engels had given him an advance on his pension, Marx was able to travel in some comfort. He crossed the frontier safely; he thought the police had failed to recognize him but in fact they were watching him closely, keeping him under continual surveillance. He brought Eleanor with him, and sometimes he would say that her illness was the real reason why he set out on this arduous journey.

36228

3000 12 | 73 – McC. – P. 2058) 36228

Detective Officer's Special Report

Metropolitan Police Office,

SCOTLAND YARD.

17th August 1874.

Carl Marx, – Naturalization.

With reference to the above I beg to report that he is the notorious German agitator, the head of the International Society, and an advocate of Communistic principles. This man has not been loyal to his own King and Country.

The referees Messrs "Seton," "Mathesen," "Manning," and "Adcock," are all British born subjects, and respectable householders. The statements made by them with reference to the time they have known the applicant are correct.

W. Reimers,
Sergeant.

F. Williamson
Supt.

They stayed at the elegant Germania Hotel, which lies on the hill overlooking the town. In the *Karlsbader Kurliste* he entered his name as "Mr. Charles Marx, gentleman, and daughter Eleanor, London." This was done deliberately in the hope that the police would not confuse him with the considerably more eminent Dr. Karl Marx. As a private person without credentials of any kind, he was compelled to pay double the *Kurtaxe*. He paid it willingly in the belief that these payments proved that he was a private person so insignificant that he was beyond the attentions of the police, and he would amuse himself by writing letters explaining how he had outwitted the police.

Life at Karlsbad proceeded according to a fixed regimen. He was up at five or half past five in the morning, taking the waters. He had to drink six glasses of water at fifteen-minute intervals, and then walk for an hour. Then he had breakfast, more walks, a bath, lunch, more walks, a light supper, and then to bed, after taking one last glass of cold mineral water. Sometimes he walked for twelve hours a day through the surrounding countryside, and it was remembered that he was especially interested in the legends associated with the places he visited and would ask endless questions about them. Along the river were some strangely shaped rocks believed to represent the people who had once attended the wedding of Hans Heiling. There were rocks shaped like musicians playing on their horns and trumpets, there was a bride's coach, and an old woman festively attired could be seen gathering her skirts to enter the coach. Marx learned that all these people had been turned into stone because the nymph Eger bewitched Hans Heiling when he married a girl from the local village. It was the kind of story Marx liked, for the youthful lover had brought upon himself a fearful vengeance.

In those hot summer days, walking slowly along the winding pathways, sometimes leaning on the arm of Eleanor, Marx felt his spirits reviving. He still suffered from insomnia, the glasses of mineral water had not yet cured his liver complaint, his temper was as erratic as ever. The fact that he was continually asking questions was a good sign. Another good sign was that he was keeping away from books and smoking less, unlike Eleanor who was smoking interminably. It was still unusual for women to be seen smoking.

Karlsbad was famous for its fine clay and world-renowned pottery works. Marx decided to make a careful study of pottery. The shaping, baking and painting of porcelain especially fascinated him, and he spent many hours in the large, well-lit factories. One day, watching a workman making very delicate cups on a kind of spinning wheel, he said: "Do you always do this work, or do you have another job as well?"

"No," answered the workman. "For many years I have been doing only this work. It is only by practice that one learns to run the machine so that this difficult shape comes out smoothly and faultlessly."

"So division of labor makes a man an appendage to the machine," Marx commented. "The power of thinking is changed into muscular memory."

He bought some of the delicate cups and went on to examine more factories. Even if he was not permitted to read he could still take notes and study the processes of manufacture.

The Kugelmanns were staying at the Germania Hotel, having arranged to take their holiday at the same time as Marx. They found him little changed; he still amused himself by giving nicknames to everyone he encountered; he was still the brilliant conversationalist, learned in half a dozen languages and capable of throwing off a jolting epigram or a gallant phrase; and they introduced him to their friends. They liked Eleanor, but they were puzzled by her smoking and her abrupt manner. She dressed tastefully, even strikingly. Marx evidently approved of her clothes, for he remarked: "Young women need to prink themselves." Gertrud Kugelmann had the feeling that she was the spoiled darling of the family and was permitted to follow her own caprices like a pampered child. Intelligent and warmhearted, Eleanor had a disturbing habit of saying the first thing that came into her mind, with absolutely no thought of the consequences. She was only nineteen, but she sometimes behaved like a woman of the world. Once she showed Gertrud Kugelmann a letter she had received from Lissagaray. The opening words were: "*Ma petite femme.*"

The Marxes and the Kugelmanns were inseparable companions, taking the waters together and wandering together along the footpaths of the surrounding forests. In the evenings they would attend the concerts given by the famous conductor Josef Labitzky, or there would be long discussions with Otto Knille, a famous Berlin painter of historical subjects. Dr. Kugelmann observed with amusement that Marx had not lost his predilection for aristocratic women. A young Russian countess captivated him, and he would watch out for her eagerly. She was a striking figure with her blond hair cut short, dressed always in black, a dagger at her waist. She paid no attention to anyone, walked with rapid strides, and was always followed by a gigantic, dark-bearded Cherkess servant in a black uniform. In Marx's eyes she had breeding and energy, two qualities which he regarded as eminently desirable in young women, and the Russian countess may have reminded him of the summer day in London which he spent tête-à-tête with the young Elizabeth von Puttkamer.

Although Marx seemed to have recovered from his nervous collapse the previous year, he was still a very sick man. Outwardly calm, he was boiling with inner excitement. In various little ways the Kugelmanns annoyed him: their wealth, their fine manners, their "so very pedantic-bourgeois-small trader" attitude toward life oppressed him, and he began to wonder why he had put up with them for so long. One day he went for a long walk in the woods with Dr. Kugelmann and the conversation turned, as so often before, to the subject of the remaining volumes of *Das Kapital.* Once again Dr. Kugelmann expressed the hope that Marx would be able to complete his great work, if necessary by the sacrifice of all political propaganda. It was one of those arguments which had been carried on so many times that they could have recited it in their sleep. This time there was a slight change, for the doctor impatiently added some remarks about Marx's lack of organizational talent. In another year Marx might have laughed the remark away, for how could anyone say he was lacking in organizational talent when he had directed the affairs of the International for so long and had acted as the leader of at least three separate political parties? But this year Marx's nerves were stretched to the uttermost. He flew into a tantrum, and all his long-concealed distaste for the doctor came out into the open. How dare he speak in this way? What did the doctor know about politics? about revolution? about propaganda? The doctor was ten years younger than Marx, a mere tyro. In violent and explosive language Marx went through the long history of the grievances he had suffered at the doctor's hands, and then made his way back to the hotel alone.

The break between Marx and Dr. Kugelmann was now complete. In his unforgiving way Marx wiped the doctor off the list of his friends and acquaintances, and his name was never mentioned except in terms of opprobrium. In a letter to Engels Marx raged against the man "from whom I have at last emancipated myself by raising myself to a higher level."

Dr. Kugelmann was deeply hurt, and looked forward to an eventual reconciliation, but there was none. Marx remained impenitently silent, and only a few brief messages came from Eleanor. The Kugelmann family continued to remember him with affection, rejoicing in the knowledge that they had entertained him while he was reading the proofs of *Das*

Kapital. Many years later the doctor said: "Marx was a hundred years ahead of his time. Those who march with their time are more likely to enjoy immediate success, while those who see too far ahead miss the things which shortsighted people see more clearly."

No doubt the break with Dr. Kugelmann was brought about by the accidents of ill-health, but it followed a familiar pattern. Marx was constitutionally incapable of argument; he was the dictator laying down the law, and anyone who opposed him must be permanently exiled from his presence. Those sudden estrangements occurred frequently; one by one he lost nearly all his friends. Rejection became a habit. It was a ritual to be repeated at suitable intervals to enable him to maintain his position of proud isolation.

THE PROMISED LAND

FROM TIME TO TIME Marx liked to return to Karlsbad, always traveling incognito, though he was well known to the authorities. The police were perfectly aware that Herr Charles Marx, staying at the Germania Hotel, was the celebrated Dr. Karl Marx, the revolutionary leader who until recently had presided over the destinies of the International. In his conspiratorial way he liked to play tricks on the police, and when he was accompanied by Eleanor he would ask his correspondents to address their letters to her; inside the letter there would be another addressed to him. He assumed that the police were stupendously stupid and would never dream of opening a letter addressed to Fräulein Eleanor Marx.

The police did not trouble him, but the reasons were not those which would have given him any satisfaction. They regarded him as harmless. Joseph Veith, the head of the local *gendarmerie,* knew exactly what he was doing, sent reports regularly to his superiors, and came to the conclusion that he should be permitted to enjoy the cure in peace. On September 1, 1875, he wrote: "Charles Marx, doctor of philosophy, from London, the well-known leader of the Social Democratic Party, is now in Karlsbad taking the cure. He has given us no cause for complaint, lives quietly, has very little intercourse with the other guests, and frequently goes on long walks alone."

In fact he saw a good deal of the other guests and enjoyed their company. Into the world of the bourgeoisie, the Austrian aristocracy and the Russian Grand Dukes he entered as though he were one of them. He spoke their language and affected their manners, their rages and their authoritarian speech, and he was on terms of intimacy with them. Wearing a long black frock coat, the monocle dangling at the end of a silk ribbon, he looked exactly like a rich Jewish merchant from some large industrial town in central Europe, who was making his annual pilgrimage to a spa.

He enjoyed Karlsbad, that remote and improbable town set in a small valley and cut off from the rest of the world by thick forests. In 1875 he visited Karlsbad alone; in the following year he was accompanied by Eleanor. He would have come again in 1877, but was told that he might be arrested. Instead he spent the summer with his wife and Eleanor at the little watering place of Neuenahr in the valley of the Ahr, " a village not pretending even to the dignity of a market town." After 1878 the law forbidding socialists to enter Germany prevented any further travel in his homeland. Thereafter he visited watering places in England and France.

What he especially liked about these watering places was the opportunity to seek out men of culture and breeding. He enjoyed club life, and the watering places were select clubs, where men of intelligence could discuss matters decorously. At Karlsbad, for example, he met Heinrich Graetz, the great chronicler of Jewish history. He was also on terms of intimacy with Count Wladislaw Plater, who had taken a heroic part in the Polish uprising of 1831 and once addressed Marx as "the leader of the Russian nihilists." The aristocratic Maxim Kovalevsky, jurist and sociologist, became a close friend.

In 1875 Maxim Kovalevsky occupied the place in Marx's affections previously occupied by Dr. Kugelmann. Almost every day they took walks along the forest pathways, while Marx practiced the Russian he had begun to learn five years previously, and asked innumerable questions about Russia, a country which had once exasperated him and now seemed to please him because he discerned the revolutionary violence below the surface. Kovalevsky was a man of great charm and distinction, a liberal who abhorred violence, but he genuinely admired Marx and would never permit anyone to say a word against him. Marx's didactic tone, he felt, was due to his uncompromising faith in the dialectical method; for Marx there could be no other method, and therefore he spoke with superb arrogance. "His repulsive coarseness has its roots in his self-assurance," Kovalevsky wrote, and though he knew Marx's failings, he found enough virtues to admire.

In his travels across Europe—for he was an inveterate traveler—Kovalevsky frequently visited Marx in London, and was treated as an honored guest. At such times Marx would show himself *en pantoufles,* humorous and at ease. One day Marx's sister Luise and her two sons, all recently arrived from South Africa, were staying for dinner. Kovalevsky found himself sitting beside Luise. She had never reconciled herself to Marx's career as a revolutionary. She could not understand how her brother became a socialist, for everyone knew he came from a respectable family in Trier, and was the son of a distinguished lawyer. Marx overheard his sister, and burst into joyful laughter. He could not stop laughing, and to Kovalevsky it seemed like the laughter of a young man.

It is from Kovalevsky too that we learn about Marx's taste in the theater. There was a cult of Shakespeare in the family, and Marx made a point of seeing all the best Shakespearean productions. He especially admired the acting of Tommaso Salvini in *Hamlet;* it was said of that exuberant actor that he thought he had delivered a bad performance unless everyone in the audience was in tears by the end of the play. But on reflection Marx would say that the performances of Henry Irving were incomparably more brilliant, for grandeur took the place of exuberance. Marx also liked to attend the performances at the Egyptian Hall where John Nevil Maskelyne was imitating the tricks of the spiritualists. Tables floated in the air, spirits spoke, ectoplasmic forms appeared out of nowhere. There were also conjuring tricks with beautiful girls cut in half and rabbits pouring out of hats. Maskelyne had also introduced one of the most satisfying automata on record, a life-size figure called Psycho who played cards and performed simple mathematical calculations. In this world of spirits and automata Marx was perfectly at home.

While Kovalevsky never lost his high regard for Marx, he had no illusions about his inordinate pride and self-will. After giving an account of his own relations with Marx, he adds that it is only fair that he should relate a story told to him by the great geographer Élisée Reclus. There had been a bitter argument in Marx's study, and suddenly a strange and disturbing thing happened. Without a word to anyone Marx marched out of the argument and assumed a pose directly below the great statue of Zeus Otricoli. It was as though he were saying: "We, the gods, have ordered it."

On the autumn day in 1874 when Marx left Karlsbad, he may have thought again about the statue given to him by Dr. Kugelmann, whom he now regarded as a mortal enemy. Now all that remained were Marx's letters, which the doctor treasured, and the bronze bust which had pride of place in Marx's study.

Marx spent a day with Eleanor in Dresden, and then went on to Leipzig to visit the faithful Wilhelm Liebknecht, whom he cherished for his loyalty, though he had no high opinion of his natural ability. The day Marx arrived in Leipzig there came the announcement that Wilhelm Blos, a young communist revolutionary, was about to be released from prison. Liebknecht thought it would be a fine gesture if Marx would welcome the revolutionary at the prison gate. Marx agreed. Blos was told that a great surprise would await him the next morning, but he was told nothing more. He spent the night in a fever of expectation, and when at last he crossed the prison yard he could make out four people waiting for him. He wrote later: "I saw Liebknecht and his young son, and there was a pretty young lady on the arm of a tall, slender gentleman in his fifties with a long white beard, but the mustaches were jet black. His complexion was florid, and one would have taken him for a jovial old Englishman."

Wilhelm Blos, who became the Socialist Minister-President of Württemberg following World War I, wrote his reminiscences fifty years after his meeting with Marx. This explains why the short and rather plump Marx became "a tall, slender gentleman." Marx had lost two pounds at Karlsbad as a result of his daily walks, but he still retained his portly figure.

As Blos remembered him, Marx was in an excellent mood, continually engaging him in discussion or delving into his rich store of reminiscences. They went to Liebknecht's lodgings and talked over cups of coffee. Once Blos made some remark about atheism and the quarrels of the freethinkers. Marx said that the "lieber Gott" must possess a rich store of gaiety to be able to look down on everything going on in the world with such calm. When Liebknecht complained about the insufferable behavior of the poet Georg Herwegh, who set himself apart from other men and claimed the divine right of poetry, Marx chided him gently, saying that poets are not like other men and besides Herwegh had acquired indisputable merit in the fight for freedom.

In the afternoon they took a walk across the fields, Marx deliberately walking behind Blos, who was a good listener, openmouthed with admiration for the old man at his side. Marx talked about Lassalle and told the story of his rise to power in the workers' movement. "He played a thoroughly infamous role," Marx said, his voice rising in anger, and then he added, as though Lassalle were an albatross hanging round the neck of the workers' movement, "and we have no way of disavowing him."

A little while later Marx, in a gentler mood, told a story about the early days in his revolutionary career, when he was living in Cologne and editing the *Neue Rheinische Zeitung*. The copy had to be taken to the censor each evening before going to the printer, when it was usually covered with red ink. In Marx's view it was necessary to punish the censor, and the opportunity occurred one evening when the censor was invited with his wife and daughter to a ball given by the governor of the city. On ordinary evenings the copy would be sent to the censor's office about seven o'clock, but on this particular evening it failed to arrive. Hours passed; the censor waited. When no copy arrived by ten o'clock, he decided to send his wife and daughter to the ball, intending to follow them later. A servant was sent to the printer's office, but the servant returned empty-handed. Finally he decided to take a carriage and go to Marx's apartment in a distant part of the city. It was now nearly eleven o'clock. After a good deal of bell-ringing, he succeeded in waking Marx whose head appeared at a third-story window. "Where's the copy?" the censor shouted. "There isn't any," Marx replied. "We are not publishing an edition tomorrow!" Thereupon Marx shut the window, and the infuriated censor went off to the ball.

Marx liked telling stories about the past, for he no longer possessed any overwhelming interest in the present. Only occasionally could he stir himself sufficiently to take a deep interest in political affairs. In 1874 the Social Democratic Workingmen's Party led by Liebknecht had polled 170,000 votes. The General Association of German Workers, led by followers of Lassalle, polled 180,000. It was clear that the two socialist groups could survive only by combining their forces. Accordingly the two parties sent delegates to the ancient Thuringian town of Gotha and hammered out a program which satisfied both of them.

The Gotha program did not satisfy Marx, who flew into a violent rage as soon as he received it and wrote a savage criticism, in which he pointed out that all that was good in the program was derived from the *Communist Manifesto* and all that was bad derived from Lassalle. He objected to elementary education by the state, insisting that neither the state nor the Church had the right to teach. The Gotha program prohibited child labor, and Marx regarded such a prohibition as "incompatible with the existence of large-scale industry and hence an empty, pious wish." The Gotha program called for freedom of science, and he noted that this was also guaranteed in the Prussian Constitution, and therefore had no place in a revolutionary program. But what especially troubled him was that the program did not look to the future and had nothing whatsoever to say about the emergence of the communist state.

Marx himself had said very little about the nature of the communist state. He had never been able to envisage it except in vague generalities. Now once more, with a sense of exalted destiny, he pronounced judgment on the world, declaring the path it must follow. First there would come the revolutionary dictatorship of the proletariat, and then this would vanish, giving way to the communist society in all its purity:

> In a higher phase of communist society, after the enslaving subordination of the individual to the division of labor, and with it also the antithesis between mental and physical labor, has vanished, after labor has become not only a livelihood but life's prime want, after the productive forces have also increased with the all-round development of the individual, and all the springs of cooperative wealth flow more abundantly—only then can the narrow horizons of bourgeois rights be crossed in its entirety and society inscribe on its banners: From each according to his ability, to each according to his needs!

Such was the revelation he offered to the world, after a lifetime of thought and struggle. In "The Civil War in France" he had described the crucifixion and resurrection of the proletariat, and in the "Critique of the Gotha Program" he offered his Book of Revelation. The millennium would come, man would no longer suffer the servitude of labor, the distinction between mental and physical labor would vanish, there would come about the all-round development of the individual, and there would be more abundant flowings of cooperative wealth. These things because they were desirable were equated with "the higher phase of communist society," and it seems never to have occurred to Marx that they might come about in another kind of society altogether.

At the end of his "Critique of the Gotha Program" he wrote: "*Dixi et salvavi animam meam.* (I have spoken and I have saved my soul.)"

These small crumbs fell on the tables of the German socialists, who promptly swept them away. Marx's ill-tempered and inadequate criticisms would have been completely forgotten if Engels had not published them in an abbreviated version in 1891. The complete text was not published until 1932.

The "Critique of the Gotha Program" was the last important statement made by Marx in his public life. Never again would there be any attempt to speak prophetically, and there would be no more laying-down of the law. He had dreamed of combining the roles of Moses and Isaiah and ushering in the new revolutionary world with its "abundant flowings of cooperative wealth." No doubt the phrase had slipped in by accident. Somewhere behind all Marx's theories there lay a child's dream of a land flowing with milk and honey.

One further pleasure remained to him. In the following year he was able to hold in his hands the French translation of *Das Kapital,* which had been many years in the making. At first the task was entrusted to Élie Reclus, the brother of Élisée Reclus, the anarchist and geographer. Nothing came of this venture. From time to time other Frenchmen showed interest in translating the work, but they always recoiled when confronted with Marx's demands for literal accuracy. Finally, with much prompting from Marx, Joseph Roy, who had previously translated Feuerbach, embarked on the task and succeeded in completing it, his own rather graceful style making it far more palatable than the German or English version. Marx declared that he "did a devil of a lot of work on it," but if so, he concealed his style behind Roy's. The book was published by Maurice Lachatre, who was living abroad, for he had been condemned to twenty years' imprisonment for his part in the Commune. It was necessary to deal with the legal administrator of his estate, who felt that the book would be improved by well-selected lithographic designs. Accordingly the title page was ornamented with a lithograph of the Pantheon in Rome, and at intervals throughout the book there may be found wreaths, flowers, and fruit, Romulus and Remus, a winged Mercury with a fig leaf, and an Etruscan carriage. Toward the end of the book the reader may pause over a lithograph of Justice gazing at her scales while absent-mindedly wringing the neck of an ostrich.

THE OLD LION

In the late seventies of the last century there could sometimes be seen a small round-faced man in a frock coat taking the air in Hampstead Heath with his grandchildren, and very occasionally people would point at him, saying that he had once been a famous revolutionary. Fame, however, had passed him by. Very few knew his history, and there were fewer still who guessed that his name would one day become a household word, that the world would be divided between those who claimed to be his followers and those who obstinately refused to follow the path he laid out for them. He lived very quietly and unpretentiously. He rarely did any serious work, and sometimes he complained that he suffered from a nervous disease which made concentrated work of any kind impossible for him.

After the Hague Congress he had relapsed into a kind of dotage, and seemed content to live on Engels' pension, which enabled him to satisfy most of his creature comforts. It was, in fact, a considerable income for the time, equivalent in purchasing power to the income of a well-placed civil servant. He had an expensive taste in wine, which was supplied from Engels' capacious cellars; his only expensive luxury was his cigars. Even when the doctors were most insistent, he was never able to stop smoking for long, and he still smoked from morning to night. Jenny was ill and spent a good part of the day in bed. There was therefore very little entertaining.

In this way, very quietly, Marx sank into obscurity. Here and there people still mentioned the name of the old social philosopher, once so fiery, now vanishing into the limbo of forgotten things. One of those who remembered him with a little shiver of apprehension was no less a person than the eldest daughter of Queen Victoria, a serious and gifted woman, deeply interested in social affairs. She had married into the Prussian royal family, and was known as the Crown Princess Victoria, her husband, the Crown Prince Frederick William, being heir to the throne. One day the princess was talking to Sir Mountstuart Grant Duff, a Liberal Member of Parliament who had served as Gladstone's Under-Secretary for India and who had been Governor of Madras. She asked him whether he knew anything about Karl Marx. Grant Duff replied that he knew nothing about him but offered to find out. He knew everybody of importance in London, and he thought it would be a fairly simple matter to arrange a meeting with Marx.

As it happened, it proved to be more difficult than he thought. Many weeks passed before he found someone who claimed to know Marx. Finally he met Leonard Montefiore, a young Oxford graduate interested in University extension lectures, who seems to have met Marx through Professor Beesly. Montefiore and Marx were invited to lunch at the Devonshire Club on St. James's Street. This rather ornate club, formerly a gambling house, was especially favored by the Liberal aristocracy.

Marx's impressions of the meeting have not survived, but Grant Duff described it in a long letter to the Crown Princess, and more briefly in his published *Notes from a Diary.* The letter to the princess shows that he was favorably impressed. Far from being a great fire-eater, Marx emerged as a kindly, adroit, humorous old scholar, sometimes caustic, but always good-natured. The lunch took place on January 31, 1879, and on the following day Grant Duff described him in a letter to the princess:

> He is a short, rather small man with grey hair and beard which contrasts strangely with the still dark moustache. The face is somewhat round; the forehead well shaped and filled up—the eye rather hard but the whole expression rather pleasant than not, by no means that of a gentleman who is in the habit of eating babies in their cradles—which is I daresay the view which the police take of him.
>
> His talk was that of a well-informed, nay learned man—much interested in Comparative Grammar which had led him into the Old Slavonic and other out-of-the-way studies and was varied by many quaint turns and little bits of dry humour, as when speaking of Hezechiall's "Life of Prince Bismarck," he always referred to it, by way of contrast to Dr. Busch's book, as the *Old* Testament.
>
> It was all very *positif,* slightly cynical—without any appearance of enthusiasm—interesting, and often, as I thought, showing very correct ideas when conversing on the past and the present, but vague and unsatisfactory when he turned to the future.

Three hours were spent over lunch, and the conversation ranged over many subjects. Grant Duff was a formidable interlocutor, and he was determined in the short time available to sound out Marx on as many subjects as possible, so that he could write an extensive report to the Crown Princess. Marx, of course, was left in ignorance about the purpose of the meeting.

Marx talked about Russia, saying that he expected "a great but not distant crash," which would come about when the government instituted reforms so sweeping that they would have the effect of breaking up the structure of government power. He thought the Russians would be unable to exercise any influence in Europe for a long time. Many people were expecting "a great but not distant crash" in Russia, and Grant Duff found nothing unreasonable in Marx's opinions.

When they turned to the subject of Germany, which Grant Duff knew well, Marx's opinions seemed less reasonable, for he thought there would be a revolt against the existing military system, with the soldiers rising against their officers.

"How can you expect the army to rise against its commanders?" Grant Duff asked.

Marx, who also knew Germany well, thought the soldiers would rise against their officers out of sheer desperation.

"These Socialists you hear about are trained soldiers like anybody else," he replied. "You must not think of the standing army only. You must think of the Landwehr—and even in the standing army there is much discontent. Never was there such an army in which the severity of the discipline led to so many suicides. The step from shooting oneself to shooting one's officer is not long, and an example of the kind once set is soon followed."

For many years Grant Duff had been proclaiming the need for a reduction of armaments by the European powers. It occurred to him that if the standing army was reduced, then there would be less possibility of a revolutionary outbreak.

"Supposing," he suggested, "the rulers of Europe came to an understanding amongst themselves for a reduction of armaments which would greatly relieve the burden on the people, what would become of the revolution which you expect it one day to bring about?"

Marx was not to be diverted from his purpose; and he had a pessimistic, and wholly accurate, view of the feasibility of reducing armaments.

"Ah," he said, "they can't do that. All sorts of fears and jealousies will make that impossible. The burden will grow worse and worse as science advances, for the improvements in the art of destruction will keep pace with its advance, and every year more and more will have to be devoted to costly engines of war. It is a vicious circle—there is no escape from it."

Grant Duff thought that even if armaments were not reduced, it was inconceivable that a revolution would break out in Germany. The country was too rich, social insurance too widespread, for revolutionary hotheads to take over the government. He said: "You have never yet had a serious popular uprising unless there was really great misery."

Marx knew a good deal more about popular uprisings than Grant Duff, and he could have pointed out that there are many reasons for revolutions, and not all of them derive from the misery of oppressed people. Instead, he answered lamely, speaking of the crisis in Germany.

"You have no idea," he said, "how terrible has been the crisis through which Germany has been passing in these last five years."

"Well, supposing that your revolution has taken place and that you have your republican government—it is still a long way to the special ideas of yourself and your friends."

"Doubtless," Marx answered, "but all great movements are slow. It would merely be a step to better things, as your revolution of 1688 was—a mere step in the road."

This, of course, represented the view which Marx held always in reserve to explain the failures of so many revolutionaries, the disastrous outcome of so many revolutions. It was not however the view which held pride of place in Marx's mind. He looked forward to convulsions and cataclysms, not the slow march of social improvement. For once he was being disingenuous, throwing out a sop to the reactionaries.

It was probably at this point that Grant Duff brought up the subject of Marx's contacts with revolutionaries abroad, or at least with one famous and unsuccessful revolutionary who had committed suicide in prison the previous year. This was Karl Eduard Nobiling, an obscure statistician, who had shot at the Emperor William I from a window in the Unter den Linden on June 2, 1878. The Emperor, contrary to his usual custom, was wearing a helmet, which deflected the bullet. He was wounded, but not gravely, and survived for another ten years. Nobiling was arrested, and in his confession he mentioned that he had recently visited England with the intention of meeting Karl Marx, but for some reason the meeting had not taken place. Grant Duff wondered aloud what would have happened if Nobiling had requested an interview with Marx.

"If he had done so," Marx said, "I should certainly have admitted him, for he would have sent in his card as an employe of the Dresden Bureau of Statistics, and as I occupy myself with statistics, it would have interested me to talk with him." Then he laughed and said: "What a pleasant position I should have been in, if he *had* come to see me!"*

This was the conversation which Grant Duff reported to the Crown Princess. It has been quoted in full, because it offers one of the rare occasions when we can watch Marx in a prolonged discussion. Grant Duff observed that there was no bitterness or savagery in Marx—"nothing of the Marat tone." When he mentioned the Crown Prince and the Crown Princess, Marx spoke of them with respect and propriety.

Grant Duff evidently enjoyed his lunch. His final conclusion was that Marx was an agreeable fellow, whom he would gladly meet again. And with a monumental lack of prophetical gifts, he announced: "It will not be he who, whether he wishes it or not, will turn the world upside down."

On the whole Marx had behaved very mildly at the Devonshire Club.

* Marx was evidently hiding his real thoughts about Nobiling. Maxim Kovalevsky, the Russian historian and jurist, was talking to Marx in his study when news of the attempted assassination reached them. Kovalevsky was surprised by Marx's sudden outburst of fury. "Marx reacted to the news by heaping curses on this terrorist who had failed to carry out his act of terror," Kovalevsky wrote. "He went on to explain that this criminal attempt to accelerate the course of events could only lead to new persecutions of the socialists. Unfortunately this prophecy was soon fulfilled: Bismarck introduced the well-known laws which considerably delayed the successful development of German Social-Democracy."

He was old now, and his revolutionary temper did not often flare up. Perhaps he felt that he was out of his element in the ornate club with its liveried servants and gilded walls; perhaps he was too busy studying Grant Duff, the man about town who was also a distinguished pillar of empire; perhaps, too, he felt there was some ulterior motive in this confrontation, and was puzzled that Leonard Montefiore should have brought them together. He seems to have been a little subdued in the presence of Grant Duff, knowing that it is always necessary to walk warily in the sight of the rulers of this world.

Marx was not always the mild philosopher; sometimes even now the embers would burst into flame. In the following year he met Henry Mayers Hyndman, whose chief claim to fame is that he was the founder of English socialism. They had much in common. Hyndman had an autocratic temper, was proud and resentful of criticism. Like Marx, he had many vanities. He was intellectually intolerant and enjoyed abusing his intellectual inferiors. He wore a frock coat and top hat when he was distributing inflammatory leaflets. Dressed in the height of fashion, he would address meetings of workingmen in Trafalgar Square and taunt the audience with being so poor that they could not dress as well, but spent their lives in slavery supporting the rich. He was rich, handsome, and brilliant, and in the nineties he would dominate the socialist movement in England as leader of the Social Democratic Federation.

In October 1880, in the company of the Social Democratic journalist Karl Hirsch, Hyndman paid a visit to Marx who, he knew, was favorably disposed to him because of some articles he had written denouncing British colonial rule in India. Hyndman had read *Das Kapital,* and was immensely impressed by Marx's fundamental analysis of capitalism, telling Hirsch that he was eager to sit at Marx's feet. Marx welcomed the English socialist with open arms, and they spent the better part of a day together. Hyndman has described their first meeting:

> The first impression of Marx as I saw him was that of a powerful, shaggy, untamed old man, ready, not to say eager, to enter into conflict, and rather suspicious himself of immediate attack. Yet his greeting to us was cordial, and his first remarks to me, after I had told him what a great pleasure and honour I felt it to be to shake hands with the author of *Capital,* were agreeable enough; for he told me that he had read my articles on India with pleasure and had commented on them favorably in his newspaper correspondence. . . .
>
> When speaking with fierce indignation of the policy of the Liberal Party, especially in regard to Ireland, the old warrior's small deep-sunk eyes lighted up, his heavy brows wrinkled, the broad, strong nose and face were obviously moved by passion, and he poured out a stream of vigorous denuncia-

tion which displayed alike the heat of his temperament and the marvellous command he possessed over our language. The contrast between his manner and utterance when thus deeply stirred by anger, and his attitude when giving his views on the economic events of the period, was very marked. He turned from the role of prophet and violent denunciator to that of the calm philosopher without any apparent effort, and I felt from the first that on this latter ground many a long year might pass before I ceased to be a student in the presence of a master.

I had been surprised in reading *Capital* and still more when perusing his smaller works, such as his pronouncement on the Commune of Paris and his *Eighteenth Brumaire,* how he combined the ablest and coolest examination of economic causes with the most bitter hatred of classes and even individual men such as Napoleon III, and Monsieur Thiers, who, according to his own theories, were little more than flies upon the wheels of the great Juggernaut car of capitalist development. Marx, of course, was a Jew, and to me it seemed that he combined in his own person and nature, with his commanding forehead and great overhanging brow, his fierce glittering eyes, broad sensitive nose, and mobile mouth, all surrounded by a setting of untrimmed hair and beard, the righteous fury of the great seers of his race, and the cold analytical powers of Spinoza and the Jewish doctors. It was an extraordinary combination of qualities, the like of which I have known in no other man.

Such was the impression which Marx produced on Hyndman at their first meeting. Marx had good reason to display himself to advantage, for he recognized in Hyndman a potential ally, even a potential disciple. To capture Hyndman, to ensure his obedience and acquiescence, and through him to capture the English socialists became his aim, and at first he was remarkably successful. Hyndman was converted to Marxian socialism, and for about nine months they were continually in each other's company. When leaving Marx after that first meeting, Hirsch had turned to Hyndman and said: "What do you think of him?" "Well," replied Hyndman, "I think he is the Aristotle of the nineteenth century." Later, when he had time to set his impressions in order, Hyndman slightly revised his verdict. If Marx was Aristotle, then he was certainly an Aristotle who would never have served as a courtier in the palaces of Alexander the Great. But Marx also had defects: he was not capable of that complete detachment which was the supreme gift of Aristotle. When Marx denounced capitalism and the exploitation of the workingman, he showed only too clearly that he was moved by a hatred so bitter and so personal that it prevented him from any detachment at all.

But this was a small fault in Hyndman's eyes, to be weighed against the vast scope of his knowledge and the range of his passion. In England men fought with buttons on the points of their rapiers, and there was something refreshing in Marx's vigorous onslaughts with naked steel.

Once Hyndman remarked that he thought he grew more tolerant as he grew older. "Do you?" Marx said. "*Do* you?" It was obvious that Marx regarded tolerance as a disease from which he was permanently immune.

Throughout the winter of 1880 and well into the spring of the following year they were continually exchanging visits, and in the comparative quiet of Marx's study in Maitland Park Road they often found themselves talking late into the night. Hyndman relates that they conducted their discussions in the manner of peripatetic philosophers:

> Our method of talking was peculiar. Marx had a habit, when at all interested in the discussion, of walking up and down the room, as if he were pacing the deck of a schooner for exercise. I had acquired on my long voyages, the same tendency to pacing to and fro when my mind was much occupied. Consequently, master and student could have been seen walking up and down on opposite sides of the table for hours in succession, discussing the affairs of the past and the present.

Marx's friendships with Englishmen rarely lasted, and eventually there was bound to be a clash of wills between two men so temperamentally alike. The break came in the summer of 1881 with the publication of Hyndman's book *England For All,* which presented the program of the Social Democratic Federation, an association of English and Scottish radical societies. The two chapters on labor and capital were largely based on *Das Kapital,* which Hyndman had read in the French translation. Whole paragraphs followed closely on the arguments of Marx, and while there was no exact verbal plagiarism, there was not the least doubt that Hyndman was writing with Marx's work open in front of him. In his preface Hyndman remarked that he was indebted to the work of a great thinker and original writer for many of the ideas included in the book. Marx's name was not mentioned.

As Hyndman must have known, Marx was not inclined to take plagiarism lightly. He was bitterly aware that his name was still little known in England, and he had hoped through Hyndman to exercise some influence on the thinking of English socialists. Hyndman was immediately called to account. He replied that the interests of the cause demanded that he should be silent, for the English did not like to be taught by foreigners and Marx's name was still detested and feared. Marx thereupon broke off all relations with Hyndman. Six months later he was still smarting from the blow, for in December he gave Sorge a long account of the affair. "Many evenings this fellow has pilfered from me," he wrote broodingly, "in order to take me out and learn in the easiest way."

To younger and lesser men he would sometimes show indulgence.

Among those who came to pay their respects to him in the spring of 1881 was the young Karl Kautsky, later to become a leading Marxist. Marx received him kindly, asked about his mother who had written romances published in socialist newspapers, and gently encouraged him to talk about his favorite subject, ancient history. Kautsky had prepared to be intimidated, but was soon at his ease. When he mentioned that he hoped for nothing so much as the early completion of the second volume of *Das Kapital,* Marx said curtly: "I, too," and there seemed to be a trace of bitterness in his voice.

While they talked Kautsky would sometimes peer up at the bronze statue of Zeus Otricoli, and it seemed to him that there could be only one explanation for the presence of the statue: a friend who had noted the strange resemblance between the god and Marx must have given it to him. He noted, too, the huge disorder in the room, with the tables piled with mountains of books, papers everywhere, Marx very quiet in the midst of the hurricane. Kautsky's dominant impression was of a kindly gentleman with a high forehead and piercing eyes that commanded respect, a gentleman of orderly habits, vast erudition and great gentleness. Marx explained that he worked most of the day, took his dinner at six in the evening, then slept for a while and received visitors at nine. Since Kautsky had presented himself at four in the afternoon, would he have the kindness to come at nine o'clock in the future?

Kautsky was a frequent visitor to Marx's house. Many years later he was genuinely surprised to learn that Marx had written caustically about him, describing him as a mediocrity, an inveterate drinker and a *Kauz,* which means "screech owl." In a letter to his daughter Jenny Longuet shortly after his first meeting with Kautsky, Marx wrote:

> When this charmer first appeared at my place—I mean little Kauz—the first question which escaped me was: Are you like your mother? Not in the very least, he assured me, and I silently congratulated his mother. He is a mediocrity with a small-minded outlook, superwise (only 26), very conceited, industrious in a certain sort of way, he busies himself a lot with statistics but does not read anything very clever out of them, belongs by nature to the tribe of the Philistines, but is otherwise a decent fellow in his own way. I turn him over to Engels as much as possible.

When Marx wrote this, his wife was dying of cancer and he was himself suffering from a racking cough and a variety of complaints. Moods of intense bitterness would alternate with acts of kindness and generosity; he was in so much pain that he sometimes scarcely knew what he was saying.

When he chose, he could be kind and tolerant. In the late summer of 1880 his old friend Charles Dana, then the editor of the *New York Sun,* sent a reporter to interview him. John Swinton knew very little about the real Marx, but he had heard just enough about the legendary Marx to look forward pleasurably to the encounter. Marx was staying at the seaside resort of Ramsgate with almost his entire family. Engels was there; so was Frau Marx; Laura and Paul Lafargue, Jenny and Charles Longuet and their three children were all in attendance. Only Eleanor was absent at this last reunion of the family. When John Swinton arrived at the small rented cottage, Marx's children and grandchildren were at the beach and for a while he talked with Marx alone.

John Swinton was one of those men who are passionately addicted to hero worship. He saw in Marx a presence of stupendous power, a revolutionary who still convulsed nations and destroyed thrones. "Is this massive-headed, generous-featured, courtly, kindly man of sixty, with the bushy masses of long revelling grey hair, Karl Marx?" he exclaimed in the article he wrote later. Marx put him at his ease, happy to be in the presence of a worshiper, speaking in vast generalities about the revolutionary movements in Europe and the wayward impulses of the European governments. "He spoke hopefully of Russia, philosophically of Germany, cheerfully of France, and sombrely of England—referring contemptuously to the atomistic reforms over which the Liberals of the British Parliament spend their time." Evidently England received the harshest treatment, but that was to be expected—it was, after all, the country Marx knew best.

There followed a long monologue in which Marx dilated on the future course of Europe, whose destiny he controlled. He informed the breathless reporter that Europe was honeycombed with his spies and agents; he had a finger in every pie, and knew all the secrets of the chancelleries; he was preparing the way for a new advent. John Swinton continues:

> Surveying the European world, country after country, indicating the features and the developments and the personages of the surface and under the surface, he showed that things were working toward ends which assuredly will be realized. I was often surprised as he spoke. It was evident that this man, of whom so little is seen or heard, is deep in the times, and that from the Neva to the Seine, from the Urals to the Pyrenees, his hand is at work preparing the way for the new advent. Nor is his work wasted now any more than it has been in the past, during which so many desirable changes have been brought about, so many heroic struggles have been seen, and the French Republic has been set up on the heights. As he spoke, the question I had put, "Why are you doing nothing now?" was seen to be a question of the unlearned, and one to which he could not make direct answer.

As John Swinton understood him, Marx was far too busy manipulating revolutionary movements from the Neva to the Pyrenees to address himself to theoretical problems; he stood at the center of the whirlwind, with all men's destinies in his hands. It was of course the same flattering self-portrait which Marx had often painted of himself, and now in his premature old age it returned to haunt him like a ghost from the past. Thirteen years before he had spoken of having all the revolutionary parties under his command, and it needed only a small turn of the wheel of fortune to bring him to a position of stupendous power and influence.

Those days had passed, and he was powerless now, lost in his dreams. He had only his dreams to offer the American reporter as they walked through a crowded seaside town on a summer evening to the beach where the family was sitting in the last rays of the sunset. They stayed by the sea until it grew dark, when the women and children left, but the men remained. Then in the darkness, drinking beer, they talked "of the world, and of men, and of time, and of ideas," until John Swinton remembered he had a train to catch and hurried away.

THE SLOW DEATH

JENNY MARX SPENT the last years of her life in seclusion. She rarely appeared in society, and rarely left the house in Maitland Park Road. She would sometimes accompany her family to the seaside, but those visits were rare. She had long ago retired from the scene, leaving the stage to Marx.

Since the pension from Engels came regularly, there was no longer any need for her to support and comfort her husband in his trials, for his trials were over. He had attained the respectability she desired for him; he had achieved a measure of recognition; and was sometimes seen in the London clubs. In his immaculate frock coat, toying with his monocle, his great mane of hair combed and curled, so that he resembled an Assyrian monarch, he had at last entered the world she regarded as her own. At long last the improvident young revolutionary had been transformed into a kind of aristocrat, a man of the world.

In his service she had grown old and gray, and little remained of her former beauty. She had always prized her beauty, her fine clothes, her gentle manners. For a long time she had known she was dying, but she had successfully hidden this knowledge from her husband, believing that he must be preserved from all unpleasantness. When the time came to put her beauty away, she did so quietly and uncomplainingly, like someone folding away the clothes she had worn long ago and would never wear again.

In the last surviving photograph, taken about four years before her death, she already has the appearance of withdrawing from the world. Her cheeks were sunken, her eyes were hollows, and no emotion could be detected on those worn features, which seemed to have been carved out of stone. She sits in a high-backed chair with one elbow resting on a small table in an attitude of indifference, as though she had no thought in her mind except that the photographer would soon go away. Yet something of her ancient beauty and of her love for fine dresses remains. Her hair is ringleted, a lace fichu lies around her neck, and more lace protrudes at her wrists. She wears a bustle, following the fashion of the time, and the voluminous folds of her silk skirt are gathered in monumental waves around her feet. From the top of an immense silken pyramid there emerges a face as silent and expressionless as the moon.

She was dying of cancer of the liver, a particularly painful and debilitating disease. She bore the pain unflinchingly, pretending it was a secret she shared only with the doctor, Eleanor, and Helene Demuth. On no account must her husband know the full extent of her agony.

In the summer of 1881, when the disease was already approaching its terminal phase, when she could walk only with difficulty, and was no longer certain she could survive a long journey, she decided that the time had come to pay a last visit to France to see her daughter Jenny Longuet, who was living at Argenteuil. She especially wanted to see her grandchildren, for there was now a small brood of them: five-year-old Johnny, three-year-old Harry, two-year-old Edgar, and a baby boy called Marcel, who had been born in April. As always, she would come laden with presents.

There were continual delays, for the doctors were watching her closely. She had thought of leaving London in June, for we find Marx writing urgently to his daughter on June 22: "Answer immediately, for Mama will not leave until she knows what you would like her to bring you from London. You know she loves doing such things." But she did not leave for France until the end of July. They had hoped to spend a month or six weeks at Argenteuil, but she was rapidly growing weaker and the visit was cut short after three weeks. She had become very frail. When she reached London, she took to her bed and never left it again.

Marx, too, was exhausted by the journey. A savage attack of pleurisy, due, according to the doctors, to his absolute refusal to look after his many ailments, brought him closer to death than he had ever been before. Jenny lay in the big front room, Marx in the small adjoining room; it was painful for them to be separated even by so short a distance. Marx seemed to be coughing his life away, and Jenny was fading visibly before their eyes. For three weeks Helene Demuth and Eleanor, who had only just recovered from an illness, looked after them, preparing their medicines, seeing that they were fed and washed, changing the bedclothes, doing everything that was necessary to bring them back from the brink of death. As one crisis followed another, they watched and waited. "For those three weeks neither Lenchen nor I went to bed," Eleanor wrote later in a letter to Liebknecht. "We were on our feet day and night, and when we were too exhausted we would take turns to rest for an hour."

Marx recovered from his latest attack of pleurisy, but never completely recovered his strength. He was very white, very drawn. He had just strength enough to totter into his wife's room, to sit with her. Eleanor remembered that morning many years later. "Never shall I forget the morning when he felt strong enough to go into mother's room. They were young again together—she a loving girl and he a loving youth, entering into life together—not an old man racked with disease and an old dying woman bidding farewell to one another forever."

They both knew that the end was not far away, and so they clung together. Marx spent most of his waking hours by her bedside. At rare intervals he would bestir himself sufficiently to continue his correspondence, but his heart was not in it. To dull his brain he would sometimes compile endless lists of dates, telling himself it was necessary to collect them in order to understand world history; and now more than ever it seemed to him that world history was important. It was his first love, and long ago in his early essays he had appealed to *Weltgeschichte* as though it were the name of a god, a talismanic force which knitted the universe together. So he wrote down the dates of Assyrian invasions, Egyptian pharaohs and Roman emperors in long, thin, empty columns, and it pleased him to see history pouring out of his fingertips.

In those days very few pleasures disturbed the monotony of ill-health. One great pleasure came at the end of November with the publication of a long article on Marx in a literary and philosophical journal called *Mod-*

ern Thought, edited by John Charles Foulger. It was a weighty journal with a considerable following in the universities and clubs. It printed such articles as "The Religious Development of India, or the Religion of Abstract Monism," by Eduard von Hartmann; and "The Secret of Aerobates, or Secularism in Colonos," by W. M. W. Call. The article which particularly interested Marx was "Leaders of Modern Thought: No. XXIII —Karl Marx," by Ernest Belfort Bax, in the issue of December 1881. In eleven columns Bax presented a general survey of Marx's life and opinions, with quotations from *Das Kapital.* Since this was the first favorable review of Marx ever to appear in an English journal, he was understandably overjoyed, especially since the article, as he wrote to his friend Friedrich Sorge a few days later, was pervaded by "a real enthusiasm for the new ideas themselves and boldly stands up against British philistinism."

He read the article aloud to Jenny on her sickbed, and she too was pleased that he had received this critical acclaim in England. Previous articles on leaders of modern thought included Victor Hugo, Richard Wagner, Shelley and Ralph Waldo Emerson, and he may have felt that he was being assured his proper place among the immortals. Indeed, no other article written in his lifetime gave him so much joy, so much unalloyed pleasure. Bax had not been afraid to use superlatives, and from time to time there could be heard the organ note of triumph. He wrote:

> Karl Marx, the greatest living exponent of the economical theory of Modern Socialism, was born at Trier (Treves) on the 2nd of May, 1818, his father, a baptised Jew, holding a high official position in that city. He studied for the law at the University of Bonn, and passed his examination with high honours about the year 1840, after which he returned to his native town, where he appeared to have lived the life of a private gentleman for some three years. In 1843 he married Jenny von Westphalen, a sister of the well-known Herr von Westphalen, subsequently member of the Manteuffel Ministry. Philosophy and political economy, with special reference to the great social problems of the age, became his chief studies on leaving the University, and in his views he rapidly approached that spectre of the *Bourgeois* politician and economist, "extreme Socialism." This enabled him to renounce a splendid opening in the Government service (which considering the nature of his genius and acquirements must inevitably have brought him to the highest posts), and resolve to devote himself to the cause of the revolution he saw approaching. Shortly after his marriage, accordingly, he repaired to Paris and became co-editor with the late Arnold Ruge of the *Deutsch-Französische Jahrbücher.* He also edited the Socialist journal *Vorwärts.* But in less than a twelve-month he was compelled to leave France, and take up his residence in Brussels. There he remained for four years, occupying himself chiefly with literary work, till in March, 1848, he was driven from Belgium, and after another short visit to Paris, found a temporary resting-place at Cologne, where the revolutionary ferment was at its height. There he again undertook the editorship of a paper, the *Rheinische Zeitung,* but the severity

> of his criticisms, and the disasters of the revolutionary party, caused its suppression the following year (1849). He returned to Paris, remained there for a short time, and subsequently came to London, where he has resided ever since. . . .

Such was the preamble to that long, informative, and oddly inaccurate article written by the twenty-seven-year-old Belfort Bax. What is odd about the inaccuracies is that they fall into a conventional pattern: the statements that are wholly wrong seem designed to emphasize his *respectability*. So we learn that when he left the University of Bonn with high honors, he returned to his native town and lived the life of a private gentleman for three years. We learn, too, that he renounced a splendid opening in government service which would have brought him to high office, and that in Belgium he occupied himself with literary pursuits. None of these statements were true, but they were exactly the kind of statements which might have been made by close friends in an effort to present Marx in a favorable light.

There is some mystery about this article, and it is tempting to inquire whether Eleanor Marx had some connection with it. She was a close friend of Dr. Edward Aveling, who was making a living as a scientific journalist and professional atheist. He was a frequent contributor to *Modern Thought*. In December 1880 he had written "Leaders of Modern Thought: No. XVIII—Percy Bysshe Shelley." He was a friend of Belfort Bax, an economist and student of German philosophy, and therefore well equipped to write about Marx's theories, although he evidently knew very little about Marx's life and activities. It is likely, therefore, that Bax consulted Aveling, who in turn consulted Eleanor. In later years Bax liked to remember that on the publication of the article Marx "sent me his thanks and many appreciative messages in a letter written by his daughter Eleanor."

Although Marx wrote to his friend Friedrich Sorge that the biographical sketch was "mostly wrong" and that the exposition of his economic principles was "confused," he found only one criticism to address to Bax. In the article it was stated that *The Eighteenth Brumaire* had been published anonymously. The next issue of *Modern Thought* included the correction that "Dr. Marx has never published anything of the nature of a personal attack without appending to it his own name." This could only have come from Marx himself.

The article exhilarated Marx. He wrote to everybody about it, gave many copies of *Modern Thought* away, and felt that he had at last broken through the walls of British reserve. He was also especially pleased that there had been posters announcing the forthcoming article all over the West End of London.

Marx read the article to Jenny on the last day of November. Two days later she was dead. She died very quietly, without pain. "Her illness," he wrote, "took on the character of a total decline due to the weakness of her great age.* Until the last moments there was no death struggle, only a slow fading away, while her eyes grew larger, more beautiful, more shining than ever."

Her last words were in English. Holding her husband's hand, she said: "My strength is broken," and then fell asleep. In the Marx household the word "broken" was used in the sense of "shattered" or "destroyed."

Some days before her death, Jenny had asked for a very simple funeral, saying: "We are no such external people," meaning that they were not given to outward show. Engels made all the funeral arrangements, and it was decided that she should be buried on unconsecrated ground at Highgate Cemetery.

On the doctor's advice Marx did not attend the funeral, which took place on the afternoon of December 5, 1881. It was a bitterly cold day, and he was still suffering from the bronchitis which had affected him all through the summer and autumn. Although he did not attend, he sometimes believed he had been present when Jenny's coffin was lowered into the ground. Some months later he told a friend that he would have fallen headlong into her grave if Engels had not snatched him back in time.

At the graveside Engels read the funeral oration. In the German fashion he recited her life history and pronounced a long eulogy. He spoke of her noble descent, of her father, Baron von Westphalen, who had occupied the post of Government Councilor at Trier, and of the close friendship between the Marxes and the Westphalens. Then he spoke of their years of exile, and how the British government and the bourgeois opposition had oppressed them:

> For Jenny Marx this was real exile with all its terrors. She might have overcome the material hardships of her life, and the sight of her two sons and a little daughter sinking into the grave, but the Government and the bourgeois opposition, from the vulgar liberals to the democrats, combined in a great conspiracy against her husband, and showered on him the most wretched and base calumnies; the entire press united against him; every means of defence was denied to him, so that for a time he was helpless against the enemies whom he and she could only despise. And all this wounded her deeply. And it lasted a long time.
>
> But not forever. The European proletariat once more secured conditions of existence, which allowed it a certain liberty of movement. The International

* Jenny Marx was sixty-seven when she died.

> was founded. The class struggle of the proletariat spread from country to country, and her husband, who was the foremost, fought among the foremost. Thus there began for her a time which compensated her for many of her cruel sorrows. She lived to see the calumny which had showered down upon her husband scattered like chaff before the wind, and to see his doctrines, which all reactionary parties, feudal as well as democratic, had gone to such immense pains to suppress, preached from the roof-tops in all civilized countries and in all cultivated tongues. She lived to see the proletarian movement, which had become one with her own existence, shake the old world from Russia to America to its foundations, and press forward against all resistance ever more confident of victory.

It was strange that he should have singled out the British government and the opposition as being chiefly responsible for her husband's miseries, and stranger still that "the entire press" should be incriminated—that press which scarcely knew of Marx's existence. There had been no "great conspiracy" against Marx, and it was not true that his doctrines were being "preached from the roof-tops in all civilized countries and in all cultivated tongues." This was the sterile language of communist apologetics, with its meaningless claims and abject recital of imaginary calumnies. This language was to become commonplace in later years, and Engels must share with Marx the responsibility for inventing it.

The funeral oration was intended for the archives rather than for the three or four family friends who gathered round the grave. In the following week it appeared in *L'Égalité* in Paris, and with some slight changes in *Der Sozialdemokrat* in Zurich. They were papers with very small circulations, but the only ones which were sympathetic to Marx's cause.

The oration was a disservice to Jenny, who deserved better. She was a warm, complicated, brilliant, tireless woman who adored her husband in spite of everything, and sometimes quarreled with him violently, and knew him too well for her own comfort. As Marx's father had foreseen, it was a tragic marriage, and she never quite reconciled herself to the sleepless nights of exile. When she lay dying at the age of sixty-seven, no more than the shell of her remained. Yet to the end she remained the aristocrat, calm and restrained in the midst of struggle.

THE LAST DAYS

Marx died on the day Jenny died. He did not die physically, but the life had gone out of him. He felt old now, and stumbled a little when he walked, and seemed not to belong to the world. On rare occasions, as though by magic, he would revive, and for a brief while he would speak in that rough, heavily accented voice about battles fought long ago, or about the attention which was now being paid to his works, or about his grandchildren, but he usually preferred to be silent, alone with his own thoughts.

As usual, Eleanor looked after him, attending to his least wishes. Her greatest desire was still to perform on the London stage, but she dared not leave her father's side. He wrote to Engels not long after his wife's death: "Not for anything in the world would I have the child imagining that she is being sacrificed on the family altar as the nurse of an old man." But Eleanor remained his nurse, keeping her thoughts to herself, determined to serve her father faithfully to the end.

The weather was atrocious; the coal fire was kept burning at night; and Eleanor was always there. She read to him, saw that there was a rug round his knees and a shawl round his shoulders, and watched him with as much solicitude as Helene Demuth, who had grown gray and old and fat in his service. Helene had her own artificial resources: when the dreariness and misery of the London winter became too much for her, she would vanish into the kitchen and consume enormous quantities of beer. Eleanor permitted herself no stimulants; it was enough that she should be beside her father. There had been a bitter quarrel in the past, and the memory of the quarrel hung over their long silences. Meanwhile she was content to pour her energy into him in the hope of keeping him alive.

That winter was one of the grimmest he had ever lived through, with the snow mounting in the streets and the fog clinging to the window-panes. By January he was coughing so violently, and in such danger of another attack of pleurisy, that it was decided to send him to the Isle of

Wight. He stayed there less than three weeks, hating his loneliness, spending most of the time indoors, and sometimes walking through the streets of Ventnor "wearing a respirator and an overcoat like a rhinoceros hide." Soon he was back in London, still coughing, while the doctors begged him to seek a warmer climate in the south. It was decided that he should go to Algiers, where at least the sun could be expected to shine. The route to Algiers led through France, and accordingly he made the journey in slow stages, spending a week with his eldest daughter in Argenteuil, meeting Jules Guesde and other socialist politicians in Paris, pretending that he was well enough to endure the winter rains of Paris better than the London snow. He did all the wrong things, caught cold, took a train which arrived in Marseilles at two o'clock in the morning, and reached Algiers toward the end of February in worse health than he had ever been. He had another attack of pleurisy, and seemed to be dying. Within a week he was rallying. The hot African sun revived him, but it had scarcely brought him back to life when it hid behind the clouds. Algiers experienced its coldest winter on record.

As he walked about Algiers after recovering from pleurisy, the Arabic world, which he had rarely contemplated and never seen before, opened out to him in all its brilliant colors. Suddenly he was overwhelmed with a desire to know everything there was to be known about the Algerians and their history. Albert Fermé, a kindly Frenchman who had been exiled to Algeria by Napoleon III, became his mentor. Fermé was an astute and intelligent observer; he knew Marx by reputation; and he shared Marx's new-found enthusiasm for Islamic history. On the rare days when the sun shone they would go out together in a carriage and study the natives.

March was a disaster; in April the sun came out again. It came out with so much force that Marx suffered from heat rash, a novel addition to his many infirmities. The rash lingered, and on the advice of his doctor he decided to cut off his bushy mane of hair and his vast flowing beard, or at least to reduce them to manageable proportions. Before this final sacrifice he went to a photographer, according to the old custom by which he was usually photographed at solemn and critical moments in his life. The photograph, the last one taken of him, survives. It shows him in his black silk morning coat, with a starched shirt and heavy black tie. The white beard, seen against the sunlight, resembles silk floss, but the mustache is still dark and tobacco-stained; but what is especially notable is that he is smiling so broadly that deep wrinkles appear on his nose. He looks like Father Christmas.

The *bonhomie,* the generosity, the kindness he showed to his daughters and his grandchildren during this last year of his life are all present in the photograph. Of the many photographs taken in his lifetime it is the only one which presents him laughing. Each of his daughters received a copy of the photograph. They were all signed "Old Nick."

A day or two later the beard and the mane fell to the barber's scissors. Thus was formed Marx's last face—a face which bore no resemblance to the great bearded prophet: beardless, covered with sores, with watery eyes and heavy lips. It was a face which very few people saw, and none remembered.

The face which Marx showed to the photographer was not acquired without effort. He was acting a role. There was little laughter in him, for he was still consumed with grief over Jenny, suffered atrociously from insomnia, had no appetite, and was helplessly aware that something was wrong with his bronchial tubes. The nights were unbearable, and all the days were somber. Dr. Fermé might regale him with stories about the court of justice over which he presided, and hold forth about the property rights of Arabs and the sinister influence of the police who tortured prisoners to extract confessions, but as the days passed Marx lost interest in Algeria and the Algerians. He was lonely for his daughters.

As April came to an end, the weather grew worse, and it was decided to send him to the south of France. At the beginning of May he sailed for Marseilles. He thought he would settle down in Nice, but forty-eight hours later he was in Monte Carlo, suffering a third attack of pleurisy. He had brought the bad weather with him from Africa. Cloudy skies and whistling winds disturbed him; it seemed that a chill had descended on the earth, and there was no escape from it.

There was some irony in the fact that Marx, the enemy of capital, should have found himself in this hotbed of capitalism, among the Russian grand dukes and the spendthrift millionaires. He observed them with a wary eye when he visited the gaming tables. Though dependent on Engels' charity, he bore himself with the air of a man born to great wealth, dignified and portly, immaculately dressed. He told himself he had escaped from Algiers to avoid the heat of the Algerian summer, but Monte Carlo had rarely been so bitterly cold. Still, there were no more attacks of pleurisy and he was gaining a little weight. His doctor pronounced him well enough to face a Parisian summer at the beginning of June. He left Monte Carlo and went to stay with Jenny at Argenteuil.

For once the skies lifted and Argenteuil basked in the sun. In the sunlight he expanded, became loquacious, and played with the children, never letting them out of his sight. Paul Lafargue, who came for a visit, reported that Marx looked better than he had been for some months, and was more garrulous than ever. He wrote to Engels:

> Marx's appearance has given me great pleasure; he holds himself straight, his eyes are sparkling with life, in short he looks stronger than when he left London, although he is much thinner. I lent my sustained attention to his conversation, which was very long and went on for several hours; he talked all the time and he never made a mistake or hesitated over the choice of words. What is troubling him at this moment is his throat. He coughs in the evening and the morning, and this tires him a great deal. He is very excitable in the evening and he sleeps badly if he has seen people in the evening.

Lafargue lived in Paris, and Marx accompanied him to the station, happy to have someone who would listen unprotestingly to his accounts of Algiers and Monte Carlo, whose history he had studied at length and whose gaming machines he had observed with stupefaction. He was full of Africa and the Arabs, and Lafargue was of the opinion that there could not have been a book on Islam which Marx had left unread, for he quoted them at immense length. So in the darkness, with the wind rising, they reached the little country station. Just before the train was pulling out, Marx said: "But you haven't told me anything!" *"Pardieu!"* exclaimed Lafargue. "You didn't give me a chance to say a word!"

The coughing went on—a deep, racking, tumultuous coughing, which left him breathless and dispirited. There were sudden bursts of anger, but they seemed to be directed more at himself than at the household, and he was always calm in the presence of the children. "I am so busy doing nothing that I am approaching imbecility," he told Lafargue, who returned to Argenteuil a few days later. "Well, that's a new horizon," Lafargue commented. It was, however, a horizon that made Marx shudder, and sometimes he would go to his notebooks and fill them with facts and statistics, pretending to be hard at work.

He was careless of his health, but deeply solicitous of Jenny's. She was thin and drained of energy, no more than a ghost of herself, and she was having trouble with the maidservant, so much trouble that she seemed permanently on the edge of hysteria. When he played in the garden with the children, he was able to forget his miseries. He would play with them even when the rain and the chill wind swept over the garden, for he hated the confinement of the house and enjoyed the sight of the children running around like young savages, whatever the weather. The first sunlit days at Argenteuil gave way to leaden skies; the wind howled; summer became winter; it was the worst summer on record. Soon he would have to think of moving to a warmer climate again, but he found it difficult to tear himself away from his grandsons.

One day Helene Demuth and Eleanor came to Argenteuil ostensibly for a family reunion, but chiefly because they were disturbed by reports of Marx's terrible fits of coughing. But he seemed well enough, with a fine color, still sun-tanned from the Algerian sun, looking more like a Moor than ever. They returned to London, pleased with his progress. He was taking sulphur baths at nearby Enghien-les-Bains; distinguished politicians from Paris came to visit him; he held court. In his appalling Germanic French, with the verbs sometimes running to the end of the sentence, he liked to expatiate on French politics at formidable length, taking especial pleasure in trouncing the deputies who showed no interest in communist ideas.

At Enghien-les-Bains Marx was at ease among the *haute bourgeoisie,* taking the requisite walks round the lake and from time to time permitting himself to be robed in rubber sheeting and then plunged into a steam bath. The cure did him no harm, but the doctors felt he would have a better chance of recovery if he went to a warmer climate. There were clear skies over Lake Geneva. Perhaps Vevey would be better. Anything was better than rainy, windy Argenteuil, where he was always in danger of another attack of pleurisy. He had little confidence in the weather of Switzerland. Wherever he traveled, it rained. "It's all my fault," Marx commented. "I bring the bad weather with me." It occurred to him that in the Middle Ages he would probably have been burned at the stake as a sorcerer, for the thunderclouds had become his companions, arising, it seemed, at his bidding.

Some weeks before he had written to Laura, saying that he feared to make any more railroad journeys alone. *"Ich wurde in der Tat kaum mehr alone auf das Reisewagnis ausgehn. Du siehst, dass es so plus ou moins votre devoir d'accompagner le vieux de la montagne."** It was one of those variegated sentences in German, English and French, which were becoming more common as he grew older, especially in his letters to his children. *"Le vieux de la montagne"* was a happy touch, deriving from his study of the Arab world—the Old Man of the Mountain was the king of the Assassins, who sent his hashish-eating warriors down into the valleys of Syria to kill Christians and Arabs alike.

Toward the end of August, with Laura as his traveling companion, he

* Indeed I scarcely ever again want to travel alone in a railroad car. So you see, it is more or less your duty to accompany the old man of the mountain.

was off to Switzerland, visiting Lausanne and Geneva before settling in Vevey, where, though there had been no rain for weeks, it began to rain interminably. He looked well; his cheeks were glowing; he had put on weight. Sometimes the skies would clear, and he would walk with Laura beside the lake, talking endlessly about his plans. In the six weeks he spent at Vevey, according to Laura, he talked as much as he talked during the six remaining months of his life. Garrulity had become his passion.

He talked about the forthcoming third edition of *Das Kapital* which would be brought out in Germany, about a history of the International, and about his work in mathematics. He decided that Laura would become his secretary and they would spend the winter on the Isle of Wight together. The documents would be collected, the books would be written, in a few months the remaining volumes of *Das Kapital* would be ready for the press. It was a beguiling, an entrancing prospect, and it pleased him that Laura immediately offered to accompany him to the Isle of Wight, sacrificing herself for him and abandoning her husband for the duration. Laura was quieter than Eleanor, more determined in her socialist faith, and more reliable. Eleanor was like himself, volatile and highstrung, while Laura more closely resembled his beloved Jenny. Now that the plans were made, he seemed more hopeful, more in command of himself. Only one thing troubled him. "It seems to me," he said, "that in all of Vevey I am the only one who keeps on coughing."

Because the coughing went on relentlessly, Laura began to think it would be better if they spent the winter in Italy. It was a wise idea, but Marx was in a hurry to get back to his books, and in any case he had no particular liking for Italy. It was decided that they should spend a few days with the Longuets in Paris and then go straight to London. But first they must call on the old revolutionary Johann Philip Becker, because he was ailing and very close to Marx's heart. This was another mistake, for Becker, who was living in poverty in Geneva, sent them confusing instructions about his address, and they found themselves wandering through the driving wind and a blinding rain in search of his lodgings. Laura wondered how Marx could have survived that cold, stormy day. "If we had stayed in Geneva another day," she wrote to Engels, "Papa would have had a relapse and all the good work done at Vevey would have been in vain."

Soon, however, the miseries of that last day on Swiss soil were forgotten in the contemplation of the children in the garden at Argenteuil. It was only a fleeting visit, long enough for a checkup by the local doctor, who pronounced that there had been considerable improvement; there was less coughing than he had expected; the important thing was to concentrate on getting rid of the catarrh. Marx seemed to regard the doctor's verdict as a clear bill of health, but when he arrived in England, he looked, according to Eleanor, "so poorly that we began to fear the worst." He spent a few days in London, and there were some convivial evenings with Engels spent over a bottle of rum. Then once again he went to the Isle of Wight in search of the sun.

All the plans for a busy autumn and winter came to nothing. No Laura came to help him complete the remaining volumes of *Das Kapital;* he was alone in the cold boardinghouse at Ventnor once more, still complaining about the weather, too ill to take his daily walks by the sea. He kept to his room, and thought himself lucky if he could sleep four hours a night. He who had once commanded a great revolutionary party and spent his life pondering the uses of revolutionary power now found himself confronted with problems of considerably less magnitude. What puzzled and perplexed him was the behavior of an old spinster in the boardinghouse, who was perfectly well but insisted on calling in the doctor three times a week. Why did people behave like this? What purpose was served by these constant visits from the doctor? It never occurred to him that the sprightly old woman liked the company of her doctor and was prepared to pay for it. He railed against her, as though she had become an enemy, the last of the long catalogue of enemies who had plagued him remorselessly.

If he could no longer concentrate on his books, he could still write letters. They poured out of him in profusion, and sometimes we hear the authentic note of pride and self-congratulation. On December 14, 1882, exactly three months before his death, he wrote to Laura: "Some recent Russian publications, printed in Holy Russia, not abroad, show the great run of my theories in that country. Nowhere is my success more delightful; it gives me the satisfaction that I damage a power, which, besides England, is the true bulwark of the Old Society."

It was a memorable and prophetic utterance, but it was also a puzzling one, for he had rarely regarded Russia as "the true bulwark of the Old Society." For him Russia had always been a half-barbarian state living in feudal bondage, remote from the main currents of European history. He would have been happier if his revolutionary doctrines had been welcomed in Germany.

His daughter Jenny was dying in Argenteuil, but the news was kept from him. She was his favorite, and it was feared that he would suffer a relapse if he knew the truth. In the first days of the New Year Eleanor, alarmed by the sadness of his letters, came down to Ventnor to visit him, bringing Johnny Longuet with her. No visit could have been more welcome, for his favorite grandson had the power to waken him from his lethargy and revive his spirits. Though continually coughing, he was in good humor, telling stories, laughing and joking. Once more they walked together arm-in-arm along the sea front, the old man huddled in his greatcoat and a mountain of scarves. Eleanor came for only two or three days, just long enough to observe that he had grown strangely frail, and then, because she had to return to London to give the lessons on which she depended for her livelihood, she left him. Then once again he was an old man alone with his grief, doing nothing in a small rented room in a Victorian lodginghouse, the books unwritten, the papers gathering dust.

The fatal blow came a few days later. Jenny's illness, following the birth of her last child, had grown progressively worse during the winter, and though for a few days she seemed to be recovering, the doctors held out little hope for her. She died on January 10. A telegram was sent to Eleanor. No telegram was sent to Marx, for obvious reasons. The burden of telling Marx rested on Eleanor, who knew exactly what she must do. After a sleepless night she took the train to Ventnor, racking her brains for some way to console and comfort her father. She knew it would be a deathblow. She would phrase the words cautiously and hesitantly, in exactly the right tones of affection and warning. But when she reached him, she found that there was no need to tell him. He had read it on her face. "Our Jennychen is dead," he said.

For himself there could be no question of remaining in the lonely boardinghouse: he would go at once to London to be close to Helene Demuth, who alone could console him. Eleanor offered to stay with him at Ventnor, but he would have none of it. Her task, he explained, was to go to Argenteuil and look after Jenny's children, and she must do this at once, without wasting a moment, taking the first boat to France. Within half an hour Eleanor was on her way back to London, to pick up Johnny and take him to France.

Marx returned alone to London to spend the remaining days of his life in his own house. Jenny's death brought on an acute attack of bronchitis, and he was coughing more violently than ever. A day or two later laryngitis set in, so that he was unable to eat solid food and was reduced to drinking milk, which he had always hated. Helene Demuth fussed over him, Eleanor read to him, and Engels came nearly every afternoon to bring some cheer to a cheerless household. In February an abscess developed in his lung. He could not speak and seemed withdrawn from the world, growing more emaciated every day. He could still write, and sometimes he would force himself to his desk in the front room overlooking the tree-lined street. Spring was late that year, and there seemed to be no end to the falling snow and the roaring of the east wind. When he looked out of the window there was nothing to see except the snow, the dark winter trees and the sparrows.

For most of the day he lay in bed, propped up by pillows, for the doctors were anxious that he should lie down at full length as little as possible. He had no appetite, and often refused to drink milk. They gave him soup and a little wine, and from time to time he seemed to rally. On the evening of March 9 the doctor announced that, if anything, he had taken a turn for the better, the abscess in the lung was healing, and if he would only bring himself to eat and drink, there would be a good chance of recovery.

In the early afternoon of March 14 Engels arrived at the house to find Eleanor and Helene Demuth in tears. They told him that in the morning Marx had drunk milk, soup and wine, but afterward there had been a slight hemorrhage and he seemed very weak and frail; they were sure the end was near. Helene Demuth went upstairs to see him and returned two minutes later. "Come up," she said. "He is half asleep." The three of them then went to the bedroom and found him sitting in his armchair. He was dead at the age of sixty-five.

The doctor who signed the death certificate wrote that his death was due to "laryngitis." It was more likely that he died of heart failure.

Marx died peacefully. There was no crisis, no agony. It was the death he had hoped for, and it came like the touch of a feather. The last person to see him alive was Helene Demuth, the faithful Lenchen, the servant who had cared for him and his family for forty years and had given birth to his surviving son.

Legend embroidered on his death. One story had it that in the last moments of his life he had clambered out of bed, gone to his study and sat down at his worktable in a rage to complete some unfinished work. Such heroic gestures are demanded of heroes, and it was felt that Marx must conform to the heroic pattern. But in fact he died in his bedroom, sitting alone in his dressing gown beside the fire.

Many years before he had written to his friend Arnold Ruge all he had to say on the subject of death. The letter was written a few days before his marriage, when the world was full of bright hopes, and there was no thought of bitterness and despair:

> And when it is all over we shall hold hands and begin again from the beginning. Let the dead bury the dead and weep over them. And yet for us it is an enviable fate to enter the new life; and that fate is ours.

Although he was a proud and despotic man, with a hankering to be remembered, he could never have guessed that he would enter a new life so soon after his death. In the eyes of millions he would become a legend, another Moses pointing toward the promised land.

The tablets of the law were enshrined in the *Communist Manifesto* and *Das Kapital.* These two books were to be his passport to the future, but it was not their substance so much as their passion and willfulness, their savage indignation, which was enduring. He left no clear-cut system, no program of action, no large body of followers. Others would come after him, choosing among his ideas as they pleased, selecting whatever was most useful for a revolutionary occasion, employing his voluminous thoughts with a fine disregard for his essential humanity. He was a man whose deepest concern was the loss of human freedom in an industrialized and alienated world, and by a supreme and terrible irony he became the legendary founder of a form of government which denied to men their most elementary liberties.

Marx would not have recognized the Russian Revolution as a product of his thought, and he would have been among the first to protest against the anarchic government of a self-appointed bureaucracy, and among the first to be killed. Some phrases and ideas were seized upon by Lenin to demonstrate that the Bolshevik revolution arose logically out of the concepts which Marx had been the first to employ, but there were other phrases and ideas which might have been employed to show that the Bolsheviks were perverting his doctrines by reducing the dictatorship of the proletariat to a dictatorship of one man or a small body of men. After the Russian Revolution only two classes were permitted to remain: the bureaucrats and their servants. This was not the revolution which Marx had hoped to bring about.

To the end Marx remained the creature of his age. He was the child of the eighteenth century with its romantic dreams of a golden age achieved by the use of the intelligence alone, and at the same time he was the inheritor of the Judeo-Christian myth which announced the coming destruction of the kings of the earth and the emergence of a golden age, when the lion would lie down with the lamb, and the riches of the earth would be distributed equally among the earth's children. This dream was as old as history. Marx translated the dream into the language of Victorian sociology which he wrote with the fervor of a

Hebrew prophet. He pointed unerringly at the doom which awaits the worshipers of the golden calf, and the salvation which attends the chosen ones, the proletariat, who are innocent and long-suffering, and therefore entitled to their place in the sun.

Again and again Marx spoke of the corrupting power of money, which turns loyalty into treachery, love into hate, virtue into vice, intellect into imbecility. The evil lay at the heart of society: the slow poison of gold turned men into slaves, or beasts, or worse. Like the prophets he saw the world in black and white, good and evil in mortal combat, the blessed and the damned at each other's throats. Ultimately, if one followed his teachings, the good would triumph, and in the last days after fearful sufferings there would be redemption for all. Then at last the children of God would come into their inheritance.

The dream of the golden age is an act of faith unsubstantiated by reasonable hopes, but Marx was supremely uninterested in reasonable hopes. He looked for miracles, and thought he detected miraculous powers in the proletariat. He charged his writings with so much power and energy, so much violence and vituperation, that sometimes the pages seem to catch fire. What was enduring in him was not his philosophy, and still less was it his studies of revolutionary power. What was enduring was the thunder of his voice and his curse on those who had committed a crime on the human race by amassing the wealth which should be the common property of all. All the rest—the senseless quarrels, the devious stratagems, the bigotry and dogmatism, the fierce pride and the yearning for power—all these fall away. The thunder and the curse remain.

The frail old man who died in a bourgeois house in the early afternoon of March 14, 1883 was born again as a legend.

THE LEGEND

According to the practice of the time, Marx's body was "laid out," which meant that he was undressed and washed and placed on the bed in his best clothes to await the arrival of the undertaker. The fire in the bedroom was put out, the curtains of all the windows were drawn. When Engels returned to the house in the evening after dispatching telegrams to Marx's friends in Germany, France and America, he found Marx already laid out, clothed in a black frock coat and black trousers, lying at full length on the bed. He had hoped to detect some expression on the dead face, but there was none. In the blue light of the gas lamps there was only a frozen mask.

Engels' telegrams were terse. To Sorge in Hoboken, he wrote: "Marx is dead. Engels." The words—the endless torrent of words—would come later.

Engels took charge of the funeral arrangements. He sent out all the funeral notices, bought the coffin, attended to the needs of Eleanor and Helene Demuth, and did all that had to be done. Marx had died on a Wednesday; and it was decided that the funeral should take place on Saturday to allow time for the delegations to arrive from France and Germany. Engels expected a large concourse of people at the graveside, and he intended to make a speech extolling the dead leader. His sorrow was great, and he was able to come to grips with it only by being constantly busy and by writing a formidable number of letters.

In the upstairs bedroom Marx lay in state. A few friends of the family were permitted to see him lying there. Among the few who saw him dead was Edward Aveling. He had been invited by Eleanor, who had become his mistress and had never dared to bring him into the house while her father was alive.

At midnight on the day of Marx's death Engels was still writing letters. In a letter to Eduard Bernstein he wrote that only those who had been close to Marx could judge the immense services he had rendered to the revolutionary movement, and to Liebknecht he wrote that it was beyond belief that Marx would never again "fertilize with his mighty thoughts the proletarian movement of two continents." At the time of his death Marx's influence was in eclipse. It was like a flame that had gone out. Engels blew on the embers, and the flame came to life again.

Within a few hours the processes of deification were already at work. Engels assumed the role of advocate of the Holy Sepulcher, the inheritor of the doctrine, and the sole trustee. The books would be edited and interpreted, his ideas would be disseminated, vast claims would be made for his towering brilliance, his understanding of the disciplines by which revolutions are brought about, and his eminence as a philosopher. The portrait of Marx as it finally emerged in the communist textbooks was largely the work of Engels.

Marx left no will, no literary testament, no instructions to be opened after his death. His small estate amounted to £250, and this figure was based on the reputed value of his furniture and books. Engels became the administrator of the estate, and inherited the responsibilities which went with it. Most of the books and much of the furniture, including Marx's armchair, passed into his possession. He inherited Helene Demuth, who became his housekeeper, and for the rest of his life he supported Marx's surviving children. He became a kindly autocrat ruling over the descendants of Marx.

On the afternoon of Saturday, March 17, 1883, a small procession arrived at the gates of Highgate Cemetery. They had come to bury Marx beside Jenny, whose grave had been opened, and to listen to Engels' funeral oration, which was longer and even more inaccurate than the one he had delivered fourteen months before. Altogether only eleven people came to the cemetery. The mourners were Engels, Eleanor, Edward Aveling, Friedrich Lessner, Georg Lochner, Ray Lancaster, Karl Schorlemmer, Charles Longuet, Paul Lafargue, Gottlieb Lemke, Wilhelm Liebknecht. In his oration Engels described Marx in ceremonial tones. He was the greatest revolutionary and philosopher of his age, a master mathematician, the supreme scientist of his time. Speaking in English for the benefit of the two or three Englishmen present, Engels acclaimed him as a world leader whose death was mourned by millions of revolutionaries all over the world. He said:

> On March 14, at a quarter to three in the afternoon, the greatest living thinker ceased to think. For scarcely two minutes he had been left alone, and when we came back we found him in his easy-chair peacefully sleeping —but forever.

> No one can measure the loss which has been sustained by the aggressive proletariat of Europe and America, and by historical science, in the death of this man. Soon enough men will come to feel the void which the death of this powerful spirit has torn into the fabric of things.
>
> Just as Darwin discovered the law of the development of organic nature, so Marx discovered the law of the development of human history: the simple fact, hitherto obscured by an overgrowth of ideology, that man must first of all eat, drink, have a roof over his head and clothe himself before he can pursue politics, science, art, religion etc., and therefore the production of the immediate material means of subsistence and consequently the degree of economic development of a people or of a period of time form the base on which state institutions, legal conceptions, art, and even the religious ideas of the people concerned have been evolved, and in the light of which they must therefore be elucidated—not, as previously, the other way round.
>
> But that is by no means all. Marx discovered also the special law of motion governing contemporary capitalist methods of production and the bourgeois society which was created out of it. With the discovery of surplus value a light was suddenly created, while all earlier investigations, both those of bourgeois economists and socialist critics, were gropings in the dark.
>
> Two such discoveries would have been enough for one lifetime. Happy the man to whom it is granted to make one. But in every single field which Marx investigated—and he investigated many fields, none of them superficially—in all of them, even in mathematics, he made independent discoveries.
>
> Such was the man of science. But this was not even half the man. For Marx science was a historically dynamic and revolutionary force. He experienced a pure joy over the discovery of any theoretical science even when its practical application could not yet be envisaged, and he experienced a totally different kind of joy when the discovery involved immediate revolutionary impact on industry, and on historical development in general. In this way he followed closely the development of the discoveries in the field of electricity and the recent experiments of Marcel Deprez.
>
> For Marx was above all a revolutionary. His real mission in life was to contribute in one way or another to the overthrow of capitalist society and the state institutions which it brought into being, and to contribute to the liberation of the modern proletariat, which *he* was the first to make conscious of its own position and its own needs, conscious of the conditions of its emancipation. Battle was his element. And he battled with a passion and a tenacity which few could rival.

As Engels spoke beside the grave, reading carefully from his notes, he must have known that many of these exalted claims were unfounded and rested on nothing more substantial than piety. Marx was not the first to assert that the material things of life "form the base on which state institutions, legal conceptions, art, and even the religious ideas of the people concerned have been evolved." The discovery of surplus value had not bathed the world in a new light. Newton's revolutionary laws of motion were nicely balanced against Marx's revolutionary laws of society, but Marx himself had never dared to compare himself with Newton. Nor was Marx the first to make the proletariat conscious of its own position and its own needs. Engels was describing a man whose greatness was almost beyond human conception, possessing the lineaments of divinity, utterly devoid of human qualities, and he seems to have known that he was overreaching himself, for he turned sharply away from the spectacle of the scientist to the embattled revolutionary. Battle was his element—*Der Kampf war sein Element.* Then at last, although very briefly, Engels described the man as he was in the years before lassitude overcame him, and all battles were abandoned.

By describing Marx in this way Engels was performing a disservice to his memory. The grandiloquent claims were no more credible than the claims made by the princes of the Church in the seventeenth century over the mortal remains of earthly princes. "Wings shall be given unto them; they shall become as angels; this very moment, now, immediately, they shall enter into God's presence." The funeral *éloge* has a respectable ancestry and usually follows a well-worn and recognizable pattern. When Bossuet announced that a prince of the blood was stepping over the threshold of heaven to the music of massed choirs of angels, he was under no illusions about the real state of affairs. He was consoling the bereaved. Engels, describing Marx's achievements, was consoling himself.

Having extolled Marx as the first champion of the proletariat and the founder of a new dispensation of society, Engels mentioned the newspapers he had worked on, giving the appropriate dates, not forgetting the *New York Daily Tribune.* He spoke very briefly of the organizations in Paris, Brussels and London which Marx had commanded, and the crowning achievement of the International Working Men's Association, of which he was the sole founder. Then came the peroration:

> And so it happened that he was the most hated and most calumniated man of his time. Governments, whether absolutist or republican, deported him, and the bourgeois, whether conservative or ultra-democratic, vied with one another in heaping abuse on him. All this he brushed aside as though they were spiders' webs, paying no attention to them, answering them only under the direst compulsion. And he is dead, revered, beloved and mourned by millions of fellow-workers from the mines of Siberia and the whole length and breadth of Europe and America as far as California, and I make bold to say: Although he had many adversaries, he had scarcely a single personal enemy.
>
> His name will endure through the centuries, and so will his work!

It is strange that Engels should have depicted Marx as a man without personal enemies, brushing aside abuse as though it fell lightly upon him, sweet-tempered and incapable of anger. The pacific Marx was added to the other portraits in the gallery of saints and scientists, all labeled with his name. As Engels well knew, Marx gloried in making enemies and practiced the fine art of bludgeoning them with every weapon that came to his hands. Nor was it true that all the governments had deported him, for he had traveled freely in his later years through France and Germany, two countries in which he had hoped to bring about revolutions, and no one in England had ever thought of deporting him.

In describing Marx, Engels sought deliberately to efface his human characteristics. The man of flesh and blood became an abstraction, and a ghostly, unrecognizable sage was offered to the worship of the proletariat.

When Engels had finished speaking, Charles Longuet stepped forward, but instead of delivering a speech he read out a letter composed by the veteran Russian revolutionary Peter Lavrov and two telegrams from French and Spanish socialist parties lamenting the cruel loss which had fallen on them. Lavrov reminded the audience that the first translation of *Das Kapital* from the original German had been made into the Russian language, and that Russian university students had the honor of being the first to acclaim Marx's genius. It was not quite true, for the first Russian Marxist group was not organized until the year of Marx's death. An unauthorized Russian translation of *Das Kapital* had appeared in 1872, and it was this volume which was studied and eagerly discussed by Russian students. In Russia *Das Kapital* fell on fertile ground.

Finally Liebknecht spoke in German, saying that Marx was immortal, that God was dead, that science had no frontiers, and that Social Democracy would conquer the world. It was a strangely stilted speech, and since Liebknecht usually spoke well, the explanation would seem to be that he was overcome by grief. "We do not mourn," he said through his tears. "Dead and living friend, we shall follow to the very end the way you have pointed out to us. We swear it on your grave!"

After Liebknecht had spoken there were no more speeches, and at about two o'clock in the afternoon the small procession of mourners left the cemetery. It was a cold blustery day with low clouds scudding across the sky.

On that morning *The Times* had come out with a belated report of Marx's death from its correspondent in Paris. The brief obituary was remarkable for its inaccuracy. It was stated, for example, that Marx was born in Cologne, that he was imprisoned in Paris, and became in 1866 the acknowledged chief of the Socialist Party in Europe. He was described in the subdued tones reserved for men who have outlived their time.

From that day there began the innumerable confusions and misunderstandings which have accumulated around his name. The man drowned in the legend, the legend was drowned in the propaganda. Ideas which he had never held were credited to him, and opinions he had thrown off in passing were regarded as dogma. In the eyes of the Russian communists he was the founder and guardian of a new science for interpreting the movements of history; one had only to learn the science, and immediately one became a prophet. But in fact there was no clear-cut vision, his own prophecies were rarely fulfilled, and he possessed none of the detachment of the scientist. His temper was hot-blooded, romantic, visionary. His followers invented something they called "scientific Marxism," which was so cold, so abstract, so divested of all human emotion that it reduced man to the level of a statistic and the state to a machine for repression.

Marx had his own way of dealing with his followers. "I, at least," he said, "am not a Marxist."

EPILOGUE

THE SURVIVORS

When Marx died, he left behind a small close-knit family. They were his daughters Laura and Eleanor and the five surviving children, Johnny, Harry, Edgar, Marcel and Jenny, of his favorite daughter Jenny. Within a few days of Marx's death Harry, a bright-eyed five-year-old, suddenly died, and the family was once more in mourning. There remained Friedrich Engels and Helene Demuth, who both regarded themselves as members of Marx's family. Overnight Engels became the new head of the family.

Engels took his new duties seriously, and indeed he welcomed them, for he was a lonely man who felt lost without the comforting presence of his friend. At first his friends in Germany had hoped he would move to Zurich, where he would be closer to the German revolutionary movement, but he was too old to start life afresh, and although he had few English friends, he regarded England as his home. His task, as he saw it, was to preside over the legacy of Marx and to enjoy his declining years as much as possible.

As he grew older, Engels became warmer. The cold authoritarian strain, which had been so pronounced a part of his character, gave way to a studied conviviality. It was as though Marx's death and the hopelessness of any further revolutionary upsurge had liberated him from some deep-seated and primitive fear. He was no longer in the shadow of another man, and no longer bore the responsibility for revolutions. He liked to regard himself as the guardian of the faith and keeper of the treasure, and it pleased him that he was in a position to receive from the European comrades the letters which would once have been sent to Marx. He answered them all, mildly encouraging their revolutionary fervor, explaining over and over again that there was no easy path to the revolution and the days of a great conflagration blazing across Europe from Spain to Russia were over.

He still lived at 122 Regent's Park Road, one of those houses which, according to Eduard Bernstein, were made in identical groups of eight, ten, or twelve, as though they were so many sausages. But when Bernstein examined the house further, he discovered to his surprise that the undistinguished exterior concealed a multitude of strangely proportioned rooms each fulfilling a peculiarly English need. The breakfast room, the front and back parlors, the lumber room, the basement, the hall—all these were rooms which seemed to have no German equivalent, and were therefore very nearly incomprehensible. Into that extraordinary machine, the English house, Engels, who somewhat resembled a lean English officer long retired from service in distant colonies, fitted perfectly. He had become more English than the English. Unlike Marx, who spoke a gravelly kind of English and often got his prepositions wrong, Engels spoke the language perfectly: not London English, but the sharply accented and billowing English spoken in the Midlands.

He especially enjoyed the Christmas season, when the rooms were decorated with green branches of all kinds and the mistletoe hung from the ceiling. Bernstein, who was present at one of these Christmas festivities, records gravely that the purpose of the mistletoe was to give any man the right to kiss any woman who stood under it or walked near it. There were wassail bowls, tipsy cakes and plum puddings glowing with blue brandy flames, and there were presents for everyone. Engels had a fine taste in wines, and these would be brought up from his capacious cellar. About two weeks before Christmas the ladies of his acquaintance would be invited to spend their days from early morning to night preparing the great Christmas feast. There would be mountains of apples, nuts, raisins, almonds and orange peel, and they would all be poured into a great tub. Finally the gentlemen would be invited to stir the pudding by means of a long wooden ladle. Engels superintended these frolics and acted as master of ceremonies. Those who were too old or too weak to drive the ladle three times round the tub were formally excused, while the younger ones, exerting their utmost strength, would receive the applause of the women. All would receive a glass of vintage champagne, and toasts would be drunk to a merry Christmas and many more Christmases to come. Nothing could be more bourgeois, or more convivial.

At such festivities all the survivors, or as many of them as could reach London, were present. Helene Demuth had become Engels' housekeeper after the death of Marx, and she adapted herself quite happily to the new dispensation. She was growing old, complained of pains in her legs and back, and drank a good deal of fourpenny ale. She had lost her pretty looks and grown stout, but she was still the presiding force in the kitchen. Charles Longuet, Laura and Paul Lafargue, and the Longuet children might be present, and Karl Schorlemmer usually came down from Owens College in Manchester to spend the Christmas holidays with Engels. Samuel Moore, a former mill-owner and high court judge in Nigeria, also joined them. He was to become the translator of *Das Kapital,* and one of Engels' stanchest defenders.

Moore was something of a character, ponderous and heavy in a German way, possessing some malice and much kindness. He did not know German very well, with the result that the translation reads nearly as ponderously as the original. The translation was completed with some help from Edward Aveling, about whom there will be more to be said later, and with the general editorial assistance of Engels. *Das Kapital* appeared in English for the first time twenty years after the publication of the original German edition.

At one time Engels hoped to write a biography of Marx, and he collected a vast amount of material for the project. The biography would crown their lifelong labors and become the authoritative record of Marx's life. Unhappily it was never written, chiefly because Engels spent so much of his time collating Marx's unpublished manuscripts, editing them, and preparing them for publication. A few days after Marx's death Helene Demuth discovered among his papers about five hundred folio pages, which at first were thought to be the second volume of *Das Kapital.* Later it was discovered that these pages were merely a fragment of the whole and nearly a thousand more pages were found. Altogether there were twenty-three notebooks, from which Engels was able to compile the huge second volume concerned with the circulation of capital. It was a labor which might have defeated a team of editorial giants, for Marx had the greatest difficulty in setting out his ideas in logical order and all these pages were in a chronic state of disorder. Fragments from one notebook had to be spliced into fragments from another notebook. It was like a jigsaw puzzle: one of those immense jigsaw puzzles made up of thousands of strangely shaped pieces.

As he worked over Marx's posthumous papers, Engels made many surprising discoveries. It was not only that Marx had left his papers in disorder, but they were written in an oddly disjointed manner, full of colloquialisms and coarse humor, with whole passages written in English, and the German text peppered with English and French words. At the conclusion of a chapter there might be a few jagged sentences suggesting an outline of the argument he intended to pursue, but written so vaguely that it was impossible to fathom his real intentions. The style was careless, the handwriting nearly illegible. The carelessness of the style was so alarming that Engels made a special point of it in his introduction to the

CAPITAL:

A CRITICAL ANALYSIS OF CAPITALIST PRODUCTION

BY KARL MARX

TRANSLATED FROM THE THIRD GERMAN EDITION, BY SAMUEL MOORE AND EDWARD AVELING

AND EDITED BY

FREDERICK ENGELS

VOL. I.

LONDON:
SWAN SONNENSCHEIN, LOWREY, & CO.,
PATERNOSTER SQUARE.
1887.

Title page of the first English edition of Capital.

book he was able to construct out of so many scattered notes. It was as though he could not quite forgive Marx, who had always prided himself as a stylist, for such a grave dereliction of duty.

Anyone who has worked over Marx's manuscripts knows the appalling difficulty of reading that handwriting, which seemed to be designed for keeping secrets. It may take an hour to puzzle out a single paragraph. Engels was confronted with thousands of pages as he worked through the vast disorderly mass of the posthumous papers. He took some comfort from the fact that Marx sometimes had the greatest difficulty in reading his own handwriting, which resembled strings of barbed wire waving in the wind.

There was some question whether Marx really wanted these works published, for it seems likely that he had abandoned them long ago to "the criticism of the mice," to whom he had abandoned the vast compilation known as *The German Ideology.* Although Engels claimed that he rewrote little, no more than ten pages, there is some evidence that he rewrote about a quarter of the whole, that in fact the second volume of *Das Kapital* is very largely a thorough reworking of the manuscripts by a devoted and painstaking disciple. It might have been better if he had retained the coarse jokes and brutal sarcasms, for what finally emerged was nearly six hundred pages of overwhelming prolixity and dullness.

The second volume of *Das Kapital* is not a work of any enduring worth; it can be of interest only to that relatively small body of economic historians who are devoted to the task of understanding the economic theories of the early sixties of the last century. The third volume, on which Engels worked from 1885 to 1893, is far more entertaining, for it purports to be a leisurely survey of all the aspects of capital omitted in the two previous volumes. From time to time the old fire returns, and there are occasional peals of sardonic laughter. Marx demolishes his enemies with his customary cutlass.

The third volume of *Das Kapital* was in fact a giant notebook in which Marx wrote his disorderly contemplations, copied out extracts from parliamentary papers, and argued with political economists of all ages. A quite disproportionate amount of space is devoted to usury, and Marx quotes with some amusement the calculations of the eighteenth-century economist Richard Price, who worked out that a penny invested at 5 per cent compounded interest at the time of Christ would amount to 150 million earths of solid gold, while a shilling invested at 6 per cent compound interest at the same time would have become a ball of gold larger than the entire solar system. "Price," Marx comments, "was simply dazzled by the gargantuan dimensions obtained in a geometrical progression." But Marx himself was dazzled by geometrical progression and continually returned to it. Capital's power to increase, as though it were some living thing, alarmed him, as it had alarmed Martin Luther, who spoke of the medieval moneylenders earning as much interest in a year as a whole province might earn. "If he has 1,000,000 florins, then he takes 400,000 annually, which means devouring a mighty king every year. And he does not risk either his person or his wares, does no work, sits near his fireplace and roasts apples, so might a lowly robber sit at home and devour a whole world in ten years."

Engels did his best to edit the vast array of notebooks into some semblance of order. When he found there was only the heading of a chapter, he wrote the entire chapter himself. One chapter entitled "Confusion" consisted of parliamentary reports extracted over a period of ten years and merely held up the argument. Engels omitted it entirely. By omitting, stitching, interpolating and rewriting he was able to put together a volume of nearly a thousand pages. Marx had written both the second and third volumes at the same time that he was wrestling with the first, most of the three massive volumes being composed between 1862 and 1864. During this period he had been suffering from the attacks of nervous prostration which became especially acute toward the end of 1864, when he was superintending the work of the International; and Engels noted that he could tell from reading the manuscript when the attacks came on and when they ended. All three volumes of *Das Kapital* were written by a man who was physically exhausted and spiritually drained.

Marx once told his son-in-law Paul Lafargue that he "would prefer to burn the manuscripts than leave them behind unfinished." But he appears to have changed his opinions often. Not long before his death he told Eleanor that he was leaving Engels "the task of completing my work," and in Eleanor's eyes this could only mean the completion of *Das Kapital.*

According to Rosa Luxemburg, the most heroic of the German revolutionaries, the three volumes must be understood as one continuing examination of the processes of capital and exploitation. The first volume is devoted to the factory, which is the source of capitalist wealth. The second and third volumes bring the reader to "the surface of society," to the mysterious world of credit and finance, where the workers no longer play a conscious role. "We see the workers in the noisy mob of business people only when they troop off to the factories in the gray light of the early morning or hurry home again in the dusk when the factories eject them in droves after the day's work." In fact, the workers play only a minor role in all three volumes, and most of what Marx had to say about them is reserved for his most famous chapter "The Working Day." His approach is always theoretical.

As Engels toiled over these manuscripts, sometimes quarreling with Marx's verdicts and methods—he noted, for example, that Marx knew virtually nothing about business accounts—his eyes began to fail. The doctors ordered him to stop working by gaslight; at most he might spend three hours of reading and writing a day; he could work for ninety minutes in the morning, and again for another ninety minutes in the afternoon. Somehow, in those three hours, he proposed to continue his work as Marx's literary executor and carry on a formidable correspondence. Since he always seemed to be writing articles, reissuing old books and supervising translations, it is clear that he rarely obeyed his doctors' orders. He had some help from Samuel Moore, who went patiently through Marx's mathematical calculations in the third volume of *Das Kapital,* and from his friend Edward Aveling, who could always be prevailed upon to act as a reliable workhorse. Aveling was on terms of close intimacy with Engels, who always defended him against the slanders and rumors which gathered around him. No one ever had a more untiring defender.

Edward Aveling was the son of a London Congregational minister. He was a scientist, playwright, brilliant political speaker, author of many books, actor, and critic. He was also a scoundrel, unreliable whenever questions of money were involved, a notorious seducer, and a man of surpassing ugliness. "No one can be as bad as Aveling looks," one of Eleanor Marx's friends said, disapproving of the association between them, for Eleanor had become Aveling's mistress. The association was formed long before Marx's death and continued until Eleanor's death fifteen years later.

It was not a happy association, nor was it entirely unhappy. Eleanor, like many daughters of authoritarian fathers, possessed a desperate need for affection, and Aveling in his cruel demanding way would sometimes give it to her. Although repulsively ugly, he was eloquent and charming, and few women could resist his recital of Shelley's "Ode to the West Wind." Hyndman said of him that "he needed but half an hour's start of the handsomest man in London" to fascinate any woman at all, and he was especially notable for his successes among actresses. Eleanor had always wanted to be an actress, and with Aveling and George Bernard Shaw she took part in what was probably the first private reading of Ibsen's *A Doll's House.* Shaw read the part of Krogstad, Aveling was Helmer, and Eleanor, inevitably, was Nora. Shaw was half in love with her, but he soon decided that she was too neurotic and too strong-willed to be worth pursuing, and he abandoned her to Aveling without any qualms, knowing that he would be unable to endure living with her.

Yet she was not unattractive. The photographs show lively features, fine eyes, a warm mouth, a look of transparent honesty and eagerness. She knew how to make herself appealing, and though she had inherited her father's rather heavy nose, she could make the best of her other features. Havelock Ellis, who sometimes took her on long country walks, found her an intelligent companion and he praised especially her eagerness for experience and her devotion to her father's causes. He noted, too, that there came from her "a potent axillary fragrance." Such phrases belonged to the medical romanticism of the time, and Eleanor would probably have been pleased to learn that her fragrance was recorded for posterity.

Others found her slightly alarming, as though she had maintained in adult life the habits of an unruly childhood. Beatrice Potter, later to become Mrs. Sidney Webb, met her one afternoon in 1883 in the refreshment room of the British Museum, and found her unpleasantly opinionated on the subject of religion—Eleanor announced that Jesus was a weak-willed, unheroic individual, and went out of her way to impress the socially minded Miss Potter with her lack of knowledge of the social sciences. Evidently Miss Potter had not read Marx, and was not prepared to assent to his universal genius. In her diary Miss Potter recorded her impressions of her brief meeting with Marx's daughter:

> In her person she is comely, dressed in a slovenly picturesque way, with curly black hair flying in all directions. Fine eyes full of life and sympathy, otherwise ugly features and expression, and complexion showing the signs of an unhealthy excited life, kept up with stimulants and tempered by narcotics. Lives alone. . . .

The last two words were untrue, and the stimulants and narcotics were probably coffee and tobacco, for she smoked nearly as much as her father. "Otherwise ugly features and expression" may have been merely a conventional feminine rebuke; no one else found her ugly, though it is likely that she wore a strained, hard, nervous expression when she proclaimed her more outrageous opinions, for she did not really believe in them. What she wanted above all was a calm domestic life, a faithful husband, and many babies, and she may have known that none of these would ever be given to her.

She saw herself as "the new woman," the disciple of Ibsen and of Marx, free to fulfill her destiny in her own way. Accordingly, not long after Marx's death, she began to live openly with Aveling, entering into a "free marriage" with him and calling herself Mrs. Eleanor Marx-Aveling. In August 1883 they rented a cottage at Bole Hill near Wirksworth in Derbyshire for an extended "honeymoon." Engels, who approved of such marriages, wrote off a conspiratorial note to Bernstein explaining the situation:

> Aveling and Tussy, without the aid of officials, etc. are married, and now bathe in bliss in the mountains of Derbyshire. *Nota bene:* about this there must be no public report. The fact is that Aveling already has a legal wife which he cannot get free from *de jure* although he has for years been so *de facto*. This is fairly well known and even among the literary Philistines fairly well accepted.

The surprising thing was Engels' request that there should be no public report of the marriage. Neither Aveling nor Eleanor did anything to conceal their relationship; in his articles on socialism Aveling would speak about his wife, and Eleanor always insisted on being addressed by her hyphenated name.

Since they were thoroughly undisciplined people, living on occasional articles and lectures, with some reviewing and editing, they were often in financial difficulties. They lived on the edges of bohemia, in the seedy backstreets where down-at-heel actors, journalists and political agitators met. Eleanor had a small allowance from Engels, and from time to time there came small payments representing royalties on her father's books. But worse than the financial difficulties were the emotional upsets, the loneliness when Aveling went in search of other women, the greater loneliness when he was "in one of his moods," present in the same room but terrifyingly withdrawn, with the accusing look in his eyes. He could reduce her to terror by his silences. She knew the "marriage" was a mistake, but she clung to it with desperation.

Many women felt an unreasoning fear and horror of Aveling, and many men simply dismissed him as a "ruffian" and refused to have anything to do with him. Many who were invited to Engels' Sunday lunches refused to return, because Aveling was always there. Olive Schreiner, the South African novelist who became Eleanor's closest woman friend, suspected that Eleanor would break under the strain, and she was not particularly surprised when she heard that Eleanor tried to kill herself with an overdose of opium. She was rescued just in time. Exactly what Aveling had done or said to bring about this attempted suicide is unknown, but it is not difficult to guess.

From time to time Eleanor would write brief articles in the socialist press about her father. These articles are full of her overwhelming affection for her father: his gentleness, his kindness, his delight in having children around him, and his strange way with animals, which always trusted him implicitly. She described how when she was five or six years old she was deeply moved by the beautiful music in a Roman Catholic Church, and went to her father, who at once gave her a sermon about the carpenter "whom the rich men killed," so that everything was made clear to her; and she remembered her father saying: "After all, we can forgive Christianity much, because it taught us to love children." In these articles, too, she spoke movingly about the way her father introduced the children to great literature, reading aloud to them *Don Quixote,* Homer, the *Nibelungenlied,* the *Arabian Nights,* all of Shakespeare, Marryat, James Fenimore Cooper, and Scott. There was a veritable cult of Scott in the house, drawing its strength from the knowledge that Jenny von Westphalen was descended from the ferocious clan of Campbell.

But these brief memoirs told only half the story, and when Eleanor in her loneliness opened out her heart to Olive Schreiner she would speak haltingly, and always a little evasively, about the other, darker half. "If you had ever been in our home," she wrote, "if you had ever seen my Father and Mother, known what *he* was to me, you would understand better both my yearning for love, given and received, and my intense need for sympathy. Of my father I was so sure! For long miserable years there was a shadow between us—I must tell you the whole story some day (if it will not be too much worry for you)—yet our love was always the same, and despite everything, our faith and trust in each other." What was the shadow which lay between them "for long miserable years"? Eleanor does not say, but it appears to have been Marx's absolute refusal while he was living to let her lead her own life. She was tied to him by chains of iron, and could never escape from him. After his death, she was tied by equally strong chains to Aveling, who resembled her father in that he was learned, charming, brutally sarcastic, and utterly unscrupulous, possessing the same ferocious hot temper and the same incapacity to earn any money.

There were other shadows in the family, and these too Eleanor would describe hesitantly in her letters to Olive Schreiner. "My mother and I loved each other passionately," Eleanor wrote, "but she did not know me as Father did. One of the bitterest of many bitter sorrows in my life is that my mother died thinking, despite all our love, that I had been hard and cruel, and never guessing that to save her and Father sorrow I had sacrificed the best, freshest years of my life. But Father, though he did not *know* till just before the end, felt he must trust me—our natures were so exactly alike!" Eleanor was wrong when she described herself as having the same nature as her father.

But if there were heavy shadows over her life with her parents and with Aveling, there were also moments of intense pleasure. She enjoyed making rousing speeches at workers' clubs with Aveling at her side to explain that she was the dedicated daughter of Marx, the standard-bearer of the coming revolution. She enjoyed her amateur theatricals, and she was observed to be especially happy during the "brief jaunt" to the United States and Canada which took place in 1887. Engels had at first decided to make the journey alone, but later decided to take his friend Karl Schorlemmer with him, and later still it occurred to him that Eleanor and Aveling would like to accompany him. As one might expect, Engels cast a disapproving eye on America. New York, in particular, disgusted him with its noise and vulgarity, its *nouveaux riches* and the worn faces of the poor. He complained about "the hideous sounds on water and on land," which were so different from the sounds he heard in his own quiet residential district of London, and he was appalled by the omnipresent "advertising, puffing, and croupier faces." He came to the odd conclusion that "the Americans have no faculty for enjoyment," and explained that this was due to the fact that the melting pot had not yet assimilated the various elements which had gone into it, although he recognized that the country was obviously on the eve of vast strides and would become the greatest power in the world. His journey to America was not made in a serious spirit of inquiry; he wanted a change of atmosphere; and it delighted him to see old friends like Friedrich Sorge, who lived in Hoboken. And when he spent a few days in Canada, he announced that it was a decaying and retrogressive country, ripe for dissolution.

As usual, Aveling behaved abominably. He was insolent and corrupt, stealing money from the American socialists, living extravagantly, parading his liaison with Eleanor as though it was some special grace granted to him by Marx, whom he had met only once in his lifetime and then only briefly. Soon rumors of his odd behavior reached Europe, and Engels found himself in the strange position of having to defend his closest confidant from the charge of theft and Eleanor from the charge of living luxuriously. To some he would say that these charges were nonsense, to others he would say that Aveling "had brought it on himself through his weakness for poetic dreaming." To Sorge he wrote in August 1887: "I have given him a good shaking up, and Tussy will do the rest. He is very gifted and useful, and thoroughly honest, but as gushing as a boy, and always inclined to some absurdity. Well, I still remember the times when I was just such a noodle."

He was continually defending Aveling out of loyalty to Eleanor, and it seems never to have occurred to him that Aveling was more a liability than an asset. "When we run down Marxism, we mean Aveling," Sidney Webb once remarked to Bernstein. Sometimes Engels would ponder why the English socialists came so rarely to his house, and Aveling would explain it away with amusing tirades against the inadequacy and folly of English socialists, who had never appreciated the mighty works of Marx.

From time to time Engels would grow restless and he would be overcome by a strange wanderlust. In the summer of 1890 he toured Scandinavia up to the North Cape with Karl Schorlemmer as his sole companion. He found Norway "in some respects like Switzerland," and complained about Norwegian beer. As a scientist, he was puzzled to discover that the Norwegians built their houses of wood, "although they have 1,000,000 times more stone." It was a very brief tour, and he was glad to return to the comfort of his London house, the books and letters arriving with every post, the good meals provided by Helene Demuth, the work on the third volume of *Das Kapital* still uncompleted, Aveling and Eleanor in constant attendance.

Helene Demuth was ailing. She suffered from arthritic pains in her legs and hips; and sometimes Paul Lafargue would wonder whether her arthritis did not come from her heavy drinking. He thought it would be better if she diluted her wine and drank less beer. He recommended magnesium citrate at every meal, a cruel punishment for someone who had such a fondness for food. She had spent part of the preceding winter with the Lafargues in Paris in the hope of escaping from the chills of an English winter, but it had rained miserably and she returned to England more arthritic and asthmatic than ever. All that summer she was in failing health, and when the autumn came she was obviously dying.

She had pains in the groin, began to menstruate again, and complained of numbness in her legs. The doctors examined her and found a suspicious spot at the orifice of the uterus and some evidence of spreading septicemia; they prescribed quinine. She lived on nothing but beef tea and milk. The thrombosis in the left leg seemed to take its natural course, the pains subsided, she became drowsy and listless, her face yellow, her pulse rapid and feverish. From time to time she regained consciousness, looked weakly round the bedroom, and then fell asleep again.

She died on November 4, 1890. A few hours before her death she signed her will with an X, leaving everything to her son. When the doctors examined the body, they learned that she had died of cancer of the bowel and perforative peritonitis. On the death certificate she was described as a "housekeeper and domestic."

So she was, but she was also very much more. "We were the last two of the pre-1848 old guard," Engels wrote in a letter to Sorge. "If Marx, for many years, and I, for the last seven years, have found the quiet required for work, it was largely her doing. I don't know what will become of me now. And I shall miss her wonderfully tactful advice on party affairs." With Eleanor's approval, it was decided to bury her in the Marx family plot at Highgate Cemetery. Various tentative ideas were proposed for the inscription on the revised tombstone. Finally it was decided that all phrases like "the beloved servant" and "dear faithful Lenchen" could be dispensed with, and she appears simply as "Helena Demuth Born January 1st 1823 Died November 4th 1890."

In her last years she grew heavy and stout, and all traces of her earlier beauty vanished. She spent her days in the kitchen, keeping close to the fire. She had helped Marx in more ways than he ever admitted, and when Engels spoke of "her wonderfully tactful advice on party affairs," he was saying no more than the truth. She was Marx's touchstone, the only proletarian he came to know well. As she lay dying on that dark November afternoon, she may have found some gratification in the thought that she had protected him and made his work possible. She had been his slave, and willingly accepted the yoke.

Engels did not wait long before acquiring a new housekeeper. Louise Strasser, the divorced wife of Karl Kautsky, was living nearby. A delicately worded note was sent to her, and she immediately came to live with him as his housekeeper. She was vivacious, intelligent, and good-looking; and soon she became his secretary, mistress of the house, and archivist. She became so indispensable that when she married Dr. Ludwig Freyberger in 1894, Engels decided to move into a larger house and invited her and her husband to stay with him. By training she was a midwife; and sometimes it amused Engels to think that with a doctor and a midwife in the house, every eventuality had been provided for.

With his vast correspondence, his friendships extending across the whole of Europe, and visitors coming every day to report on the Social Democratic movement, he needed the comfort of her protection. He was endlessly busy: books, articles, pronunciamentos, flowed from his pen. The work on the remaining volumes of *Das Kapital* went on unabated. All this work was necessary because he felt that he alone, as the appointed successor of Marx, could give guidance and direction to the communist movement.

Throughout his life his sympathies were with Germany, and he was continually pressing the claims of the German Social Democratic party. Consciously or unconsciously, he permitted his German sympathies to color his writings, so that the French communists were sometimes puzzled by his insistence that they should submit their own interests to Germany's. He protested vigorously against the Franco-Russian alliance on the grounds that Russia and France could easily destroy Germany and with it the most powerful Social Democratic party in Europe. At the same time he maintained that the position he had earned by fifty years of work gave him an independence of outlook which permitted him to regard all the European socialist parties with detachment. He claimed to be the arbiter of all disputes, the sole repository of communist truth, but there were very few who relished his claim. Like Marx he was continually announcing that great crises were at hand, and sometimes his interpretation of history as a series of imminent crises which must be turned to the advantage of the working class had a hollow ring about it. By constantly repeating the same theses he came finally to weary of them, and toward the end of his life he took some small comfort in admitting his errors.

In July 1893 he wrote to Franz Mehring that historical materialism, by which history was interpreted merely as an accumulation of economic forces, was merely a propagandist's device. It had been a necessary device, but he admitted now that it had given the enemies of communism many opportunities for distorting communist doctrine. Historical materialism was the keystone of the arch; he found it wanting.

He explained the method by which Marx had arrived at historical materialism:

> Ideology is a process accomplished by the so-called thinker consciously, it is true, but with a false consciousness. The real motive forces impelling him remain unknown to him; otherwise it simply would not be an ideological process. Hence he imagines false or seeming motive forces. Because it is a process of thought it derives its form as well as its content from pure thought, either his own or that of his predecessors. He works with mere thought material, which he accepts without examination as the product of thought, and does not investigate further for a more remote source independent of thought; indeed this is a matter of course to him, because, as all action is *mediated* by thought, it appears to him to be ultimately based on thought.

In this labored fashion Engels came to terms with the mystery which lay at the heart of Marx's thinking. Too late he admitted that he was mistaken, but the consequences of that error were to be felt in all the elaborations of Marxist doctrine. "The mistake has always struck me only later," he wrote in the same letter. There were many mistakes which struck him "only later," but the damage had already been done. Armed with the simplicities of historical materialism, revolutions would be waged, and the people who suffered these revolutions would see their civilization uprooted and replaced by one more in conformity with the science of historical materialism. Historical materialism was an error, but it had come to stay.

In August 1893 the International Socialist Congress met in Zurich, and Engels was elected honorary chairman. He made the journey with Louise Strasser and Dr. Freyberger, with frequent stops in Germany and the Rhineland to see the places he had known and loved. It was a triumphal progress, and he was keenly aware that he was the center of a cult. He would speak about himself deprecatingly, saying that he owed whatever renown he possessed to the fact that he had been the humble assistant of Marx. In Vienna he declared that he had never hoped for any reward, but it had been abundantly given to him in the triumph of the Social Democratic movement. "We are a great power now," he said. "We are to be feared. More depends on us than on the other great powers. This is my real pride!"

In Vienna he was especially attracted to the women, who reminded him of the Parisian *grisettes* he had known fifty years before. He met Adelheid Dvorak, "a delicious little factory girl," and he would elope with her whenever the conversation became too exhausting. Under the name of Adelheid Popp she became one of the leading Austrian Socialists. He met the Russians Vera Zasulich and Clara Zetkin, admiring them at a suitable distance, for they lacked the charm of the Viennese.

He was glad when all the festivities were over, and he was back again in the spacious house on Regent's Park Road, with a doctor and a midwife attending him. He suffered from an inexplicable lameness, bronchitis, pneumonia, occasional attacks of giddiness, but all these would pass, leaving him shaken but still capable of working for a few hours each day. For fifteen years he had had trouble with his sight, but Dr. Freyberger hovered over him and permitted him to read for a few hours each day. In June 1895 he wrote to Marx's old friend Nikolay Danielson that he felt poorly, but it was nothing serious; he would soon recover. He suffered from a strange soreness of the throat which grew progressively worse. Dr. Freyberger never told him the name of the incurable disease he was suffering from. Unable to talk, Engels was reduced to conversing with the help of a slate. He died quietly on the evening of August 5, 1895, with Louise and Dr. Freyberger at his side. The disease he was suffering from was a progressive cancer of the throat.

On the death certificate he was described as a man of independent means. He was in fact much richer than anyone had guessed, for the gross value of his personal estate was £25,267.

In his will he divided his estate into eight parts: two parts went to Louise Freyberger, three parts to Laura, three parts to Eleanor. The daughters of Karl Marx received about £7,000 each, a sum which, if wisely invested, would have permitted them to live in comfort for the rest of their lives. Strangely nothing was left to the children of Jenny Marx and Charles Longuet. Samuel Moore, Eduard Bernstein and Louise Freyberger were appointed executors. To August Bebel and Eduard Bernstein he bequeathed his correspondence with Marx, and Eleanor inherited Marx's family papers, which had been entrusted to Engels. The documents bequeathed to Bebel and Bernstein survived, but many of the papers inherited by Eleanor vanished or were destroyed.

Engels had asked that his body should be cremated and his ashes thrown into the sea. On August 27, more than three weeks after his death, Aveling, Eleanor, Bernstein and Friedrich Lessner placed the urn containing his ashes in a hired rowboat at Eastbourne, the seaside resort on the south coast of England which Engels had particularly liked, and when they were about two miles out to sea they dropped the urn into the English Channel.

ELEANOR MARX-AVELING

WITH THE DEATH of Engels, Eleanor Marx gradually became a shadow of herself. Like many women who have grown up under the domination of a strong-willed father, she seemed incapable of leading a normal life. She had no sense of money, no sense of ordinary human behavior. She had inherited all her father's worst qualities and little of her mother's gentleness. For the rest of her life she would live in the shadow of Edward Aveling.

She continued to write books and to edit her father's papers, but there was little market for them. She continued to make political speeches, and she still occasionally acted in private performances for workingmen, but as she grew older she gave herself up to long fits of brooding and took little part in affairs. Once Hyndman had described her as a young woman with "a broad low forehead, dark bright eyes, with glowing cheeks and a brisk humorous smile," but she rarely smiled now, as she fell into her premature old age. No longer the dauntless young woman who took the world in her stride, she appeared wan and listless, in fear of the world and especially in fear of Aveling.

William Morris, who knew him well, once called Aveling "a disreputable dog," and there were many others who shared this opinion. Some thought he was in league with the devil, for it was inconceivable that an ordinary man should be capable of creating so much evil. Only in the last months of her life did Eleanor realize that he suffered from an ineradicable moral sickness, for which there was no known cure.

In the years after Engels' death Aveling felt little need to be with her. He had once, after his graduation, been in charge of a group of strolling players who toured England, and he now spent most of his life among actors and actresses. From time to time he would visit her, demand money, speak of his conquests, and menace her in other ways. He seemed to delight in tormenting her. She lived alone with a maidservant in a small cottage in Sydenham.

In the autumn of 1897 there seemed to be a sudden change in his manner toward her. He took her to Lancashire on a propaganda tour, and for a few brief days they were happy together. When Aveling caught influenza and was on the edge of death from pneumonia, she nursed him back to health, but he had scarcely recovered when he fell victim to the same malady which had so often struck Marx. A huge fistula appeared in his groin. It was not the first time he was plagued with fistulas; there had been a smaller one four years before. The doctors were convinced that to save his life they must operate. Some days passed while arrangements were made to find a suitable hospital. Finally, it was decided to place him in Middlesex Hospital, and the operation was performed by Dr. Christopher Heath. Eleanor took up lodgings on Gower Street nearby. She was determined to do everything to bring him back to health. She convinced herself that his menaces, his ill temper, his bouts of self-pity, even his dallyings with other women, sprang from his ill-health. Once he had recuperated, there would be harmony and peace in the household.

So she believed, but sometimes she found it difficult to sustain her belief. The Hyndmans had helped her to find a doctor, and they were with her as she paced up and down the corridor, waiting to learn the outcome. Suddenly she broke down and began to tell Mrs. Hyndman about all the humiliations and miseries she had suffered at Aveling's hands. It was a torrential outpour, and Mrs. Hyndman listened in astonishment. She knew exactly what must be done—Eleanor must break immediately with Aveling, or if not immediately, then as soon as he had recovered from the operation. Eleanor, distraught, promised to make a complete break. Hyndman, who knew Aveling and detested him, hoped the knife would slip; and when Aveling recovered, he was inclined to blame the doctor. He had no illusions about Eleanor. He knew she would never be able to escape from him. The day after the operation she took him back to the house in Sydenham. The doctors suggested that as soon as he was well enough, she should take him to Margate.

She enjoyed Margate, for it reminded her of a visit many years ago with her father. But Aveling was a demanding patient. The wound in his groin had to be bathed and bandaged twice a day; there were medicines to give him; he had to be coaxed into being fed. She lived among bandages, salves, medicine bottles, the foul-smelling pus which had to be continually drawn out of the wound. A doctor helped her in the morning. In the evening she had to do the work alone. "It is a terrible business," she wrote to her old friend Wilhelm Liebknecht, who was in prison in Germany. "It means forcing a syringe into the open wound and batting it out, squeezing it (the wound) from all sides. And then *forcing* by a sinus forceps a 'plug' into the wound. You can think what pain this is to Edward, and how awful it is to have to do this."

She would have been happier, she wrote, if she had herself been in Edward's position, for she thought she could bear intense suffering bravely. He complained of the pain, and demanded her absolute attention. When the pain was endurable, he would permit her to wheel him up and down the esplanade in a wheelchair.

Despair was the landscape in which she moved, and there was no end to it. She knew that Aveling would abandon her the moment he recovered. He did not love her. She was merely someone he used for his own purposes. Sometimes she would confide her doubts and fears to Frederick Demuth, her half brother. She had come to know him well after Engels' death, and she trusted him implicitly. Some of her letters to him have survived. They portray a woman drained of energy, without spiritual resources, living out her ghostly life in fear and trembling. One of the few things that sustained her was the knowledge that Liebknecht would soon be released from prison.

"You would not know my poor Edward if you saw him now," she wrote. "He is a very skeleton and can hardly walk a few yards." So she wrote to Liebknecht at the beginning of the month, when he was still weak following the operation. He seemed to recover very slowly, and he was continually demanding that she wheel him up and down the esplanade. All through their life together he had dominated her ruthlessly. It remained for him now to perform the last service he could render her —to kill her.

The rest of the story can be told simply. On March 28, 1898, they returned from Margate to Sydenham. Eleanor seems to have been in better spirits than for many weeks. She invited friends to visit her during the early part of April, accepted an invitation to attend a banquet given in honor of Hyndman, and spent some time searching in Sydenham for someone who might be able to lend them an invalid chair, for Aveling was still bedridden and she wanted to take him out in the open air now that fine days were coming.

On March 31, with the first post, there came a letter which put an end to her brief contentment.

Exactly what the letter contained is unknown, because Aveling destroyed it. It has been supposed that it was a cutting from a newspaper announcing the marriage before the Chelsea Registrar on June 8, 1897, between a certain Alec Nelson and a twenty-two-year-old actress called Eva Frye. Alec Nelson was one of the pseudonyms of Aveling.

What is certain is that Eleanor was confronted with a sudden overwhelming crisis. Her world collapsed. She had spent the previous day hunting for an invalid chair for her beloved, thinking only of the time when he would be well again, and she saw now with piercing clarity that he would never be well, that he would continue to deceive her until the end of her life, and that all her worst fears were well-founded. Aveling, too, was confronted with a crisis. He had known it would come, and was well prepared for it. He suggested that there was a supremely simple solution to their problems—they should both commit suicide. They would die together in each other's arms, and in this way he would prove his eternal devotion to her. Moreover he was bedridden, slowly dying of a nauseating disease, with nothing to live for, and death would be a solace to both of them. The maid Gertrude Mary Gentry was sent off to the chemist with a note. It read: "Please give the bearer chloroform and a small quantity of prussic acid for the dog.—E.A." With the note went Aveling's card. The maid returned with the poison and the poison book: against the entry relating to the prussic acid someone, probably Aveling, wrote the initials "E.M.A." He knew how to forge her initials, for forgery was one of the minor arts he had cultivated. He also knew a good deal about poisons, and in the past he had had several discussions about them with the chemist.

Eleanor prepared herself for death by putting on a white dress, perhaps remembering Flaubert's *Madame Bovary* which she had translated into English twelve years before. After Madame Bovary's death, her husband insisted that she should be dressed completely in white. Madame Bovary, too, had written a brief note to her husband after taking the poison. Eleanor offered to be the first to take the poison, which came in a small bottle. There was no one else except Aveling in the house, for the maid had returned to the chemist with the poison book.

Aveling had accomplished his purpose almost too neatly. For many days he had been shamming weakness; he had no need of an invalid chair. While Eleanor was dying, he rose, dressed, and left the house. He took the next train for London, walked to the office of the Social Democratic Federation, and remembered to call the secretary's attention to the time of his arrival. He arrived there shortly after eleven o'clock. At a quarter of eleven Gertrude Mary Gentry, surprised by the long silence of her mistress, entered the bedroom. Eleanor was still breathing faintly, but when the servant talked to her there was no reply. The bottle of prussic acid stood on the table, and nearby there was a note reading: "Dear, it will soon be over. My last word to you is the same that I have said during all those long sad years—love."

There was another note addressed to her nephew Johnny Longuet, her favorite among Jenny's children. It read: "My dear, dear Johnny. My last word is for you. May it be your task to be worthy of your grandfather. Your *tante* Tussy."

A few days later there was a coroner's inquest. Since Aveling had not been in the house at the time of her death, the question of murder did not arise. The coroner was troubled by the behavior of Aveling and found him an uncooperative witness. An account of the inquest was published on April 8, 1898, in the *Forest Hill and Sydenham Examiner*. In those fading pages we learn all we shall probably ever know about Eleanor's death:

TRAGIC SUICIDE AT SYDENHAM REVELATIONS AT THE INQUEST

Considerable interest was manifested at the inquest of the body of Eleanor Marx Aveling of the Den, Jew's Walk, Sydenham, who committed suicide on Thursday morning of last week, the inquiry into the circumstances being conducted by Mr. E. N. Wood, the deputy coroner, at the Park Hall, Sydenham, on Saturday night.

The first witness was Mr. Edward Aveling, better known as Dr. Aveling, who described himself as an author residing at the Den, Jew's Walk.

Coroner: Was the deceased your wife?

Witness: Legally do you mean?

Coroner: You are a most difficult man. Were you married to the deceased?

Witness: Not legally.

Coroner: She lived with you as your wife, do you mean?

Witness: Yes.

Coroner: What was her age?

Witness: I believe she was about forty, but I am not sure.

Coroner: Was her health good usually?

Witness: Very.

Coroner: Had she had any medical attendance?

Witness: Not professionally, but Dr. Shackleton had seen her from time to time.

Continuing, witness stated that it was not until five o'clock on Thursday afternoon that he had heard that she was dead. The last time he saw her alive was at 10.10 the same morning. He told her that he was going to town. She however did not want him to go on account of his health having been so bad lately.

Coroner: Had you any idea that she would destroy herself?

Witness: She had threatened to do so several times.

Coroner: Did you consider that the threats were intentional?

Witness: I regarded them as idle because they were so frequently expressed.

Coroner: Had you any quarrel before you left in the morning?

Witness: None whatever.

Questioned by the Foreman, Witness stated that they had had slight differences, but had never had any serious quarrel. The deceased was of a morbid disposition and had several times suggested that they commit suicide together. When they had difficulties, it was not infrequent for her to say, "Let us end all these difficulties together."

Coroner: Do you mean pecuniary difficulties?

Witness: Yes—pecuniary. Not, however, so much recently as in the past.

Gertrude Gentry, the deceased's servant, said Mrs. Aveling had been much worried lately in consequence of Dr. Aveling's illness. On Thursday morning, just before ten o'clock, Mrs. Aveling sent her with a note to Mr. Dale, the chemist, and she took back a small white parcel and a book for Mrs. Aveling to sign. Deceased took the book into the front room and witness believed she signed it. After Dr. Aveling had gone, Mrs. Aveling went upstairs. About 10.45 witness went upstairs and on entering Mrs. Aveling's bedroom, she saw the deceased who was undressed in bed. She was just breathing and witness asked her if she was not well, but she made no reply. She called Mrs. Kell and went for the doctor.

Dr. Aveling was recalled.

Coroner: You say you were not married to the deceased. Tell me what was her name.

Witness: Her proper name was Eleanor Marx, but she adopted my name.

Mrs. Ellen Florrie Kell, wife of Mr. Frederick John Kell, an artist, said that when she entered the bedroom the deceased was quite dead.

Mr. George Edgar Dale, Chemist, 92 Kirkdale, Sydenham, was now called.

Coroner: I am not sure you have exceeded the Act of Parliament, so you can please yourself whether you answer any of the questions I might put. You must bear in mind that in answering my questions, should any proceedings be taken against you, they might be used against you. Were you acquainted with the deceased?

Witness: Slightly, as a customer.

Coroner: Did you receive a letter and a card?

Witness: Yes, on Thursday morning.

Coroner: Did the letter say "Please give bearer chloroform and a small quantity of prussic acid for a dog. E.A."

Witness: Yes, and Dr. Aveling's card was enclosed.

Coroner: What did you do?

Witness: I hesitated whether I would send the prussic acid, and after deliberation, and as I thought Dr. Aveling was a qualified man, I thought it would be allowable to send it.

Coroner: Did you think the note was in Dr. Aveling's handwriting?

Witness: Yes, and particularly as his card accompanied it.

Further questioned, Mr. Dale said he sent 2 oz. of chloroform and one dram of prussic acid, that being the quantity for poisoning a dog.

Coroner: Comparing the signature in the poison book with that in the note he noticed that the initials simply contained E.A., the signature in the book was E.M. Aveling.

Witness: I did not notice that at the time.

Coroner: You knew that Mr. Aveling was not a qualified practitioner?

Witness: I always understood he was. In my conversation with him I always addressed him as "Doctor" and believed he was a qualified man.

Further questioned by a juryman, Mr. Dale said he had supplied Dr. Aveling with chloroform, laudanum and poisons.

Coroner: He is not registered. I am afraid you have acted very wrongly. Of course I do not want to prejudice your case, but it will be necessary to report your conduct to the Public Prosecutor. It is no use having acts of parliament if they are to be treated in this perfunctory manner.

Dr. Shackleton deposed to having made a post mortem examination and formed the opinion that death was due to poisoning by prussic acid.

The jury returned a verdict of suicide whilst in a state of temporary insanity.

Dr. Aveling after the verdict had been returned stated to the coroner and to the jury that he had been married before and that was the reason he was not married to the deceased.

If the coroner had spent more time examining Dr. Aveling, and less in censuring the chemist, he might have learned more about the death of Eleanor Marx. In particular he might have asked why he had wanted the chloroform, and whether there was a dog in the household, and why he had needed poisons in the past. He had said that Eleanor was suicidal: why give her the opportunity to kill herself? He was morally responsible for her death, even though it might have been impossible to bring a charge of murder against him.

Eleanor died on Thursday, March 31. On the following Tuesday a few friends and members of the Social Democratic Federation met at the Necropolis Station at Waterloo, and Will Thorne, the labor leader, delivered the address over her coffin, while Aveling indulged in histrionic grief. Eleanor's body was shipped by train to Woking to be cremated, and her ashes were given to the Social Democratic Federation and kept in their offices just off Fleet Street. They remained there for some years until they became the property of the Socialist Party, and the urn decorated their headquarters in Maiden Lane. In 1920, when the Communist Party of Great Britain was formed, the urn was claimed by the communist leaders as their legitimate property, and so it was transferred to their new headquarters in King Street, Covent Garden, not far from Eleanor's birthplace.

The adventures of Eleanor's ashes were not yet over. For a while it was thought that they might be sent to Moscow: later it was decided to keep them in the Marx Memorial Library on Clerkenwell Green. The library was small and shabby, reached by a long flight of rickety wooden steps; it stood over a teashop and a furniture manufacturer. Here Harry Quelch, the English socialist, edited *Justice* at the turn of the century, and Lenin had used a little back room, scarcely larger than a cupboard, when he was editing *Iskra*. Felix Barker, who was the first to inquire seriously into the circumstances of Eleanor Marx's death, visited the Marx Memorial Library in 1953. He had been wondering what had happened to Eleanor's ashes. He knew they were no longer at the headquarters of the Communist Party. The librarian smiled slowly, and said: "We have them right here."

In 1956 the ashes of Eleanor Marx came to their last resting place. The Communist Party decided that Marx deserved a more prominent tombstone, and accordingly a new site for the grave was found halfway up the cemetery slope. The original tombstone was a small one, lying in an obscure and desolate place, flat against the earth, crowded among a thousand similar tombstones. The new stone was a granite monolith ten feet high topped with a singularly ugly bust of Marx of hammered iron. Below the granite monolith there lie the mortal remains of Jenny and Karl Marx, Helene Demuth, and Harry Longuet, the child who died in the same week as Marx. There, too, is the small urn containing the ashes of Eleanor.

The iron Marx is depicted as a man of grave ferocity, with jutting brow and thickly tangled beard. He gazes up the hill at a forest of advancing angels, and towers above the stone crosses at his feet. Not far away lies the tomb of Herbert Spencer, who once declared that socialism was slavery.

When Eleanor died, Aveling returned to his twenty-two-year-old bride. He had become the heir of all those possessions of Marx which had fallen to Eleanor, the royalties on his books, the papers and documents which had once filled a large library, for Eleanor had left him everything she owned. It was in his power to proclaim himself the leader of the Communist Party, the heir by direct line of descent, the legislator of the new doctrines. Instead, that role passed to Eduard Bernstein, who hated him. Bernstein was a close friend of Hyndman, and both of them believed that Aveling was responsible for Eleanor's death.

On April 16, eleven days after she had been cremated, the will of Eleanor Marx-Aveling "of the Den, Jew's Walk, Sydenham in the County of Kent, Spinster" was probated. The administration of the estate was granted to Aveling as sole executor. The gross value of the estate was £1,909 3s. 10d. It was a welcome windfall for a man who was close to bankruptcy.

The death of Eleanor shook the Social Democratic Federation. At meetings which took place in the Federation headquarters off Fleet Street, Eleanor was remembered. They spoke in hushed tones of her intelligence, her buoyancy, her love for the working class, and her unhappy relationship with Aveling. They remembered other things. Lee, the secretary, remembered that Aveling had pointedly called his attention to the exact time of his arrival at the office on the fatal day. They learned that on the day before Eleanor had been hunting all over Sydenham for an invalid chair for a man who was perfectly capable of walking. They learned too that the post-mortem showed that Eleanor was in sound health before she took the poison. They knew more about her way of life than the coroner. Hyndman, Will Thorne, and many others were sure she had been murdered. None of them knew that Aveling had been secretly married to Eva Frye; if they had known, they would have been even more convinced that it was murder.

Someone pointed out to Aveling that it was no longer required of him that he attend meetings of the Federation. Ostracized by his friends, he took no further part in the labor movement. With Eleanor's legacy he could pay off his debts and live quietly with his wife. He abandoned Sydenham, and set up house in Stafford Mansions in Albert Bridge Mansions Road, Battersea, and there, four months later, he died at the age of forty-seven. According to his doctor he died of a kidney disease which had been troubling him for many years. According to Eduard Bernstein he died quite suddenly one afternoon while sitting in the sunshine and reading a book.

Eduard Bernstein had excellent reasons for inquiring into the circumstances of Aveling's death. Originally he had been named as the executor of Eleanor's will drawn up in October 1895. In this will she left the royalties from her father's books to the children of her sister Jenny Longuet. By a codicil drawn up in November 1896 the royalties reverted to Aveling, who also inherited all the rest of her property and was appointed sole executor. Bernstein was to have received all her books and twenty-five pounds "for the trouble he shall have in carrying out the trusts of this my will." By the terms of the codicil he received nothing.

Although Aveling received nearly two thousand pounds by the terms of Eleanor's will, he seems to have spent the money prodigally. His own will, written less than a month before his death, left his entire estate to Eva Nelson, the former Eva Frye. The gross value of the estate of "Edward Aveling professionally known as Alec Nelson" was £852. The possessions of Eleanor Marx became the property of a young actress, and vanished. Somewhere in London, hidden among theatrical trunks in an abandoned loft, there may one day be found the books and papers which had once belonged to Eleanor Marx.

It was the fate of all Marx's legitimate children to die tragically. Thirteen years after Eleanor's suicide, Laura and Paul Lafargue committed suicide. They had been living quietly at Draveil, a small town on the outskirts of Paris, but they had little to live for. Once rich, Lafargue had lost most of his money. Sometimes visitors came to see them, and there would be talk of the great days long ago when Marx had held the International in the palm of his hand. Lenin came to visit them, accompanied by his wife Nadezhda Krupskaya, who found Laura strangely remote. Once, speaking of her husband, she said: "He will soon prove the sincerity of his philosophical opinions." Nadezhda Krupskaya was puzzled, but she understood the meaning of the words a year later. In November 1911 they entered into a pact to commit suicide, because old age had come and they had no strength left for the struggle. "No, I cannot approve it," Lenin wrote. "They could still write, they could still accomplish things, and even if they could no longer work efficiently they could still observe and give good advice." At the funeral, as the representative of the Russian Social Democratic movement, he delivered a speech in their honor, prophesying that within a few years the revolutionary ideas of Marx would receive their triumphant vindication.

Of the legitimate descendants of Marx there remained the children of his eldest daughter Jenny Longuet. Three sons and a daughter survived. Jean (Johnny), the eldest, grew up to become a lawyer, and in 1914 he was elected a socialist deputy, becoming, after the murder of Jean Jaurès, one of the leaders of the left wing of the French socialists. He showed little interest in Marxism, regarding himself as the heir of the French revolutionary tradition. Edgar, the second son, became a doctor, while his younger brother Marcel grew up to become a journalist of impeccable bourgeois leaning. Jenny, the only daughter, never married. She died at the age of seventy in 1952, having outlived all her brothers.

The third generation of Marx's descendants included a sculptor, a landscape painter, a planter in Madagascar, an automobile salesman, and a socialist lawyer, Robert-Jean, who never married. He was the last of the revolutionary descendants of Karl Marx, for all his cousins became solid middle-class citizens. Today there are fourteen descendants of Marx, all living in France.

FREDERICK DEMUTH

THERE REMAINED one survivor about whom, until recently, very little was known. This was Frederick Demuth, Marx's illegitimate son, who survived well into the present century, living in such complete obscurity that his traces were always difficult to follow. He would emerge briefly, say a few words, and then vanish again. After another long interval the dusty records would reveal some small detail about his life and character, and for another brief moment he would walk across the stage. Sometimes, as I followed him, I had the illusion that I was following in the path of a ghost who deliberately concealed himself in the shadows.

Marx had hoped that the existence of his illegitimate son would never become known. Yet no one lives on this earth without leaving some traces of himself. There are always documents, letters, birth certificates, death certificates, wills, entries in municipal registers. If he died less than fifty years ago, it might be possible to find people who remembered him; and if he died long ago, there might be people who remembered others speaking about him. In the end it was possible to find seven people who remembered him vividly. His birth and death certificates were found, and the electoral rolls showed where he lived during the later years of his life. The records of many of the factories where he worked have been destroyed, and all references to him in the letters of Marx and Engels have been suppressed, but there exist the letters written to him by Eleanor Marx and there is enough material to provide a rounded portrait of the man.

The following account of Frederick Demuth is based on the recollections of people who knew him and surviving documents.

Of his early years we know nothing. According to Louise Freyberger, who was close to Engels, Marx refused to have any part in his upbringing. Helene Demuth may have given the child to a foundling home, but it is much more likely that she found a working-class family in London who would bring up the child. She was not an irresponsible woman, and she evidently watched over her son. In the correspondence between Laura Lafargue and Engels, Freddy's name appears for the first time on February 1, 1887, as someone who is in need. "I spoke to Longuet again on the subject of Freddy," Laura writes. "He renewed his former promises to send him something."

We are not told why Frederick Demuth was in need, or why Longuet, who was far less wealthy than Engels, should have been asked to send him something. In a letter to Paul Lafargue two days earlier, Engels wrote: "Nym wants to know if Laura had spoken to Longuet and what was his reply." The request for help had therefore come from Helene Demuth. Engels, Laura Lafargue, Paul Lafargue, Jenny Longuet, and Charles Longuet all knew a good deal about Freddy, but we have no means of knowing how much they knew or what role he played in their lives.

If Frederick Demuth was in need in 1887, he was no longer in need the following year, for on February 18, 1888, he was admitted into the

Associated Society of Engineers as a skilled fitter and turner in the King's Cross (London) Branch. He was evidently a highly skilled workman, for he was admitted into what was known as "Section 1," which was reserved only for the most qualified workmen. He was entitled to unemployment, sickness and superannuation benefits. At the time he claimed that he was 35 years and 8 months old. He had knocked one year off his real age, and as we shall see later he liked to give out that he was younger than he was.

For the rest of his life he was to remain a member of the union. The son of Karl Marx was a skilled workman who served the standard six-year apprenticeship and was sufficiently proficient at his job to be admitted into the highest section of his union. He lived in London, and could therefore visit his mother whenever he pleased.

On November 4, 1890, Helene Demuth died in Engels' house in London. Shortly before her death, when she was very weak and nearly unconscious, she was able to write her mark on her will. She left "all my monies effects and other property to Frederick Lewis Demuth of 25 Gransden Avenue London Lane Hackney and being too weak bodily to sign my name have affixed hereto my mark in the presence of the undersigned witnesses." The witnesses were Engels, Edward Aveling, and Eleanor Marx-Aveling. Ten days later the will was probated, and Frederick Demuth, described as "an engineer," became the universal legatee of an estate which amounted to £95. This was all the money she was able to accumulate during all the years she had served Marx and then Engels.

Gransden Avenue, London Lane, Hackney might suggest a very large and spacious street with middle-class houses. In fact the avenue is a small, pathetic little alleyway of workmen's dwellings now scheduled for demolition. London Fields Railway Station stands a few hundred yards away, and the clatter of the railway can be heard in the dismal alleyway. It is one of those lost and shadowy alleyways where life seems to have come to a stop, and it cannot have been much more agreeable in the Victorian age than it is today. No. 25 is exactly like all the other houses, with its bay windows, lace curtains and tiny front gardens, no more than a few square feet of soot-blackened soil with a few straggling plants. There is a low wall protecting the garden from the street, and at one time an iron gate led up to each house. The iron gates have gone, and with them there vanished the last vestiges of respectability. The houses are very small, and one can imagine that two or three people might have lived in them comfortably, but five or six people would have found it unendurable.

In 1890, the year of Helene Demuth's death, 25 Gransden Avenue was occupied by at least seven persons. They were Henry Clayton, his wife, his two daughters, his son Charles, Frederick Demuth and his son Harry. Frederick Demuth had been a lodger in the house since about 1880. His son was born about 1883, and was apparently illegitimate.

Both Henry Clayton and Frederick Demuth were machinists, highly skilled men at the lathe, and together they earned a fair income. The two men admirably complemented each other, for Clayton was heavy-set and expansive, with an explosive temper, and Frederick Demuth was reserved and gentle, incapable of anger. They usually worked at the same machine shops, and they would set out for work with their dinner pails at the same time. Henry Clayton was a few years younger than Frederick Demuth, but he gave the impression of being about the same age, for Frederick Demuth looked younger than his years.

The two men were inseparable. They worked together, shared the same enthusiasms, and slept under the same roof. They were both socialists, but neither of them were revolutionaries. What they hoped for was social change achieved by legislation. Their heroes were not the Chartists of an earlier generation, but Tom Mann, Keir Hardie and Cunninghame Graham, who were emerging as the leaders of the Socialist Party. A good deal of the talk in the house was about politics.

Frederick Demuth had a way with children, and his favorite among the Clayton children was young Charles, who was born in 1891. As soon as the boy could talk, Frederick Demuth became his companion and friend, and they spent long hours together.

Charles Clayton is still living, and he remembers Frederick Demuth with the affection and respect reserved for a close family friend. He said recently: "Uncle Fred was a neat, dapper little chap with bright-blue eyes and a thick mustache. When his hair started to turn gray, he used to scrape walnut shells to make a reddish dye, and he dyed his hair and mustache with it. He was very quick in his movements and smiled a lot. He always held himself upright, and when he went to work he always carried a gladstone bag, and I had the feeling that it was empty. It was just something he liked to carry. He always wore a Muller hat—something like a derby—which workmen didn't wear very often. They wore caps.

"My father was the Paganini of the band, always up to mischief. He was a member of the union, and soon he got together with the other workmen to found the Hackney branch of the Labour Party. The founders were Fred Demuth, Henry Clayton, Jimmy Hill, Swedy Andersen and Alfred Payne, who later became Mayor of Hackney and died in office. They would go round and address meeings, and they were known as the

Musketeers. You don't hear much about them nowadays, because Herbert Morrison became Mayor of Hackney after Alfred Payne, and things began to change after that.

"Uncle Fred had a son Harry, but we never saw the boy's mother. Harry was apprenticed to an instrument maker called Harling, who made slide rules, but he did not get on well with his dad. One day they had a falling out, and the next we heard of the boy he had gone down to Portsmouth and joined the Navy. We never heard from him again, and Uncle Fred didn't talk about him."

One day in the eighties Karl Marx appears to have slept in the small house on Gransden Avenue. Charles Clayton was not yet born, but he remembers vividly an incident which occurred about 1905. Marx's name was becoming well-known in working-class circles, and Henry Clayton, who had once invited Marx to spend a night at his house, decided to honor the occasion by putting up a cast-iron plaque, reading: "Karl Marx slept here." It was a simple matter for him to hammer out the plaque, which was accordingly placed on the wall near the doorway. The owner of the house and much of the adjoining property was a certain Fortescue, whose name is still commemorated in the nearby Fortescue Road. The landlord was enraged when he saw the plaque, and ordered it taken down.

"That set off a terrible war between my father and Mr. Fortescue," Charles Clayton continued. "He wanted the plaque down, and my father wanted it up. Finally my father was forced to take it down, and on the same day he took a sledge hammer and smashed the iron gate. These gates were made of nicely curved bits of iron, and Mr. Fortescue said my father had done something very wrong and if he couldn't replace the gate exactly as it was, he would have to leave the house. My father, being a good workman, had no difficulty making another iron gate exactly like the one he had smashed, and so matters rested for a while. A year or so later we left the house for a better one, and then my father got his sledge hammer again and smashed the gate for good. We had no more trouble with Fortescue."

When Charles Clayton told this story, he did not know that Frederick Demuth was Marx's son, and imagined that the invitation to Marx had come about because Henry Clayton was prominent in Labour Party circles. But it is more likely that Marx came to Gransden Avenue to spend at least one night of his life under the same roof as his son. The strange meeting probably occurred in 1882, the year when Marx was suffering from intolerable loneliness after the death of his wife.

Charles Clayton can remember a good deal about Frederick Demuth, who pronounced his name *Deemoth* with the accent on the first syllable. He remembers, for example, that he was quiet and meticulous in manner, wore his clothes well, and was generally regarded as a cut above the other workmen. He worked at many engineering firms, never staying very long at a job. He worked at the London Small Arms, Old Ford, Thomas De la Rue, and many others. "He was a damn good turner, working on a lathe, and that's better than a fitter who spends most of his time at a bench using a file. He was nearly as good as my dad, and they were bosom friends, both rebels in their own way. Where Uncle Fred was subtle and could reason, dad was belligerent and would sooner have a fight than his dinner, for something he felt was right."

Engels, too, was a man who would "sooner have a fight than his dinner." There was a core of belligerence in him, and when he lay dying of cancer of the throat, unable to speak, writing out messages on a slate, he was in no mood to be evasive. A week or so before his death Samuel Moore, one of the translators of *Das Kapital,* came to visit him. The question of Freddy's parentage arose—that question which had been discussed secretly by so many people over so many years. Samuel Moore seems to have felt that the question should be decided once and for all by the only survivor who could speak with authority. On the slate Engels wrote that Freddy was the son of Marx. Samuel Moore then went to Orpington in Kent, where Eleanor Marx was living. He told her what Engels had said, but she protested that it was not true, that Engels himself had confessed that he was the father, and that it was necessary that Engels should make a final confession exonerating her father. Once more Samuel Moore went to the house in Regents Park Road, and once more the question was put to the dying man. Engels wrote on the slate: "Freddy is Marx's son. Tussy wants to make an idol of her father."

All this we learn from a recently discovered letter written by Louise Freyberger, the secretary and housekeeper of Engels, who was present throughout his last illness. She had met Freddy, and she felt there was not the least doubt that Marx was the father, for they were "laughably alike," and Freddy had Marx's Jewish cast of countenance and dark hair. Laura, she says, had long ago suspected it, and the secret was known to Karl Pfänder and Friedrich Lessner. As Engels' secretary, she had the free run of his correspondence and she had seen a letter written by Marx to Engels in Manchester, in which he apparently discussed Freddy at some length. As far as she was concerned, there was not the least doubt about the matter. Her final conclusion was a very simple one: Marx had refused to accept responsibility for the child because he would have had to divorce his wife the moment he accepted it. "Before Marx's eyes," she wrote, "there stood always the prospect of divorcing his wife, who was fearfully jealous. He had no love for the child, the scandal would have been too great, and he dared not do anything for the child."

This was an opinion which Eleanor, determined to uphold the family honor, was not likely to share. She hurried to London for a last meeting with Engels, arriving on Sunday, August 4, 1895, the day before his death. Once again Engels wrote on the slate that Freddy was Marx's son. Eleanor was so shattered by the news that she wept bitterly on the shoulders of Louise Freyberger. She was not weeping because Engels was dying, but because he had confirmed those suspicions which had been growing in her for many years. Her father, whom she had always thought of as a man of imperturbable moral rectitude, was now seen to be a man who would father a child on a servant girl.

Eleanor was an impulsive woman, and she did exactly what might have been expected of her. She sought out her half brother, and became very attached to him. She paid many visits to the small house in Gransden Avenue and came to know the Claytons well. On one occasion she gave Henry Clayton's wife a brooch of polished granite and two garnet earrings, saying, according to the Clayton family tradition, that they were fashioned by Karl Marx while in prison. Since Marx spent only about twelve hours of his life in prison, and was moreover quite incapable of fashioning brooches or earrings, it is more likely that the gifts came ultimately from the jewel case of Jenny Marx.

Eleanor's belated recognition that Frederick Demuth was her half brother came at a time when she was in desperate need of someone she could confide in. Edward Aveling was treating her abominably. It was not only that he continually ran after other women, but he was attempting to destroy her in every possible way, apparently in the hope of laying hands on the money left by Engels. She needed someone of her own blood, whom she could trust completely, and she found in Freddy the perfect confidant.

Nine of Eleanor's letters to Freddy have survived, all dating from the last seven months of her life. These letters are all distraught appeals for help. She begs him to see Aveling at a meeting of the Socialist Society; she wants news about the man she regards as her husband; if only Freddy will bring him back to her! She has a bed ready for Freddy at the Den, Jews Walk, Sydenham, where she is living in loneliness and misery, and what distresses her is that Freddy cannot come out and stay with her because he must be up early for work in the morning. When she learns that Aveling is about to descend on her, there is another letter to Freddy, urging him to come at once so that they can together confront the enemy, because he was threatening to sell off the house and furniture and leave her destitute and disgraced before the world. Aveling was practicing the fine art of blackmail, and she wanted Freddy to be present when Aveling made his final demands. She wrote to Freddy:

> I am so lonely, and I am faced with a fearful situation—extreme ruin—everything to the last farthing—or utter disgrace before the whole world. It is terrible. Worse than I ever imagined. And I need someone to advise me. I know I must make the final decision, and I have undertaken this responsibility—but a little advice and sympathy would be of immeasurable worth to me.
>
> So dear, dear Freddy come. I am broken.
>
> Your Tussy

The letter was written at the beginning of September 1897. Freddy immediately took the train to Sydenham, and there was the long-awaited confrontation with Aveling, who was quietly domineering, contemptuous of their arguments, and determined to have everything his own way. He was a more forceful person than Freddy could ever be, and he was able to show that Eleanor had grossly exaggerated her financial losses at his hands. Freddy told Eduard Bernstein, who later published Eleanor's letters, that Aveling produced documents and contracts showing that he was completely innocent of fraud, and he appears to have acted like a professor of economics addressing children. Nevertheless Freddy was convinced that Aveling was blackmailing Eleanor, and begged her to break off all ties with her lover. Aveling's will prevailed. With his promise to mend his ways, he was restored to her affections.

In December he caught a chill, which turned into influenza and pneumonia. Eleanor hurried him off to Hastings to recuperate, and toward the middle of January, when they returned to Sydenham, Freddy was invited to join them on the following Sunday. There would be another confrontation, another attempt to lay the ghosts of the past. Freddy wrote that he was unwell and could not come; even if he had been well, it is unlikely that he would have made the journey. He had no desire to see Aveling again, and he loved Eleanor too much to reproach her for her many weaknesses. Toward her he felt an abiding affection in which no shadow of pity was permitted to enter, but sometimes in spite of himself he found himself lamenting the hopelessness of their situation. It seemed as though nothing would ever go right for them, and he said as much in a letter declining the invitation. Eleanor wrote back on January 13, 1898, in a letter filled with brooding:

> Sometimes I have the same feeling as you, Freddy, that nothing will ever come right for us. I mean you and me. Naturally poor Jenny [Longuet] had her share of trouble and grief, and Laura [Lafargue] has lost her children. But Jenny was glad to die, and it was so sad for the children, but sometimes I think it was all for the best. I would not have wished for Jenny that she should go through the life I have had to go through. I don't think you and I have been particularly bad people—and yet, dear Freddy, it really seems as though we are being punished.

She was writing as though a curse had been visited upon the children of Marx for some crime committed in the past. Jenny's terrible illnesses, Laura's children dying in their cradles, her own interminable sufferings, even Freddy's sickness were being weighed in the balance. Soon it transpired that Aveling was suffering from a huge fistula in the upper thigh, and once more she was filled with brooding fear, and once more Freddy was invited to Sydenham. "Dear Freddy," she wrote, "you have your young one, but I have nothing, and I see nothing worth living for."

Freddy replied to her invitation with a blunt refusal. Aveling, too, wanted to see Freddy, who said he would have nothing to do with Aveling under any conditions. "Besides," he added bitterly, "Edward only wants to see me when he wants money." This was no more than the truth, for Aveling was perfectly capable of demanding loans from the poorest of his friends, even from Freddy, who earned a laborer's wage. In fact he had borrowed all of Freddy's life savings, and it was becoming increasingly clear that the loan would never be repaid.

Eleanor replied to his letter with the news that Edward was about to go into a hospital for a serious operation. He had not wanted money; on the contrary he had made the invitation with the best of motives: the operation was dangerous; he might not survive; and he wanted to see Freddy for the last time. In her anguish Eleanor found herself defending Aveling's behavior:

> More and more I realize that wrong behavior is simply a moral sickness, and the morally healthy people like yourself are not qualified to judge the condition of the morally sick, just as the physically healthy can scarcely realize the condition of the physically sick.
>
> There are people who lack a certain moral sense, just as many are deaf or short-sighted or in other ways afflicted. And I begin to realize that one is as little justified in blaming them for the one sort of disorder as the other. We must strive to cure them, and if no cure is possible, we must do our best. I have learned to understand this through long suffering—suffering whose details I could not tell even to you—but I have learned it, and so I am endeavouring to bear all these trials as well as I can.

Dear, dear Freddy, don't think I have forgotten what Edward owes you (I mean in money, for what concerns a cherished friendship passes all reckoning), and you will naturally receive your share—about that you have my word. I think Edward will go into the hospital the first half of next week. I hope he can go in as soon as possible, for I dread the waiting. I will let you know the definite date, and with all my heart I hope you will soon be well.

Your TUSSY

Freddy was probably among the many who hoped, for Eleanor's sake, that Aveling would not survive the operation. He replied to her letter by asking how she could defend such a monster, but she was in no mood to argue with him. "To understand is to forgive," she wrote. "Much suffering has taught me to understand—and so I do not need to forgive. I can only love."

After the operation she wrote again, saying that it had been successful and she was hoping to take him to Margate for his convalescence. She complained bitterly of her poverty. "The little that remains to me will be used up," she wrote, and once more she seemed to be resigning herself to the inevitable.

Her last letter to Freddy was written from Margate on March 1, 1898. Strangely, she spoke about her duty to remain by Aveling's side, and she felt encouraged by some small gifts given by the miners. She wrote:

DEAR, DEAR FREDDY,

Please don't regard my failure to write as negligence. The trouble is that I am depressed, and often I have not the heart to write. I cannot tell you how pleased I am that you do not blame me too severely, for I regard you as one of the greatest and best of the men I have known.

It is a bad time for me. I fear there is little to hope for, and the pain and suffering are great. Why we go on like this I do not understand. I am ready to go and would do so with joy, but as long as he needs help, I have a duty to remain.

So there it is, and the only thing that helps me are the testimonies of affection that come from all sides. I cannot tell you how good people are to me. Why? I really don't know. The Miners' Union and the Miners' Confederation have sent me a lovely little writing cabinet and a stylograph pen, because I could not accept payment for my services as translator at the International Miners' Congress. I am ashamed to take such a present, but I cannot refuse. And it really did please me.

Dear Freddy, how I wish I could talk with you. But I know it cannot be.

Your TUSSY

These letters provide a map of the spiritual landscape through which Eleanor moved like a sleepwalker, white-faced and drained of energy, not knowing where to turn, drawn to Aveling as by a magnet, incapable of performing the one act of renunciation which would have saved her life. She was far beyond Freddy's help. Within a month she was dead.

Freddy continued to live at Gransden Avenue for seven or eight more years. About 1906 the Claytons abandoned the house on the avenue, and went to live in Rushmore Road nearby, while Freddy took a basement apartment in Dunlace Road a few streets away. The long friendship with the Claytons had not come to an end, but he was no longer a member of the family. Every Sunday young Charles Clayton would spend the day with Freddy.

During a political campaign in 1902 in Germany there appeared an anonymous pamphlet attacking Eduard Bernstein, the socialist leader. Among the many charges leveled against him was that he had slandered Marx and Engels for having left illegitimate children without support. There is no reason to believe that Freddy ever saw the pamphlet; and if he had seen it, he would not have cared. About the same time Bernstein published in the socialist magazine *Die neue Zeit* a long article entitled "What Drove Eleanor Marx to Her Death?" with the texts of the letters Eleanor had written to Freddy. In the article he gave reasons for believing that Aveling was responsible for her death. He had evidently met Freddy, for he discusses Freddy's reactions to her letters, describing him as "a simple workman."

Meanwhile Freddy continued to live in Hackney and to practice his trade. He was a Londoner by birth, and he would remain a Londoner for the rest of his life. As far as we know he spent the greater part of his life in Hackney within an area of three or four square miles. Hackney is in the East End of London, traditionally a working-class district. This was his home, and he never showed any desire to leave it.

On June 8, 1914, he was engaged as a leading fitter and deputy for the foreman at Bryant and May's Match Factory in Fairfield Road, in the borough of Bow. It was a time when jobs were hard to get, and for old men they were particularly hard to get. Freddy lied about his age, saying he was forty-five. George Ayres, the assistant chief engineer, who engaged him, remembers that he was a small man, and therefore he was provided with a small wooden platform when he was working at his bench. He was about five feet three inches tall. He was neat and well-dressed, and the apprentices liked him and went to him with their problems. Because he was especially skilled, his hourly rate of pay was two pennies per hour above that of the other mechanics in the machine shop. And when George Ayres discusses Freddy, he uses a phrase which is heard again and again from the lips of the people who remember him—"He was a cut above the average skilled workmen of that time."

There seems to have been a pride in him: a quietness, a reserve. He rarely discussed his private affairs. He lived quietly, read a great deal, and carried himself with a strange elegance, so that the young apprentices were a little afraid of him, scenting something foreign in his manner. Some of the men who were apprentices under him are still living, and they remember him as a thin, slight man with a gray mustache, drooping shoulders, his head bowed with age. They remember, too, that he had small and beautiful hands, and was sometimes seen to rub charred paper onto them because he wanted them to look more like workmen's hands. They speak of his extraordinary kindness, and how he would go out of his way to help anyone who needed help. He was always properly dressed, with a hard white collar, a knotted tie, and his boots were polished and shining. His speech matched his immaculate dress, being precise and well modulated, if a little high-pitched. During the lunch break he would pull out a drawer of his bench, put a bar of wood across it, rest a book on the wood, and spend his time reading.

He was a very good craftsman, but he was not strong and he did not tackle the heavy jobs. He did the light, intricate jobs. He was so neat and tidy that no one ever dared to borrow a spare nut or a screw from his bench. If there was a nut on the floor and an apprentice kicked it, he would say tartly: "You wouldn't have kicked that if it were a penny, would you? You'd have picked it up. So pick up the nut and don't waste it!"

He worked on the third floor of the factory, and his mates at the bench were men with typically English names like Billy Crouch, Jack Watts, Tom Pike, Walter Jones, and Rowland Lord. They are names which can be found in the earliest records of the East End of London. They are all dead now, and the apprentices who served under him will soon be retiring.

He was still interested in socialism and the trade-union movement, but never sought public office. In 1919, when a bonus scheme was introduced, he spoke against it, saying that it was against trade-union principles to invest in something which gave a 15 per cent rate of interest. Yet it was remembered that he later invested in the scheme and reinvested the interest as long as it was permitted. In this way he became a capitalist.

He was a man who regarded money with a proper seriousness, and saved as much as he could. He had a reputation for being reliable on money matters, and when his friend Alfred Payne, the Mayor of Hackney, wrote his will in 1919, Frederick Demuth was named as a witness.

In that year he moved to a new apartment at 54 Reighton Road, where he remained for the next six years. His wages were three pound ten shillings a week, and he received extra payment on Wednesdays when the foreman was absent and he became acting foreman; he could afford a few minor luxuries. The house on Reighton Road had decorative carving round the door, and was far more respectable than the one on Dunlace Road. He was moving up in the world.

On September 28, 1924, he retired from Bryant and May's Match Factory, and received a pension. In October he also began to receive a pension from the Amalgamated Engineering Union, to which he had belonged for most of his working life. When he was applying for his pension from the match factory, it was learned that he had told a white lie when applying for a job; he was clearly much older than he claimed to be. He was ordered to produce a birth certificate. George Ayres saw the certificate, and his pension was worked out on the basis of his proper age.

He had not desired to retire. It was simply that he was growing old, and was no longer capable of carrying out his work properly. From time to time he would drop in to see his workmates, and then he ceased coming. With George Ayres he had sometimes talked about his son, who had come to no good, and of his wife, who had died long ago in childbirth, or perhaps there had never been a wife. He was a reticent man, and George Ayres never thought of probing into his private affairs.

For ten years Frederick Demuth had worked at Bryant and May's. It was a legendary place, for the match girls had once come out on strike and startled all England, and the great comedian Albert Chevalier had celebrated the factory in one of the most famous of his songs:

> Woh Liza, where d'ye get your clothes na'?
> Woh Liza, you got a turned-up nose na'!
> Strike me, ain't you altered
> Since the good old dyes
> When you used to go to work'a
> Down at Bryant and My's.

Now there were no more songs, and he was an old man living alone with his housekeeper, Laura Ann Payne. Two years later, in need of some comfort, he left Reighton Road and took up lodgings in a house at 13 Stoke Newington Common. It is a well-designed middle-class house with three stories, overlooking a small common. Trees wave in front of the house, and ivy grows over the walls. It has a look of solid gentility.

Here he died on January 28, 1929. The death certificate records that he died of "old age" and "cardiac failure." There was no post-mortem, and his housekeeper was present at his death. Three days later his body was cremated at Golders Green crematorium, and the ashes were strewn over the crematorium flower garden.

In his will, written in 1926, he left a tenth of his estate to his old friend Jimmy Hill, a quarter to his housekeeper, and the remainder to "Mr. Harry Demuth, my nephew, known as my son, of 91 Great Dover Street, Southwark, S.E. 1." His gross estate was £1,971 12s 4d. It was a surprisingly large sum for an English workman to leave. The 1920s were hard times, and most workmen found it hard enough to leave a sum of money which would cover their funeral expenses. Unlike his father, he had managed his financial affairs well. In the currency of the time he had left a small fortune.

It was an obscure and unspectacular death, and no newspapers recorded his passing. He died as quietly as he lived, being one of those calm and gentle people who pass through life without throwing any shadows. The son of a German peasant woman and a Jewish intellectual descended from a long line of rabbis, he became an English workman admired for his skill. He showed no interest in his father's doctrines, and followed the ideas of the English Labour Party.

His long life spanned an age. Born a few years after his father published the *Communist Manifesto,* he was the only one of Marx's children to see the coming of the Russian Revolution. When he died, Stalin was consolidating his power and Russia was being transformed into an iron-bound communist state obedient to the laws first announced by his father.

APPENDIXES

GENEALOGICAL TREE OF KARL MARX

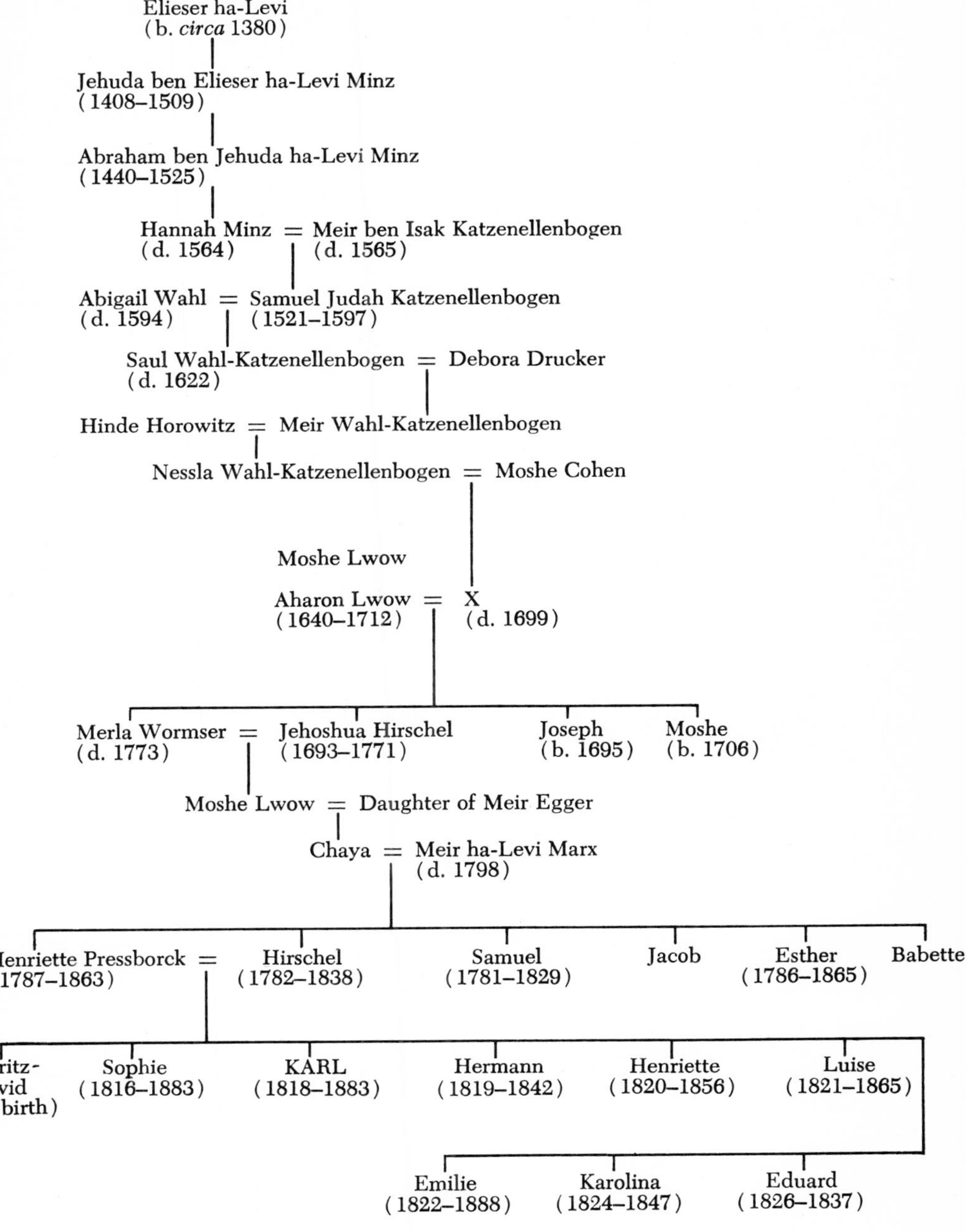

GENEALOGICAL T

COLIN, LORD CAMPBELL
first Earl of Argyll, d. 1493

ARCHIBALD CAMPBELL
second Earl of Argyll, killed at Battle of Flodden 1513

ARCHIBALD CAMPBELL = JANET STUART
of Skipnish, second son
of second Earl

A DAUGHTER = DONALD CAMPBELL
of Ardentinny, Provost
of Inveraray 1556-7

ARCHIBALD CAMPBELL
of Ardentinny

DUNCAN CAMPBELL
of Ardentinny in 1581

JOHN CAMPBELL
Apparent of Ardentinny in 1606

ANNE LINDSAY = COLIN CAMPBELL

ANNE McAULAY = JOHN CAMPBELL

JEAN CAMPBELL = ROBERT CAMPBELL OF ORC
second son of James Campbell
of Ardkinglas

JOHN CAMPBELL OF ORCHARD
served heir to his parents 1703-5
sheriff substitute of Argyll 1720
the Duke's factor of Kintyre 1727
d. 1768 *aetat.* 86

ANNE CAMPBE
Received disposition of
Orchard from her father i
1737. d. 17 November 17
aetat. 72

BARON CHRISTIAN HEINRICH PHILI
VON WESTPHALEN, Secretary to Duke
Ferdinand von Braunschweig-Lüneburg-
Wolfenbüttel
b. 24 April 1724, d. 21 September 1792

BARON JOHANN LUDWIG VON WESTPHALE
his second son, b. 11 July 1770, d. 3 March 1842

ENNY MARX

JAMES WISHART OF PITARROW
d. 1491

JOHN WISHART OF PITARROW

JANET LINDSAY = JAMES WISHART OF PITARROW
of Edzell — received Charter of Carnbege in 1511, Justice Clerk in 1513

JAMES WISHART OF CARNBEGE

ELIZABETH WOOD = JAMES WISHART OF BALFEITH
his second son, d. 1575

SIR JOHN WISHART = JEAN ANGUS
succeeded to Pitarrow in 1576, d. 1607 — daughter of William, ninth Earl of Angus

CATHERINE KERR = ALEXANDER WISHART OF PITARROW
daughter of Rev. Robert Kerr, Minister of Linton

CHRISTIAN BURNE = REVEREND WILLIAM WISHART
Minister of Kinneil, Linlithgowshire, b. December 1621, d. February 1692

NET MURRAY = WILLIAM WISHART, D.D.
Principal of University of Edinburgh 1710
b. 1660, d. 1729

RGE WISHART, D.D.
er of St. Cuthbert's Church,
urgh, in 1726, and of Tron
h, Edinburgh, in 1730

E WISHART
nburgh 20 September 1742
zwedel 31 July 1811

)LINE AMALIE JULIE HEUBEL
'5, d. 23 July 1856

NNA BERTHA JULIE JENNY = KARL MARX
zwedel 12 February 1814
ndon 2 December 1881

THE DESCENDANTS OF KARL MARX

JENNY VON WESTPHALEN (1814–1881) = KARL MARX (1818–1883) = HELENE DEMUTH (1823–1890)

- Karl Marx = Helene Demuth:
  - Frederick Demuth (1851-1929)
- Jenny von Westphalen = Karl Marx:
  - Jenny (1844–1883) = Charles Longuet (1833–1903)
    - Harry (1873–1874)
    - Jean (1876–1938) lawyer
      - Robert Jean b. 1899 lawyer
      - Karl b. 1904 sculptor
    - Edgar (1879–1950) doctor
      - Charles b. 1901 automobile salesman, has four children
      - Frédéric b. 1904 landscape painter
      - Jenny (1906–1939)
      - Paul b. 1909 planter in Madagascar Councilor of the French Union, has two children
    - Harry (1878–1883)
    - Marcel (1881–1949) journalist
      - Marcel-Charles b. 1909
    - Jenny (1882–1952)
  - Laura* (1846–1911)
  - Edgar (1847–1856)
  - Guido (1849–1850)
  - Franziska (1851–1852)
  - Ele… (1856–

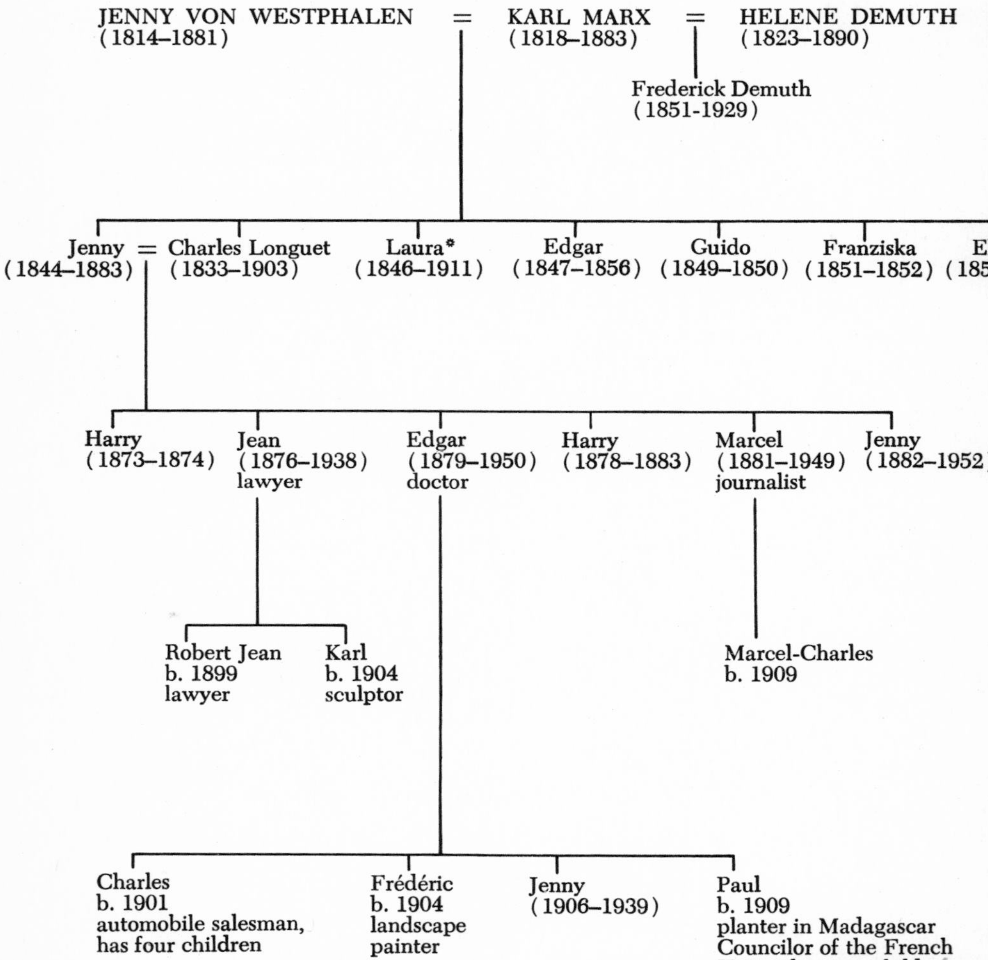

* Laura Marx married Paul Lafargue in 1868 and had three children, all of whom died in infancy. Étienne, known as Schnapps, was born in 1868 and died in 1872. Another child born in January 1870 died three months later, and the third child born in 1871 died a few weeks after birth.

SELECTED BIBLIOGRAPHY

My chief debt is to the compilation of documents known as the *Marx Engels Werke,* which at the time of writing had reached thirty-four massive volumes. Within the limits of Soviet scholarship, which permits and encourages omissions whenever it is felt that there are politically sound reasons for concealment, this is an impressive work provided with a formidable array of notes, cross references and chronological tables, admirably printed and intelligently edited by an anonymous committee appointed by the Central Committee of the German Communist Party. Marx's early writings, his bitter attacks on Russian tyranny, and his "Economic and Philosophical Manuscripts of 1844" are omitted, but these can be found elsewhere. The early writings including the 1844 manuscripts can be found in the *Gesamtausgabe,* published in the twenties and thirties, while the files of the British Museum contain Marx's articles in the *Free Press* and other ephemeral publications. The early volumes of the *Gesamtausgabe* edited by David Ryazanov are the most satisfying and authoritative, and deserve to be reprinted.

Mohr und General: Erinnerungen an Marx und Engels, published by Dietz Verlag in 1965, contains many of the contemporary reminiscences of Marx, and in addition there is the full text of Jenny Marx's *Short Sketch of an Eventful Life.* The texts are accurate and authoritative with no editorial scoring of the occasional damaging reminiscences. Between them the *Werke,* the *Gesamtausgabe,* and *Mohr und General* provide a reasonably complete portrait of Marx, and I have relied heavily on them.

Aberdare, Lord. *Letters of the Rt. Hon. Henry Austin Bruce, G.C.B.* Oxford, printed for private circulation, 1902.

Adams, Henry Packwood. *Karl Marx in His Early Writings.* New York, Russell & Russell, 1965.

Andreas, Bert. *Briefe und Dokumente des Familie Marx aus den Jahren 1862–1873.* Hanover, Archiv für Sozialgeschichte, 1962.

Andrews, Wayne, editor. *The Autobiography of Carl Schurz.* New York, Charles Scribner's Sons, 1961.

Bakounine, Michel. *Oeuvres.* Paris, P. V. Stock, 1908.

Barker, Felix. "The Life and Strange Death of Eleanor Marx," *The Cornhill Magazine,* Autumn 1955, and *The New Yorker,* November 27, 1954.

Basyn, Thomas. "Karl Marx à Bruxelles," *La Revue Générale,* November 1927; and "L'Arrestation de Karl Marx" in the same magazine, September 1928.

Beer, Max. *The Life and Teaching of Karl Marx.* Boston, Small Maynard and Co., 1924.

Berlin, Isaiah. *Karl Marx: His Life and Environment.* London, T. Butterworth, 1939.

Blackstock, Paul W., and Hoselitz, Bert F. *The Russian Menace to Europe, by Karl Marx and Friedrich Engels.* Glencoe, The Free Press, 1952.

Blumenberg, Werner. *Marx.* Hamburg, Rowohlt, 1962.

Bober, M. M. *Karl Marx's Interpretation of History.* New York, W. W. Norton, 1965.

Bottigelli, Emile, editor. *Karl Marx: Lettres et documents 1856–1883*. Milan, Instituto Giangiacomo Feltrinelli, 1958.
Bottomore, T. B. *Karl Marx: Early Writings*. London, C. A. Watts, 1963.
———, and Rubel, Maximilien. *Karl Marx: Selected Writings*. London, C. A. Watts, 1963.
Buber, Martin. *Paths in Utopia*. Boston, Beacon Press, 1958.
Carr, E. H. *Michael Bakunin*. New York, Vintage Books, 1961.
———. *Karl Marx: A Study in Fanaticism*. London, J. M. Dent, 1934.
Christman, Henry M. *The American Journalism of Marx and Engels*. New York, New American Library, 1966.
Collins, Henry, and Abramsky, Chimen. *Karl Marx and the British Labour Movement*. London, Macmillan & Co., 1965.
Cornu, Auguste. *Karl Marx, l'homme et l'oeuvre*. Paris, Félix Alcan, 1934.
———. *The Origins of Marxian Thought*. Springfield, Charles C Thomas, 1957.
Demetz, Peter. *Marx, Engels und die Dichter*. Stuttgart, Deutsche Verlags Anstalt, 1959.
Documents of the First International. London, Lawrence and Wishart, n.d.
Doerig, J. A., editor. *Marx vs. Russia*. New York, Frederick Ungar, 1962.
Dornemann, Louise. *Jenny Marx*. Berlin, Deutscher Frauenverlag, 1953.
Dragomanov, Michel. *Correspondance de Michel Bakounine*. Paris, Perrin et Cie., 1896.
Engels, Frederick, and Lafargue, Paul and Laura. *Correspondence*. Moscow, Foreign Languages Publishing House, 1960.
Feuer, Lewis S. "Marxian Tragedians," *Encounter*, November 1962.
Footman, David. *The Primrose Path, a Life of Ferdinand Lassalle*. London, Cresset Press, 1946.
Fromm, Erich. *Marx's Concept of Man*. New York, Frederick Ungar, 1963.
Gay, Peter. *The Dilemma of Democratic Socialism*. New York, Collier Books, 1962.
Gerth, Hans, editor. *The First International*. Madison, University of Wisconsin Press, 1958.
Graetz, H. *History of the Jews*. Philadelphia, The Jewish Publication Society, 1894.
Guillaume, James. *L'Internationale: Documents et souvenirs*. Paris, Société Nouvelle, 1905–1910.
Haubtmann, Pierre. *Marx et Proudhon, leurs rapports personnels 1844–1847*. Paris, Economie et Humanisme, 1947.
Heine, Heinrich. *Sämtliche Werke*. Munich, Rosl & Cie, 1923.
Heinzen, Karl Peter. *Erlebtes*. Boston, privately printed, 1864.
Hepner, Benoit P. *Karl Marx: La Russie et l'Europe*. Paris, Gallimard, 1954.
Hook, Sidney. *From Hegel to Marx*. New York, The Humanities Press, 1950.
Horne, Alistair. *The Fall of Paris*. New York, St. Martin's Press, 1965.
Horowitz, H. "Die Familie Lwow," *Monatsschrift für Geschichte und Wissenschaft des Judentums*, Frankfurt, 1928.
Hyndman, H. M. *Further Reminiscences*. London, Macmillan & Co., 1912.
———. *The Record of an Adventurous Life*. London, Macmillan & Co., 1911.
Jackson, J. Hampden. *Marx, Proudhon and European Socialism*. New York, Collier Books, 1962.
Jellinek, Frank. *The Paris Commune of 1871*. London, Victor Gollancz, 1937.
Karl Marx Album. Berlin, Dietz Verlag, 1953.
Kautsky, Karl. "Hours with Karl Marx," *The Modern Thinker and Author's Review*, May 1933.
Kenafick, K. J. *Michael Bakunin and Karl Marx*. Melbourne, privately printed, 1948.
Kisch, Egon Erwin. *Karl Marx in Karlsbad*. Berlin, Aufbau Verlag, 1953.
Landshut, Siegfried, editor. *Karl Marx: Die Frühschrifte*. Stuttgart, Alfred Kröner, 1953.
Lehning, Arthur, editor. *Michel Bakounine et les conflits dans l'Internationale*. Leiden, J. Brill, 1965.

Lewin-Dorsch, E. "Familie und Stammbaum von Karl Marx," *Die Glocke, Berlin,* 1923.

Lewis, John. *The Life and Teaching of Karl Marx.* London, Lawrence and Wishart, 1965.

Lichtheim, George. *Marxism.* London, Routlege and Kegan Paul, 1961.

Liebknecht, Wilhelm. *Briefwechsel mit Karl Marx und Friedrich Engels.* The Hague, Mouton, 1963.

London Landmarks: A Guide to Places where Marx, Engels and Lenin Worked. London, The Communist Party, n.d.

Loria, Achille. *Karl Marx.* New York, Thomas Seltzer, 1920.

Ludwig, Emil. *Bismarck.* Boston, Little, Brown & Co., 1927.

Maenchen-Helfen, Otto, and Nicolaievsky, Boris. *Karl Marx, Man and Fighter.* London, Methuen, 1936.

Marx, Eleanor, editor. *Karl Marx: Revolution and Counter-Revolution.* Chicago, Charles H. Kerr, 1896.

Marx, Karl. *Capital, A Critique of Political Economy.* Vols. I, II, III. Moscow, Foreign Languages Publishing House, 1961–1962.

———. *Secret Diplomatic History of the Eighteenth Century.* London, Sonnenschein, 1899.

———. and Engels, Frederick. *Selected Correspondence 1846–1895.* New York, International Publishers, 1936.

———. *Selected Correspondence.* Moscow, Foreign Languages Publishing House, n.d.

———. *Selected Works.* Moscow, Foreign Languages Publishing House, 1953.

———. *On Britain.* Moscow, Foreign Languages Publishing House, 1962.

Mayer, Gustav. *Friedrich Engels.* New York, Alfred A. Knopf, 1936.

Mayhew, Henry. *Mayhew's London.* London, Spring Books, n.d.

Mehring, Franz. *Karl Marx.* Ann Arbor, Michigan University Press, 1962.

———, editor. *Aus dem literarischen Nachlass von Karl Marx, Friedrich Engels und Ferdinand Lassalle.* Stuttgart, J. H. W. Dietz, 1902.

Miller, Sepp, and Sawadzki, Bruno. *Karl Marx in Berlin.* Berlin, Das Neue Berlin, n.d.

Mins, L. E., editor. *Founding of the First International.* New York, International Publishers, 1937.

———. *Karl Marx and Frederick Engels: Letters to Americans.* New York, International Publishers, 1958.

Mohr und General: Erinnerungen an Marx und Engels. Berlin, Dietz Verlag, 1965.

Müller, Manfred, editor, *Familie Marx in Briefen.* Berlin, Dietz Verlag, 1966.

Pascal, Roy. *Karl Marx: Political Foundations.* London, Labour Monthly, 1943.

Postgate, R. W. *Karl Marx.* London, Hamish Hamilton, 1933.

———, editor. *The Civil War in France, by Karl Marx.* London, Labour Publishing Co., 1921.

Regnault, Dr. Felix. "Les Maladies de Karl Marx," *Revue Anthropologique,* Vol. XLIII, 1933.

Rubel, Maximilien. *Bibliographie des oeuvres de Karl Marx.* Paris, Rivière, 1956.

———, editor. *Karl Marx: Oeuvres.* Paris, Bibliothèque de la Pleiade, 1963.

Rühle, Otto. *Karl Marx, His Life and Work.* New York, The New Home Library, 1943.

Rutson, A. O. "Opportunities and Shortcomings of Government in England," *Essays on Reform.* London, Macmillan, 1867.

Ryazanoff, David. *The Communist Manifesto.* New York, Russell & Russell, 1963.

———. *Karl Marx and Friedrich Engels.* New York, International Publishers, 1927.

———, editor. *Karl Marx, Man, Thinker and Revolutionist.* New York, International Publishers, 1927.

Schwartzschild, Leopold. *Karl Marx, the Red Prussian.* New York, Grosset and Dunlap, n.d.

Schwerbrock, Wolfgang, editor. *Karl Marx Privat.* Munich, Paul List Verlag, 1962.
Serebryakova, Galina. *Marks i Engels.* Moscow, Molodaya Gvardiya, 1966.
Somerhausen, Luc. *L'Humanisme agissant de Karl Marx.* Paris, Richard-Masse, 1946.
Spargo, John. *Karl Marx, His Life and Work.* New York, B. W. Huebsch, 1910.
Sprigge, C. J. S. *Karl Marx.* New York, Collier Books, 1962.
Stekloff, G. M. *History of the First International.* London, Martin Lawrence, 1928.
Stepanova, Helena. *Frederick Engels.* Moscow, Foreign Languages Publishing House, 1953.
Sue, Eugène. *The Wandering Jew.* New York, The Century Company, 1903.
Testut, Oscar. *Le Livre Bleu de l'Internationale.* Paris, E. Lachaud, 1871.
Thompson, E. P. *William Morris: Romantic to Revolutionary.* New York, Monthly Review Press, 1961.
Thorne, Will. *My Life's Battles.* London, George Newnes, 1925.
Tucker, Robert. *Philosophy and Myth in Karl Marx.* Cambridge, Cambridge University Press, 1961.
Victor, Walther. *General und die Frauen.* Berlin, Büchergilde Gutenberg, 1932.
Vogt, Karl. *Mein Prozess gegen die Allgemeine Zeitung.* Geneva, Selbst-Verlag des Verfassers, 1859.
Wachstein, B. "Die Abstimmung von Karl Marx," *Festkrift i anledning af Professor David Simonsens 70-aarige fødseldag.* Copenhagen, 1923.
Webb, Beatrice. *My Apprenticeship.* London, Longmans, Green, 1926.
Wilson, Edmund. *To the Finland Station.* New York, Anchor Books, 1953.
Woodcock, George, *Pierre-Joseph Proudhon.* London, Routlege and Kegan Paul, 1956.

CHAPTER NOTES

A Nest of Gentle Folk

Marx's ancestry has been carefully studied in three monographs noted in the bibliography. A good deal is known about the long-lived Jehuda Minz, the most eminent of his ancestors. He has been described by the historian Heinrich Hirsch Graetz as "most inimical to any liberal manifestation within Judaism and most strenuously opposed the advocates of freedom." His quarrel with Elias del Medigo was connected on a plane of ferocious recrimination. Except for a few *responsae,* all Jehuda Minz's writings were destroyed during a siege of Padua. From the surviving *responsae* we learn that he disapproved violently of the increasingly lax morals of the Jews in Italy. He was the stern patriarch, dominating his flock and refusing to permit anyone to deviate from the path he had chosen. His son Abraham was equally violent and self-opinionated. There is no evidence that Marx was aware of his descent from Jehuda Minz, but there is enough similarity between the behavior of Karl Marx and Jehuda Minz to suggest that Karl Marx was a throwback, reviving in himself the quarrels of a much earlier generation.

Marx descended from Jehuda Minz through a great-great-great-granddaughter who married into the rabbinical family of the Lwows, refugees from a Cossack uprising in Poland. With the son of Rabbi Moshe Lwow begins the family connection with Trier. Thereafter some member of the family was always a rabbi in Trier. The name Marx appears for the first time with Meir ha-Levi Marx, who was Karl Marx's grandfather. It is known that during his youth he was called Meir ha-Levi, but there is no known explanation for his adoption of the name Marx.

Jenny von Westphalen

The family tree of Jenny von Westphalen was drawn up at my request by Mr. David C. Cargill. It presented unusual difficulties, because at first it appeared to be impossible to trace a connection between Ann Campbell of Orchard and the family of the Earl of Argyll. It seemed that Jenny Marx's often repeated claim to be descended from the Scottish nobility would have to be rejected.

Mr. Cargill discovered the connection while going through the John Macgregor collection of documents in the Scottish Record Office. He found a manuscript note by John Macgregor, a Writer to the Signet and a prominent genealogist, to the effect that a daughter of Archibald Campbell of Skipnish married Donald Campbell of Ardentinny. John Macgregor did not quote his authority, but he was a man of impeccable scholarship, and Mr. Cargill was inclined to accept his note without question. With this discovery the pieces in the jigsaw fell into place. Jenny's family tree shows that she was descended from Colin, Lord Campbell, first Earl of Argyll. She was not, as she thought, descended from a later Earl who was beheaded at Edinburgh Castle for high treason.

The ancestors of both Jenny and Karl Marx can be traced to the middle of the fifteenth century.

In the following chapter notes MEGA refers to the *Marx Engels Gesamtausgabe,* MG to *Mohr und General,* and volume numbers and pages (e.g. XVI, 545) refer to *Werke.*

Three Essays

PAGE

32 (Nature has given) MEGA, I, 1 (2), p. 164

33 (Our imagination may be) Id. pp. 164–5

34 (The chief directing) Id., p. 167

37 (His reign) Id., p. 169

38 (The genius of Augustus) Id., pp. 169–70

39 (The alluring voice) Id., pp. 171–72
40 (Our heart, reason) Id., p. 172
41 (Thus union with Christ consists) Id., p. 173
41 (Thus union with Christ contributes) Id., p. 174

THE STRUGGLE WITH THE FATHER

PAGE
45 (What is all this) Id., p. 192
47 (I have spoken) Id., p. 198
49 (It should be an honorable) Id., p. 204
50 (When I left you) *Die Frühschriften,* pp. 2–3
51 (A curtain had fallen) Id., p. 7
52 (I proceeded to seek) Id., p. 7
52 (My heart must) Id., p. 10
52 (A deep unrest) Id., p. 11
53 (God help us) MEGA, I, 1(2), p. 226
53 (Meanwhile my clever Karl) Id., pp. 227–28
54 (We are now in the fourth) Id., p. 229
54 (I am not blind) Id., p. 229
54 (She is a darling child) Id., p. 229
55 (Dear Karl) Id., p. 231

THE POEMS OF KARL MARX

PAGE
61 (Never can I be at peace) Mehring, *Aus dem literarischen Nachlass,* I, p. 28
62 (The player strikes) MEGA, I, 1(2), p. 147
63 (He pressed her violently) Id., p. 148
66 (Kant and Fichte) Id., p. 42
66 (The soul has no existence) Id., p. 16
66 (I have taught) Id., p. 42
67 (Goethe, too,) Id., p. 43

OULANEM, A TRAGEDY

PAGE
68 (A rare alliance) MEGA, I, 1(2), p. 61
70 (Come with me) Id., p. 67
71 (Ruined! Ruined!) Id., pp. 68–69
72 (My God, your virtue) Id., p. 71
73 (*Alles, was besteht*) *Faust,* Part I, "Studien-Zimmer"

THE YOUNG EDITOR

PAGE
77 (Let me know) MEGA, I, 1(2), p. 233
81 (Who comes rushing in) *Karl Marx in Berlin,* p. 75
82 (You will be delighted) MEGA, I, 1(2), p. 260
84 (I am humorous) I, 6, 14
85 (the smuggling) XXVII, 412
86 (The savages in Cuba) I, 147
86 (The undersigned) I, 200

THE HONEYMOON

PAGE
90 (I think) *Familie Marx in Briefen,* p. 40
91 (I can assure you) XXVII, 417
92 The account of the honeymoon comes from Franziska Kugelmann in MG, pp. 294–95.
93 (The monotheism of the Jews) I, 374–75
95 (Judaism reaches its peak) I, 376
95 (It is not only in the Pentateuch) I, 377
97 (*Religious* suffering) I, 378
97 (the task of history) I, 379
98 (*Reply:* In the creation) I, 390
98 (the proletariat is only just) I, 390
99 (the *head* of this emancipation) I, 391
99 (Philosophy can be realized) I, 391
99 (When all the inner conditions) I, 391
100 (Your bride is quite) MG, p. 395

HEINRICH HEINE

PAGE
102 (Although little discussed) Heine, *Sämtliche Werke,* VII, p. 209
103 (In the second act) Id., pp. 210–11
104 (In those days Marx) K. J. Kenafick, *Michael Bakunin and Karl Marx,* pp. 25–26.
106 (Without a tear) MEGA, IV, 342
107 (We talk far too much) *Familie Marx in Briefen,* p. 51
107 (Please don't write) Id., pp. 51–52
108 (Man returns to living in a cave) MEGA, I, 3, p. 87
111 (Proletariat and Wealth) II, 37–38
113 (I see from the announcement) XXVII, 22

113 (Nevertheless, the book is) XXVII, 26
113 (*Socialism* cannot be brought) I, 409
114 (Dearest Marx!) Heine, *Sämtliche Werke*, X, 142–44
117 (I have often pondered) Id., V, 189

THE LEAGUE OF THE JUST

PAGE
118 (Your Majesty's most respectful) XXVII, 601
119 (In this document) II, 692
119 (The essence of man) III, 6, 7
120 (All social life) III, 7
121 (In *The Essence of Christianity*) III, 5
122 (A quarter of a century) XXVII, 510
125 (of great talent) XXVII, 13
125 (his philosophical lack) III, 435
125 (Once upon a time) III, 13, 14
127 (communism is empirically) III, 35
127 (the proletariat can only) III, 36
127 (In all revolutions) III, 69–70
128 (the communists are the only) III, 238
128 (The Holy Father) III, 70, 71

THE FIRST PURGE

PAGE
134 (Marx was a type of man) Edmund Wilson, *To the Finland Station*, p. 166
136 (These last words of Weitling) Id., p. 168
137 (Kriege's childishly pompous) IV, 3

PROUDHON

PAGE
140 ("Proudhon," wrote Marx) II, 33
141 (My Dear Proudhon) Pierre Haubtmann, *Marx et Proudhon*, pp. 58–59
141 (I hereby denounce) Id., pp. 61–62
142 (As for me) Id., p. 62
143 (Let us, if you wish) Id., 63–65
143 (I have also) Id., pp. 67–68
144 (My dear Monsieur Marx) Id., p. 70
145 (M. Proudhon has the) Marx, *Oeuvres* (Pleiade), p. 7
146 (M. Proudhon's work) Id., p. 8
146 (M. Proudhon knows no more) Id., p. 81
147 (The thought, opposed) Id., p. 77
148 (There is a continual) Id., p. 79
148 (*Mortalem vitam*) Lucretius, *De rerum natura*, III, 882

ON THE EVE

PAGE
151 (We are watching people) Eugene Sue, *The Wandering Jew*, Part II, The Street of the Milieu-des-Ursins, XVI
154 (Thou sodden-witted Lord) *Troilus and Cressida*, Act II, scene i
154 (He had wildly disheveled) Carl Heinzen, *Erlebtes*, II, 423
155 (I have never seen a man) *The Autobiography of Karl Schurz*, p. 271
157 (We would also be empowered) VIII, 585
157 (The aim of the League) IV, 596
159 (in no social order) Ryazanoff, *The Communist Manifesto*, p. 292
159 (*Question One*) IV, 363
160 (will be taught) IV, 376
160 (behind the backs) XXVII, 98
161 (We shall have it all) XXVII, 104
161 (Even the devil) XXVII, 98
161 (The old Poland has gone) IV, 416–17

THE COMMUNIST MANIFESTO

PAGE
166 (Ha, no salvation) MEGA, I, 1(2), p. 66
167 (The bourgeoisie, historically) IV, 464–65
168 (In these crises) IV, 468
169 (What the bourgeoisie therefore) IV, 474
169 (They destroy imported wares) IV, 470
170 (a small section of the ruling) IV, 472
170 (the self-conscious, independent movement) IV, 473
170 (They have nothing of their own) IV, 472
170 (Communism deprives no man) IV, 477
172 (Bourgeois marriage) IV, 479
172 (Expropriation of property) IV, 481
174 (Communists scorn to hide) IV, 493

THE STORM BREAKS

PAGE
175 (Dear and brave Marx) John Lewis, *The Life and Teaching of Karl Marx*, p. 98
176 (Real ill-treatment) IV, 611
178 (The magistrate was somewhat) IV, 537
180 (This measure is ultimately) V, 4

THE MAD YEAR

PAGE
183 (The organization of the) Marx-Engels, *Selected Works,* II, 330–31
184 (When we founded) Id., p. 329
185 (They will ask) V, 136–37
185 (Scandinavianism is merely) V, 394
185 (Who has been from the) V, 396
185 (Precisely such a war) V, 397
188 (I have spoken to hundreds) V, 474
189 (Those who are without means) VI, 33
189 (The question whether) VI, 242
190 (The Code Napoléon) VI, 245

THE RED NUMBER

PAGE
191 (In its recent articles) VI, 503
192 A facsimile of the "red number" of the *Neue Rheinische Zeitung* is given in *Karl Marx Album,* opposite p. 92.
192 (*We are ruthless*) VI, 505
218 (Engels: Aged 26–28) VI, 590
219 (Never play with insurrection) Karl Marx, *Revolution and Counter-Revolution,* p. 161
219 (The petty bourgeoisie) Id., p. 169
220 (*Le choses marchent*) XXVII, 506
221 (I tell you) XXVII, 500
221 (*Il faut nous lançer*) XXVII, 141
221 (I have been banished) XXVII, 142

THE SATANIC MILLS

PAGE
223 (*One comes to see*) XXVII, 186
228 (The poor little angel) XXVII, 608
229 (He would come to visit me) MG, 212
229 (a beautiful, noble-minded) MG, 47
231 (In clothes torn to shreds) VII, 546
232 (The following day) XXVII, 609

A LETTER FROM THE EARL OF WESTMORLAND

235 (There exist here) The photocopies of the Manteuffel report were communicated to me by Mr. C. J. Child, Deputy Librarian of the Foreign Office Library. The text is an English summary, evidently made in Berlin. The complete German document is in the Public Record Office.
239 (It is obvious) VII, 249
240 (*The battle cry must be*) VII, 254
241 (The aim of the society) VII, 553–54

A DUEL AT ANTWERP

The account of the duel is based chiefly on Liebknecht's *Erinnerungen* given in MG, 93–95, and Lieutenant Techow's letter quoted at length in Karl Vogt, *Mein Prozess,* pp. 156–60. Marx discusses the incident in *Herr Vogt* (XIV, 443–45) and there are occasional muted references in the Marx-Engels correspondence.

PAGE
244*n* (Barthélemi's end is glorious) XXVII, 420
246 (You are insisting) VIII, 598
246 (In these moments of crisis) VIII, 575
247 (This open and authentic) XXVII, 184–85
247 (All the world must suffer) VII, 355
248 (Before the proletariat) VII, 416

THE HOUSE IN DEAN STREET

PAGE
250 (My wife is in a truly dangerous) XXVII, 144
251 (At the head of the party) *Archiv fur Geschichte des Socialismus,* X, (1922) pp. 56–58
252 The story about Louis Blanc is told by Liebknecht in MG, 83–84.
254 (Marx is, after Mazzini) *Archiv fur Geschichte des Socialismus,* X, (1922) pp. 58–59

DEAR, FAITHFUL LENCHEN

PAGE
259 (Marx submitted like a lamb) MG, 109–10
261 (Marx is living in) Karl Marx, *Oeuvres*, (Pleiade), LXXX
262 (and in spite of all their claim) XXVII, 198
263 (The delivery was easy) XXVII, 227
264 (To round off) XXVII, 227
264 (I am saying nothing) XXVII, 228
265 (an event which I shall not) MG, 216
266 (And you know) XXVII, 293
266 (the unspeakable infamies) XXVII, 565

THE EIGHTEENTH BRUMAIRE

PAGE
269 (Because my hands) XXVII, 314
270 (So little time) XXVII, 317
271 (Days of general election) English text given in Marx-Engels, *On Britain*, p. 373
271 (His whole life) Id., p. 448
271 (a pastime expressly) Id., p. 409
273 (After what we have seen) XXVII, 381
273 (Hegel observes) VIII, 115
273*n* (The last phase) I, 382
274 (Bourgeois revolutions) VIII, 118
274 (At long last) VIII, 132
275 (Neither a nation nor a woman) VIII, 119
275 (an adventurer whose trivial) VIII, 117
275 (Together with decayed *roués*) VIII, 161
275 (the only class) VIII, 161
276 (The entire people) VIII, 117
277 (Men make their own history) VIII, 115

THE BOURGEOIS GENTLEMAN

PAGE
279 Liebknecht tells the story of Marx's blushes in MG, 102–3.
280 (*Hol' mich der Deuwel!*) MG, 104
280 (It began one evening) MG, 129
282 (We had now had enough) MG, 133–34
283 (I tried to hold him back) MG, 99
284 Liebknecht tells the story of the Sunday excursions in MG, 110–16.
288 (Suddenly there was a shock) MG, 125–28

THE DEATH OF THE LITTLE FLY

PAGE
290 (a little goblin) XXVII, 610
291 (Is Mr. Marx at home?) XXVIII, 645
292 (My wife is marching) XXVIII, 422
292 (my wife gave birth) XXVIII, 423
292 (Today I am sending you) XXVIII, 436
293 (The disease has finally) XXVIII, 442
294 ("Mohr," he said) MG, 118–19
295 (The house is desolate) XXVIII, 444
295 (Bacon says) XXVIII, 617
297 (There is an old) XI, 322
298 (These unwilling) XI, 325
298 (In the eighteenth century) XI, 323
299 (Last Sunday) XI, 343
300 (This Jew is making) XXVIII, 415

THE HOUSE ON GRAFTON TERRACE

PAGE
305 (if conditions permit) XXIX, 29
305 (*Wir, die* so) XXIX, 47
306 (The so-called revolutions) The original English text in Marx-Engels, *Selected Correspondence 1846–1895*, pp. 90–91; German text in XII, 4
309 (The overwhelming influence) *Secret Diplomatic History of the Eighteenth Century*, p. 74
310 (We spent that winter) MG, 221–22
311 (It is truly disgusting) XXIX, 102
312 (Physically the crisis) XXIX, 211–12
313 (I am working like mad) XXIX, 225
313 (Last Saturday I went fox hunting) XXIX, 245
313 (I have overthrown) XXIX, 260
314 (If this condition) XXIX, 267

THE DEMONS

PAGE
316 (He also enjoyed making) MG, 272–73
317 (It concerned an imaginary) MG, 273–74
319 (Marx *(with great solemnity)*) XXX, 17
319 (From what I hear) XXX, 22
320 (It is nothing but shit) XXX, 38
321 (First we drank port) Karl Vogt, *Mein Prozess*, pp. 151–52
323 (By means of) XIV, 599–600
324 (There was a Greek) XIV, 601–2

325 (She pointed out to me) XXX, 110
326 (Everywhere in Germany) XXX, 565
327 (I got worse) MG, 257–58
327 (pure thought and pure being) XXX, 117

Ferdinand Lassalle

PAGE
329 (The book contains the basis) XXX, 131
330 (I was born) XV, 635
331 (I thank you) David Footman, *The Primrose Path*, p. 127
332 (And now, *mon cher*) XXX, 604
332 (Lassalle is so dazzled) XXX, 163
333 (If the New Year) XXX, 212
333 (Take all in all) XXX, 214
333 (Every day my wife) XXX, 248
333 (it is quite extraordinary) XXX, 248
334 (He is now posing) XXX, 25
334 (In July 1862) MG, 233–35
335 (As for the Yankees) XXX, 286–87
336 (The funeral) XXX, 303

Marx and Engels

PAGE
339 (Dear Engels) XXX, 310
340 (Dear Marx) XXX, 312
340 (How freshly and passionately) XXX, 343
341 (That men of genius) XXX, 338

The Boils

PAGE
343 (My face has reached) XXVIII, 362
344 (I myself have one foot) XXX, 376
346 (So you see, *mon cher*) XXX, 386
347 (I have had the pleasure) XXXI, 368
348 (Mon cas) XXXI, 369
348 (really a form of) XXXI, 533
348 (Cut, lanced) XXXII, 535
349 (Whatever happens, I hope) XXXI, 305

Deaths and Entrances

PAGE
352 (This is the last will) The will was dated 31 December, 1863, and probated June 1, 1864. I have drawn on the copy in Somerset House.
352 (has been bequeathed to me) XXX, 656
353 (The Philistines here) XXX, 422
353 (which this year) XXX, 665
354 (If I had had) XXX, 417
355 The ball is mentioned by Jenny Marx in *A Short Sketch*, MG, 232.
356 (He was shot) XXX, 671–72
356 (He was certainly) XXX, 429
357 (L.'s misfortune) XXX, 673
357 (You are quite right) XXXI, 419

The Birth of the International

PAGE
364 (Sir, The Committee) *Founding of the First International*, pp. 57–58
366 (A Public Meeting) XXXI, 10–13
368 (On October 20) XXXI, 15
370 (In olden times) *Founding of the First International*, p. 35
370 (In all countries) Id., p. 33
371 (The fight for such a) Id., pp. 38–39
371 (*Considering*, That the) Id., p. 39
373 (Things are moving) XXXI, 342–43
373 (If I were to leave here) XXXII, 540
373 The facsimile of the Address to President Lincoln has been taken from the original manuscript in the National Archives, Washington, D.C.

The House on Maitland Park Road

The house and Marx's work room have been described by many visitors, notably Lafargue and Maxim Kovalevsky. Most of the descriptions are brief and rather perfunctory, perhaps because there was nothing unusual about them; and the extraordinary disorder of Marx's work room, which is mentioned by nearly everyone who visited it, was also regarded as natural and inevitable.

From 1 Maitland Park Road, where he lived from March 1864 to March 1875, he moved to No. 41, where he remained for the rest of his life. The houses appear to have been very nearly identical. The house where Marx died no longer exists. It was shattered by a bomb in World War II.

A Short Sketch of an Eventful Life

PAGE
384 (June 19, 1843) MG, 204
385 (At Easter 1852) MG, 217
386 (There came a fairly) MG, 229

The Birth Pangs

PAGE
389 (As regards my work) XXXI, 132
389 (If I had more money) XXXI, 178
390 (He must have been wearing) XXIX, 217
391 (I told this Creole) XXXI, 253
392 (Nor can I leave) XXXI, 281
392 (An irrepressible hurrah!) XXXI, 283
393 (Thereupon we clinked) XXXI, 288
394 (He is a fanatical) XXXI, 290
394 (It has always seemed) XXXI, 292
395 (I hope and am firmly) XXXI, 296–97
395 (The Kugelmanns) XXXI, 297
396 (It is certainly) XXXI, 541
396 (You ask why) XXXI, 542
397 (in order to raise) XXXI, 561
399 (Fire, fire) XXXI, 595
399 (the scholar compared) XXXII, 787
399 (The classical gods) MG, 293
400 (*La vida es sueño*) MG, 291
402 (I learned that) XXXI, 551
403 (Dear Fred) XXXI, 323

Das Kapital

PAGE
410 (Modern society) *Capital,* I, 132–33
410 (In order, therefore) Id., 103
411 (*Excellently have you*) *Paradiso* XXIV, 83–85
411 ("Jerome," he wrote) *Capital,* I, 103
412 (If money) Id., 760
412 (Englishmen, always) Id., 249
413 (Bentham is a purely) Id., 609
414 (Dear child) XXXII, 545

The Paris Commune

PAGE
420 (If you will take a look) XXXIII, 205–6
421 (justified, even necessary) Gustav Mayer, *Engels,* p. 220
422 (The war was merely) *La Critique Sociale,* December 1931, pp. 189–90
422 (the greater part) Postgate, *Civil War in France,* p. 47
423 (A master of small state roguery) Id., p. 21
423 (The Paris of M. Thiers) Id., p. 39
424 (essentially a working-class) Id., p. 23

A Letter to the Home Secretary

PAGE
426 (It is making) XXXIII, 238
426 (The work of the International) XXXIII, 252
427 (I like Rutson) Aberdare, *Letters,* I, 260
427 (Dear Sir) XXXIII, 246–47
429 (The danger of the enfranchisement) *Essays on Reform,* p. 285
431 (There have been many misunderstandings) XVII, 433

A Letter from Nechayev

PAGE
435 (Leaving aside) Bakounine, *Correspondence,* p. 390
436 (*To the student Lyubavin*) Lehning, *Michel Bakounine et les Conflits dans l'Internationale,* p. 473

The Hague Congress

PAGE
439 (and therefore a ship's) XXXIII, 389
440 The Danielson letters are taken from the original manuscripts in the British Museum.
444 (The international congress) XXXIII, 505
444 (He is not one of the) Gerth, *The First International,* p. 186
446 (We would rather) Id., 211
448 (Ich bin so overworked) XXXIII, 477
449 (We do not deny) Gerth, *The First International,* p. 236
450 (I regard Marx) Bakounine, *Oeuvres,* IV, 350–51
450 (Whereas citizen Bakunin) Gerth, *The First International,* p. 226
451 (Marx does not believe) Bakounine, *Oeuvres,* IV, 444
453 (Longuet is the last) MEGA, III, 4, 569

The Cure at Karlsbad

PAGE
458 (If this man) XXXIII, 96
458 (You shouldn't worry) XXXIII, 611
460 (Carl Marx—Naturalization) From the original manuscript in the Public Record Office
463 (Do you always do this) MG, 314

464 (from whom I have at last) XXXIII, 117
465 (Marx was a hundred) MG, 316

THE PROMISED LAND

PAGE
465 (Charles Marx, doctor) Schwerbrock, *Karl Marx Privat*, p. 79
467 (His repulsive courseness) MG, 403
467 The bitter argument is described by Kovalevsky in MG, 396.
468 (I saw Liebknecht) MG, 348
468 (He played a thoroughly) MG, 351
469 (Where's the copy?) MG, 352
470 (In a higher phase) XIX, 21
470 (I have spoken) XIX, 32

THE OLD LION

PAGE
473 (He is a short) *Times Literary Supplement*, 15 July, 1949, in a long letter to the Editor from Mr. Andrew Rothstein
475*n* (Marx reacted) MG, 398
476 (The first impression) Hyndman, *The Record of an Adventurous Life*, pp. 247–48
478 (Our method of talking) Id. 250–51
478 (Many evenings) *Letters to Americans*, p. 130
479 ("I, too") Karl Kautsky, "Hours with Karl Marx," in *The Modern Thinker and Author's Review*, III, 2, p. 107
479 (When this charmer) Marx-Engels, *Selected Correspondence*, p. 389
480 (Is this massive-headed) *New York Sun*, September 6, 1880

THE SLOW DEATH

PAGE
483 (For those three weeks) MG, 153
483 (Never shall I forget) MG, 153
484 (Karl Marx, the greatest) *Modern Thought*, December 1, 1881, p. 349
486 (Her illness took on the character) *Familie Marx in Briefen*, p. 153
486 (We are no such external) *Familie Marx in Briefen*, p. 152
486 (For Jenny Marx this) XIX, 291–92

THE LAST DAYS

PAGE
491 (Marx's appearance) Engels-Lafargue, *Correspondence*, I, 82
491 (I am so busy doing nothing) Id., I, 87
493 (If we had stayed in Geneva) Id., I, 100
494 (Some recent Russian publications) Marx to Laura, December 14, 1882
497 (And when it is all over) I, 338

THE LEGEND

PAGE
500 (On March 14) XIX, 335
502 (And so it happened) XIX, 336–37

THE SURVIVORS

PAGE
511 (Price was simply dazzled) Capital, III, 387
512 (If he has 1,000,000) Id., III, 597
512 (We see the workers) Mehring, *Karl Marx*, p. 377
514 (In her person) Beatrice Webb, *My Apprenticeship*, pp. 258–59
515 (Aveling and Tussy) Engels to Bernstein, August 6, 1883
516 (If you had ever) Eleanor Marx to Olive Schreiner, June 16, 1885, in *The Modern Monthly*, IX, 1935, p. 290
516 (My mother and I) Lewis S. Feuer, in "Marxian Tragedians," *Encounter*, November 1962, p. 24
517 (I have given him a good) Engels to Sorge, August 8, 1887, in *Labour Monthly*, February 1934
519 (We were the last two) *Letters to Americans*, p. 232
520 (Ideology is a process) Engels to Mehring, July 14, 1893. *Selected Works*, II, 497–98
521 (We are a great power now) Mayer, *Friedrich Engels*, p. 323

ELEANOR MARX-AVELING

PAGE
524 (It is a terrible business) Liebknecht, *Briefwechsel*, p. 464
525 (You would not know) Id., p. 434

FREDERICK DEMUTH

PAGE

533 (I spoke to Longuet again) Engels-Lafargue, *Correspondence,* II, 2

538 (Before Marx's eyes) The full text of the letter, as quoted by Werner Blumenberg (*Marx,* 115–17), reads:

I learned from General [Engels] himself that Freddy Demuth is Marx's son. Tussy had pressed me so hard on the matter that I asked the old man directly. General was very surprised that Tussy maintained her belief so stubbornly and gave me the right, if gossip made it necessary, to assert categorically that he denied paternity. You will remember that I gave you this information a long time before General's death.

A few days before his death General again confirmed the fact that Frederick Demuth was the son of Karl Marx and Helene Demuth to Mr. Moore, who then went to Tussy at Orpington and told her so. Tussy insisted that General was lying, and that he had always said he was the father. Moore came straight back from Orpington, and again put the question forcibly to General, but the old man stood by the assertion that Freddy was the son of Marx, and said to Moore: "Tussy wants to make an idol of her father."

On the Sunday, the day before his death, General wrote it out on the slate for Tussy, and Tussy left the room so shattered that she forgot all the hate she had for me and wept bitterly on my neck.

General empowered us (Mr. Moore, Ludwig and me) to make use of the information only if shabby inferences should be made against Freddy; he said he would not have his name disgraced, especially when it benefited no one any more. This had in fact preserved Marx from a difficult domestic conflict. Apart from us and Mr. Moore, I believe that Laura was the one among Marx's children who guessed at the story, even if she had no direct knowledge of it, while Lessner and Pfänder also knew about the existence of Marx's son. Sometime after the publication of the letters to Freddy, Lessner told me: "We were fully aware that Freddy is Tussy's brother; but we could never discover where the boy was brought up."

Freddy was laughably like Marx, and one really had to suffer from a blind conviction to see any resemblance between him and General, for he had distinctly Jewish features and blue-black hair.

I have seen a letter which Marx wrote to General, who was then living in Manchester. General had not yet moved to London, and I believe he destroyed this letter, as he destroyed so many of the letters they exchanged.

This is all I know about the matter. Freddy never found out either from his mother or from General who his father was . . .

I have just been reading once more the lines in your letter concerning this question. Before Marx's eyes there stood always the prospect of divorcing his wife, who was fearfully jealous. He had no love for the child, the scandal would have been too great, and he dared not do anything for the child . . .

The letter was written by Louise Freyberger to August Bebel on September 2, 1898, and is among the documents preserved in the International Institute of Social History at Amsterdam.

539 (I am so lonely) *Die Neue Zeit,* XVI, II, 1897–98, p. 485

540 (Sometimes I have) Id., p. 486

540 (More and more I realize) Id., pp. 487–88

541 (Dear, dear Freddy) Id., p. 489

542 (Among the many charges) A brief discussion of the pamphlet can be found in Peter Gay, *The Dilemma of Democratic Socialism,* p. 257.

CHRONOLOGICAL TABLE

1814	February 12	Birth of Jenny von Westphalen.
1818	May 5	Birth of Karl Marx.
1823	January 1	Birth of Helene Demuth.
1824	August 26	Karl Marx baptized in the Evangelical Church.
1830	Autumn	Karl Marx attends the Gymnasium at Trier, where he remains until September 24, 1835.
1834	January 20	Heinrich Marx delivers a subversive speech at the Casino Club in Trier.
	March 23	Karl Marx is confirmed.
1835	October 15	Karl Marx enters Bonn University.
1836	October 22	Karl Marx enters Berlin University, where he remains until March 30, 1841.
1837	November 10	Karl Marx writes a long letter to his father, examining his own life.
1838	May 10	Death of Heinrich Marx.
1841	January 23	Marx's "Savage Songs" published in the *Berlin Athenaeum*.
	April 15	Marx receives his doctorate from Jena University.
1842	March 3	Death of Baron von Westphalen.
	May	Marx contributes to the *Rheinische Zeitung*, becoming editor in October.
1843	March 18	Marx resigns from the *Rheinische Zeitung*.
	June 19	Marx marries Jenny von Westphalen.
	Summer and autumn	Marx at Kreuznach, writing "On the Jewish Question" and "Introduction to a Criticism of Hegel's Philosophy of Law."
	October	Marx goes to Paris and edits the *Deutsch-Französische Jahrbücher*, which appears in February 1844. He meets Heinrich Heine.
1844	May 1	Birth of Jenny Marx.
	Early September	Marx meets Engels, and they work together on *The Holy Family*.
	Autumn	Marx meets Proudhon, Bakunin and other revolutionaries. In the winter writes "Economic and Philosophical Manuscripts."

1845	January 16	Marx receives order of expulsion from France, and leaves for Brussels, where he remains until March 1848.
	Spring	Marx writes *Theses on Feuerbach.*
	July	Marx pays a brief visit to England in the company of Engels. Works with Engels on *The German Ideology* for about a year.
	September 26	Birth of Laura Marx.
1846	January	Marx sets up correspondence committee.
	March 30	Marx attacks Weitling: the first purge.
	December	Birth of Edgar Marx.
1847	January–June	Marx writes *La Misère de la Philosophie,* attacking Proudhon.
1848	End of February	Marx publishes his *Manifesto of the Communist Party* in London.
	March 4	Marx is arrested in Brussels and expelled. Leaves for Paris, where the abortive February Revolution has broken out, and stays less than a month.
	June 1	In Cologne Marx begins publication of the *Neue Rheinische Zeitung.*
	September 17	Demonstration at Worringen.
1849	February 8	Marx on trial for subversion, is acquitted.
	May 19	The "red number" of the *Neue Rheinische Zeitung* appears. Marx is expelled from Prussia and leaves for Paris.
	August 16	French police write order banishing Marx to Brittany.
	August 26	Marx arrives in London.
	November 5	Birth of Guido Marx.
1850	March–November	Marx and Engels publish six numbers of the *Neue Rheinische Zeitung, Politisch-ökonomische Revue.*
	May 24	The Earl of Westmorland receives confidential report that Marx and others are preparing to assassinate Queen Victoria.
	September 3	Konrad Schramm and August von Willich fight duel at Antwerp.
	November 18	Death of Guido Marx.
	December 2	Marx takes his family to live at 28 Dean Street, Soho, where they remain until September 1856.
1851	March 28	Birth of Franziska Marx.
	June 23	Birth of Frederick Demuth.

	August	Marx writes articles for *New York Daily Tribune*, continuing to write them until 1862.
	December 2	*Coup d'état* of Louis Napoleon.
1852	March	Marx writes *The Eighteenth Brumaire of Louis Napoleon.*
	April 14	Death of Franziska Marx.
	November 17	Marx dissolves the Communist League.
1855	January 16	Birth of Eleanor Marx.
	April 6	Death of Edgar Marx.
1856	April 14	Marx delivers a fiery speech to a Chartist gathering.
	July 23	Death of Baroness Caroline von Westphalen.
	Summer	Marx writes *Secret Diplomatic History of the Eighteenth Century.*
	October	Marx moves his family to a new house on Grafton Terrace.
1859	June	Marx publishes his *Critique of Political Economy.*
1860	December 1	Marx publishes *Herr Vogt.*
1861	February 28–April 29	Marx goes on extended visit to Holland and Germany, where he is entertained by Lassalle.
1862	July	Lassalle is entertained by Marx in London.
1863	January 6	Death of Mary Burns, the mistress of Engels.
	November 30	Death of Henrietta Marx at Trier.
	December	Marx travels to Trier.
1864	March	Marx moves his family to a new house on Maitland Park Road.
	May 9	Death of Wilhelm Wolff.
	August 31	Death of Ferdinand Lassalle.
	September 28	Foundation of International Working Men's Association.
	October 12	Jenny Marx gives her first ball in England.
1865	Summer or autumn	Jenny Marx writes *A Short Sketch of an Eventful Life.*
1867	April 10	Marx journeys to Hamburg to prepare *Das Kapital* for the press, and stays with Dr. Kugelmann in Hanover for a month.
	August 16	Marx finishes proofreading *Das Kapital* and writes to thank Engels.
	September 14	Publication of *Das Kapital.*
1868	April	Laura Marx marries Paul Lafargue.

1869	September 18	Engels retires from the Manchester cotton mill and establishes himself in London.
1870	February 25	Nechayev writes a letter to Lyubavin, threatening him with death unless Bakunin is released from the task of translating *Das Kapital.*
1871	March 18	Paris Commune established.
	June–July	Marx publishes *The Civil War in France.*
	July 12	Marx delivers documents of the International to the private secretary of Lord Aberdare, the Home Secretary.
1872	April	Publication of Russian translation of *Das Kapital.*
	September 1–7	The Hague Congress.
	October	Jenny Marx marries Charles Longuet.
1874	August 26	Marx's request for British citizenship is rejected.
1875	May 5	Marx writes his *Critique of the Gotha Program.*
1876	July 1	Death of Mikhail Bakunin.
1879	January 31	Marx meets Sir Mountstuart Grant Duff.
1880	October	Marx meets H. M. Hyndman.
1881	December 2	Death of Jenny Marx.
1882	February–October	Marx in ill-health. Goes to Algiers, Monte Carlo, Enghien-les-Bains, Vevey for his health.
1883	January 11	Death of Jenny Longuet.
1883	March 14	Death of Marx.
1890	November 4	Death of Helene Demuth.
1895	August 5	Death of Engels.
1898	March 31	Suicide of Eleanor Marx.
1911	November 26	Suicide of Laura Lafargue.
1929	January 28	Death of Frederick Demuth.

ACKNOWLEDGMENTS

My chief debt is to my father, Mr. Stephen Payne, of the Royal Corps of Naval Constructors, who assisted me throughout, not least in the long and difficult search for Frederick Demuth. Miss Gwyneth Morris led us sure-footedly through the endless complexities of London life, with grace and humor. Mr. Joseph Carter, bookman extraordinary and perennial student of Marx, first set me on the trail which led to Freddy, though he could not have guessed how many years would pass before we found our quarry.

I am also indebted to Mr. C. J. Child, Deputy Librarian of the Foreign Office Library, for the Manteuffel report, and to Mr. H. G. Pearson, Record Officer at the Home Office, for the documents concerning Marx's attempt to become a naturalized British citizen.

Mr. G. S. Aitken of the Amalgamated Society of Engineers kindly searched for the records concerning Frederick Demuth in the society's archives.

Mr. Charles Clayton gave me his recollections of Frederick Demuth in many letters and interviews.

To Mr. David C. Cargill I am indebted for the genealogical tree of Jenny von Westphalen.

Miss Lucile Kohn, the impeccable Latinist, translated Marx's Latin essay, not without some qualms over his disorderly grammar.

I am grateful to Mr. Peppino Leoni for letting me examine what remains of Marx's apartment at 28 Dean Street.

Not the least of my debts is to the anonymous officers of the Marx-Engels-Lenin-Stalin Institute in Moscow, who never replied to my inquiries and by the vehemence of their silence led me to undertake researches which I would not otherwise have attempted.

INDEX